The Poetry of
THOMAS HARDY

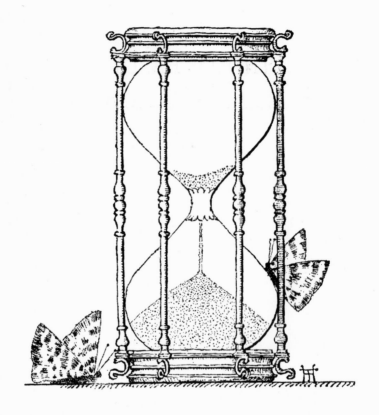

The Fleeting of Time—
The Hovering of the Soul—
The Coming of Death

Hardy's drawing to illustrate "Amabel" in Wessex Poems.

The Poetry of
THOMAS HARDY

A HANDBOOK
AND COMMENTARY

by

J. O. Bailey

THE UNIVERSITY OF NORTH CAROLINA PRESS · CHAPEL HILL

To
My Wife Mary and
My Daughter Nancy.

Preface

The Poetry of Thomas Hardy: A Handbook and Commentary
is an attempt to provide readers, students, and critics with data they
need to understand a body of poems often misinterpreted. The poems
and the poet were misunderstood during Hardy's lifetime in ways
that both dismayed and amused him. He stated this fact in the poem
"So Various." The "new critics" of recent years have continued to
misunderstand the poems through ignorance of the facts Hardy had
in mind when he wrote.

He put himself intimately—his personal experiences and his ob-
servations—into his poetry, but (except briefly, now and then) he did
not supply footnotes. The present Handbook and Commentary sup-
plies factual notes and even, where facts are not available, surmises
intended to throw light on meaning.

Professor Richard Purdy's Thomas Hardy: A Bibliographical Study
offers many hints of the relation between Hardy's life and his poetry,
but his book is devoted chiefly to manuscripts and publication facts.
His notes are limited to citing, for a few poems, the persons or occa-
sions treated or biographical parallels in The Early Life or The Later
Years. The commentaries of the present book, recognizing Purdy's
first-hand source of information (his friendship with Mrs. Florence
Hardy), tend to rely upon this information as authentic and then to
fill in the gaps wherever factual data are available.

My method has been first-hand exploration. I visited the places
Hardy names in his poems, talked with elderly citizens of Dorchester
who knew Hardy personally, read what remains of Hardy's notebooks
and as many letters as possible, and considered almost everything in
print.

In my search for elusive facts I have been aided by institutions
and individuals who have heartened me with their faith in the value
of this work. I am grateful to the Cooperative Program in the Hu-

manities of Duke University and The University of North Carolina at Chapel Hill for a grant that helped me spend the summer of 1965 exploring the Hardiana in the Colby College Library; I am grateful to The University of North Carolina at Chapel Hill for a seven-months' leave-of-absence in 1966, to live in Dorchester, read the documents in the Dorset County Museum, and explore Hardy's Wessex, Cornwall, and London. I am grateful to the University Research Council of The University of North Carolina at Chapel Hill for assistance in travel to distant libraries, for stenographic help, and for aid in the publication of this book.

Libraries and museums in both the United States and England have offered every friendly service within their power. I offer thanks to the staffs of the libraries listed here. In the United States: the Colby College Library, the Library of Congress, the New York Public Library (the Berg Collection), the Yale University Library, the Princeton University Library, the Lilly Library of the University of Indiana, and the Miriam Lutcher Stark Library of the University of Texas; and in Great Britain: the Dorset County Museum (custodian of the Max Gate papers, the Sanders Collection, etc.), the Dorset County Library in Dorchester, the Weymouth Public Library, the British Museum, the Bodleian Library in Oxford, the Fitzwilliam Museum and the University Library in Cambridge, the National Library of Scotland in Edinburgh, the County Archives for Wiltshire in Trowbridge, and the Public Records Office in London.

I wish to thank again, in this public statement, the many friendly people who have helped, often with information not to be found in libraries. Dr. George M. Harper, then Chairman of the English Department of The University of North Carolina at Chapel Hill, approved my leave-of-absence for the work in England. The late Professor Carl J. Weber of Colby College gave me, in many conversations and letters, the benefit of his career as a Hardy scholar. Curator Richard Cary, Albert Howard, and Mrs. Mary Wandersee of the Colby Library looked up for me every scrap of information in the Hardiana there. Professor Siegfried Wenzel of The University of North Carolina at Chapel Hill gave me help with problems involving Latin and Greek.

In Dorchester, where I was a stranger, I asked questions of people who had known Hardy and found everyone glad to help. Curator Roger Peers and his assistants, Miss Maureen Samuel and A. T. Stangrom of the Dorset County Museum, found for me obscure documents collected there. Lieutenant-Colonel D. V. W. Wakely of the Military Museum ransacked files for information about the old soldiers of

Hardy's poems. Assistant Librarian Miss B. M. Betts and County Archivist Miss Margaret Holmes helped me find old deeds and records. Francis Dalton, retired Curator of the Dorset County Museum, pointed out personally known facts about Hardy's poems. Good friends Ernest and Lillian Burt, living in Dorchester in 1966, took me to "Hardy places" all through Wessex. Miss May O'Rourke, a secretary for Hardy in the 1920's, provided personal data about a number of poems. Frank Southerington, Jr., Hardy scholar from nearby Abbotsbury, went with me to explore parish records in the villages where Hardy's ancestors had lived. Mr. and Mrs. J. P. Skilling, caretakers of the Hardy Birthplace, led me to spots on "Egdon" Heath mentioned in Hardy's poems. Mr. Beauchamp of Damers Hospital (formerly the "Union" of several Hardy poems) guided me through the Hospital and told me its history. Mrs. Vera Mardon, pianist for Hardy and the Hardy Players, showed me a number of letters and recalled her experiences of the 1920's.

Outside Dorchester, friends were equally generous. Frank Pinion of Sheffield University, then preparing *A Hardy Companion*, welcomed my company on several excursions and allowed me to read his manuscript. Mrs. Gertrude Bugler of Beaminster, who played Tess in the Hardy Players' production of *Tess of the D'Urbervilles*, showed me letters from Hardy and Mrs. Florence Hardy and guided me to sites of poems near her home. Mr. and Mrs. J. Stevens Cox, now of Guernsey, publishers of the Hardy monographs, showed me their collections of material. Miss Lois Deacon let me read the documents upon which *Providence and Mr Hardy* rests and discussed her theories with me. Hugh G. Brasnett of Wimborne showed me photographs he had made to illustrate Hardy's works and guided me to places of interest in Wimborne. The late Miss Verena Acland of West Stafford told me the facts underlying Hardy's "Timing Her." Mr. Gell, living in Woodsford Castle, took me through the Castle and discussed the scenes of "A Sound in the Night." Mrs. Joan Cochrane of Milton Abbas told me the story of her niece Lorna, of Hardy's "Lorna the Second." Mrs. Gwendolen Bax of the Old Rectory, St. Juliot, gave me information valuable in understanding the poems laid there. Reverend Allen G. Watling, vicar of Melbury Osmund, helped me discover facts in the parish records. Mrs. P. F. Chapman, archivist for Madame Tussaud's in London, provided information for understanding "At Madame Tussaud's in Victorian Years." Miss Joan Brocklebank of Affpuddle helped with problems of Hardy's "old folk tunes." Dean S. Evans of Gloucester Cathedral gave me information concerning "The Abbey Mason." Monica Hutchings, author of *In-*

side Dorset, helped with information about places. Bernard Jones of Sturminster Newton, editor of William Barnes's *Poems*, "translated" for me a number of Hardy's words from Dorset dialect. Arthur Oswald of *Country Life* furnished facts for interpreting "The Flirt's Tragedy." Mrs. Muir of Fawley made available the parish records there. To these and others of a list too long for citation, I am grateful for the help mentioned and many interesting suggestions.

I am grateful for permissions that I wish to acknowledge. Macmillan and Company of London has given me permission to quote portions of Hardy's *Collected Poems* needed in commentary upon them. Professor Richard Purdy of Yale University, who holds the rights of publication of Hardy's letters, has allowed me to quote from them whatever is needed in discussion of a poem. H. P. R. Hoare and the National Trust and Maurice P. Rathbone, County Archivist for Wiltshire, gave me permission to publish quotations from the letters of Mrs. Florence Hardy to Alda, Lady Hoare. Miss Irene Cooper Willis, representing the Trustees of the Hardy Estate, showed me her copies of letters in the Library of the University of Leeds and gave me permission to publish for the first time three of Hardy's poems, hitherto withheld: the early poem, not titled, that begins "When wearily we shrink away," and two poems Hardy wrote (or dictated) on his death-bed: "Epitaph" (for G. K. Chesterton) and "Epitaph" (for George Moore). Mrs. Hardy evidently refrained from publishing the latter two poems because the men attacked were living. Surely Hardy meant the poems to be published at some time. The notes on these poems indicate their importance.

Contents

The Poetry of
THOMAS HARDY

Introduction

A professor teaching a course in the interpretation of poetry had adopted an anthology without footnotes, and assigned Hardy's "The Phantom Horsewoman." Then he studied the poem himself by examining the point of view, the diction, the expected ironies, the rhythms, the figures of speech, and the supposed symbolism, but the "ghost-girl rider" baffled him. "What does she symbolize?" he asked me. "Death, riding the pale horse of Revelation? Is she luring the man into the sea?" He thought of every possibility except a fact he did not know because he was unfamiliar with Hardy's life-story. I told him that the ghost is Hardy's memory in 1913 of Emma Gifford as she was when he had courted her in Cornwall in 1870. With this fact he was able to march to his classroom beaming.

I. A. Richards, to discover whether students can judge poetry without some hint, at least, of facts the poet had in mind, conducted an experiment among his undergraduates reading English for an Honors Degree at Cambridge University. He distributed on printed sheets poems without title, author's name, or other facts external to the poem itself. One of the poems was Hardy's "George Meredith." Richards asked the students to write critical evaluations. The responses exhibited complete confusion about what the poem said, and the evaluations ranged from condemnation of the poem as worthless to extravagant praise. Students said: "It arouses no emotions in me. I understand what it says, but feel no interest in it." "I feel there is something wrong with this poem. Perhaps it is that the poet plunges too quickly into his subject; he does not pause to create an atmosphere." "The second verse is nonsense. The second line of verse four is particularly poor, only excelled perhaps by the second line of the last verse. Who ever heard of anything so strained, so artificial as 'The world's vaporous vitiate air'? The effort was not worth the ink it used."[1] If the students had known even the title and the author their judgments would have been different. If they had known of Hardy's long friendship with Meredith some who supposed the poem ludicrous might have found it an interesting critical estimate and tribute.

Except when Hardy was presenting matters so personal that he felt concealment necessary, he had no intention of being obscure. He said in 1918: "It is unfortunate for the cause of present day poetry that a fashion for obscurity rages among young poets, so that much good verse is lost by the simple inability of readers to rack their brains to solve conundrums."[2] He said again in 1920: "I am very anxious not to be obscure. It is not fair to one's readers. . . . Some of the younger poets are too obscure."[3] Hardy's poetry is obscure only when he wrote of persons, places, events, or philosophical views that he could not explain except in a long footnote or did not care to explain because of the intimate material.

Since he did not state backgrounds, poems that some reviewers, critics, and scholars have called masterpieces of structure, music, or philosophic statement, were called by others trivial, trite, rough, or melodramatic. In my observation, the more a critic has known of the backgrounds of the poems, the more just his judgments. For example, a recent book on Hardy's poetry assumes that "My Cicely" is fiction and dismisses it as one of Hardy's "canned melodramas." Examination of the poem as possibly a reflection of Hardy's journey to Topsham when he heard a false rumor of the death of Mrs. Tryphena Gale at least removes it from the category of canned melodrama. Knowledge of the places mentioned along the route illuminates Hardy's interest in history and geography.

An understanding of backgrounds is especially important in reading Hardy's poems. Florence Emily Hardy's *The Later Years* says: "Speaking generally, there is more autobiography in a hundred lines of Mr. Hardy's poetry than in all the novels."[4] He wrote to Clive Holland in August, 1923: "If you read the . . . 'Collected Poems' you will gather more personal particulars than I could give you in an interview, circumstances not being so veiled in the verse as in the novels."[5]

These statements are all the more impressive in view of the fact that Hardy's novels contain a good deal of his experience and observation. Doris Arthur Jones records that "Hardy told my father that he had never put an incident or a character in one of his books that he had not warranty for in real life."[6] Weber, analyzing *Jude the Obscure*, traces in some detail the extent to which Hardy put

[4]

himself into his fiction.[7] Thus we may suspect that a poem may be related to Hardy's life and that the key to its meaning may lie in knowledge of the facts, besides the light that seeing this connection may throw on details only hinted at in Hardy's biography.

The personal story underlying a poem may be psychological rather than physically factual. For example, when a boy, Hardy had a brief, sentimental affection for a neighborhood girl, Louisa Harding. During most of his life, he more or less forgot her; though she never married, but lived her long life in Dorchester, it is recorded that Hardy never spoke to her. After her death Hardy, in his old age, wrote two poems about her, "Louie" and "To Louisa in the Lane," which must be considered love-poems. He took guests to Stinsford Churchyard to visit her grave. In the sense that a vivid daydream is a biographical fact, the poems to Louisa are autobiographical.

On the other hand, Hardy did mingle fiction with fact. In his poems more than in his novels, he used actual place-names but sometimes used a fictional name for an actual place (as "Durnover" for Fordington) and sometimes so concealed a place that not even his friend Hermann Lea could identify it. He sometimes used actual persons' names but sometimes disguised persons with fictional names. He assumed fictional personalities. "We have Hardy's insistent warning not to assume that all his poems with 'I' as their apparent speaker are in any way autobiographical."[8]

Some poems may deal with personal matters even when there is no external evidence of the fact. It seems that Hardy felt some compulsion to express himself in poetry about matters he did not wish known. The poems that deal with Tryphena Sparks illustrate this tendency. He deliberately destroyed many records. He cut pages from his notebooks; he wrote instructions on them in red ink to his wife and his executor, Sir Sydney Cockerell, that they go through his papers and destroy certain documents. After Hardy's death, Cockerell "was much at Max Gate, sorting and burning papers," for he had "promised to prevent the publication of any of Hardy's early letters that might come to light after his death."[9] There were bonfires of papers at Max Gate. "Mrs. Hardy stood by the whole time and watched, presumably to ensure that nothing escaped the flames. . . . Mrs. Hardy herself burnt, on another bonfire, baskets full of the letters and private papers that I [the gardener] had carried down from the study to the garden under her supervision and watchful eye. She would not let me burn these, but insisted upon doing it herself, and after all the papers had been destroyed, she raked the ashes to be sure that not a single scrap or word remained."[10] These facts make documented explanation of the backgrounds for many poems impossible.

Therefore, in the present *Handbook and Commentary*, I have thought it reasonable, when a poem *seems* related to known facts in Hardy's life, to surmise the missing facts. (Every surmise is stated to be so.) I have tried to make sense of each poem but also to avoid any unwarranted inference that a statement is biographical because it occurs in a poem. Hardy did write fiction.

It may be of interest to glance at some features of his temperament as revealed in his poems. He seems to have lived as vividly in his memory as in the present, perhaps even more vividly. He tended to idealize and romanticize the images of memory. J. C. Squire wrote: "It is characteristic of Mr. Hardy that only the landscapes of his past are ever sunny; when he is writing in the present tense the chances are a hundred to one that it will be raining hard, on window-pane and bereaved tree, and there is quite a strong probability that he will actually find himself in a churchyard where the natural inclemency of the weather is re-inforced by the rain-worn cherubs on the tombstones, the half-effaced names, the dripping moss and the direct reminders of the dead." Hardy clipped this statement from a review, pasted it in his scrapbook, and opposite it wrote in pencil: "good!"[11] This tendency is portrayed in "The Old Neighbour and the New," where Hardy, calling on William Barnes's successor, scarcely sees the new rector to whom he is talking because he sees sitting in the rector's chair a vivid mental image of his old, dead friend. The tendency is allowed free rein in his "Poems of 1912-13" concerned with his memories of his first wife Emma, after her death. The mental process suggests an analogy with photography: the actual exposure is vivified, enriched, and colored when it is "developed" in the memory. Such idealizations may be mingled with remorse, where Hardy's actions, as in his married life with Emma, had brought pain not realized at the time.

An aspect of his memory is that it included much he did not himself experience. The poem "One We Knew" presents Hardy's grandmother, Mary Hardy, who, until her death in 1857, would sit by the fire with Tommy at her knees, talking of the experiences and observations of a long and eventful life. The poem says that she spoke "not as one who remembers, / But rather as one who sees." Tommy apparently saw all she told him so vividly that it seemed his own experience. The tales, legends, and facts of history poured into the ears of the eager boy are reproduced in dozens of poems of country folk who lived in Wessex villages before Hardy's birth. Ballad-like in structure, often tragic in outcome, permeated with folk-lore, such tales appear vividly in poems like "The Dark-Eyed Gentleman" and "The Bride-Night Fire." Hardy was careful to make his country people authentic in person, place, and lore. Writing in 1903 to John Pascoe, who had asked whether the legendary matter and folk-lore of his books was "traditionary and not invented," he said that this was "a point on which I was careful not to falsify local beliefs & customs."[12]

Seeming to think of the past as present and of the dead in their graves as somehow alive, Hardy not only wrote "Friends Beyond" to tell stories of the dead, but also spent much time visiting churchyards, "Paying Calls" (as a poem is titled) on dead friends. He saw nothing lugubrious in this interest but said: "I used to spend much time in such places sketching, with another pupil, and we had many pleasant times at the work. Probably this explains why churchyards and churches never seem gloomy to me."[13] There is another explanation. A broken stone skull in Stinsford Church fascinated Hardy when he was a boy. In June, 1926, when Sir Sydney Cockerell visited Max Gate, Cockerell wrote in his diary: "We went after breakfast for a motor drive, first to Stinsford Church where T. H. pointed out the place where he sat in a pew as a boy under the skull at the base of the monument to Audley Grey. The skull used to frighten him on dark days."[14] The feeling of fright disappeared when Hardy, reading the scientists (Huxley's "On the Physical Basis of Life," for instance), came to see that death is a process going on all through life and that from the corrupted body new life grows, as in "Voices from Things Growing in a Churchyard." Thus, in Hardy's poems, death haunts life in a friendly way.

Hardy described places in a double vision of their present and their past, often giving them names suggesting their past: he wrote of Puddletown but called it "Weatherbury" for the nearby ancient British hillfort of Weatherby; he called the village of Yetminster by its medieval name of Estminster. Perhaps to suggest more of the Roman "castra," he renamed Dorchester "Casterbridge" and emphasized that it "announced old Rome in every street, alley, and precinct. It looked Roman, bespoke the art of Rome, concealed dead men of Rome."[15] The places are real, described with the accuracy of an architectural draftsman, and identifiable, in spite of the changes of the present century, for he pictured their permanent aspects. The past in Hardy's poems and novels haunts the present.

His reading in the scientists during the 1860's caused him to abandon the religious faith of his boyhood and hence the concept of God as a manlike Father. Yet he could not abandon his wonder at the riddle of life and a strong feeling for religion. He expressed his wonder in a series of fantasies that personify the unknowable Power underlying existence and his feeling of compassion for all living and suffering things. The personifications of the powers of nature took various forms which by 1900, under the influence of Schopenhauer, Von Hartmann, and other philosophers, had merged into the Immanent Will of *The Dynasts*. Essentially the Will is a symbol for the mysterious, underlying, motivating forces and processes of the universe. These processes seem to have no consciousness, feeling, or morality. They are the processes of J. S. Mill's "Nature." Hardy spoke of the varying aspects of this symbol in the last sentence of the Preface of his last volume of poetry, *Winter Words*: "I also repeat what I have often stated on such occasions, that no harmonious philosophy is attempted in these pages—or in any bygone pages of mine, for that matter."

Hardy's religious feeling, deeply implanted in his youth and supported by his extreme sensitivity, was broadened by his reading *The Origin of Species* and related works. Christian teaching suggested loving-kindness and compassion as the basic virtues, and the facts of evolution indicated that all sentient life is akin. Therefore men owe loving-kindness to birds, beasts, and even trees and flowers (often personified in Hardy's poetry).

In this thinking, natural processes will forever be what they are, but men may ameliorate the conditions of life through compassion that, difficult in the present state of the world, may through the ages become instinctive and replace the self-regarding impulses of human nature. Hardy saw the process as a long one: he called it "evolutionary meliorism." Now and then, at least, he expressed belief in it, as in "A Plaint to Man" and the conclusion of *The Dynasts*.

Thus, though many of Hardy's poems are light, his subjects often trivial incidents and observations, he did have a "message." He considered his poetry as a whole to be, in Matthew Arnold's term, a "criticism of life." He spoke scornfully of the arty poetry popular in the 1890's (as in *The Yellow Book*) as "the art of saying nothing with mellifluous preciosity."[16] Depressed by the "irremediable ills" of indifferent natural law, he would look straight at remediable ills; he would take "a full look at the Worst," and set about reform. Besides his emphasis upon loving-kindness and compassion, he attacked a variety of evils. He wrote with pity of the farm boys—the expendable drummer Hodge and the "mouldering soldier" dead in Durban—sacrificed for English prestige in the South African war. Though he supported England in World War I, for the Germans were the aggressors, he expressed "The Pity of It" that "kin folk kin tongued" should be led to war by dynasts, "gangs whose glory threats and slaughters are." Beyond the slaughters he deplored the psychological consequences of violence: the "dark madness of the late war" and the "barbarizing of taste in the younger minds, the unabashed cultivation of selfishness in all classes."[17] These post-war phenomena nearly stifled his hope for meliorism. He nearly became (what he was too often called) a pessimist. By no means active in politics, he expressed some basic principles of democracy in many poems, as in "A Man" and his sympathetic treatment of ordinary village folk. He bitterly satirized social snobbery and the pretentious idle rich, as in "A Leader of Fashion." Among lesser objects of scorn, he attacked social conventions and pruderies that stifle self-expression and self-development.

Comments on other aspects of his poetry as an expression of his temperament are more the task of the critic than of a *Handbook*: his variety of poetic forms, often ballad-like, dramatic, or purely lyric; his humor, often overlooked by those who persist in regarding him as a hopelessly sad man; his fresh and indeed eccentric diction, with frequent disregard for the pretty, conventional phrase in favor of the word (a coined word where needed) that states precisely what he meant; and his use of irony in word and structure because he habitually observed the contrast between the romantic and the factual, the ideal and the real.

This *Handbook and Commentary* will by no means replace criticism in these and other fields but may supply critics with a basis for just criticism of Hardy's poems: an understanding of the facts upon which they rest.

1. Richards, *Practical Criticism*, pp. 146-53.
2. Meynell, ed., *Friends of a Lifetime*, p. 299.
3. Collins, *Talks with Thomas Hardy at Max Gate*, p. 21.
4. P. 196; *Life*, p. 392.
5. In the Dorset County Museum.
6. *The Life and Letters of Henry Arthur Jones*, p. 360.
7. *Hardy of Wessex*, 2nd ed., Chapter XVI.
8. Blunden, *Thomas Hardy*, p. 96.
9. Blunt, *Cockerell*, pp. 213-14.
10. Stephens, *Thomas Hardy in His Garden*, pp. 15-16.
11. "Thomas Hardy's Verse" pasted in "Reviews of T. H.'s Books (Poetry)," in the Dorset County Museum.
12. In the Weymouth Public Library.
13. Meynell, ed., *Friends of a Lifetime*, p. 291.
14. Blunt, *Cockerell*, p. 213.
15. *The Mayor of Casterbridge*, Chapter XI.
16. Letter to Edmund Gosse, Dec. 12, 1898; copy in the Colby College Library.
17. "Apology" for *Late Lyrics and Earlier*.

Explanatory

This *Handbook and Commentary* presents those facts in Hardy's life needed to understand his poems. As some facts underlie many poems, full presentation with each poem of the facts upon which it rests would require continual repetition. To avoid this, I am presenting below three keys for ready reference: a chronology of major events in Hardy's life, a key to persons prominent in several poems, and a key to places frequently mentioned. These keys attempt to tell, of such persons as Mrs. Emma Hardy or such places as Higher Bockhampton, only what is needed for understanding the poems.

The basic biography is Mrs. Florence Hardy's *The Early Life of Thomas Hardy* and *The Later Years of Thomas Hardy*. Because of frequent reference to these volumes, I am calling them *The Early Life* and *The Later Years* (without *The* in footnotes). Recent republication in one volume as *The Life of Thomas Hardy* necessitates in the footnotes a double reference, as *"Early Life,* p. 35; *Life,* p. 27."

As Hardy's novels are published in numerous editions, quotations from them are cited by chapter. Since the same source of information is cited in various footnotes, citations are abbreviated to author's last name, title of the book or article, and the page numbers. Full data appear in the Bibliography. Information concerning dates and other facts of publication is taken from Professor Richard Purdy's *Thomas Hardy: A Bibliographical Study.* Where the published poem is followed by a date or a place, I have omitted repetition of these facts. Much of the same information appears in many places. I have thought it sufficient to cite one source. In reading the scholarship, I have found some studies helpful in pointing to material I then looked up. For example, Copps's "The Poetry of Thomas Hardy" points to dozens of passages of the Bible quoted or echoed in Hardy's poetry. I have cited only the Bible.

Hardy's letters are scattered all over the world. I have examined as many as I could. Also the collection of letters to Hardy in the Dorset County Museum includes many of Hardy's replies in the form of his pencil-draft on the back of a letter. I have assumed that the pencil-draft in Hardy's handwriting is essentially the reply that was typed and mailed. To save space, I have referred to Hardy's letters that I have seen only in draft as "In the Dorset County Museum." Hardy's habit of close revision suggests that the letter may exist elsewhere with some differences in wording.

In Part One, the comments on Hardy's *Collected Poems* are arranged in the order of the poems as published in the 1962 edition by Macmillan and Company, Ltd., of London, which contains the poems of *Winter Words*. (The arrangement in the American edition, published by the Macmillan Company of New York, is essentially the same, but the volume does not include *Winter Words*.) Part Two treats poems not published in the *Collected Poems*, alternate titles of poems, etc. It includes several poems here published for the first time. The arrangement is alphabetical by title.

A CHRONOLOGY OF MAJOR EVENTS IN HARDY'S LIFE

This chronology is designed to show the relationships among major facts in Hardy's life and thus among biographical items in the poems. The chronology omits many of Hardy's movements—for instance, his frequent illnessess, short trips to London (often several times a year), and brief visits to persons and places in Wessex.

1840: June 2, Thomas Hardy was born at Higher Bockhampton.

November 24, Emma Lavinia Gifford was born in Plymouth.

1841: December 23, Hardy's sister Mary was born.

1844: Hardy's father gave Tommy an accordion and taught him to play the fiddle; through boyhood, Hardy played at country dances.

1845: April, Julia Augusta Martin, wife of Francis Pitney Martin, moved to Kingston Maurward as "lady of the manor."

1847: The railroad from London was extended to Dorchester.

1848: Hardy, as the first pupil, entered the village school established by Mrs. Martin at Lower Bockhampton.

1849: He was transferred to a school in Dorchester.

1851: March 20, Tryphena Sparks was born in Puddletown.

July 1, Hardy's brother Henry was born.

1852: Hardy began the study of Latin.

1853: October, Mrs. Martin and her husband left Dorset for London.

1855: Hardy's schoolmaster, Isaac Last, gave him Beza's *Latin Testament* as a "reward for diligence in studies."

He began to teach in the Stinsford Sunday School.

1856: July 11, he was apprenticed to the architect John Hicks of 39 South Street, Dorchester, next door to the school kept by William Barnes. He continued to live in Higher Bockhampton and in the early morning hours to study Latin; he took up Greek.

August 9, he witnessed in Dorchester the execution of Martha Brown for the murder of her husband.

September 2, his sister Katharine was born.

1857: January 9, Hardy's paternal grandmother, Mary Head Hardy, died.

He came under the friendly tutelage of Horace Moule of Queen's College, Cambridge. (Moule was born May 30, 1832, a son of the Vicar of Fordington.)

1859: Hardy purchased Griesbach's Greek New Testament, which he read regularly throughout his life.

1860: Horace Moule introduced him to *Essays and Reviews* and other religious, philosophic, and scientific writings.

1862: Hardy proposed to Mary Waight of Dorchester, but was rejected.

April 17, he went to London to continue architecture "on more advanced lines." He took up residence at Clarence House, Kilburn, but in 1863 moved to 16 Westbourne Park Villas.

May 5, he began work as assistant architect in the office of Arthur Blomfield.

He called on Julia Augusta Martin in London.

1863: March 16, his essay "The Application of Coloured Bricks and Terra Cotta to Modern Architecture" won a medal offered by the Royal Institute.

He spent much time in this and following years in reading the poets: the Elizabethans, Shelley, Keats, Browning, Tennyson, *et al.*

1864: He read the works of Darwin, Spencer, Huxley, and Mill, as well as the poets.

1865: March, Hardy's "How I Built Myself a House" appeared in *Chambers's Journal*, his first published fiction.

Autumn, he enrolled in an evening course in French at King's College and continued this study until March, 1866.

Autumn and early winter, he supervised the removal of coffins and bones from Old St. Pancras Churchyard for a railway cutting.

]

He inquired about matriculation at Cambridge University to prepare to become a country curate but gave up the plan because of uncertainty in his religious views.

He began writing verses.

1866: Hardy sent poems to editors of magazines, but none were accepted.

He read with enthusiasm Swinburne's *Poems and Ballads*.

1867: He thought of going on the stage and appeared at Covent Garden in a pantomime but gave up the idea.

Late July, in ill health, he went home to Higher Bockhampton.

His health improved in the country, and he resumed work with the architect Hicks in Dorchester.

He fell in love with a cousin, Tryphena Sparks of Puddletown, to whom he later became engaged.

1868: July 25, he posted the manuscript of *The Poor Man and the Lady* to Alexander Macmillan.

1869: March, in London, Hardy talked with George Meredith, reader for Chapman and Hall, about *The Poor Man and the Lady*.

April, he returned to Higher Bockhampton to work for the architect G. R. Crickmay of Weymouth.

September 14, he moved to lodgings at 3 Wooperton Street, Weymouth. He worked on a new novel, *Desperate Remedies*.

Tryphena Sparks entered Stockwell College in Clapham, London.

1870: Early February, he moved from Weymouth to Higher Bockhampton, to concentrate on *Desperate Remedies*.

Monday, March 7, he went to St. Juliot in Cornwall on an architectural errand for Crickmay, and there met Emma Lavinia Gifford; he returned to Higher Bockhampton on Friday, March 11.

April 5, he resumed lodgings in Weymouth.

Monday, May 16, he left Crickmay and went to London to assist Blomfield and the architect Raphael Brandon.

August 8, he visited Emma Gifford in Cornwall.

1871: March 25, *Desperate Remedies* was published.

March 30, Hardy took up lodgings in Weymouth to help Crickmay with church restorations.

May through June 3, he visited Emma Gifford in Cornwall.

Summer, he began writing *Under the Greenwood Tree* in Weymouth and at Higher Bockhampton.

Autumn, Tryphena Sparks completed her two-year course at Stockwell College.

October, Hardy visited Emma Gifford in Cornwall. When he was discouraged by the apparent failure of his literary efforts, Emma assured him literature was his "true vocation." About this time he began making notes for *A Pair of Blue Eyes*.

1872: He was in London much of the year helping the architect T. Roger Smith design schools.

January, Tryphena Sparks became headmistress in the Plymouth Public Free School (Girls' Department). In this year or early in 1873, Hardy broke his engagement to Tryphena, and about this time, perhaps, became engaged to Emma Gifford.

June, *Under the Greenwood Tree* was published.

August 7, Hardy visited Emma Gifford in Cornwall.

September to July, 1873, *A Pair of Blue Eyes* was published serially.

1873: May, *A Pair of Blue Eyes* was published in book form.

June 9, Hardy went to London. There he dined with Horace Moule on June 15.

June 20, he visited Moule in Moule's Cambridge rooms.

June 23 to July 2, he visited Bath, where Emma Gifford was staying with friends. He then returned to Dorchester.

September 21, Sunday, Horace Moule killed himself in his rooms in Queens' College, Cambridge.

September 24, Hardy learned of Moule's suicide.

September, he secluded himself at Higher Bockhampton to work on *Far from the Madding Crowd*.

1874: January to December, *Far from the Madding Crowd* was published serially, Hardy's first notable success.

September 17, Hardy married Emma Gifford at St. Peter's Church, Elgin Avenue, London.

November 23, *Far from the Madding Crowd* was published in book form.

After a honeymoon in France, the Hardys took up lodgings for the winter at St. David's, Hook Road, Surbiton, London.

1875: March, they moved to Newton Road, Westbourne Grove, London.

July, they moved to lodgings in Swanage. There Hardy wrote *The Hand of Ethelberta*, completed in January, 1876.

1876: March, they moved to lodgings at 7 Peter Street, Yeovil.

April 3, *The Hand of Ethelberta* was published.

Late May, they visited Holland, Belgium, and the Rhine country.

Midsummer, they moved to Riverside Villa in Sturminster New-
ton, their first separate house.

1877: Hardy began *The Return of the Native*.
June, he made notes toward treating the Napoleonic wars as
a "grand drama."
December 15, Tryphena Sparks married Charles Gale.

1878: January to December, *The Return of the Native* was published
serially.
March 18-22, the Hardys moved from Sturminster Newton to 1
Arundel Terrace, Trinity Road, Upper Tooting, London.
June, Hardy was elected a member of the Savile Club.
November 4, *The Return of the Native* was published in book
form.

1879: January 12, Florence Emily Dugdale was born.
Hardy began writing *The Trumpet-Major*.
Late August, the Hardys took lodgings in Weymouth but re-
turned to London in the autumn.
December, Hardy was elected to the Rabelais Club of "virile"
authors.

1880: January to December, *The Trumpet-Major* was published
serially.
Hardy began *A Laodicean* at Upper Tooting, London.
July 27, the Hardys took an extended trip to France.
October 23, Saturday, Hardy was taken ill, with internal bleed-
ing, but continued *A Laodicean* by dictating from his bed.
October 26, *The Trumpet-Major* was published in book form.
December to December, 1881, *A Laodicean* was published
serially.

1881: April 10, Hardy was able to go outdoors for the first time since
October.
June 25, the Hardys moved to "Llanherne" on the Avenue in
Wimborne Minster. There Hardy began writing *Two on a
Tower*.
August 23, the Hardys took a trip to Edinburgh.
November 25, *A Laodicean* was published in America in book
form; a week later, in England.

1882: May to December, *Two on a Tower* was published serially.
Late October, it was published in book form.
Winter, Hardy began work on *The Romantic Adventures of a
Milkmaid*.

1883: June 25, it was published in the *Graphic*.
June, the Hardys moved from Wimborne to 7 Shire Hall Lane

in Dorchester and purchased land for building Max Gate. Construction was begun on November 26.

1884: Late March or early April, Hardy began *The Mayor of Casterbridge*.

1885: June 29, the Hardys moved into Max Gate.

1886: January 2 to May 15, *The Mayor of Casterbridge* was published serially.

May 10, it was published in book form.

Hardy spent much time in the British Museum reading toward *The Dynasts*.

July, he was at work on *The Woodlanders*, the first of his novels to show clearly the influence of Schopenhauer's *The World as Will and Idea* (translated into English in 1883).

May to April, 1887, *The Woodlanders* was published serially.

October 7, William Barnes died.

1887: March 14, the Hardys began an extended trip to Italy: Genoa, Florence, Rome, Venice, and Milan, returning to London in April and to Max Gate in August.

March 15, *The Woodlanders* was published in book form.

1888: May 4, *Wessex Tales* was published.

May 28, the Hardys began a visit of several weeks to Paris.

1889: August, Hardy was writing *Tess of the D'Urbervilles*.

1890: March 17, Mrs. Charles Gale (*née* Tryphena Sparks) died.

July, Hardy and his brother Henry went to Topsham, near Exeter, to place a wreath on the grave of Mrs. Gale and called briefly at the home of Charles Gale.

August, Hardy took a trip to Paris with his brother Henry.

1891: May 30, *A Group of Noble Dames* was published.

July 4 to December 26, *Tess of the D'Urbervilles* (somewhat bowdlerized) was published serially.

November 29, it was published in book form.

1892: July 20, Hardy's father died.

October 1 to December 17, *The Well-Beloved* was published serially.

Hardy made a trip to Great Fawley in Berkshire, the village from which his paternal grandmother, Mary Head Hardy, had come.

1893: Spring, the Hardys took a house, 70 Hamilton Terrace, in London and, because of the fame of *Tess*, were invited to many "crushes, luncheons, and dinners."

May 18, they departed for Dublin to visit Lord Houghton.

May 19, they met Mrs. Arthur Henniker, Lord Houghton's sister.

May 29, they returned to London.

December, in London, Hardy revised with Mrs. Henniker "The Spectre of the Real" but returned to Max Gate for Christmas.

1894: February 22, *Life's Little Ironies* was published.

April 15, the Hardys moved into a house in Pelham Crescent, South Kensington, London.

August, they returned to Max Gate.

December to November, 1895, *Jude the Obscure* was published serially.

1895: November 1, it was published in book form.

1896: Spring, the Hardys returned to the house in South Kensington.

September, they went to Belgium, especially to visit Brussels and the field of Waterloo, with plans for *The Dynasts* in mind.

1897: March 2, Lorimer Stoddard's adaptation of Hardy's dramatization of *Tess of the D'Urbervilles* was produced in New York.

March 16, *The Well-Beloved* was published in book form.

Mid-June, the Hardys visited Switzerland, being in Lausanne on June 27, the anniversary of Gibbon's completing *The Decline and Fall* there.

1898: December 11, *Wessex Poems* was published.

1899: Late June, Hardy with some friends "rambled in Westminster Abbey at midnight by the light of a lantern."

1901: November 17, *Poems of the Past and the Present* (dated 1902) was published.

1902: Late September, Hardy sent *The Dynasts*, Part First, to Macmillan's.

1904: January 13, *The Dynasts*, Part First, was published.

April 3, Easter Sunday, Hardy's mother died.

Mrs. Arthur Henniker, visiting at Max Gate, brought with her Florence Emily Dugdale, who ten years later became the second Mrs. Hardy.

1905: First week in April, Hardy went to Aberdeen, Scotland, to receive the honorary degree of LL.D. from the University.

1906: February 9, *The Dynasts*, Part Second, was published.

May 30, Mrs. Hardy had a fainting fit while gardening at Max Gate, a warning of heart disease.

1907: February 8, Mrs. Hardy went to London alone to march in a suffragette parade.

Late April, the Hardys moved to London for the spring and summer.

June 22, they were guests at King Edward's Garden Party at Windsor Castle.

1908: February 11, *The Dynasts*, Part Third, was published.

November 24, Hardy's edition of *Select Poems of William Barnes* was published.

1909: May 18, George Meredith died.

June, Hardy succeeded Meredith as President of the Society of Authors.

December 3, *Time's Laughingstocks* was published.

1910: June, the King conferred on Hardy the Order of Merit.

November 16, he was presented "the freedom of Dorchester."

1912: June 1, Henry Newbolt and W. B. Yeats visited Hardy at Max Gate to present him the gold medal of the Royal Society of Literature.

July 16, after a trip to London, Hardy was at Max Gate to attend the last garden party his wife Emma gave.

November 27, Emma died.

1913: March 6, Hardy went alone to Cornwall to revisit the scenes of his courtship of Emma Gifford.

June, he received the honorary degree of Litt.D. from Cambridge University. He was made an Honorary Fellow of Magdalene College.

October 24, *A Changed Man and Other Tales* was published.

1914: February 10, he married Florence Emily Dugdale at St. Andrew's Church, Enfield.

November 17, *Satires of Circumstance* was published.

1915: November 24, Hardy's sister Mary died.

1916: September, Hardy and his wife Florence visited Cornwall.

October 3, *Selected Poems* was published.

Autumn, he visited the English wounded and also the camp of 5,000 German prisoners in Dorchester.

1917: November 30, *Moments of Vision* was published.

1920: February 10, he received an honorary degree of Litt.D. from Oxford University and attended a performance of a part of *The Dynasts* by the Oxford University Dramatic Society.

April 21, he made his last visit to London, staying for two nights at J. M. Barrie's flat.

1922. May 23, *Late Lyrics and Earlier* was published.

Hardy was made an Honorary Fellow of Queen's College, Oxford.

He was awarded an honorary degree of LL.D. by St. Andrew's University.

1923: April 1, Mrs. Florence Henniker died.

June 25, Hardy and his wife visited Queen's College, Oxford, for two nights, the last time he slept away from Max Gate.

July 20, the Prince of Wales visited Dorchester and was the guest of the Hardys.

November 15, *The Famous Tragedy of the Queen of Cornwall* was published.

1925: July 15, a deputation from Bristol University came to Max Gate to confer on Hardy the honorary degree of Litt.D.

November 20, *Human Shows* was published.

1926: November 1, Hardy paid his last visit to his birthplace at Higher Bockhampton.

1927: December 11, his final illness began.

1928: January 11, he died.

January 14, after his heart was removed, his body was cremated.

January 16, his heart was buried in Stinsford Churchyard, and his ashes in the Poet's Corner, Westminster Abbey.

October 2, *Winter Words* was published.

November 2, *The Early Life of Thomas Hardy* was published.

1930: April 29, *The Later Years of Thomas Hardy* was published.

A KEY TO PERSONS PROMINENT IN HARDY'S POEMS

This key provides background concerning persons prominent in several of the poems. If a person is prominent in only one poem or the facts about him are knit into its substance, the person is treated in the notes on the poem, as Julia Augusta Martin is treated in the notes on "Amabel." The arrangement is alphabetical by the last name.

WILLIAM BARNES, to whom a statue stands in the churchyard of St. Peter's, Dorchester, was born on February 22, 1800 (or 1801?), in Blackmoor Vale. After education at a dame school, he entered a lawyer's office, first in Sturminster and later in Dorchester. Married in 1823 to Julia Miles, he moved to Mere in Wiltshire and became a schoolmaster. He took up the study of languages, including Latin, Greek, French, Italian, and German, to which he later added Old English, Persian, and Welsh. He also practiced drawing and engraving, collected pictures, and played the organ and other instruments.

In 1835 he moved to Dorchester, set up a school there, and became recognized as a superb teacher.[1] In 1845 he helped establish the Dorset County Museum. He registered at St. John's College, Cambridge, as a "ten years' man," an adult scholar who would, in the midst of other activities, do the work for a degree. He was ordained in 1847 and became a curate at Whitcombe, near Dorchester. He received a Bachelor of Divinity degree in 1850. Three years later he published a *Philological Grammar*, drawing material from sixty languages. In 1862 he became Rector at Winterborne-Came, a parish about a mile south of Dorchester. He was also a poet, writing some poems in standard English and some in Dorset dialect. After publishing many in the *Dorset County Chronicle*, he issued *Poems of Rural Life in the Dorset Dialect* in two series, 1844 and 1862; *Hwomely Rhymes*, 1859; and *Poems of Rural Life in Common English*, 1868. When his poems were collected in 1879, Hardy reviewed the volume for the *New Quarterly Magazine*.[2] Barnes died on October 7, 1886. (See also the notes on "The Last Signal," "The Collector Cleans His Picture," and "The Old Neighbour and the New.")[3]

1. See *Early Life*, p. 211; *Life*, p. 162.
2. In Orel, *Thomas Hardy's Personal Writings*, pp. 94-99.
3. Zietlow, "Thomas Hardy and William Barnes: Two Dorset Poets," studies the influence of Barnes's poetry upon Hardy's.

ELIZABETH ("LIZBIE") BROWNE is mentioned twice in *The Early Life*, though "Lizbie" may be Hardy's pet name, and it is not certain that Browne was her family name. When Hardy was about fourteen, he had a series of boyhood sweethearts who knew little or nothing of his fancy. Among them was a "young girl, a gamekeeper's pretty daughter, who won Hardy's boyish admiration because of her beautiful bay-red hair. But she despised him as being two or three years her junior, and married early. He celebrated her later on as 'Lizbie Browne.' " He wrote in his notebook for March 1, 1888: "Youthful recollections of four village beauties: 1. Elizabeth B——, and her red hair."[1] These passages suggest that after her marriage she went away somewhere.

1. *Early Life*, pp. 33, 270; *Life*, pp. 25-26, 206.

LOUISA HARDING was the fourth daughter of Stephen Toghill Harding, a gentleman-farmer of Stinsford. Born on August 9, 1841, she was more than a year younger than Hardy. She was "short and tubby and anything but dignified. She had a round, jolly face and from youth to old age had always been full of fun and mischief, although very religiously minded." Her hair in youth was "medium brown" and her eyes were "grey flecked with green." "It has been well known in the Harding family that Thomas Hardy when he was fifteen years old had been in love with Louisa, but her parents would not permit her to have anything to do with him. Louisa never once spoke to Hardy. Louisa, herself, told me this."[1]

Miss Harding (who never married) lived most of her adult life at No. 4 Maumbury Road, Dorchester. May O'Rourke, Hardy's part-time secretary in the 1920's, as a child knew Miss Harding. She says that Miss Harding's house was shaggy with ivy, "But once inside, her warm and buoyant personality thawed away any chill from her surroundings; her fine dark eyes sparkled with welcome, and her face, furrowed as much by laughter lines as the chisellings of age, had that inner glow of fun which is a sure passport to any child's heart."[2] Miss Harding died on September 12, 1913, at the age of seventy-two; she was buried in an extension of Stinsford Churchyard.

1. O. E. Harding, relative of Louisa, as reported in O'Rourke, *Thomas Hardy: His Secretary Remembers*, p. 50. A photograph of Louisa when she was about nineteen is reproduced as the frontispiece.
2. Ibid., p. 16.

MRS. EMMA HARDY was born Emma Lavinia Gifford on November 24, 1840, the daughter of a solicitor, John Attersoll Gifford of Plymouth. She met Hardy on March 7, 1870, at St. Juliot Rectory in Cornwall, where she was then living with her sister Helen and her brother-in-law, the Reverend Caddell Holder. The story of Hardy's courtship of Emma is told so fully in all biographies of Hardy and in so many of his poems that it need not be sketched here.[1] Emma married Hardy on September 17, 1874, at St. Peter's Church, London, with her uncle, Dr. E. Hamilton Gifford, Canon of Worcester, officiating.

The marriage was a true-love match. Hardy was attracted by Emma's vitality, daring on horseback, compassion for animals, quaintness of imagination, talent as pianist and painter in water colors, and honey-colored hair and peony complexion. She was attracted to him as a scholar, writer of promise, and ardent admirer. When, before the marriage, he wavered between architecture and literature, she encouraged him to continue writing and labored to make fair copies of his manuscript for the printer. After marriage, the pair lived in various places in Wessex and London; in 1887, they took an apparently happy journey to Italy. Until about 1890, in spite of differences now and then (as when they moved from Sturminster Newton to London in 1878),[2] Hardy and Emma lived in harmony, though he was disappointed that they had no child.

Emma's tendency toward snobbery was a factor in a rift that developed in the 1890's. The niece of an archdeacon, she considered that she had married beneath her rank;[3] she often reminded Hardy that he had "married a lady." [As Hardy became famous, women ran after him, and (though no evidence exists of infidelity in the legal sense) he was attentive to more than one admirer. "Emma was wounded, jealous, and scandalized. . . . She grew bitter and queer in her behaviour to him, slighted him in public and complained of his neglect of her to her friends. She rubbed into him what she considered her indisputable social superiority."[4] She disdained his family. Whenever Hardy was in Dorchester, he paid a weekly visit to his parents, but Emma did not go with him; fond of social life, she gave many lawn parties, but there is no record that she invited Hardy's parents even to call. Florence Hardy wrote to Rebekah Owen on April 5, 1914, concerning Hardy's sisters, Mary and Kate: "I am sure you would like his sisters, but for the twenty years preceding Nov. 1912 they had not been allowed inside Max Gate, so I am not surprised that you never met them."[5] Perceptive visitors to Max Gate noticed Emma's attitudes. On September 25, 1895, George Gissing, after a weekend with the Hardys, wrote to his brother Algernon that Emma was "an extremely silly & discontented woman, to whom, no doubt, is attributable a strange restlessness & want of calm in Hardy himself."[6]

Emma had the fixed idea that she was superior to her husband in birth, education, talents, and manners. "She could not, and never did, recognize his greatness."[7] Her feeling is defined in a letter to Rebekah Owen on March 4, 1902: "I can scarcely keep a 'mere' cat to say nothing of a 'mere man' whom all the world claims, which would not so much matter if his later writings were of a more faithful truthful, & helpful kind. Do not read, or at least accept, as anything but fiction some of the poems. . . . Written 'to please' . . . others! or himself— but not *ME*, far otherwise."[8] Emma wrote verses that were published in the *Dorset County Chronicle*. Hermann Lea wrote to E. N. Sanders on January 12, 1947, that Emma "took me up to the top of the house (Max Gate) and showed me a lot of wooden boxes in which she said her unpublished poems were stored. She also told me once that she had inspired Tess!"[9] She wrote sentimental novels, one of which survives in typescript in the Dorset County Museum. Hardy's comments upon religion in *Tess of the D'Urbervilles* and *Jude the Obscure* outraged her. She replied with *Spaces*, treating "The High Delights of Heaven" and describing in detail the events of the Judgment Day, which will be heralded by a trumpet blast "in the East at 4 o'clock a.m. according to western time," etc.[10]

Her literalness in matters of piety must have irritated Hardy; certainly his unconventional views hurt her. Regarding *Jude the Obscure* as a personal affront, she wrote to Rebekah Owen on April 24, 1899: "He should be the last man to disparage marriage! I have been a devoted wife for at least twenty years or more—but the last four or five, alas! . . . The *thorn* is in my side still."[11] On December 27, 1899, Emma wrote again to Miss Owen, this time about "Omar Kayám" (as she spelled it) : "Of course I think the poetry excellent in style . . . but in sentiment pernicious, though it is rampant everywhere; such literature being no doubt a factor in the accumulation of despairs, miseries, & sorrows, to be heaped up in the latter days. . . . I still think the Bible *unmatchable.*"[12] When visitors questioned Hardy about views expressed in his works, Emma did what she could to make him seem respectable. Madame Sarah Grand and Clive Holland dined with the Hardys on March 21, 1903, and discussed religion. The next morning at his hotel, Holland "received—as he did on several other occasions—a note from Mrs. Hardy, stating that she hoped that neither he nor her visitor would regard what her husband said on religious matters as serious, adding the information that he regularly read his Greek testament."[13]

Besides these evidences of immaturity, Emma exhibited a variety of delusions, scarcely noticeable to guests at a tea, but a damper upon interchange of ideas with her husband. Mabel Robinson wrote to Irene Cooper Willis about Emma as she was in the 1880's: "Mrs. Hardy was inconsequent. Her thoughts hopped off like a bird on a bough, but never then nor at any other time did the idea cross my mind that her mind (such as it was) was unhinged. . . . she was a perfectly normal woman without much brain power but who wanted to be a poet or novelist."[14] Hardy came to look upon Emma as a child. Drawing upon a letter Hardy wrote to Kate Gifford on November 23, 1914, Henry Gifford comments that Emma had been " 'most childlike and trusting formerly.' This becomes a dominant note in the [Hardy's] poems—she has a 'child's eager glance' ('Lament') , 'the heart of a child' ('Found Her Out There'), 'a child's pleasure All her life's round' ('Rain on a grave')."[15]

Hardy had no recourse in middle age, when Emma's youthful charm had withered, except withdrawal from evenings alone with her. Her feelings about this arrangement are indicated in a letter to Alda, Lady Hoare on April 24, 1910. The letter speaks of "so much endured" since her marriage "in this town in which I have been *un-*

happy." While Hardy was in London, she invaded his study: "I am ensconsing myself in the study in *his* big chair foraging—he keeps me *out* usually—as *never* formerly—oh well! I have my private opinion of men in general & of him in particular—grand brains—much power —but too often lacking in judgment of ordinary matters."[16] As Florence Dugdale wrote to Edward Clodd on January 13, 1913: "Of course nothing can be more lonely than the life he used to lead— long evenings spent alone in his study, insult & abuse his only enlivenment! It sounds cruel to write like that, & in atrocious taste, but truth is truth, after all."[17]

Most people who knew Emma did not describe her as insane, but various letters suggest that her mind was disturbed. Hardy wrote to Mrs. Arthur Henniker on December 17, 1912: "In spite of the differences between us, which it would be affectation to deny, & certain painful delusions she suffered at times, my life is intensely sad to me now without her."[18] He wrote to Emma's cousin Kate Gifford on November 23, 1914: "In later years an unfortunate mental aberration for which she was not responsible altered her much, & made her cold in her correspondence with friends & relatives, but this was contrary to her real nature, & I myself quite disregard it in thinking of her."[19] (See the notes on "The Interloper.")

After Emma's death, Hardy discovered among her papers two personal manuscripts. One of them titled "What I Think of My Husband" he read and burned.[20] The contents of the manuscript may be surmised from letters of Florence Dugdale, later Mrs. Hardy. She wrote to Edward Clodd on January 16, 1913, that Hardy "spends his evenings in reading & re-reading voluminous diaries that Mrs. H. has kept from the time of their marriage. . . . He reads the comments upon himself—bitter denunciations, beginning about 1891 & continuing until within a day or two of her death—& I think he will end of [*sic*] believing them."[21] She wrote to Rebekah Owen on January 18, 1916: "I remember the *awful* diary the first Mrs. T. H. kept (which he burned) full of venom, hatred & abuse of him & his family."[22] The other manuscript, *Some Recollections*, is a childlike but appealing record of Emma's girlhood and youth up to the time of her marriage. Reading it "threw Hardy back to that joyful enchanted time, forty years earlier, when they had met and become engaged. He revived memories, which had lain dormant, with amazing fervour. . . . *Some Recollections*, too, seems to have set him searching for the house in which she had been born, the places she had known as a child, the churchyard where her ancestors lay and where she herself had once wished to be buried. He revisited such places in Devon and Cornwall—Plymouth, Tintagel, Boscastle, and St. Juliot—on more than one occasion."[23] To a large extent, "Poems of 1912-13" were inspired by this manuscript.

Hardy found in Emma's manuscripts a picture of himself as he and his behavior seemed to her. His poems were, as he said, an "expiation"[24] for his neglect and even his self-protective, exasperated unkindness toward her. Florence wrote to Sir Sydney Cockerell on November 26, 1922, that "the 24th was the anniversary of . . . his first wife's birthday—always forgotten during her lifetime."[25] Though Emma had wished Hardy to take her on a visit to Plymouth and Cornwall, he did not do so. As several poems say, he ignored such gestures intended to revive his love as her playing her piano and singing the songs that had attracted him during courtship. He went on walks without asking her company, leaving her lonely. In "When Oats Were Reaped," he wrote of Stinsford Churchyard: "I wounded one who's there, and now know well I wounded her." He knew, when it was too late, that Emma's abuse of him "was of course sheer hallucination in her, poor thing, & not wilfulness."[26] It is clear that he felt himself guilty of hurting a child. Though he might have detailed how Emma had failed him, he did not do so. As he wrote to Edward Clodd on December 13, 1912: "One forgets all the recent years and differences, & the mind goes back to the early times when each was much to the other—in her case & mine intensely much."[27]

Hardy did what he could to carry out wishes Emma had expressed. On March 6, 1913, he set out for Boscastle, imagining, the poems say, her spirit by his side. He went to Plymouth also, to search out her girlhood home and the other scenes of *Some Recollections*. The result was a startling revival of his vision of youthful, vital Emma in her old haunts, with the graces, the high spirit, and the glamor of "Lyonnesse" he had idealized forty years earlier.

Hardy wrote the "Poems of 1912-13" to express his feelings, but offered none of these poems to a magazine. When he went to Cambridge to receive an honorary degree on November 2, 1913, he told A. C. Benson that he did not know whether to include them in a book in preparation; they were, he said "very intimate, of course—but the verses came; it was quite natural; one looked back through the years and saw some pictures; a loss like that just makes one's old brain vocal!"[28] He wrote to Mrs. Arthur Henniker on July 17, 1914: "Some of them I rather shrink from printing—those I wrote just after Emma died, when I looked back at her as she had originally been, & when I felt miserable lest I had not treated her considerately in her later life. However I shall publish them as the only amends I can make."[29]

1. This sketch is devoted chiefly to phases of their married life not fully treated in the biographies but important in understanding many poems.

2. Hardy called the years at Sturminster Newton "Our happiest time." *Early Life*, p. 156; *Life*, p. 118.

3. Dr. Gifford, the uncle who had performed the marriage ceremony for Hardy and Emma, became Archdeacon of London. *Early Life*, p. 133; *Life*, p. 101.

4. Willis, *Thomas Hardy*, p. 7.

5. In the Colby College Library.

6. In the Yale University Library.

7. Homer, *Thomas Hardy and His Two Wives*, p. 12.

8. In the Colby College Library.

9. In the Dorset County Museum.

10. Most of Emma's writings were destroyed. Of what remains, her *Poems and Religious Effusions* were published by J. Stevens Cox in 1966.

11. In the Colby College Library.

12. In the Colby College Library.

13. Holland, *Thomas Hardy, O. M.*, p. 179.

14. In the Dorset County Museum. For the nature of Emma's delusions, see her *Poems and Religious Effusions* and the notes on "At a Fashionable Dinner."

15. "Thomas Hardy and Emma," p. 119.

16. In the Stourhead Collection, County Archives in Trowbridge, Wiltshire.

17. In the Brotherton Library Collection, Leeds.

18. In the Dorset County Museum.

19. Gifford, "Thomas Hardy and Emma," p. 117.

20. Flower, *Just As It Happened*, p. 96. Evelyn Hardy, *Thomas Hardy*, p. 276, gives the title as "What I thought of my Husband."

21. In the Brotherton Library Collection, Leeds.

22. In the Colby College Library. The other, *Some Recollections*, he read with great care, annotated in matters of fact, and partly published in *Early Life*, pp. 88-96; *Life*, pp. 67-73. All of *Some Recollections* has been published by Evelyn Hardy and Robert Gittings.

23. Evelyn Hardy and Gittings, eds., *Some Recollections*, p. x.

24. Purdy, *Thomas Hardy: A Bibliographical Study*, p. 166.

25. Meynell, ed., *Friends of a Lifetime*, p. 308.

26. Hardy as quoted in a letter of Florence Dugdale to Edward Clodd on January 1, 1913, in the Brotherton Library Collection, Leeds.

27. In the British Museum.

28. Lubbock, ed., *The Diary of Arthur Christopher Benson*, pp. 260-61.

29. In the Dorset County Museum.

—— MRS. FLORENCE HARDY was born Florence Emily Dugdale on January 12, 1879, the daughter of Edward Dugdale, headmaster of a school at Enfield. As a young woman, she was a writer of books for children. In 1904, Mrs. Arthur Henniker, on a visit to Max Gate, brought Miss Dugdale with her. Hardy was working on *The Dynasts*, and Miss Dugdale volunteered to help in his research. He was pleased to have her do some quasi-secretarial work for him in the British Museum. In gratitude, he made her presents of books, including inscribed copies of his own works, and contributed poems to introduce some essays in her books for children. (See the notes on "The Calf," "The Lizard," and "The Yellow-Hammer.")

When Max Gate was in confusion after the death of Emma, who had run the household, Hardy turned to Florence for help. In December, 1912, she came and restored order there, and served (in Hardy's words) as "chucker-out" of many unwanted visitors.

On February 10, 1914, Hardy met Florence in Enfield, and they were married. The witnesses were Hardy's brother Henry and Florence's sister Margaret. The bride of thirty-five and the groom of nearly seventy-four went straight to Max Gate for the placid years suggested in Hardy's "A Jog-Trot Pair."

MARY HARDY, Hardy's favorite sister, was born on December 23, 1841. She was only a year and a half younger than Thomas, while more than ten years separated him from his brother Henry and his sister Kate. A letter from Florence Hardy to Edward Clodd, written the day of Mary's death on November 24, 1915, reports her feelings and what Hardy must have said about his childhood with Mary: "We shall miss her so much—she was the dearest & kindest sister to us both, & my husband's earliest playmate—a kind little sister sharing with him, gladly, all she had, proud of him beyond words."[1] Mary was her brother's intellectual and artistic comrade in his youth; his letters to her from London in the 1860's exhibit a free-and-easy discussion of his doings, their mutual friends and mutual tastes, and books they were both reading.[2] In middle age, they rambled together the fields, woods, and hills. Fond of literature and talented in music and painting, Mary was close to her brother in temperament. (See "Middle-Age Enthusiasms.")

His obituary article for her sums up her career. She received a teacher's certificate from Salisbury Training College in April of 1863, and then was for many years headmistress of the Dorchester Elementary Girls' School. She was endowed with "a large share of the family taste and talent for art and music." She was a church organist and had a "lifelong devotion to sketching and painting." At the time of her death, in her seventy-fourth year, she was living with her brother Henry and sister Kate at "Talbothays" near West Stafford, about three miles from Dorchester. She was buried in Stinsford Churchyard.[3]

Hardy said of her often, as in a letter to Sir George Douglas on December 7, 1915: ". . . as a painter of portraits she had a real skill in catching the character of her sitter."[4] When she painted Hardy's portrait in oils, he hung it in the dining room at Max Gate. She also painted one of her father and one of her mother. Of the latter

Hardy said, comparing it with other portraits, that it was best of all, showing their mother with "a face of dignity and judgment."[5] Her real though modest talents gained for her no wide fame; perhaps she did not seek it. Hardy wrote of her ten years after her death: "Mary's birthday. She came into the world . . . and went out . . . and the world is just the same . . . not a ripple on the surface left."[6]

1. In the Brotherton Library Collection, Leeds.
2. *Early Life*, pp. 50-53, 67-69; *Life*, pp. 38-41, 51-52.
3. "Death of Miss Mary Hardy," pp. 8-9.
4. Parker, "Hardy's Letters to Sir George Douglas," p. 223.
5. These portraits are now in the Dorset County Museum.
6. *Later Years*, p. 245; *Life*, p. 430. Clive Holland reported that Hardy said, "Mary might be considered the original of Bathsheba in Far from the Madding Crowd." "When I Cycled and Talked with Hardy," p. 474.

MRS. ARTHUR HENNIKER was born in 1855 as the Hon. Florence Ellen Hungerford Milnes, a daughter of Richard Monckton Milnes, the first Lord Houghton.[1] In 1882, she married Lieutenant Arthur Henry Henniker of the Coldstream Guards. She was in Dublin in 1893 as hostess for her brother, the second Lord Houghton, Lord Lieutenant of Ireland. Having "some slight acquaintance with Mrs. Hardy (and possibly Hardy himself),"[2] she invited them for a visit that lasted from May 19 to 25. *The Later Years* quotes from Hardy's diary for May 19: "We were received by Mrs. Arthur Henniker, the Lord-Lieutenant's sister. A charming, *intuitive* woman apparently." The diary for May 20 presents Emma as Mrs. Henniker's companion: "To Dublin Castle, Christ Church, etc., conducted by Mr. Trevelyan, Em having gone with Mrs. Henniker, Mrs. Greer, and Miss Beresford to a Bazaar." On May 22, Mrs. Henniker entertained with music: "A large party at dinner. Mr. Dundas, an A. D. C., played banjo and sang: Mrs. Henniker the zithern." On the 25th, the Hardys went with her to a brewery: "Went over Guinness's Brewery, with Mrs. Henniker and several of the Viceregal guests. . . . On the miniature railway we all got splashed with porter, or possibly dirty water, spoiling Em's and Mrs. Henniker's clothes."[3]

Hardy was more attracted to this "charming, *intuitive*" woman, then thirty-eight years old while he was nearly fifty-three, than these records indicate. During the week of June 8, when Mrs. Henniker was in London, he joined her in a theatre party: "In the week he still followed up Ibsen, going to *The Master Builder* with Sir Gerald and Lady Fitzgerald and her sister, Mrs. Henniker, who said afterwards that she was so excited by the play as not to be able to sleep all night." He went also to another play and wrote Mrs. Henniker an amusing letter: "The evening of yesterday I spent in what I fear you will call a frivolous manner. . . . Barrie had arranged to take us and Maarten Maartens to see B.'s play of *Walker, London*. . . . Mr. Toole heard we had come and invited us behind the scenes. We accordingly went and sat with him in his dressing-room, where he entertained us with hock and champagne, he meanwhile in his paint, wig, and blazer, as he had come off the stage, amusing us with the drollest of stories about a visit he and a friend paid to the Tower some years ago: how he amazed the custodian by entreating the loan of the crown jewels . . . offering to deposit 30s. as a guarantee that he would return them, etc." This letter exhibits the tone of many that Hardy wrote to Mrs. Henniker.

She made her home in Southsea, about seventy-five miles east of Dorchester. She was a writer, publishing six novels and three volumes of short stories and writing one play that reached production. In October, 1893, Hardy began collaborating with her on a short story, his only collaboration except in dramatizations of his works. At this time he would go about once a week to Salisbury, Winchester, or London to meet Mrs. Henniker. This collaboration was completed in December: "Finishing his London engagements, which included the final revision with Mrs. Henniker of a weird story . . . entitled 'The Spectre of the Real,' he spent Christmas at Max Gate as usual."

In November, 1911, the "Dorchester Debating and Dramatic Society gave another performance of plays from the Wessex novels. This time the selection was . . . *The Three Wayfarers*; and a rendering by Mr. A. H. Evans of the tale of *The Distracted Preacher*. The Hardys' friend, Mrs. Arthur Henniker, came all the way from London to see it, and went with his wife and himself." Here and there *The Later Years* quotes a bit from a letter to Mrs. Henniker, as on June 5, 1919, a response to a birthday greeting: "Sincere thanks for your good wishes, my dear friend, which I echo back towards you. . . . Do you mean to go to London for any length of time this summer? . . . Florence sends her love, and I am, Ever affectionately, Th. H." In July, 1920, the Hardys went "motoring about Dorset, showing some features of the country to their friend, Mrs. Arthur Henniker, who was staying at Weymouth, and at that time had ideas of buying a house in the neighbourhood." In July, 1922, "Florence Henniker came early in the month, and went for a delightful drive with him and his wife in Blackmore Vale, and to Sherborne." The closing record reads: "*April 5*. In to-day's *Times*. 'Henniker.—on the 4th April, 1923, of heart failure, the Honourable Mrs. Arthur Henniker. R. I. P.' After a friendship of 30 years! *April* 10. F. Henniker buried to-day at 1 o'clock at Thornham Magna, Eye, Suffolk."[4]

This record is sketchy and restrained in tone perhaps because the friendship was closer than Hardy wished to exhibit. He (or perhaps Mrs. Hardy) even cut out a passage written for *The Later Years* which says that Mrs. Henniker was the subject of a number of poems. The passage, written for insertion under the date of June, 1893, reads: "The chief significance of Hardy's visit to Dublin was his meeting there with Mrs. Arthur Henniker (Florence Henniker) who became afterwards one of his closest and most valued friends, remaining so until her death many years after. As befitted the daughter of Monckton Milnes (Lord Houghton) she had a love of the best in literature, and was herself a writer of novels and short stories, none of which, unfortunately, ever received the recognition which, in Hardy's opinion, they undoubtedly deserved. Some of his best short poems were inspired by her, and the only time he ever wrote in collaboration was with her in a short story, 'The Spectre of the Real.' "[5] Hardy's "best short poems . . . inspired by her" seem to include "The Division," "A Broken Appointment," "A Thunderstorm in Town," "At an Inn," "In Death Divided," "He Wonders about Himself," "The Coming of the End," "The Month's Calendar," "Last Love-Word," "Alike and Unlike," and possibly "The Recalcitrants" and "Come Not; Yet Come!"[6]

In addition to Hardy's inscribing a number of his books to Mrs. Henniker and her dedicating her volume of stories *Outlines* (1894) to him, he wrote a sketch to recommend her books, "The Hon. Mrs. Henniker," published in the *Illustrated London News* for August 18, 1894. The sketch speaks of her "emotional imaginativeness, lightened by a quick sense of the odd" and "touches of observation lying midway between wit and humour."[7]

The most revealing record of this friendship is a large number of letters from Hardy to Mrs. Henniker, now in the Dorset County Museum. Though not all the letters are dated, twenty-three seem to belong to 1893; they continue in diminishing numbers until 1922 (two letters and a card). The letters make clear that Hardy was emotionally attracted to Mrs. Henniker. A letter of "Saturday" in 1893 says: "I sincerely hope to number you all my life among the most valued of my friends." One of July 13, 1893, says: "You seem quite like an old friend to me, and I only hope that time will bear out the seeming." Many letters are evidently written for the purpose stated in one of "Thursday" (August, 1893?): "for the pleasure of sending you a letter apropos of nothing in particular." A letter of September 9, 1893, thanks Mrs. Henniker for the gift of an inkstand engraved "T. H. from F. H., 1893," now on Hardy's table in the Dorset County Museum; it speaks of Mrs. Henniker as "almost a sister." Warmth of this kind is evident through 1896. Yet the letters contain nothing improper. Many offer literary criticism and encouragement; they include invitations to theatre parties or other gatherings and chit-chat. When Arthur (then General) Henniker died in 1912, Hardy wrote a poem "A. H., 1855-1912" to praise him, and Mrs. Henniker published it in her *Arthur Henniker: A Little Book for His Friends.*

1. These facts are largely from Purdy, "A Note on the Hon. Mrs. Arthur Henniker" in *Thomas Hardy: A Bibliographical Study,* pp. 342-48.
2. Ibid., p. 343.
3. Pp. 18-20; *Life,* pp. 254-55.
4. Pp. 20, 21-22, 27, 150, 191-92, 213-14, 227, 230; *Life,* pp. 256-57, 261, 356-57, 389, 406, 416, 419.
5. In the typescript labelled "T. H. Vol. II. . . . Mrs. Hardy (Personal Copy)," in the Dorset County Museum.
6. This list agrees with that in Purdy's "Note," pp. 345-46.
7. P. 195. The article is illustrated with a portrait. See Orel, *Thomas Hardy's Personal Writings,* p. 244. Lois Deacon in *The Chosen* has a full-page portrait of Mrs. Henniker, p. 4. Purdy says that "Mrs. Hardy is my authority . . . that Sue Bridehead [in *Jude the Obscure*] was in part drawn from Mrs. Henniker." P. 345.

HORACE MOSLEY MOULE was the fourth son of the Reverend Henry Moule, vicar of the church of Fordington St. George in what is now a part of Dorchester. As a youth Hardy sometimes attended services at this church and visited at the vicarage. Though Moule, born in 1832, was eight years older than Hardy, from about 1860 until Moule's death in 1873 Hardy regarded him as his adviser, teacher, and friend—the term he always used in referring to Moule.

A basis for this friendship is suggested in the reminiscences of Bishop Handley C. G. Moule, Horace's brother. He mentions Horace's gaiety of spirit, his "leading the family singing," his playing the organ in the church at the age of twelve, and his "interesting and teaching me, alike in scholarship and in classical history. He would walk with me through the springing corn, translating Hesiod to me."[1]

Horace was a student at Trinity College, Oxford, in 1851-54, but left without a degree. He was admitted as pensioner to Queens' College, Cambridge, in 1854, but, though he won the Hulsean Prize in 1858, he still did not take a degree.[2] He came home in this year full of literary knowledge and eager to impart it. Hardy, though working at architecture for John Hicks, was giving himself a strenuous course in the classics, and he gladly accepted Moule's help. They walked and read together whenever they were both in Dorchester. Nine letters in the Dorset County Museum from Moule to Hardy define their relationship of willing teacher and ardent student. A letter of July 2, 1863, tells Hardy: "The grand object of all in *learning to write well* is to gain or generate *something to say*." A letter of February 21, 1864, lectures Hardy learnedly on the use of "if" with the subjunctive.

Hardy went to London in 1862, where Moule was earning his living partly by writing for the *Saturday Review*, the *Literary Gazette*, and other quarterlies, and partly by serving as assistant Local Government Poor Law Inspector. In 1865-68, Moule was assistant Master at Marlborough College. He and Hardy met from time to time, though not frequently, if at all, between July, 1870, and September, 1872.[3] When Hardy began to publish fiction and was discouraged by a "slating" in the reviews, Moule encouraged him to persevere. Belatedly Moule sought to rescue *Desperate Remedies* by writing a long article in the *Saturday Review*.[4] In the same journal, he wrote a review of *Under the Greenwood Tree* that opened: "This novel is the best prose idyll that we have seen for a long while past." He had much to say, from his first-hand knowledge, of the "power and truthfulness shown in these studies of the better class of rustics."[5] He reviewed *A Pair of Blue Eyes* in 1873.

In that year (continuing occasional meetings), Hardy dined with Moule on June 15, before Moule had to leave for Ipswich on Poor Law duties. On June 20, Hardy went to Cambridge to visit Moule and spend the night. Next morning they climbed to the roof of King's Chapel, "where we could see Ely Cathedral gleaming in the distant sunlight. A never-to-be-forgotten morning. H. M. M. saw me off for London. His last smile." Then in September: "On the 24th he [Hardy] was shocked at hearing of the tragic death [suicide] of his friend Horace Moule, from whom he had parted cheerfully at Cambridge in June."[6] The body was brought to Fordington St. George for burial; Hardy attended the funeral. (The coroner had ruled "temporary insanity," which allowed burial in consecrated ground.) In the *London Mercury* for October, 1922, Hardy published "Ave Caesar," a poem of six stanzas by Moule. To accompany the poem, he wrote a brief biographical sketch which said, "It is hoped that this may be printed in any new edition of the Oxford Book of English Verse. T. H."[7]

This record of a friendship offers no explanation for Moule's suicide.[8] The writings of Moule's family say nothing on this topic. At the inquest, Charles Moule said that, having heard that his brother was ill, he was visiting in Horace's rooms at Queens' College on the evening of Sunday, September 21. After about three hours of conversation, Horace had gone into his bedroom, saying, "I shall lie down now." Charles, on hearing a trickling noise, went into the bedroom and found Horace in bed, bleeding from a gash in his throat. The physician who was summoned could do nothing. Horace articulated "Love to my mother. Easy to die," and died. Charles deposed that Horace "had been ill, and had suffered for some time past from exceeding depression of mind . . . extreme beyond any adequate cause. He had been liable to fits of depression for many years past, and sought relief in stimulants. . . . Years ago he had been in the habit of talking about suicide, but not of late. . . . He was perfectly sober on Sunday night." The physician stated that "For the last 13 months deceased's state of mind had been such that witness [the physician] feared he might commit suicide, but he was not in such a state as to call for his being put under restraint. His work was very laborious, and he had great anxiety in getting through it."[9]

Hardy's relations with Moule and other possible causes for his suicide are discussed in the notes for "A Confession to a Friend in Trouble," "Before My Friend Arrived." "The Five Students," and "Standing by the Mantelpiece."

1. *Memories of a Vicarage*, pp. 21, 34-35.
2. An excellent scholar in the classics, he had trouble with mathematics, but in spite of doing other work in the meantime, he was able to take his A.B. in 1867.
3. Deacon, *The Moules and Thomas Hardy*, pp. 125-26.
4. The article is not signed, but Rutland, Purdy, and other scholars agree that the author was probably Moule, who was writing for the *Saturday*.
5. XXXIV (1872), 417.
6. *Early Life*, pp. 123, 126; *Life*, pp. 93, 96. Most of this sketch is summarized from these volumes, *passim*.
7. Various critics have insisted that Henry Knight in *A Pair of Blue Eyes* is a portrait of Horace Moule, among them F. A. Hedgcock. In his copy of Hedgcock's *Thomas Hardy: Penseur et Artiste* Hardy wrote in the margin: "T. H. never learnt the classics by correspondence or of any person like Knight—who was not drawn from any friend of his." (Copied from V. H. Collins's copy of the novel, in which Collins had copied Hardy's comment, now in the Colby College Library.) The disclaimer is not altogether convincing in regard to some of Knight's traits.
8. Hardy's papers in the Dorset County Museum show several directions to his wife and his literary executors, especially in notebooks from which pages have been cut, to go through the papers and destroy anything about "M——."
9. The *Dorset County Chronicle*, September 25, 1873, p. 3.

LADY SUSAN O'BRIEN, daughter of the first Earl of Ilchester, became the wife of William O'Brien. She is buried with her husband in Stinsford Church in a vault built by Hardy's grandfather, Thomas Hardy the First. The couple are commemorated by linked plaques mounted in the south wall of the chancel. They read: "To the Memory of William O'Brien, Esqre Late Receiver General of the County of

Dorset. ob. Sep. 2, 1815. Aet 77. His Amiable Disposition, Cultivated Mind, and Worthy Character Endeared Him to All Who Knew Him!" and "To the Memory of Susanna Sarah Louisa Eldest Daughter of Stepn. First Earl of Ilchester. ob. August 9, 1827. Aet 83. of William O'Brien, Esqre the Faithful Wife and Inseparable Companion."

The Early Life, in describing Stinsford Church, indicates Hardy's lifelong interest in the O'Briens. In this church "lies the actor and dramatist William O'Brien with his wife Lady Susan, daughter of the first Earl of Ilchester, whose secret marriage in 1764 with the handsome Irish comedian . . . caused such scandal in aristocratic circles. 'Even a footman were preferable,' wrote Walpole. 'I could not have believed that Lady Susan would have stooped so low.' . . . O'Brien, besides being *jeune premier* at Drury, was an accomplished and well-read man, whose presentations of the gay Lothario in Rowe's *Fair Penitent,* Brisk in *The Double Dealer,* Sir Harry Wildair in *The Constant Couple,* Archer in *The Beaux' Stratagem,* Sir Andrew Aguecheek, the Prince in *Henry the Fourth,* and many other leading parts, made him highly popular, and whose own plays were of considerable merit. His marriage annihilated a promising career, for his wife's father would not hear of his remaining on the stage. The coincidence that both young Hardy's grandmothers had seen and admired O'Brien, that he was one of the Stinsford congregation for many years, that young Thomas's great-grandfather and grandfather had known him well, and that the latter as the local builder had constructed the vault for him and his wife . . . lent the occupants . . . a romantic interest in the boy's mind at an early age." In his journal for December 23, 1883, Hardy recorded further: "Death of old Billy C—— at a great age. He used to talk enthusiastically of Lady Susan O'Brien. . . . 'She kept a splendid house—a cellarful of home-brewed strong beer that would a'most knock you down; everybody drank as much as he liked.' "[1] And again, commenting in his journal for September 17, 1892, on the burning of Stinsford House, Hardy wrote: "I am sorry for the house. It was where Lady Susan Strangways, afterwards Lady Susan O'Brien, lived so many years with her actor-husband, after the famous elopement in 1764."[2]

Essential facts underlying these allusions are: The first Earl of Ilchester held Stinsford House among his properties. Lady Susan met William O'Brien during private theatricals at Holland House. Though her father disapproved, Lady Susan, on becoming twenty-one in 1764, eloped with O'Brien. The couple went to Canada for some years. Presumably the old Earl partly forgave his daughter in view of

O'Brien's pledge never again to act on a public stage. After the Earl's death, Lady Susan's brother, then Lord Ilchester, gave the house beside Stinsford Church to the O'Briens and secured O'Brien an appointment as Receiver General for Dorset. Lady Susan lived there with her husband, in an affectionate attachment mentioned in all accounts, for the rest of their lives. Horace Walpole's *Letters* (mentioned by Hardy), Boswell-Stone's *Memories and Traditions*, Foster's *Wessex Worthies*, and Evelyn Hardy's *Thomas Hardy* offer additional details about the O'Briens.

1. Pp. 11-12, 213-14; *Life*, pp. 9, 163-64.
2. *Later Years*, pp. 12-13; *Life*, p. 250.

TRYPHENA SPARKS was born at Puddletown, about two miles from Hardy's home in Higher Bockhampton, on March 20, 1851. She was baptized as the daughter of James and Maria Sparks. Since Maria was the elder sister of Hardy's mother, Jemima, Tryphena was understood to be Hardy's cousin.[1] While a boy at home, he was not acquainted with Tryphena, or took little notice of her, as she was eleven years younger than he, still a child when he went to London in 1862. When he returned home in July, 1867, he found Tryphena, then sixteen, attractive and fell in love with her. Other evidence than that of Deacon and Coleman[2] indicates that before Hardy met Emma Lavinia Gifford he was tentatively engaged to another girl. In 1940, Miss Irene Cooper Willis, a friend of Mrs. Florence Hardy and lawyer for the Trustees of the Hardy Estate, speaking of Hardy's love for Emma, wrote: "Their love . . . at the beginning was so irresistible that Hardy broke off an understanding that there had been between him and a girl of his own countryside, and bestowed upon Emma the ring intended for the discarded maiden. Mrs. Hardy told me this."[3] Deacon and Coleman provide evidence that the "discarded maiden" was Tryphena Sparks.

In 1869-71, Tryphena attended Stockwell Training College for teachers in London and in 1872 became headmistress of the Plymouth Public Free School. She met Charles Gale of Topsham, near Exeter, and on December 15, 1877, married him, more than three years after Hardy's marriage to Emma.

Hardy took pains to make the break with Tryphena decisive and to conceal his romance with her. In the various printings of "Thoughts of Phena" (the only item of Hardy's extant writings that suggests her name) he blurred the name in several variations. (See the notes on this poem.) *The Early Life* and *The Later Years* published by Florence Hardy make no mention of Tryphena by name. Hardy destroyed many pages of journals, letters, and other papers in his old

[35]

age, and he wrote such instructions in his notebooks as: "Go through E's papers again. . . . Continue to examine and destroy useless old MSS, entries in notebooks, & marks in printed books."[4] Sir Sydney Cockerell, one of Hardy's executors, "promised to prevent the publication of any of Hardy's early letters that might come to life after his death."[5] The instructions were carried out.

Thus nothing was generally known of Hardy's romance with Tryphena until Miss Deacon's investigations that began in 1959. In that year she met Mrs. Eleanor Tryphena Bromell, the eighty-year-old daughter of Tryphena Sparks (Mrs. Charles Gale). Mrs. Bromell, in a series of interviews that lasted until February, 1965, told the story of Tryphena's engagement to Hardy as she had learned it from her mother and exhibited albums of photographs to corroborate what she said.[6]

On this basis, *Providence and Mr Hardy* asserts that in the late summer of 1867 Hardy became Tryphena's lover with the understanding that they would marry, and in the summer of 1868 a child "Randy" (Randal) was born to them. He was in some concealed way cared for by the Sparks family, and while quite young was sent to live in Bristol with Maria Sparks's son Nathaniel, eight years older than Tryphena. The evidence for the existence of Randy, aside from inferences drawn from Hardy's poems and novels, is Mrs. Bromell's identification of the photograph of an adolescent boy as Randy and her answers to subsequent questions. Mrs. Bromell made the identification only a few weeks before her death.[7] No record of the birth of Randy has been found in the registers of Puddletown, Dorchester, or elsewhere.

In 1869-70, Hardy was now and then in London, where Tryphena was in college preparing to be a schoolmistress. His friend Horace Moule was there also. *Providence and Mr Hardy* asserts that Hardy introduced Tryphena to Moule but did not tell him of their engagement. Moule and Tryphena became emotionally "involved," but Hardy did not break with Tryphena on this account or at this time. When she became a schoolmistress in Plymouth, she openly wore Hardy's ring. Hardy met Emma Gifford in 1870 and fell in love with her, but did not at this time break his engagement. In these years, Tryphena had not been able to see much of her son. On Christmas day, 1872, her sister Rebecca married Frederick Payne[8] in Puddletown, but left him immediately to join Tryphena in Plymouth, so that Randy could visit his mother and pass as Mrs. Payne's son. In 1873, Tryphena broke her engagement to Hardy and returned his ring. He gave Emma the ring and married her in 1874.

Presumably, after her marriage to Charles Gale, Tryphena saw little of Randy. The photograph alleged to be of him shows him in adolescence. Perhaps he died shortly afterward; neither a record of his death nor a trace of him as a man has been found. After Tryphena's death on March 17, 1890, Hardy visited her grave and left on it a card reading: "In loving memory, Tom Hardy."[9]

When we consider the startling nature of these theories, their source in the uncertain memory of an elderly woman who (born October 13, 1878) was only eleven years old when her mother died, and the extent to which they rest upon inferences from Hardy's fiction and poetry, we must conclude that there is need for cautious further investigation of Hardy's romance with Tryphena.

1. Deacon and Coleman in *Providence and Mr Hardy* surmise that Tryphena was not Maria Sparks's daughter. This surmise and others, based upon interpretations of Hardy's novels and poems, are so complex and controversial that they are not presented here.

2. See footnote 1 above.

3. "Thomas Hardy," an unpublished, signed typescript in the Colby College Library, p. 4.

4. In the Dorset County Museum.

5. Blunt, *Cockerell*, p. 214.

6. By 1965, Mrs. Bromell was eighty-six, feeble, and (as Deacon and Coleman admit) somewhat wandering in her mind. In the effort to find traces of Tryphena in Hardy's work, Deacon and Coleman have drawn inferences from his novels and poems, interpreting as autobiographical fact situations and actions that may be fiction, and reading these quasi-facts into Hardy's life story.

7. In interviews on January 17 and February 8 and 10, 1965. She died on February 24.

8. So spelled by Deacon and Coleman, but spelled "Paine" on the marriage certificate at Somerset House.

9. Deacon and Coleman, *Providence and Mr Hardy*, passim. See the notes on "My Cicely" and "Thoughts of Phena."

A KEY TO PLACES PROMINENT IN HARDY'S POEMS

This key locates some of the places named in Hardy's poems. Such well-known places as Stonehenge and Salisbury Cathedral, and such cities as Plymouth, Exeter, Bath, Sherborne, and Yeovil are not described. Such details as streets in Dorchester are treated in the notes. Hardy varied his spelling, as Blackmoor and Blackmore, Maumbury and Maembury, Frome and Froom.

BEENY CLIFF is an abrupt cliff nearly a mile long, rising 150 to 200 feet from the sea. Beginning at Pentargan Bay, about a mile northeast of Boscastle, it extends northeastward along the Cornish coast.

BLACK DOWN is a large, somewhat rounded hill 707 feet high, five miles southwest of Dorchester and three miles from the coast. On the crest a monument to Sir Thomas Masterman Hardy of Trafalgar fame is visible for many miles.

BLACKMOOR (BLACKMORE) VALE is a long, wide, somewhat triangular valley that begins some ten miles north of Dorchester. It lies north of the road along Batcombe Hill between Minterne Magna and Evershot. To the east, near Dogbury Gate, the eminence called High Stoy rises, and to the west, north of Evershot Station, is Bubb Down Hill. Blackmoor lies north and east of these hills.

BOCKHAMPTON LANE is a secondary road three and a half miles east of Dorchester, running north from Lower Bockhampton to Higher Bockhampton and into the London Road.

BOSCASTLE is a village on the crest of a steep hill about fifteen miles west of Launceston and half a mile east of the Cornish coast. Boscastle Harbour lies half a mile to the north, where the Valency River runs between cliffs into the sea. The highway through Boscastle Harbour to the village winds around the hill to provide an easy ascent for vehicles, but a narrow, steep lane leads directly to Boscastle.

BOSSINEY is a village on the coast of Cornwall about two and a half miles southwest of Boscastle. From the road between Boscastle and Bossiney, the picturesque coast and the sea are visible across the fields.

BUDMOUTH is Hardy's name for Weymouth.

CASTERBRIDGE is Hardy's name for Dorchester.

COLLITON HOUSE is a grey stone mansion situated beside Glyde Path Road in Dorchester. It faces northwest toward a square, Colliton Park, now occupied by the County Hall, and beyond that the Frome River. (It is Hardy's model for "High Place Hall" in *The Mayor of Casterbridge*.) Plate 77, page 97, of Lea, *Thomas Hardy's Wessex*, pictures Colliton House, now much altered.

CONQUER BARROW is an ancient burial mound about two hundred yards northeast of Max Gate.

DORCHESTER is the county town of Dorset, 123 miles southwest of London. A large number of Hardy's poems are set in Dorchester, with scenes in the churches, on the streets, in nearby fields, and at Max Gate. It is an ancient town, of importance before the coming of the Romans, during their occupation (as many remains testify), and ever since. An agricultural center, especially for the marketing of cattle and sheep, it has industries that include brewing and printing. Its population is now about 13,000.

DURNOVER is Hardy's name for Fordington.

EGDON HEATH is Hardy's name for several heaths or rolling hills and valleys of chalky, relatively poor land, extending eastward from the Bockhamptons to Wareham and Poole Harbour, a distance of about fifteen miles, and southward from Bere Regis to the coast, about ten miles. The western edge of Egdon lies just behind Hardy's birthplace. In his boyhood (as to some extent today) Egdon wore the somber dress of furze, scrubby bushes, and wasteland described in the opening chapter of *The Return of the Native*. Recently portions of it have been used for an Army tank camp and for Winfrith, a center for research in atomic energy; other portions have been forested with pines.

FORDINGTON now usually denotes a southeastern section of Dorchester. Formerly Fordington town and parish, a part of the Duchy of Cornwall, nearly encircled Dorchester on the east, south, and west, including the area of Maiden Castle. Hardy usually called Fordington "Durnover" and included in the term the water-meadows lying east of Dorchester along the Frome River. Fordington Field ("Durnover Great Field and Fort" in "The Alarm") seems to be the area northeast of Maiden Castle.

FROME (FROOM) RIVER, THE, has been called "Hardy's River." It is a small, swift, clear stream that originates near Evershot, about twelve miles northwest of Dorchester, flows through Maiden Newton, partly around and partly through Dorchester, mingles with the Cerne River and goes on to empty into Poole Harbour. Leaving Dorchester, it flows in a tangle of pools and bywaters south of Stinsford Church and Lower Bockhampton.

The junction of the Frome and the Cerne is not a clear one of two rivers flowing together. They join, separate, and rejoin in a maze of streamlets lacing the meadows. Directly east of Dorchester, the river is in two main streams, one through the edge of town and one a few hundred yards farther east. Everyone calls the stream through the edge of town the Frome; some people call the outer stream the Cerne; others call both streams and their bywaters the Frome.

GREY'S BRIDGE is a stone bridge on the London Road across that branch of the Frome (or Cerne) farthest east from Dorchester. (See "The Frome River.") Built by Lora Grey in the eighteenth century, it is described in *The Mayor of Casterbridge*. A photograph of this bridge is presented opposite page 302 of Pinion, *A Hardy Companion*.

HIGH STOY is a wooded hill jutting northward from Batcombe Down into Blackmoor Vale, about nine miles north of Dorchester, near the road between Minterne Magna and Evershot.

HIGHER BOCKHAMPTON is a row of scattered houses (hardly a village) along both sides of a narrow track a quarter of a mile long, leading from Bockhampton Lane to Hardy's birthplace on the edge of Egdon Heath; the birthplace is the last house on the track. It is about a mile and a half from Stinsford Church and two and a half miles from Dorchester.

KING'S HINTOCK is Hardy's name for Melbury Osmund.

KINGSTON MAURWARD was in former times the estate of the lord of the manor in the Stinsford area. It is about a mile and a half northeast of Dorchester, about a quarter of a mile east of Stinsford Church and just north of the Frome River. On the estate are two imposing houses. The older one was built in 1591 as the manor house. A few hundred yards closer to Stinsford Church, a "new" house was built of brick in 1717-20, but following a visit by King George III and his derisive "Brick, brick, brick!" the owner in 1794, William Pitt, M.P., refaced it with Portland stone. It was in Hardy's boyhood called Kingston Maurward House. In April, 1845, William Grey Pitt sold it to Francis Pitney Brounker Martin, Esq., who lived there with his wife, Julia Augusta Martin, until October, 1853, when Hardy was from five to thirteen years old. Mrs. Martin was especially attentive to "Tommy" Hardy, who nourished a romantic attachment for her throughout his adolescence. (See the notes on "Amabel," "The Harvest-Supper," and "To a Well-Named Dwelling.") Both houses are pictured opposite page 15 in Pinion, *A Hardy Companion*.

LEWSDON HILL, about eighteen miles west of Dorchester, rises to some 800 feet, towering over Marshwood Vale to the south.

LOWER BOCKHAMPTON is a village just north of the Frome River and on Bockhampton Lane, about a mile south of Higher Bockhampton; it is a mile and a half from Dorchester.

MAIDEN (MAI DUN) CASTLE is not a castle in the ordinary sense; it is a hill-fort, or extensive ancient earthwork. Located on a high hill nearly two miles southwest of Dorchester, with a commanding view in all directions, it is an oval about a half-mile long and a quarter-mile wide. Its earthworks, in three steep ramparts of sixty feet or more each with fosses between, enclose upwards of a hundred acres. Though it is perhaps 2000 years old, the work of early British tribes, the remains of a Roman temple stand near its center. The name *Maiden* is a corruption of the British *Mai Dun* meaning "strong hill." Hardy's story "A Tryst at an Ancient Earthwork" includes a fine description, and Lea has a picture of it as Plate 198, page 261, of *Thomas Hardy's Wessex*.

MAUMBURY (MAEMBURY) RING (s) is a pre-Roman earthwork shaped like a football stadium about 220 feet long and 160 feet wide. It is in Dorchester between Dorchester cemetery and the town center. The Romans adapted it to be, as Hardy says, "The Cirque of the Gladiators." The ramparts, used as seats for spectators, are mounds about thirty feet high. Besides a description in Chapter XI of *The Mayor of Casterbridge*, Hardy published "Maumbury Ring" in the *Times* on October 9, 1908, reprinted in Orel, *Thomas Hardy's Personal Writings*, pp. 225-31.

MAX GATE is the large, turreted brick house Hardy designed and had built in 1883-85 to be his home for the rest of his life. It was in an open field, but he planted several thousand trees around it that later almost hid it from sight. *The Early Life*, facing page 226, presents a photograph of the house when first built, with Conquer Barrow a few hundred yards in the background. Max Gate is located in the Fordington area of Dorchester, about a mile from town center on the road toward Wareham.

MELBURY OSMUND is a village about thirteen miles northwest of Dorchester, a quarter of a mile west of the road between Dorchester and Yeovil. It is near the park and estate of the Earls of Ilchester. Hardy's mother, Jemina, was born in this village. Lea, *Thomas Hardy's Wessex*, has photographs of Melbury Osmund as Plates 123 and 124 on pages 156 and 158.

MELLSTOCK is Hardy's name for Stinsford.

PILSDON PEN, a hill about nineteen miles northwest of Dorchester, rises to some 800 feet, towering over Marshwood Vale to the south. Its flattened peak was an ancient hill-camp about a quarter of a mile long and an eighth of a mile wide. Tumuli of ancient burials mark this area.

POUNDBURY CAMP is an ancient hill-fort on a hill half a mile northwest of Dorchester. It was the site of Henchard's ruinous "celebration of a national event" in Chapter XVI of *The Mayor of Casterbridge*.

[41]

PUDDLETOWN is a village five miles northeast of Dorchester on the London Road. It was the birthplace of Tryphena Sparks.

PUMMERY (PUMMERIE) is Hardy's name for Poundbury Camp.

RAINBARROW (S) is a group of prehistoric burial mounds or tumuli on a high part of Puddletown Heath (a part of "Egdon"). The mounds are about half a mile southeast of Hardy's birthplace, beside the course of the old Roman Road across the heath. Concerning the name Rainbarrow, "Mr. Hardy thought it had been so named because the farmers used to have their meals on top of it. 'Rain' or 'raven down' means 'to eat voraciously' in the Dorset dialect. It is more probable, however, that it means 'the Raven Hill.' "[1]

1. Zachrisson, *Thomas Hardy as Man, Writer, and Philosopher,* p. 8. Lea has a picture of Rainbarrow taken before the area was reforested, as Plate 62, p. 73, of *Thomas Hardy's Wessex.*

RIDGEWAY (RIDGE-WAY) is the central section of the main road (to some extent following the course of an old Roman Road) between Dorchester and Weymouth. From Ridgeway Hill, about halfway between the towns, one may look down on either town, each about three and a half miles away.

ROMAN ROAD, THE, usually means, in Hardy's references, the course of the old Roman Road leading from Durnovaria (Roman Dorchester) across Puddletown ("Egdon") Heath. This road ran about a quarter of a mile south of Hardy's birthplace, northeastward past Rainbarrow and Rushy Pond.

RUSHY POND is a depression about half a mile southeast of Hardy's birthplace. It is on a high part of Puddletown ("Egdon") Heath, near Rainbarrow and beside the course of the Roman Road. Perhaps the pond, nearly circular in shape, was originally some two hundred feet across, with rushes around the edges but open water in the center. Today silted up, it is little more than a bog. Remains of foundations show that a hut once stood beside it. The heath around the pond is now partly wooded with old and new growth. It seems the original for the pool at "Mistover Knap" in *The Return of the Native.* Deacon, in *Hardy's Summer Romance, 1867,* presents a photograph of Rushy Pond today.

ST. JULIOT RECTORY was the home of Emma Lavinia Gifford when Hardy met her in 1870 and until their marriage in 1874. She was living there with her sister Helen and her brother-in-law, the Reverend Caddell Holder, Rector of St. Juliot Church, which Hardy had been sent to examine for repairs. To reach this rural rectory, one follows Road 3263 northeastward from Boscastle Harbour for about a mile and a half, turns onto a narrow lane that leads easterly, and after about a mile reaches the church and the rectory nearby. Evans, in *The Homes of Thomas Hardy*, presents a photograph of the rectory.

ST. PETER'S CHURCH is the principal church in Dorchester, situated in the center of the town at the Bow, or rounded corner of High West and North Streets. At this point High West becomes High East Street. St. Peter's faces High West and, across it, looks down South Street.

STINSFORD CHURCH, or St. Michael's Church, Stinsford Parish, is about a mile and a half northeast of Dorchester. The parish contains farmlands and three tiny villages: Stinsford House, the vicarage, and a few other buildings north of the church; Lower Bockhampton on the Frome, with the school and postoffice, about half a mile to the east; and Higher Bockhampton a little more than a mile to the northeast.

UNION, THE, in Dorchester, was built in 1836 as the "workhouse" for the paupers of Dorset, governed by a Board of Guardians; in 1930 it was taken over by the Dorset County Council; and in 1948 it came under the rule of the National Health Service. It is no longer a "poorhouse," but is Damers Hospital, used as a geriatric unit (or "old folks' home") of the Dorset County Hospital. During the nineteenth century, it had a "labor ward" for the delivery of pauper children, often of unwed mothers sent there by the magistrates. This is where Fanny Robin goes in Chapter XL of *Far from the Madding Crowd*.

VALENCY (VALLENCY) RIVER, THE, is a small stream in Cornwall that runs westward between hills into Boscastle Harbour.

WEATHERBURY is Hardy's name for Puddletown.

WEST STAFFORD is a tiny village about two and a half miles southeast of Dorchester.

WEYMOUTH is a resort town or small city on the coast seven miles south of Dorchester. Hardy lived in Weymouth in 1869, visited it often, and wrote a number of poems about events there.

WINYARD'S (WYNYARD'S) GAP is a high point in a notch between hills on the road between Dorchester and Crewkerne, about sixteen miles northwest of Dorchester. This road is crossed by a road between the villages of Hallstock and Cheddington. At the crossroads is an old stone inn called Winyard's Gap Inn. Stables for horses indicate that in the nineteenth century it was a coach-stop and a gathering place for hunters and hounds. Though Hardy's "At Wynyard's Gap" says the inn is closed and "To Let," today it is a popular restaurant, with its car park filled each evening. Behind the inn a steep hill rises; its crest is now National Trust property, the site of a memorial to the men of the Wessex Division who died in World War II. Lea in *Thomas Hardy's Wessex* has a photograph of "Wynyard's Gap Inn" as Plate 224, page 297.

YELLOWHAM (YELL'HAM) WOOD is an old wood chiefly of firs, pines, and beeches on the sides and top of Yellowham Hill, about three miles northeast of Dorchester, along both sides of the London Road. It is about two miles from Puddletown and half a mile from Hardy's boyhood home. Within the wood are glades lovely with wildflowers in spring and summer. In a clearing just beyond a curtain of trees north of the road is the original of Fancy Day's home in *Under the Greenwood Tree*. Lea, in *Thomas Hardy's Wessex*, has a photograph of "The Keeper's Cottage, Yellowham Wood" as Plate 100, page 125.

Part One

~~~~~~~~~~~~

Notes on Hardy's Collected Poems

Hardy was writing verses in 1865 and sending them to editors in 1866, but not one was accepted. Perhaps, as Edmund Gosse said, they were not even comprehended: "Fifty years ahead of his time, Mr. Hardy was asking in 1866 for novelty of ideas" foreign to this high-Victorian time.[1] Hardy saved some of the poems written in his London lodgings, and after he had become famous as a novelist and Victorianism itself was looking toward the twentieth century, he published them.

In 1892, when everyone was reading *Tess of the D'Urbervilles*, Hardy was planning his first volume of poems. He entered in his journal: "Title:—'Songs of Five-and-Twenty Years.' Arrangement of the songs: Lyric Ecstasy inspired by music to have precedence." Before 1897, he "had already for some time been getting together the poems which made up the first volume of verse that he was about to publish. In date they ranged from 1865 intermittently onwards, the middle period of his novel-writing producing very few or none, but of late years they had been added to with great rapidity." On February 4, 1897, he jotted down a new title: "Wessex Poems: with Sketches of their Scenes by the Author."[2] *Wessex Poems* appeared during the week of December 11, 1898.

Seventeen of the fifty-one poems were dated in the 1860's. Five were part of a ballad-sequence he had planned in 1875 to treat the Napoleonic wars. Most of the others, no doubt, were those recently written "with great rapidity."

The poems were illustrated with thirty-one "Sketches of their Scenes."[3] Clive Holland says Hardy told him that frequently "ideas presented themselves to his mind in the first instance more in the guise of mental pictures than as subjects for writing down."[4] "Rough sketches" (as Hardy's Preface calls them) or not, the drawings both portray the scenes and express in symbols ideas or feelings essential in the poems. Hardy was not sure they would be understood or liked. He wrote to Edward Clodd on March 29, 1899: "The illustrations to the Wessex Poems, that take your fancy, had for me in preparing them a sort of illegitimate interest—that which arose from their being a novel amusement, & a wholly gratuitous performance which could not profit me anything, and probably would do me harm."[5]

1. "Mr. Hardy's Lyrical Poems," p. 273.
2. *Later Years*, pp. 3, 66, 58; *Life*, pp. 243, 291-92, 285.
3. Hardy had thirty-two drawings in the manuscript, but in publication one drawing, a tailpiece for "The Casterbridge Captains," was omitted.
4. *Thomas Hardy*, p. 60.
5. In the British Museum.

THE TEMPORARY THE ALL is illustrated in *Wessex Poems* with the picture of a sun-dial casting a long shadow. The poem states a theme of Hardy's poems as a whole, that the apparent promise of the future is denied by the realities of that future when it becomes the present. Hardy meditated in 1882, "Since I discovered, several years ago, that I was living in a world where nothing bears out in practice what it promises incipiently . . . . Where development according to perfect reason is limited to the narrow region of pure mathematics, I am content with tentativeness from day to day."[1] Chance leads men to "Mistress, friend, place, aims" they do not freely choose, as in *A Pair of Blue Eyes*: ". . . though Smith was not quite the man Knight would have deliberately chosen as a friend . . . he somehow was his friend. Circumstance, as usual, did it all. . . . Our intimate *alter ego* . . . is really somebody we got to know by mere physical juxtaposition long maintained, and was taken into our confidence, and even heart, as a makeshift." (Chapter XIII.)

The tone of this poem, its imitation of sapphics, and its similarity to poems dated in the later 1860's suggest that period of Hardy's life. If the experiences of the poem are his, the friend "unchosen" can hardly represent Horace Moule, whom Hardy admired through these years; but he may represent Henry Robert Bastow, who was thrown with Hardy in the office of the architect Hicks. Bastow encouraged Hardy in the study of Greek and Latin and perhaps stimulated him in discussions of religion, but Bastow's letters to Hardy when he had gone to London and Bastow had gone to Tasmania are so filled with pious platitudes that Hardy must have been repelled. Bastow found reason to scold Hardy for not replying to his letters.[2]

The "damsel" may be any one of a number of girls who attracted Hardy in his youth and about whom he later wrote poems, possibly Elizabeth Browne or Louisa Harding. The "Tenements uncouth" may be Westbourne Park Villas, where Hardy lived in London while working for the architect Blomfield and where his health declined; and the "visioned hermitage" may represent a vicarage.[3]

Reviewers found "The Temporary the All" puzzling in meter and diction. Hardy added the term "Sapphics" to explain his meter only after the first edition of *Collected Poems*.[4] He later commented "that he often wrote verse in sapphics but intentionally not quite correct —a bad thing to do . . . because then people thought he did not know what sapphics were."[5] The diction of the poem ("chancefulness," "fellowlike," etc.) reflects Hardy's experiments in line with his friend William Barnes's practice of building words on common roots.

1. *Early Life*, p. 201; *Life*, p. 155.

2. In the Dorset County Museum.

3. See *Early Life*, p. 35; *Life*, p. 27, for Hardy's statement that he thought of entering the Church.

4. Purdy, *Thomas Hardy: A Bibliographical Study*, p. 287. The term describes poetry in imitation of the Greek poet Sappho; in strict sapphics, the verse has five feet of which the first and two last are trochees, the second a spondee, and the third a dactyl. Three sapphic verses are followed by an adonic, or short verse with a dactyl and a spondee or trochee. The stanzas are not rimed.

5. Felkin, "Days with Thomas Hardy," p. 32.

AMABEL has been called derivative from various sources. Weber, pointing out Hardy's boyhood fondness for W. H. Ainsworth's novels, suggests that Hardy may have taken the name from "Amabel, the grocer's daughter . . . of *Old St. Paul's*."[1] Brennecke related the poem to the "Tennysonian tradition," saying that, "In its refrain, the iterated name, 'Amabel,' and in its sentimentality it reminds one somewhat of Tennyson's ballad of *Oriana*."[2] The Bible is echoed in "Till the last Trump."[3] The theme of the poem seems a contradiction of Shakespeare's Sonnet 116: "Love's not Time's fool, though rosy lips and cheeks / Within his bending sickle's compass come."

The poem, dated 1865,[4] may reflect Hardy's avid reading of poetry in the earlier 1860's. In the concept of the poem, love rests upon idealization. The parts of the name "Ama-bel" suggest the beloved-beautiful. This concept of love as subjective runs through Hardy's works.[5] The poet has been in love with the woman of his vision, but he asks immediately whether she can inhabit the aged shell he now observes. The negative answer is characteristic of Hardy, who often presents a lovely girl with the meditation that her peach-blossom complexion will fade, her full throat will become stringy, and her vibrant flesh covers a skull.[6] This idea forms the climax of *Two on a Tower* where Swithin, after an absence, is shocked and repelled when he sees that Lady Constantine is an old woman.

Another idea of the poem characteristic of Hardy is that idealization is nature's device for propagating the race. Though a lover knows that a woman's beauty fades when she is past child-bearing, the race must go on. Nature therefore impels the lover to deceive himself. Rejecting the idealistic lure, the lover looks upon Amabel's traits with disillusioned eyes.

Evelyn Hardy has suggested that the poem may be associated with Mrs. Julia Augusta Martin.[7] She was the wife of Francis Pitney Brounker Martin, who on April 23, 1845, purchased the Kingston Maurward manor house, a little more than a mile southwest of Hardy's boyhood home in Higher Bockhampton.[8] When the Martins moved into Kingston Maurward, Hardy was five years old and Mrs.

[49]

Martin was thirty-five. *The Early Life* tells the story of Mrs. Martin's affectionate interest in "Tommy." In 1848, she established a model school in Lower Bockhampton at her own expense, and Hardy "was the first pupil to enter the new school building, arriving on the day of opening" and becoming a favorite. The next year he was sent instead to a Dorchester school. Mrs. Martin was offended, for "under her dignity lay a tender heart, and having no children of her own she had grown passionately fond of Tommy . . . whom she had been accustomed to take into her lap and kiss. . . . He quite reciprocated her fondness" and "his feeling for her was almost that of a lover." He saw her again when he was about ten at a harvest-supper at Kingston Maurward, where she exclaimed, " 'O Tommy, how is this? I thought you had deserted me!' Tommy assured her through his tears that he had not deserted her, and never would desert her." In October, 1853, the Martins moved to London, and Hardy did not see her again until he was twenty-two years old.

In 1862, he paid a call "on the lady of his earliest passion as a child, who had been so tender towards him in those days, and had used to take him in her arms. . . . But the lady of his dreams—alas! To her, too, the meeting must have been no less painful than pleasant."[9]

A typescript of *The Early Life* contains a deleted passage that indicates Hardy's romantic feeling about Mrs. Martin: "Thus though their eyes never met again after his call on her in London, nor their lips from the time when she had held him in her arms, who can say that both occurrences might not have been in the order of things, if he had developed their acquaintance earlier, now that she was in her widowhood, with nothing to hinder her mind from rolling back upon her past?"[10] Evidently, during adolescence Hardy daydreamed of Mrs. Martin in lover-like fashion, and was shocked to realize in 1862, when she was fifty-two, that she was an old woman.

That Mrs. Martin sensed his shock is revealed in a one-sided correspondence—five letters from her to Hardy between his visit and May 11, 1887. The earlier letters address Hardy as "Dear Tommy" and "Dear Tom," but the last one seems to apologize for the familiarity: "Considering I taught you your letters I can't call you Mr. Hardy." Inviting Hardy to call again, the letters suggest Mrs. Martin's awareness that her age has kept him away. A letter of April 21 says: "For an old woman I am very brisk," and the last letter is signed: "Your old withered up friend, A. Martin."[11]

These facts need not suggest callousness on Hardy's part. Perhaps he was so hurt by the sight of Mrs. Martin in decay and her realization of his shock that he would not risk a repetition. If "Amabel," not published until after Mrs. Martin's death, may be associated with her, we may surmise Hardy's purpose in writing it. Perhaps to crush a feeling that it would be painful to drag out, he wrote the poem as a caricature exaggerating Mrs. Martin's symptoms of old age. It is the method of killing love in Hardy's poem "The Caricature."[12]

"Amabel" has been set to music in the series *Before and After Summer* (London: Boosey and Hawkes, 1949).

1. "Ainsworth and Thomas Hardy," p. 197.
2. *The Life*, p. 122.
3. I Cor. 15:52, ". . . at the last trump: for the trumpet shall sound, and the dead shall be raised."
4. The date on the manuscript is 1866.
5. It is stated by Fitzpiers in *The Woodlanders*, Chapter XVI, and is the theme of the novel *The Well-Beloved* and the poem "The Well-Beloved."
6. Hardy drew an hour-glass as tailpiece for the poem in *Wessex Poems*, suggesting that aging is a running out of the sands toward death, even if the soul, the pictured butterflies, is outside time. See frontispiece of this volume.
7. *Thomas Hardy*, p. 65.
8. For a picture of Kingston Maurward, see Evelyn Hardy, *Thomas Hardy*, p. 26.
9. *Early Life*, pp. 20-25, 53-54; *Life*, pp. 16-20, 41.
10. The typescript, in the Dorset County Museum, is labelled "Mrs. Hardy (Personal Copy)." The clause "now that she was in her widowhood" is puzzling. Her husband did not die until 1892. Hardy was in his eighties when he prepared notes for his biography. Perhaps he then recalled his adolescent fantasy so vividly that he forgot the facts, and then deleted the passage when he came upon a letter from Mrs. Martin dated July 16 [1875?] that said: "Mr. Martin unites in kind regards and best wishes."
11. Evelyn Hardy, *Thomas Hardy's Notebooks*, pp. 123-29.
12. The suggestion may have come from Shakespeare. Hamlet seeks to destroy his love for Ophelia by verbally caricaturing her.

HAP is a sonnet expressing an idea not entirely original with Hardy. No doubt his reading of *The Origin of Species* underlies the poem. As Lionel Stevenson says, "The Darwinian theory of 'natural selection' was generally held to be synonymous with accident, in that it proclaimed the mere freak of chance as determining who should survive and who perish."[1] Tennyson, expressing a similar reaction to evolution, had pictured a meaningless universe in which the stars run blindly and nothing in the cosmos cares for man.[2] Tennyson willed to reject this vision, but Hardy could not.

The thought of "Hap" needs to be examined in the light of Hardy's comments. The poem presents the Doomsters, Crass Casualty[3] and dicing Time[4] as mechanical processes, purposeless and "purblind" to human hope or suffering. As the opening stanza implies, these processes are not "vengeful": they are indifferent. They "had [might have] as readily strown / Blisses about my pilgrimage as pain." Hardy objected when critics read his terms to mean evil, hostile, or even stupid. In his copy of Hedgcock's *Thomas Hardy, Penseur et*

[51]

Artiste, which translated "Crass Casualty" as "stupide contingence," Hardy underscored "stupide" and wrote in the margin: "insensible ('Crass' in original)."[5] Brennecke, in *The Life of Thomas Hardy*, page 124, commented that "Hap" expressed "the essential malignity of chance and circumstance." Hardy, in his copy, underscored "essential malignity" and wrote in the margin: "false (vide supra)"—see what the poem says of "Blisses." In May, 1865, at about the period of the poem, Hardy wrote: "The world does not despise us; it only neglects us."[6]

The poem says that the poet's "best hope ever sown" still "unblooms,"[7] but does not identify this hope. Other poems of the 1860's suggest a blighted love; on June 2, 1865, Hardy wrote: "Not very cheerful. . . . Wondered what woman, if any, I should be thinking about in five years' time."[8] More likely, Hardy's disappointed hope concerned his failure to find a publisher for poems on which he "had worked long and hard. . . . His evening hours of toil had been spent with joy and gladness, with 'the best hope ever sown'—that of achieving publication and subsequent renown. But nothing 'got published.'"[9]

Probably one reason for the rejection of Hardy's poems is that, to achieve truth and strength, he adopted the cacophony of Browning's verse. "That thy love's loss is my hate's profiting" has the gnarled compactness of Browning's "Irks care the crop-full bird?" Words like "unblooms" and phrases like "for gladness" are stronger than "blooms not" and "instead of gladness," but they did not seem poetic to mid-Victorian editors.

Hardy's symbolism was unfamiliar. The image of "dicing Time" can be read today in the light of *The Return of the Native*, where "Venn, plot-wise an agent of fate, symbolically Fate itself, sits [dicing] 'with lips impassively closed and eyes reduced to a pair of unimportant twinkles.'"[10]

The poem has been set to music by Hubert James Foss in *Seven Poems by Thomas Hardy* (London: Oxford University Press, 1925).

1. *Darwin Among the Poets*, pp. 266-67.
2. *In Memoriam*, lyrics III and LIV-LVI.
3. Chance, the title of the poem in manuscript.
4. Events in a senseless sequence.
5. V. H. Collins's copy of Hedgcock's book, pp. 43-44, in the Colby College Library; Collins copied Hardy's comments.
6. *Early Life*, p. 63; *Life*, p. 48.
7. Hardy's "un-" as a prefix indicates the negative to be absolute: "unblooms" means "shows no sign of bud or bloom."
8. *Early Life*, p. 65; *Life*, p. 50.
9. Weber, *Hardy of Wessex*, 2nd ed., p. 54.
10. Anderson, "Time, Space, and Perspective," p. 201; *The Return of the Native*, Book Third, Chapter VIII.

"IN VISION I ROAMED" presents the unimportance of man in a "Universe taciturn and drear," but the poem turns from this vision to the human concern with home and a loved one.

The poem states no particular stimulus for Hardy's vision. He had seen Donati's Comet in 1858 and an eclipse of the moon in 1860. No doubt his reading in the sciences—in biology, which extended his view of human life into a shocking past, and in astronomy, which treated the "ghast" expanse of the universe—interpreted the cosmic phenomena he had seen and for a time helped him subjugate personal cares to philosophy. Swithin remarks in *Two on a Tower* that if "you are restless and anxious about the future, study astronomy. . . . Your troubles will be reduced amazingly. But your study will reduce them in a singular way, by reducing the importance of everything." Swithin goes on to say, however, that this attitude is humanly sterile: "It is better—far better—for men to forget the universe than to bear it clearly in mind!" (Chapter IV.) Hardy neither forgot the universe nor bore it unduly in mind. The sestet of the sonnet turns from the "ghast heights of sky" to the Earth, as in the Preface of *Two on a Tower* Hardy stated his intention "to set the emotional history of two infinitesimal lives against the stupendous background of the stellar universe," but to show that "of these contrasting magnitudes the smaller might be the greater to them as men."

The poem is dedicated "To——," with no indication of the person addressed. If the poem was stimulated by the memory of Donati's Comet, the person may be Hardy's mother, his sister Mary, or some Dorset sweetheart.

AT A BRIDAL appeared in *Wessex Poems* without the subtitle "Nature's Indifference," but addressed "To——." The sonnet may present an actual incident, the marriage of a woman who had jilted Hardy for a socially better match. Possibly he had in mind Mary Waight of Dorchester; it is reported that he proposed to her in 1862, but was rejected. (At that time, he was twenty-two, and Miss Waight was twenty-nine.) In 1865, she married George Stroud Oliver; it is not known that Hardy attended the wedding. That the poem mentions "Mode's decree" suggests that the bridegroom was financially better off than Hardy. After Mary Waight's marriage, "the couple first lived in Trinity Street, Dorchester, but later at 1 West Walks, Dorchester. This house was full of treasures, beautiful china, glass and antique furniture."[1]

In some theories of evolution (as Tennyson's in the "Epilogue" of *In Memoriam*) the process is Nature's device for the improvement of the race. Such was the "dream" of "At a Bridal." "I" would wed to fulfil Nature's (Love's) design for "high-purposed children." But the subtitle and Nature's answer deny that evolution is purposive.

The poem links two themes, first, that marriage according to "Mode's decree" (for wealth, rank, and fashion) defeats the dream of rationally guided evolution; and second, that Nature has no purpose—otherwise, the impulses for mating would sweep aside questions of "Mode." Thus, in spite of the subtitle and Nature's answer that concludes the poem, the event seems to present *human* indifference to eugenic mating. The poem seems to attack the class-system of Victorian society. It anticipates Hardy's *The Poor Man and the Lady*[2] and such incidents as Grace's socially motivated rejection of Giles in *The Woodlanders*. In *Jude the Obscure*, picturing Jude's thought about Sue, Hardy wrote: "He projected his mind into the future, and saw her with children more or less in her own likeness around her. But the consolation of regarding them as a continuation of her identity was denied to him, as to all such dreamers, by the wilfulness of Nature in not allowing issue from one parent alone. Every desired renewal of an existence is debased by being half alloy. 'If at the estrangement or death of my lost love, I could go and see her child—hers solely—there would be comfort in it!' said Jude." (Part III, Chapter VIII.)

1. Oliver, *Thomas Hardy Proposes to Mary Waight*, p. 8.
2. See *Early Life*, pp. 75-83; *Life*, pp. 58-63; and *An Indiscretion in the Life of an Heiress*.

POSTPONEMENT, like other poems and proposed stories,[1] projects the young man of the poem into the situation, feeling, and speech of a lonesome bird. In a conversation with V. H. Collins on December 27, 1920, Hardy explained the last stanza:

"H: You see, earlier in the poem the young man [in fact, the bird] is described as not being able to marry for want of money; and the woman as not waiting, but marrying someone else.

"C: I understand that. The 'being born to an evergreen tree' means, then, simply and solely having money?

"H: Yes."[2]

The young man presumably represents Hardy, who in 1866 was twenty-six, had courted a variety of girls, but had too little money to marry in comfort. It is not known whether the poem refers to any particular girl who proved fickle because he was poor.

1. See Number Five in Evelyn Hardy, "Plots for Five Unpublished Short Stories," p. 34.
2. Collins, *Talks with Thomas Hardy*, p. 23.

A CONFESSION TO A FRIEND IN TROUBLE was titled in the manuscript "To a Friend in Trouble (a confession of selfishness)." The friend has been identified as Horace Mosley Moule.[1] The poem reveals both Hardy's imaginative compassion that made him feel the pain of others as his own and his tendency to shrink from pain. Just as he did not like to be touched physically, he did not like to be touched emotionally by another's distress. In the original title, Hardy labelled this variety of compassion selfishness. With his moral reason he called the instinct "lawless" and found its presence in his nature a bitter fact.

The "trouble" of this poem, dated seven years before Moule's suicide in 1873, possibly concerns religion. Some evidence suggests that Moule, member of a deeply religious family, was shaken by doubt in the 1860's. Early in their acquaintance, Moule introduced Hardy to scientific and philosophical books that questioned orthodox beliefs. Hardy's copy of Jabez Hogg's *Elements of Experimental and Natural Philosophy* is inscribed "T. Hardy, from his friend Horace, 1857." In commenting upon his talks with Moule, Hardy mentions "the newly published [1860] *Essays and Reviews* by 'The Seven Against Christ,' as the authors were nicknamed."[2] Moule was a writer for the *Saturday Review*, which published a good deal on the conflict between orthodoxy and science in the 1860's. It seems that Moule, drawn toward agnosticism, sought to support his faith by turning toward the Roman Church. Hardy, in a letter to his sister Mary on August 17, 1862, wrote: "H. M. M. was up the week before last. We went to a Roman Catholic Chapel on the Thursday evening." Hardy's diary for July 2, 1865, records: "Worked at J. H. Newman's *Apologia*, which we have all been talking about lately. A great desire to be convinced by him, because Moule likes him so much. . . . Only—and here comes the fatal catastrophe—there is no first link to his excellent chain of reasoning, and down you come headlong."[3] Perhaps Moule came down headlong at this time, and "A Confession to a Friend in Trouble" may indicate his despair. The poem suggests a discussion that Hardy pursued with "zeal." At the time Hardy wrote the poem Moule was "far away," and perhaps Hardy was brooding over the fruit of his zeal.

1. Purdy, *Thomas Hardy: A Bibliographical Study*, p. 97.
2. *Early Life*, p. 43; *Life*, p. 33.
3. *Early Life*, pp. 50, 63-64; *Life*, pp. 38, 48.

NEUTRAL TONES has the effect of an etching in steel by a man trained in drawing the ruins of old churches, as Hardy was. The ruins of the poem are those of passionate love, disillusioned, embittered, and etched on the memory in images of nature in winter. The movement of the poem is from the scene as it scored its images upon the mind anesthetized by despair, to the contemplation of these images in their universal meanings—from a sun whitened "as though chidden of God" and leaves "fallen from an ash," to a "God-curst sun" and the dead leaves lying there. The ash tree (with its suggestion of ashes in the name) was an ancient symbol of happiness. But its once-green leaves have decayed into the "neutral" grayish.

The intensity of this etching and the particularity of its images suggest that it presents Hardy's actual experience. The pond seems the same as that treated in "At Rushy-Pond." Deacon and Coleman have suggested that the poem presents a crisis in Hardy's love for Tryphena Sparks. The poem is dated 1867 and, according to Purdy,[1] was written at Hardy's lodgings in London in that year, before he returned to Higher Bockhampton and met Tryphena. "But," say Deacon and Coleman, "perhaps this indicates not the year in which it was composed but the year in which Hardy and Tryphena became lovers, a year of hopefulness at first, but one which led to the despair of 1871."[2] Such evasive dating, perhaps to conceal the fact, is a possibility.

In his novels Hardy often summarized a disaster by presenting the scene etched on a character's memory. In *Desperate Remedies*, Cytherea faints when her father falls from a scaffold; as she recovers, the scene is etched on her mind: ". . . her eyes caught sight of the south-western sky, and, without heeding, saw white sunlight shining in shaft-like lines from a rift in a slaty cloud. . . . Even after that time any mental agony brought less vividly to Cytherea's mind the scene from the Town Hall windows than sunlight streaming in shaft-like lines." (Chapter I, 3.) When Elfride, in *A Pair of Blue Eyes*, confesses to Knight her former love for Stephen Smith, "The word fell like a bolt, and the very land and sky seemed to suffer. . . . The scene was engraved for years on Knight's eye: the dead and brown stubble, the weeds among it, the distant belt of beeches shutting out the view of the house, the leaves of which were now red and sick to death." (Chapter XXXIV.) On discovering the loss of his sheep, Gabriel in *Far from the Madding Crowd* "raised his head, and wondering what he could do, listlessly surveyed the scene. By the outer margin of the pit was an oval pond, and over it hung the attenuated skeleton of a chrome-yellow moon. . . . The pool glittered like a dead man's eye. . . . All this Oak saw and remembered." (Chapter V.)

1. *Thomas Hardy: A Bibliographical Study*, p. 98.
2. *Providence and Mr Hardy*, p. 82.

SHE AT HIS FUNERAL is the dramatic soliloquy of a girl at the funeral of a lover to whose family she is a stranger. Hardy's drawing in *Wessex Poems* emphasizes her isolation. She is standing outside the southwest wall of Stinsford Churchyard peering over it. Her shadow cast along the wall by the afternoon sun perhaps symbolizes her regret that "consumes like fire." The term "regret" suggests some responsibility for her lover's death.

The published date is "187–," and Hardy listed the poem under "Written in 1873" in a notebook labelled "A Chronological List of Thomas Hardy's Works."[1] This date suggests the funeral of Horace Moule, though Moule was buried in Fordington rather than Stinsford. If the funeral is that of Moule, disguised by the shift in place, possibly the girl is the "lady of title" to whom Moule is said to have been engaged, or possibly she represents Tryphena Sparks. Deacon and Coleman suggest that Moule was involved with her in a way to threaten the friendship of Hardy and Moule and perhaps to contribute to the latter's suicide. For details about these possible identifications, see the notes on "Standing by the Mantelpiece."

1. In the Dorset County Museum.

HER INITIALS condenses almost to an epigram the thought of "Amabel": that the lover idealizes, time passes, and love fades. The four concluding lines use images of light to define the process. In *Wessex Poems* Hardy pictured the "poet's page" as an open book of squiggles with two indecipherable initials in the left margin; the initials "T. H." at the end of the pages seem to be Hardy's signature on the drawing.

HER DILEMMA dramatizes the conflict between two moral rights: truth (honesty) and compassion. "The 'dilemma' which Nature has devised is the mismating of 'the human pair,' . . . which is at the center of all Hardy's fiction."[1] The Church, teaching both moralities without reconciling them, offers no help. It is a "sunless church" with "mildewed walls."

Hardy's drawing for this poem pictures in cross-section the interior of a church, the lovers, and beneath their feet, coffins, bones, and skulls, seeming to say, "What does abstract truth matter?" Thus the woman felt: " 'Twas worth her soul to be a moment kind."

The subtitle " (In ––– Church)" suggests an actual church and possibly an actual incident. Miss Deacon surmises that "Hardy's drawing is of the south aisle of Fordington St. George Church" and that "the man and the woman of Hardy's poem are Horace Moule and Tryphena [Sparks]." She surmises that when Tryphena went to London to attend Stockwell Training College in 1869, Hardy confided her "to the care and tutelage of his old bachelor friend, Horace

Moule, who . . . about twenty years Tryphena's senior, could guide her in her reading and generally help her" and that Moule fell in love with Tryphena, who did not love him. In this theory, the scene takes place in the church where Moule's father was vicar, at some time after Moule had determined upon suicide.

Hardy's date for the poem, 1866, contradicts this theory, but Miss Deacon says that "several poems in this first volume of Hardy's are ante-dated by about one to ten years" to conceal the identity of the characters.[2] (See the notes on "Standing by the Mantelpiece.")

1. Tuttleton, "Thomas Hardy and the Christian Religion," p. 80.
2. *The Moules and Thomas Hardy*, pp. 130, 125.

REVULSION is evidently a sonnet of self-analysis; it states in part a thought and feeling that runs through Hardy's poetry and fiction. For him, love begins in the sight of beauty, impulse, idealization, and dream, but ends in the decay of beauty, pain and death. The young man's problem is whether the ecstasy of love is worth the probable pain of love's decay.

THE "SHE, TO HIM" SONNETS

These sonnets were "part of a much larger number which perished."[1] The intensity and coherence of the sonnets suggest that the "perished" ones might have filled out an interesting story.

In *Wessex Poems*, Hardy introduced them with a drawing of the eastern slope of a darkening hill topped by a monument; behind the hill the sun is sinking. In the foreground two dim figures follow a winding path downward. The hill resembles Black Down. A road winds down its eastern slope in fact as well as in the symbolism of Hardy's drawing.

Critics have commented upon the "She, to Him" sequence as written under the spell of Shakespeare's sonnets, with some differences from Shakespeare's concluding couplets; "it was wanton of Hardy to refuse the couplet" in three of the four poems.[2] The substance is characteristic of Hardy in its analysis of a woman's emotions and (if he may be considered the false lover) an instance of his tendency to feel more the pain of others, especially when responsible for it, than his own.

Lois Deacon has identified the woman of the poems as Tryphena Sparks, the lover as Hardy, and the situation as his rejection of Tryphena when he discovered she had allowed the advances of his friend Horace Moule. In this pattern sonnet IV represents Tryphena's reaction to Hardy's courtship of Emma Gifford.[3] This identification requires the assumption that Hardy predated the sonnets 1866 to conceal events of his personal life that occurred later.

1. *Early Life*, p. 71; *Life*, p. 54.
2. Duffin, *Thomas Hardy*, p. 330.
3. Deacon, *Hardy's Sweetest Image*, pp. 21-22.

She, to Him, I presents a woman forsaken by her lover, remembering the terms in which he "lauded" her beauties. She shares with Hardy a typical thought: in the lonely years to come her beauties will fade. She does not plead for renewal of love, for pity, or even for compassion, but feels that she deserves friendship on the sunless downward way.

She, to Him, II does seem to ask for pity, not while the woman lives and may feel its condescension, but when she is dead. It will be a step toward justice if her lover will then understand that she loved more deeply than the thin impulse which prompted his "I do," and will grant her a sigh: "Poor Jade."

Purdy says that "The MS. adds at the end, 'Prosed in "Desperate Remedies." ' "[1] The passage seems to be that in which Miss Aldclyffe, describing to Cytherea man's fickleness in love, says: "You, as the weary, weary years pass by will fade and fade—bright eyes *will* fade—and you will perhaps then die early. . . . Whilst he, in some gay and busy spot far away . . . will long have ceased to regret you . . . will say, 'Ah, little Cytherea used to tie her hair like that.' " (Chapter VI, 1.)

1. *Thomas Hardy: A Bibliographical Study*, p. 98. See also the August, 1912, Preface of the novel.

She, to Him, III is more than the woman's vow to be faithful to her fickle lover. It is a statement that she cannot be otherwise. The intensity of her feeling is expressed in the image of her heart "Numb as a vane that cankers on its point." Blackmur called this "one of the best tropes Hardy ever produced and perhaps the only one of similar excellence in its kind."[1]

1. "The Shorter Poems," p. 26.

She, to Him, IV presents the jilted woman's bitter reflection that her successful rival cannot feed the heart of her lover as she, the speaker, might do. It is an interesting rationalization that jealously on this basis is a virtue.

DITTY is inscribed with the initials of Emma Lavinia Gifford, whom Hardy met in March of 1870, and with whom he promptly fell in love. He described his state of mind during the following months in London: "He seems to have passed the days in Town desultorily and dreamily—mostly visiting museums and picture-galleries, and it is not clear what he was waiting for there. In his leisure he seems to have written the 'Ditty' in *Wessex Poems*."[1]

The poem presents the rural isolation of St. Juliot, its tiny church (which Hardy, as architect's assistant, had gone to St. Juliot to "restore"), and its rectory with "walls of weathered stone," where Miss Gifford lived with her sister and brother-in-law. Hardy was attracted to Miss Gifford by her painting, her music, and most of all her vitality —her daring horsemanship along the picturesque cliffs of Cornwall.[2] " 'She was so living,' he used to say. In the poem 'Ditty' he called her 'a Sweet,' not a Beauty."[3]

The poem, in which there is no pain, lacks the intensity of passion of the "She, to Him" sequence or the later "Poems of 1912-13" concerned with Emma. It is characteristic of Hardy in meditating the slender chance that led him to her door: "What bond-servants of Chance / We are all." Various critics have called this early poem derivative from Hardy's reading: Duffin, that it "is in a Browning measure,"[4] and Brennecke that William Barnes's " 'Maid o' Newton' may well have provided its formal inspiration."[5] In his copy of Brennecke's book Hardy wrote opposite this passage: "untrue."[6]

"Ditty" was set to music by Gerald Finzi in *A Young Man's Exhortation* (Oxford University Press, 1933).

1. *Early Life*, p. 101; *Life*, p. 76.
2. Elfride in *A Pair of Blue Eyes* reflects the traits in Emma that attracted Hardy.
3. Weber, *Hardy's Love Poems*, p. 16.
4. *Thomas Hardy*, p. 304.
5. *The Life of Thomas Hardy*, p. 135.
6. In the Dorset County Museum.

THE SERGEANT'S SONG, with the date 1803 under the title, is assumed to have been sung then, when Englishmen feared that Napoleon would invade and derided the idea. Hardy's drawing in *Wessex Poems* presents the head-and-shoulders of Napoleon in a cloud that looms above a rank of bayonets.

The poem was first published in Chapter V of *The Trumpet-Major*. There, at a jolly party, Sergeant Stanner of the —th Foot, who was recruiting at Budmouth, sang the first three stanzas of the song. (It is stated that he sang thirteen stanzas, though they are not given.) Then Festus Derriman entered and sang the fourth stanza, "which had been omitted by the gallant Stanner, out of respect for the ladies." In this way, the song serves to characterize the brash Festus.[1]

The refrain imitates that of early English folk-songs. When the

Dorchester Debating and Dramatic Society produced *The Trumpet-Major* as a play in London in 1912, "The Sergeant's Song" was set to music by Harry Pouncy and Boynton Smith; the song and music were printed in the program and later in *The Yearbook of Dorset Men in London* for 1913-14. (Pp. 130-31.) Other musical settings for the song are by Gustav Holst (London: Edwin Ashdown, 1923), Hubert James Foss (in *Seven Poems by Thomas Hardy*, London: Oxford University Press, 1925), Gerald Finzi (in *Earth and Air and Rain*, London: Boosey & Hawkes, 1936), Frederick Keel (London: J. B. Cramer & Co., 1938), and Christopher Fleming (London: Novello & Co., 1963).

1. Purdy points out that in *The Trumpet-Major* as published in 1880, "only the first stanza (sung by Sergeant Stanner. . .) and the last (sung by Festus Derriman) were given then. . . . Stanzas 2 and 3 were added in later editions." *Thomas Hardy: A Bibliographical Study*, p. 99.

VALENCIENNES reflects Hardy's lifelong interest in the French Revolution and the Napoleonic wars. As a boy, he heard the stories told of his grandfather, Thomas Hardy the First, who had served as a Volunteer, and read an illustrated periodical discovered in a closet, *A History of the Wars*. This interest bore its most substantial fruit in *The Dynasts*, but this epic-drama was the climax of a number of earlier poems and stories and one novel, *The Trumpet-Major*, that treated these wars.

The earlier poems sprang from tales told Hardy by old soldiers. When he was about ten years old he attended a Harvest Supper at Kingston Maurward, and here "began Thomas's extensive acquaintance with soldiers of the old uniforms and long service, which was to serve him in good stead when he came to write *The Trumpet-Major* and *The Dynasts*." When he was thirty, Hardy visited Chelsea Hospital and talked with "old asthmatic and crippled men, many of whom in the hospital at that date had fought at Waterloo, and some in the Peninsula." In June, 1875, he again visited the hospital "and made acquaintance with the Waterloo men still surviving there." During that month he entered in his journal: "Mem: A Ballad of the Hundred Days. Another of Moscow. Others of earlier campaigns—forming altogether an Iliad of Europe from 1789 to 1815." In June of the next year, he visited Chelsea, "where, in the private parlour of 'The Turk's Head' over glasses of grog, the battle [of Waterloo] was fought yet again by the dwindling number of pensioners who had taken part in it."[1] Hardy wrote, as part of his original plan for a series of ballads, "Valenciennes," "San Sebastian," "Leipzig," "The Peasant's Confession," and "The Alarm."

The dates at the end of "Valenciennes" indicate that he began the poem in 1878, perhaps while planning *The Trumpet-Major*, and completed it in 1897, when turning his attention toward *The Dynasts*. As the headnote suggests, the story of the poem is told by "Corp'l Tullidge" in *The Trumpet-Major*. There the corporal, "on the shady side of fifty" about 1803, attends Miller Loveday's entertainment. He is "hard of hearing, and sat with his hat on over a red cotton handkerchief that was wound several times round his head." He keeps his hat on "because his head was injured at Valenciennes, in July, Ninety-three. 'We were trying to bomb down the tower, and a piece of shell struck me. I was no more nor less than a dead man for two days. If it hadn't a been for that and my smashed arm I should have come home none the worse for my five-and-twenty years' service.'" Presumably he had seen service before the French Revolution began and was forty or more at Valenciennes. Anthony Cripplestraw comments upon the surgery that "morticed" the corporal's skull as "a beautiful piece of workmanship." Tullidge returned home in "Ninety-four." (Chapter IV.)

Hardy's inspiration for a story of a deafened soldier may have come from a visit on October 27, 1878: "To Chelsea Hospital and Ranelagh Gardens: met a palsied pensioner—deaf. He is 88—was in the Seventh (?) Hussars." This man was not deafened at Valenciennes in 1793. "He enlisted in 1807 or 1808, served under Sir John Moore in the Peninsula, through the Retreat, and was at Waterloo."[2] Perhaps Hardy combined this pensioner's deafness with some other old soldier's tale of Valenciennes.

His dedication of the poem "In Memory of S. C. (Pensioner). Died 184—" offers a puzzle. Apparently relying upon a footnote identifying an officer's servant at Waterloo as "Samuel Clark; born 1779, died 1857. Buried at West Stafford, Dorset," Purdy identifies "S. C. (Pensioner)" as Samuel Clark of West Stafford,[3] but this man would hardly have fought at Valenciennes in 1793, at the age of fourteen; even if so, he would not have returned to England deaf in 1794, as "Tullidge" did, and then fought at Waterloo in 1815. Hardy says that "S. C. Died 184—." West Stafford is little more than a mile from Kingston Maurward House. Perhaps Samuel Clark attended the Harvest Supper there in 1849 and told tales of the wars that fascinated young Hardy, who perhaps lost sight of Clark after that, supposed he may have died shortly afterwards, and gave the date of the supper as the date of Clark's death. Clark's tales may not have been about Valenciennes. "In Memory of" need not mean "This is his experience." It seems likely that "Valenciennes," the first war-ballad in Hardy's first volume of poems, was the first written, and fitting that it should be dedicated to an old soldier who "began Thomas's extensive acquaintance with soldiers of the old uniforms."

In *Wessex Poems,* Hardy illustrated the poem with a headpiece showing the English fortifications with their cannon turned toward Valenciennes. By 1793, French revolutionary armies had begun attacks upon neighboring nations, and England in alliance with German states and Austria had come to the rescue. This action was not universally approved, as the fourth stanza suggests.

After a defeat at Famars, French forces retired to Valenciennes, and the allied armies followed, built fortifications around the city, and established batteries like those pictured. On June 14, 1793, the allies, under the command of the Duke of York, called upon the French to surrender. When the terms were rejected, the allies began an incessant bombardment. "From the beginning of July, two hundred pieces of cannon played on the town without intermission, and the greater part of it was speedily reduced to ashes."[4] Both sides burrowed under fortifications to plant underground mines. On July 25, at a signal given by the explosion of their mines, the allies launched a major assault. By July 26, so much of Valenciennes was in the hands of the allies that the Duke of York called for the French to surrender, and after a truce of two days they did so.

"Valenciennes" seems a rousing battle-poem, but the aging storyteller is stone deaf and "O' wild wet nights, when all seems sad, / My wounds come back." He fought and lost his hearing for no principle that he understood, but felt "that's not my affair." Feeling alive only in his memory of glorious excitement, he is weary of the world, ready for "Heaven wi' its jasper halls." Subtly, Hardy criticizes war as an evil in which the common soldier is a dupe.

The old soldier is a Dorset countryman who versifies in the singsong stanza of Dorset balladry. An interesting feature of the verse is the dual stanza-form. Alternate stanzas rime aaab and abab—with every stanza ending in the same b, "Valencieën." The words are those of Dorset dialect: "A-topperen" (killing with a blow on the head), "snocks and slats" (smart blows and slaps), and "slent to shards" (smashed to pieces).

When *The Trumpet-Major* was produced by the Dorset Debating and Dramatic Society in 1912, stanzas 2, 7, 8, and 13 of "Valenciennes" were inserted into the play and sung to music written by Boynton Smith.[5]

1. *Early Life,* pp. 25, 103, 139, 140, 146; *Life,* pp. 19, 78, 106, 111.
2. *Early Life,* p. 161; *Life,* p. 123.

3. *The Dynasts*, Part Third, VII, v. Purdy, *Thomas Hardy: A Bibliographical Study*, p. 99.

4. McGregor, *History of the French Revolution*, III, 171. The summary here was taken from pp. 170-75.

5. The music, printed in the program, is in the Dorset County Museum.

SAN SEBASTIAN was one of the "ballads" in Hardy's early plan for treating the Napoleonic wars. (See the notes on "Valenciennes.") It is a retrospective dramatic monologue, except for the first eight lines that ask the question which causes the sergeant to tell his story.

The notation "With thoughts of Sergeant M—— (Pensioner), who died 185—," the setting on the "Ivel Way," and the mention of a "Hintock maypole" suggest that the story is based upon the life of a local veteran, perhaps Sergeant C. Matthews, who "served through the war" in the Dorset Regiment and was awarded a Waterloo Medal. (A "proud career" is mentioned twice in the poem.)[1] The questioner of the first eight lines may represent Hardy himself, fascinated during his teen-age years by stories of the Napoleonic wars. In *The Woodlanders* and elsewhere, the "Hintock" villages include Melbury Osmund, about thirteen miles northwest of Dorchester and near the "Ivel Way," Hardy's name for the road to Yeovil. Parish records do not show that Sergeant Matthews was born or died in Melbury Osmund, though he may have lived there for a while and gone at last to a home for old soldiers.

Or the questioner may represent the Reverend John Jenkins Matthews, rector of the Melbury Osmund church for sixteen years. His name suggests some relationship to Sergeant Matthews. If related, the rector in his double role of relative and parson may well have questioned the sergeant and heard his confession. Coincidentally, the rector had one child, Sabine, who was born in 1838 and lived until 1871, but, as he died in 1855 at the age of fifty-two, he could not have taken part in the battle of San Sebastian. Hardy may have heard the sergeant's story from John Jenkins Matthews, either directly or through his mother, whose family had lived in Melbury Osmund and who had relatives there. Then for dramatic purposes, he may have awarded to the sergeant the one child who was the daughter of the rector. "With thoughts of Sergeant M———" seems flexible enough to allow this surmise.

The scene of the maypole dance is probably "Fiddler's Green" near the "watersplash," a shallow ford where the village road crosses a stream.

In *Wessex Poems*, Hardy illustrated the poem with a drawing of San Sebastian and Mount Urgull seen in the "baffling gloom" of the poem. His account of the battle seems filled out from Napier's *His-*

tory of the War in the Peninsula.[2] A few sentences from this history give details of the kind Hardy used in the poem. Napier defines Hardy's "woe within" that opened the way for the English victory: "A number of powder barrels, live shells, and combustible materials, which the French had accumulated behind the traverses for their defence, caught fire. Soon a bright consuming flame wrapped the whole of the high curtain, a succession of loud explosions were heard, hundreds of the French grenadiers were destroyed, the rest were thrown into confusion. . . . Five hours the dreadful battle had lasted at the walls, and now the stream of war went pouring into the town . . . and a thunder-storm . . . added to the confusion of the fight. This storm seemed to be a signal from hell for the perpetuation of villany [sic] which would have ashamed [sic] the most ferocious barbarians of antiquity. . . . At San Sebastian, the direst the most revolting cruelty was added to the catalogue of crimes,—one atrocity of which a girl of seventeen was the victim, staggers the mind for its enormous, incredible, indescribable barbarity." (Pp. 276-78.)

In the first edition of *Wessex Poems*, Hardy did not include the next-to-the-last stanza, "Maybe we shape our offspring's guise / From fancy . . ." which both introduces the folk-idea of prenatal influence and partly states the theme of the poem: "We are left with the suggestion that his [the sergeant's] tortured conscience is to blame for the fancied resemblance."[3] The theme as a whole, however, includes "the deep melancholy of war, its bestiality, its remorse."[4] In retrospect, perhaps in "confession" to his rector, the sergeant feels himself marked "with a God-set brand / Like Cain's."[5] A review of *Wessex Poems* in the Glasgow *Herald* for January 4, 1899, said: "It is only a poet like Mr. Hardy who could have thought of touching such a curious point in moral physiology."[6] Someone, presumably Hardy, underscored this sentence in red.

1. Information from Lieutenant-Colonel D. V. W. Wakely of the Military Museum in Dorchester.
2. The edition of Napier that was in Hardy's library and is now in the Dorset County Museum is dated 1892. Hardy may have written the poem before this date, using an earlier edition not his own, or he may have written or revised it after 1892. In a letter of January 26, 1918 (in the Dorset County Museum), Edmund Gosse asked Hardy: "Am I right in conjecturing that 'Leipzig' and 'San Sebastian,' which are not dated, were written in 1878 or '77?" I have seen no reply.
3. Firor, *Folkways in Thomas Hardy*, p. 122.
4. Duffin, *Thomas Hardy*, p. 319.
5. Gen. 4:15, "And the Lord set a mark upon Cain, lest any finding him should kill him."
6. In the scrapbook labelled "Reviews of T. H.'s Books Poetry" in the Dorset County Museum.

THE STRANGER'S SONG was first published as part of the short story "The Three Strangers" in *Longman's Magazine* for March, 1883. It was then extracted and published as "The Hangman's Song" in W. D. Adams, ed., *Songs from the Novelists* (London: Ward and Downey, 1885).

In the story, the song reveals to a convicted sheep-stealer the identity of the hangman. Timothy Sommers, sentenced to be hanged, has escaped from jail and, not recognized, found refuge from a storm in a shepherd's house. The hangman, on his way to Casterbridge to hang Sommers the next morning, also comes in from the storm. As the two men, who have never seen one another, carouse together, the hangman sings the song. Shortly afterward, Sommers's brother enters, recognizes both Sommers and the hangman, and flees. Supposing the brother to be the sheep-stealer, the hangman and the shepherd's guests go in search of the brother, and Sommers escapes.

Hardy dramatized the story as *The Three Wayfarers*, which was produced by Charles Charrington at Terry's Theatre in London on June 3, 1883. For the play, the tune of the song was "a traditional one in the County of Dorset, and very old."[1] Later, H. Balfour Gardiner published music for *The Stranger's Song* (London: Boosey and Co., 1903).

1. Davis, "The Music of Thomas Hardy," p. 73. The Dorset County Museum has Hardy's typed "correct private copy" of *"The Three Wayfarers Play in One Act* by Thomas Hardy, with tune of song; & dance figures."

THE BURGHERS, dated "17——" and set in Dorchester, may be based on fact. G. S. Churchill of London, on October 6, 1921, wrote to Hardy: "With reference to your poem 'The Burghers' (Casterbridge 17——) I should be very greatly obliged if you could kindly let me know if the poem is founded on fact and, if so, were any of the Churchills of Colliton House, Dorchester, involved in this episode?" Hardy's reply, to be signed by Mrs. Hardy, said: "He [Hardy] is sorry to say that his poem 'The Burghers' having been written between 20 & 30 years ago he can only recall in the vaguest manner the circumstances connected with his writing it. All he can remember is that Colliton House was in his mind as the scene of the enactment. It is quite possible that the story was an invention; yet after reading it over at this distance of time there seems to be some slight tradition associated with C. H. at the foundation of it."[1]

In presenting the action, Hardy almost maps out Dorchester. The drawing that precedes the poem, in *Wessex Poems*, shows a man in eighteenth-century costume, perhaps the "nearing friend" of the second stanza, walking up High West Street toward Glyde Path Road at sunset.[2] High West Street runs from the center of Dorchester straight west, with Glyde Path Road running off from it to the north about halfway between St. Peter's Church and the "Top o' the Town."

The opening line means from sunrise over Grey's Wood about two miles east (and slightly north) of Dorchester to sunset over Damers Hill (so spelled now, without the apostrophe) directly west of Dorchester on the edge of town. In the third line, the speaker leaves Colliton House and walks a few yards along Glyde Path Road to High West Street.

In the sixth stanza, the "Froom's mild hiss" refers to the River Frome,[3] which semicircles the town, flowing into Dorchester from the base of Poundbury[4] and around the east side of Gallows Hill. The "Gibbet" once stood on Gallows Hill[5] in the Fordington area of southeast Dorchester, near the junction of South Walks and Icen Way.

The "pleasaunce hard by Glyd'path Rise" is the garden of the mansion called Colliton House, situated on a hill beside Glyde Path Road. Formerly an arched door in a side-wall opened onto Glyde Path Road.[6] The latter half of the poem mentions the doorway and suggests the wealth of the family living in Colliton House. At the end the lovers go northward and then westward on curving Glyde Path Road and vanish across a field (a "haw").

The time of the lovers' rendezvous is indicated by "Three hours past Curfew" and "Eleven strokes." The bells of St. Peter's Church formerly rang curfew at eight o'clock and struck the hours.

In the second stanza the Old Testament attitude of "an eye for an eye" is suggested in the reference to "those the furnace held unshent," from the Book of Daniel.[7] St. Peter's bells, perhaps, form part of the "something" that held the husband's arm and drew him toward the merciful attitude of the New Testament. Perhaps Hardy, who in 1921 had forgotten his source for the poem written "between 20 & 30 years ago," wrote the poem when he was working on *Jude the Obscure*, in which the characters Phillotson and Gillingham belong to the class of burghers. Gillingham's attitude is that of the "friend" in the poem, and Phillotson's is that of the husband—attained in somewhat the same way. Phillotson tells Gillingham: ". . . in the first jealous weeks of my marriage, before I had come to my right mind, I hid myself in the school one evening when they were together there, and I heard what they said. I am ashamed of it now, though I suppose I was only exercising a legal right. I found from their manner that an extraordinary affinity, or sympathy, entered into their attachment, which somehow took away all flavor of grossness. Their supreme desire is to be together—to share each other's emotions, and fancies, and dreams." (Part IV, Chapter IV.) The last line of the poem expresses an attitude Hardy attributed to Grace Melbury in an earlier novel, *The Woodlanders.* Grace says to Mrs. Charmond: "O, I do pity you, more than I despise you! For *you* will suffer most!" (Chapter XXXIII.)

1. Churchill's letter and a draft of Hardy's reply are in the Dorset County Museum.

2. The main east-west thoroughfare was formerly called East Street and West Street, meeting in the center of the town at South Street. These parts of High Street are now called High East Street and High West Street.

3. The river is now usually spelled Frome.

4. "Pummery-Tout" is now named Poundbury, though locally still called Pummery.

5. The name continues in local usage, though no gallows has stood there for more than a century.

6. This door is described in Chapter XXI of *The Mayor of Casterbridge.*

7. 3:25: "Lo, I see four men loose, walking in the midst of the fire, and they have no hurt."

LEIPZIG is illustrated in *Wessex Poems* with two drawings, a full-page picture of the Markt-Platz of Leipzig seen at dusk, and a tailpiece of a fiddler on the street outside the "Master-tradesmen's Parlour" of the Old Ship Inn in Dorchester ("Casterbridge"), also at dusk. One character seen in silhouette through the lighted window is wearing a flat visored cap and may represent "old Norbert." The poem does not name the tune the fiddler plays reminding Norbert of the song his mother sang and her story of the battle of Liepzig, but, to celebrate the allied victory over Napoleon, it was perhaps "The Fall of Paris."

The Old Ship Inn in Dorchester is a "pub" and small hotel on the south side of High West Street near the Top o' the Town, with its principal bar next to the street. Norbert's "flat blue cap" suggests that he had seen military service and continued to wear this part of his uniform, but, though Norbert is called "old," he had not been born at the time of the battle of Leipzig; his mother "as simple maid / . . . saw these things." The cap may be one his father wore in the years after Waterloo when, as a member of George III's German Legion (the York Hussars), he was stationed near Dorchester.[1] Whether or not Norbert was a real person, the particularity of the narrative suggests Hardy's imaginative interpretation of historical records. The frame (Norbert, his mother, the fiddler, the haunting song) gives romantic distance to the battle. The poem belongs to Hardy's planned ballad-sequence on the Napoleonic wars. (See the notes on "Valenciennes.")

The battle of Leipzig was a great, complex battle, sometimes called "The Battle of the Nations." A defeat for Napoleon, it was a turning point in his career. Since 1808 the German states had been subject to Napoleon; in 1813, led by Prussia, the Germans were in revolt. The King of Saxony, however, had submitted to Napoleon, and before marching to Leipzig to meet the allies, Napoleon had "sat down" in Dresden.[2] The battle is skilfully outlined in the poem.[3] Aside from preliminary skirmishes, it was fought between Napoleon and the allied forces of Russia, Prussia, and Austria, on October 16-19, 1813.

The geography of Leipzig had much to do with the outcome. Leipzig is in a depression just east of the Elster River where it is joined by the Pleisse in some miles of water-meadows, marshes, and bogs. The only effective crossing to the west was a bridge over the river-lands to Lindenau. Napoleon's forces were centered in Leipzig, on which city three hostile armies converged. The "Three Chiefs-at-arms" were Prince Karl Philip Schwarzenberg, field marshal and commander of the Austrian forces; Gebhard Leberecht von Blücher, field marshal and commander of the Prussian forces; and Charles John Bernadotte, Crown Prince of Sweden, in command of the Russian and other northern forces. The combined troops of the allies numbered 325,000, against Napoleon's 214,000.[4] The allies approached Leipzig to surround it in a near-circle extending from the northwest, around the east, and to the southwest. At dusk on October 15, three white rockets were sent up from Schwarzenberg's forces in the southwest, and they were answered with four red ones[5] from Blücher's forces in the northwest. The rockets signalled readiness for the attack that, at 9:00 on the morning of October 16, opened with a furious cannonade. At the end of the first day, losses were perhaps 25,000 men on each side. The nearly equal losses increased the ratio of numerical superiority of the allies, and allied reinforcements were arriving. Victory for the French seemed unlikely, yet the "French held all at bay."

The second day was devoted chiefly to skirmishing, but on the third the French fought stubbornly, a fact Hardy sums up in epic fashion by reciting the names of leaders: Ney; the "true Bertrand," Count Henri Bertrand, an aide-de-camp to Napoleon;[6] Victor, Duke of Bellune; Augerau, Duke of Castiglione; Polish Prince Joseph Poniatowski; and Jacques Law, Marquis of Lauriston (an aide-de-camp).

By the night of October 18, the French were in retreat along the only way open, the bridge across the rivers and marshes to Lindenau. Napoleon had mined this bridge to blow it up when the last French forces had crossed. The colonel of engineers in charge of the operation went to Lindenau to inquire what corps would form the French rear and left the mine in charge of a corporal. Seeing allied troops near-by, even though several divisions of the French remained in the city, he ignited the fuse and blew up their only route of escape. The French troops still in Leipzig fell into panic and plunged by thousands into the river. Some succeeded in crossing, among them Alexandre MacDonald, Duke of Taranto and Marshal of France; others drowned, among them Poniatowski. The remnant of Napoleon's army re-treated toward France.

Characteristically, in the midst of his description of the battle, Hardy inserted a "chorus" of the "old folks" of Leipzig to comment on a battle in which they played no part. He phrased their comment to echo the words of Isa. 2:4, "And he shall judge among the nations . . . and they shall beat their swords into plowshares . . . nation shall not lift up sword against nation, neither shall they learn war any more."

Hardy retold the story of the battle of Leipzig in *The Dynasts*, Part Three, Act Third. In doing so, he made use of stanzas 26 and 27 of the poem as Semichoruses I and II of the Pities in Scene IV; and stanzas 30, 31, 32, and 33 as Semichoruses of the Pities in Scene V. In addition, he used scattered lines from stanzas 6, 11, and 16 in the choruses of Scene II. The wording is altered only slightly.

1. Hardy's "The Melancholy Hussar of the German Legion" tells a story of this Hanoverian regiment in the 1790's before the wars with Napoleon.

2. Saxon allegiance, however, was so lukewarm that on October 18, during the battle of Leipzig, about 35,000 Saxon troops left Napoleon's army and joined the allies.

3. For a military analysis, see Dodge, *Napoleon*, IV, 246-81.

4. The number is uncertain, and it varied as reinforcements arrived. In *The Dynasts* (Part Three, III, i) Murat reports to Napoleon that the French number 190,000, and the allies 350,000.

5. *The Dynasts* says three red ones.

6. Called "true" because he accompanied Napoleon to Elba, returned with him to Waterloo, and went with him to St. Helena.

THE PEASANT'S CONFESSION belongs to Hardy's ballad-sequence on the Napoleonic wars. (See the notes on "Valenciennes.") *The Later Years* says that in the spring of 1898, "Hardy did some reading at the British Museum with a view to *The Dynasts*, and incidentally stumbled upon some details that suggested to him the Waterloo episode embodied in a poem called 'The Peasant's Confession.' "[1]

He indicated a source for the poem in the quotation from Thiers in the headnote.[2] This source raises the question of what happened to a messenger from Napoleon's army to Marshal the Marquis de Grouchy, commander of Napoleon's Third and Fourth Corps (the right wing), but Thiers does not suggest that the messenger was murdered by a peasant. Passages that precede and follow the quotation explain that after Napoleon had crippled the Prussian forces under Field Marshal Gebhard von Blücher, at Ligny on June 16, and the Prussians had withdrawn, Napoleon on June 17 ordered Grouchy to pursue the Prussians and prevent their joining the English. When Grouchy's generals, on June 18, learned of the battle of Waterloo, they wished to go to Napoleon's aid, but Grouchy insisted on following the Prussians as Napoleon had ordered.

On April 20, 1926, Brigadier-General J. H. Morgan wrote Hardy about "Lord King's book on the Comte de Flahault." He said: "In reading De Flahault's own account, my mind constantly went back to . . . 'The Peasant's Confession'. . . . I see that you base your poignant verses on a chapter in Thiers and it may interest you to know that De Flahault . . . wrote to Thiers approving his narrative as correct. In a hitherto unpublished letter he (De Flahault) wrote: 'Grouchy was, as you say, *under some kind of illusion* during those two days, for he had it in his power to save France . . . and his action is the more difficult to understand in view of the words which the Emperor used as he left him . . . I heard them myself and they are graven in my memory.' Is your poem—'The Peasant's Confession'—wholly imaginative or had you some oral tradition to go upon?" Hardy replied on April 24: "I fear my memory does not enable me to say what foundation I had for that legend I called 'The Peasant's Confession' beyond the passage in Thiers prefixed to the verses. Of course Thiers says a great deal more about the mystery of Grouchy's movements than I quoted from him—in fact he argues it out at length if I remember, so as to prove if possible that it was not Napoleon's fault the battle was lost."[3] Unless Hardy's "legend" refers to a source he had forgotten or wished to conceal, the story that a peasant murdered Napoleon's messenger would seem his invention, suggested by Thiers's questions.

Possibly Hardy's legend came from Hugo's *Les Misérables*. In this novel, just before the battle of Waterloo begins, Napoleon examines the plateau of Mont St. Jean: ". . . the slopes . . . the ascents . . . the tufts of the trees, the square rye field, the footpath. . . . He bent over and spoke in an undertone to the guide Lacoste. The guide made a negative sign of the head, probably treacherous."

When the battle for the plateau has begun, the French advance in a furious cavalry charge, but suddenly ". . . the cuirassiers saw between themselves and the English a ditch, a grave. It was the sunken road of Ohain.

"It was a frightful moment. There was the ravine, unlooked for, yawning at the very feet of the horses, two fathoms deep between its double slope. The second rank pushed in the first, the third pushed in the second; the horses reared, threw themselves over, fell upon their backs, and struggled with their feet in the air, piling up and overturning their riders; no power to retreat; the whole column was nothing but a projectile. . . .

"Here the loss of the battle began. . . . It may almost be said that from this shake of a peasant's head came the catastrophe of Napoleon."[4]

Hugo's summarizing statement would have interested Hardy, who constantly in his fiction pivots a disaster upon some little, unnoticed incident. But the battle swayed back and forth long after Napoleon lost his cuirassiers. Most readers would question the sunken road as the pivot and would point to Grouchy's failure to arrive as decisive. For this reason, perhaps, Hardy shifted the role of the treacherous peasant from Napoleon's guide to one who misled an officer in search of Grouchy. The point is the same in either story: the fate of Europe turned on a peasant's treachery.

Hardy adroitly selected the form of a dramatic monologue spoken by the peasant to a priest. As the priest could not divulge secrets told him in confessional, the facts are not to be expected in historical records.

In *Wessex Poems,* Hardy illustrated "The Peasant's Confession" with a full-page night-scene of cultivated fields during a rain. Distant buildings near some poplar trees represent the peasant's hut.

Within the frame that gives the narrative the human interest of remorse, Hardy sketched the battle of Waterloo in epic fashion. Perhaps it is hard to believe in the peasant's detailed knowledge of events, though the man responsible for Napoleon's defeat might have informed himself of the details.

The course of events in the poem may be compared with historical facts. In the beginning there seems some confusion in dates. If the "eve in middle June" is that when the officer calls the peasant to the door, it must be the evening of June 17, for the battle of Waterloo takes place on the next day, June 18. Then "Three nights ere this" is a mistake, for Napoleon had crossed the Sambre River at Charleroi on June 15. It was about midnight before news reached the Duke of Wellington in Brussels that Napoleon's forces were approaching. (The English indeed "Dallied in Parc and Bois" and ball until this news arrived.) Then hastily mustered English forces advanced to meet the French under Ney at Quatre Bras, a village about ten miles north of Charleroi, and the Prussians under Blücher to meet the French under Napoleon at Ligny, about ten miles northeast of Charleroi and some eight miles east of Quatre Bras. The "gloomy gun" the peasant had heard "Growl through the long-sunned day" was the fierce battles fought at these villages "yestertide," June 16. The fighting at Quatre Bras ended in a stalemate, but at Ligny Napoleon forced Blücher to retreat.

On June 17, Napoleon ordered Grouchy with his 30,000 men to follow the Prussians to prevent their joining Wellington's forces; Grouchy was to base his army at Gembloux, about ten miles northeast of Ligny. But the Prussians had turned northwestward to concentrate at Wavre—closer to Waterloo than Grouchy's forces following them. To prevent a junction of the Prussians and the English, Grouchy should have marched farther to the northwest to a position between Wavre and Waterloo, where the English were preparing to fight. The poem says that Napoleon sent orders "To strike between the double host ahead"—between Wavre and Waterloo—but Grouchy, who would not disobey orders to *follow* the Prussians (not head them off), did not receive the new orders.

The peasant's farm is not located, but his fear of a battle there suggests an area southeast of Wavre. From this point the peasant led the officer toward Joidoigne, some ten miles east of Wavre. Then the peasant turned southwest to Ottignies on the Dyle River, crossing Grouchy's line of march between Gembloux and Wavre. (Perhaps Hardy misplaced these villages.) Wandering at random, the peasant turned east again toward Perwez (ten miles southeast of Ottignies) and distant Noville (some sixty miles farther southeast— a direction, not a destination). This wandering was sufficient to arouse the officer's suspicion.

Apparently, perhaps to allay suspicion, the peasant turned westward again, and before noon of June 18 had led the officer close enough to Mont-Saint-Jean, about three miles south of Waterloo, to hear the artillery there and to see in the distance the arrival of Blücher's van at Chapelle-Saint-Lambert, between Wavre and Waterloo. The murder ends the peasant's story except for the remorse expressed in the confessional frame.

The poem turns to the battle of Waterloo, outlined by the battlefronts from Hougoumont ("Goumont"), about three miles southwest of Waterloo, to Papelotte and Smohain, about three miles to the southeast. As his Imperial Guard wavers, Napoleon sees the advance of Blücher's van and, to hearten his men, lies: "Grouchy is now at hand!"

Perhaps because it was a convention of epic poetry (and Hardy was planning *The Dynasts*) the poet presents the magnitude of Waterloo in a catalogue of the heroes and the fallen on both sides. Some names are world-famous; others are obscure.[5] Perhaps Hardy intended the lists of heroes to develop a characteristic theme, that great consequences may flow from petty motives. The peasant's action is not to be read as chance or fate. It was chance that the officer knocked at the peasant's door, but it was the peasant's fear for his little properties that caused him to deceive the officer. His remorse at last does not cancel out the "dykes of dead," Napoleon's defeat, or the ignominy of the French flight at Genappe Bridge across the Dyle River, for all of which the peasant feels responsible.

In *The Dynasts*, Hardy devotes Acts VI and VII of Part Third to the battle of Waterloo. In VII, ii, Napoleon expects Grouchy, who does not arrive. Apparently Napoleon himself had not sent for Grouchy, for he asks Marshal Soult, his Chief-of-Staff, whether a messenger has been sent. When Soult replies, "I sent a messenger," Napoleon says, "A messenger! Had my poor Berthier been here / Six would have insufficed!" Later in the battle (VII, viii), when the Prussians are seen arriving, Napoleon sends word to his troops that what he knows to be the "dim Prussian masses" are "Grouchy's three-and-thirty thousand, come / To clinch a victory." In Hardy's treatment, as perhaps in history, the battle of Waterloo hinged upon Grouchy's failure to receive an order to head off the Prussians and hasten to Napoleon's aid.

In "The Peasant's Confession," not only the peasant's detailed historical knowledge, but also his somewhat formal language, have been criticized. To this criticism Hardy replied: "Concluding that the tale must be regarded as a translation of the original utterance of the peasant, I thought an impersonal wording admissible."[6]

1. P. 74; *Life*, p. 298.
2. The quotation is from M. A. Thiers, *Histoire du Consulat et de l'Empire*, Paris, 1884, XX, Book LX, "Waterloo," p. 258. This edition, which was in Hardy's library, is now in the Dorset County Museum. Purdy, in *Thomas Hardy: A Bibliographical Study*, p. 100, points out that "Hardy has marked the passage in his copy of the English translation by D. Forbes Campbell (London, 1862), p. 144."
3. General Morgan's letter is in the Dorset County Museum; Hardy's is in the Berg Collection, the New York Public Library.
4. Hugo's French reads: "Ceci commença la perte de la bataille. . . . On pourrait presque dire que de ce signe de tête d'un paysan est sortie la catastrophe de Napoléon." The English passages are quoted from Vol. I, The Valjean Edition, New York and London, [1862], Chs. VIII and IX, pp. 334-37; and the French from Vol. III, *Cosette*, Paris, 1862, Ch. IX, pp. 72-73. I am indebted to Dr. George Taylor, Professor of History at the University of North Carolina, for suggesting Hugo. Hardy certainly read *Les Misérables*. He wrote a tribute to Hugo, saying: "His works are the cathedrals of literary architecture." *Later Years*, p. 92; *Life*, p. 311.

5. Those readily identified are as follows, here alphabetized in groups according to nationality and fate: English heroes: Major-General Sir James Kempt, commanding the 8th Brigade of Picton's Division; Major-General Sir Peregrine Maitland, commanding the 1st British Brigade of Guards; Major-General Sir John Vandeleur, commanding the 4th Cavalry Brigade; and Major-General Sir Richard Hussey Vivian, commanding the 6th Cavalry Brigade. English wounded: Captain (Lieutenant-Colonel?) Henry D'Oyley of Wellington's 1st Guards; Lieutenant-Colonel James Hay of the 16th Light Dragoons; Major-General Sir Dennis Packe of the 9th Brigade of Reserves; Lieutenant-Colonel Sir Frederick Cavendish Ponsonby, commanding the 12th Light Dragoons; and Lieutenant William Smith of the Royal Artillery. English killed or missing: Captain George Battersby of the 1st Dragoon Guards; Lieutenant John Blackman of the 2nd Battalion of Coldstream Guards; Lieutenant-Colonel Charles Fox Canning, aide-de-camp to Wellington; Colonel Sir William Delancey, Deputy Quartermaster-General; Lieutenant-Colonel William Fuller of the 1st Dragoon Guards; Lieutenant-Colonel Sir Alexander Gordon, aide-de-camp to Wellington; Lieutenant (Captain?) Edward Grose, 3rd Battalion of 1st Guards; Major Hon. F. Howard, the 10th Hussars; Major L'Estrange, aide-de-camp to Major-General Sir Dennis Packe; Captain Montague Lind, 1st Life Guards; Lieutenant-Colonel (Colonel?) Charles Morice, 69th Infantry; Colonel Baron Charles Ompteda, commanding the 5th and 6th Battalions of Wellington's German Legion; Lieutenant-General Sir Thomas Picton, commanding the 5th Division of Reserves; and Captain (Lieutenant-Colonel?) Edward Stables, 2nd Battalion of the 1st Guards. English unidentified: Phelips may be a member of the Phelips family of Montacute House in Somerset. French heroes: Lieutenant-General Drouet d'Erlon, commanding the 1st Corps of Napoleon's Army under Ney; Lieutenant-General Count Reille, Marshal of France, commanding the 2nd Corps under Ney; and General Travers, commanding a brigade of Cuirassiers. French wounded: General Blancard; Edouard de Colbert; General Delord (or Delort?) of Napoleon's Cavalry; General Dnop (or Donop?) of Napoleon's Cavalry; Lieutenant-General Louis Friant, commanding the 3rd Grenadiers of Napoleon's Imperial Guard; General Guyot of Napoleon's Cavalry; General L'Heritier of Napoleon's Cavalry; and Lieutenant-General Count Lobau, commanding Napoleon's 6th Corps. French killed or missing: Lieutenant-General Count Duhesme, commanding Napoleon's Young Guard (called "wronged" because, when wounded, he fell into enemy hands and was killed by a Prussian); Lieutenant Legros; and Lieutenant-General Michel, commanding the 1st Battalion of the 3rd Chasseurs under Ney. Prussians not identified: Boek, Von Schwerin, and Watzdorf.

6. Blunden, *Thomas Hardy*, p. 104.

THE ALARM has a headnote giving its source as "Traditional." This term replaces "1803" in the first edition of *Wessex Poems*, and it replaced "1804" in the manuscript.[1] "Traditional" and the dedication to "One of the Writer's Family Who Was a Volunteer During the War with Napoleon" indicate that Hardy heard the story from his paternal grandmother Mary Head Hardy (the wife of the poem), the speaker was his grandfather, Thomas Hardy the First, the poem was based on fact, and the date of the action was uncertain in Hardy's mind.[2]

From the beginning of the war with Napoleon, England feared that the French would invade across the Channel and land somewhere near Weymouth (Hardy's "Budmouth"); then they could attack Plymouth to the west or Portsmouth to the east, both naval arsenals.[3]

The Earl of Dorchester, Lord Lieutenant of the County of Dorset, made plans to meet an invasion. A "Plan of the County of Dorset Shewing the Divisions along the Coast alloted [sic] for the Troops of Yeomanry . . . and the Depots to be removed to" is dated August, 1801. A map of 1804 shows a "Plan of the County of Dorset, Divided into Divisions, Shewing the Beacons fixed on, Signal Posts erected by Government, Depots, & Places of Assembly of Volunteer Corps."[4] This map includes orders for the troops to aid the civilian population in case of invasion, to drive wagons, to care for stock, etc. Many of the troops were regulars, but as the poem says, they included "Yeomen / Militia, Fencibles and Pikemen." The militia were volunteers more or less drilled; the "fencibles" were men intended for defensive service only, and the pikemen were civilians instructed to fight with whatever they had. It was arranged for news of an invasion to be flashed from the beaches to the hilltops by beacon-fires. In 1803, "Beacons were erected on Badbury Rings, Woodberry [sic for Woodbury] Hill, Piddletown Heath, Blackden Hill, and others further Eastwards and Westwards, to communicate from Winchester through the whole district."[5]

Perhaps all the characters of the poem were actual persons. Hardy wrote of his grandfather Thomas Hardy the First that "he had been a volunteer till the end of the war, and lay in Weymouth with his company from time to time, waiting for Bonaparte who never came."[6] This Thomas Hardy, who was born in 1778, married Mary Head at the age of twenty-one, settled in Higher Bockhampton in 1801,[7] and enlisted as Volunteer 34 in the Dorset Muster.[8] In the poem his wife, Mary, called "Molly," is pregnant with a child expected in July, evidently their first child, John, baptized on August 21, 1803. The "neighbour-natives" include Captain W. Smith of the Dorset Volunteer Rangers, Captain Percival Meggs of the Dorsetshire Militia in command of a division to protect the area from Poole to Wimborne, and Colonel Richard Bingham of the Third Foot, drillmaster for the Dorset Militia.[9]

The geography of the poem is precise. The "ferny byway" describes the track that leads from Bockhampton Lane eastward a few hundred yards to Hardy's birthplace. The Volunteer had come in haste from Weymouth on the coast, called "royal George's town" because George III had been accustomed since 1789 to spending his vacations there. The "halterpath and wood" may be the short cut across the Heath through Puddletown Forest to Puddletown; the path may be the "Snail Creep" to the Hardy homestead which smugglers used.

[76]

The "Road" in which Napoleon might anchor is the outer harbor at Weymouth, deep enough for naval transports. The Volunteer advises Molly, if in danger, to flee to "Kingsbere," Hardy's name for Bere Regis, about nine miles further inland.[10] Then he turns to the "eastward lanes," or short cuts across fields toward Dorchester; when he gets out of the hollow in which the homestead nestles, he looks eastward and sees "above He'th Hills" the Barrow-Beacon burning low, as if lighted some time previously. This beacon was on the hill called Rainbarrow about half a mile southeast of the homestead.[11]

In *Wessex Poems*, Hardy illustrated this scene with a headpiece showing the Volunteer in early morning dusk silhouetted against the eastern sky, the barrow, and the low flame of the beacon.

When the Volunteer reaches the highway and continues toward Dorchester, he goes downhill to an eastern by-water of the Frome and there falters; releasing a bird entangled in the tufts on the bank, he lets the direction of the bird's flight guide him to turn back or go forward. The bird flies due south across the Frome and "Durnover Great Field and Fort." "Durnover" is Hardy's name for Fordington, and the Great Field is the moor-and-meadowland around Dorchester.[12] The Fort directly south of where the Volunteer stood is Conquer Barrow. He does not follow the bird due south, but goes through Dorchester and then southward toward Weymouth along the highway that runs about half a mile east of Maiden Castle or Mai-Dun.[13] About half-way between Dorchester and Weymouth he climbs the spine of hills called Ridgeway, and from that height he can see the coast and harbor of Weymouth three or four miles to the south, and beyond the harbor the rocky peninsula of Portland. The full-page drawing in *Wessex Poems* pictures the soldier standing on the road as it crosses Ridgeway and gazing toward Weymouth.

Hardy's manuscript dated the alarm as 1804. In his short story, "A Tradition of 1804," he described the gravest threat of invasion as in this year. A fishing fleet that came to Portland in a fog on May 1, 1804, was taken for the French. "Weymouth was in a state of confusion and uproar . . . the Troops there were all under Arms, and every possible measure of defence taken."[14] But Hardy's "Notes taken for 'Trumpet-Major'" read: "N. B. The autumn of 1804 was one of alarm at the expected invasion, equally with 1803, though perhaps not to such an intense degree. So that the beacon-firing may be in either year."[15] Possibly Hardy chose 1803 to make his poem more dramatic by having his Volunteer drawn toward desertion in the months just before his first child was to be born.

The conflict between domestic love and military duty was perhaps actual, narrated by Hardy's grandmother; it reflected an attitude widespread among Dorset volunteers. During one alarm, "The volunteers were called out to march to Weymouth, but declined to go farther than South Street, saying they would stop at that point and defend their native town."[16] The Volunteer in the poem lets God decide the conflict. To him "a thought of Holy Writ occurred,"[17] he uttered a prayer for guidance, and followed the guidance given.

Hardy's care for historical and geographical accuracy is matched by his care in other details. In spring, the country people of Dorset breakfasted early enough for the Volunteer to leave home in time to walk the ten miles to Weymouth by the "assembly-hour" of "six that morn." The equipment he must carry for battle-array is precise according to lists and pictures—perhaps the "melodramatic prints" Hardy found in *A History of the Wars*.[18]

He was fond of the story of the alarm. Besides its appearance in *The Trumpet-Major* and "A Tradition of Eighteen Hundred and Four," Granfer Cantle in *The Return of the Native* boasts of his valor at the time: "In the year four 'twas said there wasn't a finer figure in the whole South Wessex than I, as I looked . . . the day we ran out o' Budmouth because it was thought that Boney had landed round the point." (Book Second, Chapter VI.)

1. Purdy, *Thomas Hardy: A Bibliographical Study*, p. 100.

2. An additional source is mentioned in Hardy's biography: "He also found in a closet *A History of the Wars*—a periodical dealing with the war with Napoleon, which his grandfather had subscribed to at the time, having been himself a volunteer." *Early Life*, p. 21; *Life*, pp. 16-17.

3. See Wheeler and Broadley, *Napoleon and the Invasion of England, passim*, which Hardy owned.

4. In the Dorset County Archives.

5. Thompson, *Records of the Dorset Yeomanry*, p. 62. The beacon on "Piddletown Heath" was the beacon of the poem, on Rainbarrow.

6. *Early Life*, p. 14; *Life*, p. 12.

7. [Bartelot], "Stinsford and the Hardy Family," p. 109; *Early Life*, p. 10; *Life*, p. 8.

8. Sparks, "Piddletown Volunteer Broadside," p. 58.

9. See Thompson, *Records of the Dorset Yeomanry, passim*, and Copps, "The Poetry of Thomas Hardy," pp. 383-84. I have found no identification for Michel, Gambier, and Cunningham, but suppose that Hardy got the names from his grandmother and knew the families. In *The Trumpet-Major*, Hardy refers to the "Longpuddle volunteers, sixty rank and file, under Captain Cunningham." Chapter XXVII.

10. "Kingsbere" is named in Chapter XXVI of *The Trumpet-Major* as a place of refuge for Miller Loveday's womenkind, if Napoleon should invade.

11. From this point, before the present forests were planted, a beacon-fire would be visible to beacon-keepers on other hills in all directions. The actual names of the beacon-keepers, the "old men" Jems Purchess and John Whiting, are given in *The Dynasts*, Part First, II, v.

12. Usually, when Hardy says "Durnover," he means either the part of Fordington now within the town of Dorchester (east of the town-center and along the Frome River) or the water-meadows lying across the Frome.

13. Mai-Dun tops a high hill about a mile and a half southwest of Dorchester.
14. Thompson, *Records of the Dorset Yeomanry*, p. 70. On another occasion, "One of the signal beacons on Abbotsbury beach was by some accident set alight during the night, and the whole chain of beacons of course followed suit." Mc-William, "In Thomas Hardy's Wessex," p. 44.
15. P. 44. In the Dorset County Museum.
16. Boswell-Stone, *Memories and Traditions*, p. 52. South Street in Dorchester leads into the Weymouth Road.
17. As in Job 12:7, "But ask now the beasts, and they shall teach thee; and the fowls of the air, and they shall tell thee."
18. For definitions of these antiquated items see Copps, "The Poetry of Thomas Hardy," pp. 380-81.

HER DEATH AND AFTER was one of Hardy's favorite poems. He wrote, in April of 1901, to Sir George Douglas: "I shall ask you when I see you what you think of my opinion that 'Her Death and After,' & 'The Dance at the Phoenix' . . . are two as good stories as I have ever told?"[1] Edward Clodd, writing to Hardy on December 5, 1909, refers to the poem as one that Hardy selected for reading to his friends at Strafford House, Aldeburgh.[2]

He told the story as the central character's retrospective monologue that, in its conclusion, seeks to justify the sin he confesses. The verse-technique is intricate, with stanzas linked in pairs by opening lines that rime. He gave the story a suitable time-setting by laying the death scene in winter, picturing the weather in images the narrator would notice in his agitated states of mind. Before the dying woman's declaration the trees "shed on me their rime and hoar," but afterwards "the swinging trees / Rang above me." He set the poem in well-known places in Dorchester, each presented in words that give the familiar fact symbolic value.

The narrator goes to his loved one's "tenement"—without the warmth of "home"—"by the way of the Western Wall so drear." This wall running beside Albert Road, along what was once the western boundary of the town, extends from West Walks to the upper end of High West Street at the roundabout (traffic circle). The wall, partly of modern brick and stone, includes a portion of the original Roman Wall. In *Wessex Poems*, Hardy followed the poem with a drawing of ice-laden trees interlacing over West Walks under wintry moonlight. From the end of the Walks, the narrator crosses to a house that Lea identifies as "a solidly built house known as Top o' Town,"[3] which faces directly down High West Street. This house, which now holds military recruiting offices and an office of the Ministry of Labour, was in 1841 known as Grove House (in an area then known as The Grove) and was occupied by Charles Burt Henning; and after 1844 to about 1903, by Arthur E. Mansell, J. P.[4] Whether Hardy's story concerns either Henning or Mansell,[5] or is fictional, the man of the house is so devoted to business that he is absent in the City (the financial district of London) while his wife lies dying in childbirth.

He takes "heed," however, enough to bury her next night in "the Field of Tombs where the earthworks frowned." This Field is Dorchester Cemetery south of town on Weymouth Avenue, beyond Maumbury Rings.[6] In *Wessex Poems*, Hardy illustrated the poem with a full-page drawing of Dorchester Cemetery viewed from the south. Maumbury Rings is seen beyond the cemetery wall, and the towers and housetops of Dorchester lie beyond the Rings.

Maumbury Rings is both a reality and, in the poem, a symbol. Situated on Weymouth Avenue a few hundred feet from the cemetery, between this place of burial and the town center, its ramparts "frown" over the cemetery. It is a pre-Roman earthwork, adapted by the Romans to be, as Hardy says, "the Cirque of the Gladiators." In *The Mayor of Casterbridge*, Hardy established it as a symbol of malign influences: to the imagination it is watched over by the ghosts of Hadrian's legions; though isolated, it is not a place where lovers care to meet. (Chapter XI.) It has a similar significance in "Her Death and After." When the narrator retreats from the cemetery to Maumbury Rings, the husband follows. There the lie is told, accompanied by the conditional challenge to a duel "with ball or blade . . . here." The place seems to invoke the judgment of time upon the conduct of the men.

The poem presents a conflict between conventional, legal right and the morality of the heart. The dying wife says that the husband "has not been kind"; that the child is lame suggests brutality. The husband's attitude toward his wife's grave suggests respectable "decency" as his standard of morality. He gives up the little girl for self-righteous spite rather than either poverty or generosity. The narrator, who accepts the girl out of compassion and love, is not entirely at ease. To outweigh his wrong to the loved woman's name, he can offer only his feeling: "She forgives, or would, / If only she could know!"

1. Parker, "Hardy's Letters to Sir George Douglas," p. 221.
2. In the Dorset County Museum.
3. *Thomas Hardy's Wessex*, p. 262.
4. Information from Miss Margaret Holmes, Dorset County Archivist.
5. It would hardly concern Mansell, alive when the poem was published.
6. In *The Mayor of Casterbridge*, Mrs. Henchard was buried in this cemetery, "the still-used burial-ground of the old Roman-British city. . . . Mrs. Henchard's dust mingled with the dust of women who lay ornamented with glass hairpins and amber necklaces, and men who held in their mouths coins of Hadrian, Posthumus, and the Constantines." Chapter XX.

THE DANCE AT THE PHOENIX was one of Hardy's favorites as a story told in verse. (See the notes on "Her Death and After.") Purdy's bibliography points out that "Hardy wrote to Edmund Gosse that the poem 'is based on fact' " and that the "MS. reads 'Nelly' for 'Jenny' throughout" (p. 100). That Hardy changed his heroine's name suggests that in fact it was Nelly. In the poem, not even Jenny's husband knew the story, and "The King's said not a word." Perhaps the story came to Hardy from his grandmother.

The dance takes place in Dorchester ("Casterbridge"). Jenny's husband came there from "inland leazes" north of Dorchester, in the area of the Parrett, Yeo, or Tone Rivers. Aging Jenny sees the King's Own Cavalry as the troops pass up High West Street past St. Peter's Church; she rests her head on the iron railing that separates the church from the street. The Phoenix Inn is a very old inn on High East Street, about three hundred yards east of St. Peter's on the opposite (southern) side. It has always been a favorite gathering place for the soldiers quartered in Dorchester barracks.[1] Jenny's direction of walk to the Phoenix and mention of the moorland and Standfast Bridge indicate that her home was in the lower part of the Fordington area of Dorchester, close enough to High East Street for her to hear the music of the dance. When she leaves her house she descends to a by-street and from it goes westward up High East to the inn. A few hundred feet in front of her, on the same side of High East Street, stands All-Saints' Church, over whose towers she sees the star Sirius, and, looking northwest over the buildings around North Square, the constellation Charles's Wain (the Dipper). North Square ("Bullstake")[2] widens out from narrow North Street about a hundred yards from the junction of this street with High East, High West, and South Streets. All-Saints' Church and "Bullstake" Square both define the direction from which Jenny comes to the Phoenix and suggest her meditation in the light of the stars before she makes her "sinful" entry.

When the soldiers have escorted Jenny home, their footsteps die away toward dawn; the morning star (Phosphor) shines on Fordington Moor (across the Frome) and the elms beside the London Road. From Poundbury ("Pummery Ridge") in the northwest, Maumbury Ring ("Maembury Ring") in the southwest, and Standfast Bridge over the Frome near Jenny's house—that is, throughout the town as outlined by this triangle—no life stirs.[3]

The King's Own Cavalrymen take the London Road and pass from sight over Stinsford Hill ("Mellstock Ridge"), a mile from the town. In *Wessex Poems*, Hardy drew a tailpiece for the poem showing the cavalry crossing this hill just past the first milepost.

The King's Own Cavalry were temporary visitors. Until a few years ago, infantry and artillery of the Dorset regiments were regularly stationed in Dorchester in barracks just northwest of Top o' the Town. No regiment officially called the "King's Own Cavalry" ever had a permanent station there,[4] but regiments passing through Dorchester from time to time were entertained. Several cavalry regiments of the late eighteenth century had the word "King's" in their title. Seeking to identify Hardy's cavalry, J. F. Ware, Research Assistant for the Imperial War Museum, wrote on July 11, 1966: "The most appropriate appears to be the Third, King's Own, Regiment of Dragoons (later Light Dragoons). From their history I can confirm that the regiment were stationed in Dorchester in 1777 and on 7th December 1818 marched from Canterbury to Bristol. It seems unlikely that they would have passed through Dorchester on this march, but the dates do fit the two episodes in the poem." Hardy's name for the regiment may be fictitious even in a poem he said was "based on fact."

The music of the poem seems drawn from the repertory of Hardy's family. "Soldier's Joy" is No. 24 in the manuscript music book belonging to Hardy's father and grandfather.[5] Apparently Hardy considered this tune conducive to "convulsions, spasms, St. Vitus dances, and fearful frenzies" of the kind to lure Jenny to the Phoenix. It is the dance tune played at the harvest supper and dance after the marriage of Bathsheba and Sergeant Troy in *Far from the Madding Crowd*.[6] To illustrate "The Dance at the Phoenix" in *Wessex Poems*, Hardy drew a scroll of music showing this tune as a headpiece. Firor lists "Maiden Coy" as a "fine old tune."[7] "Speed the Plough" is No. 40 in the Hardys' music book, and "The Triumph, or Follow My Lover" is No. 98. It is one of the country dances at Tranter Dewy's Christmas party in *Under the Greenwood Tree*. (Chapter VII.) John Masefield made a model of a "full-rigged" sailing ship, named it "The Triumph" because of Hardy's fondness for this tune (mentioned also in "One We Knew"), and gave it to Hardy. It is now in the Dorset County Museum. "The Sylph" is No. 94 and "The Row-dow-dow" is No. 78 in the Hardys' music book. Firor calls the latter a tune with a rhythmic drum-roll at the beginning of each phrase. "The Duke of York's Reel" is No. 123, and "The Fairy Dance" is No. 12 in the music book. "The Bridge of Lodi" is not a folk-tune; it was introduced from France at Vauxhall Gardens, but Hardy loved the tune "as he loved brilliant uniforms, for . . . dash and glamour."[8] "The Fall of Paris" was used as a military march by the Germans and

English in the war with Napoleon; Hardy treats it in *The Dynasts*. (Part Third, II, iii.) For its connotation, perhaps, it is used as a kind of "Good Night, Ladies" in the poem, as St. Peter's clock chimes four.[9]

The almost hypnotic power of music, especially the tunes of "The Dance at the Phoenix," is prominent in Hardy's fiction. The effect of "Soldier's Joy" in *Far from the Madding Crowd* is mentioned above. In the short story "The Fiddler of the Reels," Car'line Aspent goes into a frenzy and loses all self-control when Mop Ollamoor plays "Fancy Lad" and "The Fairy Dance." In "The Dance at the Phoenix," Jenny, with an innate taste for pleasure in the opening of the poem, becomes a sedate wife for most of a lifetime; she is given dignity by this fact and by her communion with the stars before and after the dance, but under the spell of dance music, moral responsibility, her age, and her husband's trust are temporarily forgotten. Though the Phoenix is an actual inn, the name seems to have symbolic significance in the poem. As the fabled bird the phoenix dies in flame, Jenny at nearly sixty re-enacts the follies of her youth, and burns herself out in a single evening.

1. Lea has a photograph of High West Street and of the Phoenix Hotel as Plates 197 and 199 in *Thomas Hardy's Wessex*, pp. 261 and 263.

2. It was formerly called Bullstake because bulls were baited there. In a letter to Pearce Edgcumbe dated "Saturday" [1895?], Hardy expressed his fondness for the "old names" of places in Dorchester. He wrote: "Three of particular historic importance are, to my mind, 'The Bow' (the curved wall of St. Peter's Churchyard); 'Bull Stake'; & 'Bowling Alley Walk' (opposite your south front). But how about the respectabilities of 'North Square'? Of course, if the people who live there have a grain of sense, they will know that Bull Stake is worth ten North Squares." In the Miriam Lutcher Stark Library, University of Texas.

3. Standfast Bridge in the poem is not the present bridge of that name, built about 1962. Hardy's reference is to a bridge now called Prince's across a branch of the Frome at the end of Mill Street near a group of cottages called Standfast Cottages on an Ordnance Map of 1888. See Lea, *Thomas Hardy's Wessex*, p. 264.

4. Information from Lieutenant-Colonel D. V. Wakely, Curator of the Military Museum in Dorchester.

5. In the Dorset County Museum.

6. The quotation is from this novel; see Chapter XXXVI.

7. *Folkways in Thomas Hardy*, p. 196.

8. Ibid., pp. 196, 191. See the notes on the poem "The Bridge of Lodi."

9. Hardy's music for "Speed the Plough," "The Triumph," and "The Duke of York's Reel" has been published by Sherman in *Wessex Tune Book*, and for "The Triumph" and "The Fairy Dance" in "Thomas Hardy: Lyricist, Symphonist."

THE CASTERBRIDGE CAPTAINS is Hardy's only poem that touches upon the English wars in India. Even this poem is not about a war; it is about a soldier who escaped death when two friends gave their lives in their country's service.

The poem is set in All Saints' Church on High East Street in Dorchester ("Casterbridge"). The captains of the poem had apparently attended this church as boys and carved their names on a panel; Hardy's drawing of this panel provides a headpiece for the poem in *Wessex Poems*. It is no longer in the church, since its "reseating." The captains were John Bascombe Lock (1808-42), Thomas Henry Gatehouse Besant (1806-84?), and J. Logan (?-1842).[1] Lock and Logan lost their lives in the battle for Khyber Pass. On the north aisle of nearby St. Peter's Church, a wall-tablet reads: "To the Memory of John Bascombe Lock (a Native of this Town) Captain in the 5th, Bengal Native Infantry, Who died in the Khybur [*sic*] Pass, Upper India, January 24th, 1842, Aged 54 years. *He fell in an action with the Affreedies, whilst bravely struggling to convey the succour so much needed by the British forces in Affghanistan.* His afflicted relatives thus record their sorrow, affection, and esteem." Captain Besant escaped, returned, and heard a sermon on a text from Matt. 16:25, "For whosoever will save his life shall lose it," whereupon, according to the poem, he ceased to feel exultant at his escape, but felt that the glory of "Transcendent triumph" belonged to the men who died. The poem is "a delicate study in compunction"[2] under the influence of religious emotion.

1. Purdy, *Thomas Hardy: A Bibliographical Study*, pp. 100-101.
2. Gosse, "The Lyrical Poetry of Mr. Hardy," p. 225.

A SIGN-SEEKER states Hardy's position in a fundamental intellectual conflict of the nineteenth century. The conflict was between the rationalist view that trusted the senses and the methods and conclusions of science as the way toward truth, and the romantic view that trusted the feelings and traditions, especially in religion. Hardy's position in the poem was that of many an honest doubter in a time when advances in science were constantly bringing into question the explanations of the universe offered by the churches. The discoveries listed in the third and fourth stanzas are not his discoveries, but he had read astronomers' conclusions as he had read the books of the biologists, and his poem speaks for all men of religious temperament who must accept demonstrable fact, however shocking, to be fact. The fact seems to deny not only the personal immortality promised by faith, but also the dream of ultimate justice to a world in which pain and evil are often triumphant.

The stanza-form resembles that of Tennyson's *In Memoriam*, and the tenth stanza seems a reference to the trance described and trusted as evidence of immortality in lyric XCV. Hardy's poem treats a basic issue of Tennyson's, but with an opposite conclusion. However much he wished to do so, Hardy could not "faintly trust the larger hope" of lyric LV without demonstrable evidence.

In *Wessex Poems*, he illustrated "A Sign-Seeker" with a drawing of a comet and a few bright stars flaming in a black sky over what seems to be the rooftops and towers of Dorchester. This drawing introduces five stanzas that both present the observed powers and magnitudes of earth and sky and interpret the findings of astronomers. The imagery is animistic: the months wear liveries (as lackeys, perhaps, of Time); hours "clang negligently by";[1] mist has an "eyeless countenance"; and the earthquake has a "lifting arm." Human reason has wrung from all this quasi-living Nature no evidence that man is other than a tiny part of the whole, ever-mysterious cosmos, and no promise of a spiritual life beyond the grave, "Of heart to heart returning after dust to dust."

All his life Hardy continued to look for God, "As an external personality, of course—the only true meaning of the word," he said.[2] If he could not see God himself, he would accept any tangible, visible, or audible evidence of His existence. He told Hermann Lea and others, "I have always wanted to see a ghost. . . . I would willingly concede ten years of my life if I could see any supernatural thing that could be proved to me to exist by any means within my capacity."[3]

It was said that he did see a ghost long after "A Sign-Seeker" was published. In a letter to Sir Sydney Cockerell, December 27, 1919, Mrs. Florence Hardy wrote: "He saw a ghost in Stinsford Churchyard on Christmas Eve, and his sister Kate says it must have been their grandfather upon whose grave T. H. had just placed a sprig of holly— the first time he had ever done so. The ghost said: 'A green Christmas' —T. H. replied 'I like a green Christmas.' Then the ghost went into the church and, being full of curiosity, T. followed, to see who this strange man in 18th century dress might be—and found no one. That is quite true—a real Christmas ghost story."[4]

1. An image perhaps suggested by the clang of the clock in the tower of the Corn Exchange, Dorchester; a silhouette of this tower appears in the drawing.
2. Duffin, *Thomas Hardy*, p. 196.
3. Lea, *Thomas Hardy Through the Camera's Eye*, p. 30. See a more detailed discussion in Archer, "Real Conversations. Conversation I."
4. Meynell, ed., *Friends of a Lifetime*, p. 305. *Later Years*, p. 259; *Life*, p. 441, mentions another apparition Hardy thought he saw.

MY CICELY is unusually complex in geographical and historical interest, theme, verse-form, and possible relation to Hardy's life. He especially wished the geography and the versification to be appreciated. On December 29, 1908, he wrote to a Mr. Pouncy, who was planning some lectures about Hardy: "By the way, if you wanted more views, or rather new things to say, the poem 'My Cicely' in the 'Wessex Poems' would afford a capital panoramic treatment of the Great Western Road from London to Exeter—accompanied by your recitation of the journey with the galloping movement of the verses."[1]

Two drawings in *Wessex Poems* picture the mid-journey near Dorchester, and the end of the journey near Exeter. A headpiece shows a solitary horseman riding westward on a road across a heath just northeast of "Triple-ramparted Maidon." Some distance in front of him, beside the road, a body is hanging from a gibbet (as in stanza twelve), and the distant horizon is humped with five barrows or burial mounds. A tailpiece shows the tops of the towers of Exeter Cathedral as they look from the southeast, as on Topsham Road.[2]

The journey of the poem is a dual one, westward from London through Wessex to Exeter, and backward in time from the eighteenth century into prehistory. The narrator identifies the places along his route by referring to their past. The journey begins as the narrator leaves London on horseback "for the ancient West Highway / To far Exonb'ry" (Exeter). This "Highway" is the course of a series of those Roman roads, shown on the Ordnance "Map of Roman Britain,"[3] that lead most directly from London to Exeter. The route of the rider is west from London for a few miles, then southwest through Staines to Silchester, then in a more southerly direction to Old Sarum, then still more southerly to Badbury, then more westerly to Dorchester, and then west, but bending slightly to the north to join a road from Lincoln in the north, and then running southwesterly to Exeter. The rider could not have followed these Roman roads exactly, for they no longer exist as roads, except in stretches that coincide with later roads. The points of view from which he saw the places mentioned suggest that he sometimes followed a road, but, being on horseback, sometimes cut across country, perhaps more along the *course* of a straight Roman Road than along the winding modern highways through villages and towns.

Besides heaths, the first place mentioned along his route is "the House of Long Sieging." This "House" is a ruin in the village of Basing, about two miles from Basingstoke, which is about thirty-five miles southwest of London. Basing House was the fortified castle of John, fifth Marquis of Winchester, loyal to King Charles in the Civil War. It withstood siege by the Parliamentary forces from the summer of 1643 until October, 1645, when it fell to Oliver Cromwell.[4]

The "thin steeple / That tops the fair fane of Poore's olden / Episcopal see" is the spire of Salisbury Cathedral. Presumably the rider, following the course of the Roman Road, did not enter Salisbury, but saw the steeple from Old Sarum, about two miles north of the Cathedral. Since leaving Basing House he not only has come about thirty-five miles southwest, but has reached ruins four and a quarter centuries farther in the past. Richard Poore, Bishop at St. Osmund's Cathedral in Sarum, on April 28, 1220, laid the cornerstone for the present cathedral, where he presided as bishop until 1228.

On Salisbury Plain, dotted with barrows (not to mention Stonehenge), the rider passed many "bleak hill-graves of Chieftains" of prehistoric times. The Roman Road from Sarum to Dorchester was called the Icen Way (Via Icenia) because it was part of a road-system that began in Norfolk and took its name from the Iceni, the people living there in Roman times. The course of this road is a "pale riband" because long stretches of it across ridges and fields, by "lynchet and lea," are not now visible. About half-way from Sarum to Dorchester he rode through Blandford Forum, important in Roman times as a market place at a ford on the River Stour, and as a halting place for legions on the march.

After leaving Blandford, the rider followed the course of the Roman Road somewhat parallel to the modern highway, but about two miles south of it; in doing so he passed within half a mile of Weatherby Castle, spelled by Hardy as "Weatherbury." It is not a castle in the usual sense, but is a small hill-fort of the pre-Roman Britons, with ramparts and fosses still in existence. It is about three miles northeast of Puddletown.[5]

Following the Roman Road, the rider passed through Dorchester ("Casterbridge")[6] and then to the scene just southwest of Dorchester pictured in Hardy's drawing, with "Triple-ramparted Maidon" (Maiden Castle) to the left of his route.

The next three places, "Eggar," "Pummerie," and the "Nine-Pillared Cromlech," are not presented in the order of the rider's journey; perhaps they are scrambled to suggest the behavior of memory. All three are monuments of pre-Roman Britain. In the order of the rider's journey, he first passed Poundbury Camp ("Square Pummerie") but, taking the Roman (and approximately the present) Road west, saw it on his right, to the north.

The rider next passed the "Nine-Pillared Cromlech," a miniature Stonehenge, on the left (southern) side of Road 35 about five miles west of Dorchester, but about a mile south of the course of the Roman Road.[7] As the Nine Stones are small, to see them the rider at this point must have followed the present Road 35. The "hill-fortress of Eggar" is Eggardon Hill,[8] about nine and a half miles northwest of Dorchester. It is a pre-Roman fort on a hill that rises 828 feet above sea-level just north of the course of the Roman Road. As it is nearly two miles north of Road 35, the road the rider was following at this point is not clear.

Apparently in the latter part of his journey he abandoned any particular road. On the Roman Road, he would have been some miles to the north of the "Bride-streams," if they are the River Bride and its tributaries. This river runs parallel to the sea-coast about four miles inland, from the village of Little Bredy in the east to Burton Bradstock (some three miles southeast of Bridport), where it "modestly hides itself beneath the shingle, and trickles gently through the pebbles into the sea at Freshwater Bay." [9] The rider's route westward crossed the Rivers Axe and Otter, which, lying farther west, flow southward into the sea at Seaton and Budleigh Salterton, respectively.

Apparently he approached Exeter from the southeast, where the "Exe [River] scents the sea" in the broad, navigable bay south of Topsham, a suburb of the larger city. It is not stated that he rode all the way into Exeter. The "graveacre" may have been Topsham cemetery, from which neighborhood the towers of Exeter Cathedral look as they do in Hardy's drawing.

The "famed Lions-Three" where the rider's former sweetheart was barmaid offers a puzzle. Lea states that it stood "about ten miles back from the city [Exeter] on the Taunton Road." [10] Whatever route the rider chose he would hardly have arrived by the Taunton Road running north from Exeter. Perhaps the inn name is fictional, with its inn sign derived from the coat of arms of the town of Dorchester, which shows three lions. [11]

Besides the journey into the west and the past, "My Cicely" presents a complex theme of idealism, disillusion, and the rejection of disillusion for a preferable hallucination. The third and fourth stanzas establish the narrator as an idealist engaged in the commercial life of London, but scornful of its "frenzy-led factions" and regretful that he had "squandered" his youth in worship of "Baals illusive and specious." The rumor that one formerly beloved is dead revitalized her ideal image "To full apogee." Later phrases suggest that the narrator associated the girl not only with youth and beauty, but also with superior rank and high morality; she was the "Canon's kinswoman." Disillusion came when he discovered that she had debased herself morally and socially; with her idealized image in his mind he had not recognized her as the drunken barmaid of the "Lions-Three." His first reaction was an impulse toward cynicism. [12] To preserve his "choice vision," he wilfully embraced the hallucination that his Cicely was not the barmaid, but was the dead woman.

The ballad-like "My Cicely" is complex also in its experimentation with verse-forms. Weber has pointed out that the poem has the "rapid anapestic rhythm," as in its journey it has a theme, of Browning's "How They Brought the Good News from Ghent to Aix."[13] In other features it is closer to the poetry of Hardy's friend William Barnes. Rutland has pointed out that "My Cicely" resembles Barnes's "Woak Hill" in stanza-form, meter, and the single rime of the last line of each stanza throughout the poem.[14] The opening stanza of "Woak Hill" will illustrate the similarity in stanza-form and meter:

> When sycamore leaves wer a-spreaden,
> Green-ruddy, in hedges,
> Bezide the red doust o' the ridges,
> A-dried at Woak Hill. . . .[15]

Hardy's use of dialect also suggests Barnes's influence in such words as "lynchet" (flint slope), "jee" (gee, turn right), and "graveacre," "garth," and "church-hay" (cemetery). His opening the poem at its crisis and then cutting back to begin the action in the third stanza is also unusual.

Deacon and Coleman have suggested that "My Cicely" may narrate in fantasy an event in Hardy's relations with Mrs. Tryphena Sparks Gale. On March 8, 1888, old Mrs. Gale, Tryphena's mother-in-law, died in Topsham. Hardy recorded in his journal for March 9 that he was in London in the British Museum Reading Room. The next published entry in the journal is dated March 28. It opens: "On returning to London after an absence," with no hint of where he had been. Deacon and Coleman theorize that, as the poem says of the narrator in stanzas 5 and 6, Hardy heard a "chance . . . death-rumour" concerning a Mrs. Gale of Topsham,[16] supposed her to be Tryphena, went to Topsham, and there discovered that the dead woman was the mother-in-law, and that Tryphena, alive and well, "although not selling liquor like the Cicely of the poem, was sometimes helping at the South Western [Hotel] owned by Charles," her husband.[17] When Tryphena did die in 1890, Hardy and his brother Henry visited her grave in Topsham. If Hardy made the surmised trip in 1888, probably he went by train. The setting of the poem in the eighteenth century and the journey on horseback disguise any personal meaning in the poem and develop the theme of the journey into the west and the past.

1. Photostat of the letter in the Colby College Library.
2. Purdy, *Thomas Hardy: A Bibliographical Study*, p. 101, says "from the north-

west." The slanting view could be from either, but the traveller in the poem approaches Exeter from an easterly direction, and the discussion below will indicate another reason for regarding Topsham as the viewpoint.

3. Third edition, Chessington, Surrey: The Ordnance Survey, 1956.

4. See *The Great Siege of Basing House,* a pamphlet with maps, on sale at the gateway. Lea, *Thomas Hardy's Wessex,* has a picture of "The Gateway, Basing House" as Plate 200, p. 263.

5. In presenting Puddletown in *Far from the Madding Crowd,* Hardy called it "Weatherbury," taking the name from nearby Weatherby Castle.

6. A street in Dorchester is named Icen Way.

7. The cromlech is described by the plaque put there by the Ministry of Works: "A small stone circle about 25 feet in diameter. Constructed in the Bronze Age about 1500 B.C. and used for religious purposes."

8. Presumably Hardy took the fictional name "Egdon Heath" from Eggardon, though "Egdon" is some miles away, east of Dorchester.

9. Daniell, *The Valley of the Bride,* p. 3.

10. *Thomas Hardy's Wessex,* p. 265.

11. Pictured in Hutchins, *History of Dorset,* II, 335.

12. Stanzas 21 and 22 resemble Jude's discovery that Arabella had become a barmaid in Part III, Ch. VIII of *Jude the Obscure.*

13. *Hardy of Wessex,* 1st ed., pp. 270-71.

14. *Thomas Hardy,* pp. 11-12.

15. Jones, ed., *The Poems of William Barnes,* I, 378.

16. *Dorset County Chronicle* did not record Mrs. Gale's death. Some London newspaper may have listed the name without fully identifying details.

17. *Providence and Mr Hardy,* pp. 122-23.

HER IMMORTALITY is illustrated in *Wessex Poems* with a drawing of the scene vaguely described in the opening stanza. This drawing presents a view that resembles the fields and rolling hills extending from a point in front of Kingston Maurward Park, on the Dorchester-Tincleton Road, toward the lane to Hardy's boyhood home in Higher Bockhampton. A path (not now existent) takes a short-cut across the fields. An iron railing shown in the picture does not, as one might suppose, enclose a grave; such a railing separates the road from the fields. Thus the scene of the poem is the lovers' trysting-place. The "I" of the poem may be Hardy, and the dead woman may be Mrs. Tryphena Sparks Gale, who died in 1890.[1]

The poem dramatizes an idea in "Thoughts of Phena," in which the poet retains in memory the "phantom" of Tryphena, perhaps "the best of her." In "Her Immortality" this phantom speaks to explain that life in her lover's memory is a kind of immortality. (The trance of the poem is not literally the vision of a spirit; it is a point of the poem that "A Shade but in its mindful ones / Has immortality.") Hardy treats this theme in "His Immortality" and "The To-Be-Forgotten."

1. The pictured scene resembles in some features that of "The Mound," which seems to treat Hardy's meeting-place with Tryphena. Deacon and Coleman say that, in spite of differences, the scene is that of "In a Eweleaze near Weatherbury," which seems to treat Tryphena. See *Providence and Mr Hardy,* p. 71.

THE IVY-WIFE is a parable of the clinging, possessive woman. The ivy that grows abundantly in English woods damages certain trees. Hardy, a close observer of natural phenomena and a convert to Darwin's principle of struggle for survival, commented in *The Woodlanders*: "The leaf was deformed, the curve was crippled, the taper was interrupted; the lichen ate the vigour of the stalk, and the ivy slowly strangled to death the promising sapling." (Ch. VII.) Certain trees resist ivy. It is seldom found under beech trees; it has difficulty with plane trees because they shed bark to which ivy might cling, a fact that enables them to thrive in cities, as they regularly shed the overcoat of grime which might make breathing difficult.

Mrs. Emma Hardy read the poem as having some application to herself. In a letter of December 27, 1899, she wrote to Rebekah Owen: "Of recent poetry perhaps you admire 'The Ivy Wife.' Of course my wonder is great at any admiration for it, & *some* others *in the* [*sic*] same collection." The *"some* others" are not named, but a later comment in this letter about "Omar Kayám" [*sic*] as "in sentiment pernicious" suggests poems expressing unorthodox views on religious subjects.[1]

1. In the Colby College Library. Zietlow, in "Thomas Hardy and William Barnes," pp. 295-96, contrasts "The Ivy-Wife" with Barnes's "The Weather-Beäten Tree," which compares ivy to true love.

A MEETING WITH DESPAIR had in the manuscript the explanatory note " (Egdon Heath)." In the opening chapter of *The Return of the Native*, Hardy treats Egdon as a vast, ancient, brooding, living presence, as it seems to those who live on it, some loving it for its austerity, and some hating it. A similar suggestion of animism underlies treatment of this "land . . . like a tract in pain" of the poem. Hardy describes the many moods of the Heath through his own feelings about it, but does not identify himself with it, as in the poem: a "scene, like my own life." Though he tells himself that he is like Egdon only in a passing mood, the poem concludes with the realization of a temperamental affinity.

In *The Return of the Native*, Egdon is presented as a microcosm, the world of those who live on it. Its apparent cruelties frustrating human desire are the merciless processes of nature. On the Heath are Rainbarrow and tumuli, the burial mounds of prehistoric men now returned to mould. Perhaps the visible "Thing" that, in the poem, rises on the horizon is a barrow croaking to the poet the futility of human life and its brevity: the vanity of human hope.

UNKNOWING presents the naiveté of young lovers who plan their future without realizing their helplessness to control circumstances.

If the speaker may be Hardy, the loved woman may be Tryphena Sparks. That Tryphena, who died in 1890, had been dead for eight years before the poem was published fits the concluding stanza.

FRIENDS BEYOND treats the dead who lie in Stinsford Churchyard. The frontispiece in *Wessex Poems* is a drawing of the entrance gate seen at dusk. The pillars for the gate are topped by urns, each adorned with a "face" and drapes that suggest a ghost or a moth. Beyond the gate are tombs under the branches of yew trees, and beyond them the church silhouetted against a darkening sky lighted by a half-moon. The drawing is captioned with two lines from "Friends Beyond": "At mothy curfew-tide / They've a way of whispering to me." Curfew in old Dorchester was eight o'clock. Except for the moth-like faces on the urns, no moths appear in the drawing, but the suggestion in the poem, as in Dorset folk-belief, is that moths, emerging at night-fall, are souls of the dead.[1]

The core of "Friends Beyond" is a dialogue among the dead. They were based on actual people, Hardy's "friends"—even those dead before his birth—with whom he often communed in imagination (see "Paying Calls"). In the dialogue each speaker characterizes himself and his interests in the life he is glad to have laid aside. The leader of the chorus is William Dewy, who appears in *Under the Greenwood Tree* and elsewhere as the 'cellist in the Mellstock choir. He is the father of Reuben Dewy and the grandfather of Dick.[2] As leader of the choir old Dewy was called by reviewers a portrait of Hardy's grandfather, but *The Early Life* says ". . . this was not the case; he [Hardy's grandfather] died three years before the birth of the storyteller, almost in his prime, and long ere reaching the supposed age of William Dewy."[3] Yet similarities are evident. Hardy's grandfather organized the string-band of Stinsford Church and in it played the violincello; he led the Christmas carolling and played at dances, christenings, weddings, and harvest- and wedding-suppers. In the poem, Dewy's "old bass-viol" was the central interest of his life. According to *Tess of the D'Urbervilles*, his grave in Mellstock Churchyard is "just between the second yew-tree and the north aisle" (Chapter XVII) in the area of the Hardy graves.

The Squire of the poem may be based on any one of several men of this rank buried at Stinsford. He may be Squire Audeley Grey (see "Voices from Things Growing in a Churchyard") , or William O'Brien, the husband of Lady Susan. In the list of names that opens and closes the poem and in the dialogue, the Squire is placed next to Lady Susan. More likely he unites the traits of several squires. The Squire suggests his lifetime interest in his "manse" without naming either Kingston Maurward or Stinsford House. His permission, "You may wed my spouse," suggests Squire Francis Martin, for whose wife Hardy had an adolescent dream of love, but Martin had no children.[4]

Lady Susan of Stinsford House was the daughter of the first Earl of Ilchester and the wife of William O'Brien. She is buried in a vault with her husband in Stinsford Church. Her speech suggests the dead woman's anticipation that after her death her possessions, especially her journal and her letters, would be "conned" by relatives.[5]

Farmer Ledlow, speaking in Dorset dialect, expresses his present carelessness about his farm. It was the first one visited by the Mellstock Quire for their Christmas carolling in *Under the Greenwood Tree*. During the services in Mellstock Church, members of the Quire observed that "Mrs. Ledlow, the farmer's wife, counted her money and reckoned her week's marketing expenses during the first lesson." (Part the First, Chapters IV and VI.) Ledlow's wife is mentioned in *The Mayor of Casterbridge*. There Mrs. Cuxsom speaks of going to a Christmas party at Mellstock, "at old Dame Ledlow's, farmer Shinar's sister, do ye mind? —she we used to call Toadskin, because her face were so yaller and freckled, do ye mind?" (Chapter XIII.) These references give dimension to the wife's anxiety about her "best blue china."

The other characters named in the opening stanza speak only in the chorus. Tranter (carter) Reuben was the son of William Dewy in *Under the Greenwood Tree*. "He was a stout florid man about forty years of age, who surveyed people up and down when first making their acquaintance" and who played the tenor violin in the Mellstock Quire. (Part the First, Chapter II.)

Robert was in actual life a boot-maker named Robert Reason, but in *Under the Greenwood Tree* was called Robert Penny. *The Early Life* says of him: "He, like the Tranter and the Tranter's wife, is buried in Stinsford Churchyard near the tombs of the Hardys, though his name is almost illegible. Hardy once said that he would much have preferred to use the real name, as being better suited to the character, but thought at the time of writing that there were possible relatives who might be hurt by the use of it, though he afterwards found there were none."[6] These relatives are "Robert's kin" of the poem.

John and Ned are, like many tombstones in Stinsford Churchyard, not identifiable.

The theme of "Friends Beyond" is a complex of attitudes characteristic of Hardy. Primarily, perhaps, the poem presents one of his frequent visits to "friends" still alive in his imagination. He had not known the characters of the poem in actual life, but he had known them in the tales of his grandmother (see "One We Knew"). These friends represented a permanence and stability he did not find in the ever-changing world around him. They symbolized a village life, customs, order, and ritual—the Christmas carol singing, for instance—that Hardy found richly satisfying. They were real: there they lay asleep in the churchyard, serene, free, and equal, amused, if anything, by the vanities of the world, their own vanities when alive.

The verse-form of the poem fits its subject. The long lines suggest the measure of "Locksley Hall," but the short lines, in Hardy's terza-rima pattern, slow down the rush of Tennyson's poem. The varied line-length lets the speakers' voices sound in the rhythms of colloquial talk, with some suggestion of antiphonal chanting. Hardy's use of rare and learned words in descriptive lines: "stillicide" (the drip of water) and "Trine" (the Trinity); of feudal words: "in fee" (in hereditary possession); and of Dorset dialect: "mid" (may), "zell" (sell), "charlock" (wild mustard), and "grinterns" (bins in a granary) —both gives variety to his verse and suggests the social levels of a vanished time.

In addition to the appearance of the characters of "Friends Beyond" in the prose pieces mentioned above, they appear in other poems: "The Dead Quire," "The Rash Bride," and "The Paphian Ball"; and in the short-stories: "The Fiddler of the Reels" and "The Grave by the Handpost." Echoes of the thought of the poem are scattered throughout Hardy's works. For instance, Lady Susan's speech is echoed in another key in *The Mayor of Casterbridge*, where Mother Cuxsom, mourning the death of Susan Henchard, says: "And all her shining keys will be took from her, and her cupboards opened; and little things a' didn't wish seen, anybody will see; and her wishes and ways will all be as nothing!" (Chapter XVIII.)

"Friends Beyond" has been set to music by Hubert James Foss in *Seven Poems of Thomas Hardy* (London: Oxford University Press, 1925).

1. In a letter to E. B. Poulton on May 20, 1924, Hardy wrote that the "miller moth," supposed to fly out of a man's mouth at the moment of death and "supposed to be his soul—is or was a belief of this country. . . . How old the superstition may be I do not know. . . . The common white moth is still called a 'miller's soul' by the peasantry for obvious reasons." In the Dorset County Museum.

2. He is the subject of a humorous legend in *Tess of the D'Urbervilles*, Chapter XVII.

3. P. 122; *Life*, p. 93. The Dewys' house as described in the novel resembles Hardy's birthplace. Hardy possibly took the name from Joanna Dewey (*sic*), his

maternal great-great-great grandmother, the wife of the Joseph Childs who was born about 1670. In a partial identification of Reuben Dewy, Hardy said, "He had been the many years' neighbour of the Hardys, and did the haulage of building materials for Hardy's father, of whom he also rented a field for his horses." In another memorandum, he seems to identify this man as James Dart, "one of the old Mellstock fiddlers." *Early Life*, pp. 13, 121, 127; *Life*, pp. 11, 92, 97.

4. Unless illegitimate ones as suggested by Deacon and Coleman, *Providence and Mr Hardy*, pp. 170-72. Hardy's phrasing seems to hint at this circumstance.

5. Hardy read Lady Susan's journal some time after "Friends Beyond" was published. Letters from Dowager Lady Ilchester to Hardy, dating from February 19, 1914, to November 6, 1915, tell of her sending Hardy piecemeal a typed copy of Lady Susan's journal. One letter says, "I know I need not ask you not to lend it to anyone out of your House," and a final letter says, "I am at last sending you the end of Lady Susan." In the Dorset County Museum.

6. P. 122; *Life*, p. 92.

TO OUTER NATURE is illustrated in *Wessex Poems* with a headpiece picturing a vase with wilted flowers dangling down its sides. The decay of these flowers, once fresh and lovely, symbolizes the decay of Hardy's once hopeful view of nature.

His boyhood, though strenuous, was not somber. Thrilled by the beauty of woods, fields, and flowers, he was Wordsworthian in his feeling. He called his "Domicilium," written between his seventeenth and twentieth year, "Some Wordsworthian lines." "To Outer Nature" states young Hardy's view: Love had wrought the world for human pleasure; natural beauty made life "Iris-hued."

Time, personified in the poem as a cynic that scorns human hope, brought disillusion. In his maturity Hardy substituted the Darwinian view of nature for the Wordsworthian. His observation of life led him to write of Wordsworth in *Tess of the D'Urbervilles*: "Some people would like to know whence the poet whose philosophy is in these days deemed as profound and trustworthy as his song is breezy and pure gets his authority for speaking of 'Nature's holy plan.'" (Chapter III.)

Blunden points out an influence from Browning's "A Pretty Woman" on Hardy's verse-form. He says that "the metrical discipleship can hardly be denied."[1]

1. *Thomas Hardy*, p. 261.

THOUGHTS OF PHENA presents Hardy's only surviving mention of Tryphena Sparks by name. The obscure background of the poem demands cautious attention to every detail.

Hardy wrote of the composition of this poem in his journal for March 5, 1890: "In the train on the way to London. Wrote the first four or six lines of 'Not a line of her writing have I.' It was a curious instance of sympathetic telepathy. The woman whom I was thinking of—a cousin—was dying at the time, and I quite in ignorance of it.

She died six days later. The remainder of the piece was not written till after her death."[1] "Thoughts of Phena" was in the manuscript titled "T——a. At news of her death. (Died 1890)." When published in *Wessex Poems*, it bore the title "Thoughts of Ph——a," but when republished in *Selected Poems*, the title was "At News of a Woman's Death."[2] These facts indicate that Hardy was writing of an actual woman, Tryphena Sparks Gale, though her death on March 17, 1890, was more than Hardy's "six days later" than March 5.

Hardy's full-page drawing for the poem in *Wessex Poems* shows the shrouded body of a woman laid out on a sofa. Purdy says that the picture represents "a sofa formerly in the dining-room at Max Gate,"[3] but there is some ground for modifying this statement. I see little reason to doubt evidence presented by Deacon and Coleman that in July, four months after Tryphena's death, Hardy and his brother Henry visited her home, talked with her eleven-year-old daughter "Nellie" (Eleanor) Tryphena Gale, and afterwards visited Tryphena's grave in Topsham cemetery; and that, in *Wessex Poems*, the body of Tryphena is pictured lying on a divan drawn from a monument just two graves distant from Tryphena's simple tombstone. Their argument says: "It is to Lieutenant Francis Ross, who was killed on H. M. S. *Tremendous* on June 1, 1794, and shows a shrouded figure with his arms folded across his chest in such a way that at first glance the figure appears to be that of a woman. The figure is laid out on a classical divan, like the one in the [Hardy's] sketch. The monument is so unusual, and so conspicuously next to Tryphena's grave, that this must be evidence that Hardy visited her grave, and corroborates Nellie's account of the visit."[4] Possibly he got the idea for his drawing from Ross's divan and then, when he prepared *Wessex Poems* for publication eight years later, used a sofa at Max Gate for a model.

Some of the recent discoveries of Deacon and Coleman clarify much that has been vague about Tryphena and Hardy's life between 1867 and 1874. The discoveries rest largely upon Miss Deacon's conversations with Mrs. Nellie Tryphena Bromell, Mrs. Tryphena Sparks Gale's daughter, from 1959 to 1965, upon photographs in Mrs. Bromell's album, and upon records in her family Bibles.[5] A summary of Miss Deacon's findings is presented under "A Key to Persons" in the introduction of this book.

The opening lines of "Thoughts of Phena," "Not a line of her writing have I, / Not a thread of her hair," imply that Hardy had received love-letters from Tryphena and had treasured a lock of her hair, as he treasured a lock of Emma's hair,[6] but in loyalty to Emma had either returned them or destroyed them. According to the poem and all known facts, he neither saw Tryphena nor communicated with her after her marriage to Charles Gale.[7] Remembering her only as she was in her youth, he finds it impossible "To conceive my lost prize / At her close." The second stanza is made up of questions that wonder what changes the conditions of her life and the passage of time may have wrought. She remains in his mind only the "phantom" of the maiden he had loved, which (the poem says) may be a finer picture than knowledge of the reality would sustain.

Phrases like "lost prize," "gifts and compassions," and "sweet ways" evaluate Tryphena tenderly. They present Hardy's feeling, about which allowance must be made for his idealizing tendency and his nostalgia; they do not describe her. A statement in the Preface of *Jude the Obscure* reads: "The scheme was jotted down in 1890, from notes made in 1887 and onward, some of the circumstances being suggested by the death of a woman in the former year." This seems to imply that the character of Sue Bridehead may be to some extent drawn from Hardy's memory of Tryphena. Deacon and Coleman point out many similarities between what is known of Tryphena's character and career and Sue's.[8]

1. *Early Life*, p. 293; *Life*, p. 224.
2. Purdy, *Thomas Hardy: A Bibliographical Study*, p. 102. In *Tess of the D'Urbervilles*, Chapter IX, Hardy gave one of Mrs. d'Urberville's chickens the name Phena.
3. Ibid.
4. *Providence and Mr Hardy*, pp. 64, 73. See the illustrations facing p. 113, which present Hardy's drawing and a photograph of Lieutenant Ross's monument.
5. Mrs. Bromell died on February 24, 1965. Miss Deacon has the photographs and the Bibles in her possession.
6. See "On a Discovered Curl of Hair."
7. The implication of the poem "My Cicely" that Hardy saw Tryphena on a visit to Topsham is not evidence that he did so.
8. See also Evelyn Hardy, *Thomas Hardy*, pp. 244-45.

MIDDLE-AGE ENTHUSIASMS is addressed to Hardy's favorite sister, Mary, in comment upon a temperament they shared. In middle-age together they were stirred to youthful joy at a party on a lawn, at a bird-scene in a wood, and in a "sweet" shady nook. Like young people, they promised each other to repeat these pleasures, but both knew in sober middle age that in neither life nor death could they repeat the thrill of the moment. The humorous lines that mock their make-believe are more reflective than cynical.

IN A WOOD was begun in 1887 and completed in 1896. The first of these dates, as well as the headnote, indicates a relationship to *The Woodlanders*, first issued in book form on March 15, 1887. The notation "From 'The Woodlanders'" printed in the *Collected Poems* is misleading: the poem is not in the novel, which contains only a prose statement paralleling its picture of strife among the trees.

The headnote seems the result of a series of editor's errors. In *Wessex Poems*, the notation was "See 'The Woodlanders,'" thus calling attention to the passage in the novel. On examining Hardy's manuscript, Weber discovered that Hardy had written *"Vide* 'The Woodlanders,'" the Latin of which an editor, presumably, translated as *"See."* In the Wessex Edition of 1914, someone changed the *"See"* to *"From,"* and this term was copied into the *Collected Poems*.[1]

The passage in *The Woodlanders* reads: "They went noiselessly over mats of starry moss, rustled through interspersed tracts of leaves, skirted trunks with spreading roots whose mossed rinds made them like hands wearing green gloves; elbowed old elms and ashes with great forks, in which stood pools of water that overflowed on rainy days and ran down their stems in green cascades. On older trees still than these huge lobes of fungi grew like lungs. . . . The leaf was deformed, the curve was crippled, the taper was interrupted; the lichen ate the vigour of the stalk, and the ivy slowly strangled to death the promising sapling." (Chapter VII.)

Just as the passage in the novel is Hardy's description of the wood, the "I" of the poem is Hardy. "He is the one who was 'spirit-lame.' Hardy himself is the one who felt 'city-opprest' and who came to 'this wood' in search of 'release from men's unrest.'"[2] Perhaps, in a general way, the poem presents his development from the period of his youthful Wordsworthian view of nature to his mature, Darwinian view. He went to the wood to learn its secret of "sylvan peace," and questioned the trees, but found "no grace . . . / Taught me of trees." In turning back to man, where, "now and then, are found / Life-loyalties," he advanced toward his later "evolutionary meliorism" which found hope for the betterment of the world in human resistance to the impulses of nature.[3]

To some extent, the verse resembles that of Tennyson's "The Charge of the Light Brigade."[4] Dactyllic rhythms are unusual in Hardy's poems. Perhaps he wished to suggest a strenuous inner struggle against disillusion. The verse-form allowed him to place in ironic balance apparent "sweet comradeship" and the fact of "poison-drip," apparent "brave hollies" and their fear-filled "twitch / Sidelong from thorn."

Gustav Von Holst set "In a Wood" to music. This music in manuscript is now in the Dorset County Museum.

1. See Weber, "Thomas Hardy's 'Song in the Woodlanders.'"
2. Weber, *Hardy of Wessex*, 2nd ed., p. 163.

TO A LADY was titled in the manuscript "To Lady ———. Offended by something the Author had written." This suggests that the person who took offence at "something" was a member of the titled aristocracy, but Hardy may have intended to conceal the person he rebuked. The revised title widens the list of persons to be considered.

The novel most offensive to the largest number of ladies was *Jude the Obscure*. The lady of the poem might be Mrs. Emma Hardy, who made a trip to London to ask Dr. Richard Garnett at the British Museum to help her persuade Hardy not to publish his "vicious manuscript" of *Jude*.[1] She might be Jeannette Gilder, who in "Thomas Hardy Makes a New Departure" called *Jude*, "almost the worst book I have ever read," spoke of its "coarseness, which is beyond belief," and said of Jude, "he is a beast." Or she might be Mrs. Margaret O. W. Oliphant, who denounced *Jude* in a review titled "The Anti-Marriage League." Certain phrases in the poem suggest that Weber was right in identifying Rebekah Owen as the lady Hardy had in mind.[2]

Rebekah Owen was a woman from New York who, after discovering Hardy's novels, became an ardent disciple, visited England and met Hardy in 1892, thereafter spent a good deal of time in England, was welcomed at Max Gate, and became intimate with Hardy, Emma, and, later, Florence.

Miss Owen's discipleship did not include agreement with all Hardy's ideas. Independently wealthy, she shared some of Emma Hardy's pride of social position and looked with disfavor upon Hardy's fellow-feeling for the underprivileged and his thrifty habits, and also she shared Emma's distaste for *Jude the Obscure*. She had been accustomed to bring Hardy her copies of his books as they appeared for him to autograph, as he willingly did. On November 12, 1896, she brought three volumes for his signature, but *Jude* was not among them. Sensitive about *Jude* because of the abuse in many reviews, he noticed the omission. She returned to Max Gate on November 23, with *Life's Little Ironies* for his signature, but again without *Jude*. There is no record of what he said, but shortly before leaving for New York on December 12, she sent *Jude* for his autograph. He took his time about signing it, but did dispatch it to her on January 10.

Apparently Miss Owen felt herself rebuked, and repented in writing, at least, but incurred Emma Hardy's displeasure in doing so. In a letter of February 19, 1897, Emma lectured her: "One thing I abhor in authors. It is their blank materialism. . . . I get irritated at their pride of intellect, & as I get older I am more interested in ameliorations & schemes for banishing the thickening clouds of evil advancing. . . . I do not want T. H. to be hand in glove with Zola. Alas, that *you* are a Jude-*ite*."[3] Miss Owen secretly continued to disapprove. A review of *Jude* in the *Pall Mall Gazette* for November 12, 1895, was captioned "Jude the Obscene," and the punning phrase was widely echoed in other reviews. Miss Owen wrote a doggerel verse about it:

"Anent 'The Simpletons—Hearts Insurgent—
Jude the Obscure'
The vex't question of title may now, I submit,
Be settled at last, with small straining of wit.
Change two letters only [,] the u r I mean,
And you better the sense, for Obscure, read Obscene."[4]

Yet Miss Owen did not discontinue her visits to Max Gate, with perhaps more attention from Emma than from Hardy. Only a few hours before Emma's death, Rebekah and her sister Catharine Owen visited there.[5]

The phrases of "To a Lady" express what Hardy must have felt when Miss Owen, long an ardent disciple with "ready Yeas," disapproved of the most earnestly provocative book he had written. His phrase "cosy cushions" expresses some sense of the petted luxury to which Miss Owen was accustomed. The phrase "as flambeaux banish eve" pictures how showy, artificial lights banish dark truths—the truths of the stars. The sestet answers the lady in terms that echo St. Jerome: "If an offence come out of the truth, better it is that the offence come than that the truth be concealed."[6]

1. Weber, *Hardy of Wessex*, 2nd ed., p. 214.
2. *Hardy and the Lady from Madison Square*, pp. 113-16.
3. In Colby College Library.
4. The title of this verse refers to titles given *Jude* as it was being published in *Harper's Magazine*, Dec., 1894–Nov., 1895. The verse is pencilled on p. 239 of Miss Owen's copy of Israel Zangwill's review of *Jude*, "Without Prejudice," in the *Chap-Book*, Jan. 15, 1896. It is in Colby College Library. See Slack, "The Text of Hardy's *Jude the Obscure*," p. 261.
5. Weber, "From Belmount Hall to Colby," pp. 91-92.
6. Chew, *Thomas Hardy*, p. 143.

TO A MOTHERLESS CHILD has in *Wessex Poems* the title "To an Orphan Child," with the subtitle "A Whimsey." Hardy must have changed the title because the child was only half an orphan; her father was still alive. Perhaps he deleted "A Whimsey" because, though the idea of asexual birth is fanciful, the wish expressed in the poem was an earnest one.

The poem presents his meditation when he and his brother Henry visited Topsham in July, 1890, four months after the death of Tryphena Sparks Gale. They went first to Topsham Cemetery to lay a wreath on Mrs. Gale's grave. Then they called at her home, where they were entertained by her eleven-year-old daughter "Nellie" (Eleanor) Tryphena, the child of the poem.[1] Hardy did meet Nellie's father, but briefly and formally. The father is reported to have told Nellie, "I don't want to see Tom Hardy. You can entertain him," and then to have stayed in the pantry while Nellie served a lunch. As Hardy and his brother left the house, Charles Gale did walk with them to the end of the courtyard. Nellie went on with them to the end of a field. Perhaps the idea for the poem came from their parting. "As they were saying goodbye Henry said she was exactly like her mother, and kissed her. Thomas did not kiss her, but drew away with what Nellie later called a wry expression."[2]

It is not clear that Hardy felt any aversion for Charles Gale. The poem concerns only the fact that Nellie was not an exact replica of her mother. In blaming "niggard Nature's trick of birth," he implied his characteristic charge that the "mechanic artistry" of natural law tends to frustrate human dreams. He expressed this thought in other poems and in *Jude the Obscure*. (See the notes on "At a Bridal," including the quotation from *Jude*.)

1. Nellie Gale, later Mrs. Bromell, was the woman who told Lois Deacon the story of Hardy's youthful romance with Tryphena Sparks.
2. Deacon and Coleman, *Providence and Mr Hardy*, pp. 64-65.

NATURE'S QUESTIONING is illustrated in *Wessex Poems* with a headpiece picturing a door-key broken in the neck between the handle and the head. In addition to the symbolism of the snapped key to represent human inability to unlock the mystery of existence, a broken key had for Hardy a special significance. In *Far from the Madding Crowd*, Maryann says: "an unlucky token came to me this morning. I went to unlock the door and dropped the key, and it fell upon the stone floor and broke into two pieces. Breaking a key is a dreadful bodement." (Chapter XXXIII.) Florence Hardy wrote to Rebekah Owen on May 5, 1916: ". . . my husband says that the breaking of a *front* door key is a sign of death—that some time before his father died their front-door key, at Bockhampton, fell out of the lock and was broken."[1]

The poem opens with the poet looking out a window at early dawn, for Hardy a period of depression. In *The Woodlanders* he describes a dawn: "There was now a distinct manifestation of morning in the air, and presently the bleared white visage of a sunless winter day emerged like a dead-born child." In another chapter, "the tones of morning were feeble and wan. . . . The tree-trunks, the road, the out-buildings, the garden, every object, wore that aspect of mesmeric passivity which the quietude of daybreak lends to such scenes. Helpless immobility seemed to be combined with intense consciousness; a meditative inertness possessed all things." (Chapters IV and XXIV.) The poem likens this "intense consciousness" and "meditative inertness" seen in "Field, flock, and lonely tree" to that of "chastened children" in a school, cowed by their "master's ways," but seeming to ask questions of the human mind.[2] The questions they ask, each implying an answer, are those asked by eighteenth- and nineteenth-century thinkers.

The first question, suggesting the Creator to be "some Vast Imbecility, / . . . impotent to tend" His creation, takes the Deistic view of God as like a watchmaker who created the universe, wound it up, and lets it run by means of natural law. The Deistic God is outside the world, so that, as Hardy phrased it in "Hap," life is left to "Crass Casualty" and "dicing Time," hazardry. The second question implies the Creator to be an unconscious Automaton, and life to be meaningless process, like the bubbling of what Hardy called in *The Dynasts* "some sublime fermenting vat." (Part First, VII, iii.) The concept resembles Schopenhauer's Will, which thrusts blindly in each individual against all others. The third question seems to image the fading of God as an omniscient, omnipotent Person into the misty Deity of the transcendentalists and metaphysicians—Carlyle's "Divine Idea" or Arnold's "Power not ourselves." Swinburne's "Hertha" suggests this God as dying: His "twilight is come on him, / His anguish is here." The fourth question considers the purposive evolution of Tennyson's *In Memoriam* as modified by J. S. Mill's essay on "Nature." Mill argues that the "Principle of Good *cannot* at once and altogether subdue the powers of evil," but must struggle to do so. The Creator needs human help in this struggle. There may be ultimate victory in some evolutionary future. In the meantime, men fare like expendable soldiers in a battle they do not understand.

The questions are left questions, with Hardy's response: "No answerer I." Though agnostic in reasoning, he was religious in feeling. He continued to question all his life. He wrote to Alfred Noyes on December 19, 1920: "A poem often quoted against me . . . is the one called 'Nature's Questioning,' containing the words 'some Vast Imbecility,' etc.—as if these definitions were my creed. But they are merely enumerated in the poem as fanciful alternatives to several others, having nothing to do with my own opinion."[3] His opinion is suggested in his drawing of the broken key and in the last two lines of the poem.

1. In Colby College Library.
2. Hardy wrote in his journal for February, 1897: "In spite of myself I cannot help noticing countenances and tempers in objects of scenery, *e.g.*, trees, hills, houses." *Later Years*, p. 58; *Life*, p. 285. Sherman, in "A Note on One of Hardy's Poems," points out that Hardy's simile of children in a school resembles his "description of the school children of migratory agricultural laborers in his 'Dorsetshire Labourer' essay." See this essay in Orel, *Thomas Hardy's Personal Writings*, especially pp. 182-83.
3. *Later Years*, p. 218; *Life*, p. 409.

THE IMPERCIPIENT is titled in the manuscript "The Agnostic (Evensong:——Cathedral.)"[1] Hardy's full-page drawing in *Wessex Poems* pictures the nave of Salisbury Cathedral during a religious service.

Hardy spoke of himself as "churchy; not in an intellectual sense, but in so far as instincts and emotions ruled."[2] He attended services with some frequency all his life. One statement about his attitude is that in church "we have to sing, 'My soul doth magnify the Lord,' when what we want to sing is 'O that my soul could find some Lord that it could magnify!' "[3] His wish to believe, his sense of isolation from the "bright believing band," was not strong enough to make him *will* to believe in spite of the evidence as he saw it. The poem expresses his distress that both the critics, who attacked him for unbelief, and his friends, whom his agnosticism hurt, did not fully see that he could not accept their faith. A large part of the shocked horror in reviews of *Jude the Obscure* concerned its treatment of orthodoxy. Hardy's friend, Rev. H. J. Moule, wrote to him on June 16, 1903: "But 'The Impercipient'! Of that there is no more to be said than that I can hardly write—I could not speak—without tears. It goes to my heart of hearts that my dear old friend (for it can only be T. H. who mourns) should be so craving for assurance of a Father."[4]

No doubt Hardy did consider whether his inability to believe was a lack in himself. In the first stanza he, "far from claiming any superiority as an 'emancipated' modern, recognizes the extent of his losses while refusing to allow these to lure him into a faith his mind has already rejected."[5] There is irony in his use of "shortcomings" in the stanza that turns upon his critics; by implication, the "glorious distant sea" they saw was a mirage they wished to see, while he saw the fact of a "dark / And wind-swept pine." Yet "the pathos is not weakened by the suggestion that the speaker's vision may be the truer—

the nostalgia and the isolation are still present."[6] The ambivalence is clear in the tight-lipped lines that conclude the poem.

The poem is in the common meter of many hymn-tunes and ballads, with the peculiarity that alternate lines rime with *ee*.

1. Purdy, *Thomas Hardy: A Bibliographical Study*, p. 102, reprints a discarded fourth stanza that states in other words the gist of the present fifth stanza.
2. *Later Years*, p. 176; *Life*, p. 376.
3. *Later Years*, p. 121; *Life*, p. 332.
4. In the Dorset County Museum.
5. Howe, *Thomas Hardy*, p. 177.
6. Perkins, "Hardy and the Poetry of Isolation," p. 156.

AT AN INN, Hermann Lea says, was written at the George Inn, Winchester,[1] presumably on the basis of Hardy's statement, though Hardy more likely meant that the poem concerned an incident there. Some evidence supports Purdy's belief that "The poem is, perhaps, to be associated with Mrs. Henniker."[2]

In the mid-1890's Hardy became very friendly with Mrs. Arthur Henniker, whom he had met in 1893. The poem presents an afternoon meeting, presumably for tea, under such circumstances that a flush of feeling could not be hidden. Possibly "that which chilled the breath / Of afternoon" was realization that they could not be lovers. Later, the final stanza suggests, they suffered from the separation in obedience to the "laws of men."

Perhaps just because the poem described an emotional incident, Mrs. Henniker did not "notice" it in writing to Hardy. He took occasion to point it out to her, writing on February 15, 1899: "Did I tell you that I have had an application for leave to set 'At an Inn' to music? You have never noticed that one, by the way." Mrs. Henniker's reply is not available—it was perhaps destroyed—but he mentioned the poem to her again in a letter of April 13: "I, too, was surprised that 'At an Inn' was asked for and set to music. I almost rejected it when scraping together the pieces [for publication in *Wessex Poems*.]"[3]

1. *Thomas Hardy's Wessex*, p. 267.
2. Purdy, *Thomas Hardy: A Bibliographical Study*, p. 103.
3. I have not seen the music mentioned in these letters.

THE SLOW NATURE is noted as "An Incident of Froom Valley," specifically "Moreford Rise."

"Moreford" is a shallow, unbridged crossing over the Frome River on an unpaved road running north from the village of Moreton, about seven miles east of Dorchester. The "Rise" is a hill beyond the Frome. Presumably, Mistress Damon's house was on the heath, not in Moreton village. Families named Damen (so spelled) have lived for generations in this area.[1] Lea, however, who talked with Hardy about his identifications, called the poem a "fictitious presentment,"[2] and an elderly Mr. Damen now living at Moreton Station and formerly verger of Moreton Church told me that he had never heard of a bull goring a Damen. Hardy's 1894 may date the composition of the poem, rather than a real incident.

As the title suggests, the theme of the poem is the psychological trait of delayed reaction illustrated in Mistress Damon's attention to trifles at the news of her husband's death. Possibly the poem reflects Hardy's meditation upon a trait observed in himself and expressed in many personal poems of remorse for attitudes and actions he regretted when he later reconstructed them imaginatively.

1. Perhaps Hardy named Damon Wildeve in *The Return of the Native* in view of this fact.
2. *Thomas Hardy's Wessex*, p. 267.

IN A EWELEAZE NEAR WEATHERBURY is set in a meadow called Coombe Eweleaze less than half a mile southwest of Puddletown. It is on a secondary road from Puddletown to Beacon Corner, where it turns southward; at Beacon Corner, a pathway continues across Puddletown ("Egdon") Heath to Hardy's boyhood home in Higher Bockhampton. The distance from the Hardy homestead to Coombe Eweleaze along this pathway and road is less than two miles. Hermann Lea says that "This field . . . was at one time a favourite spot for village festivities."[1]

In *Wessex Poems*, Hardy illustrated the poem with a drawing of the eweleaze,[2] the gently sloping and partly wooded hill south of it, and the trees along the course of the present road, though Hardy drew the road across the meadow instead of beside it and a row of three trees instead of the actual four. He drew his spectacles as laid upon the picture, perhaps to symbolize the memory of past years through which he viewed the scene.

The poem recalls Hardy's romance with Tryphena Sparks of Puddletown, perhaps late in the summer of 1867 and (if the last two lines of the poem may be taken literally) at the time of a mutual declaration of love.

The poem is dated 1890. Tryphena's death on March 17 of that year evidently stirred in Hardy memories to which he, then fifty years old, looked back through the "spectacles" of age. Under the spell of revived memories, the first stanza says, he felt himself essentially what he had been twenty-three years earlier. The second stanza, personifying Time as a sculptor, reflects upon the chisel of the years so destructive that, in the defiant fantasy of the third stanza, Beauty (or Tryphena) would scorn his present "worshipping." The spectacles cannot be removed from the scene; the romance must remain a memory.

1. *Thomas Hardy's Wessex*, p. 267.
2. A part of a sheep-pasture where, at lambing time, ewes are kept separate from other sheep.

THE BRIDE-NIGHT FIRE under the title of "The Fire at Tranter Sweatley's"—the title in *Wessex Poems*—was Hardy's first poem to be published. It was written in 1866, but was rejected for publication at that time.[1] When Hardy had made a reputation as a novelist, Richard Gowing of the *Gentleman's Magazine* asked him on September 11, 1875: "Could you favour me with a short sketch, or brief story, or an article on some literary, art or social subject for my next January number?" Hardy sent "The Fire at Tranter Sweatley's." It so pleased Gowing that he wrote on September 30: "Many thanks for the Ballad which I think is full of freshness, vigour and picturesqueness." He did not hold it for January, but said, "It is just what I want to give variety to my November number," in which he published it.[2]

The poem tells its story in the manner of a folk-ballad and to some extent in the Dorset dialect found in the poems of Hardy's friend William Barnes. It is a humorous poem, a fact misunderstood by critics who insisted on regarding Hardy as a writer of tragedies. To some extent, he intended humor in the dialect, which was so little understood that he provided the present glossary for editions after *Wessex Poems*. The rollicking tone of the poem, its almost farcical characterizations, its "junketings, maypoles, and flings" and the "custom-kept rout, shout, and flare / Of a skimmity-ride" are fun. Typically, chance plays a part in the poem (if Sweatley's drunken carelessness is chance), and Sweatley does lose his life, but he, elderly, stingy, and a drunkard, is the villain; in the pattern of folk-tales, he *should* die to make way for the happiness of Barbree and her "true love" Tim.

The Later Years says: "Hardy had a born sense of humour, even a too keen sense occasionally: but his poetry was sometimes placed by editors in the hands of reviewers deficient in that quality. . . . Hence it unfortunately happened that verses of a satirical, dry, caustic, or farcical cast were regarded by them with the deepest seriousness. In one case the tragic nature of his verse was instanced by the ballad called 'The Bride-night Fire,' . . . the criticism being by an accomplished old friend of his own, Frederic Harrison, who deplored the painful nature of the bridegroom's end in leaving only a bone behind him. This piece of work Hardy had written and published when quite a young man, and had hesitated to reprint because of its too pronounced obviousness as a jest."[3] As late as 1920 Hardy commented to Robert Graves about the critics' misunderstanding of it: "Hardy was at the critics again. . . . One man had recently singled out as an example of gloom a poem he had written about a woman whose house was burned down on her wedding-night. 'Of course it is a humourous piece,' said Hardy, 'and the man must have been thick-witted not to see that.' "[4]

The source of the story is "A Wessex Tradition." Edmund Gosse surmised that Hardy heard it from his grandmother: "Was it she who told him . . . that incomparable comedy in verse, 'The Fire at Tranter Sweatley's,' with its splendid human touch at the very end?"[5] While Barbree and Tim may be presented with farcical exaggeration, the event of the fire that burned down Sweatley's house before he, reeling drunk, could escape is realistic for Dorset; only a spark was needed to cause many a roof thatched with straw to flare into holocaust. The skimmity-ride that concludes the poem, though humorously described, is realistic as "A Wessex Tradition." A skimmity-ride "was reported as late as 1884 as having occurred at Whitchurch Canonicorum, between Lyme and Bridport."[6] The anapestic meter of the poem gives it racy animation.

1. Hardy said of it that, "as with his other verses, he had been unable to get [it] into print at the date of its composition by the rather perfunctory efforts he made." *Early Life*, p. 141; *Life*, p. 107.
2. In the Dorset County Museum.
3. P. 80; *Life*, p. 302.
4. *Good-Bye to All That*, pp. 364-65.
5. "Mr. Hardy's Lyrical Poems," p. 290.
6. Heath, *Dorchester*, p. 73. The parallel with Chapter XXXIX of *The Mayor of Casterbridge* is obvious.

HEIRESS AND ARCHITECT is a philosophical allegory that makes use of Hardy's experience as architect's assistant. It is inscribed "For A. W. Blomfield," his employer in 1867, when the poem was written.

Arriving in London in 1862 to seek a position as architectural draughtsman, Hardy was recommended to Arthur William Blomfield and went to work for him on May 5. "Blomfield was the son of the recently deceased Dr. Blomfield, Bishop of London; a Rugbeian, a graduate of Trinity College, Cambridge, where he had been a great boating man; and a well-known church-designer and restorer. . . . Hardy found him . . . a lithe, brisk man of thirty-three, with whom Hardy was to keep up a friendship for near on forty years."[1] Even at the time of Hardy's employment, Blomfield was distinguished, the

President of the Architectural Association. A specialist in "modern Gothic," he devoted himself chiefly to church restoration. Later he became Official Architect to the Bank of England, winning such distinction that he was knighted in 1889. Blomfield's career, as well as Hardy's mentions of merrymaking in Blomfield's office, suggests that the grim architect of the poem is not a portrait of Blomfield.

Possibly Hardy wrote this poem "For" Blomfield to explain to this son of a bishop some of his drift from a "Wordsworthian" to a "Darwinian" point of view in the years 1862-67, when he was reading the scientists. Or possibly he expressed some visionary ideas for buildings that Blomfield found impractical, and the poem may have been in part a mild protest against his veto of Hardy's dreams.

"Heiress and Architect" has a decremental structure found in folk-ballads and many of Hardy's poems. The house of which the heiress dreams progressively shrinks. She would build to welcome nature's beauty, then joy, then love, and finally meditation, but the "arch-designer" reminds her step by step that she must build for security, suffering, disillusion, and death.

The poem is an allegory of human dreams and hopes crushed by realities. The heiress may be considered a romantic inheritor of life and hope, and the "arch-designer" (surely a pun) a master of the real conditions of existence. The debate opens, after the architect's warning about "such vicissitudes as living brings," with the heiress's Wordsworthian assumption that life open to nature will bring happiness. The architect counters with the Darwinian reminder that nature can be cruel. The debate continues on these terms, the romantic dream *versus* the realistic fact, with the house reduced to a coffin at the end.

In *Wessex Poems*, Hardy illustrated "Heiress and Architect" with a page-drawing of figures in outline trying to take a coffin down a stairway without up-ending it. Perhaps this drawing came from a memory of his home in Higher Bockhampton, where the stairs were narrow to save space, perhaps were built against walls in a corner, and turned sharply half-way up.[2]

The poem contains a few technical terms from architecture: inter-volve (complexity of proportion), ogive-work (pointed archways with perforations), and engrailed (having an ornamental border).

1. *Early Life*, p. 48; *Life*, p. 36.
2. The stairs now in this "cottage" have been rebuilt, and no one seems to know just how they were altered.

THE TWO MEN was titled in the manuscript "The World's Verdict. A morality-rime."[1] Though the poem is dated 1866, possibly

Hardy had been considering its underlying problem for some time in relation to his own career. *The Early Life*, speaking of the summer of 1865, says: "About this time Hardy nourished a scheme of a highly visionary character. He perceived from the impossibility of getting his verses accepted by magazines that he could not live by poetry, and (rather strangely) thought that architecture and poetry . . . would not work well together. So he formed the idea of combining poetry and the Church—towards which he had long had a leaning—and wrote a friend in Cambridge for particulars as to matriculation at that University . . . his idea being that of a curacy in a country village." He abandoned this scheme because he felt "after some theological study, that he could hardly take the step with honour while holding the views which on examination he found himself to hold."[2] Perhaps in his indecision—drawn toward penniless poetry that would not "work well" with architecture—he pondered a verse from Ecclesiastes that parallels the thought of the poem: "In the morning sow thy seed, and in the evening withhold not thine hand: for thou knowest not whether shall prosper, either this or that, or whether they both shall be alike good."[3] He dramatized the situation by sketching the life-stories of two men so alike in all except moral aims as to seem two aspects of the same man. He exaggerated tendencies that might have been his own by giving one man ideal or spiritual, and the other crassly selfish aims.

The "views which on examination he found himself to hold" also enter the poem. These views postulate the mechanistic world of "Hap." In this world of chance, nature is indifferent equally to idealism and selfishness. Both men come to what the world judges a bad end; under other circumstances both might have come to a good end. The contrasts of the poem are reflected in Hardy's fiction, as in the equally ineffective careers of the idealist Clym and the sensualist Wildeve in *The Return of the Native*, or the chivalric Giles and the predatory Fitzpiers of *The Woodlanders*.

1. Purdy, *Thomas Hardy: A Bibliographical Study*, p. 104.
2. P. 66; *Life*, p. 50. Dr. Elsie Smith, Librarian of Salisbury Cathedral, told me she had documentary evidence that Hardy applied for admission to a theological school or university, but was rejected. She did not exhibit the evidence, as she wished to publish it herself. In *Jude the Obscure*, Jude's application to Christminster and his rejection (Part II, Chapter VI) are suggestive.
3. Eccles. 11:6. The phrase "much corn and wine" echoes Gen. 27:28: "God give thee of the dew of heaven, and the fatness of the earth, and plenty of corn and wine."

LINES, as the headnote indicates, was written to help raise money for Mrs. Francis Jeune's Fund to give children in London a holiday in the country. Called upon to write this poem on an assigned topic, Hardy completed it at his club just before it was to be recited on the stage. The lines were spoken as an epilogue to a special matinee performance of *As You Like It*, in which the speaker, Ada Rehan, played the role of Rosalind.[1]

The sponsor of the Holiday Fund, Mary Jeune, was a close friend of Hardy's; he had made her acquaintance in the 1880's and had been a guest in her home in London. She was the wife of Francis Henry Jeune, who was knighted in 1892 and became Judge-Advocate-General. His knighthood accounts for the "Lady Jeune" in the headnote.

Ada Rehan was an American actress (born in Ireland in 1860, but brought to America in 1865) in the theatrical company of Augustin Daly, whose production of *As You Like It* was the occasion of the poem. In his journal for July 9, 1888, Hardy wrote a paragraph in praise of Miss Rehan's acting in *The Taming of the Shrew*. In June of 1890, he met Miss Rehan and described her as "A kindly natured, winning woman with really a heart." Evidently she was touched by his "Lines." He was not present, but Mary Jeune reported to him: "Miss Rehan's hand shook so much when she read them that she seemed scarcely able to follow the lines."[2]

Hardy's poem expresses several characteristic ideas: the child is the victim of "unwitting Time's design" and "Nature's quandary"; life is such that, if given a choice before birth, the child might not choose to be born. (See "To an Unborn Pauper Child.") The emphasis of the poem is upon the guilt of society in "immuring" children in city streets and walls, and upon the plea to help them to a holiday on "The down, the cornland, and the stretching green" in open "Space—the child's heaven."

Perhaps because of its intellectual appeal, the newspapers criticized Hardy's "Lines." He wrote to his wife on July 24: "The *Daily News* says they are spirited; the *Globe* that they are poor stuff."[3] He even wrote to the *World* a defensive explanation: that the lines "were written for a charitable purpose, and . . . in great haste, while the accomplished Lady who recited them was waiting for the manuscript."[4]

1. Weber, *Dearest Emmie*, p. 6.
2. *Early Life*, pp. 277, 298, 299; *Life*, pp. 211, 228.
3. Weber, *Dearest Emmie*, p. 6.
4. Bowden, "The Thomas Hardy Collection," p. 9.

"I LOOK INTO MY GLASS" fittingly closes *Wessex Poems*, which opens with "The Temporary the All," expressing the illusions of Hardy's "flowering youthtime." "I Look Into My Glass" asserts the "throbbings of noontide" beneath the "wasting skin" of a man nearly sixty.

A pen-portrait by Henry Nevinson, drawn on May 30, 1903, shows what distressed Hardy when he looked into his glass: "Face a peculiar grey-white like an invalid's or one soon to die; with many scattered red marks under the skin, and much wrinkled—sad wrinkles, thoughtful and pathetic, but none of power or rage or active courage. Eyes bluish grey and growing a little white with age, eyebrows and moustache half light brown, half grey. Head nearly bald on the top, but fringed with thin and soft light hair. The whole face giving a look of soft bonelessness, like an ageing woman. Figure spare and straight; hands very white and soft and loose-skinned."[1] Hardy's pen-portrait offers fewer particulars but more deductions and his typical protest against the ravages of time. "I look in the glass. Am conscious of the humiliating sorriness of my earthly tabernacle, and of the sad fact that the best of parents could do no better for me. . . . Why should a man's mind have been thrown into such close, sad, sensational, inexplicable relations with such a precarious object as his own body!"[2]

His protests sprang from his feeling young inside, where his sensitivity to beauty and to pain still thrilled and shocked him. In the images of his memory, Time stood still. When, after Emma's death, he visited Sturminster Newton, he was amazed at the size of the monkey-puzzle tree he had planted: "He waited a moment as if thinking. Then: 'I suppose that was a long time ago. I brought my first wife here after our honeymoon. . . . She had long golden hair. . . . How that tree has grown! But that was in 1876. . . . How it has changed. . . .' He paused, still staring at the tree—then remarked: 'Time changes everything except something within us which is always surprised by change.' "[3]

The poem laments that his heart has not shrunk as his features have. Hardy was as sensitive to pain as to beauty, and in the 1890's, it seemed to him, Emma had "grown cold" toward his dreams, his ideas (as in *Jude*), and himself. The constantly abrasive pain of loneliness muted every joy. That his distress at remaining young in heart while growing old in body was more than a fleeting fancy is suggested in *The Well-Beloved*. There Pierston's meditations upon this theme parallel the poem: "When was it to end—this curse of his heart not ageing while his frame moved naturally onward? Perhaps only with life." Pierston sees the fact in his glass: "The person he appeared was too grievously far, chronologically, in advance of the person he felt himself to be. . . . Never had he seemed so aged by a score of years as he was represented in the glass in that cold grey morning light. While his soul was what it was, why should he have been encumbered with that withering carcase, without the ability to shift it off for another. . . ?" In this novel Hardy fulfils the wish of his poem: "Would God it came to pass / My heart had shrunk as thin!" After an illness, Pierston loses his sensitivity to beauty, the source of his inspiration as artist, and in the loss finds "equanimity": "The artistic sense had left him, and he could no longer attach a definite sentiment to images of beauty recalled from the past. . . . 'I don't regret it. That fever has killed a faculty which has, after all, brought me my greatest sorrows, if a few little pleasures. . . . Yes. Thank Heaven I am old at last. The curse is removed.' "[4]

"I Look into My Glass" is written in the stanza and meter of the "short-metre doxology" of Hardy's copy of *Hymns Ancient and Modern*. The poem has been set to music by Gerald Finzi in *Till Earth Outwears* (London and New York: Boosey and Hawkes, 1958).

1. *Changes and Chances*, pp. 807-8.
2. *Later Years*, pp. 13-14; *Life*, p. 251.
3. Flower, *Just As It Happened*, p. 97.
4. Part II, Chapter XII, and Part III, Chapters IV and VII.

POEMS OF THE PAST AND THE PRESENT

Following the date July 8, 1901, *The Later Years* says: "During the seven weeks ensuing he [Hardy] was preparing for the press a number of lyrics and other verses which had accumulated since *Wessex Poems* appeared, and sent off the manuscript to the publishers at the end of August. It was published in the middle of November under the title of *Poems of the Past and the Present*."[1] Evidently because reviewers had treated *Wessex Poems* harshly and because he had put into the new volume a good deal of himself in his darkest moods, Hardy was nervous about its reception. On September 17, he wrote to Edmund Gosse: "Alas for that volume! I feel gloomy in the extreme when I think of it, & hope they will let it down easily. Can there be anything more paralyzing than to know that features, subjects, forms, & methods, adopted advisedly, will be set down to blundering, lack of information, pedantry, & the rest."[2]

Poems of the Past and the Present, with a hundred poems, was nearly twice as long as *Wessex Poems*. A few of the poems had been written many years earlier, but most of them shortly before the volume was prepared for publication. Four ("At a Lunar Eclipse," "Her Reproach," "The Widow Betrothed," and "The Ruined Maid") were either written or sketched in the 1860's, and two ("To Lizbie Browne" and "The Levelled Churchyard") seem to date from the 1880's. Most of the "War Poems" treated the early months of the Boer war, in 1899. The "Poems of Pilgrimage," treating journeys of 1887 and 1897, were written long after Hardy's return, perhaps about 1900.

The "War Poems" present no martial glories, but the soldiers as they leave for the far South or as they lie lonely in their foreign graves. "Poems of Pilgrimage" present visits to shrines known to Hardy through his reading, rather than interest in foreign peoples. Among the "Miscellaneous Poems," those on philosophic subjects ("The Mother Mourns." "The Lacking Sense," etc.) exhibit Hardy at work on *The Dynasts*. They represent early stages in his development of the Immanent Will and the Spirits of this epic-drama. With the "In Tenebris" triad, they suggest that the period from the mid-1890's to 1901 was for Hardy one of difficult labor and depression of spirits. A source of depression was his intellectual separation from his wife.

1. P. 91; *Life*, p. 310.
2. In the Dorset County Museum.

v. r. 1819-1901 is Hardy's poetic comment on Queen Victoria, who died on January 22, 1901. He wrote it on January 27 and published it in the London *Times* on January 29. It fittingly opens *Poems of the Past and the Present*. Victoria had been queen through all Hardy's past, and at the time of her death he was composing poems of the present for his new volume.

A letter to Mrs. Arthur Henniker on February 15 suggests his regret that the poem does not express all he felt about the fatefulness of transition from the Victorian time to an uncertain present: "I wonder if you saw some lines I wrote about the Queen. . . . I wrote them during a bad headache, & posted them immediately, & they came out the next day—so that they have all the crudeness of an unrevised performance."[1]

Fatefulness is a theme of the poem. In 1901, Hardy was working out his symbolism of the Will set forth in *The Dynasts*, and the poem presents the Queen as the agent of this Will in Its shaping of an era. Though describing Victoria as personally "Serene, sagacious, free," the poem is no conventional laureate's tribute; it suggests her as symbol of a predestined epoch in human history.

Because it is built upon this deterministic basis and implies more than it states, the poem needs to be read in relation to Hardy's thought as a whole. "The mightiest moments pass uncalendared" suggests that Victoria had not done any great deed, but had in quiet ways, as in the moral earnestness of her life, shaped the era that bears her name. The "deedful word" of the Absolute appointed Victoria to this task. Her "mould" was the pattern she set for her nation; with every "royal-reckoned attribute," she was all a queen was then expected to be.

Hardy expressed his opinion of Victoria in a letter to her biographer, Lytton Strachey, dated April 20, 1921: "I was deeply interested in reading the book, notwithstanding that your subject was a most uninteresting woman. . . . Perhaps I ought not to be quite so absolute as to hold that she was uninteresting all through, since during the 20 years of her married life she was certainly more attractive. . . . However, Victoria was a good queen, well suited to her time and circumstances, in which perhaps a smarter woman would have been disastrous."[2]

The twelfth line of the poem so puzzled N. R. Harihara of India that he wrote Hardy in 1921: "I have not been able to find from reference books 'the deed of hers most bright in eyes to be.' "[3] The deed may be one not now known; it may be the "impulse" or "intent" of Hardy's poem "A Commonplace Day."[4] His conclusion means, I think: let us wait to judge the era she ruled by its ripened fruit.

1. In the Dorset County Museum.
2. In the Miriam Lutcher Stark Library, University of Texas.
3. In the Dorset County Museum; I have not seen Hardy's reply, if he replied.
4. Frank R. Southerington wrote to me: "Isn't the point of this line simply that the most obvious glories of Victoria in the eyes of her subjects may actually be less important than something of which her subjects were ignorant?"

WAR POEMS

The "War Poems" were written about the South African (or Boer) War of 1899-1902. Before 1899, British and Dutch settlers in South Africa contended not only for land but for control of gold and diamond mines. Dreams of South Africa united under the British Crown were contested by President Kruger of the South African Republic, who undertook to squeeze British settlers out of the country. As early as February, 1899, various troubles gave promise of war. Hardy's views at this time are perhaps partly echoed in a letter by Mrs. Emma Hardy to Rebekah Owen, dated February 27. Forecasting war, she said: "The battles will be on a huge scale that's certain—& a terrible ending it will all have. But the Boers fight for homes & liberties—we fight for the Transvaal Funds, diamonds, & gold! is it not so? . . . . Why should not Africa be free, as is America?"[1] Hardy was dismayed by the war, which broke out on October 12, as one of imperial conquest. Troops began to leave for South Africa during the week of October 15, and he went to Southampton to see them embark. Describing the scene, Philo Calhoun wrote: Hardy "had no friend or kin embarking that day: Southampton Docks was just one of many objectives in one of many days of cycling. Nevertheless, his sensitive nature was absorbing not only all the heart-aches of parting, but all the inexorable senseless tragedies which were in store for many of those who stood on the docks with him."[2] It is not clear whether Hardy made more than one trip to Southampton. On November 9, he wrote to Mrs. Arthur Henniker: "I was not at Southampton on the Saturday when you were there—I went Friday, & saw off 5000 altogether." On November 24, he wrote regarding the departure of the artillery from Dorchester: "I am sending with this the sonnet which I wrote on the departure of the troops which I wrote for the Daily Chronicle. . . . It was almost an exact report of the scene & expressions I overheard."[3]

Though the dated poems all belong to 1899, those undated indicate that Hardy was much troubled by the war until its end on May 31, 1902.

1. In the Colby College Library.
2. "An Old Architect's Last Draft," p. 61.
3. In the Dorset County Museum.

EMBARCATION identifies Southampton with three wars of imperial conquest. In 43-44, during the reign of the Emperor Claudius, Roman legions under Vespasian (later Emperor) landed on the southwestern coast of Britain and in some thirty battles fought their way as far northwest as modern Somerset, thus establishing the basis for Roman colonization in Hardy's Dorset. When the Romans had left Britain in the fifth century, the Saxon leader Cerdic, in 495, landed in Southampton water, fought a number of battles with the British, and by 519 established himself as the King of the West Saxons, though in 520 he was temporarily defeated at Badbury (near Wimborne) in Dorset. In turn, the English became invaders. Henry V sailed from Southampton on August 11, 1415, to prove his claim to the French throne by defeating the French at Harfleur and Agincourt. In numbers, at least, the present embarcation is one of "Vaster battalions . . . for further strands." By November 30, 58,000 men and 9,000 horses had left Southampton for South Africa.

The list of invasions introduces Hardy's theme, that even in this "late age of thought, and pact, and code" men still "argue in the selfsame bloody mode." The victims are both the soldiers bound for the "tragical To-be" and their "Wives, sisters, parents" who suppress their tears and smile. Among them are "None dubious of the cause, none murmuring." In 1920, after a war Hardy thought necessary, he selected this line as the motto for the plaque in the Dorchester post-office in memory of the postal workers who died in World War I. In the context of "Embarcation" the line is ironic. That Hardy parallels the South African war with the invasions of Vespasian and Cerdic indicates that he was dubious of the cause and perhaps thought the men should have murmured. His friend Edmund Gosse saw that the poem was not jingoistic and approved. He wrote on October 25: "You are the only poet, up to date, who has said anything worth singing. They all make the blunder of trying to translate our emotion into rhetoric, whereas in this period of suspense rhetoric . . . is monstrously out of place."[1]

1. In the Dorset County Museum.

DEPARTURE expresses the essence of Hardy's lifelong protest against war, and of his remedy: internationalism. Though his statements quoted below were written in reference to World War I (in which he saw England justly fighting a brutal aggressor) they define the feeling that runs through "Departure." In reply to a letter from the "Committee for Promoting an Intellectual Entente among the Allied and Friendly Countries," Hardy wrote on February 8, 1917: "That nothing effectual will be done in the cause of peace till the sentiment of *Patriotism* be freed from the narrow meaning attaching to it in the past (& still upheld by Junkers & Jingoists) & be extended to the whole globe. On the other hand, that the sentiment of *Foreignness* . . . attach only to other planets & their inhabitants, if any." Referring specifically to "Departure," he wrote to John Galsworthy on April 20, 1923: "The exchange of international thought is the only possible salvation for the world: & though I was decidedly pessimistic when I wrote at the beginning of the South African War that I hoped to see patriotism not confined to realms but circling the earth, I still maintain that such sentiments ought to prevail."[1]

Hardy's compassion was for the common soldiers, used "as puppets in a playing hand," considered expendable, and destroyed by power-mad rulers engaged in a selfish game. He pointed out that war-makers consider anyone expendable, men of genius along with "Hodge." Speaking to M. Frederic Lefevre in 1925, he said of World War I: "Many young writers were killed, and I frankly do not see how their intellectual wealth can have found its way to those who survived. . . .

War is a fatality. It has nothing to do with either reason or intelligence."[2]

In imagery "Departure" is worth analysis. The soldiers boarding the ships are pictured (and heard) as "the late long tramp of mounting men"; the dominant races of the Western World, engaged in "wroth reasonings" (words that comment upon each other ironically) are personified in their tribal pride as "Teutons, Slavs, and Gaels."

1. In the Dorset County Museum.
2. Copps, "The Poetry of Thomas Hardy," pp. 416-17, quoting from the *Living Age*, April 11, 1925.

THE COLONEL'S SOLILOQUY is a dramatic meditation, perhaps suggested to Hardy as he heard the forced "Hurrah!" of an aging officer waving farewell to his "Girl," now a grandmother. He wrote to Sir George Douglas on October 26, 1904: "The colonel was meant to be merely an ordinary man of a romantic turn."[1] But in view of his typical realism, Hardy may have had in mind Lieutenant-Colonel Cecil Henry Law, in command of the Dorsetshire Regiment. That Hardy's colonel had served "In Eastern lands and South" matches the fact that Colonel Law had served in India in the 1870's.[2] He may have had in mind Major Arthur Henniker, who had served in Egypt. On October 19, 1899, just before Major Henniker departed for South Africa, Hardy wrote him expressing wishes for his "good fortune out there & speedy return."[3]

The professional soldier, now aging and saddened, half-realizes the folly of war and, in thinking of the role he must play, struggles against self-mockery.

1. In the National Library of Scotland.
2. See Atkinson, *The Dorsetshire Regiment*.
3. In the Dorset County Museum.

THE GOING OF THE BATTERY presents the departure of the 73rd Field Artillery from Dorchester Barracks, on November 2, 1899, for the South African War. The subtitle "Wives' Lament" and the substance of the poem express Hardy's reflections upon this stirring, yet pathetic event. To witness the scene, he stayed up till the last group entrained at 4:45 in the morning. He wrote to Mrs. Arthur Henniker on November 9 of ". . . the going of our Battery of Artillery (stationed in this town) & as they left at 10 at night, & some at 4 in the morning, amid rain & wind, the scene was a pathetic one." He said of the poem, "It was almost an exact report of the scene & expressions I overheard."[1]

The pathos of the departure is evident in various reports. A long article in the *Dorset County Chronicle* for November 9 begins on an ardent note, but modulates into a somber portrayal: *"The Artillery Off for the War. An Enthusiastic Send Off.* Nothing could have exceeded the heartiness with which the 73rd Field Artillery were sent off on Thursday night by the people of Dorchester. The scene owed nothing to that picturesque and imposing appearance presented by a battery of artillery in review of marching order. There was nothing to impress the senses like the prancing of horses, the rattling of the long train of gun-carriages and waggons"—and so on, as the men marched to the railway station, where their guns were ghostly under tarpaulins. The article then makes an effort toward heartiness by describing the surging crowd, the band music, and the pealing of bells, but in describing the farewells of wives and sweethearts comes close to Hardy's picture.

The rhythm of the poem, with its internal rimes ("O it was *sad enough*, weak enough, *mad enough*") , represents the swinging march of the soldiers mingled with the equally rhythmical lament of the wives. The concert pianist Isaac Levine wrote to Hardy on January 11, 1911: "I know of no poem in the same metre—since Hood's 'Bridge of Sighs' that has so much natural pathos. In it I hear . . . the voices of sorrowful wives, and the heavy, dull, indifferent tread of the soldiers."[2] The poem has been set to music by Alfred Hale in *Five War Poems* (London: Goodwin & Tabb, 1926) .

1. In the Dorset County Museum.
2. In the Dorset County Museum.

AT THE WAR OFFICE, LONDON deceptively suggests that Hardy witnessed the clerks of the War Office "Affixing the Lists" in December, 1899. He wrote to Mrs. Arthur Henniker on December 19: "I have not run up to London after all, this month: but I have written a little poem, of 2 stanzas only, on the scene at the War Office after a battle, which, though I have not witnessed it, I can imagine with painful realism."[1]

The opening phrase of the poem, "Last year," when Hardy "called this world . . . / The darkest thinkable," may refer to "A Meeting with Despair," published in *Wessex Poems.*

When the poem appeared in the *Sphere* on January 27, 1900, the word *unshent* created a commotion among reviewers. "Some critics asserted that Hardy had invented it. But they were wrong. *Unshent* is a perfectly good word, with a record dating back to the 14th century, and it has been used effectively by both Keats and Browning. Its meaning, as given in the Oxford Dictionary, is 'Uninjured, unharmed, unspoiled.' "[2]

1. In the Dorset County Museum.
2. Flower, *Just As It Happened,* p. 233.

A CHRISTMAS GHOST-STORY was attacked editorially, and the attack brought forth, in Hardy's reply, a statement of his attitude toward war. The attack and reply are involved with the history of publication of the poem.

Though he dated the poem "*Christmas-eve* 1899," it was printed in the *Westminster Gazette* on December 23, 1899. As first published the poem was only eight lines long. The last four lines were added after the attack on the poem;[1] they develop, in a slightly argumentative tone, a point in Hardy's reply.

The location of the poem, "inland from far Durban," and the identification of the "mouldering soldier" as "your countryman" suggest that Hardy may have found his inspiration in a news-story in the *Dorset County Chronicle* for November 30, 1899, "The Somersets At Durban," announcing the arrival of the Somersetshire Light Infantry.[2]

On Christmas Day an editorial in the *Daily Chronicle* attacking the pacifistic feeling expressed in the poem, concluded: ". . . we fear that soldier is Mr. Hardy's soldier, and not one of the Dublin Fusiliers who cried amidst the storm of bullets at Tugela, 'Let us make a name for ourselves!' " Hardy responded that day; his letter is dated December 25, and the editor of the *Chronicle* printed it on December 28. It argues essentially that, though the living soldier may have had the physical courage of a Dublin Fusilier, it is not likely that a disembodied spirit, "an entity which has passed into a tenuous, impartial, sexless, fitful form of existence, to which bodily courage is a contradiction in terms," would be concerned with making a name. He then goes on to surmise that a ghost might share some of his internationalism: "His views are no longer local; nations are all one to him; his country is not bounded by seas, but is co-extensive with the globe itself, if it does not even include all the inhabited planets of the sky. He has put off the substance, and has put on, in part at any rate, the essence of the Universe." With some humor, Hardy points out that the ghosts of Greek, Roman, Hebrew, and Christian literature—from Homer to Dante—rose to a "level of serenity" in the spiritual world above fear or courage. In his conclusion, he perhaps overlooked the phrase "your countryman" in his poem, or perhaps meant it to be read in the sense of the poem "His Country." He said: "Thus I venture to think that the phantom of a slain soldier, neither British nor Boer, but a composite, typical phantom, may consistently be made to regret on or about Christmas Eve (when even the beasts of the field kneel, according to a tradition of my childhood) the battles of life and war in general, although he may have shouted in the admirable ardor and pride of his flesh-time, as he is said to have done: 'Let us make a name for ourselves!' "

The editor, in printing this reply, added: "Mr. Hardy's dead soldier is rightly admitted to the best company of Christmas ghosts, and we feel the pathetic beauty of the conception, whatever we may think of its metaphysics."[3]

Hardy's definition of the unworldly serenity of ghosts was not altogether made up for the occasion. Throughout his works his ghosts exhibit detachment.

In "A Christmas Ghost-Story," as in other poems treating Christian holy-days, his theme is the disparity between the teachings of the Prince of Peace and the behavior of Christian nations. Honoring this point of view in Hardy's writings, Dr. Nevile Lovett, Lord Bishop of Salisbury, in a Hardy Memorial service at Stinsford Church on June 2, 1940, said: "May we not say that we honour him . . . that he did valuable service by his blows at the distortions of Christianity to which we Christians have become all too complacent."[4]

1. Purdy, *Thomas Hardy: A Bibliographical Study*, p. 108.
2. Somerset, northwest of Dorset, is a part of Hardy's Wessex. Durban is a port in Natal, from which troops would march inland to seek the enemy. A soldier killed there would lie under Canopus, a bright star of the Southern heavens.
3. Orel, *Thomas Hardy's Personal Writings*, pp. 201-3.
4. "The Hardy Centenary," the *Western Gazette*, Yeovil, June 7, 1940, p. 2.

DRUMMER HODGE, on its first printing in *Literature*, November 25, 1899, bore the title "The Dead Drummer," with the note: "One of the Drummers killed was a native of a village near Casterbridge [Dorchester]." Then Hodge is no abstraction, but a boy whom perhaps Hardy knew. It seems impossible, however, to identify him. As Colonel D. V. W. Wakely of the Military Museum in Dorchester said, "He may be any boy from Dorset, who may have joined the Dorset Regiment or the Dorset Volunteers for the war in South Africa."[1] In naming the boy[2] Hodge, Hardy used a nickname for yokel or country bumpkin to represent the attitude of the war machine toward country boys as cannon fodder. This attitude is indicated in the opening line of the poem: "They throw him in . . ." *they* being the burial-detail of the Quartermaster Corps who treat Hodge as rubbish.

Hardy protested this attitude vigorously. In *Tess of the D'Urbervilles*, he sought to lead readers to understand Hodge as a person by showing how Angel Clare came to revise his unusually liberal, but still snobbish view: "The conventional farm-folk of his imagination—personified by the pitiable dummy known as Hodge—were obliterated after a few days' residence. At close quarters no Hodge was to be seen. . . . He had been disintegrated into a number of varied fellow creatures—beings of many minds, beings infinite in difference; some happy, many serene, a few depressed, one here and there bright even to genius, some stupid, others wanton, others austere; some mutely Miltonic, some potentially Cromwellian; into men who had private views of each other, as he had of his friends; who could applaud or condemn each other, amuse or sadden themselves by the contemplation of each other's foibles or vices; men every one of whom walked in his own individual way the road to dusty death."[3] Drummer Hodge is no yokel, but a callously sacrificed unknown soldier of the Boer War.

Hardy underrated the poem. He wrote of it to Mrs. Arthur Henniker on November 24, 1899: "The thought it embodies is a mere passing one of no profundity, but it happens to be curiously apposite to the moment."[4] It is eloquent in its picture of a farm-boy sacrificed for nothing he understood. To home-loving Hardy, bred in the Wessex tradition and fond of "paying calls" on departed friends in the churchyard, Hodge's eternal hole in the loam ("uncoffined") of an alien land added insult. An archetypal feeling runs through the poem that the soul must wander lost forever when the body lies in an "unknown plain" under "strange-eyed constellations." The foreignness of that fate is emphasized by Hardy's use of Dutch words, "kopje" instead of the Wessex downs, "veldt" instead of grazing land, and the Karoo instead of the familiar heath.

The poem has been set to music by Alfred Hale in *Five War Poems* (London: Goodwin & Tabb, 1926).

1. In a conversation on April 21, 1966. Colonel Wakely consulted records and found several possibilities.
2. Drummers were usually teen-agers.
3. Chapter XVIII. Hardy's essay "The Dorsetshire Labourer," reprinted in Orel, *Thomas Hardy's Personal Writings*, pp. 168-91, defines the conventional view of Hodge as a bumpkin and protests that this view is a libel and a lie.
4. In the Dorset County Museum.

A WIFE IN LONDON, Hynes says, "provides a simple example of the way in which Hardy's ironic view determined the structure of his work."[1] Another critic finds the "presentment here too raw, and too obviously raw. . . . True irony would demand—would it not?—the impact of the sharp ill upon the comfortable good news; but for a woman already sea-deep in woe, ironic contrast is lost."[2] This critic is demanding artifice for effect. In view of his frequently factual sources, possibly Hardy knew the woman. Certainly the event was likely in days when letters were carried by ship.

1. *The Pattern of Hardy's Poetry*, p. 44.
2. Freeman, "Thomas Hardy," p. 132.

THE SOULS OF THE SLAIN appeared in the *Cornhill Magazine* in April, 1900, with a note longer than the present one: "The spot indicated in the following poem is the Bill of Portland, which stands, roughly, on a line drawn from South Africa to the middle of the United Kingdom; in other words, the flight of a bird along a 'great circle' of the earth, cutting through South Africa and the British Isles, might land him at Portland Bill."[1] This note says nothing of the peculiar geography of which Hardy makes symbolic use in the poem. The Isle of Portland (or peninsula, with a narrow neck of pebbles connecting it to the mainland) is a promontory of stone (lightly covered with topsoil), shaped like the neck and head of a bird jutting out about five miles into the ocean. The Bill, as the outer tip is called, is a jumbled mass of great rocks, falling sheer into the sea, among them a towering cube called Pulpit Rock. In the ocean beyond the Bill is the Race, between the land and a shallow area called the Shambles three miles to the southeast. The Race is turbulent, for currents from French shores and the south clash there with currents from the northeast. Weymouth Bay and Portland Harbor lie northeast of the Bill, above the neck of the "bird," and Deadman's Bay (where part of the Spanish Armada was wrecked) lies northwest, under the throat. Conflicting currents in the Race "cause a continual bubbling and rippling of the water," and the Race is dangerous for the "foulness and rockyness of the ground, which makes that space of the sea boil like a pot, and drives vessels on shore on the beach west of the island," in Deadman's Bay.[2] In stormy weather the sea beats against the Bill with a force that sends geysers fifty feet into the air. This beating of the sea has worn great caverns, one of them called Cave Hole, into the clifflike rocks, wherein the sea booms like a drum. The "turreted lantern" of the poem is a lighthouse on the Bill; a lightship floats above the Shambles.[3]

Hardy's setting for the poem is accurate, atmospheric, and symbolic. The spirits arrive and depart on no natural wind—"No wind fanned the flats of the ocean"—but "Like the Pentecost Wind."[4] They cross the Race and light "On the ledge by the turreted lantern," on or near Pulpit Rock. There, "On a dim afternoon in November one can listen to sermons of excellent import."[5] This is near Cave Hole, which, along with the Race, "That engulphing, ghast, sinister place," seems in the poem to symbolize Hell. In terms of folk-lore rather than the Bible, the souls are compared with night-moths. The General who arrives, though "Of the like filmy hue," is a "senior soul-flame," like the Holy Ghost that appears in "cloven tongues like as of fire" at Pentecost. (Acts 2:3-4.)

Friedman analyzed the poem in detail as a "dream vision." The dream begins as "The thick lids of Night closed upon" the narrator, "an old man caught in a dilemma, a conflict; the spectres whose talk he overhears externalize his internal brooding." The landscape is "an elaborate psychic metaphor defining the state of his *persona*. Its features have the qualities of human features. The ground on which the narrator ostensibly finds himself is 'Many-caverned, bald, wrinkled of face.' The slope of the land is 'bent-bearded.' " Hardy's image of the ocean suggests the human psyche. "Hardy strengthens the psychic association of his sea by characterizing the submergence of the souls as a forgetting. He means in one way that these unfortunates, having left only bitterness behind them, disappear from the memories of their acquaintances. But he means in another way that the attitudes they bespeak form the consciousness of his *persona*, that they are repressed." Friedman compares the idea of the poem, that the dead live only in men's memories, with that of "His Immortality." Ironically, in view of the glory for which they gave their lives, "No one . . . remembers the spirits as warriors, except perhaps the girls who would exploit their fame. The captain [General] has . . . heard no martial music, no glorification of the battles they fought."[6] Men *are* long-remembered for their homely, kindly deeds. In something like the Last Judgment, "those of bitter traditions" plunge into the Hell of the Race, but "Those whose record was lovely and true" depart to the Heaven of home—for as long as their deeds are remembered.

Hardy may be considered the dreamer-narrator, but no other identifications are possible. Various generals were killed in the Boer War before December, 1899; though Portland is in Dorset, Hardy's note with the first publication speaks of "the middle of the United Kingdom."

Unusual words include "bent-bearded" (covered with stiff grass), "mighty-vanned" (with great wings), "mould" (flesh, form), "nether bord" (Southern shores, Africa), and "Under Capricorn" (in Southern tropics).

1. Purdy, *Thomas Hardy: A Bibliographical Study*, p. 109.

2. Hutchins, *History of Dorset*, II, 827.

3. In *The Well-Beloved*, set on Portland, Hardy described the Bill and the Race; see the opening chapter and Part III, Chapter VI. Lea's *Thomas Hardy's Wessex*

has a picture of "Cave Hole, Portland" as Plate 157, p. 207; of "Hope Cove, Portland" as Plate 162, p. 211; and of "The Pulpit Rock, Portland Bill" as Plate 203, p. 269.

4. "And when the day of Pentecost was fully come . . . suddenly there came a sound from heaven as of a rushing mighty wind." Acts 2:1-2.

5. Powys, *Dorset Essays*, p. 105.

6. "'When There Is Nothing': Hardy's *Souls of the Slain.*"

SONG OF THE SOLDIERS' WIVES AND SWEETHEARTS was first printed in the *Morning Post* for November 30, 1900, with the title "Song of the Soldiers' Wives." In sending the poem to the editor, J. Nicol Dunn, on November 28, Hardy wrote that it was in celebration of the return from Africa of the Household Cavalry, adding: "If too late for the homecoming of the Household Cavalry, it might be later on."[1] "Household Cavalry" is a term used for the Royal Horse Guards (also known as "The Blues") and the Life Guards, the special troops who escort the King or Queen in London.

In a letter to Mrs. Arthur Henniker on Christmas Eve, 1900, Hardy said, "My Soldiers' Wives' Song finished up my war effusions, of which I am happy to say that not a single one is Jingo or Imperial."[2] Consistent with this statement, the happy welcome says not a word of heroism or glory.

The meter and the repetitions, as of "home again," have the lilt of song, along with a definition of what home means to the soldiers as well as to the wives and sweethearts. The poem has been set to music by Alfred Hale in *Five War Poems* (London: Goodwin & Tabb, 1926).

1. McCutcheon, *The Renowned Collection of First Editions of Thomas Hardy*, p. 65.

2. In the Dorset County Museum.

THE SICK BATTLE-GOD fittingly closes the War Poems with a sketch of the sickening unto death of the old romantic war-idol. In *The Dynasts*, the Spirit of the Pities, observing the Battle of Waterloo, pictures the barbaric attractiveness of this god:

> Behold the gorgeous coming of those horse,
> Accoutred in kaleidoscopic hues
> That would persuade us war has beauty in it!—
> Discern the troopers' mien; each with the air
> Of one who is himself a tragedy:
> The cuirassiers, steeled, mirroring the day;
> Red lancers, green chasseurs: behind the blue
> The red; the red before the green:
> A lingering-on, till late in Christendom,

> Of the barbaric trick to terrorize
> The foe by aspect! (Part Third, VII, iv.)

Hardy defines the eras of the battle-god's reign in the realities of rape, raid, bruise, blood-hole, and corpse. Viewing these realities through modern meditation, penmen's pleadings, thought on "The mournful many-sidedness of things," and realization that the enemy is no Devil but a companion on the road to dusty death, civilized men reject the battle-god. The poem expresses Hardy's faith that war is an anachronism in the twentieth century. In 1901, he said to William Archer: "Oh yes, war is doomed. It is doomed by the gradual growth of the introspective faculty in mankind—of their power of putting themselves in another's place. . . . Not to-day, nor to-morrow, but in the fulness of time, war will come to an end, not for moral reasons, but because of its absurdity."[1] He held this view until 1914: "A long study of the European wars of a century earlier had made it appear to him that common sense had taken the place of bluster in men's minds . . . and as long before as 1901 he composed a poem called 'The Sick Battle-God,' which assumed that zest for slaughter was dying out." Then World War I disillusioned him: "It was seldom he had felt so heavy of heart as in seeing his old view of the gradual bettering of human nature . . . completely shattered by the events of 1914 and onwards."[2]

Besides the general references to nations and rulers that had caught the "sheen" of the battle-god, Hardy names celebrated heroes who sacrificed themselves in quixotic homage to this god. Major-General James Wolfe died in the rash (though successful) capture of Quebec from the French in 1759. The French Marshal Michel Ney, though he did not die in battle, led Napoleon's troops in suicidal assaults upon the British squares at Waterloo. Admiral Horatio Nelson was picked off by a French sharpshooter at Trafalgar because he insisted upon wearing his martial decorations into battle.[3]

"The Sick Battle-God" presents one of Hardy's "richest examples of internal rhyme . . . in a regular pattern throughout the poem. . . . In the exact middle of the last line of the stanza occurs the rhyme of the preceding line, which is not repeated elsewhere. The scheme might be designated as *aabb-a*."[4]

1. Archer, "Real Conversations: Conversation I," p. 317.
2. *Later Years*, p. 162; *Life*, pp. 365-66.
3. In *The Dynasts*, Part First, V, ii, Nelson refuses to remove his "stars and orders," saying: "They were awarded to me as an honour, / And shall I do despite to those who prize me, / And slight their gifts? No, I will die with them, / If die I must."
4. Vinson, "Diction and Imagery in the Poetry of Thomas Hardy," p. 171.

Eight of the "Poems of Pilgrimage" treat the Hardys' trip to Italy in the spring of 1887; two of them treat their visit to Switzerland in 1897; and the final one presents Hardy's reason for not visiting America. He devoted Chapter XV, "Italian Journey, 1887," of *The Early Life* and *The Life* to a narrative of the trip to Italy, and pages 67-70 of *The Later Years* (pages 293-95 of *The Life*) to the visit to Switzerland.

His attitude toward these trips is stated as a "pilgrimage." The term indicates no tourist's jaunt to gaze at curiosities and pass on. His trip to Italy was made somewhat holy to Hardy by his study of Latin classics and his visions based upon them. None the less, for finding his way around, identifying what he saw, and even writing his poems "a long time after"[1] the journey, he found useful Baedeker's *Handbook for Travellers*.[2]

Baedeker's descriptions treat chiefly Christian Italy and monuments of the Middle Ages and the Renaissance. It is characteristic, however, that Hardy's poems set in Italy treat chiefly Shelley, Keats, and the ruins of pagan Rome; even the poem about a room in the Vatican is devoted to the pagan Muses. *The Early Life* and *The Life* state this interest: "But he was on the whole more interested in Pagan than in Christian Rome, of the latter preferring churches in which he could detect columns from ancient temples. . . . So that, for instance, standing on the meagre remains of the Via Sacra then recently uncovered, he seemed to catch more echoes of the inquisitive bore's conversations there with the poet Horace than of worship from the huge basilicas hard by, which were in point of time many centuries nearer to him."

1. *Early Life*, p. 246; *Life*, p. 187.
2. The editions of Baedeker cited in the bibliography are those of 1886 for the "First Part" and 1881 for the "Second Part," presumably those Hardy used.

GENOA AND THE MEDITERRANEAN presents the Hardys' first impression of Genoa. From his reading in the classics, Hardy brought to Genoa the dream of a multimarbled "Queen" enthroned beside the "epic-famed, god-haunted Central Sea." His copy of Baedeker's *Handbook for Travellers* supported this dream; Baedeker called Genoa "La Superba," a term used in the poem.[1] But from a train window and the railroad station the Hardys saw the city in the "squalid undress" of gaudy wash hung across the narrow streets. Emma Hardy wrote in her diary, "When we came to Genoa caught peeps of the Mediterranean & shipping dull weather, no blue sea."[2] The poem rebukes "Genova the Proud" for thus greeting guests in negligee: "clad—not as the Beauty but the Dowd."

Baedeker's details explain what happened. The Hardys travelled from Turin to Genoa by way of Alessandria, crossing the Ligurian Apennines. The train ran through eleven tunnels, the last of them, the Galleria dei Giovi, nearly two miles in length; it entered the city through a tunnel. On exit from the final "deep-delved way" the Hardys arrived at the Station Piazza Principe. Toward the sea, they had to look across railroad yards and dockyards, where construction work was in progress. "The Duke of Galleria . . . having presented twenty million francs for the improvement of the harbour, on condition that the government and the city would advance the remainder of the required sum, extensive alterations have begun to take place." Baedeker recommended that visitors avoid the streets near the harbor, which he called "noisy and bustling." [3]

Later, Hardy observed the marble in Genoa, "so pre-eminently the city of marble—everything marble . . . even little doorways in slums." [4] Baedeker likewise mentioned marble in nearly every building he described. The poem echoes this fact in the term "multimarbled." One item in the poem owes nothing to Baedeker. Hardy was impressed by his first sight of orange trees. Baedeker's description of the Palazzo Doria[5] spoke of "The garden of the palace, extending towards the harbour" and the "gardens on the hill opposite," but made no mention of the orange bowers that in the poem "Went far to mend" the Hardys' first impression.

1. Baedeker, *Italy. First Part: Northern Italy*, p. 78.
2. In the Dorset County Museum.
3. Baedeker, pp. 72-80.
4. *Early Life*, p. 246; *Life*, p. 187.
5. A palace in the Piazza del Principe presented to Andrea Doria in 1552 as a reward to Genoa's "greatest citizen after Columbus and Mazzini." Doria "freed his country from the rule of Charles V and then from the rule of Francis I, swept the Barbary corsairs from the seas, and beat the Turks in battle on shore and seas." Copps, "The Poetry of Thomas Hardy," p. 427.

SHELLEY'S SKYLARK is a tribute to Shelley rather than Italy. From Genoa, the Hardys travelled to Pisa, where they "saw the sun set from one of the bridges over the Arno, as Shelley had probably seen it from the same bridge many a time." [1] The prose account makes no mention of a side-trip to nearby Leghorn, but "Shelley's Skylark" suggests a ramble "Somewhere afield here."

Viewing the Italian journey as a pilgrimage, Hardy visited shrines associated with Shelley's life and poetry. In 1866, as a young man in London, he read with absorption Shelley's *Queen Mab and Other*

Poems. "Mrs. Hardy tells us that he cherished even the most remote approaches he had made to the footsteps of Shelley: as the fact that in childhood he and his mother had once put up at the Cross-Keys, St. John Street, Clerkenwell, where Mary Godwin and Shelley used to meet.[2] He cherished the one meeting he had with Sir Percy and Lady Shelley, the visit he had paid to Mary Shelley's grave in Bournemouth, and to Shelley's grave in Rome. At Max Gate he kept a portrait of Shelley near the chimney-piece. Sir James Barrie . . . speaking of the copy of Shelley's poems that Hardy carried in his pocket when a young man, declared: 'There are a hundred, a thousand, pencil marks.' "[3] Hardy absorbed Shelley's thought and quoted liberally from Shelley's poems.[4]

Shelley wrote "To a Skylark" in 1820, while living at Casa Ricci at Leghorn. In it he was "moved . . . to prophecies" that had inspired young Hardy. Besides thinking with reverence of the skylark's poetic immortality, Hardy thinks of the bird's death in relation to his own experience and to the scientifically based idea[5] that the perished bird has been absorbed into the organic life of the place. An incident in his childhood experience is echoed in the image of the dead bird as "A little ball of feather and bone." He "remembered . . . being in the garden at Bockhampton with his father on a bitterly cold day. They noticed a field-fare, half-frozen, and the father took up a stone idly and threw it at the bird, possibly not meaning to hit it. The field-fare fell dead, and the child Thomas picked it up and it was as light as a feather, all skin and bone, practically starved."[6] That the dead bird may live in other forms—a Shelleyan idea—is found in a number of Hardy's poems, for instance, "Voices from Things Growing in a Churchyard."

1. *Early Life*, p. 246; *Life*, p. 188.
2. See *Early Life*, pp. 21-22; *Life*, p. 17.
3. Bartlett, "Hardy's Shelley," p. 15.
4. Hardy's works contain many references to Shelley and quotations from his poems. For instance, *Desperate Remedies* quotes from "To ——," concluding Chapter II, and from "Lines: 'When the Lamp Is Shattered' " in VI; *Far From the Madding Crowd*, from "Ode to the West Wind" in XLIV; *The Hand of Ethelberta*, from "Adonais" in XVII; *The Mayor of Casterbridge*, from "The Revolt of Islam" in XLIV; *The Woodlanders*, from "The Revolt of Islam" in XVI; and *The Well-Beloved*, from "The Revolt of Islam" on the title page and in I, i, and from "Prometheus Unbound" in I, i. See Weber, *Hardy of Wessex*, 1st ed., p. 244, for additional quotations.
5. As in the laws of conservation of energy and matter; see FitzGerald, "Science in the Poetry of Tennyson, Hardy, and Meredith," p. 49.
6. *Later Years*, p. 263; *Life*, p. 444.

IN THE OLD THEATRE, FIESOLE is not in chronological order among the poems of pilgrimage. The Hardys visited Fiesole on their return to Florence after their trip to Rome. In Florence, Hardy renewed his acquaintance with a friend of his boyhood, who had been living in Florence for some time. She was "Miss Lucy Barnes of Dorchester, afterwards Mrs. S. T. Baxter of Florence, known to readers as 'Leader Scott.' I [Hardy] can first remember her as an attractive girl of nineteen or twenty, living at the house of her father, William Barnes, the poet and philologist. . . . During our stay in Florence in 1887 my wife and I saw her almost every day; and we made pilgrimages together to many spots of interest."[1]

In the afternoon of Easter Monday[2] the Hardys journeyed to the foot of the hill on which Fiesole stands and there engaged an omnibus for the top. The driver "went to have a drink before starting, and left the omnibus untended"; the horse ran away toward Florence, till stopped by some workmen. Then the Hardys and Mrs. Baxter "climbed up—this time on foot despite all invitations from flymen." There, "while Hardy was sitting in the stone Amphitheatre on the summit of the hill,"[3] a child showed him a coin "That bore the image of a Constantine."

Among Roman coins found near Dorchester and preserved in the Dorset County Museum an especially interesting one bears this image. "In case XV, in the Fordington find, is a 3rd brass of Constantine I. (marked IV.) which had evidently been put in the mouth of a corpse, probably for Charon's fee."[4] According to the poem, the sight of the child's coin opened the poet's mind to "The power, the pride, the reach of perished Rome."

Baedeker's description of Fiesole indicates other similarities between Fiesole and Dorchester. This description of Fiesole (then about the size of Dorchester) says that the "Cyclopean walls" of this "ancient Etruscan town . . . are still partly preserved. . . . We first reach a well-preserved fragment of the *Ancient Etruscan Wall*, and next the entrance of an *Ancient Theatre*, excavated since 1873. Sixteen tiers of stone seats, in a semicircle 37 yds. in diameter, are visible." Nearby, on the ground floor of the Palazzo Pretorio, "is the *Museo Fiesolano*, containing the yield of the excavations mentioned above."[5] The presence of Mrs. Baxter there, perhaps with talk of her childhood home; crumbling boundary walls, "Where Rome and dim Etruria interjoin," like the crumbling walls of the Roman outpost of Durnovaria (Dorchester) ; the Old Theatre like Maumbury Ring at Dorchester; the "Museo" like the Dorset County Museum, with similar "yield" of excavations—all would suggest to Hardy how similar the two towns had been under the Caesars. The surmise is supported by a comment he made in his journal in Venice: "Yes: here to this visionary place I solidly bring in my person Dorchester and Wessex life. . . . The bell of the Campanile of S. Marco strikes the hour, and its sound has exactly that tin-tray *timbre* given out by the bells of Longpuddle and Weatherbury, showing that they are of precisely the same-proportioned alloy."[6] The coin brought Hardy's distant home to his mind and presented Dorchester and Fiesole as twin-parts of the Rome of the Constantines.

1. Hardy, "Recollections of 'Leader Scott.' " See Orel, *Thomas Hardy's Personal Writings*, p. 255. His "Recollections" was written as an obituary. He wrote to Mrs. Arthur Henniker on November 28, 1902: "A friend of ours has lately died at Florence. Having known her in early life I wrote a little obituary notice of her. She was a gentle & charming woman, & had lived in Florence between 30 & 40 years." In the Dorset County Museum.

2. Dated in Emma Hardy's diary in the Dorset County Museum.

3. *Early Life*, p. 251; *Life*, pp. 191-92.

4. Moule, *Dorchester Antiquities*, p. 70.

5. *Italy. First Part: Northern Italy*, pp. 458-59.

6. *Early Life*, pp. 252-53; *Life*, p. 193. "Longpuddle" and "Weatherbury" are Hardy's fictional names for Puddlehinton-Puddletrenthide and Puddletown, villages near Dorchester.

ROME: ON THE PALATINE pictures the Hardys on a tour, Baedeker in hand. In Rome, they "put up at the Hôtel d'Allemagne, in the Via Condotti, a street opposite the Piazza di Spagna. . . . Hardy's notes of Rome were of a very jumbled and confusing kind."[1] This fact, with the suggestion that the poem was written long after the tour, suggests that he turned to Baedeker to refresh his memory, but still recalled that he explored the Palatine independently.

If the opening stanza traces the Hardys' route, they began near the middle of the tour prescribed for "The Palatine" and proceeded irregularly toward Baedeker's starting point, the "Ingresso."[2]

In the poem, the tour begins with the shrine to "Victor Jove," which Baedeker described: "From the Academia a few steps descend to the flight of steps by which an ancient temple was approached. This, according to Rosa, was the temple of *Jupiter Victor.* . . ."

Baedeker described the next exhibit as *"Private House,* excavated in 1869 . . . believed to have been the house of Tiberius Claudius Nero the father of Tiberius, to which his mother Livia also retired. . . . Adjoining the right side of the court is the Triclinium . . . with walls painted bright red." Hardy condensed this and more to a single image: "Livia's rich red mural show." From this point the Hardys went "thridding cave and Criptoportico," as detailed by Baedeker: "Returning . . . to the above-mentioned passage, which was once entirely covered by the buildings of Tiberius *(Cryptoporticus),* and following it to the right to the end . . . we perceive the continuation of the passage to the left . . . a second covered passage is reached on the right."

The Hardys then turned to "Caligula's dissolving pile," which Baedeker had designated as the start of the tour. There they heard "a waltz by Strauss." Hardy was a dancing man, and "The love of Strauss's waltzes long burned bright in Hardy's breast; back in 1869 he first heard the *Morgenblätter* at Weymouth."[3] Perhaps at about the time he wrote "Rome: On the Palatine," he wrote to Sir George Douglas, on May 30, 1897: "I shd. like to meet you any afternoon at the Imperial Institute at 1/2 past 4 & hear the Strauss band."[4] In the sonnet, the waltz-tune mingles with meditations of old Rome to suggest that time is an illusion; it "blended pulsing life with lives long done."

1. *Early Life*, pp. 246-48; *Life*, pp. 188-89.
2. *Italy. Second Part: Central Italy and Rome*, pp. 241-49. Quotations below are from these pages, *passim*.
3. Sherman, "Music in Thomas Hardy's Life and Work," p. 427.
4. Parker, "Hardy's Letters to Sir George Douglas," p. 220.

ROME: BUILDING A NEW STREET IN THE ANCIENT QUARTER treats the erection of houses, "a frail new mansion," rather than street-construction. The site may have been near the Colosseum. The Hardys were in Rome "not so long after the peeling of the Colosseum and other ruins of their vast accumulations of parasitic growths. . . . This made the ruins of the ancient city . . . more gaunt to the vision and more depressing to the mind than they had been to visitors when covered with greenery, and accounts for [Hardy's] allusions to the city in poems on Rome written after his return, as exhibiting 'ochreous gauntness,' 'umbered walls,' and so forth."[1] The poem may bring together his observations of building throughout the city. Emma Hardy wrote in her diary: "A great many dangers in Rome streets. So much building going & materials carried along, nearly had something down upon us from scaffolding at Capitol."[2] In a letter to Edmund Gosse, dated from Rome, Hardy stated the theme of the poem: "I am so overpowered by the presence of *decay* in ancient Rome that I feel it like a nightmare in my sleep. Modern Rome is full of building energy—but how any community can go on building in the face of the 'Vanitas vanitatum' reiterated by the ruins is quite marvellous."[3]

1. *Early Life*, p. 247; *Life*, p. 188. The quoted phrases do not occur in the poems on Rome, but "gaunt anatomy" and "umbered cliffs" are a close approach.
2. In the Dorset County Museum.
3. In the British Museum.

ROME: THE VATICAN: SALA DELLE MUSE describes an experience, expresses Hardy's attitude toward the arts, and seems to owe some of its phrasing to Baedeker. According to *The Early Life*, his "nearly falling asleep in the Sala delle Muse of the Vatican was the source of another poem, the weariness being the effect of the deadly fatiguing size of St. Peter's."[1] A later experience (but probably before the poem was written) furnished a theme for the poem. When *Wessex Poems* appeared critics attacked Hardy-the-novelist for taking up "a hitherto uncared for art" at the "eleventh hour." The theme, a meditation upon the unity of the arts, seems a justification of his switch from fiction to poetry and of his writing poetry in lyric, epic, and dramatic forms. *The Later Years* says: "But probably few literary critics discern the solidarity of all the arts. Curiously enough Hardy himself dwelt upon it in a poem that seems to have been little understood. . . . It is called 'Rome: The Vatican: Sala delle Muse.' "[2] He has the composite goddess of all the Muses state the theme (including his favorite aphorism from Marcus Aurelius: "Be not perturbed")[3] that all the arts "are but phases of one."

The phrasing suggests that in visiting this hall of the Muses Hardy consulted Baedeker to identify the statues before he sat down to rest. Baedeker's description reads: "The magnificent Sala itself . . . derives its name from the statues of the Muses preserved here. . . . To the right of the Apollo: Calliope (Muse of epic poetry); Terpsichore (dancing); Erato (erotic poetry); Euterpe (music). Then, on the other side: Melpomene (tragedy); Thalia (comedy); Urania (astronomy); Clio (history); Polyhymnia (higher lyric poetry)."[4] The poem does not follow Baedeker's list exactly. In speaking of Form, Hardy may have meant any one of several; the synthesis of the Muses into "One" is a point of the poem. In omitting "lyric poetry" and using the word "Hymn," he must have had "Polyhymnia (higher lyric poetry)" in mind, as well as church-music.

1. P. 248; *Life*, p. 189.
2. P. 77; *Life*, p. 300.
3. "On the last day of the year 1885 he wrote in his journal: 'This is the chief thing: Be not perturbed.' . . . He copied these words into the thirty-ninth chapter of *Tess of the D'Urbervilles*." Weber, *Hardy in America*, p. 252.
4. *Italy. Second Part: Central Italy and Rome*, pp. 309-10.

ROME: AT THE PYRAMID OF CESTIUS NEAR THE GRAVES OF SHELLEY AND KEATS records a visit to the graves of Shelley and Keats in the Protestant Cemetery. Baedeker's description of this cemetery says: "Amongst many illustrious names the eye will fall with interest upon that of the poet *Shelley* (d. 1822), 'cor cordium,' whose heart only was buried here (near the upper, or Eastern, wall). . . . The tombstone of *John Keats* (d. 1821), who also rests here, bears the melancholy inscription, 'Here lies one whose name was writ in water.' " Then Baedeker devotes a paragraph to: "The *Pyramid of Cestius* . . . the tomb of Caius Cestius, who died within the last thirty years before Christ." Perhaps the irony of this juxtaposition—Keats's great name "writ in water" beside unknown Cestius's bragging bid for fame—inspired the wry humor of Hardy's poem.

Emma Hardy's diary tells how the Hardys reached the cemetery from their hotel. "Thursday [March 31]. Went to Colliseum [*sic*] driving there, then to English cemetery, visiting Shelley & Keats' grave. . . . The road to the English cemetery Via St. Paolo. . . . Gathered violets off graves of Shelley & Keats."[1] "Driving," no doubt, means being driven in a cab; therefore the Hardys did not need Cestius's pyramid "With marble finger high" to guide their "pilgrim steps." Hardy found the finger useful in mocking Cestius, who "Maybe / Slew, breathed out threatening."[2] His "Maybe" reflects even Baedeker's ignorance of why Cestius had a towering monument. The *Handbook* identifies Cestius only by describing the pyramid and translating the inscription. It "is built of brick and covered with marble blocks; height 116 ft., width of each side of the base 98 ft. According to the principal Inscription on the E. and W. sides (C. Cestius L. F. Pob. Epulo. Pr. Tr. Pl. VII. vir Epulonum), the deceased was praetor, tribune of the people, and member of the college of Septemviri Epulonum, or priests who superintended the solemn sacrificial banquets. . . . Alexander VII. caused the somewhat deeply embedded monument to be extricated in 1663, on which occasion the two columns of white marble and the colossal bronze foot now found in the Capitoline Museum were found. According to the inscription on the pedestal, the foot appears to have belonged to a colossal statue of Cestius."[3] In the poem the "marble finger" served as a beacon to "where two immortal Shades abide," but perhaps the foot amused Hardy, whether or not he saw this monstrosity. Fittingly this mockery is the same as that of Shelley's "Ozymandias."

Though mocking Cestius, the poem is reverent toward Shelley and Keats. Hardy copied in pencil the inscription on Keats's grave.[4] On September 17, 1901, when Edmund Gosse was visiting Rome, Hardy wrote asking him to visit Keats's and Shelley's graves to ". . . tell me exactly how it all looks there, & whether any 'improvements' have done harm to the spot."[5]

1. In the Dorset County Museum. In a letter to Edmund Gosse from Rome, Hardy wrote: "I send you a violet or two which I gathered from Keats's [grave] —He is covered with violets in full bloom just now, & thousands of daisies stud the grass around." In the British Museum.

2. From Acts 9:1: "And Saul, yet breathing out threatenings and slaughter against the disciples of the Lord."

3. *Italy. Second Part: Central Italy and Rome*, p. 253.

4. In the Dorset County Museum, with the notation "Copied on the spot. Rome, 31 March 1887."

5. In the British Museum.

LAUSANNE: IN GIBBON'S OLD GARDEN: 11-12 P.M. treats an incident of the Hardys' visit to Switzerland in the summer of 1897. They "stopped at the Hôtel Gibbon, Lausanne, Hardy not having that aversion from the historian of the *Decline and Fall* which Ruskin recommended. He found that, though not much might remain of the original condition of the building or the site, the remoter and sloping part of the garden, with its acacias and irregular contours, could not have been much changed from what it was when Gibbon haunted it, and finished his history. Accordingly his recaller sat out there till midnight on June 27, and imagined the historian closing his last page on the spot, as described in his *Autobiography*:

" 'It was on the day, or rather the night, of the 27th of June 1787, between the hours of eleven and twelve, that I wrote the last lines of the last page, in a summer house in my garden. After laying down my pen I took several turns in a *berceau*, or covered walk of acacias, which commands a prospect of the country, the lake, and the mountains.'

"It is uncertain whether Hardy chose that particular evening for sitting out in the garden because he knew that June 27th was Gibbon's date of conclusion, or whether the coincidence of dates was accidental."

The last two lines of the poem, stating its theme, summarize a passage from John Milton's *The Doctrine and Discipline of Divorce*, quoted in *The Later Years*: "Truth is as impossible to be soiled by any outward touch, as the sunbeam; though this ill hap wait on her nativity, that she never comes into the world, but like a bastard, to the ignominy of him that brought her forth; till Time, the midwife rather than the mother of truth, have washed and salted the infant and declared her legitimate."[1]

Hardy's message is related to his feeling of need for courage as he wrote *Jude the Obscure* and his sense of outrage when this attack upon pruderies and social conventions was libeled as "Jude the Obscene." Gibbon and Milton were in his mind as he wrote *Jude*. Among the "Christminster Ghosts" that Jude "sees" is "the smoothly shaven historian so ironically civil to Christianity," Gibbon. Just after her daring purchase of the statuettes of Venus and Apollo, Sue "began reading a book she had taken from her box, which Miss Font-over knew nothing of. It was a volume of Gibbon, and she read the chapter dealing with the reign of Julian the Apostate."[2] A sentence from Milton's *The Doctrine and Discipline of Divorce* is quoted as the motto for Part IV: "Whoso prefers either Matrimony or other Ordinance before the Good of Man and the plain Exigence of Charity let him profess Papist, or Protestant, or what he will, he is no better than a Pharisee." Hardy expressed his outrage at the reception of *Jude* in an inscription he wrote in a first edition: "The criticisms which this story received in England & America were a monumental illustration of the crass Philistinism of the two countries, & were limited to about 20 pages out of more than 500. It was left to the French and Germans to discover the author's meaning, through the medium of indifferent translations. October: 1904. Thomas Hardy."[3]

His protest was not limited to attacks on *Jude*. As early as January, 1890, he pled for sincerity in fictional treatment of the passions, in "Candour in English Fiction."[4] Since *The Woodlanders* and especially since *Tess of the D'Urbervilles*, he had been castigated by the reviewers because he departed from the sentimental pattern for Victorian fiction, its childlike heroine, idealized hero, idyllic love not overtly concerned with sex, optimistic concepts of progress, patriarchal family, orthodox piety, and happy ending.[5]

While the poem expresses Hardy's own opinion, it is interesting that he chose as his "authorities" Gibbon and Milton, and dramatized his statement as one made by Gibbon quoting Milton: mighty voices from the grave. The poem exhibits some subtle symbolism. That "far lamps fleck him through the thin acacias" may be both factual and a suggestion that distant truth shines dimly through the shadows. Gibbon's turn at an "alley's end" suggests the seer's lonely way.

1. *Later Years*, pp. 67-69; *Life*, pp. 293-94.
2. Part II, Chapters I and III.
3. Newton, *Thomas Hardy, Novelist or Poet*, p. 26.
4. In the *New Review*. Reprinted in Orel, *Thomas Hardy's Personal Writings*, pp. 125-33.
5. See Hodgins, "A Study of the Periodical Reception of the Novels of Thomas Hardy, George Gissing, and George Moore."

ZERMATT: TO THE MATTERHORN treats a tragic event recalled to Hardy by his visit to Zermatt. This town is at the foot of the Matterhorn, a rugged mountain 14,782 feet high, on the border between Switzerland and Italy. On July 14, 1865, seven men, led by E. M. Whymper, reached the summit of this mountain, the first to do so. On the way down, four of the men, Lord Francis Douglas, Rev.

Charles Hudson, and Robert Hadow, Englishmen, and Michael Croz of Chamonix, their guide, lost their lives. Hadow slipped against Croz, and the two falling together dragged down Hudson and Lord Francis, attached to them by a rope. The four fell over a series of precipices, a distance of some 4,000 feet. Three of the bodies were found, but that of Douglas was not. The others of the party, Whymper, a guide Taugwalder, and his son escaped because the rope linking all together broke between Taugwalder and Douglas.

Hardy read of this event in the newspapers. Then in 1894 he visited Edward Clodd in Aldeburgh, Suffolk, and there met "Whymper, the mountaineer, who told of the tragedy on the Matterhorn in 1865 in which he was the only survivor of the four Englishmen present—a reminiscence which specially impressed Hardy from the fact that he remembered the particular day, thirty years before, of the arrival of the news in this country. He had walked from his lodgings in Westbourne Park Villas to Harrow that afternoon, and on entering the place was surprised to notice people standing at the doors discussing something with a serious look. It turned out to be the catastrophe, two of the victims being residents of Harrow. The event lost nothing by Whymper's relation of it. He afterwards marked for Hardy on a sketch of the Matterhorn a red line showing the track of the adventurers to the top and the spot of the accident—a sketch which is still at Max Gate with his signature."[1]

The Hardys visited Zermatt in 1897, arriving on June 28. "That night Hardy looked out of their bedroom window in the Hôtel Mt. Cervin, and 'Could see where the Matterhorn was by the absence of stars within its outline,' it being too dark to see the surface of the mountain itself. . . . He meant to make a poem of the strange feeling implanted by this black silhouette of the mountain on the pattern of the constellation; but never did, so far as is known." The mountain brought Whymper's story to his mind. Emma Hardy's diary for June 30 records: "Fine day at Zermatt. . . . T. H. talked of Whimper [sic] —he knows him."[2] Hardy began the poem at this time: "the mountain inspired him to begin one sonnet, finished some time after—that entitled 'To the Matterhorn'—the terrible accident on whose summit, thirty-two years before this date, had so impressed him at the time of its occurrence."[3]

Though The Later Years says that Hardy "never did" write a poem to express his "strange feeling" aroused by the mountain silhouetted against the stars, the sestet of "Zermatt: To the Matterhorn" seems partly to express it. Like Egdon Heath in The Return of the

Native, the Matterhorn is "A Face on which Time Makes but Little Impression." While the human centuries have run like sands, and men-shaking events (including the disaster of the octave) have come and gone, the granite block of the mountain has stood unmoved. Miltonic in its high seriousness, the sestet marks off ages by citing human crises which, it is said, stirred the heavens themselves. In Old Testament times, Joshua gave orders: "And the sun stood still, and the moon stayed, until the people had avenged themselves upon their enemies." (Josh. 10:13.) In Roman times, according to Shakespeare, cosmic forces struggled for the life of Caesar: "Fierce fiery warriors fight upon the clouds, / In ranks and squadrons and right form of war, / Which drizzled blood upon the Capitol." (*Julius Caesar,* II, ii, 19-21.) In the Gospels, as Christ died: "And when the sixth hour was come, there was darkness over the whole land until the ninth hour." (Mark 15:33.) Through these crises the Matterhorn stood unmoved.

1. *Later Years,* pp. 30-31; *Life,* p. 264.
2. In the Dorset County Museum.
3. *Later Years,* p. 69; *Life,* p. 294.

THE BRIDGE OF LODI has this note in the manuscript: " (Visited 23 April, 1887: Battle fought May 10, 1796.) "[1] *The Early Life* says that this "pleasant jingle" was "written some time after the excursion to the scene."[2]

In their pilgrimage of 1887 the Hardys, after visiting Venice, on the way home stopped in Milan. There, sunning on the roof of the cathedral, Hardy "thought in after years, though he was not quite sure, that he conceived the Milan Cathedral scene in *The Dynasts.*"[3] The vicinity turned his mind to the battle of Lodi.

In his interpretation, Napoleon's victory in this battle convinced him that he was a genius destined to rule an empire. The Austrians had fortified the bridge over the Adda; they swept it with artillery fire as Napoleon's troops sought to take it. Napoleon sent in his grenadiers, who drove the Austrians to retreat without being able to set fire to the bridge as planned. Napoleon's victory fired all France with enthusiasm. "Long afterward Napoleon himself declared: 'That evening, after the battle of Lodi, I first became aware that I was an exceptional man; from then I date the awakening of an ambition to do the great things which hitherto had existed for me as the fantasies of a dream.' "[4] In *The Dynasts,* Hardy interprets this statement as defining Napoleon's first awareness that he was guided by the Immanent Will. Refusing mercy toward Louisa, Queen of Prussia, he said to her: "Some force within me, baffling mine intent, / Harries me

onward, whether I will or no. / My star, my star is what's to blame—
not I." The Spirit of the Years commented upon this speech: "He
spoke thus at the Bridge of Lodi. Strange, / He's of the few in Europe
who discern / The working of the Will." Again, as omens threaten
Napoleon's venture into Russia, Napoleon said: "That which has
worked will work!—Since Lodi Bridge / The force I then felt move
me moves me on, / Whether I will or no; and oftentimes / Against
my better mind."[5]

In addition to these thoughts, Lodi reminded Hardy of a dance-
tune in his father's music-book, "The Bridge of Lodi"—not a folk-
air, but a boy-time tune he loved "as he loved brilliant uniforms, for
their dash and glamour."[6] "Hence," the poem says, "the tune came
capering to me." *The Early Life* tells an amusing story of Hardy's
making the acquaintance of a Scot to whom he described the battle of
Lodi, and with whom he went to visit the bridge across the Adda,
though the Scot's enthusiasm was "somewhat damped at finding that
the most persevering inquiries at Lodi failed to elicit any tradition
of the event."[7] This fact is echoed in the poem, wherein "the wives
of Lodi" know nothing of the battle, and "heed but transitory /
Marketings in cheese and meat."

Hardy's phrase describing the transience of worldly glory is echoed
from Baedeker's sketchy mention of Lodi, a single paragraph, contain-
ing the following sentences in sequence: Lodi "is celebrated as the
scene of Napoleon's storming of the bridge over the Adda, 10th May,
1796. Excellent Parmesan cheese is made in the neighbourhood."[8]
This is the amusing juxtaposition of Hardy's poem, the basic ironic
joke.

In this humorous poem, "The rhyming of the word 'Lodi' [rimed
with "body"] . . . is whimsical. We find eight rhymes with this word
in seventeen stanzas: 'body,' 'god he,' 'toady,' 'anybody,' 'nod he'
(twice) , 'trod he' and 'palinody' [palinode].' "[9]

1. Purdy, *Thomas Hardy: A Bibliographical Study*, p. 111.
2. P. 257; *Life*, p. 196.
3. *Early Life*, p. 256; *Life*, p. 195. The Cathedral Scene is Part First, I, vi.
4. Copps, "The Poetry of Thomas Hardy," pp. 441-42.
5. Part First, I, viii; Part Third, I, i.
6. Firor, *Folkways in Thomas Hardy*, p. 191.
7. *The Early Life*, pp. 256-57; *Life*, pp. 195-96.
8. *Italy. First Part: Northern Italy*, p. 293.
9. Vinson, "Diction and Imagery in the Poetry of Thomas Hardy," p. 173.

ON AN INVITATION TO THE UNITED STATES may be a response to
various invitations. Possibly Rebekah Owen invited Hardy to visit

America. In 1892, she had purchased a Romano-British skull which she named Metellus and proposed to take to New York. When she asked whimsically whether Metellus would object to the trip, Hardy replied, "I should think he would much rather go to New York with you than stay in Fordington. I am sure I should."[1] On November 18, 1895, Mrs. Pearl Mary Craigie of New York wrote to Hardy: "I wish you would visit America. I feel sure that you and Mrs. Hardy would enjoy the place and the people."[2] William Lyon Phelps visited Hardy at Max Gate in September of 1900 and possibly invited him to visit America then, as he certainly did later.

After 1901, Hardy had many formal, written invitations, which he either ignored[3] or refused. To one such in July, 1906, he replied: "The handsome invitation of the Trustees of the Pittsburgh Institute that I should attend the dedication with wife or daughter, free of expense to us from the time we leave home till we return again, is a highly honouring and tempting one. But I am compelled to think of many contingent matters that would stand in the way of my paying such a visit, and have concluded that I cannot undertake it."[4] In September, 1907, he replied to John Moule of New Brunswick, Canada, a former neighbor, who asked him to visit Canada: "I have never visited Canada and suppose that I shall never do so now, but the spectacle of a Continent (including the United States) developed by people from this side of the Atlantic . . . is one that would be deeply interesting to a visitor who should have the leisure to examine it."[5]

None of Hardy's letters of refusal state the reasons given in the poem. Instead, he wrote to John Galsworthy, then in California, on February 7, 1921: "How I should like to be in California all of a sudden—say for a week or two, borne thither on the magician's carpet. But to travel all the way there to see and experience its climate, and through a country where 'only the language is different,' as somebody says—no thank you."[6] It is not likely that he held back because Mrs. Florence Hardy was reluctant to take the trip. Speaking to Katharine Adams in 1920, "She said she longed to go to America—'but I never shall,' she said with a deep sigh."[7]

Perhaps the poem states the truth. Hardy made with eagerness his pilgrimage to the ancient shrines of Europe; perhaps (his letters seem to say) he now and then had a fancy for visiting a "modern coast," but he shrank from the positive action necessary to visit America. Purdy suggests that Hardy's feeling may have been fixed by a passage in Henry James's *Hawthorne* that Hardy copied into his notebook in 1879: "History, as yet, has left in the United States so thin and impalpable a deposit that we very soon touch the hard substratum of nature; and nature herself, in the western world, has the peculiarity of seeming rather crude and immature."[8] The passage perhaps rationalized a dread that had roots in Hardy's temperament. When Life had "bared its bones," he apparently found in tragic contemplation something like a satisfactory catharsis. Instead of seeking to escape realization of the human struggle as futile by turning to a land of promise, he preferred, like an antiquarian, to pore over the palimpsest of Wessex.

1. In the margin of p. 194 of Miss Owen's copy of *The Return of the Native* in the Colby College Library. Hardy autographed this book, and Miss Owen signed it "Rebekah Owen, Casterbridge, August 6, 1892."

2. In the Dorset County Museum.

3. I have found no answers to a number of invitations in the Dorset County Museum.

4. *Later Years*, p. 120; *Life*, p. 331. The "contingent matters" included Hardy's absorption in *The Dynasts* at this time.

5. Ghent, "Thomas Hardy Note Is Mainly Concerned with Canadian Babe," newspaper clipping in Colby College Library. Later invitations that Hardy rejected or ignored include one from the University of Virginia in 1908; one from Mrs. Champ Clark of Washington in 1910; one from the University of Chicago in 1917; one from William Lyon Phelps of Yale in 1919, to lecture for a fee of $1,000; and one from Nicholas Murray Butler of Columbia University in 1923.

6. Marrot, *The Life and Letters of John Galsworthy*, p. 506.

7. Meynell, ed., *The Best of Friends*, p. 25.

8. *Thomas Hardy: A Bibliographical Study*, p. 111.

MISCELLANEOUS POEMS

THE MOTHER MOURNS dramatizes the mourning of Mother Nature in contemplation of Yellowham Wood. Taking a night-walk there in autumn the poet hears the soughing of the wind in the fir trees, and as always this sound seems to him a kind of mourning.[1]

Nature, considered as the mother from whom all life comes, is presented as the living Spirit of primitive religions, more recently seen as manipulator of the processes of evolution. These processes have unwittingly produced human life with its capacity for hope, dream, frustration, and pain.

Hardy developed the lament of Nature from a meditation copied into his notebook on November 17, 1883: "Poem. We [human beings] have reached a degree of intelligence which Nature never contemplated when framing her laws, and for which she consequently has provided no adequate satisfactions."[2] He elaborated this meditation in an entry of April 7, 1889: "A woeful fact—that the human race is too extremely developed for its corporeal conditions, the nerves being evolved to an activity abnormal in such an environment. Even the higher animals are in excess in this respect. It may be questioned if

Nature, or what we call Nature, so far back as when she crossed the line from invertebrates to vertebrates, did not exceed her mission. This planet does not supply the materials for happiness to higher existences."[3] A similar thought is attributed to Sue in *Jude the Obscure*: "that at the framing of the terrestrial conditions there seemed never to have been contemplated such a development of emotional perceptiveness among the creatures subject to those conditions as that reached by thinking and educated humanity."[4] The theme of the poem is in part Hardy's interpretation of an irrational, unintended, and purposeless process of Nature. The Mother, becoming aware of the consequences of her process, mourns that the world of instinctive life she planned is judged unworthy by the critical human reason.

Nature's human children even boast that, given "the matter / And means the gods lot her," they could "evolve a creation / More seemly, more sane." The thought here is close to FitzGerald's:

Ah Love! could you and I with Him conspire
To grasp this sorry Scheme of Things entire,
   Would not we shatter it to bits—and then
Re-mould it nearer to the Heart's Desire![5]

Hardy does not entirely agree; as the Mother says of her censorious children: "My children have aped mine own slaughters" of species after species in the evolutionary struggle.

"The Mother Mourns" is notable for its single rime (the last word in each stanza) carried on through twenty-two stanzas. This rime, as well as the rhythm of the poem, is based on William Barnes's "The Knoll," which is in turn based upon a Persian measure called "ghazael."[6]

1. See "The Pine-Planters" and a corresponding passage in *The Woodlanders*, Chapter VIII, where Marty South shares Hardy's feeling that pines sigh at the prospect of life.
2. This passage is stated to be "clearly the germ of the poem entitled 'The Mother Mourns' and others." *Early Life*, p. 213; *Life*, p. 163.
3. *Early Life*, pp. 285-86; *Life*, p. 218.
4. Part VI, Chapter III.
5. *Rubáiyát of Omar Khayyám*, stanza XCIX.
6. King, "The Lyrical Poems of Thomas Hardy," p. 167.

"I SAID TO LOVE" views the lures of sexual love as a trick of nature to propagate the species. One may defy love only under the threat that "Mankind shall cease." Hardy's "So let it be" echoes Jude's doctor after Little Father Time had killed himself and the children: "The doctor says there are such boys springing up amongst us—boys of a sort unknown in the last generation—the outcome of new views of life. They seem to see all its terrors before they are old enough to have staying power to resist them. He says it is the beginning of the coming universal wish not to live."[1]

Rutland, attributing this thought to Hardy's reading Eduard von Hartmann's *The Philosophy of the Unconcious* and remarking that " 'I Said to Love' is on the conception that love is the imposition of means to ends which are not the ends of the individual," quotes a passage from Von Hartmann: "Whoever has once understood the illusory nature of successful love after union, and therewith also of that before union, whoever has come to see the pain outweighing the pleasure in all love, for that man the phenomenon of love has no more health, because his consciousness offers resistance to the imposition of means to ends which are not *his* ends; the pleasure of love has been for him undermined and corroded, only its smart remains to him unrelieved."[2]

The imagery of the poem is from Roman myth: "the Boy, the Bright, the One" is the god of love, Cupid, son of Venus, represented in art as something like a cherub, with a bow and arrows for striking the heart; swans and doves were birds symbolic of Venus.

1. *Jude the Obscure*, Part VI, Chapter II.
2. Quoted from Chapter XIII, Part 3, in *Thomas Hardy*, p. 255.

A COMMONPLACE DAY expresses a mood at the end of a dull, rainy day, during which the poet has felt listless. He turns from regret that he has done nothing, to meditate that even on such a day, someone, somewhere, may have followed an impulse of the kind "from whose maturer glows / The world's amendment flows." He saw this amendment as a minutely gradual process, "undiscerned on sea or land"; he later called his hope "evolutionary meliorism." The last stanza reflects that perhaps on such a day the kindling impulse was "benumbed at birth."

Hardy's description of a dull day in images of "ghost," "corpse-like," and "sepulchre-lid" is characteristic. The "pale corpse-like birth" of the day resembles the image of a dawn in *The Woodlanders*, where "the bleared white visage of a sunless winter day emerged like a dead-born child."[1]

In spite of the rain mentioned in the poem, the extinction of the fire at bedtime, as in the second stanza, was customary because sparks from the chimney might set a thatched roof afire during the night.

1. The opening of Chapter IV.

AT A LUNAR ECLIPSE was written in "186—."[1] The eclipse that Hardy saw was probably that of July 18, 1860.[2]

This Miltonic sonnet expresses a thought that runs through

Hardy's works. It meditates the contrast between the "ghast" cosmos of astronomy and the human world, or between vast imperturbable serenities and "Nation at war with nation" on a planet unimportant to the Will of the universe, yet important to man. In his Preface for *Two on a Tower*, Hardy stated this theme as his intention in the novel: "This slightly-built romance was the outcome of a wish to set the emotional history of two infinitesimal lives against the stupendous background of the stellar universe, and to impart to readers the sentiment that of these contrasting magnitudes the smaller might be the greater to them as men." In *The Return of the Native*, Clym Yeobright watches the moon as an eclipse begins and is led to dream of relative values: "More than ever he longed to be in some world where personal ambition was not the only recognized form of progress —such, perhaps, as might have been the case at some time or other in the silvery globe then shining upon him." (Book Third, Chapter IV.) In *Tess of the D'Urbervilles*, Hardy draws a moral lesson from the relativity presented in the poem. Angel Clare learns from a world traveller to view Tess's fault in proportion. "The stranger had sojourned in many more lands and among many more peoples than Angel; to his cosmopolitan mind such deviations from the social norm, so immense to domesticity, were no more than are the irregularities of vale and mountain-chain to the whole terrestrial curve." This view "influenced Clare more than all the reasoned ethics of the philosophers." (Chapter XLIX.) In *The Dynasts*, the Napoleonic wars are presented through the Spirits in "stellar gauge," continents lying spread to view as on a map. Apparently Hardy's meditations upon an eclipse he saw in 1860 helped shape his view of the world for the rest of his life.

"At a Lunar Eclipse" has been set to music by Gerald Finzi in *Till Earth Outwears* (London and New York: Boosey and Hawkes, 1958).

1. Purdy, *Thomas Hardy: A Bibliographical Study*, p. 111.
2. Vincent, *Haydn's Dictionary of Dates*, p. 271.

THE LACKING SENSE is a philosophical dialogue of questions and answers, between the poet and a personified "Ancient Mind" called Time. The date of publication, when he was working on *The Dynasts*, suggests that Time is another name for the Spirit of the Years, combining human experience and reason.

Waddon Vale, a deep valley about four miles southwest of Dorchester, is described as a "sad-coloured landscape." This valley, running between the villages of Upwey and Portesham, is not markedly somber. Waddon Hill (or ridge) to the north is steep and rocky, and hills to the south cut Waddon Vale off from the sea, but the prospect is generally one of green meadows and farms. At present, though off main roads, the Vale is accessible. However, Sherren reports that in earlier years it was isolated. Then, "Viewed from the chalk-scarred summit, the treeless valley, intersected as it is by dense criss-cross hedges, appears like a Titanic patch-work quilt." It may have seemed "sad-coloured" to Hardy on a dull day: "The poem . . . seems to voice the eerie atmosphere of the valley when alone with the east wind and nature's inclemencies—to picture the sad phase of it when the green robes of mead and upland have been seared, and the skeleton of its trees revealed to a neutral sky."[1] The Mother of whom Time and Hardy talk is the Mother Nature of "The Mother Mourns."

Though the Mother has wounded her creation and the term "red ravage" appears, Hardy does not present her as like Tennyson's "Nature red in tooth and claw / With ravine." (*In Memoriam*, Lyric LVI.) The Mother is not callous; she "has wounded where she loves." The explanation is that she is sightless. The term evidently means foresightless, unable to foresee the results of evolution, as indicated in a later, unpublished note, dated May 29, 1922: "*Poem*. I = First Cause—omniscient, not omnipotent—limitations, difficulties, &c from being only able to work by Law (His only failing is lack of foresight.)"[2]

Like the general philosophic basis of the poem, Time's plea to man to assist the Mother "where thy creaturely dependence can or may" reflects J. S. Mill's essay on "Nature." Postulating a benevolent Deity and reasoning that "the Principle of Good *cannot* at once and altogether subdue the powers of evil," Mill wrote that "man's duty would consist . . . in standing forward a not-ineffectual auxiliary to a Being of perfect beneficence." Time, in the last two lines of the poem, tells the poet that man, as a son of the Mother, "of her clay," owes her this help. The thought leads toward the evolutionary meliorism of *The Dynasts*, that in the course of many ages the human mind may develop both the knowledge to guide evolution and loving kindness as an instinct. Men may thus guide the Mother toward goals she cannot foresee.

1. *The Wessex of Romance*, pp. 73-74.
2. In the notebook "Memorandum II," in the Dorset County Museum.

TO LIFE presents a masquerade. Life appears to the poet mouthing the "too-forced pleasantry" of a clown to mask the "sad seared face" of a lame beggar. The clown's performance is boring, for the truth he would tell is that of "Death, Time, Destiny." The poet asks for a more convincing masquerade, to "feign like truth" that Life is made for joy; in this mumming he would like to join till "maybe" he could believe it true. The third stanza may be considered a petition if not a prayer: the poem is written to a hymn tune in short-meter doxology.

"To Life" has been set to music by Hubert James Foss in *Seven Poems by Thomas Hardy* (London: Oxford University Press, 1925), and by Isaac Levine (in manuscript, in the Dorset County Museum).

DOOM AND SHE presents an overheard conversation between Doom representing fate, and She, evidently the blind Mother Nature of "The Lacking Sense." Doom, who has neither feeling nor moral sense, may represent the quasi-mechanical operation of natural laws, especially those of cause and effect producing what is usually called fate. Doom and Mother Nature dwell in the "vague Immense," which seems to be the Will of *The Dynasts*. Though the poem seems a by-product of Hardy's thinking about the Spirits of this epic-drama, one of his notebooks suggests that its underlying concept had been in his mind for some time: "The whole construction of the world (so stupidly does it work) would be an unpardonable crime did it issue from a power that knew what it was about. . . . 'In sober truth,' says Mill, 'nearly all the things which men are hanged or imprisoned for doing to one another, are Nature's everyday performances.' "[1]

Observing the relation of the poem to *The Dynasts*, Wright says: "The World-weaver can make patterns; all around him Hardy saw them. . . . They were orderly enough, despite the endless variations. But when Hardy reflected on human fate, he found in the patterns no purpose as men understand purpose. The weaver was ever busy, but her fingers were unguided by sight. The supernatural pair do not match any two supernatural beings in *The Dynasts*; but 'It' creates patterns in networks and webs, there are hints of Doom in the Spirit of the Years, and, of course, the consequence for man is the same."[2]

Purdy notes that in the manuscript of "Doom and She" the penultimate line first read "On High-stoy Hill or Pilsdon Peak" and then "On Pilsdon Pen or Lewsdon Peak."[3] Hardy's manuscript thus placed the scene of his sensing the conversation between Doom and She on hills in Wessex that, high above the inhabited valleys below, were favorite places for his meditations. Perhaps he decided upon "Alpine height or Polar peak" to suggest universality.

1. P. 177 of "Literary Notes I" in the Dorset County Museum. The source and date of the note are given: "Quot in Spec. from Rev. H. Footman's book. 21. 4. 83." The sentence from J. S. Mill is in the essay "Nature."
2. *The Shaping of "The Dynasts,"* p. 66.
3. Purdy, *Thomas Hardy: A Bibliographical Study*, p. 112.

THE PROBLEM poses the "Case" of whether the novelist, poet, essayist, lecturer, or teacher ("We" in the poem) is morally right to state for the general public rationalistic conclusions that would undermine belief in the creeds of the churches. It is the problem that faced Angel Clare in *Tess of the D'Urbervilles*. Angel, remembering Tennyson's *In Memoriam*, concludes that he would be wrong to disturb Tess's faith by stating his own beliefs: "He himself knew that, in reality, the confused beliefs which she held, apparently imbibed in childhood, were, if anything, Tractarian as to phraseology, and Pantheistic as to essence. Confused or otherwise, to disturb them was his last desire:

> Leave thou thy sister, when she prays,
> Her early Heaven, her happy views;
> Nor thou with shadow'd hint confuse
> A life that leads melodious days.

He had occasionally thought the counsel less honest than musical; but he gladly conformed to it now."[1]

On the other hand, writing less of religion than of prudery, Hardy said in his "Explanatory Note" to the first edition of *Tess*: "I would ask any too genteel reader, who cannot endure to have said what everybody nowadays thinks and feels, to remember a well-worn sentence of St. Jerome's: If an offense come out of the truth, better it is that the offense come than that the truth be concealed."

The poem treats only the question of happiness, peace, and comfort to be found in belief, but in *The Later Years* Hardy raised the question of whether rationalists have a monopoly on truth: "Rationalists err as far in one direction as Revelationists or Mystics in the other; as far in the direction of logicality as their opponents away from it."[2]

The "pigment" and the "painting" of the last line seem to mean, respectively, the truth and the effect upon a reader. The line may be read as an ironic comment upon the stanza.

1. Chapter XXVII. *In Memoriam*, Lyric XXXIII.
2. P. 121; *Life*, p. 332.

THE SUBALTERNS presents a series of messages from personified natural forces. Since the forces are those of earth and since Hardy was working on *The Dynasts* when the poem was published, some light is cast upon his meaning by the role of the Shade of the Earth in this epic-drama. There this Shade is a "subaltern" among the Spirits. She calls herself "the ineffectual Shade / Of her the Travailler." She opens the play by asking the question: "What of the Immanent Will and

Its designs?"—for she does not see purpose in Its manipulation of her processes. Suffering from this manipulation, she asks the Spirit of the Years: "What boots it, Sire, / To down this dynasty, set that one up, / Goad panting peoples to the throes thereof, / Make wither here my fruit, maintain it there. . . ?" In the clash of opinion among the Spirits, she is on the side of the Pities. When this Spirit would like to see the earth produce kindly men instead of tyrants, she is "not averse," but she is "curbed and kinged" by the Will.[1] As the earth is subject to the Will, the four subalterns of the poem are subject to the earth, sharing its compassion for man and its helplessness. They speak in the worsening series of dull weather, freezing temperatures, sickness, and death—two conditions of outer nature and two forces of human decay.

Though, except for expressions of compassion, the poem is not Christian, it is written in the "Common Measure" of church hymns. Each subaltern speaks in the language of faith. The leaden sky speaks of "laws in force on high." As Ransome phrases it: "North is going to turn his blast upon one who is like a shorn lamb; he is thinking of the Christian proverb, 'God tempers the wind to the shorn lamb.' . . . Sickness is about to invade his victim's little ark, despite what has been said about the Covenant, the promise of security. . . . And Death will end his victim's pilgrimage."[2] The Will to which these forces are subject is the mysterious, unconscious force that established natural laws and manipulates them to create non-moral "Eternal artistries in Circumstance." This It (Hardy's capitalization) is described at length in *The Dynasts*. Thus the subalterns that seem to be malicious forces are fellow-slaves with man.

In the final stanza the poet is reconciled to the conditions of life because he understands the "passiveness" of natural laws. This conclusion is contrary to that of his earlier poem "Hap," in which there is no "vengeful god" to laugh at human suffering. In "The Subalterns," life loses its fell look just because nothing can be blamed.

1. Fore Scene and Part First, I, ii.
2. "Thomas Hardy's Poems and the Religious Difficulties of a Naturalist," p. 176.

THE SLEEP-WORKER is a philosophic sonnet that asks three questions of "O Mother," presumably Mother Nature, though Hardy blurs her identity. She may be either the Shade of the Earth of *The Dynasts* or the Immanent Will. Her traits suggest a fusion of Mother Nature as a "subaltern" (see "The Subalterns") and as an unconscious Will operating through nature.

The poem asks three questions: when may the Mother wake to awareness? if she wakes, what will be her reaction? and will she then destroy the universe or heal its ills? The first possibility of the final question reflects Hardy's reading in Von Hartmann's *Philosophy of the Unconscious.* "Von Hartmann surmises that the Will made conscious would relieve pain by ceasing to will and hence to exist—that is, by annihilation of the world. He suggests that this is the only way the Unconscious may achieve this end: 'Were now this end *attainable without consciousness,* or did such a consciousness in the sense of an emancipation of the Idea from the will exist at the beginning of the world-process in God, the whole cosmic process would be *foolish* and *aimless,* in that it would be struggling to attain somewhat that either is *not at all requisite* for the object, or that *existed long ago.*'"[1] The second possibility seems Hardy's hope as expressed by the Spirits who sing the final chorus of *The Dynasts*: "Consciousness the Will informing, till It fashion all things fair!"

"The Sleep-Worker" has been set to music by Hubert James Foss in *Seven Poems by Hardy Set to Music* (London: Oxford University Press, 1925).

1. Bailey, *Thomas Hardy and the Cosmic Mind,* p. 159, quoting Von Hartmann, II, 274-75.

THE BULLFINCHES is a philosophical fantasy of Mother Nature's blindness, as told to the leader of the bullfinches by the fairies of Blackmoor Vale. In *Tess of the D'Urbervilles,* "Marlott" (based on Marnhull), Tess's girlhood village, is in this Vale.

Besides the locality, "The Bullfinches" seems to have some relation to *Tess,* the meaning of which is not entirely clear. The mother of Alec Stoke-D'Urberville is blind; she lives in a mansion that is called "ornate and imposing"; she has a number of bullfinches of which she is fond; she handles her birds with loving but groping hands; she employs Tess to teach them to whistle tunes. In saying "He! Pooh!" when Tess reports that Alec whistled to the birds, she implies, with her "face creased into furrows of repugnance," that he is their enemy. (Chapter IX.) In "The Bullfinches," the Mother of whom the fairies told is blind; she lives in a "handsome house / Known as Space"; she works with "groping hands"; she is not able to protect her birds from "Fiends"; her work is "hussif'ry" (housewifery).

In the opening of the poem, the "Bulleys" are exhorted to sing joyfully through the day in the hope that when the day is done (their short lives over) they will go "Where they be that sang of old"—to the bullfinches' heaven. After the leader tells them the tale of the blind Mother who is unable to prevent "havoc in her bands," they sing again, in the last stanza, the refrain of the first, slightly changed; but in context "Where those be that sang of old" seems this time to mean

[148]

extinction. The fairies suggested no power in the Mother to care for them; the Mother is making all things "for Death's taking"; and they will sing all their brief lives because there is no other life. The sadness of tone in the poem, which suggests "birds warbling faintly in the sunset,"[1] and the tenuous relation to *Tess* support this interpretation.

The poem has been set to music by Alys F. Serell (*The Bullfinches,* London: West & Co., 1914).

1. Gosse, "The Lyrical Poetry of Thomas Hardy," p. 245.

GOD-FORGOTTEN is a philosophical fantasy. The opening "I towered far" seems to begin a dream, and "Homing at dawn" to represent the wakening.

To explain why God has forgotten the earth, Hardy makes some use of the Biblical story of the fall of man. In the poem, however, God was partly responsible for the fall: the earth, He says, "lost my interest from the first." Man was partly responsible, too, for "Of its own act the threads were snapt" that tied the earth to God. The poem does not specify what act—except "doing as it durst"—alienated the earth from God so completely that He forgot its existence. Hardy expected his readers to understand the fall from the Scriptures. There is no suggestion that the fall is fortunate; not even the Messenger (the angel) comes, much less the Messiah. That the speeches concerned with the fall are colloquial in tone and mildly humorous suggests that Hardy was as incredulous of the concept as the Spirit of the Years in *The Dynasts,* who says:

> Some, too, have told at whiles that rightfully
> Its warefulness, Its care, this planet lost
> When in her early growth and crudity
> By bad mad acts of severance men contrived,
> Working such nescience by their own device.—
> Yea, so it stands in certain chronicles,
> Though not in mine. (The Fore Scene.)

The idea that the Prime Cause is unconscious runs all through Hardy's notebook, as well as his fiction, poems, and *The Dynasts.* This idea included the remorse God would feel if He knew. On December 10, 1888, he wrote in his notebook: "He, she, had blundered; but not as the Prime Cause had blundered. He, she, had sinned; but not as the Prime Cause had sinned. He, she, was ashamed and sorry; but not as the Prime Cause would be ashamed and sorry if it knew."[1] In *The Dynasts* and elsewhere he developed God's statement that *"Not to Mend* / For Me could mean but *Not to Know."*[2] That, in this poem, man informs God of the existence of earth and its suffering is paralleled in other poems, for instance, "God's Education."

1. *Early Life*, p. 282; *Life*, p. 215.
2. Perrine suggests that *"to Mend"* is to be interpreted as "put an end / To what men undergo" or annihilate the earth. "Thomas Hardy's 'God-Forgotten'," pp. 187-88.

THE BEDRIDDEN PEASANT dramatizes an idea Hardy expressed in a note on February 5, 1898: "Write a prayer, or hymn, to One not Omnipotent, but hampered; striving for our good, but unable to achieve it except occasionally."[1] He may have drawn the peasant from life or from some such source as a letter from Lady Catherine Milnes Gaskell describing a peasant over eighty years old: "Poor old soul he was just waiting for death. I went and sat with him in his bare bedroom whilst the 'jeunesse' of the place in the form of his 3 gt-grandchildren fought over some cakes I had brought them. . . . How little happiness there seems to be in many of those lives and yet they don't regret life & then their faith is so wonderful. . . . Many of them have minds & minds without culture is an excellent change to culture without minds which is what one so often gets in society."[2]

The philosophy of the peasant as well as his diction ("deem . . . succour") suggests that he is one of those who "have minds" and some culture. The peasant philosophizes toward Hardy's conclusion that God cannot be aware of needless human suffering or He would not allow it. Like Hardy, he feels a need for believing in a benevolent God, but unlike Hardy, he lets his feeling override his reasoned conclusion. Hardy commented in *The Return of the Native*: "Human beings in their generous endeavour to construct a hypothesis that shall not degrade a First Cause, have always hesitated to conceive a dominant power of lower moral quality than their own; and, even while they sit down and weep by the waters of Babylon, invent excuses for the oppression which prompts their tears." (Book Sixth, Chapter I.) He found a basis for this statement in J. S. Mill's "Nature": "But those who have been strengthened in goodness by relying on the sympathizing support of a powerful and good Governor of the World, have . . . never really believed that Governor to be . . . omnipotent. They have always saved his goodness at the expense of his power."

1. *Later Years*, p. 73; *Life*, p. 297.
2. The letter, dated Sept. 6 [1893?], is in the Dorset County Museum.

BY THE EARTH'S CORPSE is less a dialogue than a one-stanza question by Time and a three-stanza answer by the Lord. When the poem was published, Hardy was working on *The Dynasts*. Then Time may be the Spirit of the Years under another name. As this Spirit is equated with the rational interpretation of human experience, it is reasonable that he should question the Lord at the conclusion of this experience. The source for the Lord's answer is Gen. 6:6, "And it repented the Lord that he had made man on the earth, and it grieved him at his heart." In the poem, the question is "O Lord, why grievest Thou?" and the reply refers to "Noë's days," with which Genesis 6 is concerned.[1] The theme of the poem was in Hardy's mind on May 9, 1881, when he was using the word Law for what he later called Will; he wrote in his journal: "The emotions have no place in a world of defect, and it is a cruel injustice that they should have developed in it. If Law itself had consciousness, how the aspect of its creatures would terrify it, fill it with remorse!"[2] The vision of the earth as cold and lifeless may owe something to *fin du globe*, a phrase common at the close of the nineteenth century, along with *fin de siècle*, or to the picture of the cold, dying world of H. G. Wells's *The Time Machine*.

Fairchild says: "Still more surprisingly, the indifferent Will has a heart, and can speak the language of the Biblical Jehovah, for in *By the Earth's Corpse* 'the Lord' is 'grieved' at the final liquidation of the world. . . . The same poem suggests that Hardy's God, usually regarded as omnipotent, is subservient to *Time*. There are too many radically different myths."[3] Hardy does mingle theological, philosophic, and scientific images and names, but the poem presents only one "myth." Hardy extends a passage in Genesis into the future foreseen by science.

1. "Noë" is an archaic spelling for Noah.
2. *Early Life*, p. 192; *Life*, p. 149. Hardy may have derived his idea of "Law" from J. S. Mill's definition of natural law in "Nature," "such as the laws of motion, and of gravitation . . . the observed uniformities in the occurrence of phenomena."
3. *Gods of a Changing Poetry*, p. 248.

MUTE OPINION uses the pronoun I; in the second stanza the poet has "grown a Shade." The poem seems to represent Hardy in his sixties looking back upon the world he knew in his twenties. In the 1860's, "spokesmen" for popular opinion "spake out strong" against Darwin's theory of evolution and against J. S. Mill's *The Subjection of Women*, while Darwin, continuing research in his laboratory, remained "mute" in the controversy. By 1901, the theory of evolution was generally accepted, and ultimate victory for the suffragettes (including Mrs. Hardy) was a foregone conclusion.

Aside from attacks by reviewers who condemned *Jude the Obscure* for its unconventional views, Hardy's memory of principles set forth in Mill's *On Liberty* may have influenced "Mute Opinion." In a letter to the *Times* published on May 21, 1906, Hardy described hearing Mill make a speech in 1865 and mentioned "the treatise *On Liberty* (which we students of that date knew almost by heart)."[1] Chapter II of *On Liberty* contains many passages that express the thought of Hardy's poem. One passage reads: "Yet it is as evident in itself, as any amount of argument can make it, that ages are no more infallible than individuals; every age having held many opinions which subsequent ages have deemed not only false but absurd; and it is as certain that many opinions, now general, will be rejected by future ages, as it is that many, once general, are rejected by the present." Hardy wrote to Mrs. Arthur Henniker on October 22, 1893, when he was writing *Jude the Obscure*: "If you mean to make the world listen to you, you must say now what they will all be thinking and saying five and twenty years hence: and if you do that you must offend your conventional friends."[2]

1. *Later Years*, pp. 118-19; *Life*, p. 330.
2. In the Dorset County Museum.

TO AN UNBORN PAUPER CHILD adds in the manuscript: " 'She must go to the Union-house to have her baby.' Casterbridge Petty Sessions."[1] This notation suggests that Hardy was present in the Dorchester ("Casterbridge") magistrate's court when a pauper-mother was ordered to the Union-house.

The idea of the poem, that it is better, especially for paupers, not to be born is expressed in several of Hardy's works, as in the protest of Little Father Time in Part VI, Chapter II, of *Jude the Obscure*: "I think that whenever children be born that are not wanted they should be killed directly, before their souls come to 'em, and not allowed to grow big and walk about." Chapter III of *Tess of the D'Urbervilles*, commenting on Tess's brothers and sisters, suggests Hardy's opinion that it would be better even for children who are wanted in a poverty-stricken household not to be born: "All these young souls were passengers in the Durbeyfield ship—entirely dependent on the judgment of the two Durbeyfield adults for their pleasures, their necessities, their health, even their existence. If the heads of the Durbeyfield household chose to sail into difficulty, disaster, starvation, disease, degradation, death, thither were these half-dozen little captives under hatches compelled to sail with them—six helpless creatures, who had never been asked if they wished for life on any terms, much less if they wished for it on such hard conditions as were involved in being of the shiftless house of Durbeyfield."

The poem expresses Hardy's opinion that life, especially for the poor, offers more pain than pleasure, and his compassion. The conclusion of the poem, however, expresses the hope that, even to the pauper child, life may offer "Joys seldom yet attained by humankind!"

1. Purdy, *Thomas Hardy: A Bibliographical Study*, p. 112.

TO FLOWERS FROM ITALY IN WINTER, following "To an Unborn Pauper Child," suggests Hardy's extension of compassion to organic nature, imagined, "as some men say," to be sentient. It seemed important to him, as in "Drummer Hodge," whether the dust of the dead lies at home or abroad. Whimsical when applied to flowers, the thought is characteristic of his imagination.

ON A FINE MORNING is dated in February, when fine mornings are rare in Dorchester. Perhaps the feeling of relief from dull weather, his sight of the sun on the meadows near Max Gate, gave Hardy a feeling of zest. His negative statements indicate his underlying awareness of "Life's conditions" and "Time's monitions." The lovely morning *is* a "specious show." The solace of religion, the view that the world is "Part of a benignant plan," is an escape from reality, but for "this heyday" the poet wills to believe what nature seems to say.

TO LIZBIE BROWNE addresses one of Hardy's boyhood sweethearts. She had red hair that he admired, but she "despised him as being two or three years her junior, and married early."[1] After marriage, it seems, she moved away from the Dorchester area. The colloquial yet tender tone of the poem indicates the reality of the boyhood experience, recollected with nostalgia. The poem has been set to music by Gerald Finzi in *Earth and Air and Rain* (London: Boosey & Hawkes, 1936).

1. *Early Life*, p. 33; *Life*, pp. 25-26.

SONG OF HOPE is written in a folk-rhythm, with an allusion to the country dancing that Hardy as a youth enjoyed, but references to the present "sense of sorrow" and "Sighs from the Gone" suggest that the gaiety is forced. Humorously, but with insight into the pretense of the poem, Blunden said that "it has the lugubrious hopelessness of one of those gentlemen who, having been drinking, beset the approach to public-houses with renderings of 'Abide with Me.' "[1] The poem seems a companion-piece to "On a Fine Morning."

1. *Thomas Hardy*, p. 245.

THE WELL-BELOVED and the novel of the same title express a persistent theme in Hardy's works. *The Later Years* says: "The theory on which this fantastic tale of a subjective idea was constructed is explained in the preface to the novel, and again exemplified in a poem bearing the same name, written about this time. . . . The theory of the transmigration of the ideal beloved one, who only exists in the lover, from material woman to material woman." The novel, though a fantasy in its story, presents the "truth that all men are pursuing a shadow, the Unattainable."[1] Hardy's journal for October 28, 1891, comments on this idealization, saying: "It is the incompleteness that is loved, when love is sterling and true. That is what differentiates the real one from the imaginary, the practicable from the impossible, the Love who returns the kiss from the Vision that melts away. A man sees the Diana or the Venus in his Beloved, but what he loves is the difference."[2] For love to be "sterling and true," then, the lover must see through the imagined Diana or Venus to the real woman. Hardy's novels illustrate this idea: love for the vision is disastrous. In domestic life the real replaces the vision. Then perhaps "substantial affection," like that between Bathsheba and Gabriel in *Far from the Madding Crowd*, "arises (if any arises at all) when the two who are thrown together begin first by knowing the rougher sides of each other's character, and not the best till further on, the romance growing up in the interstices of a mass of hard prosaic reality." (Chapter LVI.) Against this background, "The Well-Beloved" presents a disillusionment that *may* have a happy sequel. After the marriage the next morning, the husband may find the actual woman more "sterling and true" than the vision.

Hardy's view that romantic love is subjective may owe much to Shelley. The novel *The Well-Beloved* quotes as motto Shelley's "One shape of many names."[3] The pursuit of the Unattainable in the novel is summarized in Shelley's "In many mortal forms I rashly sought / The shadow of that idol of my thought." ("Epipsychidion," lines 267-68.)

The concept plays an important role in bringing about disaster in Hardy's novels. In *Far from the Madding Crowd*, Boldwood's passion for Bathsheba is based upon an idealization from a Valentine-card sent as a jest. Though he goes mad for love of her, Boldwood knows little of Bathsheba as a woman, but only as a dream. In *The Return of the Native*, Eustacia is in love with Clym before she ever sees him, and she dreams of him as a knight with visor down whose face she cannot see; and Clym, idealizing Eustacia, will not listen to the truth about her even from her own lips. She says of his plan for opening a school on the heath, "I am aware that there are Boulevards in Paris," but he goes away thinking "that his scheme had somehow become glorified. A beautiful woman had been intertwined with it." (Book Third, Chapter III.) In *The Woodlanders*, the trifler Fitzpiers is aware that his passion for Grace Melbury is based upon a vision. He says to Giles: "Human love is . . . joy accompanied by an idea which we project against any suitable object in the line of our vision, just as the rainbow iris is projected against an oak, ash, or elm tree indifferently." (Chapter XVI.) In *Tess of the D'Urbervilles*, Angel sees Tess as "no longer the milkmaid, but a visionary essence of woman—a whole sex condensed into one typical form. He called her Artemis, Demeter, and other fanciful names half teasingly, which she did not like because she did not understand them." (Chapter XX.) His cruel rejection of her is based upon this idealization; he says, "You were one person [Artemis, Demeter]; now you are another [the flesh-and-blood Tess]." (Chapter XXXV.) Jude's marriage to Arabella in *Jude the Obscure* is based upon a difficult idealization: "He knew well, too well, in the secret centre of his brain, that Arabella was not worth a great deal as a specimen of womanhood. . . . For his own soothing he kept up a factitious belief in her. His idea of her was the thing of most consequence, not Arabella herself." (Part I, Chapter IX.)

"The Well-Beloved" is localized near "Kingsbere," Hardy's name for Bere Regis, about twelve miles northeast of Dorchester. The lover of the poem seems to come from the northeast, perhaps from near Salisbury. He does not follow a main road, but, guiding himself "by star and planet shine," cuts across meadows, "On gravel and on green." He follows roughly the course of the old Roman Road, the "Ikling Way," which runs north of Bere Regis. There a goddess appears, "Nigh where the Pagan temple stood." There is no authentic record of a temple to Venus along the course of the Roman Road from Salisbury (or Old Sarum) to the scene of the poem.[4] The "ancient hill and wood" he passes may refer to Woodbury Hill (with an ancient hill-fort and tumuli) and Bere Wood, less than a mile east of Bere Regis, but more distant from the Roman Road. The goddess disappears "by the lane / Adjoining Kingsbere," apparently a path from Woodbury Hill to the town center.

In the Wessex edition, Hardy shifted the scene from Bere Regis to Jordon Hill, near Weymouth, about seven miles south of Dorchester. This was the site of the Roman station Clavinium. This shift suggests that he had no factual basis for the incident, but provided geographical particulars only to give the sense of fact. The area near Weymouth is the site of the novel *The Well-Beloved*, and at Jordon Hill, a mile to the northeast, "the important find of a Roman temple was made in 1834, although Roman coins had been turned up on this site many years before. This hill, overlooking the sea, was laid out as a Romano-British temple set in a spacious courtyard."[5]

The poem expresses much of Hardy's view of the world: as the poem begins the bridegroom is on his way to his wedding. His disillusionment is too late for him to change his mind. In the third stanza he sings "to sky and tree," and thus calls upon the forces of nature; Venus, a goddess derived from nature, appears when called.

1. P. 59; *Life*, pp. 285-86.
2. *Early Life*, p. 314; *Life*, p. 239.
3. "The Revolt of Islam," Canto I, Stanza XXVII.
4. Ordnance maps mark the site of a Roman well near this road, a little more than a mile north of Bere Regis, and a "Roman Burial found A.D. 1858" at a point nearly two miles northeast of the village. Hardy's "men say," in the penultimate stanza, suggests that the existence of a temple is only a local tale.
5. Hutchings, *Inside Dorset*, p. 106.

HER REPROACH is a sweetheart's rebuke for her lover's neglect of her in order to study and (the sweetheart says sarcastically) strive toward some empty fame. Possibly Hardy, living and studying in Westbourne Park Villas until late in July, 1867, made the poem by paraphrasing a letter from a sweetheart in Dorchester, but no sweetheart of this date is known. After returning to Dorchester later in this month, Hardy fell in love with Tryphena Sparks. Both "Westbourne Park Villas" appended to the poem and a statement in *The Early Life* indicate that the poem was written before he left London, to which he returned during the year only on a "flying visit . . . to fetch his books and other impedimenta."[1] Possibly the poem develops a reproach from Hardy's sister Mary about his immersion in study. The poem may be fictional, treating Hardy's own feeling, which debated the worth of ambition against the loss of present joys.

The poem has been interpreted by critics who seem not to have read *The Early Life*. Vinson, for instance, says that the "dead page" is "the past of two lovers."[2] In view of Hardy's life in 1867, it is the printed page: Greek, Latin, the English poets, etc.

1. *Early Life*, pp. 71, 75; *Life*, pp. 54, 57.
2. "Diction and Imagery in the Poetry of Thomas Hardy," p. 133.

THE INCONSISTENT may be entirely imaginary. If it is Hardy's personal expression, it may represent his mood at the time he visited Topsham cemetery after the death of Mrs. Tryphena Sparks Gale in 1890 and was "standing by her mound." The expression of regret in the last two lines may refer to Hardy's jilting Tryphena in order to marry Emma Gifford. Three years after this marriage Tryphena signed "Her name upon a faded book" with that of Charles Gale.

A BROKEN APPOINTMENT probably "is to be associated with Mrs. Henniker" and "The scene is the British Museum."[1] As Hardy first met Mrs. Arthur Henniker in May, 1893, the poem must be dated some time later. The evidence indicates that his feeling for Mrs. Henniker was, as the poem suggests, warmer than hers for him. Though he may have had Mrs. Henniker in mind, the lines also express a general human experience of disappointed expectation.

On a casual reading, the poem seems to treat an elderly lover's pique that his beloved did not keep her appointment, but the poem says that this feeling is less than the poet's grief at discovering—or inferring—that she lacks "high compassion."

Critical appraisal of this poem has been varied. Murry found it "one of the finest of modern lyrical poems. . . . The language in which the emotion is expressed could hardly be more direct and simple. In the first verse there is . . . one simple yet tremendous metaphor—'And marching Time drew on, and wore me numb.' "[2] Duffin said that "The thought in the poet's mind was not a simple one, but it is expressed with absoluteness and economy, and yet without obvious effort at compression."[3] Hynes admires the images of "marching Time" and the "time-torn man." These images "modify each other, since Time in the first image is, at least superficially, the time spent waiting for the woman who doesn't come, while in the second it is time in larger terms, Time-the-destroyer, Hardy's old enemy, with whom the woman is now in league." Hynes does not approve the "pace" of the poem for its "sheer oral difficulty; it is hard to read, and impossible to read musically."[4] Brown finds the poem too much in the "grand manner," for "along with the pathos goes the gesture of importance, behind the eloquence stand Shakespeare—and Swinburne."[5]

1. Purdy, *Thomas Hardy: A Bibliographical Study*, p. 113.
2. *The Problem of Style*, pp. 24-25.
3. *Thomas Hardy*, p. 301.
4. *The Pattern of Hardy's Poetry*, pp. 127 and 60.
5. *Thomas Hardy*, pp. 178-79.

"BETWEEN US NOW" may represent Hardy and his first wife. The lines "Let there be truth at last, / Even if despair" are characteristic of Hardy's insistence upon frankness as a basis for love or friendship. Gustav von Holst set the poem to music (in manuscript in the Dorset County Museum) .

"HOW GREAT MY GRIEF," unless it refers to Mrs. Emma Hardy, is presumably without personal application, but is an exercise in writing in the graceful, amusing, fixed verse-form called the triolet. This form, invented in thirteenth-century France, consists of eight short lines with two rimes, as abaaabab. The first line is repeated as the fourth line, and the first two lines as the seventh and eighth. The name triolet comes from the fact that the first line appears three times, but in the second and third appearances in a context that alters its meaning.

"I NEED NOT GO" concerns a dead woman called "my Love" whose identity is not clear. Lea's identification stops with the assertion that "Stinsford Churchyard holds the tomb in which *She* lies."[1] She cannot be Hardy's wife, mother, or sister, still living when the poem was published. Possibly Hardy was thinking of Mrs. Tryphena Sparks Gale, who was buried in Topsham cemetery.

1. *Thomas Hardy's Wessex*, p. 270.

THE COQUETTE, AND AFTER is written in two triolets, which are ingenious in the shifting of meaning in their repeated lines. (See the notes on "How Great My Grief.") Hardy selected this graceful verse-form to express both a thought he had in mind when drawing Sue's flirtatious character in *Jude the Obscure*, and a comment upon Victorian moral codes. To explain her caprices to Jude, Sue says: "I feel that I shouldn't have been provided with attractiveness unless it were meant to be exercised! Some women's love of being loved is insatiable." Later, when she has come to love Jude, Sue uses almost the words of the first triolet to tell how her love began: "At first I did not love you, Jude; that I own. When I first knew you I merely wanted you to love me. I did not exactly flirt with you; but . . . the craving to attract and captivate, regardless of the injury it may do the man—was in me. . . . But, you see, however it ended, it began in the selfish and cruel wish to make your heart ache for me without letting mine ache for you."[1]

The second triolet recalls the fate of Tess in *Tess of the D'Urbervilles*.

1. Part IV, Chapter I, and Part VI, Chapter III.

A SPOT seems to be set in the sheep pasture called Coombe Eweleaze near Puddletown. (See the notes on "In a Eweleaze Near Weatherbury.") Deacon's suggestion seems tenable that the lovers are Hardy and Tryphena Sparks.[1]

Firor points out that the poem makes use of the folk-belief in the power of shepherds to perceive emanations from a place that was the scene of strong emotional disturbance.[2] Hynes has identified the verse-form as drawn from Nahum Tate's and Nicholas Brady's *A New Version of the Psalms of David*, where "Psalm 148 is written in stanzas of eight lines, four three-stressed lines followed by four two-stressed lines, rhyming ababcddc"—though Hardy varies the pattern somewhat.[3]

Russell Boughton, in his operatic version of Hardy's *The Queen of Cornwall*, with Hardy's approval omitted the epilogue and substituted "A Spot," sung by a chorus of Shades at the end of the opera.[4] More recently the poem, under the title "In Years Defaced," has been set to music by Gerald Finzi in *Till Earth Outwears* (New York and London: Boosey and Hawkes, 1958).

1. *Hardy's Sweetest Image*, pp. 9-10.
2. *Folkways in Thomas Hardy*, p. 70.
3. *The Pattern of Hardy's Poetry*, p. 87.
4. Roberts, *Hardy's Poetic Drama and the Theatre*, p. 100.

LONG PLIGHTED seems an elaboration of the ending of Hardy's short story "The Waiting Supper." In this story, circumstances have caused Nicholas Long and Christine Everard, "plighted" for many years, to postpone marriage until both are past middle age. When at last free to marry, Christine says to Nicholas: "Is it worth while, after so many years? . . . We are fairly happy as we are—perhaps happier than we should be in any other relation, seeing what old people we have grown. . . . Let us be joyful together as we are, dearest Nic . . . and 'With mirth and laughter let old wrinkles come.'" The first line of each stanza of the poem repeats Christine's question, with "after so many years" changed to "now," "when," and "since." In the story, Christine and Nicholas remain close friends, but do not marry. The poem states in more detail than the story how they can be happy as companions roaming "Yell'ham's wooded mounds" and coming to lie at last "As mates in Mellstock churchyard."

Apparently Hardy drew the theme for "The Waiting Supper" from Browning's "The Statue and the Bust"; the story quotes lines 138-40 of this poem. He localized the story in the Frome Valley near Casterbridge (Dorchester), with references to Athelhall (Athelhampton), five miles from Dorchester; the manor-house of the story, Froom-Everard, resembles Kingston-Maurward. Though the story does not mention rambles in Yell'ham Wood, it does refer to the Mellstock (Stinsford) fiddlers. It would seem Hardy began with an idea from Browning, developed it into "The Waiting Supper," and then wrote the poem to expand its conclusion into Christine's vision of how she and Nicholas, too weary of life for marriage (in a sense, looking forward to death), might find "mirth and laughter" in companionship.

THE WIDOW BETROTHED seems to be a fiction inspired by an actual setting. On February 18, 1918, Hardy wrote to Edmund Gosse about this poem: ". . . though I thought of it about 1867 when looking at the house described, which is near here, it must have been written after I had read Wordsworth's famous preface to Lyrical

Ballads, which influenced me much, and influences the style of the poem, as you can see for yourself."[1]

In the first edition of *Poems of the Past and the Present*, the opening line of the poem read "By Mellstock Lodge and avenue." In revising, Hardy removed the place-name. As "Mellstock" is Stinsford, the "fair tenement" of the widow would seem to be Stinsford House, just northwest of Stinsford Church. It was formerly a manor house with a gatekeeper's lodge at the end of an avenue.[2] Stinsford House was partly burned on September 17, 1892,[3] but the present house has the gable ends and creeper mentioned in the poem. If this identification is right, the poem may present an imaginary incident in the widowhood of Lady Susan O'Brien. It would be entirely fictional: no child or post-marital lover is suggested in her life story.

The influence of Wordsworth is evident in the theme and language of the poem. The theme is the subtle destruction of a romantic dream, but without lasting harm to the possibility of domestic happiness. The lover may find his life enriched by the child. The poem is written, according to Wordsworth's prescription, in everyday language.

1. Purdy, *Thomas Hardy: A Bibliographical Study*, p. 113.

2. The old avenue leads to an unused gatehouse about halfway to Dorchester; the manor house, approached by another road, is now a school. The "Mellstock House" on the way from Bockhampton Lane to Hardy's birthplace is a new house, not that of the poem.

3. *Later Years*, p. 12; *Life*, pp. 249-50. Though Hardy said he thought of the poem about 1867, he may not have written it until after the fire.

AT A HASTY WEDDING is a triolet (see the notes on "How Great My Grief"), first published in Hardy's short story "A Changed Man" on April 21, 1900. In the story, the poem is attributed to a somewhat cynical guest at the wedding of Captain Maumbry of the Hussars and the town belle, Laura. This guest "could on occasion do a pretty stroke of rhyming in those days, and he beguiled the time of waiting by pencilling on a blank page of his prayer-book a few lines," the poem.

Though the story falsifies the prediction of the wedding guest, the sentiment of the poem is constant in Hardy's writing: a hasty marriage to "solace swift desire" is likely to be disastrous. The disasters that follow the marriages of Bathsheba to Troy in *Far from the Madding Crowd* and of Jude to Arabella in *Jude the Obscure* represent Hardy's usual feeling.

THE DREAM-FOLLOWER presents a complex view of illusion and disillusion with the speed of flashing pictures: an idealized "old Love," the lover's pursuit of the ideal, his sight of the reality as mortal woman subject to age and decay, the death of his dream, and his shocked flight. This view is characteristic of Hardy as temperamentally a dreamer, but intellectually a realist who often, unwillingly and unhappily, saw through youth and beauty to the skull beneath.

HIS IMMORTALITY may be considered a companion-poem to "Her Immortality." Both poems assume that the only life after death is in the memories of the living. In "Her Immortality" this thought holds a bereaved lover back from suicide: he will live to give his beloved even this spectral life. In the last stanza the thought crosses his mind that when he dies, she will die a second and final death. This thought is the theme of "His Immortality," which traces the fading of memory as time passes, the friends who remember die, and the "I" of the poem only now and then recalls in a "feeble spark, / Dying amid the dark."

THE TO-BE-FORGOTTEN had in the manuscript an identifying note and a motto: " (In Stourcastle Churchyard.) 'Neither have they any more a reward, for the memory of them is forgotten.' " The poem was dated "Feb. 9, 1899?"[1] "Stourcastle" is Hardy's name for Sturminster Newton,[2] where the Hardys lived from July, 1876, until March 18, 1878. The questioned date suggests that he went to Sturminster Newton in early February of 1899, and the poem suggests that he called upon "old friends" there and found some of them in the churchyard. Perhaps as he saw the inscriptions on their tombstones so weathered that they could hardly be read, the quoted verse from Eccles. 9:5, came to mind.

In the poet's question and a reply from the tombs, the poem develops the theme of this verse. The reply includes phrases from other portions of the Bible: the "second death" from Rev. 20:14, "This is the second death," and "Things true, things lovely, things of good report" from St. Paul's words in Phil. 4:8, "Finally, brethren, whatsoever things are true . . . whatsoever things are lovely, whatsoever things are of good report, if there be any virtue, and if there be any praise, think on these things." The evidence of the tombstones from which the names were fading indicated that St. Paul's recommendation, "neither shunned nor sought" by the ordinary man, would not keep the dead alive in memory after their names had faded.

The poem is to be associated with "Her Immortality" and "His Immortality," setting forth the concept that man's only immortality exists in the memory of the living, which perhaps fades faster than the tombstones and brings about the "second death . . . oblivion's swallowing sea."

1. Purdy, *Thomas Hardy: A Bibliographical Study*, p. 114.
2. Lea, *Thomas Hardy's Wessex*, p. 6.

WIVES IN THE SERE develops the theme that though time and cares decay youth and beauty a husband may still glimpse in an aging wife "some early light or pose" that moved him to choose her.

Critics have disagreed about the quality of the verse. Ransome says: "Logically the stanzas are two, but so far as the rhyme-system goes they might as well be one. The eight odd-numbered lines of the poem rhyme together in a masculine ending, and the eight even-numbered lines in a feminine ending. The feminine rhymes are not very choice. . . . It was pedantic of Hardy to try for technical success by forcing his native language to such rude measures."[1] Grew, considering the poem as a song, disagrees: it "might almost have come from a book of Elizabethan lute-songs."[2]

1. *Selected Poems*, xxviii.
2. "Thomas Hardy as Musician," p. 124.

THE SUPERSEDED seems a personal expression. Living and laboring until 1928, Hardy undoubtedly felt full of vigor and promise at sixty-one, but found himself both revered as a kind of classic and pushed aside by the younger novelists and poets of the new century. His meditation was "expressed with poignant brevity by Oscar Wilde when he said, 'The worst of old age is not that we are old, but that we are young.' "[1]

1. Nevinson, *Thomas Hardy*, p. 41.

AN AUGUST MIDNIGHT casts light upon Hardy's writing habits. On July 26, 1884, he wrote: "Mr. Thomas Hardy begs to state in reply to Dr. Hugo Erichsen's circular that he prefers night for working, but finds daytime advisable as a rule."[1]

The poem pictures Hardy at his work-table, distracted enough to reflect upon the darkness, the quiet (except "the beat of a clock from a distant floor") , and the insects that had come as if to visit him. The reflections have his peculiar blend of humor, compassion, and philosophic thought. The insects are a bother, but they are "guests." With a charity as all-embracing as that of St. Francis, he (presumably) did not swat the insects (all were harmless) , but treated them with respect as fellow creatures.

Hardy's reverence for all life had some basis in his readings in science; in evolutionary theory, all living beings are akin. "Hardy had so completely assimilated the theory of evolution and harmonized it with an increase of sensibility that he based thereupon the conception of morality itself not only in relation to man, but to the entire world of conscious, sentient beings."[2] He reflected upon how the world might seem through senses different from those developed in man, in some respects more acute. On another occasion he remarked to Newman Flower: "Flower, I often wonder how much animals know—about things—things of which we are 'ignorant.' "[3] The "Earth-secrets" that he supposed the insects might know are not earth's meaning. They do not know more than the poet does, but each perceives something the other does not.

1. In the Harvard University Library.
2. Chakravarty, *"The Dynasts" and the Post-War Age in Poetry*, p. 23.
3. Flower, *Just As It Happened*, p. 104.

THE CAGED THRUSH FREED AND HOME AGAIN is written in the form of a villanelle, a verse-form developed from a round song that originated in the rustic dances of medieval France. Later the form became fixed as a poem in five tercets closed with a quatrain. Two rimes run throughout the poem, the first and third line of every tercet having the same rime, the second line of each riming, and the last two lines of the quatrain repeating the first and third lines of the opening tercet. Perhaps Hardy chose the villanelle to represent the repetitive song of a bird.

Speaking in the voice of a thrush allowed him to rebuke man's arrogance in caging song birds, by presenting in graceful irony the discovery by the thrush that mighty "Men know but little more than we." He did not take the caging of a thrush lightly. In reporting a visit to him in the summer of 1909, Arthur Compton-Rickett wrote: "A thrush broke out into song outside, and the smile faded from Hardy's face. 'An hour before you came,' he said vehemently, 'I saw a horrible sight—a thrush in a cage. Canaries and finches are bad enough, but a thrush! How can people do it?—The cruelty of it!' His eyes blazed with anger, and for the rest of that visit there was little else discussed except the treatment of birds and animals."[1]

1. "Thomas Hardy, O. M.," p. 23.

BIRDS AT WINTER NIGHTFALL was written in December, 1899, and the Hardys used it as a Christmas card in 1919[1]—perhaps as "propaganda" for kindness to birds. The notation "Max Gate" suggests that the "crumb-outcaster" was Hardy. Like other statements in prose and verse (for instance, "The Reminder"), the poem makes clear that, when falling snow made it impossible to feed the birds, he thought of the birds without berries and unable to find food on the snow-covered ground. The poem is a triolet. (See the notes on "How Great My Grief.")

1. Purdy, *Thomas Hardy: A Bibliographical Study*, p. 114.

THE PUZZLED GAME-BIRDS bore the title "The Battue" in the Wessex Edition of Hardy's works. This term means that the game-birds on a gentleman's estate were protected and fed until the hunting season. Then, for sport and as a social event, the birds were driven from cover by "beaters" in order that ladies and gentlemen might shoot them for the pleasure of "bagging" as many as possible.

Clive Holland tells a story about Hardy's feeling for wounded birds. When Holland was bicycling with him and they stopped to rest, ". . . a blackbird with a broken wing fluttered out of the hedge onto the road. Hardy shuddered on seeing it. Then he said, 'I cannot bear such a sight, poor thing! Could you put it out of its misery? If left, a cat or a stoat will get it and torture it.' He turned away his head while I did as he wished. It was not merely a common humanitarian instinct that had been aroused in him, I could see; but a sheer sickness and revulsion against a helpless thing suffering."[1]

Hardy's revulsion at the suffering of birds extended to active and scornful hostility toward the breeding and shooting of game-birds for sport. He wrote in his notebook in January, 1882: "Next day I met with a keeper—tells me that one day this season they shot (3 guns) 700 pheasants in one day—*a battue*—driving the birds into one corner of the plantation. When they get there they will not run across the open ground—rise on the wing—then are shot wholesale. They pick up all that have fallen—night comes on—the *wounded* birds that have hidden or risen into some thick tree fall & lie on the ground in their agony—next day the keepers come and look for them. (They found 150, on the above occasion, next day.) Can see the night scene —moon—fluttering & gasping birds as the hours go on—the place being now deserted of humankind."[2] When W. L. Phelps went on a bicycle tour with Hardy in 1900, Hardy "spoke of the wickedness of shooting game birds, or killing any animals: 'wickedness' was the word he used."[3] The year before he died Hardy sent a check to the League for the Prohibition of Cruel [blood] Sports, writing "sorrowfully that the human race is practically still barbarian and man's delight in cruel sport can be lessened only by slow degrees: 'to attempt even this is, however, a worthy object which I commend.' And out of the profits arising from the productions of the Hardy Players donations were set aside to assist the work of the R.S.P.C.A."[4]

Hardy expressed his feeling for birds throughout his novels, as in the instance of the starved goldfinch in *The Mayor of Casterbridge* (Chapter XLV) and Jude's letting the birds eat Farmer Troutham's wheat in *Jude the Obscure* (Part I, Chapter II). Possibly drawing from the page of his notebook quoted above, Hardy has a scene in

Tess of the D'Urbervilles that pictures a consequence of the actions that puzzle the game-birds. After sheltering herself in a wood for the night, during which she hears sounds of gasping, gurgling, and falling, Tess awakes to find that the sounds come from wounded pheasants. "Under the trees several pheasants lay about, their rich plumage dabbled with blood; some were dead, some feebly twitching a wing, some staring up at the sky, some pulsating quickly, some contorted, some stretched out—all of them writhing in agony. . . ." Tess, understanding that the birds had been wounded by a shooting party, wrings their necks to end their suffering. Then she recalls hunters she had seen "peering through bushes, and pointing their guns, strangely accoutred, a blood-thirsty light in their eyes." In certain weeks of autumn and winter "they ran amuck, and made it their purpose to destroy life—in this case harmless feathered creatures, brought into being by artificial means solely to gratify these propensities—at once so unmannerly and so unchivalrous towards their weaker fellows in Nature's teeming family." (Chapter XLI.) These thoughts, in character for Tess, also represent Hardy's feeling. Speaking to Henry Nevinson, he "described the indignation of the neighbouring landowners because he had described *their* pheasant plantations in 'Tess,' after which they had long refused to call on him."[5]

1. Holland, "The Thomas Hardy I Knew," p. 14.
2. This page from Hardy's notebook is in an envelope in the Dorset County Museum.
3. Phelps, *Autobiography with Letters*, p. 390.
4. Hansford, "A Heart of Pity," p. 573.
5. Nevinson, *More Changes More Chances*, p. 179.

WINTER IN DURNOVER FIELD probably presents a scene near Max Gate. The "stage-direction" for the little "play" Hardy thus observed presents a typical winter scene in Dorset; the birds, the pigeon being a wood-pigeon, are among the most common residents in this area.[1] Though Hardy presents no denouement, his lifelong compassion for suffering birds suggests that he felt the scene as a tragedy.

1. See Moule, *A Revised List of the Birds of Dorset*, pp. 11, 13, 18.

THE LAST CHRYSANTHEMUM opens with a question typical of Hardy's pondering the mystery of life, that of plants as well as of animals. He surely knew the scientific answer to the question, ecological adaptation, for in *The Mayor of Casterbridge* Elizabeth-Jane finds a "latitude of calm weather" as a result of the process: her "cunning enlargement, by a species of microscopic treatment, of those minute forms of satisfaction that offer themselves to everybody not in positive pain." (Chapter XLV.) Plants adapt in the same way. Some flowers attract and feed bees and wasps, others butterflies, others moths; they disperse their seeds in a fantastic variety of ways, as if to escape competition; they blossom in a seasonal procession. Adaptation is forever going on, apparently toward the end that every species shall win an ecological niche where it may thrive.

Knowledge of the process does not explain the "Great Face behind," the force that established the laws of nature that operate as evolution, adaptation, etc. As Hardy was working on *The Dynasts* when the poem was published, the "Great Face" would seem to be another name for the Immanent Will.

THE DARKLING THRUSH in the *Collected Poems* is dated "31st *December* 1900," but Hardy wrote the poem before this date. It was published in the *Graphic* on December 29 as "By the Century's Deathbed." Purdy says, "The date '31st December 1900' in Hardy's final revision he may have felt necessary in view of the altered title."[1] He intended the poem as a comment upon the dying century, to be read as if written as darkness fell in the evening of the century's last day.

The change of title added much to the connotations of the poem. The word *darkling* is a poetic word with the general meaning of "shrouded in darkness." It had been used in three great poems known to Hardy, in two of them in connection with a bird's song, and in the third in connection with the intellectual confusions of the nineteenth century. In Milton's *Paradise Lost*, the blind poet, speaking of inspiration, says: "Then feed on thoughts, that voluntary move / Harmonious numbers; as the wakeful Bird / Sings darkling, and in shadiest Covert hid / Tunes her nocturnal Note." (Book III, 37-40.) These lines suggest a flow of music more from feeling than from reason. A few lines later, Milton speaks of his blindness, saying that he finds "Nature's works to me expunged and razed, / And wisdom at one entrance quite shut out." Both intuitive song and human limitations are echoed in Hardy's poem. Keats's "Ode to a Nightingale" also uses the word *darkling*. As the nightingale sings, the poet says, "Darkling I listen."[2] Matthew Arnold's "Dover Beach" uses *darkling* to characterize the "plain" where intellectual struggles of the nineteenth century were fought out: "And we are here as on a darkling plain / Swept with confused alarms of struggle and flight, / Where ignorant armies clash by night." Hardy's poem implies that the poet is in despair because these struggles are still unresolved.[3]

The thrush of the poem is evidently a missel-thrush, which sings cheerfully in winter. Among other inspirations for the poem, Hardy may have read Hudson's *Nature in Downland*, published in 1900, containing this passage: "Mid-winter is the season of the missel-thrush.

. . . But when it is too gloomy for even his [the song-thrush's] fine temper, when there is no gleam of light anywhere and no change in that darkness of immense ever-moving cloud above; and the south-west raves all day and all night, and day after day, then the storm-cock [missel-thrush] sings his loudest from a tree-top and has no rival. . . . If you should observe him in rough or gloomy weather, perched on an elm-top, swayed about this way and that by the gusts, singing his best, you must believe . . . that his pleasure in life . . . must greatly exceed in degree the contentment and bliss that is ours." (Pp. 251-52.)

The earlier title, "By the Century's Deathbed," indicates the meaning of Hardy's symbols. The poem laments the dying century, for him a time when science and rationalist philosophies undermined man's religion and sense of divine purpose, and left man in a bleak world where basic forces were unintelligible to the mind. This lament is followed by the song of a thrush, which is no exotic from a land of dreams. He is "aged . . . frail, gaunt, and small," subject to all the pangs of hunger, decay, and death. His feathers (his only shelter) are "beruffled" by the wintry wind. The thrush withstands the blast and sings. In the last four lines of the poem Hardy expresses a characteristic thought. The poet "could think" (imagine, speculate) that the thrush "knew" (in an instinctive knowledge more basic than reasoning) of a "blessed Hope" for which the poet's reason saw no evidence. This Hope may be an irrational, intuitive certainty that the world and life have meaning and purpose similar to that attributed to it by religious faith.[4]

The imagery of the poem pictures the thought-movement of the theme. In the first two stanzas, the images build a picture of death and desolation; the third stanza dares death with an "evensong"—a quasi-religious hope in the tones of a thrush; the last stanza poses reason against instinct. The images that suggest death are remarkable: the gathering frost has the pallor of a spectre; the winter day remains only as dregs; the setting sun is a "weakening eye"; stems of vines against the sky seem broken strings of lyres as imaged on tombstones; men "haunt" rather than dwell nearby. Similar images symbolize the corpse of the Victorian century, with a crypt of clouds and a death-lamenting wind. Against this picture is thrown the image of a thrush that, under the circumstances, should be desolate, but is upheld by a force suggested to be akin to religion. In an "evensong / Of Joy" he chooses to "fling his soul" against the darkness in the poet's mind. The poem is in the "common meter" of many ballads and hymns.

"The Darkling Thrush" has been set to music for violin and orchestra by Robin Milford (Oxford University Press, 1930).

1. Purdy, *Thomas Hardy: A Bibliographical Study*, p. 114.
2. Other phrases in this ode are echoed in "The Darkling Thrush": Hardy's "spectre-gray," "full-hearted evensong," "fling his soul," and "ecstatic sound" echo Keats's "spectre-thin," "full-throated ease," "pouring forth thy soul," and "such an ecstasy." See Perkins, "Hardy and the Poetry of Isolation," pp. 151-54.
3. Hardy used *darkling* again, in connection with a "twilit plain," in "God's Funeral."
4. Hardy's capital letter for Hope suggests that it is religious.

THE COMET AT YELL'HAM is based on an actual experience. When Dr. T. Herbert Warren quoted the poem in a speech, Hardy wrote to him on October 24, 1909: "I have read the proof of your interesting & able address at the celebration of the Jubilee of the Oxford Museum, & am much honoured by your quoting my little poem about the comet. It appeared, I think, in 1858 or 1859—a very large one—& I remember standing and looking at it as described."[1] The comet was Encke's Comet, brilliant in England in September and October, 1858. According to the poem, Hardy watched the comet from the top of Yellowham Hill. The "sweet form" who was with him may have been either a boyhood sweetheart or his mother or sister.

The poem, in comparing the comet's return "long years hence" with the brevity of human life, suggests a theme of *Two on a Tower*, Hardy's wish "to set the emotional history of two infinitesimal lives against the stupendous background of the stellar universe." (Preface.) Looking at both the novel and the line "It will return long years hence," Weber says: "For fictional purposes . . . Hardy transferred to Encke's Comet the characteristics of the comet he had seen on June 25, 1881. We now know this comet as Tebbutt's. . . . Of course no one then knew its name, for no one then living had seen it before. The last time it had been visible was in 547 B.C. . . . It will not be back until A.D. 4309."[2]

1. In the Colby College Library.
2. *Hardy of Wessex*, 2nd ed., p. 133.

MAD JUDY is a grimly humorous poem that presents the radical pessimism of a woman considered mad by her neighbors, but implied, by the irony between the first muted "we knew" and the same phrase at the end, to be rational in her view that life is a curse and death a blessing. In view of Hardy's many expressions of the idea that life is a curse, as in "To an Unborn Pauper Child," and his sense of isolation from more hopeful men, as in "The Impercipient," Judy would seem to represent an aspect of Hardy himself.

A WASTED ILLNESS perhaps treats Hardy's dangerous illness, with internal bleeding, from October, 1880, to May, 1881,[1] but the addition of "(Overheard)" to the title in the Wessex Edition indicates that he either was writing of someone else's illness or intended the reader to think so.

In the poem, death is presented as a release from life, as a goal to be attained, but only by passing through the "vaults of pain" described in images of physical suffering and mental horror. The illness of the poem was "wasted" because the speaker recovered from it. Stanza six presents the "dews of comfort" on recovery, but the stanza is ironic: to reach the goal of death he must again pass through the pain of illness.

1. See Chapter XI in *Early Life* and *Life*.

A MAN is set in "Casterbridge" (Dorchester). The Elizabethan House that "smiled the long street down for near a mile" was on the upper part of High West Street. The view from this house would extend down High West and High East Streets to the Frome River. This location fits that of the "fine mansion of the Trenchards at the corner of Shirehall Lane" and High West Street, which Hardy mentioned among old buildings, long ago demolished, in his speech accepting the Freedom of the Borough on November 16, 1910.[1] This identification agrees with that of Herman Lea.[2]

The house is partly described in L. C. Boswell-Stone's *Memories and Traditions*, as "a handsome stone house in the High Street, belonging to the Trenchards of Wolverton. . . . It was built of stone, grown gray with age. It had carved stone balustrades, some of which remain now, and have a very odd effect in a side street [Shirehall Lane]." A room on the second floor "had a wide fireplace, opposite to which was a splendid bay window filling nearly all the north end of the room. Mr. and Mrs. Henning and their son and daughter lived in this house." The account says that the house should not have been destroyed, but restored; it was an ornament to the whole town. "I remember hearing that Lucas, the builder, who purchased this one [the Trenchard house], said he had made a bad bargain; it took so much time and labor to destroy the solid masonry."[3] As this description indicates, the "Trenchard mansion" passed out of the possession of the Trenchards early in the nineteenth century. No clear record tells when the house was demolished. The building now on the site is referred to in a deed of 1849 as "now being erected" and in another deed of 1855 as "newly erected." The present building is occupied by the Dorset County Council, a Civil Defense organization, the Dorset Marriage Guidance Council, and a barber shop. On the east side of the present building at the rear along Glyde Path Road what seems a portion of the original house remains, with walls topped by a stone balustrade, perhaps removed there when the front was torn down.

Hardy must have seen this balustrade many times. At the end of June, 1883, the Hardys moved from Wimborne Minster to Dorchester and lived there in a rented house on Shirehall Lane while Max Gate was being built.[4] He had to walk past the balustrade to get to High West Street.

The "Man" of the poem is less clearly identifiable. The subtitle "In Memory of H. of M." gives initials; the poem indicates that he was an itinerant laborer who proudly "packed his tools and went." If the mansion was demolished before 1822, "H. of M." may refer to George *H*and of *M*elbury Osmund (about fifteen miles northwest of Dorchester), Hardy's maternal grandfather, of whom little is known but that he was a laboring man who died in 1822 in poverty. The "H. of M." may refer to Hardy's father or paternal grandfather, *H*ardy of *M*ellstock (Stinsford), not as the laborer of the poem, but as the teller of the anecdote.

The anecdote expressed in a dramatic decision two views with which Hardy agreed, that laboring men are not to be looked upon as clowns without intelligence, taste, or pride, and that it was wrong to destroy a beautiful and historically valuable building to carry out some utilitarian end. His attitude is expressed in the closing line: "His protest lives where deathless things abide!"[5]

1. *Later Years*, p. 145; *Life*, p. 352.
2. *A Handbook to the Wessex Country*, p. 43. Lea's Glyde Path Road is the present name for the narrow street formerly called Shirehall Lane.
3. Pp. 39-41. See also Moule, *Dorchester Antiquities*, p. 94.
4. Weber, *Hardy of Wessex*, 2nd ed., p. 139.
5. See "The Dorsetshire Labourer" and "Memories of Church Restoration" in Orel, *Thomas Hardy's Personal Writings*, pp. 168-89, 203-17.

THE DAME OF ATHELHALL is set at Athelhampton Hall, a fifteenth-century mansion less than a mile east of Puddletown. This mansion was the ancient seat of the Martyn family, descendants of Martin of Tours who entered England with William the Conqueror. It is "traditionally said to have been erected on the site of a castle, once a stronghold of King Athelstan. In recent years it has been considerably altered and enlarged."[1]

The word *Dame* in the title suggests a connection with Hardy's *A Group of Noble Dames*; possibly Hardy found the story in the manuscript from which he drew the *Noble Dames*. In the Sanders Collection, "Extracts from Books, 2" (in the Dorset County Museum) is an unpublished typescript by Sidney Heath titled "How Thomas Hardy Offended the County Families of Dorset." Heath says that Hardy obtained material for *A Group of Noble Dames* "from his old friend, Harry Moule . . . Curator of the newly-founded County Museum. Soon after his appointment Harry Moule unearthed in the basement of the Museum some very ancient, but authentic, documents relating to the old Dorset families, which records had somehow got mixed up with old municipal deeds and records which had been presented to the Museum. Thinking they might form the basis for some good plots he copied them out and took them to Max Gate. The result was 'A Group of Noble Dames,' every story of which is based on facts."[2] Neither the present Curator of the Museum, Roger Peers, nor the Dorset County Archivist, Margaret Holmes, was able to find the manuscript Heath mentions.

The ironic theme of the poem is the misery that results from sentimental loyalty.

1. Lea, *Thomas Hardy's Wessex*, p. 271. See Plate 204 on p. 269 for a picture of Athelhampton Hall.
2. P. 3 of Heath's typescript.

THE SEASONS OF HER YEAR had, in the manuscript, the title "The Pathetic Fallacy."[1] This original title is based upon John Ruskin's definition in *Modern Painters*.[2] Ruskin discusses "the difference between the ordinary, proper, and true appearances of things to us; and the extraordinary, or false appearances, when we are under the influence of emotion," and states that violent feelings "produce in us a falseness in all our impressions of external things, which I would generally characterize as the 'pathetic fallacy.' " Movingly simple, direct, and poignant, "The Seasons of Her Year" is an illustration of Ruskin's theory. The poem presents the pathetic fallacy in two phases of external nature seen through strong emotion, the second stanza reversing both the seasons and the emotionally conditioned view of the first.

1. Purdy, *Thomas Hardy: A Bibliographical Study*, p. 115.
2. Volume III, Part IV, Chapter XII.

THE MILKMAID is a somewhat humorous study of the pathetic fallacy. (See the notes on "The Seasons of Her Year.") The scene recalls the milking scenes in *Tess of the D'Urbervilles* and Hardy's feeling for the heartaches of milkmaids. In giving his milkmaid the fancy name Phyllis, he suggests the pastoral illusion of the second stanza: "Few pilgrims but would choose / The peace of such a life in such a vale." From the entrance of the "passing train" the poem is humorous, mocking the pastoral idealization in terms of petty and passing realities.[1]

1. Zietlow in "Thomas Hardy and William Barnes," p. 292, calls "The Milkmaid" a contrasting "direct counterpart" of Barnes's idyllic "The Milk-Maid o' the Farm."

THE LEVELLED CHURCHYARD is a humorous quasi-prayer by the souls of the dead whose tombstones have been removed and their bones "mixed to human jam" during the levelling of a churchyard. In spite of the formula "Deliver us O Lord! Amen!"[1] at the end of the poem, the prayer is addressed to "O Passenger" (any passer-by). Suitably for a prayer, the poem is in the common meter of many ballads and hymns.

In the manuscript "(W——e Minster)" was added to the title.[2] At the date of the poem, 1882, the Hardys were living in Wimborne. No significant alterations in the churchyard there took place at this time, but a somewhat ruthless restoration of the Minster had been "carried out by Wyatt between 1855 and 1857."[3] No graves were disturbed and no bones disinterred, but old gravestones were uprooted and laid flat as paving stones, and much of the churchyard was levelled to make a lawn. For the graphic details of the poem, Hardy doubtless drew upon his experience as an architect in London, where he took part in removing the remains of the dead from Old St. Pancras Churchyard so that a railway might use the site. The "human jam" of the poem had some reality in this experience: "In one coffin that fell apart was a skeleton and two skulls. He used to tell that when, after some fifteen years of separation, he met Arthur Blomfield again and their friendship was fully renewed, among the latter's first words were: 'Do you remember how we found the man with two heads at St. Pancras?' "[4] Besides this experience, he may have had in mind a passage in Hutchins's *History . . . of Dorset* concerning Wimborne Minster: "It appears by one of the old churchwarden's books that there was in ancient times a charnel-house here for the reception of dead bones, but whereabouts the same was situated does not appear. Only in the year 1748, part of the ground near the middle gate of the church-yard southwards being dug for a vault, a vast quantity of human bones were discovered lying about four feet thick, which gave reason to imagine that this charnel-house must have been formerly erected on the spot. . . . In different directions, are scattered a variety of tomb-stones, loaded with a profusion of bad poetry." (III, 227.) The jesting of Hardy's poem may owe something to this "bad poetry."

Though the poem is humorous, the final stanza protesting church restoration expresses one of Hardy's convictions. In 1880, he joined the Society for the Protection of Ancient Buildings and remained a member until his death. In "Memories of Church Restoration," to be read at the meeting of the Society in 1906, he wrote: "The chancel of a church not a hundred and fifty miles from London has in one corner a vault containing a fashionable actor and his wife, in another corner a vault inclosing the remains of a former venerable vicar, who abjured women, and died a bachelor. The mural tablets, each over its own vault, were taken down at the refurbishing of the building, and refixed reversely, the stone of the theatrical couple over the solitary divine, and that of the latter over the pair from the stage. Should disinterment ever take place . . . the excavators will be surprised to find a lady beside the supposed reverend bachelor, and the supposed actor without his wife. As the latter was a comedian he would probably enjoy the situation if he could know it, though the vicar's feelings might be somewhat different. . . . And unhappily it was oftenest of all the headstones of the poorer inhabitants—purchased and erected in many cases out of scanty means—that suffered most in these ravages. It is scarcely necessary to particularise among the innumerable instances in which head-stones have been removed from their positions, the churchyard levelled, and the head-stones used for paving the churchyard walks, with the result that the inscriptions have been trodden out in a few years."[5]

1. In the litany of the Church of England, "Deliver us O Lord!" is the recurring response of the congregation to a series of pleas read by the parson.
2. Purdy, *Thomas Hardy: A Bibliographical Study*, p. 115.
3. Mills, "Thomas Hardy's Association with Wimborne," pp. 12-14.
4. *Early Life*, p. 59; *Life*, p. 45.
5. Orel, *Thomas Hardy's Personal Writings*, pp. 206-8.

THE RUINED MAID is a dramatic dialogue, humorous in tone, between a debauched town girl and an innocent friend from Dorset.[1] The "anapestic base meter is exactly right to catch the querulous, jealous whine of the girl who stayed home, and the newly acquired insolence, and as yet tentative affectation of the girl who is 'ruined.' "[2] One analysis of the poem presents it as symbolizing the ruined girl's inner debates about her way of life, "her old self conversing with the new."[3]

The poem is dated 1866, when Hardy was living in London. Prostitution at this time flourished,[4] Hardy frequented the dance halls, he states that he was accosted in Piccadilly,[5] and in *Desperate Remedies*, when Manston has to "idle about the streets" of London for a while, he observes "lost women of miserable repute looking as happy as the days are long." (Chapter XVI, Part 4.) If Hardy observed such a girl as he presents, he probably did so with more compassion than shock. His moral in the poem may be surmised in "A Daughter Returns," which poem presents a later phase of a ruined maid's story.

"The Ruined Maid" has been set to music by Walter Pierce (in manuscript in the Colby College Library).

1. The dialect-words indicate Dorset: "spudding up docks" (spading up weeds), "barton" (farmyard), "thik oon" (that one), "theäs oon (this one), and "'ee" (you).
2. Gross, *Sound and Form in Modern Poetry*, p. 43.
3. Hogan, "Structural Design in Thomas Hardy's Poetry," p. 221.
4. See Terrot, *Traffic in Innocents*.
5. *Early Life*, p. 308; *Life*, p. 235.

THE RESPECTABLE BURGHER is not dated. Blunden, discussing its relation to *Essays and Reviews* (1860), surmises that the poem was written "not long after this publication appeared."[1] The poem also echoes ideas found in Matthew Arnold's *Literature and Dogma* (1873). The thought of the poem would have been somewhat out of date, the satire irrelevant to current ideas, after 1890, but Hardy may have written it at any time as an exercise in satiric versification.

The poem is a double-edged satire, upon the excesses of the "higher criticism" and the attitude of the practical middle class toward religion. From the establishment of Christianity until the nineteenth century, biblical criticism, assuming the Bible to be the literal Word of God, had consisted chiefly of interpreting the text. With the rise of science, theologians, scholars, and critics began to test the stories of the Bible against historical, geological, archaeological, biological, linguistic, and other scientific evidence. Such criticism convinced many people that a great deal of the Bible is not literally true. Liberal clergymen, accepting some of the findings of the critics, declared that the Bible should be read as moral and ethical experience, not as history or science. A notable publication was *Essays and Reviews*, a collection of essays by the distinguished clergymen and scholars Henry Bristow Wilson, Frederick Temple, Mark Pattison, Benjamin Jowett, Rowland Williams, Baden Powell, and C. W. Goodwin. Because the essays treated the language of the Bible as figurative and questioned the authenticity of miracles, the authors were denounced by many churchmen as "the Seven against Christ," controversy arose, and respectable men, brought up to believe literally, were confused. Some became, like the burgher of the poem, agnostic. Matthew Arnold, in "The Function of Criticism at the Present Time" (1864), attacked the excesses of the critics, who presented their findings with a zeal that undermined faith in the Bible as an ethical guide. His *Literature and Dogma*, treating the Bible as a poetic record of religious experience, defined a position that allowed man to be reverently religious in feeling and belief, without accepting incredible statements as facts. Though more agnostic than Arnold, Hardy accepted Arnold's position as reasonable. "The Respectable Burgher" satirizes the higher criticism, as Arnold did, for its misleading excesses.[2]

The respectable burgher is a matter-of-fact citizen of the middle class, a Philistine by Arnold's definition in *Culture and Anarchy*. As far as literal belief in the miraculous events of the poem is concerned, Hardy agreed with the burgher. The satire concerns the burgher's downright, "practical" habit of mind that rejects the ethical truths of religion because the Biblical stories are shown to be absurd. That Hardy intended satire is clear in the witty phrasing of the poem and in such an amusing *tour de force* as carrying a single rime through all its thirty-six lines.

Annotations must be line-by-line. *1*: The "Reverend Doctors" are presumably the clergymen authors of *Essays and Reviews*. *3*: The critics, in the light of biological evolution, treated the story of Adam and Eve, in Gen. 1-3, as a myth. *4*: Geological research indicated that the whole earth had never been subjected to the flood described in Gen. 7-9. *5-7*: The critics contended that some prophecies were more historical records than inspired forecasts of the future. *8-12*: Historical records threw doubt upon the story of David and Goliath (I Sam. 17), condemned David's adultery with Bathsheba (II Sam. 11), and doubted his authorship of the Psalms. *13-14*: The Song of Solomon had been interpreted as an allegory of Christ's love for His bride, the Church; the critics found it a passionate love song. In *Jude the Obscure*, Sue echoes this view: " 'And what a literary enormity this is,' she said, as she glanced into the pages of Solomon's Song. 'I mean the synopsis at the head of each chapter, explaining away the real nature of that rhapsody. You needn't be alarmed: nobody claims inspiration for the chapter headings. Indeed, many divines treat them with contempt. It seems the drollest thing to think of the four-and-twenty elders, or bishops, or whatever number they were, sitting with long faces and writing down such misinformation.' " (Part III, Chapter IV.) *15-23*: The critics tended to interpret the stories here mentioned as fiction. See Esther 5:1-3; for Mordecai, Esther 2:5-7; for Joshua, said to have made the sun and the moon stand still, and Job, the Books of Joshua and Job; for the story of Balaam, the angel, and the talking ass, see Num. 22:20-35; for Nebuchadnezzar's fire that would not burn flesh, see Dan. 3:10-28; and for the refusal of lions to attack Daniel, see Dan. 6:16-23. *24-32*: In Luke 7:11-15, Jesus raised from the dead the only son of a widow of Nain. John 11:1-44, tells of the raising of Lazarus from the dead after four days in his tomb;

Sheol is the Hebrew land of the dead. The Italian painter called Piombo (Sebastiano Luciani) painted a celebrated "Raising of Lazarus," which was brought to England in 1792 and placed in the National Gallery, where the burgher might have seen it. The story of Jael's murder of Sisera by helping him to sleep and driving a nail through his head is told in Judg. 4:17-22. The critics tended to judge Pontius Pilate (Matt. 27:11-26) as a ruler helpless in the face of popular demand. It was doubted that Peter would have cut off the ear of Malchus, the high priest's servant, as in John 18:10. The conflicting stories told by the four Gospels of Christ's resurrection cast some doubt upon it. *33-36*: The burgher, shocked that "Reverend Doctors" could assert the truth of religion while questioning the facts of the Bible, gives up church-going and decides to read the works of the rationalist-philosopher Voltaire (François Marie Arouet, 1694-1778). He was "moderate" because consistent and urbane in his satire upon some doctrines of the church.

1. *Thomas Hardy*, p. 15.
2. See Hardy's attempt to harmonize rationality and religion in the "Apology" of *Late Lyrics and Earlier*.

ARCHITECTURAL MASKS treats two unidentified houses. Perhaps Hardy's "long dwellers" in "ivied walls" were people of aristocratic lineage whom he had found to be crassly selfish. Possibly Max Gate was the house of "blazing brick and plated show." There both Hardy and Emma busied themselves reading, writing, painting, and making music.

THE TENANT-FOR-LIFE develops the theme that all men, however they may rent, own, or tend their dwellings, are tenants-for-life only. The title refers to a specialized meaning for the term. In the English system of landholding, farms may be leased for a lifetime or a series of lifetimes, after which the property reverts to the basic owner. "Lifeholding" played a role in Hardy's family history. His "mother's grandfather was a man who worried a good deal about the disposition of his property as he grew old. It was mostly in the form of long leasehold and lifehold houses, and he would call on his lawyer about once a fortnight to make some alteration in his will. The lawyer lived at Bere Regis, and her grandfather used to talk the matter over with the man who was accustomed to drive him there and back—a connection of his by marriage. Gradually this man so influenced the testator on each journey, by artfully playing on his nervous perplexities as they drove along, that he got three-quarters of the property, including the houses, bequeathed to himself."[1] The problem of lifeholding occurs throughout Hardy's novels. In *The Woodlanders*,

Giles loses his house because his father had failed to add Giles's name to a life-copyhold. Tess's father, in *Tess of the D'Urbervilles*, "was the last of the three lives for whose duration the house and premises were held under a lease" (Chapter L) ; at his death, Tess's family was set adrift, and this fact forces Tess to return to Alec and brings on the final tragedy. The novel has a passage that presents the thought of the poem: the new residents in Tess's home-place "were in the garden, taking as much interest in their own doings as if the homestead had never passed its primal time in conjunction with the histories of others." (Chapter LIV.)

1. *Early Life*, pp. 182-83; *Life*, pp. 139-40.

THE KING'S EXPERIMENT sets forth the pathetic fallacy with more machinery than in other poems. (For the pathetic fallacy see the notes on "The Seasons of Her Year"; for Doom, on "Doom and She"; and for Hodge, on "Drummer Hodge.") The jesting of Doom in the last stanza seems more forced than humorous. Pinion relates the poem to Crabbe's "The Lover's Journey."[1]

1. *A Hardy Companion*, p. 202.

THE TREE places a story of passion, guilt, and defeat in a setting to suggest how, in mysterious ways, the forces of nature affect human life. Stanzas I and II describe the fallen tree realistically, suggest that there is something demonic about its "mad Earth-god's spiny hair," and relate it to a frustrated human love. The tree seems either the demon that influenced the murder of the story or an agent of retributive justice for the guilty woman: "Distraught went she."

The tree recalls old South's tree in *The Woodlanders*. "Its boughs, which none but darers trod, / A child may step on from the sod" echoes "The weakest idler that passed could now set foot on marks formerly made in the upper forks by the shoes of adventurous climbers only." "And twigs that earliest met the dawn / Are lit at last upon the lawn" echoes the description of a tree upon which Marty South worked, which "caught the earliest rays of the sun and moon while the lower part of the forest was still in darkness." As the felling of South's tree seems to cause his death, so the fall of the tree in the poem brings about the revelation of the woman's guilt.[1]

1. See Chapters XIV and XIX, and Kramer, "Repetition of Imagery in Thomas Hardy," p. 26.

HER LATE HUSBAND tells a story that may rest upon fact. "King's Hintock" is Hardy's name for Melbury Osmund, the home of Hardy's maternal ancestry.

An entry in his "Notebook I" under the date 1893 reads: "M——

O———: Gt. Grandfather and Gt. Grandmother Swetman [are buried] over by the Swaffields. Gt. Grandfather and Gt. Grandmother Childs near others of the Childs family. *Valeat quantum valere potest.*"[1] The "M——— O———" stands for Melbury Osmund. Hardy's great-grandfather buried there was John Swetman, husband of Maria Childs Swetman. The Latin means: "Let this be valued for what it is worth."

This notebook entry, which seems to be the basis for the poem, contains an error: "Gt. Grandfather and Gt. Grandmother Childs" were not Hardy's great-grandparents, but his great-great-grandparents. Hardy's mother's parents were George Hand (1775-1822) and Elizabeth Swetman Hand (1778-1847). Elizabeth Hand's parents (Hardy's great-grandparents) were John Swetman (1733-1822) and Maria Childs Swetman (?-1802). Maria Swetman's parents (Hardy's great-great-grandparents) were Joseph Childs (1703-?) and Mary Hurlstone Childs (?-1746).[2]

If the poem may concern John and Maria Childs Swetman, there is a discrepancy between what the poem seems to say and the facts. The poem implies that the "late husband" has died and his widow is giving directions for his burial beside the dead woman's grave "with the initialed stone," and for her own later burial under her maiden name among her "kith and kin," but Maria Swetman died in 1802 and was buried "over by the Swaffields" twenty years before her husband died in 1822.

A central question, if the poem concerns John and Maria Swetman, is why was Maria Swetman buried beside the Swaffields? A possible answer, consistent with Hardy's many concealments, is that he wished to tell the story suggested by the facts (his notebook entry), and yet to conceal the identities of his great-grandparents. It is possible to read the poem as Maria Swetman's expressed desire, before her death in 1802, that she be buried with others of the Childs family and that her husband, still alive, be buried not beside her but beside "his very Love," a Swaffield, where perhaps John Swetman had expressed a wish to be buried. In this case, one may surmise, when Maria died first, John Swetman, wishing to be buried near both the Swaffields and his wife, countermanded her directions to the sexton—perhaps without difficulty, as the poem expresses the sexton's approval of the "Hintock rule." If so, the poem is dated "182—" for 1822, the date of John Swetman's burial, for that date completes the ironic story of the "late husband." In this reading, it is an irony that Maria's generous gesture that angels might praise is wasted.

Details from local custom and folk-lore appear in the poem. The sexton had thought of burying the wife "to right, / And on the left hand he," the right being considered lucky and the left unlucky.[3] In folk-lore suggested by the Christian story, angels walk the earth on Christmas night.

1. Evelyn Hardy, *Thomas Hardy's Notebooks*, p. 68.

2. These data rest upon "The Hardy Pedigree" in Evelyn Hardy, *Thomas Hardy*, facing p. 224, corrected by reference to the parish records of Melbury Osmund. The pertinent grave-stones are no longer legible, and grave-sites are not recorded.

3. Firor, *Folkways in Thomas Hardy*, p. 20.

THE SELF-UNSEEING presents Hardy's nostalgic meditation during a visit to his boyhood home at Higher Bockhampton. The scene is the living-room, where the poet remembers a little drama of his childhood. The characters are himself, his father, and his mother. Hardy is the violinist of the drama; the "dead feet" are those of his father, who died in 1892;[1] and his mother, still alive when the poem was published, was probably present when he recalled the drama. He recalled it again in *The Early Life*: Hardy "was of ecstatic temperament, extraordinarily sensitive to music, and among the endless jigs, hornpipes, reels, waltzes, and country-dances that his father played of an evening in his early married years, and to which the boy danced a *pas seul* in the middle of the room, there were three or four that always moved the child to tears, though he strenuously tried to hide them. . . . He was not over four years of age at this date."[2]

Aside from light upon Hardy's lifelong love of music and dancing, the poem expresses his characteristic of "looking away" from the present toward something in the past or the future. The little boy, on a day when "Blessings emblazoned" his life and "Everything glowed with a gleam," failed fully to value his present joy, perhaps dreaming childish versions of the dreams suggested in "The Temporary the All."

The poem has been set to music by D. M. Steward (London: Augener, 1921) and in *Before and After Summer* (London: Boosey & Hawkes, 1949).

1. Hardy's childhood home had its front door about ten feet to the left of the present entrance as one faces the house, where there is now a window. Writing the poem after the door had been moved, Hardy recalled the "former door / Where the dead feet walked in." Mr. and Mrs. James Skilling, caretakers of the Birthplace, exhibited the evidence in the stone-and-brickwork.

2. Pp. 18-19; *Life*, p. 15.

IN TENEBRIS

The three poems now called "In Tenebris" ("In Darkness") were originally published as "De Profundis" ("From the Depths").

The Latin mottoes for the poems are from St. Jerome's version of the Psalms.

These poems express Hardy's depression in the years 1895 and 1896. "We have Hardy's insistent warning not to assume that all his poems with 'I' as their apparent speaker are in any way autobiographical; yet the small group entitled 'In Tenebris' . . . can scarcely represent anything but the spiritual anguish of the writer himself. They are, as nearly as anything can be, Hardy's parallel to James Thomson's *City of Dreadful Night*."¹ He had a variety of reasons for feeling depressed at this time. His father had died in 1892; critics had attacked *Tess of the D'Urbervilles* as an immoral book, and were attacking *Jude the Obscure* as "Jude the Obscene"; and his relations with his wife Emma were bitter and hostile in these years.²

The poems offer some justification for calling Hardy a pessimist. Though at times he resented the term, at other times he defended pessimism. In 1901, in a conversation with William Archer, he sought to define his position: "For instance, people call me a pessimist; and if it is pessimism to think, with Sophocles, that 'not to have been born is best,' then I do not reject the designation. I never could understand why the word 'pessimism' should be such a red rag to many worthy people; and I believe, indeed, that a good deal of the robustious, swaggering optimism of recent literature is at bottom cowardly and insincere. I do not see that we are likely to improve the world by asseverating, however loudly, that black is white, or at least that black is but a necessary contrast and foil, without which white would be white no longer. . . . But my pessimism, if pessimism it be, does not involve the assumption that the world is going to the dogs, and that Ahriman is winning all along the line. On the contrary, my practical philosophy is distinctly meliorist. What are my books but one plea against 'man's inhumanity to man'—to woman—and to the lower animals?"³

1. Blunden, *Thomas Hardy*, p. 96.
2. See Evelyn Hardy, *Thomas Hardy*, p. 271, and Weber, *Hardy of Wessex*, 2nd ed., p. 216, and *Hardy's Love Poems*, p. 50.
3. Archer, "Real Conversations: Conversation I," pp. 316-17.

In Tenebris I has a motto from the Vulgate Scriptures that may be literally translated as: "I am smitten like dry grass, and my heart is dry." In the King James Version, it is translated as the fourth verse of Psalm 102: "My heart is smitten, and withered like grass."

The theme is the poet's disenchantment after a series of blows that have frozen feeling and hope. (See "In the Seventies" for the hope thus chilled.) In the first line of each stanza an image from nature (wintertime, flower-petals, etc.) symbolizes each blow, which is then partly defined: old-age and bereavement, severance from beauty, loss of vitality, loss of friends, loss of feeling (love), and the coming of death. The poem offers no definite clue to the particular losses: "bereavement-pain" may mean the death of Hardy's father; the "severing scene" may refer to a break with Emma.

The symbol of winter denies Shelley's line from "Ode to the West Wind," "If Winter comes, can Spring be far behind?" Hardy's "in unhope" is an absolute negative, stronger than "without hope."

In Tenebris II has a motto from the Vulgate Scriptures. In the King James Version, it is translated as the fourth verse of Psalm 142: "I looked on my right hand, and beheld, but there was no man that would know me: . . . no man cared for my soul." From the manuscript Hardy deleted an additional Latin motto, from Psalm 2: "Quare fremuerunt gentes, et populi meditati sunt inania?" It appears in the King James Version as: "Why do the heathen rage, and the people imagine a vain thing?"[1] In the eighth line, the poem again makes use of the Bible, quoting the phrase in which St. Paul refers to himself as "one born out of due time." (I Cor. 15:8.)

The poem is an attack upon the robustious optimism of those men who hailed England's world-wide empire and material progress as utopian perfection and perhaps those who attacked Hardy's candor in *Jude the Obscure* as false and bleak pessimism; it is a defense of pessimism; and it is also his ironic presentation of himself as a pariah.

Defining the phrase used for swaggering optimists, Houghton details the background of Hardy's thought. "The 'many and strong' would not look at the other side of the picture, and labeled anyone who did—who questioned the blessings of English liberty, or the virtues of English civilization, or doubted if change was entirely progress or progress entirely upward—a pessimist. For, after all, nothing *was* much the matter for *them*. The Victorians were well off, as Kingsley dryly observed, unless they happened to be 'Dorsetshire labourers—or Spitalfield weavers—or colliery children—or marching soldiers—or, I am afraid, one half of English souls this day.' "[2] The structure of the poem suggests Hardy's view in each of the ironic last lines of the first three stanzas, and in the equally ironic fourth stanza which presents the optimists' attack upon his views.

Hardy's reliance upon taking "a full look at the Worst" as the only "way to the Better" runs throughout his works. In his early novel *Far from the Madding Crowd*, Oak undoubtedly speaks for Hardy in advising Bathsheba to be wary of Sergeant Troy: "I don't say he's such a bad man as I have fancied—I pray to God he is not. But since we don't know exactly what he is, why not behave as if he *might* be bad, simply for your own safety?" (Chapter XXIX.) He stated the same idea in his journal on January 1, 1902: "Pessimism (or rather what is called such), is, in brief, playing the sure game. You cannot lose at it; you may gain. It is the only view of life in which you can never be disappointed. Having reckoned what to do in the worst possible circumstances, when better arise, as they may, life becomes child's play." He repeated it on January 16, 1918: "As to pessimism. My motto is, first correctly diagnose the complaint—in this case human ills—and ascertain the cause: then set about finding a remedy if one exists. The motto or practice of the optimists is: Blind the eyes to the real malady, and use empirical panaceas to suppress the symptoms."[3]

As the motto of the poem suggests, Hardy's presentation of himself as a pariah for holding pessimistic views may be only partly ironic. He was hurt by attacks upon him as one who "disturbs the order here." He knew that he could have been happier as one of "the many and strong." His choice to be true to his own experience, for instance, to publish *Jude the Obscure* in the face of Mrs. Hardy's protests, could not have been a pleasure.

1. Purdy, *Thomas Hardy: A Bibliographical Study*, p. 116.
2. *The Victorian Frame of Mind*, p. 414.
3. *Later Years*, pp. 91, 183; *Life*, pp. 311, 383.

In Tenebris III has a motto from the Vulgate Scriptures that may be literally translated as: "Woe to me that my dwelling is prolonged! I have dwelt with the inhabitants of Cedar; my soul has been a long dweller." The passage in the King James Version, verses 5-6 of Psalm 120, reads: "Woe is me that I sojourn in Mesech, that I dwell in the tents of Kedar. My soul hath long dwelt with him that hateth peace." In the eighteenth line, the poem quotes phrases from a passage in Rev. 10: 9-10, in which an angel offers John a book: "And I went unto the angel, and said unto him, Give me the little book. And he said unto me, Take it and eat it up; and it shall make thy belly bitter, but it shall be in thy mouth sweet as honey. And I took the little book out of the angel's hand, and ate it up; and it was in my mouth sweet as honey: and as soon as I had eaten it, my belly was bitter." Evidently, in connection with this passage, Hardy's line means that his youthful reading, as in Greek drama or natural science, gave him pleasure at the time, but later brought the pain of disillusion.

The poem says, with instances, that Hardy was happy as a boy and that it is a pity he did not die then without growing up to discover that "the world was a welter of futile doing." Citing times when he might have died before becoming disillusioned, the poem (unless the scenes are fictional) adds to *The Early Life* some experiences of Hardy's boyhood. He was happy and hopeful of beauty in springtime flower-gardening at home in Higher Bockhampton. He was happy with his mother, somewhere on "Egdon," confident in her "watching and ward" as the evening darkened into night.[1] He was not happy, but he might have died without disillusion on a winter night when, sitting by a chimney-corner, he was overcome by drowsiness and a "baptism of pain."[2]

1. For what is perhaps the same scene of Hardy with his mother, see "The Roman Road."

2. I have seen no other record of the incident. It can hardly be Hardy's illness that began in 1880, for the scene seems to be at Higher Bockhampton during his boyhood.

THE CHURCH-BUILDER was titled in the manuscript "Nisi Dominus Frustra."[1] This phrase is from the Vulgate Scriptures, Psalm 126:1. It is translated in the King James Version in Psalm 127 as: "Except the Lord . . . in vain."[2]

The poem is spoken by the church-builder in the few minutes between his approach to the church and his suicide. Reviewing reasons for the act he is about to commit, he looks forward with wry humor to the discovery of his body "Dangling in mockery" of the church he built and of the "deeper thinkers" who sneered at his sacrifice.

Hardy may have drawn the idea for the poem from an entry in his notebook labelled "Facts": "*Hung himself.*—J. Davis of Abbotsbury, in the Independent Meeting House, of which he was the proprietor. ib. [*Dorset County Chronicle*], Sp [September] 23. 30. Cf. Rector of Stedham, Sussex—hung himself to bell rope in belfry. Apl. 1882. D. C. C. [*Dorset County Chronicle*] Also Farmer at Morcombe —lends £700 to build chapel—not repaid—kills his child. (ante)."[3]

Hardy's addition to such facts is partly grotesque humor and partly satire. The poem achieves the grotesque by surrounding the horrible with the beautiful: the corpse will be found between the "ivoried Rood" (the Cross) and the "prie-dieu, lately hewn / From woods of rarest dye." The satire seems directed partly toward the "deep thinkers" in whose "nod and wink" the church-builder read himself as "fool and blind," and partly toward the church-builder's self-deluding idealism. The items of his disillusionment indicate a theme characteristic of Hardy, that literal faith in a thankfully rewarding God is futile in a world where still "powerful Wrong on feeble Right / Tramples in olden style."

The church-builder's zeal led him to study architecture. His soliloquy includes words Hardy knew from his earlier work restoring churches: battled (battlemented, crenelated), ashlared (of hewn stone), mullions (vertical bars between panes in Gothic windows), fillet (a band to separate mouldings), ogee (a moulding of a continuous double curve), circleted (ringed, as a halo), dossal (ornamental cloth behind the altar), boss (an ornamental projection where the ribs of a vault intersect), brass (a memorial tablet), chore (the choir or chancel), prie-dieu (prayer-desk), and truss (a bracket, as under a cornice). The church-builder's prayer, "Illume this fane," asks God to bless the church with His visible presence as at the dedication of Solomon's temple: "the house was filled with a cloud, even the house of the Lord. . . . For the glory of the Lord had filled the house of God." (II Chronicles 5:13-14.)

1. Purdy, *Thomas Hardy: A Bibliographical Study*, p. 116.
2. The phrase is elliptical. The verse reads: "Except the Lord build the house, they labour in vain that build it: except the Lord keep the city, the watchman waketh but in vain." "Nisi Dominus Frustra" is the motto of the city of Edinburgh.
3. P. 173, in the Dorset County Museum. The "Sp 23. 30." refers to September 23, 1830; Hardy read through old files of the *Chronicle*.

THE LOST PYX is Hardy's poetic presentation of the basic legend about the Cross-and-Hand stone.[1] This stone column "consists of a round smooth tapering shaft, which, together with the abacus of the mutilated capital at the top, measure three feet eight inches in height from the ground, it girths thirty-four inches at the base, thirty-two inches in the middle, and twenty-eight inches immediately under the roll moulding beneath the capital; the moulding itself measuring one and a quarter inch deep. . . . The capital shows some kind of carving on the south side, said to represent a hand, but it has been much damaged on the north side, where no carving appears. The pillar is of a hard spar-like stone. . . . The origin of the stone can only be conjecture. It has stood in its present position from time immemorial, and numerous local traditions as to its origin are preserved. It possibly once formed the upper part of the tapering shaft of a cross surmounted by a ball-shaped abacus, upon which was mounted a canopy or cross . . . if the above suggestion be correct, it would be late fourteenth-century work . . . or it may be Roman."[2]

The stone is on Batcombe Hill, about eight miles north and slightly west of Dorchester. It stands just north of the road that leads westward from Road 352 (Dorchester to Sherborne) at Dogbury Gate, to Road 37 (Dorchester to Yeovil) at Evershot Station. This secondary road runs along the top of Batcombe Hill, which overlooks Blackmoor Vale. About two miles from Dogbury Gate, the stone stands on the edge where Batcombe Hill plunges downward into Blackmoor.

In the poem the priest travels on foot northward from Cerne Abbas ("Cernel's Abbey") for about two and a half miles, across a series of rugged hills (chiefly Wether Hill and Gore Hill) to Cross-and-Hand, and then farther north to "the cot on the waste" somewhere in Blackmoor Vale. At Cerne Abbas are the remains of a once large and thriving abbey. "According to William of Malmesbury's legendary life of St. Augustine, this abbey was founded by St. Augustine between 588 and 603; the abbey became important in the life of the area until the dissolution of the monastery. Now only the gate-house, the guest house, the tithe barn, and the cemetery remain."[3] According to tradition, the construction of the abbey was completed in 987. The gate-house, three stories high, bears the shields of the Earl of Cornwall. The poem suggests that the priest's bones lie somewhere in the "field that was the Cernel choir." The "Abbey north of Blackmore Vale" is evidently Sherborne Abbey, about eight miles north of Cross-and-Hand.

Regarding the story, Hardy wrote to Clement Shorter on December 10, 1900: "The tradition, I may say, is a real one."[4] Variants have sprung from this basic legend. After telling the story in some detail, H. J. Moule presents a variant: "But *(me judice)* in the last century a rider was added as follows:—The priest was much astounded at what he saw, yet not so much so but that he observed among the live-stock a black horse, kneeling, indeed, like the rest, but only on one knee. The priest said to this lukewarm beast, 'Why don't you kneel on both knees, like the rest?' 'Wouldn't kneel at all if I could help it.' 'Who, then, are you?' 'The devil.' 'Why do you take the form of a horse?' 'So that men may steal me, and get hung, and I get hold of them. Got three or four already.'"[5] Hardy knew this variant. In a letter to John Pasco on December 10, 1903, he wrote of "such supplementary detail being often added to medieval tales; as, for instance, to the legend of the Lost Pyx . . . a black-hoofed animal that would not kneel is subjoined by some tellers."[6] He mentions other variants in *Tess of the D'Urbervilles.* On her way to see old Mr. Clare, Tess "reached Cross-in-Hand, where the stone pillar stands desolate and silent, to mark the site of a miracle, or murder, or both." On her return, she meets Alec at this spot: "At length the road touched the spot called 'Cross-in-Hand.' . . . The place took its name from a stone pillar which stood there. . . . Differing accounts were given of its history and purport. Some authorities stated that a devotional cross had once formed the complete erection thereon, of which the present relic was but the stump; others that the stone as it stood was entire, and that it had been fixed there to mark a boundary or place of meeting." Alec compels Tess to swear an oath upon the stone: " 'This was once a Holy Cross. Relics are not in my creed; but I fear you at moments . . . and to lessen my fear, put your hand upon that stone hand, and swear that you will never tempt me.' " When Alec has gone, Tess asks a shepherd: " 'What is the meaning of that old stone I have passed? . . . Was it ever a Holy Cross?' 'Cross—no; 'twere not a cross! 'Tis a thing of ill-omen, Miss. It was put up in wuld times by the relations of a malefactor who was tortured there by nailing his hand to a post and afterwards hung. They say he sold his soul to the devil, and that he walks at times.' " (Chapters XLIV and XLV.) Mrs. Florence Hardy in an undated letter to the editor of *Notes and Queries*, London, stated yet another tradition about Cross-and-Hand: "But some antiquarians have from its shape conjectured its origin to be phallic, and not Christian at all."[7]

Perhaps to give a sense of authenticity to the version of the legend told in the poem, Hardy implies that he knew certain facts about the priest. He was "In later life sub-prior / Of the brotherhood" and he was buried in "Cernel choir." Early records of Cerne Abbas have been lost, and the first reliable accounts of the church there begin in 1628. Nothing is known of anyone who became sub-prior in the long demolished abbey.[8]

"The Lost Pyx," aside from exhibiting Hardy's interest in a legend, presents his characteristic attitude toward "common beasts and rare." The animals worshiping the pyx include "many a member seldom seen / Of Nature's family." The poem exhibits Hardy's skilful, free use of anapests and internal rimes.

1. Called also Cross-in-Hand, Crossy-Hand, Christ-in-Hand, and Batcombe Cross.
2. Pope, *The Old Stone Crosses of Dorset*, pp. 14-16. Lea, *Thomas Hardy's Wessex*, has a photograph of "Cross-in-Hand" as Plate 207 on p. 274.
3. Lake, *Cerne Abbas of Dorset*, a folder.
4. Colby College Library, *A Descriptive Catalogue of the Grolier Club Centenary Exhibition, 1940*, p. 43.
5. "Monolith on Batcombe Hill," pp. 247-48. See also Windle, *The Wessex of Thomas Hardy*, p. 186.
6. In the Weymouth, Dorset, Public Library.
7. The signed draft of this letter is in the Dorset County Museum.
8. R. G. B., "Cerne Abbas Church Inventory, 1634," pp. 98-99.

TESS'S LAMENT is a soliloquy spoken, crooned, or perhaps inarticulately felt by Tess of *Tess of the D'Urbervilles* during her life at Flintcomb-Ash farm or later. Possibly the idea for the poem came from Lorimer Stoddard's dramatization of *Tess*, produced in New

York in 1897. In Act I, Stoddard gave Tess a speech that is not in the novel: "I would I could write poems. I would I could express myself as the trees do when the wind makes them whisper, as the river does over the stones. They all say something that they feel. I alone, cannot. You [Angel Clare]—you have your music, but I—I feel, in silence."[1] Another possibility is that Hardy, in writing *Tess*, meditated scenes in Tess's life at Talbothays that he did not use in the novel (or after publication of the novel thought of scenes he might have drawn) and wrote the poem to use these scenes. The novel says nothing of two scenes of courtship mentioned in the poem: "The flowers we potted" and the picnic "where we had our supper-fire." Other particulars in the poem refer to scenes in the novel. The wish to be dead that opens the poem is expressed in Tess's meditation as she falls asleep in a copse on her way toward Flintcomb-Ash: "The wife of Angel Clare put her hand to her brow, and felt its curve, and the edges of her eye-sockets perceptible under the soft skin, and thought as she did so that a time would come when that bone would be bare. 'I wish it were now,' she said." The chimney-seat at Talbothays dairy, mentioned in the second stanza, refers to dairyman Crick's sense of propriety in having Angel, a gentleman, eat his meals apart from the common dairy-workers. There Angel would "sit in the yawning chimney-corner during the meal, his cup-and-saucer and plate being placed on a hinged flap at his elbow" and watch the dairymaids. He was especially attracted to Tess: "She soon finished her eating, and, having a consciousness that Clare was regarding her, began to trace imaginary patterns on the tablecloth with her forefinger with the constraint of a domestic animal that perceives itself to be watched. 'What a fresh and virginal daughter of Nature that milkmaid is!' he said to himself." The wedding of the fifth stanza was a climax of Tess's happiness. As she and Angel left the church after the marriage, "she could feel the vibrant air humming round them from the louvred belfry in a circle of sound, and it matched the highly charged mental atmosphere in which she was living." The stanza then moves back to the days of joyful labor at the dairy. When Angel was in charge of the milking, he arranged the cows so that Tess could milk her favorites, Dumpling and Old Pretty; she was milking Old Pretty when Angel first "went quickly towards the desire of his eyes, and, kneeling down beside her, clasped her in his arms."[2]

In the manuscript, the first title of the poem was "A Lament."[3] Possibly Hardy at first wished the poem to be read with application to any abandoned wife whose misery makes her wish to have her life "unbe." In Tess's case, the misery is deepened by the feeling of guilt and remorse expressed in the fourth stanza. Though innocent in Hardy's interpretation of "A Pure Woman Faithfully Presented" (Hardy's subtitle for the novel), Tess saw herself through the eyes of her husband and felt that it was she who had wronged and hurt him, she "who did it all."

Critics have found the versification of "Tess's Lament" remarkably adapted to the theme. The poem "wails in a metre which seems to rock like an ageing woman seated alone before the fire, with an infinite haunting sadness,"[4] especially in the plaintive repetition in the second line of each stanza.

1. See Roberts, *Tess in the Theatre*, p. 86.
2. Chapters XLI, XVIII, XXXIII, and XXIV.
3. Purdy, *Thomas Hardy: A Bibliographical Study*, p. 116.
4. Gosse, "Mr. Hardy's Lyrical Poems," p. 283.

THE SUPPLANTER was titled in the manuscript "At the Cemetery Lodge."[1] Details suggest Dorchester Cemetery. As in the poem, this cemetery has a gatekeeper's lodge with a "gateway-pier" at the entrance; the gates are closed to visitors in winter at 4:30 and in summer at 6:30—"when evening glooms."

The poem offers more balladry than clear theme. The abandoned mother, though guilty, is scarcely more guilty than the man; he owes her at least kindness. As she points out, his final faithfulness to a dead woman is futile and cruel to the living. Yet, seduced by the "wine of France," the dance, and the coaxing girl, he did abandon the "phantom . . . in despair," his earlier love, for which he hates himself. His "unpitying, passion-tossed" anger reflects a conflict in his conscience, symbolized in the ghost of the dead woman to whom he once swore fidelity and who will not let him go. All this, like the verse-form, belongs to the conventions of the ballad.

1. Purdy, *Thomas Hardy: A Bibliographical Study*, p. 116.

IMITATIONS, ETC.

SAPPHIC FRAGMENT is Hardy's translation of Sappho's poem given as number 71 in Edmonds's *Lyra Graeca*:

κατθάνοισα δὲ κείσεαι οὐδέ τινι μναμοσύνα σέθεν
ἔσσετ' οὐδέποτ' <εἰς> ὕστερον· οὐ γὰρ πεδ· ἔχεις βρόδων
τῶν ἐκ Πιερίας, ἀλλ' ἀφάνης κἠν' Ἀΐδα δόμοις·
φοιτάσεις πεδ' ἀμαύρων νεκύων ἐππεποταμένα!

The motto from Omar Khayyám is part of a line in stanza 47 in the first edition of *The Rubáiyát*: "Thou shalt be—Nothing—Thou shalt not be less." The motto from Shakespeare is part of line 229 in *Henry V*, I, ii: "Tombless with no remembrance over them." These mottoes state the thought of the poem.

Hardy's intention in the translation is indicated in a letter to Swinburne on April 1, 1897: ". . . one day, when examining several English imitations of a well-known fragment of Sappho, I interested myself in trying to strike out a better equivalent for it than the commonplace 'Thou, too, shalt die' &c, which all the translators had used during the last hundred years. I then stumbled upon your 'Thee, too, the years shall cover' ["Anactoria"], and all my spirit for poetic pains died out of me. Those few words present, I think, the finest *drama* of Death and Oblivion, so to speak, in our tongue."[1]

1. *Later Years*, pp. 60-61; *Life*, p. 287.

CATULLUS: XXXI is Hardy's translation of *Carmen XXXI*:

Paene insularum, Sirmio, insularumque
Ocelle, quascumque in liquentibus stagnis
Marique vasto fert uterque Neptunus;
Quam te libenter quamque laetus inviso,
Vix mi ipse credens Thyniam atque Bithynos
Liquisse campos, et videre te in tuto.
O quid solutis est beatius curis?
Cum mens onus reponit, ac peregrino
Labore fessi venimus larem ad nostrum,
Desideratoque acquiescimus lecto.
Hoc est quod unum est pro laboribus tantis.
Salve, o venusta Sirmio, atque hero gaude:
Gaudete vosque o Lydiae lacus undae:
Ridete, quidquid est domi cachinnorum.

According to the notation under the title, Hardy wrote the translation after passing Sirmione in April, 1887, presumably in a train en route from Venice to Milan, toward the end of his Italian "pilgrimage." Sirmione is a peninsula that extends two and a half miles into the southern end of Lago di Garda. On this peninsula the Latin poet Gaius Valerius Catullus (84?-54 B.C.) had a villa. For a while in 57 B.C., he was absent in Bithynia. His poem celebrates his return home. Blunden says that Hardy's translation "is remarkable for evading or obscuring all the familiar beauties of the original and for Hardy's retaining it in his collected works."[1]

1. *Thomas Hardy*, p. 58.

AFTER SCHILLER is a translation of the first stanza of Schiller's "Ritter Toggenburg." On page 6 of Hardy's commonplace book labelled "Literary Notes II," dated "188— onwards," Schiller's stanza is written on one side of the page and Hardy's translation on the other.[1] The poem reads:

Ritter, treue Schwesterliebe
    Widmet euch dies Herz,
Fordert keine andre Liebe,
    Denn es macht mir Schmerz.
Ruhig mag ich euch erscheinen
    Ruhig gehen sehn
Eurer Augen stilles Weinen
Kann ich nicht verstehn.

The translation in "Literary Notes" differs in a few words from that in *Collected Poems*. For instance, the last two lines show Hardy experimenting. They appear in ink as: "Thine eyes silent weeping / My eyes cannot know." This is corrected in pencil to: "Thy silent tearfulness / I must not know."[2]

1. "Literary Notes I" closes in " '88." Purdy, *Thomas Hardy: A Bibliographical Study*, p. 117, says that the date of Hardy's poem is 1889, and that he copied the poem from Sonnenschein and Stallybrass's *German for the English* (4th ed., London, 1878), which he "bought and annotated in an effort to learn the language."
2. In the Dorset County Museum.

SONG FROM HEINE is Hardy's translation of Heinrich Heine's "Ich stand in dunkeln Träumen" from the *Reisebilder* (*Die Heimkehr*, number 25).[1] Heine's poem reads:

Ich stand in dunkeln Träumen,
Und starrte ihr Bildnis an,
Uud das geliebte Antlitz
Heimlich zu leben begann.

Um ihre Lippen zog sich
Ein Lächeln wunderbar,
Und wie von Wehmuthsthränen
Erglänzte ihr Augenpaar.

Auch meine Thränen flossen
Mir von den Wangen herab—
Und ach, ich kann es nicht glauben,
Dass ich dich verloren hab'!

"The German original was set to music by Franz Schubert. The precise conformity of foot and meter suggests that Hardy meant the English to fit Schubert's music."[2]

1. "Hardy owned at least two volumes of Heine's verse in translation, *The Poems of Heine*, trans. E. A. Bowring (London, 1878), and *Heine's Book of Songs*, trans. C. G. Leland (New York, 1881), and in both volumes this lyric has been marked." Purdy, *Thomas Hardy: A Bibliographical Study*, p. 117.

2. Osawa, "Hardy and the German Men-of-Letters," p. 521.

FROM VICTOR HUGO is Hardy's translation of "À Une Femme," number XXII of *Les Feuilles d'Automne*, by Hugo:

Enfant! si j'étais roi, je donnerai l'empire,
Et mon char, et mon sceptre, et mon peuple à genoux,
Et ma couronne d'or, et mes bains de porphyre,
Et mes flottes, à qui la mer ne peut suffire,
    Pour un regard de vous!

Si j'étais Dieu, la terre et l'air avec les ondes,
Les anges, les démons courbés devant ma loi,
Et le profond chaos aux entrailles fécondes,
L'éternité, l'espace, et les cieux et les mondes,
    Pour un baiser de toi!

Hardy had great admiration for Hugo. In reply to a request from Dr. Mario Borsa in February, 1902, asking him to contribute a brief statement to *Il Piccolo* of Trieste, in honor of Victor Hugo on the centenary of his birth, he wrote: "His memory must endure. His works are the cathedrals of literary achitecture, his imagination adding greatness to the colossal, and charm to the small."[1]

1. *Later Years*, p. 92; *Life*, p. 311.

CARDINAL BEMBO'S EPITAPH ON RAPHAEL translates part of an epitaph by Cardinal Pietro Bembo that is carved on the painter's tomb. The last two lines of the epitaph read: "Ille. Hic. Est. Raphael. Timuit. Quo. Sospite. / Vinci. Rerum, Magna, Parens. Et. Moriente. Mori."[1]

1. Copps, "The Poetry of Thomas Hardy," p. 477.

"I HAVE LIVED WITH SHADES," written after Hardy had given up writing novels and published under the covering title "Retrospect," seems an estimate of his career among the "Shades" of his imagination. A question for interpretation is: Are the Shades characters of his fiction and poetry, memories of the dead whom he will some day join, or living people in whose minds his personality and reputation live a flickering life? They seem figments of his mind, "whence we came," curiously endowed with powers of prophecy. In some temporal

"To-be," with rooms like a Hall of Fame or Memory, they ask the poet to look at a vision of himself. They say it would be painful for him to know the authenticity of the vision.

Giving this fantasy more gravity that its vagueness and quasi-supernatural machinery supply, Hardy wrote it in the rhythms of Tate and Brady's *New Version of the Psalms of David* (1696). Hynes points out that "Psalm 148 is written in stanzas of eight lines, four three-stressed lines followed by four two-stressed lines, rhyming ababcddc."[1] The rime-scheme, not exactly that of the Psalm, is close enough to echo the solemn tone.

1. *The Pattern of Hardy's Poetry*, p. 87.

MEMORY AND I is a dialogue between Hardy as a disillusioned man of about sixty and his Memory of himself. The poet questions what has happened to the idealism of youth, joy, hope, faith, and love. In a sense, the poem is spiritual autobiography.

The man who as a boy had labored over his books searching for truth images the fruit of his search in a "crumbled cot" and a "tottering tree." The "sweet employ" of earlier days has turned into drudgery. The dreams that prompted him to write his novels have their monument: a "tomb of tomes." The faith that debated even the proper method of baptism has gone. His love for vital Emma Gifford sees her now as "an ageing shape," if not (in Gertrude Atherton's words) "an excessively plain, dowdy, high-stomached woman with her hair drawn back in a tight little knot."[1] In Memory all these good things, though they seem only phantoms, do exist in the mind.

1. Weber, *Hardy of Wessex*, 1st ed., p. 165.

ΑΓΝΩΣΤΩι ΘΕΩι ("To the Unknown God") fittingly closes *Poems of the Past and the Present*, for it suggests the meliorism that softened Hardy's pessimism in many poems of this volume. The title is from the Greek Scriptures that describe St. Paul's preaching in Athens. In the King James Bible, the phrase is found in Acts 17:23, where St. Paul "found an altar with this inscription TO THE UNKNOWN GOD."[1]

The first two stanzas refer to a variety of "weak phantasies" of the Deity presented in poems earlier in the volume, for instance, "The Mother Mourns," "The Lacking Sense," "Doom and She," "The Subalterns," "The Sleep-Worker," "God-Forgotten," and "The Bedridden Peasant." The concepts of the "Willer" in these poems, presumably written in 1900-1901, are expressed in the Will of *The Dynasts*.

The last two stanzas present the meliorism of the "After Scene" of *The Dynasts*. The Willer may be thought of as a symbol for the processes of natural law and the Mind that may be presumed to lie behind them. In *The Dynasts*, It (so-called in this epic-drama) is immanent in phenomena and so may be affected by the consciousness of the creatures It inhabits, including the human mind. Thus It may "grow percipient" and act through impulses in men to weaken selfishness and cruelty, in favor of loving-kindness. The poem suggests Hardy's perception of evidence in human history that this betterment is taking place, for which betterment the poet would "raise my voice in song."[2]

1. "Agnostoi" suggests the word "agnostic," coined by T. H. Huxley to describe his religious attitude as "unknowing."
2. See Bailey, "Evolutionary Meliorism in the Poetry of Thomas Hardy."

TIME'S LAUGHINGSTOCKS AND OTHER VERSES

THE LATER YEARS, commenting upon Hardy's activities in 1909, says: "In the meantime he had been putting together poems written between whiles, some of them already printed in periodicals—and in addition hunting up quite old ones dating from 1865, and overlooked in his earlier volumes, out of which he made a volume called *Time's Laughingstocks*, and sent off the MS. to his publishers the first week in September."[1] The volume was published on December 3.

Reviewers, looking at the volume as a whole, spoke of the poems as pessimistic. Hardy's friend Edmund Gosse shared this view, but Hardy, writing to Gosse on December 12, said: "That the verses should seem to be preponderantly sad is not quite what I intended: it comes by chance. I fancied that, bulk for bulk, there would be as many of a cheerful or neutral pattern as of a deeper shade. But possibly gloom is more telling than brightness . . . so that a great deal of the latter is required to counteract a little of the former. . . . Some writers of verse are instinctively vocal in sadness & silent in joy, just as others are vocal in joy & silent in sadness."[2] In a letter to the editor of the London *Daily News*, published on December 15, he quoted a reviewer's statement that "throughout . . . the outlook is that of disillusion and despair," and replied: "If this were true it might be no bad antidote to the grinning optimism nowadays affected in some quarters; but I beg leave to observe that of the ninety odd poems the volume contains, more than half do not answer to the description at all."[3]

The ninety-four poems of the volume are of various kinds, written at various times. When only the poems that Hardy dated are considered, six ("1967," "Her Definition," "From Her in the Country," "Her Confession," "To an Impersonator of Rosalind," and "To an Actress") are love lyrics written when he was in London in 1865-67. The humorously cynical poem "A Young Man's Epigram on

Existence" belongs also to these years. Two poems ("At Waking" and "The Dawn After the Dance"), besides others evidently of this period but not dated, are love lyrics written in Weymouth in 1869. One poem, "The Minute Before Meeting," dated 1871, seems to refer to his romance with Emma Gifford. Surprisingly classified as a love lyric, "He Abjures Love" is dated 1883. "The Division," a love lyric dated 1893, seems concerned with his feeling for Mrs. Arthur Henniker. Two other dated poems ("After the Fair," 1902, and "The Homecoming," 1901) are love poems, but they do not seem to be about Hardy himself.

The other dated poems, ranging from 1897 ("The Dead Quire") to 1909 ("George Meredith") treat a variety of subjects. Some tell ballad-like stories ("A Trampwoman's Tragedy," 1902, and "A Sunday Morning Tragedy," 1904); others concern members of Hardy's family ("Bereft," 1901; "After the Last Breath," 1904; and "One We Knew," 1902); and one ("The Rejected Member's Wife," 1906) concerns the wife of a politician. Eight other dated poems of this period present a variety of experiences, observations, and meditations.

The sixty-three undated poems treat subjects classified as "Time's Laughingstocks," "More Love Lyrics," "A Set of Country Songs," and "Pieces Occasional and Various." Some of these poems, the subjects indicate, were written in the 1860's; perhaps most were written in the period 1901-9.

Especially notable in the volume are "The Revisitation," which originally had the title "Time's Laughingstocks, a Summer Romance" and so furnished the title for the book; "Reminiscences of a Dancing Man," which presents Hardy's memories of one aspect of his youth in London; "One We Knew," about his grandmother whose memories provided material for many poems; and "Panthera," which indicates his attitude toward the supernatural elements in the Christian story.

1. P. 139; *Life*, p. 347.
2. In the British Museum.
3. Orel, *Thomas Hardy's Personal Writings*, pp. 245-46.

TIME'S LAUGHINGSTOCKS

THE REVISITATION is a retrospective narrative, first published in the *Fortnightly Review* for August, 1904, as "Time's Laughingstocks, A Summer Romance." The setting is in and near Dorchester. It begins in the military barracks at the upper end of High West Street. The narrator passes through the stone gateway of the barracks onto High West Street, down this street and High East, and then out of town on the London Road. Just outside town he crosses Grey's Bridge over the Frome River. After about a quarter of a mile he reaches a side road leading northeastward toward Waterston. Though officially Road 3143, it is locally called Slyre's Lane. He follows this road for nearly two miles to a point where it crosses Waterston Ridge.[1] There he turns eastward onto an overgrown track called Ridge Way, leading to Puddletown. In the fields along Ridge Way are numerous burial barrows and relics of ancient tribes. After about half a mile he comes to a depression in the center of which is a "Sarsen stone," presumably an ancient boundary marker.[2] It is a rough cube about two feet high, large enough to provide a seat for two people. At this point the narrator is in a rolling meadow about halfway between Dorchester and Puddletown. From a seat on the Sarsen stone, a person approaching from the east would be seen in silhouette. The figure of the poem comes from the meadowland of Pydel Vale between the stone and Puddletown. Later the morning sunlight illumines the landscape "From the Milton Woods to Dole-Hill," or Milton Park Wood about seven miles northeast of Waterston Ridge, and Dole's Hill Plantation north of the Ridge and about a mile and a half away. When Agnette leaves, she goes eastward down the slopes toward Puddletown, about two miles away.

Hardy's theme concerns the inexorable stream of Time, personified as a sculptor whose "transforming chisel" has both decayed Agnette's "peonies" into "pits" and made the soldier's ardor "lame." The setting near ancient burial barrows provides a suggestive background for the revelation of Agnette's decay. The dreams of the night disappear in the morning sunlight. "Love is lame at fifty years" suggests that the lover's attraction to woman's beauty is not strong enough to make him idealize in daylight. The realization that Agnette has "A nobler soul than mine" is not supported by the drive of passion. This theme appears in the climax of *Two on a Tower* when Swithin perceives the decay of Lady Constantine and underlies the story "The Waiting Supper." It appears also in many poems, as in "Amabel" and "The Well-Beloved."

Lois Deacon holds the theory that "The Revisitation" is an allegory of Hardy's retrospective meditation about his frustrated romance with Tryphena Sparks. In this allegory, Hardy, haunted by the memory of his "lost prize," Tryphena, imagines a meeting with her some twenty years after he had last seen her. To disguise his identity, he speaks through the persona of an aging soldier. The surmise is supported by the geography: the Sarsen stone is about halfway between Tryphena's girlhood home in Puddletown and his boyhood home in Higher Bockhampton. The poet, day-dreaming of Tryphena, who died in 1890, forces himself to face the idea that even if he had married Tryphena and she had lived, they might not have been happy. The beauty of the maiden he had known would have decayed.[3]

1. Lea, *Thomas Hardy's Wessex*, has a picture of Dorchester Barracks and of Waterstone Ridge, as Plates 220 and 221, p. 294.
2. The word "Sarsen" is a corruption of "Saracen" or foreign; the stone may have been brought from the Wiltshire Downs.
3. The theory is set forth in *Hardy's Summer Romance, 1867*, pp. 34-42.

A TRAMPWOMAN'S TRAGEDY Hardy considered "upon the whole, his most successful poem." *The Later Years* has a good deal to say of it: "In April of this year [1902] he was writing 'A Trampwoman's Tragedy'—a ballad based on some local story of an event more or less resembling the incidents embodied, which took place between 1820 and 1830." In July, 1903, "He then corrected the proofs of 'A Trampwoman's Tragedy' for the *North American Review,* in which pages it was published in November. When the ballad was read in England by the few good judges who met with it, they reproached Hardy with sending it out of the country for publication, not knowing it was first offered to the *Cornhill Magazine,* and declined by the editor on the ground of its not being a poem he could possibly print in a family periodical. That there was any impropriety in the verses had never struck the author at all, nor did it strike any readers, so far as he was aware."[1] In a letter to Edmund Gosse on November 15, 1903, Hardy says of the poem: "It was written between one and two years ago, after a bicycle journey I took across the Poldon Hill described, & on to Glastonbury. . . . 'Marshal's Elm' you will find on any map of Somerset. The circumstances have been known to me for many years. You may like to be told that the woman's name was Mary Ann Taylor —though she has been dust for half a century."[2] When the poem was published in the *North American Review,* a headnote read: " (The incidents on which this tale is based occurred in 1827.) "[3]

To dramatize the story, essentially a folk-tale, Hardy chose the form of many a ballad: a frame-story told by a remorseful narrator in a country setting with a supernatural appearance in the ending; within the ballad structure, the poem is a dramatic monologue.

The poem is more psychologically realistic than the typical ballad: as the title suggests, it approaches tragedy. The Trampwoman loved her "fancy-man." Her teasing to make her lover jealous seems a perverse manifestation of the possessive instinct, or a wish to exhibit her power over him, plus, perhaps, a desire for excitement in a life of geographically varied monotony. Telling the story from the Trampwoman's point of view, Hardy makes it clear that she knows the fault is hers, but he offers no blame. The seeds of his characters' behavior lay in their natures and their lonely, roaming lives.

Typically, he used geographical detail to give the story reality. The first two stanzas present the landscape of the trek from Winyard's Gap to Marshal's Elm Inn, approximately the area Hardy covered on his bicycle trip. Stanza IV lists the inns which the Trampwoman and her "fancy-man" had "loved." Stanzas V and VI repeat the trek to "Poldon top" and from there to Marshal's Elm, where the murder took place. Stanzas X, XI, and XIII present the scenes of the jail at "Ivel-chester," Mother Lee's death at "Glaston," and the woman's wandering on the "Western Moor."

The "cosy house" at Winyard's ("Wynyard's") Gap, a little more than fifteen miles northwest of Dorchester, is an inn which is still popular among motorists who drive from surrounding towns for teas and dinners. From this point, the Trampwoman and her companions walked north and slightly westward for about twenty miles to "sad Sedge-Moor." This is King's Sedge Moor near the village of Weston Zoyland, where the Duke of Monmouth was defeated by King James II's forces in 1685. It is called "sad," perhaps, because it is the site of a bloody battle and because it was a boggy moorland. The Trampwoman's group "skirted" it and turned northeastward toward Glastonbury to climb the ridge called Poldon crest overlooking the "inn that beamed thereby," Marshal's Elm Inn, described in Hardy's notes.

The Trampwoman at this point cuts back to mention her wanderings during previous months. The "Great Forest" is the New Forest, an area of extensive wasteland, including both woodland and pasture, within which hunting was at one time reserved to the King. "The New Forest may be described, in broad terms, as the southwestern corner of Hants [Hampshire], bounded by the Southampton water and the Solent on the east and south, and by the Dorset and Wilts borders on the west and north. Its extreme length is twenty-one miles, and its greatest width twelve miles."[4] The wanderings included Blackmoor Vale, the valley of the Parrett River, which flows northwestward across Somerset into Bridgewater Bay on the Bristol Channel, and the Mendip Hills in Somerset about halfway between Glastonbury and Bristol. The Yeo River rises in northern Dorset and flows northwestward past Yeovil into the Parrett. The phrase "every Marshwood midge" refers to insects in the Vale of Marshwood, lying south of Pilsdon Pen and close to the southern coast of Dorset.

The "Lone inns we loved" are scattered over Wessex. "King's Stag" may have been near the village of Kingstag, about twelve miles north of Dorchester. Lea says, without locating it: "King's Stag was burnt down about fifteen years ago [that is, about 1898], and its site is now filled by some modern cottages."[5] In his copy of the 1923 edition of *Collected Poems*, Hardy wrote in pencil for insertion into his notes: " 'King's Stag' (Stanza IV) was an inn down to 1829, & I know not how much later."[6] His note on "Windwhistle" adequately describes it; now modernized, it is on a high ridge on Road 30, about three and a half miles west of Crewkerne. Lea identifies " 'The Horse' on Hintock Green" as the White Horse Inn at Middlemarsh, a village about ten miles north of Dorchester on Road 352 to Sherborne. It is still a large, comfortable inn.[7] "The Hut" no longer exists. It stood on the northern side of Long Bredy Hill about seven miles west of Dorchester on the road to Bridport. Recently, when this road was being widened, the remains of the inn were uncovered and then re-covered by the roadway. It is called "renowned" perhaps because ancient tumuli and burial barrows are found nearby.

Stanza VI returns to Marshal's Elm Inn, the scene of the murder. It was located in a suburb of the town of Street, about two miles south-west of Glastonbury. Lea says, "This inn has now [1913] become a farmhouse, its licence having dropped thirty or more years ago."[8]

The Trampwoman's "fancy-man" was captured and tried, pre-sumably at Glastonbury, where Mother Lee died, and was hanged at "Ivel-chester jail," as the old, now-demolished jail at Ilchester (ten miles south of Glastonbury) was called.[9] Since then, having delivered his dead-born child, the Trampwoman strays over the "Western Moor," "haunting" there, and haunted by guilt. This moor is wild, hilly, forested Exmoor in northwestern Somerset.

The versification of the poem has been justly admired. "Monotony of pace is avoided by the internal change in timing within each stanza: the refrain-like repetition in the second line holds back the movement, which is released in the forward momentum of the tetram-eter triplets, especially effective in the 'knifing' stanza."[10]

1. Pp. 92-93, 100-101; *Life*, pp. 311-12, 317-18.
2. In the British Museum.
3. Purdy, *Thomas Hardy: A Bibliographical Study*, p. 138.
4. Cox, *The Royal Forests of England*, p. 304.
5. *Thomas Hardy's Wessex*, p. 298.
6. In the Dorset County Museum.
7. Lea, *Thomas Hardy's Wessex*, has a picture of Windwhistle Inn as Plate 226 and of the White Horse Inn as Plate 227, both on page 300.
8. *Thomas Hardy's Wessex*, p. 298. The inn now called Marshal's Elm is not the old inn of the poem. Lea's Plate 225 on p. 297 gives a picture of the farm-house into which it was converted.
9. Lea, *Thomas Hardy's Wessex*, has a picture of "The Hanging Chamber. Ilchester Gaol" as Plate 228 on p. 302.
10. Hogan, "Structural Design in Thomas Hardy's Poetry," pp. 199-200.

THE TWO ROSALINDS was first published in *Collier's* (New York) on March 20, 1909; then, together with "Reminiscences of a Dancing Man," in the *English Review* for April, under the covering title of "London Nights."[1] These poems reflect Hardy's memories of London in the 1860's, to which "The Two Rosalinds" adds a memory of an incident of 1890. The poem is a retrospective narrative monologue.

The Early Life indicates that "The Two Rosalinds" is based upon Hardy's visit to the Lyceum Theatre on July 2 to see Ada Rehan play Rosalind in *As You Like It*. "Before starting Hardy wrote: 'Am going with E. to see Rosalind, after not seeing her for more than twenty years. This time she is composed of Ada Rehan.' After going he added: 'At the end of the second act I went round, and found her alone, in a highly strung throbbing state—and rather despondent. . . . I endeavoured to assure her that it was going to be satisfactory, and perhaps succeeded, for in the remaining acts she played full of spirit.' It is possible that the dramatic poem entitled 'The Two Rosalinds' was suggested by this performance combined with some other; but there is no certainty about this, and dates and other characteristics do not quite accord."[2]

The poem says that the theatre where the "hag" was hawking the "words" was the "self-same portal" as that the speaker had entered to see Rosalind "some forty years before." All available evidence indicates that the earlier Rosalind played at the Haymarket Theatre (not the Lyceum) in 1867, only twenty-three years before.

Identification of the earlier Rosalind cannot be certain, for Hardy may have seen various actresses play this role in the 1860's.[3] In any case, "forty years" must be poetic license; Hardy did not see *As You Like It* when he was ten years old. Two other poems, "To an Actress" and "To an Impersonator of Rosalind," seem to refer to the earlier actress. Purdy identifies her as Mrs. Mary Frances Scott-Siddons.[4] Mrs. Scott-Siddons made her debut on the London stage on April 8, 1867, in the role of Rosalind at the Haymarket Theatre. A review in the *Daily News* for April 9 says: "Mrs. Scott-Siddons's neat figure, pretty face, and pleasing arch delivery, qualified her for light comedy. . . . Her reading of *Rosalind* was saucy and attractive." The *Daily Telegraph* on April 10 says: "Possessed of a fine expressive face, which may be called classical in its profile, and endowed with the advantages of a neat symmetrical figure, Mrs. Scott-Siddons effectively supplies the external requisites for this most fascinating of Shakespeare's heroines." Mrs. Scott-Siddons later acted in America with success, but when she returned to London in 1872, critics found her acting "not a satisfactory success."[5] She was acting as late as 1881, but she seems not to have appeared on the stage after this date. She died in November, 1896. These facts suggest that she could have been the "hag" of the poem, reduced to hawking copies of the text "Just without the colonnade."

The theme is characteristic of Hardy. He tended to idealize youthful beauty but, as Alfred Noyes said, "In the poetry of Thomas Hardy . . . we are shown the skull beneath the face of beauty and reminded of it with remorseless power."[6] To contrast actualities with the youth and beauty suggested by Shakespeare's play, he opens the poem with street scenes of worn and listless passers-by, goes into the theatre to seek the old illusion of his dream, fails to find it completely, and leaves the theatre to find the illusion decayed into a hag. He heightens the contrast by picturing the scenes of *As You Like It* and quoting phrases from the play: "the seasons' difference" is from "Here feel we but the penalty of Adam, / The season's difference"; "Who lived with running brooks for books in Nature's wildwood garden" recalls "And this our life exempt from public haunt, / Finds tongues in trees, books in the running brooks"; and "Come woo me," is quoted from the play.[7] He ends the poem with the irony that "the band withinside lightly / Beat up a merry tune."

1. Purdy, *Thomas Hardy: A Bibliographical Study*, p. 139.

2. P. 298; *Life*, p. 228.

3. The poem gives the date of her performance as 1863. *Early Life* says that about this date "Charles Kean and his wife were still performing Shakespeare at the Princess's Theatre." It again mentions Shakespeare following the date 1865: "During Phelps's series of Shakespeare plays at Drury Lane Hardy followed up every one." Pp. 56, 69; *Life*, pp. 42, 53. The line "Yes—in eighteen sixty-three" was perhaps written to rime with "she." As other discrepancies suggest, Hardy did not feel it necessary to give the date accurately.

4. *Thomas Hardy: A Bibliographical Study*, p. 143. Purdy cites no evidence for his statement.

5. Pascoe, *Our Actors: The Dramatic List*, pp. 299-300. Barnes, *Forty Years on the Stage*, presents a portrait of Mrs. Scott-Siddons and says: "Mrs. Scott-Siddons was a sweet little gentlewoman, with a beautiful classic set of features and a petite pretty figure. She was not a powerful actress." Pp. 30-31.

6. "The Poetry of Thomas Hardy," p. 103.

7. II, i, 5-6, 15-16, and IV, i, in prose.

A SUNDAY MORNING TRAGEDY tells the story of a fatal effort to produce an abortion. Hardy had trouble in publishing it. When he submitted it to the *Fortnightly Review*, the editor, W. L. Courtney, wrote on October 3, 1907: "You know how proud I am that you send your poems to me. . . . But I fear that I cannot possibly publish your latest poem, because of its subject. . . . Pray forgive my inability, which you must put down to the fact that the 'Fortnightly Review' circulates among families!"[1] The *Cornhill* also rejected the poem. The opinion that the poem was unsuitable for publication was not shared by all literary men. Ford Madox Hueffer [Ford] says that he established the *English Review* especially to publish it: "Arthur Marwood . . . came, then, to my house one day, his face pale with indignation and brandishing a newspaper which contained the information that 'The Cornhill Review' and every other magazine in London had refused to publish a poem by Thomas Hardy called 'A Sunday Morning Tragedy.' 'We must,' Marwood said, with a determination that there was no eluding, 'we must start a magazine where it can be printed.' And so we did."[2] Discussing the previous rejections, Hardy wrote to Hueffer on September 9, 1908: "The editor of the review, who returned it, merely said that he would have personally liked to print it, but that his review circulated amongst young people. Of course, with a larger morality, the guardians of young people would see that it is the very thing they ought to read, for nobody can say that the treatment is other than moral, and the crime is one of growing prevalence, as you probably know, and the false shame which leads to it is produced by the hypocrisy of the age."[3] The poem was published in the first issue of the *English Review*, for December, 1908.

"A Sunday Morning Tragedy" is a narrative monologue in the form of a ballad, spoken by the guilty mother in remorse and self-accusation. True to the conventions of the ballad, the poem contains folk-lore materials in the use of an aborticide that may be mandrake and in the suggestion of something like a witch's "poppling brew" in the preparation of the drug. The site of the action is the valley of the River Piddle ("Pydel") near Piddlehinton, about five miles northeast of Dorchester. Lea, in *Thomas Hardy's Wessex*, says that it was in Piddlehinton Church that the banns were called, "in circumstances reported to be veracious." (P. 303.)

The mother views the irony in the seducer's too-late change of heart with fatalism like that of Mrs. Durbeyfield in *Tess of the D'Urbervilles*: "'Tis nater, after all, and what do please God!" (Chapter XII.) If the story is based on fact, this irony, deepening the mother's remorse, is not the result of the poet's manipulation. Besides fate, the mother blames only herself, not her erring daughter, "wronged, sinless she!" In this story of an effort to avoid the consequences of violating a social convention, one may, in the light of Hardy's phrase "a larger morality," infer some effort to undermine this convention.

The repetitions of the poem, which suggest the refrain of the ballad-form, are psychologically right for the sorrowing mother; the eighteen occurrences of "alas for me," with its variants, and the use of rimes for *me* and *be* in the second and fourth lines of each stanza give the poem a haunting, tolling effect. The diction suggests a country woman's talk without being markedly in Dorset dialect: "Christendie" (Christendom), "strook" (struck), "Betimes" (early), and "picotee" (a variety of carnation). The closing line, "But pray God *not* to pity me," recalls Michael Henchard's soliloquy in *The Mayor of Caster-bridge*: "I—Cain—go alone as I deserve—an outcast and a vagabond. But my punishment is *not* greater than I can bear!" (Chapter XLIII.)

Hardy thought of dramatizing the story of "A Sunday Morning Tragedy" long before he published it as a poem. In a manuscript labelled "Possible Schemes of Dramatization," in the Dorset County Museum, he wrote out a three-page sketch-scenario for a play on the subject. Dated April 21, 1893, it is headed: "*Birthwort. A Tragedy in 2 acts by Thomas Hardy.*" Act I would treat the mother's effort to persuade the lover to marry, the lover's refusal, her appeal to the shepherd, and the preparation of the "decoction." Act II would open as church bells are ringing on Sunday morning; a friend brings news that the lover has changed his mind; neighbors coming from church enter with the news of the banns; the lover arrives, but the girl is dying. The same package of manuscript contains a later (?) scenario for a three-act play called "The Sunday Morning Tragedy." The basic action is that of the poem: Act I would treat the daughter's confession, the mother's unsuccessful effort to persuade the lover to marry, and suspicion of the neighbors regarding the daughter's pregnancy. Act II would treat the preparation of the shepherd's herb and the daughter's taking it. Act III would treat the arrival of neighbors and the lover, the death of the girl, and the mother's confession to the parson, who "tells her to kneel and pray for mercy. She kneels, prays for *no* mercy."

In "On Censorship of the Drama" Hardy stated why he did not write the play: " 'A Sunday Morning Tragedy' I wished to produce as a tragic play before I printed the ballad form of it, and I went so far as to shape the scenes, action, etc.; but it then occurred to me that the subject—one in which the fear of transgressing convention over-rules natural feeling to the extent of bringing dire disaster—the emi-nently proper and moral subject, would prevent my getting it on the boards, so I abandoned it."[4]

1. In the Dorset County Museum.
2. Ford, "Thomas Hardy, O. M. Obiit 11 January 1928," pp. 2-3.
3. Wilson, *Thirteen Author Collections of the Nineteenth Century*, p. 97.
4. The *Academy*, August 14, 1909; reprinted in Brennecke, *Life and Art*, p. 128.

THE HOUSE OF HOSPITALITIES, first published in the *New Quar-terly* for January, 1909, seems to present Hardy's memories of Christmas festivities during his boyhood, with his characteristic vision of ghosts of the dead who shared them.

Purdy says, "Hardy identified the scene as the 'house by the well,' Higher Bockhampton."[1] His birthplace had a separate well, and the caretakers, Mr. and Mrs. James Skilling, in a letter on November 13, 1966, say: "Knowing *Under the Greenwood Tree* so well and what went on here at Christmas in Hardy's boyhood, we wonder whether he was not, in fact, thinking of the birthplace as 'The House of Hospitalities.' Florence's book suggests that his parents were very hospitable and certainly the viol and the old clock fit in well here."

The "house by the well" may refer to a house opposite the old community well for Higher Bockhampton. This well, now disused but with its curbstone and iron standards for a windlass still in place, is on the right side of the track that leads from Bockhampton Lane to Hardy's birthplace, about two hundred yards from it.[2]

The house may be one that stood on the northern edge of Lower Bockhampton. In December, 1919, Hardy there ". . . opened a village war memorial in the form of a club-room." In his speech opening the club, he said that here ". . . used to be dancing parties at Christmas, and some weeks after. This kind of party was called a Jacob's Join, in which every guest contributed a certain sum to pay the expenses of the entertainment . . . . the man who used to give the house-room for the dances lived in a cottage which stood exactly where this Club house stands now."[3] This club-house no longer exists; young people of the village now motor to Dorchester for merrymaking, and the site is occupied by the Martin House.[4]

"The House of Hospitalities" has been set to music in an unsigned manuscript in the Dorset County Museum.

1. *Thomas Hardy: A Bibliographical Study*, p. 140.
2. This house seems to be the site of the "Paddock" house in Hardy's story "Enter a Dragoon." In this story, laid in "Mellstock" (Stinsford), ". . . other inhabitants of the hamlet came out to draw water, their common well being in the public road opposite the garden and house of the Paddocks." The story includes a merrymaking there.
3. *Later Years*, pp. 198-200; *Life*, pp. 394-95.
4. Zietlow, in "Thomas Hardy and William Barnes," p. 299, compares the poem with Barnes's "Herrenston."

BEREFT is the ballad-like lament of the widow of a working man who finds herself unable to give order to her life after his death. As the husband would walk almost to town to meet his wife when she tarried, the widow would now go to join him in the grave. The stanza-form sharpens the contrast: the four stanzas that picture the widow's memories are set against the refrain of the first stanza and the last.

The site of the poem is somewhere in the country east of Dorchester. "Durnover Lea" is Fordington Moor. That the husband crossed it to reach Grey's Bridge indicates that he walked from the direction of Stinsford, perhaps from Higher Bockhampton. Hardy may have had in mind the loneliness of his mother, who lived until 1904, after the death of his father in 1892.

JOHN AND JANE is humorous in tone for three stanzas, with a "surprise" ending when joy and hope "fade to a skull's grimace." The poem presents four stages in many a human life, suggested in the common names John and Jane. Its structure is in two ways incremental for three stanzas and then suddenly decremental: in progress from "boisterous," "pleasant," hopeful (suggested by "palace"), to "gruesome"; and from John; John and Jane; John, Jane, and the baby; to John, Jane, and the "worthless son." The opening "boisterous" subtly anticipates "worthless."

THE CURATE'S KINDNESS is an ironic monologue spoken in a modified Dorset dialect by an aged, indigent countryman being brought to the "Union" workhouse in Dorchester, identified by the references to "Pummery or Ten-Hatches Weir." "Pummery," or Poundbury, is an ancient hill-fort just northwest of Dorchester. Poundbury Weir is a dam in the Frome River just below the hill. Ten-Hatches Weir (a dam with ten hatches that may be raised) is on the Frome at a point about a hundred yards north of Grey's Bridge, east of Dorchester.[1]

Through mistaken compassion the "young Pa'son" persuaded the Guardians to alter their rules to allow the "Old folks" to live in the Union as man and wife. In Hardy's time, male and female paupers were housed in separate dormitories and mingled only in the dining hall. This separation was not modified until about 1942. As the dormitories had no rooms suitable for a couple, the concession of "The Curate's Kindness" would have been both inconvenient and unusual.[2]

1. Ten-Hatches Weir backs up the Frome to form the pool where Michael Henchard, in Chapter XLI of *The Mayor of Casterbridge*, contemplated drowning himself. Lea, *Thomas Hardy's Wessex*, has a picture of Poundbury Weir as Plate 231 on p. 304, and of Ten-Hatches Weir as Plate 84 on p. 103.

2. Based on a conversation with Mr. Beauchamp of Damers (Dorset County) Hospital.

THE FLIRT'S TRAGEDY is a monologue telling a dramatic story on the theme that murder will out. Hardy personifies Time as one who "twitched at" the curtain concealing the crime and slowly withdrew it.

The story is laid in Tintinhull Valley in the eighteenth century.

Tintinhull is a village about four miles northwest of Yeovil. Near the village is a seventeenth-century mansion called Tintinhull House, now a property of the National Trust. The speaker with "Wealth . . . beyond wish" would seem to represent the owner of Tintinhull House, and the woman of the poem a squire's coquettish daughter "Embowered" in a "manor" on the estate.

Hardy's localizing and dating the story suggests that he may have dramatized it from tales told about a John Napper (or Napier) of Tintinhull House, who died in 1791. "From 1576 to 1760 there was a succession of Thomas Nappers, the last of whom was succeeded by his youngest brother John. In 1791 the latter's son, another John, died deep in debt, having ruined himself in riotous and extravagant living, and the following year the manor and advowson were put up for sale and purchased by Admiral Marriot Arbuthnot." Tintinhull House itself, however, remained Napper property until 1835, when it was sold to a local farmer, Jeremiah Penny.[1] Available records concerning the John Napper who "ruined himself" make no mention of the story Hardy tells. He married Mary, the daughter of Captain Philip Walsh, R. N., and had four sons. "Mary Napper outlived her husband by some thirty years, and continued to live in Tintinhull."[2] If Hardy's story concerns John Napper and is even distantly based on fact, it must treat an earlier alliance than that with Mary Walsh.

If the story is fiction, Hardy probably placed the murder in Venice with some memory of his "pilgrimage" there in April of 1897.[3] The gloomy *calle* would seem to be an alley or street leading into the Grand Canal, the "still street of waters dividing / The city in two."

Perhaps to provide a monotony suitable to meditative despair, Hardy employs an identical end-rime for each of his stanzas, all riming with the "knew" that concludes the first stanza. Echoes from the Bible give depth to the speaker's remorse. "On new moons and sabbaths" is echoed from Isaiah 1:13: ". . . the new moons and sabbaths, the calling of assemblies, I cannot away with." "Tophet" and "Cain" echo the Bible. The concluding stanza recalls the rejection of pity found in Michael Henchard's will in *The Mayor of Casterbridge.* (Chapter XLV.)

1. Oswald, "A Somerset Village: Tintinhull and Its Houses," pp. 739, 798.
2. Rawlins, "Napper of Tintinhull," p. 284.
3. See *Early Life*, pp. 252-56; *Life*, pp. 192-95.

THE REJECTED MEMBER'S WIFE was published in the *Spectator* on January 27, 1906, under the title of "The Ejected Member's Wife" from a manuscript that bore the title "The Rejected One's Wife."[1] No doubt the successful candidate for Parliament and the rejected member occupied popular attention in the scene described, but it is characteristic that Hardy both treated the most helpless victim of a defeat and avoided comment on politics. His attitude was stated in a letter to Pearce Edgcumbe on April 23, 1891: "Moreover the pursuit of what other people are pleased to call art so as to win unbiassed attention to it as such, absolutely forbids political action. . . . I therefore never take any, beyond occasionally recording a vote."[2]

The poem concerns an election held in South Dorset on January 17, 1906. The "Declaration of the Poll" was reported in the *Dorset County Chronicle* for January 25. Colonel William Ernest Brymer of Ilsington House, near Dorchester, had been a Conservative Member of Parliament for Dorchester in the years 1874-85, and for South Dorset in 1891-1906. He was defeated for re-election by the Liberal candidate T. T. L. Scarisbrick. The *Chronicle* describes the arrival of the successful candidate at the County Hall when the poll was declared and the enthusiasm of the crowd for Mrs. Scarisbrick, who, "dressed in her husband's colours, appeared inside the window of the Hall Keeper's office, her face radiant with delight and continuously waving her handkerchief in triumph." The newspaper describes also the arrival of "the gallant Colonel," who "was greeted with mingled cheers and hooting." It comments upon the "disgraceful behaviour of a section of the Radical Party . . . in not letting Colonel Brymer speak," but it does not mention Mrs. Brymer. Evidently Hardy was present and observed her. The poem suggests that she also waved "her white-gloved hand." It was a pitiful gesture after a hard-fought contest between Colonel Brymer's "stormy sturdy band" and his opponents, "Fervid with zeal." The Liberal forces swept to victory with the song "Hang old Brymer to a sour-apple tree," to the tune of the American "Battle Hymn of the Republic."

Hardy summed up his attitude in a letter of February 11 to Mrs. Arthur Henniker: "Well, what do you think of the Elections? . . . As you know, the husbands of both Madeleine B[rymer] & Dorothy A. are out. I am sorry for them rather—I mean the wives. I had a poem in the Spectator a week or two ago on a typical Ejected Member's wife."[3]

He knew Mrs. Brymer personally and admired her enough to arouse a hint of jealousy in Mrs. Florence Hardy, who wrote to Lady Hoare on July 31, 1914: "Mrs. Brymer was telling me that she *wanted* her *portrait painted & she asked if I* knew of an artist. . . . My husband says he likes her—but I cannot see what it is that attracts him. . . . She is, to my mind, a woman who lives solely for her own gratification, & for the good things of this world."[4]

1. Purdy, *Thomas Hardy: A Bibliographical Study*, p. 140.
2. In the Miriam Lutcher Stark Library, University of Texas.
3. In the Dorset County Museum.
4. In the County Archives in Trowbridge, Wiltshire.

THE FARM-WOMAN'S WINTER was published in the *Pall Mall Magazine* in January, 1905.[1] The poem suggests the joys of farm life, which might include "bravely tilling / Long hours," but for the bleakness and cruelty of "savage winter." Where Meredith saw "the husbandman's welcome to the cheerless hardships of winter as essential for the processes of growth," Hardy saw that "the winter is more likely to kill the farmer."[2]

1. Purdy, *Thomas Hardy: A Bibliographical Study*, p. 140.
2. Stevenson, *Darwin Among the Poets*, p. 262.

AUTUMN IN KING'S HINTOCK PARK is a meditative soliloquy, ballad-like in its refrain of "Raking up leaves." On October 29, 1906, Edmund Gosse, then directing the *Books Supplement* of the *Daily Mail*, wrote to Hardy: "Will you, for old friendship's sake (and for proper payment as well, of course,) send me a Poem."[1] Hardy sent the poem, which appeared on November 17, under the title "Autumn in My Lord's Park."[2]

The theme is an aging woman's meditation that the processes of the seasons typify human life: as leaves wither and die, so do people. "Springtime deceives" the passing "Lords' ladies" as it deceived the once "fresh and free" girl now raking up leaves and memories. The refrain suggests the strokes of the rake, the circling of the seasons, and the rhythmic repetition of the woman's thought.

"King's Hintock" park is the park of the Earls of Ilchester, adjoining Melbury Osmund. After sending the poem to Gosse, Hardy wrote that "It happened in Lady L[ondonderr]y's daughter's park at Melbury by the way."[3] He wrote to Mrs. Arthur Henniker on December 21, 1906: "How *could* you guess that those lines of mine in the Daily Mail referred to the Ilchester's park? I happened to be walking, or cycling, through it years ago, when the incident occurred on which the verses are based, & I wrote them out. . . . My interest in the park arises from the fact that a portion of it belonged to my mother's people centuries ago, before the Strangways absorbed it."[4]

On September 21, 1913, Roma Green of Chelsea wrote Hardy that he had set "Autumn in the Park" to music and asked permission to publish the words with the music. Permission was granted.[5]

1. In the Dorset County Museum.
2. Purdy, *Thomas Hardy: A Bibliographical Study*, p. 140.
3. Ibid.
4. In the Dorset County Museum.
5. In the Dorset County Museum.

SHUT OUT THAT MOON suggests successive periods in Hardy's life. The first stanza, mentioning "lutes . . . strewn / With years-deep dust" and "names . . . / On a white stone," seems to refer to his joy in music-making with his father, who died in 1892. The second stanza suggests his mother, with whom he had gazed at the stars,[1] and who died in 1904, the year of the poem. The third stanza, mentioning "you and me," may refer to Hardy's courtship of Emma Gifford, now the staid Mrs. Hardy, and their dreams that love was "All it was said to be." The fourth stanza pictures the present reality.

In this poem of symbols the moon, personified as "she," seems to have a double meaning. In the first three stanzas she "wears . . . the guise" of romance, but the joy and love suggested are illusions. In Dorset folk-lore, to see the moon through glass is a portent of evil;[2] hence, the opening imperative of the poem is "Close up the casement, draw the blind." In Hardy's works generally, the moon symbolizes the coldness and remoteness of nature, which in time destroys "Life's early bloom" and brings "Too tart . . . fruit." The theme of the poem approaches that in an episode of *Far from the Madding Crowd*: "Gabriel, after losing his sheep, sees the waning moon's reflection, broken in the ripples of the pond, like an 'attenuated skeleton'; but instead of accepting this invitation to suicide, he pulls himself together, and when we next meet him he possesses a 'dignified calm he had never before known.' "[3] It is the calm of the stoic, close to the bitter acceptance of reality in the final stanza of "Shut Out That Moon."

The poem has been set to music in a manuscript signed "AM," in the Dorset County Museum.

1. The "Lady's Chair" is Cassiopeia's Chair.
2. Knott, "Dorset Superstitions," p. 73.
3. Morrell, *Thomas Hardy: The Will and the Way*, pp. 12-13. See the novel, Chapters V and VI.

REMINISCENCES OF A DANCING MAN, rejected by the *Cornhill*, was published in New York by *Collier's* on March 27, 1909. It was then published, together with "The Two Rosalinds," in the *English Review* for April under the collective title "London Nights."[1]

Hardy's interest in London dance halls was aroused before he went to live in London in 1862. While he was working with the architect Hicks in Dorchester, another pupil in Hicks's office named Fippard went to London now and then and returned "whistling quadrilles and other popular music, with accounts of his dancing experiences at the Argyle Rooms and Cremorne, both then in full swing. Hardy would relate that one quadrille in particular his precursor Fippard could whistle faultlessly, and while giving it would caper about the office to an imaginary dance-figure, embracing an imaginary Cremorne or Argyle *danseuse."* Shortly after his arrival in London, Hardy began dancing. "Balls were constant at Willis's Rooms, earlier Almack's, and in 1862 Hardy danced at these rooms, or at Almack's as he preferred to call the place, realizing its historic character. He used to recount that in those old days, the pretty Lancers and Caledonians were still footed there to the original charming tunes, which brought out the beauty of the figures as no later tunes did, and every movement was a correct quadrille step and gesture. . . . Cremorne and the Argyle he also sought, remembering the jaunty senior-pupil at Hicks's who had used to haunt those gallant resorts." In 1895, he revisited Willis's Rooms with Mrs. Hardy: "In London in December they went to see Forbes-Roberton and Mrs. Patrick Campbell as Romeo and Juliet, supping with them afterwards at Willis's Rooms, a building Hardy had known many years earlier, when it was still a ballroom unaltered in appearance from that of its famous days as 'Almack's.' "[2]

Almack's (Willis's Rooms) in King Street was opened in 1765 for an aristocratic clientele: a subscription of ten guineas admitted one to a ball and a supper once a week for three months. It became popular, but the balls were discontinued in 1863 because of "the plebeian invasion."[3]

The second stanza presents "gay Cremorne" Gardens in Chelsea, on the bank of the Thames close to Battersea Bridge, opened as a place of public amusement in 1845 and closed in 1877. The entertainments there included concerts, dancing, short plays, and the marionettes. The Argyle in Regent Street was a suite of four splendid rooms and a rendezvous of fashion.

Hardy's phrase "Who now remembers" that introduces each stanza of youthful gaiety leads into a dance of death, with some suggestion that the dances were not entirely innocent entertainments. The poem has the rhythms of waltzing figures in a mixture of iambic and anapestic meters.

1. Purdy, *Thomas Hardy: A Bibliographical Study,* p. 141.
2. *Early Life,* pp. 44-45, 56; *Later Years,* pp. 43-44; *Life,* pp. 34, 42-43, 274.
3. Copps, "The Poetry of Thomas Hardy," pp. 489-90.

THE DEAD MAN WALKING is dated in the manuscript 1896.[1] This date and the substance of the poem relate it to the "In Tenebris" poems written about this time.

Hardy's series of disenchantments are suggested to be: the loss of zest for life when, during his years in London, he lost his religious faith and observed the materialistic values of the city; the deaths of "my friend" (Horace Moule) and "my kinsfolk" (Hardy's father, among them, died in 1892); and his difficulties with Emma.

The stanzas presenting the stages of Hardy's inching toward death-in-life follow a decremental structure partly indicated in the imagery: "By equating life with 'fire' Hardy is able to talk of diminishing life in terms of lowering temperature; ambition *ices* the speaker, bereavement leaves him *bleak*, his Love's hate causes him to die one more *degree*. (Appropriately, his Love's heart *kindles* in hate of him.)"[2]

1. Purdy, *Thomas Hardy: A Bibliographical Study*, p. 141.
2. Hogan, "Structural Design in Thomas Hardy's Poetry," p. 37.

MORE LOVE LYRICS

The manuscript for the twenty-six poems called "More Love Lyrics" was entitled "Love Poems of Past [Years] Days";[1] in the first edition of *Time's Laughingstocks* the heading was "Love Lyrics."

The group includes poems written as early as 1866 and as late as the 1900's. Poems treat love's idealizations, dreams, moments of ecstasy, passions, follies, consequences, and disillusionments. Some of the poems are identifiable with Hardy's experiences of young love and his dreams, for instance, of an actress whom, presumably, he saw only from a seat in the theatre; others are reflections of his emotional experiences in mature life, long after marriage. Yet other poems seem dramatic pictures based on observation, as in a dancing class at Weymouth. A few are concerned with love in general and its "desolations," for instance, "He Abjures Love" that concludes the group. The poems are varied in form, with several Shakespearean sonnets among those written in the 1860's and 1870's.

1. Purdy, *Thomas Hardy: A Bibliographical Study*, p. 141.

1967, though classified as a love lyric, refers to love only in the mention of "me and you" and in the last line. Stevenson related the poem to the "evolutionary meliorism" expressed in Hardy's "Apology" for *Late Lyrics and Earlier*: "That this hope is not an outgrowth of his old age is aptly shown by the poem called 1967, written when Hardy was twenty-seven."[1] Sherman associated the poem with the "radicalism" of Hardy's unpublished first novel, *The Poor Man and the Lady*. He surmised that Hardy may have attended the organizational meeting of the First International in St. Martin's Hall, London, on September 28, 1864, presided over by Professor Edward Beesly, or heard Beesly on April 11, 1866, speak on the grievances of the working man: "the unequal pressure of indirect taxation . . . the operation of the game laws, the excessive expenditure on the army and navy compared with that on education, the treatment of the poor in work-houses, and the monopoly of the land by large proprietors."[2] Also in 1867 there was agitation in London for the Second Reform Bill.[3] Whatever the backgrounds for the poem, there is quasi-utopian hope in the lines saying that the next century "Will show . . . at its prime, / A scope above this blinkered time."

The violent image of the last line brings the poem to a close not entirely prepared for in "a pinch of dust or two." The image re-sembles that of Donne's "The Flea." In his copy of Chew's *Thomas Hardy Poet and Novelist* (1921 edition), Hardy underscored on page 20 the sentence "Here broodings upon death are constant" and wrote in the margin: "In this & similar criticisms it is curious that the in-fluence of Donne is not mentioned."[4] The image may have been suggested by Shelley. In the copy of Shelley's *Queen Mab and Other Poems* that he owned in 1866, commenting on *The Revolt of Islam*, "Hardy marked Cythna's resolution that, when they have accomplished all they can for freedom, they share an 'undivided tomb.'"[5]

If the "Love" of the poem is a real person, she could hardly have been Tryphena Sparks, whom Hardy did not know well until after he left London in 1867.

1. *Darwin Among the Poets*, p. 292.
2. "Thomas Hardy and Professor Edward Beesly," p. 167. *The Early Life*, p. 220; *Life*, pp. 168-69, quotes part of a letter of 1884 from Beesly to Hardy.
3. The Reform League had headquarters on the ground floor rooms under Blomfield's offices, 8 Adelphi Terrace, where Hardy was employed.
4. In the Dorset County Museum.
5. Bartlett, "Hardy's Shelley," p. 17.

HER DEFINITION seems artificial, more precious than passionate and not necessarily inspired by any particular person. Though some phrases have been judged conventional and others those of "a popular song hit," the poem has been called a "perfect sonnet."[1]

Lois Deacon says that the poem concerns Tryphena Sparks, on the basis that "maiden mine" is echoed in "Lover to Mistress," where "Maid mine" may well refer to Tryphena.[2] Unless Hardy concealed his subject by misdating the poem 1866, it cannot refer to Tryphena, whom he did not know well until late in 1867.

1. Vinson, "Diction and Imagery in the Poetry of Thomas Hardy," p. 247, and Brennecke, *The Life of Thomas Hardy*, p. 131.
2. *Hardy's Sweetest Image*, pp. 7-8.

THE DIVISION was for a long time supposed by Hardy's critics and biographers to concern only a marital rift between Hardy and his wife Emma.[1] Then Purdy in 1954 suggested that the poem is to be associated with Mrs. Arthur Henniker.[2] Much evidence indicates that the poem is addressed to her. Hardy's letters to Mrs. Henniker, especially in the years 1893-96, express a discreet but warmly emotional attraction, though her feeling for him was apparently no more than warm-hearted friendship. The feeling may have seemed like overt love to Mrs. Emma Hardy, who apparently voiced hostility toward Mrs. Henniker. Writing to Rebekah Owen on July 29, 1917, about a visit to Lady St. Helier and Mrs. Henniker, Mrs. Florence Hardy said that Mrs. Henniker "kissed me warmly and called me 'dear Florence.' How it was that the first Mrs. Hardy so much disliked these two warm-hearted, generous kind women, I cannot conceive."[3]

Despite the discretion of his letters and his meetings with Mrs. Henniker, Hardy published "The Division" among his "Love Lyrics." The scene of the poem is evidently Max Gate. The "hundred miles between" may represent the distance to Southsea, where Mrs. Henniker was living in the latter part of 1893. The phrase "that thwart thing betwixt us twain" may have meant in his mind the barrier that each was married to another, but more likely it refers to Emma's watchful and (it seemed to Hardy) unreasonable jealousy. Other poems suggest that Emma had been hostile to Mrs. Henniker from their first meeting. (See the notes on "Alike and Unlike.")

"The Division" may have been set to music. On December 19, 1910, Hardy wrote to Mrs. Henniker: "By an unfortunate accident I never replied to your question if Mr. Frank Lambert might set 'The Division' to music. Please let him know, if he is still in the mind, that he certainly may, & that it will be a great pleasure to me."[4]

1. See, for instance, Weygandt, *The Time of Yeats* (1937), p. 281; Weber, *Hardy of Wessex*, 1st ed. (1940), pp. 167-68; Collins, "The Love Poetry of Thomas Hardy" (1942), p. 81; Evelyn Hardy, *Thomas Hardy* (1954), p. 265; and Meynell, ed., *The Best of Friends* (1956), p. 200.
2. *Thomas Hardy: A Bibliographical Study*, p. 141.
3. In the Colby College Library.
4. In the Dorset County Museum.

ON THE DEPARTURE PLATFORM, Purdy says, "is to be associated with Miss Dugdale, in spite of Hardy's reference to himself as a 'young man.' "[1] Florence Emily Dugdale, who became the second Mrs. Hardy, worked with Hardy in the British Museum in his researches for *The Dynasts*.

In the poem, the crowds in which the young woman vanished suggest that the scene is in London. The date of the incident (if the poem presents a fact) must be between 1904, when Hardy met Miss Dugdale, and the late summer of 1909, when he prepared *Time's Laughingstocks* for publication. In these years he was sixty-four to sixty-nine, but did not in some moods think of himself as too old for a moment of romance. He wrote: "I was a child till I was 16; a youth till I was 25; a young man till I was 40 or 50"—and hence in spry middle age through the early 1900's.[2] His novel *The Well-Beloved*, though not autobiographical, presents Pierston as "A Young Man of Forty" (the title of Part Second) : "In his heart he was not a day older than when he had wooed the mother [Avice the First] at the daughter's present age. His record moved on with the years; his sentiments stood still." (Chapter VI.) In Part Third, titled "A Young Man of Sixty," Pierston fancies himself in love with the granddaughter of Avice the First. May O'Rourke, Hardy's secretary in the 1920's, wrote a poem "At Hardy's Birthplace," which speaks of Hardy in his eighties as "A Man with April in his eyes, / And winter on his face."[3]

"On the Departure Platform" presents this dual picture. The last stanza seems a colloquy between the Hardy with "winter on his face" (the questioner) and himself with "April in his eyes" (the "young man" realizing the facts). Gierasch shows how the realization that the flush of feeling cannot come again in quite the same way runs through the poem: " 'She left me,' 'disappear,' 'vanished'—all seem to point directly to the conclusion. . . . and although the past tense is used throughout the description of the past event, more than mere past time is indicated in 'she who was more than my life to me'—a hint that in the present she is such no longer . . . in the conclusion . . . the word 'fond' carries the meaning not only of strong attachment but also of the folly of that attachment."[4]

Weber has suggested the influence of Browning in the poem, mentioning Browning's "Any Wife to Any Husband" and "In a Year." He quotes from the latter: "Never any more . . . need I hope to see his face / As before."[5]

1. Purdy, *Thomas Hardy: A Bibliographical Study*, p. 142.
2. *Later Years*, p. 179; *Life*, p. 378.
3. *Thomas Hardy: His Secretary Remembers*, p. 8.
4. "Hardy's *On the Departure Platform*."
5. *Hardy of Wessex*, 1st ed., p. 273.

IN A CATHEDRAL CITY is set in Salisbury. The woman addressed was possibly Tryphena Sparks. Hardy's sisters, Mary and Kate, attended Salisbury Training College for teachers, whereas Tryphena took her teacher-training at Stockwell College in London. Perhaps Tryphena did not visit Salisbury at all.

The poet's resolution to "rest" in view of the "grey Cathedral" until he achieves the "spot's unconsciousness" of the woman loved and lost is characteristic. The third stanza, speaking of the woman's never having entered the Cathedral, recalls Chapter I, Part III, of

Jude the Obscure, in which "Melchester" stands for Salisbury. Jude proposes that he and Sue "go and sit in the Cathedral," but as she would "rather sit in the railway station," they do not enter it.

"I SAY I'LL SEEK HER" exhibits Hardy's sensitivity to the pain of others, evident in his vision of the woman's pain when her lover fails to appear. If the woman is Tryphena Sparks, the poet's failure to "seek her side" may reflect his indecision between her and Emma Gifford.

HER FATHER is dated in the manuscript "1869,"[1] perhaps indicating the date of the action. Hardy was working in Weymouth then.

Holmes says that the "cynic ghost" of the fourth stanza cannot stand for "Such vague meanings as the lover's 'conscience' or his intuitive perception of the father's viewpoint," but stands for "the lover's regretful realization that this love is now a thing of the past."[2] It seems more likely to stand for Hardy's characteristic idea, expressed in his novels and poems, that a lover's love depends upon the sweetheart's "pink and white," which will be despoiled by the cynic Time, as in "Amabel," "The Two Rosalinds," "Autumn in King's Hintock Park," and the climax of *Two on a Tower*.

1. Purdy, *Thomas Hardy: A Bibliographical Study*, p. 142.
2. "Hardy's *Her Father*."

AT WAKING, noted as written in "Weymouth, 1869," when Hardy was working in that city, may record a personal experience. The scene is the narrator's bedroom. Brennecke states that the woman of the poem is his wife;[1] Southworth likewise traces the mood of the poem to "physiological or biological" depletion "following the marital act."[2] Hardy was not married in 1869. Deacon and Coleman say that the narrator "on waking, sees his love," and they identify her as Tryphena Sparks because the poem calls her the narrator's "prize," a word that refers to Tryphena in "Thoughts of Phena."[3] Hardy's phrasing is ambiguous, but "seemed to behold" probably means "saw in a vision." His word is "insight," not "sight." This interpretation would neither eliminate Tryphena, to whom he was engaged in 1869, nor require her to be present.

Read as a vision, the poem expresses a mood characteristic of Hardy. He was usually depressed in the early morning. His tendency to idealize a loved one seems reflected in "The Well-Beloved" and the novel with the same name. In the depression of a grey dawn, he rejected all idealization.[4] The concluding "Off: it is not true" suggests that by evening the narrator might fall again under the spell of romance.

In imagery Hardy's association of "cold clouds" and "Dead white . . . corpse" is typical. The verse-form seems to owe something to Tate and Brady's *A New Version of the Psalms of David*.

1. *The Life of Thomas Hardy*, p. 137.
2. *The Poetry of Thomas Hardy*, p. 47.
3. *Providence and Mr Hardy*, p. 77.
4. In *The Well-Beloved* Pierston's disillusionment occurs when he sees himself in a mirror at dawn. See Part Third, Chapter IV.

FOUR FOOTPRINTS, since it follows two poems annotated "Weymouth," may be set on the beach fronting this seaside town. The poem may reflect a personal experience, and the "dutiful daughter" may be the woman of "Her Father."[1]

1. In *Jude the Obscure*, Jude returns at dawn after his first evening with Arabella to the spot of their embrace and observes their footprints: "Jude looked on the ground and sighed. He looked closely, and could just discern in the damp dust the imprints of their feet as they had stood locked in each other's arms." Part I, Chapter VII.

IN THE VAULTED WAY was published in the first edition of *Time's Laughingstocks* as "In the Crypted Way." Purdy says that the manuscript gives 1870 as the date of composition, "suggesting the poem may be an episode of Hardy's courtship at St. Juliot in Cornwall."[1] The tiny, isolated St. Juliot Church has no vaulted or crypted way, and visitors who would cause the lovers to retire "To the shadowy corner that none could see" seem unlikely. There is neither a cathedral near St. Juliot nor evidence that Hardy and Emma Gifford made extensive trips together in 1870. Lois Deacon suggests that the scene is in Winchester Cathedral and the persons are Hardy and Tryphena Sparks at a time after he had met Emma Gifford but before he had broken his engagement to Tryphena,[2] but evidence for this identification is lacking. The poem is vague concerning "the words that burned."

The poem is a monologue, but the tone is more that of a letter than anything spoken to the woman; it mentions "our parting" as an action in the recent past. The psychological probing suggests some influence from Browning.

1. *Thomas Hardy: A Bibliographical Study*, p. 142.
2. *Hardy's Sweetest Image*, p. 7.

IN THE MIND'S EYE[1] appeared in *Time's Laughingstocks* as "The Phantom" and in *Selected Poems* as "The Face in the Mind's Eye." In his copy of *Time's Laughingstocks* Hardy underscored "The Phantom" and wrote in the margin "Ghost-face."[2] The "ghost" is a memory of a dead woman, perhaps Tryphena Sparks. Fackler, characterizing the many phantoms that Hardy described, says that they are "not malign or ominous spectres but wistful, gentle shades, more dear than dreadful, of many loved long since and lost awhile."[3]

The poem has been set to music by Gerald Finzi (London: Boosey & Co., 1936). It is also in *Before and After Summer: Ten Songs for Baritone and Piano* (London: Boosey & Hawkes, 1949).

1. The New York edition of *Collected Poems* has the title "The Phantom." The index of the London edition has "The Phantom," not "In the Mind's Eye."
2. In the Dorset County Museum.
3. "Death: Idea and Image in Some Later Victorian Lyrists," p. 140.

THE END OF THE EPISODE has been generally thought to be Hardy's address to his wife Emma. Referring to "Hardy's marital situation . . . seemingly ruptured by" the publication of *Jude the Obscure*, which Mrs. Hardy tried to have suppressed, Anschutz says: "Hardy's reaction might be judged by his earlier statement that women's belief in convention, in the rightness of things you know to be 'damnably wrong,' makes the heart ache." He quotes the conclusion of the poem to define Hardy's reaction.[1] Weber supposes that the end of their affection was an episode of June 22, 1907, when he went with Emma to a Royal Garden Party at Windsor Castle, was offered a ride up a steep hill on a hot day, and was told by Emma to walk, while she took her seat in the carriage. "Hardy was now seventy years old, weary, worn, and sad. The rosy colour of the Cornish romance of forty years ago had faded. . . . The fire on the hearth at Max Gate had gone out."[2] Evelyn Hardy says, in discussion of Hardy's differences with Emma, "His doctrine was to suffer in dignified silence," and quotes the final stanza.[3]

Deacon and Coleman, however, relate the poem to Hardy's broken engagement to Tryphena Sparks: " 'The End of the Episode' is a bitter poem of [their] parting." To some extent, they rest their surmise on the fact that Russell Boughton, in his operatic version of *The Queen of Cornwall*, included "The End of the Episode" among Hardy's poems set to music as a part of the opera. " 'The End of the Episode' is important because Hardy suggested that it, like 'A Spot' [associated with Tryphena], should be included in the operatic version. . . . When he was discussing this with the composer Hardy took him not to Cornwall but to Coomb Eweleaze, a place of memories of Tryphena."[4] If this identification is right, "There shall remain no trace / Of what so closely tied us" may explain "Not a line of her writing have I, / Not a thread of her hair" in "Thoughts of Phena." On the other hand, Marguerite Roberts says that Boughton selected the poems to be included, and Hardy only "admitted that the lyrics seemed to him to have been written for the opera."[5]

1. "The Road to Nirvana," p. 134.

2. *Hardy's Love Poems*, pp. 57-60.
3. *Thomas Hardy*, p. 261.
4. *Providence and Mr Hardy*, p. 83.
5. *Hardy's Poetic Drama and the Theatre*, p. 100.

THE SIGH is a dainty poem that critics have analyzed variously. Even in the moment of yielding her first kiss, the poem suggests, a woman may pine secretly for another lover, "a commonplace of present-day literature. One has only to think of Proust's large statement of the impossibility of knowing, possessing, and uniting with the person loved—an impossibility arising from the fact that each individual . . . creates and inhabits his own universe."[1] Hogan finds the poem humorous: "Throughout each stanza the perturbed lover reassures himself of her sincerity, only to return amusingly at each final line to the most delicate of doubts."[2] Hardy expressed the idea of the poem in *Under the Greenwood Tree*: when Fancy Day seems fickle and Dick Dewy is despondent, his father Reuben says: "Now, Dick, this is how a maid is. She'll swear she's dying for thee, and she will die for thee; but she'll fling a look over t'other shoulder at another young feller, though never leaving off dying for thee just the same." (Part the Second, Chapter VIII.)

One phrase, "Till my appointed change," echoes Job 14:14, ". . . all the days of my appointed time will I wait, till my change come." The poem has been set to music by Gerald Finzi in *A Young Man's Exhortation* (Oxford University Press, 1933).

1. Perkins, "Hardy and the Poetry of Isolation," pp. 147-48.
2. "Structural Design in Thomas Hardy's Poetry," p. 219.

"IN THE NIGHT SHE CAME" expresses a theme constant in Hardy's thought, that love decays with the passage of "dull defacing Time." He wrote in a notebook entry for May, 1870: "A sweet face is a page of sadness to a man over thirty—the raw material of a corpse."[1] In the poem the lover's subconscious fear brought on a dream that he remembered on waking and that undermined love's idealization.[2]

1. Evelyn Hardy, *Thomas Hardy's Notebooks*, p. 29.
2. Dreams that give vivid, fantastic form to hopes and fears are frequent in Hardy's works, as Eustacia's dream of a faceless "man in silver armour" in *The Return of the Native*, Book Second, Chapter II; Angel Clare's sleep-walking dream in *Tess of the D'Urbervilles*, Chapter XXXVII; and Napoleon's dream before Waterloo in *The Dynasts*, Part Third, VI, iii.

THE CONFORMERS expresses the lover's fear that marriage may end romance. In *Far from the Madding Crowd*, Jan Coggan tells the story of Bathsheba Everdene's father, "one of the ficklest husbands alive," who cured his "wicked heart wandering" by making his wife "take off her wedding-ring and calling her by her maiden name as they sat together after the shop was shut, and so 'a would get to fancy she was only his sweetheart, and not married to him at all. And as soon as he could thoroughly fancy he was doing wrong and committing the seventh,[1] 'a got to like her as well as ever, and they lived on a perfect picture of mutel love."[2] *Jude the Obscure* echoes throughout Sue's feeling that the contract of marriage would chill the spontaneity, the impulsiveness, and the excitements of love.

As the two poems are printed in sequence, possibly "The Conformers" and "The Dawn After the Dance" are companion poems treating two episodes of the same story. If so, the "little fay" of "The Conformers" would follow the example of her parents in "The Dawn After the Dance," in a life of "formal / Matrimonial commonplace and household life's mechanic gear." In "The Conformers," the reluctant, mocking lover yields to her plea for marriage, but in "The Dawn After the Dance" the lovers apparently agree to break the vows "frail as gossamere."

1. Breaking the seventh Commandment, "Thou shalt not commit adultery."
2. Chapter VIII. Hardy tells a similar story related to him as fact by the judge of a divorce court. See *Later Years*, p. 110; *Life*, p. 324.

THE DAWN AFTER THE DANCE is related to a background stated in *The Early Life*. During 1869, Hardy worked for the architect G. R. Crickmay in Weymouth. The references in the poem to "this-year's end eve" must refer to the evening of December 31, 1869. In the following February "Hardy gave up his rooms at Weymouth and returned to his rural home to be able to concentrate more particularly on the MS. [of *Desperate Remedies*] than he could do in a lively town and as a member of a dancing-class where a good deal of flirtation went on, the so-called 'class' being, in fact, a gay gathering for dances and love-making by adepts of both sexes. The poem entitled 'The Dawn after the Dance,' and dated 'Weymouth, 1869,' is supposed . . . to have some bearing on these dances."[1] One may see the poem as picturing a final phase of the "flirtation" and "love-making by adepts of both sexes" that Hardy observed. The woman would seem to be a dance-hall girl with whom an "adept" solaced himself from one New Year's eve to the next. In relation to "The Conformers," which seems a companion poem, the lover dreaded the dullness of married life. By year's end he was satiated. Nothing in the poem points to Hardy as the young man. His comment suggests only that he had had enough of dancing and was making up his mind to abandon the diversions of Weymouth and get on with *Desperate Remedies*. In this period he was presumably engaged to Tryphena Sparks of Puddletown, whose parents did not live in Weymouth.[2]

The ambiguities of the poem interested V. H. Collins, who asked Hardy, "What is that which makes man's love the lighter and the woman's burn no brighter?" He replied somewhat evasively: "I suppose when they get intimate. . . . I think perhaps I originally wrote 'the brighter.' "[3] Either reading makes sense, "the brighter" as woman's hope for motherhood and marriage, and "no brighter" as the prospect of motherhood without marriage. The man's love is "lighter" after sexual satisfaction.[4]

The poem seems to imitate the metrical pattern of Poe's "The Raven."

1. *Early Life*, p. 85; *Life*, p. 64.
2. The Hardy scholar, Frank Southerington, wrote to me: "I think 'The Dawn after the Dance' does point to Hardy and Tryphena. The lines about 'That which . . . Came to pass with us inevitably' fit Lois Deacon's theory of Tryphena's becoming Thomas Hardy's mistress and fit the possibility of a weakening of Hardy's feelings as expressed in 'At Waking.' From the poems of this date I get the general impression of a firm relationship slowly crumbling, and would explain Hardy's subsequent marriage elsewhere partly on the basis of these poems. I think the reference to 'vows' also fits."
3. *Talks with Thomas Hardy*, p. 23.
4. As always in Hardy's works; see the opening of *The Mayor of Casterbridge* and Webster, *On a Darkling Plain*, pp. 68-69, 225.

THE SUN ON THE LETTER was in the manuscript titled "A Discord."[1] The sun in the poem seems a symbol of the indifference of nature to man's happiness. That its rays "beamed /As brightly on the page of proof / That she had shown her false to me / As if it had shown her true" recalls the lines in "Hap," where "purblind Doomsters had as readily strown / Blisses about my pilgrimage as pain."

As it parallels other poems, Miss Deacon has surmised that this one concerns a letter from Tryphena Sparks on July 4, 1872, declaring that their intimate acquaintance must end.[2] The poem is written in an unusual pattern: the lines of each stanza rime a-b-c with the other stanzas.

1. Purdy, *Thomas Hardy: A Bibliographical Study*, p. 142.
2. "Cross-in-Hand," unpublished manuscript, p. 292.

THE NIGHT OF THE DANCE describes the hour of preparation in a country home before a dance. The mention of "Old Robert" suggests that the home is that of Robert Reason ("Robert Penny" of *Under the Greenwood Tree*). The narrator looks forward to an evening of joy and love-making, but the poem suggests that the merriment may have sinister consequences. The "cold moon" that "centres its gaze on me" and the "stars, like eyes in reverie" seem to "Quiz" the preparations "curiously."

MISCONCEPTION portrays the masculine vanity of an old-fashioned man who supposed his "Love" would find comfort in retreating from the "moils" of the world to the shelter of the home he labored to make for her. In theme, it parallels "From Her in the Country," written before Hardy's marriage. The poem may reflect the moves of Hardy and Emma from town to town, including London, until Hardy built Max Gate, where Emma was not altogether happy.

THE VOICE OF THE THORN, portraying various attitudes toward a patch of gorse (or furze) like that on the Wessex downs, associates it with a scene of heartbreak. Lea says: "Doubtless this poem might have been suggested by any thorn on any down, but familiarity with our author's methods leads us to suppose that a particular thorn tree was before him as he wrote. This was in fact the case. From Upper Bockhampton there is a footpath leading across Kingston Park to Stinsford Church, and here we can see old thorn trees, many of which strike us as reasonably typical."[1] Miss Deacon, shifting Lea's site about a mile and a half, suggests the nature of the heartbreak. She says: "From the top of the path Cuckoo Lane leads downhill to the Yalbury [Yellowham] Bottom of *Under the Greenwood Tree*, and then you are on the Troytown-Puddletown Road, with Dorchester behind you. . . . Can it be doubted that 'She' [called "thee" in the poem] was Tryphena and 'I' was Hardy?"[2] That is, since Tryphena Sparks lived in Puddletown, the woman of the poem may be Tryphena and the thorn may be in Yellowham Wood. If so, the thorn may be the "thin thorn hedge" of "The Mound," which seems to tell the story suggested in the last two lines of "The Voice of the Thorn."

The poem has been set to music by Ivor R. Foster (London: Alfred Lengnick & Co., 1947).

1. *Thomas Hardy's Wessex*, pp. 303, 305.
2. "Thomas Hardy and Tryphena: Her Immortality," unpublished manuscript, pp. 218-19.

FROM HER IN THE COUNTRY suggests a letter to Hardy from a girl in rural Dorset. In 1866 he was corresponding with his sister Mary. Though she was a country girl, no discovered letter from her and nothing known of her suggests a longing for "city din and sin." The writer cannot be Tryphena Sparks, whom Hardy scarcely knew before the autumn of 1867. Read in connection with "Dream of the City Shopwoman," a contrasting "companion" poem on the same subject and given the same date, "From Her in the Country" seems an imaginative presentation of Hardy's view of woman's restless tendency to suppose happiness always somewhere else.[1]

1. A similar theme is found in "Misconception"; it is the attitude of Eustacia Vye in *The Return of the Native*.

HER CONFESSION presents a woman's admission to her lover of her coy maneuver for enhancing his ardor and her "bliss." Evelyn Hardy points out "that Hardy, even at this early age [twenty-five to twenty-seven], could penetrate a woman's mind and interpret her thoughts as well as he could his own."[1]

1. *Thomas Hardy*, p. 65.

TO AN IMPERSONATOR OF ROSALIND is dated *"21st April 1867,"* which identifies the actress as Mrs. Mary Frances Scott-Siddons, who played Rosalind in *As You Like It* at the Haymarket Theatre on Saturday night, April 20. (For Mrs. Scott-Siddons, see the notes on "The Two Rosalinds.") The poem exhibits Hardy's characteristic idealization of a charming woman, saying that the actress embodies the "very, very Rosalind" of Shakespeare's play. This phrase is quoted from Act IV, i.[1]

1. The title of Hardy's *Under the Greenwood Tree* is taken from a song in Act II, v, of *As You Like It*. The novel ends with a nightingale's song interpreted as "Come hither, come hither, come hither!" from the same song.

TO AN ACTRESS, dated 1867, may be addressed to Mrs. Mary Frances Scott-Siddons, whom Hardy saw act Rosalind in *As You Like It* in April of this year. She was unknown to him before this time, as she had begun to act in London only on April 8. The poem seems an idealization: it is not known that he had any acquaintance with her beyond that of a member of the audience. (See the notes on "To an Impersonator of Rosalind" and "The Two Rosalinds.")

THE MINUTE BEFORE MEETING, according to Weber, treats Hardy's third visit to St. Juliot, Cornwall, to see Emma Gifford, whom he had met in March and visited again in August, 1870. "Letters went back and forth between Dorchester (i.e., Bockhampton) and St. Juliot; and gradually, one by one, 'The grey gaunt days dividing us in twain,' and the 'slow blank months' of the winter of 1870-71 passed. In May 1871 there was another visit to Cornwall. Hardy was now almost thirty-one years old, but his desire to marry Miss Gifford was overshadowed by the thought that he had not, thus far, made a real success of anything."[1]

The sonnet portrays a lover's anticipated ecstasy in meeting his beloved, colored by the thought that "in a short space of time the meeting will be over to be followed by dividing months of despondence. He would 'rein back Time,' and love on for ever 'in close expectance, never closed' "[2]—somewhat like the lover in Keats's "Ode on a Grecian Urn."

1. *Hardy's Love Poems*, p. 19.
2. Collins, "The Love Poetry of Thomas Hardy," p. 73.

HE ABJURES LOVE concludes "More Love Lyrics," which present the ecstasies, illusions, and follies of love. Hardy rejects love's idealizations because they are followed by disillusionment.

When, in 1920, Alfred Noyes charged Hardy with pessimism and cited "He Abjures Love," he replied that "The poem called 'He abjures Love,' ending with 'And then the curtain,' is a love-poem, and lovers are chartered irresponsibles."[1] Evelyn Hardy interprets the poem as a mature view of life that Hardy had reached by 1883: "Then suddenly in 1883 we find a beautiful poem compact with certitude and decision, 'He Abjures Love' in which the writer shakes off love's enchantment. . . . Deeply romantic, he has hitherto made love the lodestar of his being: when this fails there is nothing left. . . . Lacking the consolations of religion, with a soul 'laid bare by faith's receding wave' . . . blessed, and at the same time cursed, with excessive sensitivity and compassion for human and animal life, Hardy's only escape was to live as an avowed stoic."[2]

Critics have found "He Abjures Love" "a great poem, gaunt and terrible in thought and movement."[3] Gilbert Murray wrote to Hardy on December 11, 1909: "The poem that really delights me most is 'He Abjures Love.' Perhaps it is the classical scholar that likes it specially. It is so like Horace: the thought, the severity and clearness of form, and the fine stinging rhythm."[4]

"He Abjures Love" has been set to music in *Before and After Summer: Ten Songs for Baritone and Piano* (London: Boosey & Hawkes, 1949).

1. *Later Years*, p. 218; *Life*, p. 409.
2. *Thomas Hardy*, p. 199.
3. Duffin, *Thomas Hardy*, p. 297.
4. In the Dorset County Museum.

A SET OF COUNTRY SONGS

"Let Me Enjoy," the theme-poem of "A Set of Country Songs," lures the reader to find pleasure in the things of the earth. In the seventeen poems that follow, Hardy emphasizes the pleasures of rural life in realistic portrayals of Dorset scenes, places, and experiences. Seven are scenes at Dorchester fair; the other ten remain in the country near Dorchester. The poems present rural life as Hardy knew it from youth ("To Carrey Clavel" and "The Fiddler") to reflective middle age ("The Dark-Eyed Gentleman" and "The Husband's View"). Some of the poems are ballad-like, retelling tales Hardy had heard. Not even "Julie-Jane" is pessimistic in tone, though it tells of two deaths. The series ends with the comedy of "The Homecoming."

LET ME ENJOY appeared in both the *Cornhill* and *Putnam's Magazine* (New York) for April, 1909.[1] Perhaps this poem should include "the Earth" as part of the title, for the last stanza, expressing doubt that Paradise exists, repudiates the idea of any other joy "for me" than that of earth. Life offers "loveliness" to him who, accepting its conditions, can live in dreams; Hardy acknowledges his own somber temperament, but affirms that he "takes pleasure in countless sweet things."[2]

Perhaps because the poem is both a song and a hymn to earth, it is written in the long meter of many hymns. It has been set to music by Ivor R. Foster (London: Alfred Lengnick & Co., 1947) and Gerald Finzi, in *Till Earth Outwears* (London and New York: Boosey and Hawkes, 1958).

1. Purdy, *Thomas Hardy: A Bibliographical Study*, p. 143.
2. Van Doren, "The Poems of Thomas Hardy," p. 95.

AT CASTERBRIDGE FAIR

As "Casterbridge" is Hardy's name for Dorchester, the poems under "At Casterbridge Fair" treat his observations at the annual fair held in Dorchester until the mid-1930's, when automobile traffic through the town caused it to be abandoned. It was originally called Candlemas Fair as it was held in early February;[1] later it came to be called St. Valentine's Fair and held on or near February 14.

A postcard on sale at the Dorset County Museum, picturing a fair held in Dorchester in 1835, portrays booths at the junction of South, High West, High East, and North Streets—beside and in front of St. Peter's Church in the town center.[2] In 1849 a Cornmarket building was erected at the corner of High East and North Streets. In the 1860's a clock tower was placed on this building. The poems refer to these places.

They were hiring-fairs: laboring men who wished to change employers stood on the sidewalks, each with straw, wool, or some other sign of his occupation as haymaker, shepherd, etc. in his hat, to be approached by farmers looking for help. Engagements would be made for work to begin on Lady Day, Old Style, April 6.[3] Usually the fair included a cattle sale. Merrymaking was a popular attraction. Near the Bow, the curved corner at St. Peter's Church, and up and down the streets and into North Square booths were set up for shooting galleries, hawkers, fortune tellers, and sellers of sweetmeats.

As one of the poems, "The Ballad Singer," was dated in the manuscript "1901," and another, "After the Fair," is dated 1902, probably the poems describe incidents at fairs of the period 1900-1902. The fair held in Dorchester on February 14, 1902, is described in the *Dorset County Chronicle* for February 20. "The day was unusually sunny and springlike" with daffodils and violets on sale. The fair was held on "busy, crowded streets," with "rows of canvas-covered stalls for the sale of gingerbread, china, ornaments, and other 'fairings' . . . by the kerbstone in front of St. Peter's Church and the Corn Exchange. . . . A number of cheap-Jacks as usual took their stand in Cornhill [the old name for the northern end of South Street] in front of the Town Pump. . . . The band of the 3rd Battalion Dorset Regiment . . . paraded the streets at intervals, playing lively tunes." There was a bustling sale of cattle, "70 or 80 bulls brought into the ring," besides cows, sheep, and horses.[4]

Of the seven poems under "At Casterbridge Fair," three are not obviously related to the fair, "After the Club-Dance," "The Market-Girl," and "A Wife Waits," though the incidents may be imagined as related to it.

1. Candlemas is February 2.
2. This postcard is reproduced opposite p. 270 of Pinion, *A Hardy Companion*.
3. For Hardy's description of a hiring-fair in Dorchester as held before 1874, the date of the novel, see Chapter VI of *Far from the Madding Crowd*.
4. Clive Holland, commenting upon Hardy's fondness for fairs, describes a visit with him to a fair on Woodbury Hill, near Bere Regis, in September. They bicycled to Bere Regis and walked up the hill. "On reaching the summit I soon realized that Hardy was in his element. Quite a number of the farmers, dealers, and frequenters seemed to know him, and he fell into the vernacular in talking with them. What a crowd it was with the side-shows, a strident band, fat women and a skeleton man, fortune tellers, their little booths crowded with village girls in quest of clues to possible lovers foretold by the nut-brown gipsy-women. . . . And we went to inspect some fine specimens of West of England sheep, and later on refreshed ourselves with some cider and gingerbread." "My Walks and Talks in Wessex with Thomas Hardy," p. 171. See Chapter L of *Far from the Madding Crowd*, in which "Greenhill" is Hardy's name for Woodbury Hill.

The Ballad-Singer was first published in the *Cornhill Magazine* for April, 1902, under the title "At Casterbridge Fair." The manuscript shows the deleted date "1901."[1]

The poem, with its mixture of rollicking tune and the sadness of disappointed love, resembles a ballad; it may express Hardy's feeling while listening to ballads at the fair. He was fond of the poem and suggested that it was a personal expression. In a letter to Edward Thomas on March 3, 1915, he wrote concerning an anthology: "If your book is . . . to illustrate the idiosyncrasy of each writer, I am not sure that they [Thomas's selections] are so good as would be, say, 'When I Set Out for Lyonnesse,' or 'To Meet or Otherwise,' or 'The Ballad-Singer.' "[2]

A musical setting by Angus Maclachlen is in the Dorset County Museum. Hardy wrote to him on December 20, 1910: "I duly received your setting of 'Sing Ballad-Singer' to music. . . . You have selected a poem of mine that I myself like."[3] It was also set to music by Alfred Hale in a series called *At Casterbridge Fair*. The manuscript of this series is in the Colby College Library.

1. Purdy, *Thomas Hardy: A Bibliographical Study*, p. 143.
2. In the Miriam Lutcher Stark Library, University of Texas.
3. In the Yale University Library.

Former Beauties doubtless expresses Hardy's memories as he observed aging "market-dames" at the fair and recalled his and their youth.

The theme is characteristic: the decay of beauty with the passage of time and nostalgia for vanished youth. Can the "market-dames" with "tissues sere" be the "muslined pink young things" of former trysts and dances? The mind falters to acknowledge them the same, and they, too, must have forgotten what they were, or their memory "would transfigure them" in the Biblical sense, perhaps, so spiritualizing them that inner beauty would shine through their aging faces.[1]

The poem has been set to music by Alfred Hale in *At Casterbridge Fair* (in manuscript in the Colby College Library), and Gerald Finzi in *A Young Man's Exhortation* (Oxford University Press, 1933).

1. For a sensitive analysis, see Neumeyer, "The Transfiguring Vision," pp. 263-66.

After the Club-Dance is a woman's meditation upon the sequel to a dance held in Dorchester, as she plods homeward along one of the roads running across Black Down.

The theme of the poem is the young woman's question why she and apparently nature feel shame for her love-making under the influence of the dance and wine. The birds that "eye" her "have done the same." Her meditation is that of Tess in *Tess of the D'Urbervilles*: "Walking among the sleeping birds in the hedges, watching the skipping rabbits on a moonlit warren, or standing under a pheasant-laden bough, she looked upon herself as a figure of Guilt intruding into the haunts of Innocence." Hardy's comment is: "But all the while she was making a distinction where there was no difference. . . . She had been made to break an accepted social law, but no law known to the environment in which she fancied herself such an anomaly." (Chapter XIII.)

The Market-Girl first appeared in an annual called *The Venture*. Laurence Housman, in a letter of July 18, 1903, asked Hardy for a poem for "a literary and artistic annual . . . which I am editing for publication next Christmas." Hardy replied on July 21 that he "might find a small song or poem of some sort of two or three stanzas."[1] Housman wrote again on September 1 to remind Hardy, who on September 2 sent "The Market Girl (Country Song)."

The location is Dorchester, perhaps on South Street near High West, where farmers still bring produce for sale at the "causey kerb," beside a street paved with cobblestones in Hardy's time.

"The Market-Girl" has been set to music by Arnold Bax (London: Murdock, Murdock, & Co., 1922), Gerald Finzi in *Till Earth Outwears* (London and New York: Boosey and Hawkes, 1958), and Alfred Hale in *At Casterbridge Fair* (in manuscript in the Colby College Library).

1. In the Dorset County Museum.

The Inquiry is a dramatic monologue spoken by Patty Beech to someone from "Hermitage, by Ivel Road" whom she met at a fair in Dorchester. That the poem names people and places suggests a factual basis, perhaps an overheard conversation. The names may be fictional. (I see no connection between John Waywood and John Wayward of "The Workbox.") Patty Beech's questions are those any woman might ask of an acquaintance from the village about a lover not heard from for fifteen years. Hermitage is actual, but it is not "by Ivel Road." ("Ivel" is Hardy's name for Yeovil.) It is a village in Blackmoor Vale about ten miles north and slightly west of Dorchester and about a mile west of the road from Dorchester to Sherborne. (Hardy often moved locations a few miles when he mingled fact and fiction.)

A few phrases in Dorset dialect—"sengreens" (house-leeks), "hurdled" (made sheep pens of horizontal bars interwoven with strips of hazel or willow wood), and "fag" (tiring labor) —give a sense of reality to Patty Beech's speech. The statement that "Time, that dooms man's love to die, / Preserves a maid's alive" is characteristic of Hardy.

"The Inquiry" has been set to music by Alfred Hale in *At Casterbridge Fair* (in manuscript in the Colby College Library).

A Wife Waits in the manuscript had the title "Waiting."[1] Hardy's note about "The Bow" is not now needed. At his insistence upon the value of traditional names, "the curved corner by the crossstreets in the middle of Casterbridge" has been renamed "The Bow."[2] The "Club-room below" has been identified by Hermann Lea as one now "swept away. It stood facing onto North Square," half a block from The Bow.[3] Hardy's specific locations suggest that he may have observed the waiting wife and heard her story.

"A Wife Waits" has been set to music by Alfred Hale in *At Casterbridge Fair* (in manuscript in the Colby College Library).

1. Purdy, *Thomas Hardy: A Bibliographical Study*, p. 144.
2. See a letter by Hardy to Pearce Edgcumbe, dated Saturday (1895?) in the Miriam Lutcher Stark Library, the University of Texas.
3. *Thomas Hardy's Wessex*, p. 305.

After the Fair pictures the merrymaking at the fair in Dorchester, the departure of the visitors toward midnight, and the "ghosts" that, in Hardy's imagination, haunt the ancient town and recall its merrymaking as far back as Roman times. "This Roman note at the end of the composition seems almost a 'fundamental tone' from which result the 'overtones' of later history."[1]

The fairs in Dorchester were held in Cornmarket Place at the "Cross" of the main streets in the center of town. Here the streets rang in the "treble and bass" of singers presenting "their broadsheets of rhymes" and "skits on the times"—ballads and comic songs on perhaps political subjects. The "stammering chimes" were those of St. Peter's Church which, before World War I, played secular music as well as hymns.[2] "Clock-corner steps" was across North Street from St. Peter's, where the Corn Exchange now stands.[3]

In the poem, Hardy follows the "folk" down High East Street to the "Hart" and Grey's Bridge. The "Hart" is the White Hart Tavern at the foot of High East,[4] just where the street crosses a bridge over a branch of the Frome. Beyond this bridge a few hundred yards is Grey's Bridge, and beyond that the countryside where people disperse "into byways and 'drongs' " (narrow lanes between hedgerows), each person reacting to the recent merriment as his temperament demands.

Returning to the site of the fair, the poet seems to see the ghosts of merrymakers there through the centuries back to the Roman occupation of Durnovaria (Dorchester) and shows them all "just as these."[5]

"After the Fair" has been set to music by Alfred Hale in *At Casterbridge Fair* (in manuscript in the Colby College Library).

1. Hogan, "Structural Design in Thomas Hardy's Poetry," p. 83.
2. During the war the bells were not rung for security reasons, and since the war they have been rung only for church purposes. In *The Mayor of Casterbridge*, Chapter IV, these "chimes were heard stammering out the Sicilian Mariners' Hymn."
3. Lea says: "*Clock-corner steps* . . . has been altered too completely to allow us to trace any similarity between it and the steps which now lead into the Corn Exchange." *Thomas Hardy's Wessex*, p. 307.
4. In *Far from the Madding Crowd*, Chapter LII, Troy meets Pennyways at the Hart.
5. *The Mayor of Casterbridge*, Chapter XI, presents a detailed picture of this

vision: "Casterbridge announced old Rome in every street, alley, and precinct," etc.

THE DARK-EYED GENTLEMAN is a humorous "country song," with the lilt and substance of a ballad, but with a happy ending not common in ballads of seduction. Its stanzas present three stages in the singer's life: the seduction, the consequent shame, and the later realization that the seduction brought at last the blessing of "a fine lissom lad / . . . comrade, and friend."

The singer is a country woman, a day-laborer, and her seducer a gentleman. The theme is the growth of the girl into a mature woman with the strength to recover from "ruin" and the good sense to form, from her experience, a conclusion contrary to the conventions. This theme is stated in a passage in *The Early Life* that may be Hardy's source. In December of 1882, "Hardy was told a story by a Mrs. Cross, a very old country-woman he met, of a girl who had been betrayed and deserted by a lover. She kept her child by her own exertions, and lived bravely and throve. After a time the man returned poorer than she, and wanted to marry her; but she refused. . . . The young woman's conduct in not caring to be 'made respectable' won the novelist-poet's admiration . . . . and he made use of it in succeeding years in more than one case in his fiction and verse."[1]

In spite of its tragic ending, *Tess of the D'Urbervilles* suggests that sexual misfortune *can* be a kind of fortunate fall. Tess "became what would have been called a fine creature; her aspect was fair and arresting; her soul that of a woman whom the turbulent experiences of the last year or two had quite failed to demoralize. But for the world's opinion those experiences would have been simply a liberal education." (Chapter XV.)

Crimmercrock Lane is an ancient country track leading from Kingcombe across thinly populated country to Rampisham.[2] "Crimmercrock" is a rural corruption of the medieval name, Cromlech Crock Lane.

"The Dark-Eyed Gentleman" has been set to music by Hubert James Foss in *Seven Poems by Thomas Hardy Set to Music* (London: Oxford University Press, 1925).

1. Pp. 203-4; *Life*, p. 157.
2. Kingcombe is about ten miles northwest of Dorchester on Road 356 from Maiden Newton to Crewkerne. Rampisham is about a mile northeast of Kingcombe.

TO CARREY CLAVEL is a humorous lyric monologue of the taunting trick by which a would-be lover perhaps wins a kiss from coy Carrey. The poem is given a rural flavor by the dialect words "Dew-beating" (walking with large, flapping feet) and "coll" (embrace). The poem has been set to music by Arnold Bax (London: Murdock,

Murdock & Co., 1926) and Mary Sheldon (in manuscript in the Dorset County Museum and the Colby College Library).

THE ORPHANED OLD MAID is a monologue in the speech of a country woman. The poem is "saved from sentimentality by terse treatment and from sketchiness by rural realism."[1]

1. Hogan, "Structural Design in Thomas Hardy's Poetry," p. 210.

THE SPRING CALL was first printed in the *Cornhill Magazine* for May, 1906.[1] It exhibits Hardy's interest in both dialectal accents and the songs of birds. The poem suggests that he had not listened to blackbirds in Scotland and Ireland, but had discussed their notes with friends from these lands. His interest in the songs of birds is stated in a note in *The Early Life* made in 1868: "In April he was . . . taking down the exact sound of the song of the nightingale—the latter showing that he must have been living in sylvan shades at his parents', or at least sleeping there, at the time, where nightingales sang within a yard of the bedroom windows in those days."[2]

1. Purdy, *Thomas Hardy: A Bibliographical Study*, p. 144.
2. P. 76; *Life*, p. 57.

JULIE-JANE is a dramatic monologue in which an old friend of the dead girl tells her life-story to a stranger who had known her "in maidhood."

Edmund Gosse stated Hardy's attitude toward such a girl as Julie-Jane, who on her death-bed would choose her bearers "From her fancy-men." Hardy "is pleased sometimes to act as a fiddler at a dance, surveying the hot-blooded couples, and urging them on by the lilt of his instrument, but he is always perfectly aware that they will have 'to pay high for their prancing' at the end of all."[1] The poem suggests the hypnotic power of music and dancing that Hardy treated in the short story "The Fiddler of the Reels." He felt, it would seem, that those die young to whom the gods give the gifts of ecstasy and indiscretion.

In July, 1893, when Hardy was calling on Lady Londonderry, "The Duchess of Manchester . . . called. . . . It may be mentioned here that after the Duchess of Manchester's death later Hardy described her as having been when he first knew her 'a warm-natured woman, laughing-eyed, and bubbling with impulses, in temperament very much like "Julie Jane" in one of my poems.' "[2]

The poem employs an interesting device: "Sing," "Dance," and "Laugh," introducing the first three stanzas, convey the narrator's wonder at Julie-Jane's capacity for joy which, in the final stanza, mocks at death.

1. "The Lyrical Poetry of Thomas Hardy," p. 252.
2. *Later Years*, p. 23; *Life*, pp. 257-58.

NEWS FOR HER MOTHER is a girl's song-like soliloquy as she races home after a lovers' tryst where she became engaged. Her ecstasy is mingled with two sobering questions: will beloved "Mother mine" approve my choice? and will my marriage "sunder / Her from me"? The trochaics of the poem, which Hardy seldom wrote, convey the girl's leaping ecstasy as she is bounding home "Like a ball or leaf or lamb along the ground."

THE FIDDLER expresses a fiddler's half-rueful exultation in his power to stir dancing couples to emotional madness. Elliott points out that "Music and dancing have a delirious influence on Hardy's women. Cytherea [in *Desperate Remedies*] is overcome by Manston's organ playing, and soon submits to his love entreaties. It is at an open air dance that Wildeve [in *The Return of the Native*] recaptures Eustacia's heart after she had married Clym. In 'The History of the Hardcomes' music plays havoc with four lovers, who are so acted upon by emotion that they marry the wrong cross partners, only to realize the error when it is too late. Poor Car'line cannot resist Ollamoor, 'The Fiddler of the Reels,' when he fiddles, although she despises him at all other times."[1] "The Romantic Adventures of a Milkmaid" might be added to the list.

"The Fiddler" has been set to music by Frederic Austin in *Three Wessex Songs* (London and New York: Boosey & Co., 1927).

1. *Fatalism in the Works of Thomas Hardy*, pp. 94-95.

THE HUSBAND'S VIEW presents a miniature drama, potentially tragic, but with a happy ending because the husband is unusually magnanimous. The poem may be considered a "companion" to "A Wife and Another," which reverses the situation. Duffin remarks that "These cold eugenic husbands and wives do not often get into literature, but they are as interesting as the jealous ones, and more original."[1] They are not frequent in Hardy's realistic presentation of men and women. Woman's concealment of a "past" is fatal in the cases of Elfride in *A Pair of Blue Eyes* and Tess in *Tess of the D'Urbervilles*.

1. *Thomas Hardy*, p. 322.

ROSE-ANN is a dramatic monologue spoken by a guileless man deceived by a flirt. He was deceived because of idealism like that of Clym in *The Return of the Native*, who shut his ears to all he heard against Eustacia and even, like the man in the poem, quarrelled with his mother about her. In "The Tree of Knowledge,"[1] Hardy joined a group of writers in a discussion of the need for sexual education for girls. Recommending "a plain handbook on natural processes," he said that also "Innocent youths should . . . receive the same instruction; for . . . it has never struck me that the spider is invariably male and the fly invariably female." ("At the Altar Rail" presents a similar situation.)

"Rose-Ann" has been set to music by Mary Sheldon (in manuscript dated 1925 in the Dorset County Museum and in Colby College Library), Alfred M. Hale, Opus 32, No. 7 (London: Goodwin & Tabb, 1926), and Ivor R. Foster (London: Alfred Lengnick & Co., 1947).

1. *New Review*, June, 1894, p. 681.

THE HOMECOMING, written in December, 1901, first appeared in the *Graphic* for Christmas, 1903.[1] It is a humorous, ballad-like poem "with a Teniers picture in every stanza."[2] The italicized lines provide a refrain typical of the ballad. In this refrain the wind is personified as a growling, ghostly menace: it "swears things" down the chimney. As the bride may have heard and the groom acknowledges, Toller Down is "known to be haunted."[3] This wind is the villain, supported by the lonely setting and the young bride's naïveté. But the villain is vanquished in the last stanza by the bridegroom's good nature: "That's right, my Heart!"

Lea says: "Toller Down was chosen by our author with due regard to effect. It is a lonesome spot, quite sufficient in itself to explain the utter feeling of isolation which gripped the bride on her introduction to the wind-swept upland. . . . If we visit Toller Down in the autumn or winter we shall have little difficulty in proving to ourselves the truth contained in our author's description of the spot. The boisterous wind, howling, driving before it everything movable, cutting like a knife over the ridges, forming a concentrated draught through the valleys and cuttings, hurries away down 'Crimmercrock's long lane.' "[4]

Toller Down is a ridge with a peak about 825 feet high, about half a mile west of the gap called Toller Down Gate. From its peak the Down drops gradually in every direction. The Gate is fourteen miles northwest of Dorchester on the road between Maiden Newton and Crewkerne.

Apparently the bride, married in "Ivel Church," comes to her isolated home—"how strange and far"—from the city of Yeovil, some ten miles to the north, a long way from "dear daddee" in the days before automobiles.

The winter wind blasts across Toller Down from Whitesheet Hill near Maiden Newton, six miles to the southeast, across the valleys to Benville Lane, which crosses the main road here. It seems to whirl around the house in gusts and then to plunge again southward toward "Crimmercrock's long lane."

The bridegroom's dialect, as well as his old-fashioned food and furnishings, may be part of the setting that frightens the bride. She is not used to "skimmer cake" (a pudding cooked on the utensil used for skimming milk) or to the "summat strong . . . under stairs" (probably cider). To her husband, she is a "poppet" (a doll: a rural endearment).

"The Homecoming" has been set to music by Gustav Holst (London: Steiner and Bell, 1913).

1. Purdy, *Thomas Hardy: A Bibliographical Study*, p. 144.
2. Blunden, *Thomas Hardy*, p. 253.
3. Firor, *Folkways in Thomas Hardy*, p. 75. The image of the wind as a blasphemous ghost occurs in the description of a storm in *The Woodlanders*: ". . . as the storm went on it was difficult to believe that no opaque body, but only an invisible colourless thing, was trampling and climbing over the roof, making branches creak, springing out of the trees upon the chimney, popping its head into the flue, and shrieking and blaspheming at every corner of the walls . . . a spectre which could be felt but not seen." Chapter XLI.
4. *Thomas Hardy's Wessex*, p. 307.

PIECES OCCASIONAL AND VARIOUS

A CHURCH ROMANCE first appeared in the *Saturday Review* for September 8, 1906.[1] It was later included in that portion of *The Early Life* which treats the youth of Hardy's parents, for it tells the story of their meeting.

In the early 1830's, Thomas Hardy the first, the poet's grandfather, led the choir at Stinsford Church, playing the 'cello. The other instrumentalists were his sons, Thomas and James, and a man named James Dart, all playing the violin. This choir performed twice each Sunday in the now-demolished West Gallery of the Church.

"The second Thomas Hardy, the author's father, was a man who in his prime could be, and was, called handsome. To the courtesy of his manners there was much testimony among the local county-ladies with whom he came in contact as a builder. . . . He was about five feet nine in height, of good figure, with dark Vandyke-brown hair, and a beard which he wore cut back all round in the custom of his date; with teeth that were white and regular to nearly the last years of his life, and blue eyes that never faded grey; a quick step, and a habit of bearing his head a little to one side as he walked."

Hardy's mother, born Jemima Hand, "was rather below the middle height with chestnut hair and grey eyes, and a trim and upright figure. Her movement also in walking being buoyant through life, strangers approaching her from behind imagined themselves, even when she was nearly seventy, about to overtake quite a young woman. The Roman nose and countenance inherited from her mother would better have suited a taller build. Like her mother, too, she read omnivorously. She sang songs of the date, such as the then popular Haynes Bayly's 'Isle of Beauty,' and 'Gaily the Troubadour.' "

In 1835 or 1836,[2] Miss Hand came to live near Bockhampton and attended Stinsford Church. At this time, Hardy's father was about twenty-five years old, and his mother was about twenty-three. They were married in 1839.

The Early Life gives the details of the meeting: "Mrs. Hardy once described him [Hardy's father] to her son as he was when she first set eyes on him in the now removed west gallery of Stinsford Church, appearing to her more travelled glance (she had lived for a time in London, Weymouth, and other towns) and somewhat satirical vision, 'rather amusingly old-fashioned, in spite of being decidedly good-looking—wearing the blue swallow-tailed coat with gilt embossed buttons then customary, a red and black flowered waistcoat, Wellington boots, and French-blue trousers.' "[3]

Baker calls the last five lines of the poem a tribute to "a life-loyalty which grows out of an individual dramatic vision. . . . The 'Church Romance' is notable for its success in presenting a very complicated scene and then in moving easily to the later recapitulation of it. In such a recapitulation the sheer evocatory power that comes from naming the old music is apparent. The transition, however, could never have been accomplished without the compression achieved in the one line: 'Thus their hearts' bond began, in due time signed.' Similar compression also appears in the next line, in the phrase 'when Age had scared Romance.' "[4]

Biographers have surmised that Hardy made use of the church romance in his first unpublished novel, *The Poor Man and the Lady*.[5] He published a rescued fragment of this novel as *An Indiscretion in the Life of an Heiress* in which the following sentences appear in the opening chapter: "Now a close observer, who should have happened to be near the large pew, might have noticed before the light got low that the interested gaze of the young man had been returned from time to time by the young lady, although he, towards whom her glances were directed, did not perceive the fact."

1. Purdy, *Thomas Hardy: A Bibliographical Study*, p. 144.
2. As still published in collections, the event of the poem is dated " (Mellstock:

circa 1835)," but as published in *The Early Life*, the date is corrected to " (*Mell-stock, circa* 1836)." "Mellstock" is Hardy's name for Stinsford.

3. *Early Life*, pp. 16-18; *Life*, pp. 13-14.
4. "Hardy's Poetic Certitude," pp. 60-61.
5. See Evelyn Hardy, *Thomas Hardy*, p. 10.

THE RASH BRIDE first appeared in the Christmas Number of the *Graphic*, 1902.[1] It is a reminiscent monologue by a member of the Mellstock Quire (Choir).

The Mellstock Quire is defined in *Under the Greenwood Tree*.[2] The instrumentalists of the Quire are: elderly William Dewy, leader of the Quire, who plays the bass violincello; his son Reuben Dewy, the tenor violinist; Dick Dewy, Reuben's son, the treble violinist; elderly Michael Mail, the second violinist; Robert Penny, boot- and shoemaker; Elias Spinks, a former schoolmaster; Joseph Bowman; and feeble-minded Thomas Leaf. As the action of *Under the Greenwood Tree* takes place at the time Mellstock Church abandoned instrumentalists in favor of an harmonium, the events of "The Rash Bride" took place earlier. "Mellstock" is a fictional name for Stinsford, and the instrumentalists of the Quire seem based in part upon the choir of Stinsford Church, who about 1835 were Thomas Hardy the First, Thomas Hardy the Second, James Hardy (Hardy's grandfather, father, and uncle), and James Dart. "Conducting the church choir all the year round involved carol-playing and singing at Christmas, which Thomas Hardy the Second loved as much as did his father." After the death of Thomas Hardy the First in 1837, "The practice was kept up by Thomas Hardy the Second, much as described in *Under the Greenwood Tree* . . . though its author, Thomas Hardy the Third, invented the personages, incidents, manners, etc., never having seen or heard the choir as such, they ending their office when he was about a year old," that is, about 1841.[3]

These facts suggest some basis for "The Rash Bride" in a reminiscence of Hardy's father, either of his own experience or one handed down from Hardy's grandfather. The "I" of the poem may be either man at an age to regard young John as a "boy." The geography of the poem indicates Stinsford Parish; the name Michael suggests Michael Mail, and "Our old bass player," William Dewy of *Under the Greenwood Tree*. The "Vale" is the valley of the Frome. John (a singer, not an instrumentalist) and the widow have not been identified, but Giles Swetman from "Woolcomb Way" may be a distant relative of Hardy's, whose maternal grandmother was born Elizabeth Swetman of Melbury Osmund.[4] Woolcombe (as now spelled) is a village about three quarters of a mile northeast of Evershot, and about two and a quarter miles southeast of Melbury Osmund.[5] The "Ninetieth Psalm . . . to Saint Stephen's tune" is the well-known hymn, "O, God, Our Help in Ages Past," sung at Hardy's funeral as one of his favorites.

The "sesquipedalian" meter of "The Rash Bride," with its "quasi-triple internal rhyme" has been judged "more appropriate to the idyllic beginning than to the tragic ending." [6]

1. Purdy, *Thomas Hardy: A Bibliographical Study*, p. 145.

2. In manuscript, this novel had at first the title *The Mellstock Quire or Under the Greenwood Tree*, altered to *Under the Greenwood Tree or The Mellstock Quire*. In his Preface of April, 1912, Hardy wrote: ". . . the exhibition of the Mellstock Quire in the following pages must remain the only extant one, except for the few glimpses of that perished band which I have given in verse elsewhere."

3. *Early Life*, pp. 12-15; *Life*, pp. 9-12.

4. Hardy's pedigree, listing the Swetmans among his ancestors, does not mention a Giles Swetman. See Evelyn Hardy, *Thomas Hardy*, facing p. 224. Giles is a frequent first name in the Melbury Osmund registers.

5. Woolcombe lies about twelve miles north and slightly west of Dorchester. In his diary for September 30, 1888, Hardy recorded: "In the afternoon by train to Evershot. Walked to Woolcombe, a property once owned by a—I think the senior—branch of the Hardys." *Early Life*, p. 281; *Life*, p. 214.

6. Duffin, *Thomas Hardy*, pp. 303, 322.

THE DEAD QUIRE was first printed in the Christmas Number of the *Graphic*, 1901.[1] The poem treats, as a story told by the "sad man," a ghostly reappearance of the Mellstock Quire (Choir). Hardy as a youth heard tales of this Quire from his elders. Then the poem may dramatize the sad man as an oldster with the boy Hardy as a listener. The sad man may represent Hardy himself, speaking to an unidentified listener. He is saddened by the passing of an older social order and the rise of a generation irreverent toward both their fathers' pattern of life and Christianity. That the young people in the "dormered inn" are engaged in merrymaking is not the point. The old Quire enjoyed dancing, singing, and drinking homemade mead and cider. The point is suggested by the *bawdy* revelry on Christ's birth-night, climaxed by a toast not to Christ, but to John Barleycorn. When the Mellstock Quire was alive, there was a time and place for reverence and another for merrymaking. In *Under the Greenwood Tree*, old William Dewy will not allow his grandson Dick even to tune his violin for dancing until after the festival of Christ's birth-day is over: " 'Dick! Now I cannot—really, I cannot have any dancing at all till Christmas-day is out,' said old William emphatically. 'When the clock ha' done striking twelve, dance as much as ye like.' " (Part the First, Chapter VII.)

Though the story is a fantasy, it is realistic in its persons and places. The action takes place in Lower Bockhampton, along a path beside a branch of the Frome River, and in Stinsford Churchyard.

Hardy based each member of the dead Quire upon an actual person buried there. He created old William Dewy in writing *Under the Greenwood Tree* and treated him repeatedly, in *Tess of the D'Urbervilles* and in other poems and stories. Where "The Dead Quire" reads "Old Dewy lay by the gaunt yew tree," dairyman Crick of *Tess* says: "I can tell you to a foot where he's a-lying in Mellstock Churchyard at this very moment—just between the second yew-tree and the north aisle."[2] *The Early Life* states that "tranter" Reuben Dewy, presented as William's son, was created from a person Hardy knew. In 1872, "Hardy received an account of the death of 'The Tranter,' after whom the character in *Under the Greenwood Tree* had been called, though it was not a portrait, nor was the fictitious tranter's kinship to the other musicians based on fact. He had been the many years' neighbour of the Hardys and did the haulage of building materials for Hardy's father, of whom he also rented a field for his horses."[3] Michael is Michael Mail of *Under the Greenwood Tree*. As Bowman appears in this novel, he was probably a real person presented under a fictitious name, as Robert Reason was.[4] The singers, who "had followed one by one" the instrumentalists to their graves, consisted in the novel of "four men and seven boys." (Part the First, Chapter IV.) The characters in the tavern, Eliza, Dolly, Nance, Joan, the widow, and the "sons and grandsons" of the Quire, represent the younger generation, possibly real persons.

The places are *all* actual, though Hardy gives them only descriptive names. The "Mead of Memories" must be the wide meadow beside the Frome and its bywaters down the hill below Stinsford Church. "Church-way" is Church Lane (so named in stanza XX) that winds up the hill from a branch of the Frome to the Churchyard. "Moaning Hill" seems to be the wooded ground rising northwest of Stinsford Church and House.[5] At the end of the poem the sad man presumably goes down Church Lane and across a pasture to the Mead of Memories.

The action of the story begins "three meadows off" from Church Lane at a "dormered inn." This inn is now a private dwelling, still dormered and thatched, just north of a branch of the Frome in Lower Bockhampton. It faces the road through the village (in the poem an "empty highway") that runs between Higher Bockhampton and West Stafford. A few hundred feet south of the inn, the road crosses a stone bridge over a branch of the river. Crossing this bridge the revellers turn to the right (westward) to follow the Spirits along a footpath ("Bank-walk") for about half a mile to "Bank-walk wicket," a gate at the foot of Church Lane. On the way they pass hedge-rows separating three fields.[6] They turn to the right, cross a footbridge, and go up Church Lane to the Churchyard with its old yew trees and tombstones.

This action follows that of the Mellstock Quire in *Under the Greenwood Tree*. The dead Quire is heard as only ghostly voices at midnight; in the novel, as the Quire begins its rounds, old William Dewy says, "Now mind, neighbours . . . go quietly, so as to strike up all of a sudden, like spirits." After the midnight song, the Quire of the novel goes to Mellstock (Stinsford) Churchyard for refreshments, following exactly the route of "The Dead Quire": "They now crossed Mellstock Bridge, and went along an embowered path beside the Froom towards the church and vicarage, meeting Voss with the hot mead and bread-and-cheese as they were approaching the churchyard." (Part the First, Chapters IV and V.)

1. Purdy, *Thomas Hardy: A Bibliographical Study*, p. 145.

2. Chapter XVII. In the margin of her copy of *Tess*, Rebekah Owen wrote: "Mr. Hardy said: 'There was something like this once.' William Dewy and the 'Tivity Hymn played to the bull are founded on fact." In the Colby College Library.

3. P. 121; *Life*, p. 92.

4. That Hardy used real characters in Stinsford Churchyard in his fiction is stated in *The Later Years*: "On October 9 . . . he walked to Stinsford in the morning. The bright sunlight shone across the face of a worn tomb whose lettering Hardy had often endeavoured to decipher, so that he might recarve the letters with his penknife. This day, owing to the sunlight, they were able to read: SACRED / to the memory of / ROBERT REASON / who departed this life / December 26th 1819 / Aged 56 years / Dear friend you should mourn for me / I am where you soon must be.—Although Robert Reason had died twenty years before the birth of the author of *Under the Greenwood Tree*, he was faithfully described in that novel as Mr. Penny, the shoemaker, Hardy having heard so much of him from old inhabitants of Bockhampton." Pp. 242-43; *Life*, pp. 428-29.

5. This hill rises across a road from the present farmhouse; the main approach is still through meadows. Lea says that Hardy calls it " 'Moaning Hill' . . . doubtless from the weird sound made by the wind as it passes among the twigs and branches of the clump of chestnut trees just in front." *Thomas Hardy's Wessex*, p. 309.

6. Lea has a picture of "Church Lane, Stinsford" as Plate 239, p. 311; of the "dormered inn" as "Cottage, Once an Inn, Lower Bockhampton," as Plate 236, p. 310; of "The Bridge and Riverside House, Lower Bockhampton," as Plate 97, p. 121; and of "The Path Beside the River, Lower Bockhampton," as Plate 237, p. 310, in *Thomas Hardy's Wessex*.

THE CHRISTENING opens with a question, "Whose child is this. . . ?" to which the only answer is that the mother is an unmarried girl and the father is a lover who disdains marriage.[1] The scene may be in St. Mary's Church in Puddletown, one of the few churches near Dorchester that still has, near the entrance to the church, a "gallery stair" to a musicians' gallery.[2]

One theme of the poem is implied in the action: nature does not penalize a mother for being unmarried. The child is "superb," and the mother's love and dainty care for it are evident. She states a second theme in reply to "Where is the baby's father?" This unconventional man "In the woods afar" loves the girl with a feeling that would die if he and she were "chained and doomed for life / . . . As vulgar man and wife."

Hardy understood the temperamental differences between human beings who might love one another but could not be happy if "chained" together. *Tess of the D'Urbervilles* presents Tess as spiritually deepened, rather than depraved, by her experience in bearing Alec's child. In *Jude the Obscure*, Sue expresses an idea that runs all through the novel: "If the marriage ceremony consisted in an oath and signed contract between the parties to cease loving from that day forward, in consideration of personal possession being given, and to avoid each other's society as much as possible in public, there would be more loving couples than there are now." (Part V, Chapter I. See also an amusing story told of Bathsheba's father in Chapter VIII of *Far from the Madding Crowd*.)

This is not to say that Hardy, twice married, opposed marriage. His attack is rather upon the Victorian prudery that held any unmarried mother "ruined" and shameless, and that bound together any married couple, however discordant, by the threat of public disgrace.

1. Deacon and Coleman, *Providence and Mr Hardy*, pp. 204-5, provide an identity for mother and father, but the evidence is not altogether convincing.

2. Lea pictures the gallery and stairs of this church as Plate 32, p. 39, in *Thomas Hardy's Wessex*. See also the frontispiece of Evelyn Hardy, *Thomas Hardy*. This gallery seems the one in *Far from the Madding Crowd* that Sergeant Troy said he used in attending church unseen. Chapter XXIX.

A DREAM QUESTION, stating a theological problem insoluble to logic, treats a conversation between the poet and the Lord. By presenting it as a dream, Hardy can state the question without being responsible for an answer.

As the motto from Micah suggests, the poem seems to be the fruit of his reading in the Old Testament and judging its Hebraic concepts of God as jealous and wrathful in the light of nineteenth-century rationalism. Suggesting that in the government of the world God shapes "griefs and ails untold," he asks whether, as Moses wrote, God rages at His creatures' "censure."[1] His sample of this censure paraphrases J. S. Mill's statement in the essay "Nature": "Not even on the most distorted and contracted theory of good which was ever framed by religious or philosophical fanaticism, can the government of Nature be made to resemble the work of a being at once good and omnipotent."

God denies the wrathfulness attributed to Him by the prophets. He does not care "what my creatures say," but He cannot explain the antinomy—an ethic beyond good and evil, justice and injustice—to a mind that cannot comprehend a fourth dimension.

1. Possibly Hardy had in mind Deut. 1:34, "And the Lord heard the voice of your words, and was wroth," and 9:19, "For I was afraid of the anger and hot displeasure, wherewith the Lord was wroth against you to destroy you."

BY THE BARROWS, in specifying a place "Not far from Mellstock" and stating that a woman "in our modern age" fought there "to shield a child," seems to tell a factual story.

"Mellstock" is Hardy's name for Stinsford. How far from Stinsford the battles took place and in what direction are not specified. Prehistoric hill-forts and burial tumuli are scattered throughout the countryside. One possibility is the group of barrows called Rainbarrow on Puddletown Heath. This spot is prominent in *The Return of the Native* and *The Dynasts*, but the line comparing the barrows with bosoms "Of Multimammia stretched supinely there" echoes *The Mayor of Casterbridge*. In their search for Henchard, Elizabeth-Jane and Farfrae leave the "Melchester" (Salisbury) road at Weatherbury (Puddletown) and take a forking road that goes across "Egdon" toward "Anglebury" (Wareham). They pass tumuli that are like "the full breasts of Diana Multimammia supinely extended there" (Chapter XLV)—almost the words of the poem. These tumuli may be the barrows of Southover Heath, nearly two miles southeast of Puddletown and four miles east of Stinsford. In *Tess of the D'Urbervilles*, when Tess is on her way to Flintcomb-Ash, "she reached the irregular chalk table-land or plateau, bosomed with semi-globular tumuli—as if Cybele the Many-breasted were supinely extended there." (Chapter XLII.) This is an area near Dole's Ash Farm, about six miles north of Stinsford, but the area around Flintcomb-Ash is not generally called "The He'th." Most likely, in spite of Hardy's "Multimammia" in *The Mayor* and *Tess*, he had in mind Rainbarrow.

The poem balances a battle between patriots fighting for home, it would seem, and a woman's struggle to shield a child. The theme is that the woman's selfless courage had moral value beyond all military heroism.

A WIFE AND ANOTHER moved Edmund Gosse to write: "Mr. Hardy, indeed, is not concerned with sentimental morals, but with the primitive instincts of the soul, applauding them, or at least recording them with complacency, even when they outrage ethical tradition."[1] Hardy did hold radical views about marriage, expressed in his contribution to a symposium on "How Shall We Solve the the Divorce Problem?" Hardy's statement, titled "Laws the Cause of Misery," reads: "As the present marriage laws are . . . the gratuitous cause of at least half the misery of the community, that they are allowed to remain in force for a day is, to quote the famous last words of the ceremony itself, an 'amazement,' and can only be accounted for by the assumption that we live in a barbaric age, and are the slaves of gross superstition."[2]

Concerning the story of the poem, Deacon and Coleman suggest that the wife's opening speech is addressed to her servant, the husband's mistress, and that the wife is Julia Augusta Martin.[3]

The poem may be considered a companion to "The Burghers," with the roles of husband and wife reversed. Hardy's novels contain numerous comments upon the theme of "A Wife and Another." In *The Woodlanders*, for instance, Grace feels sympathetic toward her husband's two mistresses, Suke Damson and Mrs. Charmond, when the three women come together at Fitzpiers's bedside: "A tenderness spread over Grace like a dew. It was well enough, conventionally, to address either one of them in the wife's regulation terms of virtuous sarcasm, as woman, creature, or thing. But life, what was it, after all? She had, like the singer of the Psalm of Asaph, been plagued and chastened all the day long; but could she, by retributive words, in order to please herself, the individual, 'offend against the generation,' as that singer would not?" (Chapter XXXV.) The theme is discussed at length in *Jude the Obscure*.

1. "The Lyrical Poetry of Thomas Hardy," p. 251.
2. In *Nash's Magazine*, March, 1912, and Orel, *Thomas Hardy's Personal Writings*, p. 252.
3. *Providence and Mr Hardy*, pp. 173-74. The basis for this identification seems more surmise than conclusive evidence.

THE ROMAN ROAD presents an incident of Hardy's childhood with his mother and the vision that arose when she told him the story of the half-obliterated road on which they walked across the heath. The poem is also a tribute to his mother, of whom he wrote to Rowland Grey in 1922: "I . . . still regard my mother as one whose intellect, and judgment, and character-reading powers were much above my own."[1]

The course of the Roman Road leading northeastward from Dorchester passes about a quarter of a mile south of Hardy's birthplace and then mounts the hill into Puddletown Heath (a portion of "Egdon"). Though now reforested, the Heath was largely bare during his boyhood, and the Road wherever possible was straight. His image of the Road as a "pale parting-line in hair" seems a recurrent memory, for he used it in *The Return of the Native* to describe a road across Egdon Heath; it "bisected that vast dark surface like the parting-line on a head of black hair."[2]

1. Grey, "A Letter from Thomas Hardy," p. 226.
2. Part the First, Chapter II. Hardy used a similar image in the serial version of *The Woodlanders* (removed from later editions), where the wood of the opening scene is "bisected by the highway, as a head of thick hair is bisected by the white line of its parting." See Kramer, "Repetition of Imagery in Thomas Hardy," p. 26.

THE VAMPIRINE FAIR is a reminiscent monologue that tells a ballad-like tale. The callous depravity of the narrator and the consequent horror of the story are relieved by Hardy's grotesque humor. The woman finds it only "touching" that, as her lord lay dying, he gazed "With love upon me still" while she searched for his "letters, keys, or will."

The woman's cottage on the estate of "My Lord" is evidently in the "Coomb" or valley southeast of Win Green ("Wingreen") Hill, an eminence about five miles southeast of Shaftesbury ("Shastonb'ry" in the poem).[1] The "Manor Court" is apparently Rushmore House (now a school), about two miles southeast of Win Green Hill, or a mile from the "Coomb." The "steeple-cock" that "gleamed golden" in the afternoon sunlight is the weather-vane still to be seen on an old stable behind Rushmore House, and so visible from the bedroom in which the lord lay dying. This precision in locating the action suggests that "The Vampirine Fair" tells a factual story.

The title suggests a female vampire, which in a figurative sense describes the woman. The lord of the manor, smitten by passion, is ruthless toward his tenant Gilbert's wife, but the lord meets his match in this woman, strong-minded, shallow, and vain with a morality suggested in her saying she would "give my prettiest emerald ring / To see my lord alive."

1. In *Jude the Obscure* Hardy calls Shaftesbury by its old name of Shaston. Win Green Hill is now National Trust property used for public recreation.

THE REMINDER pictures Hardy at Max Gate on a frosty Christmas evening. He is comfortable until "Something" makes him look out the window, where he observes the distress of a bird that he would prefer not to see. He wished to be a spectator of life or "a spectre not solid enough to influence my environment; only fit to behold and say, as another spectre said: 'Peace be unto you!' "[1] He could not help becoming involved in the misery of others. The stanzas of the poem outline his involvement: the comfortable poet, the distressed bird, and the misery of the two together. His sympathy with hungry birds in winter runs throughout his work, as in *Far from the Madding Crowd*, to describe a frosty evening, he wrote: "Many a small bird went to bed supperless that night among the bare boughs." (Chapter III.)

1. *Early Life*, p. 275; *Life*, p. 210.

THE RAMBLER presents Hardy on a walk through hills and fields that he does not see with the perception and zest of youth. Memories are now more full of meaning than present sights, but their meaning in "now perceived too late by me!"

NIGHT IN THE OLD HOME pictures Hardy alone in his old home at Higher Bockhampton. The "wasting embers" call to his mind "My perished people who housed them here," and in a ghostly vision they appear.

Presumably the vision occurs after the death of his mother. The ghostly visitors, the Hardys who had lived and died there, are Thomas Hardy the First (died 1837) and his wife Mary (died 1857), Hardy's grandparents; and Thomas Hardy the Second (died 1892) and his wife Jemima (died 1904), his parents. They were a "once strong stock," who (except for some fatalism in Jemima Hardy) took life as they found it, content to "watch Time away beamingly."

Hardy was dismayed that he and his unmarried brother and sisters were the last of their line; he felt himself a "pale late plant," as well as an unconventional "thinker of crooked thoughts upon Life," isolated by temperament from most men.

The "strange upbraiding smile" of the ghosts suggests that as a boy (in spite of much evidence of a happy youth) he had felt himself a lonely misfit and had been upbraided for his moodiness. Possibly the final stanza expresses not only his present wish that he had the temperament, strength, and faith of his forebears but also advice remembered from boyhood.

"Night in the Old Home" has been set to music by Hubert James Foss in *Seven Poems by Thomas Hardy* (London: Oxford University Press, 1925).

AFTER THE LAST BREATH comments upon the death of Hardy's mother, Jemima, on Easter Sunday, April 3, 1904. The title and "Blankly we gaze" suggest that the moment of the poem is just after the mother has ceased to breathe, and the poet, his brother, Henry, and his sisters, Mary and Kate, are standing nearby.[1]

Jemima Hardy, born in 1813, was almost ninety-one years old when she died. She had lived vigorously until a short time before her death. Hardy wrote to Sir Sydney Cockerell on June 3, 1917, that his mother had thought nothing of walking from her house to Max Gate, about three miles, at the age of seventy-seven: "I find from a note that she walked here from Bockhampton in that year of her life, and in slippery winter weather. On our asking her with alarm why she had ventured out she said coolly: 'To enjoy the beauties of Nature of course: why shouldn't I?'"[2] The account of her funeral in the *Dorset County Chronicle* suggests serenity, "long beautiful stages of old age," almost to the end.

The poem calls her death a "deft achievement / Whereby she has escaped the Wrongers." Critics, noting the personified "Time" and "Wrongers," have supposed that these terms expressed Hardy's "dark joy" at his mother's death.[3] Probably he had in mind only his mother's recent disabilities that made this vigorous woman's life a burden. His letters about his mother's death name such "Wrongers": On April 12, 1904, he wrote to Edward Clodd that "my mother was 90, & what the papers call an 'aged lady,' & had been, owing to her deafness & other infirmities, shut out from much intercourse with her kind of late years."[4] On April 18, he wrote similarly to Mrs. Arthur Henniker.[5]

1. The Dorset County Museum has a number of pencil-drawings of Hardy's mother by his sister Mary. One of them, dated April 4, 1904, pictures the mother after her death.
2. Meynell, ed., *Friends of a Lifetime*, p. 286.
3. See, for instance, Blunden, *Thomas Hardy*, p. 114.
4. In the British Museum.
5. In the Dorset County Museum.

IN CHILDBED expresses a message that Hardy stated in various places, as in "The Unborn": the hardships and pains of life are such that it were better not to be born. Perhaps he dramatized the poem, having the mother's ghost appear to her daughter at midnight, to give the message the authority of a voice from the grave.

THE PINE PLANTERS, Part II, was published in the *Cornhill Magazine* in June, 1903, with no reference to Marty South, but with the headnote: *"The man fills in the earth; the sad-faced woman holds the tree upright, and meditates."*[1]

The complete poem develops Marty South's unspoken thought as she and Giles Winterborne of *The Woodlanders* set out fir trees. Marty is in love with Giles, but Giles, in love with Grace Melbury, pays little attention to Marty. The scene in Chapter VIII reads: "The holes were already dug, and they set to work. Winterborne's fingers were endowed with a gentle conjuror's touch in spreading the roots of each little tree, resulting in a sort of caress under which the delicate fibres all laid themselves out in their proper directions for growth. . . .

"'How they sigh directly we put 'em upright, though while they are lying down they don't sigh at all,' said Marty.

"'Do they?' said Giles. 'I've never noticed it.'

"She erected one of the young pines into its hole, and held up her finger; the soft musical breathing instantly set in which was not to cease night or day till the grown tree should be felled. . . .

"'It seems to me,' the girl continued, 'as if they sigh because they are very sorry to begin life in earnest—just as we be.'

"'Just as we be?' He looked critically at her. 'You ought not to feel like that, Marty.'

"Her only reply was turning to take up the next tree; and they planted on through a great part of the day, almost without another word. Winterborne's mind ran on his contemplated evening-party [for Grace Melbury], his abstraction being such that he hardly was conscious of Marty's presence beside him."[2]

"The Pine Planters" develops Marty's character more fully than the parallel passage in the novel; it prepares the reader for Marty's soliloquy over Giles's grave at the end of the novel. Because the poem is thus related to the novel, Weber surmised that it "was composed at the same time as *The Woodlanders*,"[3] that is, about 1886-87. The prose passage was possibly written from the poem; it was an insertion in the manuscript of the novel: "The passage during the tree-planting scene in which Marty notices that the trees sigh when planted because 'they are very sorry to begin life in earnest' is all an addition on the verso of sheet 86 (p. 73)."[4] Hardy may have written the poem later, perhaps while preparing a late edition of the novel.

"The Pine Planters" has two themes, Marty's helpless love for Giles, and Hardy's animistic feeling that fir trees grieve and sigh. He expressed this feeling to Sir William Rothenstein: "I loved a thing he told me about young trees when first planted—how the instant their roots came in contact with the ground they began to sigh."[5] He expressed it in various other places, as in *Under the Greenwood Tree*, which opens: "To dwellers in a wood almost every species of tree has its voice as well as its feature. At the passing of the breeze the fir-trees sob and moan no less distinctly than they rock."

The verse-form of "The Pine Planters" has been compared to that of Browning's "A Woman's Last Word": "The short lines, the feminine rhymes of the odd-numbered lines, the masculine rhymes of the even-numbered ones, the quatrain divisions, are all reproduced in Hardy's poem 'The Pine Planters,' "[6]

The poem seems to have been set to music at least twice. Sylvia Townsend Warner, in a letter of October 23, 1919, asked Hardy's permission to publish a musical setting, and permission was granted. Harold Child, on July 21, 1925, wrote Hardy that Patrick Hadley had set "Marty's words to music . . . which had its first hearing last night."[7]

1. Purdy, *Thomas Hardy: A Bibliographical Study*, pp. 145-46.
2. A sentence in Chapter VIII of *A Pair of Blue Eyes* states the situation of the poem. Stephen Smith says: "My grandfather planted the trees that belt in your lawn; my grandmother—who worked in the fields with him—held each tree upright whilst he filled in the earth: they told me so when I was a child."
3. *Hardy of Wessex*, 2nd ed., p. 163.
4. Kramer, "Revisions and Vision," p. 51.
5. Hamilton, "Thomas Hardy: Fruitless Conflicts," p. 247.
6. Weber, *Hardy of Wessex*, 1st ed., p. 271.
7. In the Dorset County Museum.

THE DEAR, without the second stanza, was published in the *Monthly Review* for June, 1902.[1] On May 18, Hardy had written the editor, Sir Henry Newbolt, that the poem was "made on a real incident that seemed worth recording for its own sake."[2]

Lea says that the scene of the poem, " 'Fairmile Hill-top' is the summit of the hill on the old Sherborne Road from Dorchester. . . . It is said to derive its name from being a fair or full mile long."[3] The scene may, however, be Fairmile on a hill top about ten miles east of Exeter on Road 30 and about seven miles from Broadclyst, where Hardy often visited Eden Phillpotts.

1. Purdy, *Thomas Hardy: A Bibliographical Study*, p. 146.
2. Sotheby & Co, *Catalogue of Valuable Printed Books . . . Autograph Letters*, for sale on June 22 and 23, 1959, p. 53.
3. *Thomas Hardy's Wessex*, pp. 312-13.

ONE WE KNEW was first published in the *Tatler* on December 2, 1903, and then under the title "Remembrance" in *Harper's Weekly* (New York) on December 12.[1] The poem is a tribute to Hardy's paternal grandmother, Mary Head Hardy. She was born in Fawley, Berkshire, and baptised there on October 30, 1772, lived in Higher Bockhampton after her marriage, and died there on January 9, 1857. Describing Hardy's visit to Fawley in June of 1923, *The Later Years* says: "His father's mother, the gentle, kindly grandmother who lived with the family at Bockhampton during Hardy's childhood, had spent the first thirteen years of her life here as an orphan child, named Mary Head, and her memories of Fawley were so poignant that she never cared to return to the place after she had left it as a young girl."[2]

From Hardy's birth until he was almost seventeen, when his grandmother was sixty-eight to nearly eighty-five, she slept in the tiny bedroom next to his and, according to "One We Knew," must have sat many an evening before the fire downstairs, gazing "into the embers" and seeing, as if in them, the "dead themes" of her life, the Hardy children "seated around her knees," fascinated. He seems to have drawn another picture of her as the grandmother of Swithin St. Cleeve in *Two on a Tower*: "Inside the house his maternal grandmother was sitting by a wood fire. . . . This woman of eighty, in a large mob cap, under which she wore a little cap to keep the other clean, retained faculties but little blunted. She was gazing into the flames, with her hands upon her knees, quietly re-enacting in her brain certain of the long chain of episodes, pathetic, tragical, and humorous, which had constituted the parish history for the last sixty years." (Chapter II.)

"One We Knew" presents in summary materials Hardy used in dozens of stories and poems. The first two stanzas picture country dances like those in *Under the Greenwood Tree,* where "The Triumph, or Follow My Lover" opens the Dewys' Christmas party. It appears also in "The Dance at the Phoenix."[3] The maypole and bandsmen of the third stanza appear in the first chapter of Book Sixth of *The Return of the Native.* The grandmother's tales of the French Revolution, Napoleon, and the French threat to invade England must have stirred Hardy deeply: "The Alarm" seems to tell one of her experiences; Hardy implied that *The Trumpet-Major* owed many details to her memories,[4] as did *The Dynasts.* The crude justice of the gibbet and the child whipped at the cart-tail left impressions to be found in poems like "The Burghers" and in Hardy's illustrations for "My Cicely."

Many poems and incidents in his fiction seem to echo Mary Head Hardy's memories. Gosse says: "From her lips he heard many an obscure old legend of the life of Wessex in the eighteenth century. Was it she who told him the terrible Exmoor story of 'The Sacrilege'; the early tale of 'The Two Men,' which might be the skeleton-scenario for a whole elaborate novel; of that incomparable comedy in verse, 'The Fire at Tranter Sweatley's,' with its splendid human touch at the very end?"[5]

1. Purdy, *Thomas Hardy: A Bibliographical Study,* p. 146.
2. P. 231; *Life,* p. 420.
3. The music for "The Triumph" and "The New-rigged Ship" is in the manu-

script book that belonged to Hardy's father and is now in the Dorset County Museum. This music has been published by Elna Sherman in the *Wessex Tune Book*, London: Schott & Co., 1963. The dances mentioned are old: "poussetting" was dancing in a circle with hands joined, and "allemanding" was dancing a German dance featured in 1540 at the fêtes given by Francis I to Charles V.

4. The Preface to the 1895 edition says: "The present tale is founded more largely on testimony—oral and written—than any other in this series. The external incidents which direct its course are mostly an unexaggerated reproduction of the recollections of old persons well known to the author in childhood, but now long dead, who were eye-witnesses of those scenes."

5. "The Lyrical Poetry of Thomas Hardy," pp. 254-55.

SHE HEARS THE STORM was titled in manuscript "The Widow's Thought."[1] Details of the setting suggest Hardy's birthplace. Thorncombe Wood lies just south of the house and partly surrounds it; the Frome ("Froom") River is less than a mile to the south; and Stinsford ("Mellstock") Leaze seems to be the meadows between Stinsford and Dorchester, soggy in wet weather. The Hardy "cottage" has a roof of thatch and a "garden-hatch" that would clack when shaken. These details and its position after "One We Knew" suggest that the poem presents a meditation by either Hardy's grandmother, Mary Head Hardy, after the death of her husband, Thomas Hardy the First, in 1837, or Hardy's mother after the death of Thomas Hardy the Second in 1892.

The widow remembers her anxiety for her husband coming across meadows "bare of hedge or tree" between Dorchester and Higher Bockhampton. He is now safe from any storm in Stinsford Churchyard. The ballad-like stanza and the tone of the poem indicate a resigned acceptance of coming death, symbolized in a premonition, the "candle slanting sooty-wick'd."[2]

1. Purdy, *Thomas Hardy: A Bibliographical Study*, p. 146.
2. Firor, *Folkways in Thomas Hardy*, p. 15.

A WET NIGHT seems Hardy's memory of himself as a youth trudging home from Dorchester to Higher Bockhampton. The "moorland way, / And up the hill" suggests a path across Fordington field to Stinsford; then the "ewe-leaze gray / Into the lane" indicates a short-cut across meadows. If so, the poem pictures young Hardy's resolution to endure because of pride in the "sturdy muteness" of his physically stronger forebears.

BEFORE LIFE AND AFTER looks back to a golden age before life evolved consciousness and with it pain, and forward to some period when "nescience shall be reaffirmed." This theme rests upon Hardy's interpretation of biological evolution,, "as, indeed, earth's testimonies tell," and upon speculations found in Eduard Von Hartmann's *Philosophy of the Unconscious*, that the Immanent Will, becoming aware of suffering in Its creations, would either amend all injustice or discreate the universe.[1]

That reflective consciousness is an evil is expressed in Hardy's description of Clym in *The Return of the Native*. Clym "already showed that thought is a disease of flesh, and indirectly bore evidence that ideal physical beauty is incompatible with . . . a full recognition of the coil of things." (Book Second, Chapter VI.) The thought is allied with the "new views of life" discussed in *Jude the Obscure*, where Jude's doctor calls Father Time's suicide "the beginning of the coming universal wish not to live." (Part VI, Chapter II.) It runs throughout *The Dynasts*, in which the Spirit of the Years explains consciousness as an accident of evolution: "The cognizance ye mourn, Life's doom to feel, / If I report it meetly, came unmeant, / Emerging with blind gropes from impercipience / By listless sequence —luckless, tragic Chance." (Part First, V, iv.)

"Before Life and After" has been set to music by Benjamin Britten in *Winter Words* (New York: Boosey and Hawkes, 1954).

1. For Von Hartmann's influence upon Hardy, see Bailey, *Thomas Hardy and the Cosmic Mind*, Chapter Four.

NEW YEAR'S EVE was first published in the *Fortnightly Review* for January, 1907.[1]

The thought of the poem, like that of "The Mother Mourns" and "Before Life and After," is dramatized in the poet's colloquy with "God," not the personal, omniscient God of Christianity, but the unconscious Will of *The Dynasts* symbolized as a personality. This "God" stands for natural processes that have no consciousness of purpose, right, wrong, justice, or mercy. The poem may be considered a conversation between the questioning and answering sides of Hardy's mind.

Aware of indifference in these processes but religious in feeling, Hardy was unwilling to conceive God as consciously unjust: an unconscious Will was his compromise. The concept appears so frequently throughout his works that it cannot be regarded as a passing fancy, even though, on the defensive against the criticism of Alfred Noyes, he asserted it to be so. In a letter to Noyes on December 19, 1920, he wrote: "The other verses you mention, 'New Year's Eve,' 'His Education,' are the same fanciful impressions of the moment."[2] A letter to Edward Clodd on January 2, 1907, while ambiguous, seems closer to a definition of his attitude: "Many thanks for your letter about my New Year's fantasy or dream in the F. R. [*Fortnightly Review*]. . . . As you say, people will no doubt mistake it for a belief. It is Feuerbach who says that God is the product of man. . . . On the other hand I quite enter into Spencer's feeling—that it is paralyzing to think what if, of all that is so incomprehensible to us (the Universe) there exists no comprehension anywhere."[3] It is the poet rather than God who quotes from the Bible. The clause "who in / This tabernacle groan" echoes II Corinthians 5:4, "we that are in this tabernacle do groan."

Hardy's works offer parallels to the phrasing and the thought of the poem. The identification of the seasons as "grey, green, white, and brown" is paralleled in *The Trumpet-Major*: "The year changed from green to gold, and from gold to grey. . . ." (Chapter XXXVIII.) In *Jude the Obscure*, Sue, "in the days when her intellect scintillated like a star," thought "that the world resembled a stanza or melody composed in a dream . . . that the First Cause worked automatically like a somnambulist, and not reflectively like a sage." (Part VI, Chapter III.) In his first speech in *The Dynasts*, the Spirit of the Years says of the Immanent Will: "It works unconsciously, as heretofore, / Eternal artistries in Circumstance, / Whose patterns, wrought by rapt aesthetic rote, / Seem in themselves Its single listless aim." To this concept the Spirit of the Pities offers the objection of the poet in "New Year's Eve": "But O, the intolerable antilogy / Of making figments feel!" (Part First, IV, v.)

1. Purdy, *Thomas Hardy: A Bibliographical Study*, p. 146.
2. *Later Years*, pp. 217-18; *Life*, p. 409.
3. In the British Museum.

GOD'S EDUCATION in the first edition of *Time's Laughingstocks* bore the title "His Education." The God whom the poet addresses is evidently that of "New Year's Eve," wherein God, after listening to man, "sank to raptness as of yore." In "God's Education," God "mused" and glimpsed the idea that He might learn from "men's . . . teaching mind."

The thought underlying both poems may owe something to T. H. Huxley's statement in "Evolution and Ethics": "The cosmic process has no sort of relation to moral ends; . . . the imitation of it by man is inconsistent with the first principle of ethics. . . . Let us understand once for all, that the ethical progress of society depends, not on imitating the cosmic process . . . but in combating it." (P. 83.) Hardy rejected Huxley's "combating" in favor of "teaching" the cosmic process. His idea, fanciful as it may be in poetic imagery, persisted as a serious thought that, in the "Apology" of *Late Lyrics and Earlier*, he called "evolutionary meliorism."

The God of the poem resembles the Immanent Will of *The Dynasts*, in which the hope for teaching the Will is expressed in the chorus of Spirits that concludes the epic-drama: "Consciousness the Will informing, till It fashion all things fair!" Hardy does not mean that the human mind may bring about alterations in natural laws. He cannot seriously mean that the aging process described in "God's Education" will cease to operate. He may mean that in the slow, erratic processes of evolution, good will, unselfishness, loving-kindness, and compassion may cease to be hard-won moralities and may become instinctive. Then men may not need to combat natural impulses, as Huxley suggested, but only to follow them.

TO SINCERITY may be related to "God's Education," for it suggests a first step toward the meliorism symbolized there. Man cannot teach God truth and justice unless man develops them in his own nature. Recognizing that to do so is difficult, when selfish instincts are rationalized as "modern methods," the poem pleads for intellectual honesty. This honesty will demand some unpleasant, unpopular, so-called "pessimism"—"The exploration of reality, and its frank recognition stage by stage along the survey, with an eye to the best consummation possible: evolutionary meliorism." (Quoted from "Apology.")

PANTHERA tells an apocryphal legend of the parentage and crucifixion of Jesus. Hardy's chief sources for the story were Mary Ann Evans's (George Eliot's) translation of David Strauss's *Das Leben Jesu*, that is, *The Life of Jesus Critically Examined*, and Joseph McCabe's translation of Ernst Haeckel's *Die Welträtsel*, that is, *The Riddle of the Universe at the Close of the Nineteenth Century*. Hardy's copy of *The Life of Jesus*, now in the Colby College Library, is the edition of 1898. The legend of Panthera is told on pages 139-40. Apparently Hardy read little further: pages are cut only through page 210 of this 784-page book.[1]

The passages that tell the story of Panthera are as follows, with Strauss's footnotes in brackets: "The author of the Natural History of the Great Prophet of Nazareth . . . brings into comparison a story in Josephus [Antiq. xviii.3.4.], according to which, in the very time of Jesus, a Roman knight won the chaste wife of a Roman noble to his wishes, by causing her to be invited by a priest of Isis into the temple of the goddess, under the pretext that the god Anubis desired to embrace her. In innocence and faith, the woman resigned herself, and would perhaps afterwards have believed she had given birth to the child of a god, had not the intriguer, with bitter scorn, soon after discovered to her the true state of the case. It is the opinion of the author that Mary, the betrothed bride of the aged Joseph, was in like manner deceived by some amorous and fanatic young man . . . and that she on her part, in perfect innocence, continued to deceive others. [1ter Theil, s. 140 ff.] It is evident that this interpretation does not differ from the ancient Jewish blasphemy, which we find in Celsus and in the Talmud; that Jesus falsely represented himself as born of a pure virgin, whereas, in fact, he was the offspring of the adultery of Mary with a certain Panthera. [The legend has undergone various modifications, but the name of *Panthera* or *Pandira* has been uniformly retained. . . .] This whole view, of which the culminating point is in the calumny of the Jews, cannot be better judged than in the words of Origen. If, says this author, they wished to substitute something else in the place of the history of the supernatural conception of Jesus, they should at any rate have made it happen in a more probable manner; they ought not, as it were against their will, to admit that Mary knew not Joseph, but they might have denied this feature, and yet have allowed Jesus to have been born of an ordinary human marriage; whereas the forced and extravagant character of their hypothesis betrays its falsehood. [Orig. c. Celsus i. 32.] . . . The correct view of the narrative before us is to be found, that is indirectly, in Origen. For when at one time he places together, as of the same kind, the miraculous conception of Jesus and the story of Plato's conception by Apollo, and when at another time he says of the story concerning Plato, that it belongs to those mythi by which it was sought to exhibit the distinguished wisdom and power of great men . . . he in fact states the two premises, namely, the similarity of the two narratives and the mythical character of the one; from which the inference of the merely mythical worth of the narrative of the conception of Jesus follows; a conclusion which can never indeed have occurred to his own mind."[2]

Presumably after reading this account, Hardy read the following in Haeckel's *The Riddle of the Universe*, published in English in 1900: "Now, we find in one of these documents an historical statement, confirmed, moreover, in the *Sepher Toldoth Jeschua*, which probably furnishes the simple and natural solution of the 'world-riddle' of the supernatural conception and birth of Christ. The author curtly gives us in one sentence the remarkable statement which contains this solution: 'Josephus Pandera, the Roman officer of a Calabrian legion which was in Judaea, seduced Miriam of Bethlehem, and was the father of Jesus.' . . . The statement of the apocryphal gospels, that the Roman officer Pandera was the true father of Christ, seems all the more credible when we make a careful anthropological study of the personality of Christ. He is generally regarded as purely Jewish. Yet the characteristics which distinguish his high and noble personality, and which give a distinctive impress to his religion, are certainly not Semitical; they are rather features of the higher Aryan race, and especially of its noblest branch, the Hellenes. Now, the name of Christ's real father, 'Pandera,' points unequivocally to a Greek origin; in one manuscript, in fact, it is written 'Pandora.'" (Pp. 336-37.)

Of these two sources, Hardy evidently found Haeckel's mention of "the Roman officer of a Calabrian legion" the more satisfactory and sought to investigate the story more fully. His notebook labelled "Facts," now in the Dorset County Museum, contains three extensive notes numbered 1, 2, and 3. Notes 1 and 2 are not in Hardy's handwriting, as if he had a secretary to read and take notes for him. Note 3 is in Hardy's hand. Apparently he made no use of these notes in the poem.[3]

His motive in publishing a poem that he knew would anger some people and disturb more can be surmised.[4] Its position just after "Sincerity," which calls for men to "look at true things / And unilluded view things," suggests a motive. In the "Apology" of *Late Lyrics and Earlier* he expresses hope for "an alliance between religion, which must be retained unless the world is to perish, and complete rationality, which must come, unless also the world is to perish." He looked upon the virgin birth as a beautiful myth, but so irrational that perhaps it kept many from reverencing Jesus for His teachings. Matthew Arnold, with a point of view somewhat like Hardy's, wrote *Literature and Dogma* to *save* religion. He thought Christians should ignore "Aberglauben" (superstitions, extra beliefs) that obscure the "true greatness" of Jesus, His "sweet reasonableness" and His message for the world.

Hardy took pains to keep the story from being offensive. Though the seduction of Mary and the crucifixion must be central in the story, they are presented as only episodes in the life of a distinguished Roman soldier. The story is told as a narrative monologue within a narrative monologue, a device that holds the reader at some distance from immediate perception and certainty that the woman of the poem was Mary and the "criminal" was Jesus. (Neither Mary nor Jesus is named.) Panthera only thinks he recognizes the woman at the Cross, and the woman does not recognize him.

Panthera is not, as in some sources Hardy noted, licentious. Limited in freedom by his military duties, he is honest and chivalrous. He is brave, serene, serious-minded, truthful, and of "noble spirit." The unnamed girl is innocent at heart, meek, modest, and artless;

she "had no arts, but what out-arted all, / The tremulous tender charm of trustfulness." In short, he softened the legend and presented it with delicate ambiguity. Besides having hinted of Panthera that "shocks" had "disarranged his mind," the narrator who speaks to us doubts the woman's identity. That she "did not recognize / Her lover's face, is matter for surprise."

At the same time, Hardy gave the story reality in various ways. Panthera's campaigns are credible for the turbulent first century. His point of view is that of a conscientious Roman officer, just contemptuous enough of the Jewish rabble to pick up only scraps of the turmoil about Jesus. Ignoring the sentiments of Victorian society toward the child born out of wedlock, Hardy characterized Panthera and the girl with the finest traits usually attributed to Roman character and Hebrew religion. By implication, Jesus would inherit the best traits of two races.

It is characteristic that, as Hardy makes the legend his own, he develops the theme of Chance. Paraphrasing Bacon, he has Panthera state the ostensible moral of the story: "He who goes fathering / Gives frightful hostages to hazardry."[5] Panthera's meeting with the girl by the well is a likely chance and so is his departure before the child is born. It is less likely that, with all the years between, he should return at the crucifixion just too late to save his son.

1. Rutland, *Thomas Hardy*, p. 106, states that Hardy's edition was that of 1892 and that Hardy "must have studied it extensively if he went to the expense of buying it." Possibly he owned two copies.

2. Pp. 139-40.

3. They present various items, mentioning: "The virgin being forced by a soldier called Pandera"; "an idle and worthless debauchee named Joseph Pandera, of the fallen tribe of Judah" who "spent his time in robbery and licentiousness"; the Talmudic account "amplified & altered in the medieval 'Sepher Toldoth Jeschu' "; Mary "being big with child was divorced by her husband the carpenter for committing Adultery with one Pandera, a soldier . . . scandalous wretch"; Jesus, having learned in Egypt the "arts" of the country, "return'd into his native country, & swelling with a vain conceit of the miracles he shd. do, gave out that he was God." The notes end: "Vide also Haeckel, Strauss, etc." Nothing exclusively in these notes appears in the poem.

4. Rutland, who admired Hardy, calls "Panthera" an "offensive poem . . . the only one of his productions that dishonours him." *Thomas Hardy*, p. 106.

5. In "Of Marriage and Single Life" Francis Bacon wrote: "He that hath wife and children hath given hostages to fortune."

THE UNBORN was first published as "Life's Opportunity" in a volume of poems, *Wayfarer's Love*, edited by the Duchess of Sutherland in 1904. When Hardy discarded the original final stanza and substituted a new one, he dated the poem 1905.[1] In a dramatic vision, the poem presents a meditation on the disaster of being born.

In 1905, Hardy was working on *The Dynasts*, in which human

beings are driven or attracted to do all they do by impulses from the Immanent Will. The fantasy of "The Unborn" personifies the attractive impulses, or lovers' idealizations, of procreative love in which children are brought to life without knowing its pain or having a chance to refuse it.

The disillusioned "I" of the poem would seem to represent Hardy, who in various statements said that it is best not to be born. Clive Holland reports that Hardy asked him whether, if he had had any choice in being born, he would have been. Holland replied by asking "Would you?" and Hardy said "No, surely not."[2] When Alfred Noyes in 1920 attacked Hardy for his pessimism, he replied: "As for 'The Unborn,' to which you allude, though the form of it is imaginary, the sentiment is one which I should think, especially since the war, is not uncommon or unreasonable."[3] This idea is suggested in many compassionate passages in Hardy's works, as in "To an Unborn Pauper Child." In *Tess of the D'Urbervilles*, he pictures the birth of the Durbeyfield children as a disaster: "All these young souls were passengers in the Durbeyfield ship. . . . If the heads of the Durbeyfield household chose to sail into difficulty, disaster, starvation, disease, degradation, death, thither were these half-dozen little captives under hatches compelled to sail with them—six helpless creatures, who had never been asked if they wished for life on any terms. . . ." (Chapter III.) In *Jude the Obscure*, Little Father Time killed himself and Sue's two children because Sue had "sent for another." (Part VI, Chapter II.)

1. Purdy, *Thomas Hardy: A Bibliographical Study*, p. 147.
2. "The Thomas Hardy I Knew," p. 14.
3. *Later Years*, p. 218; *Life*, p. 409.

THE MAN HE KILLED was first published in *Harper's Weekly* (New York) on November 8, 1902[1] In this publication, the poem had a headnote: "Scene: *The settle of the Fox Inn, Stagfoot Lane*. Characters: *The speaker (a returned soldier) and his friends, natives of the hamlet*." This hamlet is the home of "Parson Tringham . . . of Stagfoot Lane," who, in *Tess of the D'Urbervilles*, tells John Durbeyfield that he is a D'Urberville. This fictional hamlet is based upon Hartfoot Lane, a village about eight miles northeast of Dorchester.

The soldier may be any Dorset countryman recently returned from the South African War. He is a friendly fellow who enjoys a drink of ale with neighbors in an "old ancient inn." When out of work, he "thought he'd 'list," without imagining he would kill a man like himself for no reason he could understand. The soldier's state of mind, baffled in his effort to grasp why his victim was his foe, is portrayed in the stumbling speech of the third stanza. ·His conclusion that war is "quaint and curious" is as far as he can go toward explaining a war fought by men like himself for national policies they do not understand.· The poem presents an aspect of Hardy's protest against imperialist war, essentially that of the Pities in *The Dynasts* at the battle of Talavera. This Spirit sees enemy soldiers, exhausted with fighting, go to a little stream between the armies to drink. There, "They get to grasping hands across the rill, / Sealing their sameness as earth's sojourners.—/ What more could plead the wryness of the times / Than such unstudied piteous pantomimes!"[2]

1. Purdy, *Thomas Hardy: A Bibliographical Study*, p. 147.
2. Part Second, IV, v. For this scene Hardy drew upon facts stated in historical records. See Wright, *The Shaping of "The Dynasts,"* p. 182.

GEOGRAPHICAL KNOWLEDGE was first published in the *Outlook* (London) on April 1, 1905.[1] Christiana C———, in whose memory the poem was written, was Mrs. Christiana Coward, the postmistress at Lower Bockhampton (for Higher Bockhampton also) in 1875 and perhaps earlier.[2] That Hardy indicates the actual name suggests that the poem states facts he observed as a young man.

The irony or joke of the poem is that Mrs. Coward, who probably sorted a good deal of mail for nearby localities, knew nothing of places that did not touch her emotionally, though these places are near Lower Bockhampton. Extensive Blackmoor Vale lies approximately twelve miles to the north; the road to Bath is Road 37 that branches from Road 356 about four miles northwest of Dorchester. The "track athwart / Froom Mead" is the secondary road that leads from Lower Bockhampton, past West Stafford, to Woodsford, about three miles from Lower Bockhampton; and "Yell'ham" (Yellowham) Wood is less than two miles north of the postoffice.

Hardy's observation of Mrs. Coward perhaps suggested a passage in *The Trumpet-Major*. When Bob Loveday has gone to sea, Anne's dreams followed him, and "all that belonged to the sea was her daily thought and her nightly dream . . . and she acquired a precise knowledge of the direction in which Portsmouth, Brest, Ferrol, Cadiz, and other such likely places lay." (Chapter XXXIV.)

1. Purdy, *Thomas Hardy: A Bibliographical Study*, p. 147.
2. *Postoffice Directory of Hampshire, Wiltshire, and Dorsetshire*, in Dorset County Archives. No earlier record was available; she was not listed for 1885.

ONE RALPH BLOSSOM SOLILOQUIZES presents a dying scamp wondering what the seven girls he has seduced will say to him when he is in Hell. The source of the poem is a quotation from the *Budmouth* (Weymouth) *Borough Minutes* in "16——," perhaps by way of now-destroyed pages in Hardy's notebook. If so, the impulse to take this note may have come to him from memory of a ballad sung at Squire Martin's Harvest Supper when Hardy was about ten years old. The ballad was "one variously called 'The Outlandish Knight,' 'May Colvine,' 'The Western Tragedy,' etc." As partly quoted in *The Early Life*, the ballad contains the lines: "For six pretty maidens thou hast a-drown'd here, / But the seventh hath drown-ed thee!"[1]

Character-reading Ralph presents swift, varied impersonations of the girls. Hardy's attitude seems amused and tolerant. Though Ralph pictures himself in Hell, like Sergeant Troy of *Far from the Madding Crowd* he "never passed the line which divides the spruce vices from the ugly; and hence, though his morals had hardly been applauded, disapproval of them had frequently been tempered with a smile." (Chapter XXV.)

1. P. 26; *Life*, p. 20.

THE NOBLE LADY'S TALE was first published as "The Noble Lady's Story" in *Harper's Weekly* (New York) on February 18, 1905.[1] Parts I and II are a reminiscent soliloquy by the Noble Lady, and Part III is the poet's commentary.

The poem narrates an imaginary incident in the lives of Lady Susan Fox-Strangways O'Brien (1743-1827) and her husband William O'Brien (1738-1815). (For details about Lady Susan, see the Key to Persons.)

Hardy disclaimed any factual basis for "The Noble Lady's Tale." In a letter to her sister on May 30, 1916, Mrs. Ethel Inglis wrote of visiting him the day before. They went to Stinsford Church, where he pointed out the tablets to Lady Susan and O'Brien: "Mr. Hardy said he had written a little poem about him in which he makes him fly up to London, but he said it was pure imagination."[2]

Though the meter of the poem is not exactly the same, critics have compared it with Browning's "Love Among the Ruins." Like various poems by Browning, "The Noble Lady's Tale" analyzes personality to the point of mystery and leaves the reader to ponder the "Riddle death-sealed for ever."

Various items in Hardy's fiction seem related to Lady Susan. "The First Countess of Wessex" in *A Group of Noble Dames* seems based on Lady Susan's mother.[3] The scene in the vault and the story of runaway Elfride in Chapter XXVI of *A Pair of Blue Eyes* suggests the vault Hardy's grandfather built for Lady Susan. The psychic phenomena suggested in "The Noble Lady's Tale" is anticipated in

Chapter XXI of *Desperate Remedies,* where the wraith of Miss Ald-clyffe appears to Cytherea.

1. Purdy, *Thomas Hardy: A Bibliographical Study,* p. 147.
2. In the Dorset County Museum.
3. See Peirce, "Hardy's Lady Susan and the First Countess of Wessex."

UNREALIZED first appeared in 1905 as "Orphaned, A Point of View," in *The Queen's (Christmas) Carol,* a gift-book in support of Queen Alexandra's Fund for the Unemployed.[1] The poem is a little girl's quasi-nursery jingle about her reactions to new freedoms. Blunden comments that Hardy "strangely" thought the poem suitable for a book intended to arouse compassion. The later title suggests Hardy's characteristic irony: the orphaned children will later realize their loss.

1. Purdy, *Thomas Hardy: A Bibliographical Study,* p. 148.

WAGTAIL AND BABY, then subtitled "An Incident of Civilization," was first printed in the *Albany Review* for April, 1907.[1]

Though the wagtail is a summer resident in Dorset, probably Hardy chose this migrant bird for its name. For the animals he chose "the fiercest of their kind: the bull, the stallion, the cur, and by contrast, the *perfect* gentleman."[2] The ironic humor of the poem is aided by the two-syllable rime that runs through the stanzas in the second and fourth lines.

"Wagtail and Baby" has been set to music by Benjamin Britten in *Winter Words* (London and New York: Boosey and Hawkes, 1954.)

1. Purdy, *Thomas Hardy: A Bibliographical Study,* p. 148.
2. Hutchings, *Dorset River,* p. 145.

ABERDEEN was first published in *Alma Mater,* the Aberdeen University Magazine, for September, 1906. Hardy gave the poem to this magazine in memory of his visit to Aberdeen to receive the LL.D. degree in April, 1905.

This was the first academic recognition of his achievement. His pleasure and pride in receiving it are set forth in *The Later Years.* A paragraph quoted from his remarks accepting the honor, reads: "I am impressed by its [the honor's] coming from Aberdeen, for though a stranger to that part of Scotland to a culpable extent I have always observed with admiration the exceptional characteristics of the northern University, which in its fostering encouragement of mental effort seems to cast an eye over these islands that is unprejudiced, unbiassed, and unsleeping."[1]

In a conversation with V. H. Collins, Hardy defined the "Queen" of the poem as "Knowledge."[2] He wrote to J. M. Bulloch on October

6, 1918: "I am glad to hear about old Aberdeen. To me it bears, &
always will, a curiously romantic aspect."[3]

1. P. 109; *Life*, p. 323.
2. *Talks with Thomas Hardy*, p. 23.
3. In the Miriam Lutcher Stark Library, University of Texas.

GEORGE MEREDITH is a tribute to an old friend and a critical
estimate of his work. When Meredith died on May 18, 1909, "Hardy
was in London, and walking along Dover Street on his way to the
Academy saw on a poster the announcement of the death of Meredith.
He went on to the Athenaeum and wrote some memorial lines on
his friend, which were published a day or two later [May 22, the day
of Meredith's funeral] in *The Times*."[1]

Hardy had known Meredith for forty years. *The Early Life* de-
scribes their meeting in 1869, when Meredith was a reader for Chap-
man and Hall, to whom Hardy had submitted *The Poor Man and
the Lady*. Meredith then cautioned him against expressing radical
opinions and advised him to write a novel with a more complex plot.
Hardy followed this advice in *Desperate Remedies*. He did not meet
Meredith again until a dinner at the Rabelais Club in the summer
of 1886. In April, 1894, he paid the first of several visits to Meredith
at his home on Box Hill, Surrey. In July, 1895, they were together
at the Omar Khayyam Club, where each made a speech referring to
their meeting in Chapman and Hall's back rooms. Hardy said that
if it had not been for Meredith's encouragement he "would probably
not have adopted the literary career."[2] He visited Meredith in Lon-
don in June, 1899, and wrote in his journal that he found Meredith
"cheerful, enthusiastic, and warm. Would gladly see him oftener, and
must try to do so." In June, 1905, after Hardy visited him at Box
Hill, Meredith wrote to Edmund Gosse: "I am always glad to see
him, and have regrets at his going; for the double reason that I like
him, and am afflicted by his twilight view of life."[3] In March of
1909, Meredith wrote Hardy thanks for a gift of *The Dynasts*, their
last correspondence.[4]

Hardy appreciated Meredith more as a man than as a novelist,
poet, or thinker. In his notebook for May 14, 1915, commenting on
Henry James, he wrote: "It is remarkable that a writer [James] who
has no grain of poetry, or humour, or spontaneity in his productions,
can yet be a good novelist. Meredith has some poetry, and yet I can
read James when I cannot look at Meredith." He felt that Meredith's
productions were more "artificial" than true to life: "Meredith was
. . . in the direct succession of Congreve and the artificial comedians
of the Restoration, and in getting his brilliancy we must put up with

the fact that he would not, or could not—at any rate did not—when aiming to represent the 'Comic Spirit,' let himself discover the tragedy that always underlies Comedy if you only scratch it deeply enough."[5] Meredith, "instinctively positive and virile, saw in the development of life from primordial matter a law of earth acting toward a beneficent end and using men as its instruments for progress; the latter [Hardy], instinctively negative and sensitive, saw in the same phenomena an Immanent Will blindly and aimlessly obeying its urgent need to appear in changing forms."[6] Though he could not agree with Meredith's views, Hardy respected them. Admiring the man, he kept a medallion-portrait of Meredith over the mantel in his study.[7]

The phrase "A morning horn" in the poem refers to Meredith's virile energy, and "trenchant" to his cutting irony. The "green hill" is a reference to Meredith's home on Box Hill. "George Meredith" is written in the terza rima that Hardy admired in Browning's "The Statue and the Bust."

A curious addition to Hardy's thought about Meredith is recorded in his description of a dream that he wrote out for Mrs. Granville Barker: "In the morning of Oct. 21: 1923 I dreamt that I stood on a long ladder which was leaning against the edge of a loft. I was holding on by my right hand, & in my left I clutched an infant in blue and white, bound up in a bundle. My endeavour was to lift it over the edge of the loft to a place of safety. On the loft sat George Meredith in his shirt sleeves, smoking; though his manner was rather that of Augustus John. The child was his, but he seemed indifferent to its fate, whether I should drop it or not. I said, 'It has got heavier since I lifted it last.' He assented. By great exertion I got it above the edge, & deposited it on the floor of the loft: whereupon I awoke."[8]

1. *Later Years*, p. 137; *Life*, p. 345.
2. Sassoon, *Meredith*, p. 229.
3. Hill, "George Meredith and Thomas Hardy," p. 69.
4. See *Early Life*, pp. 80-83, 237; *Later Years*, pp. 30, 37, 83, 135; *Life*, pp. 60-63, 181, 263, 268, 304, 344. See also Hardy's "G. M.: A Reminiscence" in Orel, *Thomas Hardy's Personal Writings*, pp. 151-55.
5. *Later Years*, pp. 169, 257; *Life*, pp. 370, 439.
6. Stevenson, *Darwin Among the Poets*, pp. 344-45.
7. This portrait is now in Hardy's study as recreated in the Dorset County Museum.
8. This note in the Dorset County Museum is labelled "Written out and sent by request to Mrs. Granville Barker" and is signed "T . . . . H . . . ."

YELL'HAM-WOOD'S STORY is a fantasy of what three woods near his boyhood home tell Hardy about the promises and processes of nature and hence of life. "Coomb-Firtrees" is a wood beside Coomb Eweleaze, about a mile and a half to the east; "Clyffe-hill Clump" is Clyffe Copse near Tincleton, two miles farther east. These woods are of firs that seem to moan as the wind blows through them. (See the notes on "The Pine Planters.")

The trees of "Yell'ham" (Yellowham, Yalbury) Wood, however, half a mile to the north, are largely of beech and other hardwoods. Its glades in spring and summer are idyllically beautiful with bluebells and other wildflowers. In *Under the Greenwood Tree*, a glade in this wood is the site of Fancy Day's home; in the nut groves nearby Fancy and Dick Dewy made up their lovers' quarrel. (Part the Fourth, Chapter I.) Thus the beauty of Yellowham Wood seems to proclaim the gladness of life, but in the autumn the leaves of hardwood trees turn brown and fall. Nature's promise of continued joy is "thwarted." The poem implies that "We see within our reach beauty and love and achievement, but before we can grasp it beauty is gone, the splendid hopes fail to realize themselves and we are left, aged, to look back to the youth and love of the past."[1]

1. Knowles, "The Thought and Art of Thomas Hardy," p. 212.

A YOUNG MAN'S EPIGRAM ON EXISTENCE was written when Hardy at twenty-six was living at Westbourne Park Villas in London. In *The Early Life* notes of this period suggest that he was somewhat torn between his appetite for pleasure, as in dancing and theatre-going, and his lonely efforts to learn and to achieve in poetry and other literary activities.

When Alfred Noyes, accusing him of pessimism, mentioned "A Young Man's Epigram" as an example, Hardy denied that the poem represented his philosophy. He wrote on December 19, 1920: "The lines you allude to, 'A Young Man's Epigram' dated 1866, I remember finding in a drawer, and printed them merely as a amusing instance of early cynicism."[1] Yet the idea of the first two lines is echoed in later writings. When Tess, in *Tess of the D'Urbervilles*, has buried her child, Hardy comments: " 'By experience,' says Roger Ascham, 'we find out a short way by a long wandering.' Not seldom that long wandering unfits us for further travel, and of what use is our experience to us then?" Angel Clare is unable to discard his prejudices until both he and Tess have suffered. Then he "began to discredit the old appraisements of morality. He thought they wanted readjusting." (Chapters XV and XLIX.)

1. *Later Years*, p. 217; *Life*, p. 409.

SATIRES OF CIRCUMSTANCE LYRICS AND REVERIES

Satires of Circumstance Lyrics and Reveries with Miscellaneous Pieces was published in November, 1914. As represented in *The*

Collected Poems (which differs slightly in the arrangement, grouping, and number of poems) it has 106 poems, grouped as "Lyrics and Reveries," 31 poems; "Poems of 1912-13," 21 poems; "Miscellaneous Pieces," 39 poems; and "Satires of Circumstance in Fifteen Glimpses," 15 poems. Most of the poems seem to have been written in the years 1910-14, though two ("The Sun on the Bookcase" and "When I Set Out for Lyonnesse") are dated as referring to events of the 1870's, and three ("A Thunderstorm in Town," "Wessex Heights," and "The Schreckhorn") to the 1890's. The leading title, *Satires of Circumstance*, was selected by the publishers, Macmillan and Company, from the title of a group of the poems.[1]

In substance, the poems vary widely. The "Lyrics and Reveries" range from comments on current events ("The Convergence of the Twain") through reviews of Hardy's personal life ("Wessex Heights") to philosophic and religious meditations ("A Plaint to Man" and "God's Funeral"). The "Poems of 1912-13" nearly all treat Hardy's memories of his courtship of Emma Gifford, though not all deal with this period, for instance, "Where the Picnic Was." The "Miscellaneous Pieces" include a variety of observations; a few that treat Hardy's courtship of Miss Gifford might have been placed among "Poems of 1912-13," for instance, "I Rose Up as My Custom Is" and "A Week." The "Satires of Circumstance in Fifteen Glimpses" present ironic snapshots of incidents.

1. Purdy, *Thomas Hardy: A Bibliographical Study*, pp. 160-72.

LYRICS AND REVERIES

IN FRONT OF THE LANDSCAPE fittingly opens *Satires of Circumstance*, which presents many memories of the past and the dead. Duffin says rightly that this poem "affords an insight into the strange double life he [Hardy] led—his body perambulating in the present and the material world, his mind occupied by visions and ghosts."[1] The poem is one of scenes and images in procession through a fog that "obscures the landscape for us just as it does for the poet. All our flounderings 'as amid waste waters'" represent "the violent flood of memories, regrets, perhaps even a brooding frustration, which has overwhelmed him as he recalls the past."[2]

Though the places, persons, and events of the poem are veiled in dream-like imagery, it is possible to infer the poet's factual references. Hardy's friend Hermann Lea, intent upon identifying the places mentioned in Hardy's works, had to guess the location of the poem. He wrote of it: "? (Seen from Came Down near Culliver Tree?)"[3] Came

[261]

Down is a rolling hill about three miles south of Dorchester. On the hill is a clump of trees called Culliver (or Culliford) Tree or Wood. A chalk-pit is near this "Coppice." Burial tumuli are scattered in all directions from this point. Though the approach to the peak from Dorchester is gentle, the hill rises sharply on the south in a series of wave-like chalky banks. These facts match the details in the second stanza.

On the other hand, the general impression is that of someone lost in a fog. It is said that on one occasion during a fog Hardy was lost on Hod Hill,[4] about a mile north of Stourpaine or seventeen miles northeast of Dorchester. The hill overlooks deep valleys on all sides; the top is surrounded by steep earthen ramparts and fosses of an ancient hill-fort. It is conceivable that Hardy could become confused in entering this place through zig-zag entrances in a fog. Possibly his memory of being lost there supplied the suggestion of one "Plunging and labouring . . . as amid waste waters," even if he transferred the experience to Came Down.

The remembered landscapes in front of the actual landscape are more difficult to identify. The "headland of hoary aspect" in the seventh stanza could be Portland Bill, but the "two friends . . . Guilelessly glad . . . touched by the fringe of an ecstasy" suggest Beeny Cliff during Hardy's courtship of Emma Gifford. The "Later images" of the eighth stanza may be any number of dead friends, but the "chiefest . . . of the broad brow" may represent Horace Moule. To some extent, Moule "shared in the dramas" of Hardy's young manhood. If the landscape is that of Came Down, he may represent William Barnes, who was Rector of nearby Winterborne-Came Church.

The poem presents the behavior of Hardy's mind in reverie when the senses drowse, but the memory calls up a train of flashing and dissolving images. They seem to stand "in front of the landscape" and to obscure it.

1. *Thomas Hardy*, p. 311.
2. Southerington, "Hardy's Poetic Vision," pp. 85-86.
3. Cox, ed., *Thomas Hardy Through the Camera's Eye*, p. 52.
4. This information came from Frank Pinion, Hardy scholar at the University of Sheffield.

CHANNEL FIRING was first published in the *Fortnightly Review* for May, 1914.[1] It tells a fantastic story in a tone humorous, but not frivolous. Though one of the speakers is God, in dialogue with the dead, and though He laughs and talks in easy colloquialisms, the poem is not blasphemous. God is compassionate: realizing that men "rest eternal sorely need," He may not "blow the trumpet" for Judgment after all.

The story is narrated by a dead man who reports the dialogue and comments upon it. Gunnery practice on battleships in the English Channel is so noisy that it sets dogs howling, frightens the church-mouse, drives worms into their mounds, scares the clergyman's ("glebe") cow, and wakes the dead. God soothes them all with an explanation and a bitter comment upon men "Mad as hatters" in their threatening. If it were Judgment Day, He would send the gunners to "scour Hell's floor" for their behavior. Through this joking, however, runs a serious theme. The ghost of Parson Thirdly laments that he had not "stuck to pipes and beer," instead of sacrificing these pleasures to a theology powerless against the evil in human nature.

When World War I broke out three months after the poem was published, Hardy admitted that he had not foreseen "the coming so soon of such a convulsion as the war, though only three or four months before it broke out he had printed a prophetic poem . . . whereof the theme, 'All nations striving strong to make / Red war yet redder,' was, to say the least, a perception singularly coincident."[2] The poem implies that both theology and human experience seem powerless to make men melt their swords into ploughshares—that men learn nothing from history. This implication is symbolized in the place-names that stand for three long-perished civilizations or dynasties, whose monuments stand within hearing distance, so the poem says, of the booming guns.

"Stourton Tower" is the Alfred Tower about three miles north of Stourton and a little more than thirty miles north of Portland Harbor on the Channel. It is a triangular brick monument about 160 feet high, erected in 1766 to commemorate the victory of Alfred the Great over the invading Danes in a battle near this spot in the year 879. Part of the inscription reads: "To him we owe the Origin of Juries / The Establishment of a Militia / The Creation of a Naval Force. ALFRED the Light of a Benighted Age / Was a Philosopher and a Christian / The Father of His People / The Founder of the English / MONARCHY and LIBERTY."

"Camelot" is the romantic name of the citadel of legendary King Arthur, who, in an earlier period, had led the Britons in temporarily victorious battles against the invading Saxons, Alfred's race. While the location of Arthur's Camelot is open to question, legend has usually placed it near Glastonbury; recent excavations at South Cadbury, about twelve miles southeast of Glastonbury, have provided some evidence that a British fort (or "castle") there was the original of Camelot.[3] Hardy evidently had this area in mind. South Cadbury is about twenty-eight miles north and slightly west of Portland Harbor.

Stonehenge represents an ancient British civilization that preceded the coming of the Celts or the Romans. It is about seven miles north and slightly west of Salisbury and some forty-five miles northeast of Portland Harbor. Whether the roar of gunnery practice actually reached these places is beside the point. They represent civilizations that rose through battle and perished as dynasties.

Mrs. Florence Hardy wrote that "The buried people at Stinsford hear the guns being fired at Portland."[4] In many references by name to the dead in Stinsford Churchyard, Hardy does not mention a Parson Thirdly. Perhaps he had in mind St. Mary's Church in Puddletown. A Parson Thirdly appears in *Far from the Madding Crowd*, with its setting at "Weatherbury" (Puddletown). Thirdly, as in the poem, is a self-sacrificing man. Coggan says of him: "Why, neighbours, when every one of my taties were frosted, our Pa'son Thirdly were the man who gave me a sack for seed, though he hardly had one for his own use, and no money to buy 'em. If it hadn't been for him, I shouldn't hae had a tatie to put in my garden."[5]

"Channel Firing" is something like a ballad on the level of a country tale. It treats the dead, grave-worms, and even God's voice speaking of the Judgment in everyday language, with no striving for weird effect. The final stanza sweeps the narrative suddenly upward and backward through time to provide the comment of history upon the disturbing, roaring guns and the folly they represent.

"Channel Firing" has been set to music in *Before and After Summer* (London: Boosey & Hawkes, 1949).

1. Purdy, *Thomas Hardy: A Bibliographical Study*, p. 160.
2. *Later Years*, pp. 161-62; *Life*, p. 365. Hardy did not suppose the gunnery practice incited the German attack. On September 28, 1914, he wrote to F. A. Duneka: "You will know what a man of peace I am, & how ugly a thing war at its best is to me; but events proved to me with startling rapidity that there was no other course for us but to fight. The transparent falsity of the charge that we purposed war, and might otherwise have prevented it, is shown, in a dozen ways— not the least of which was our being so unprepared." In the Dorset County Museum.
3. Ashe, *King Arthur's Avalon*, p. 16.
4. To Rebekah Owen, April 5, 1914, in the Colby College Library.
5. Chapter XLII. See also Moon's similar comment in Chapter XXXIII.

THE CONVERGENCE OF THE TWAIN, completed on April 24, 1912, was first published in the program of the "Dramatic and Operatic Matinée in Aid of the 'Titanic' Disaster Fund," given at Covent Garden Theatre on May 14.[1]

The poem treats the sinking of the White Star liner *Titanic* on

April 15, 1912, on her maiden voyage across the Atlantic, with the loss of 1,513 persons of the 2,224 aboard. The ship went down at 2:20 A.M., two and three quarter hours after smashing into an iceberg at full speed. The passengers included men of great wealth, high office, and world fame. The heavy loss of life was the result of the belief that the ship was unsinkable and the consequent neglect to provide enough lifeboats.

The theme of the poem, the rebuke of the "Pride of Life" in collision with a great natural force, parallels the publicity given this subject after the disaster. A news-story in the *Dorset County Chronicle* of April 18, which Hardy probably read, is typical. It emphasized the luxury of the ship, the rank and wealth of the passengers, and the pride that dared the elements. It spoke of members of the peerage aboard, "more than one millionaire," and scores "prominent in New York society." The ship was "the most luxuriously appointed vessel that had ever left a port." The article mentioned Turkish baths, an elaborate gymnasium, a palm court "with real ivy and crimson ramblers," mahogany panelling, bandstands and organs, and immense stores of wines, cream, and foods of all kinds. It contrasted these features with the "field of icebergs . . . of mountainous character" with surfaces "smooth as glass." Publicity was given to a question Mrs. Albert Caldwell asked when she boarded the *Titanic*: "Is this ship really unsinkable?" A deck-hand replied: "Yes, lady, God himself could not sink this ship."[2] "The Convergence of the Twain" is something like a rebuke to the deck-hand's arrogant quip.

Hardy had a personal as well as a general interest in the disaster. In a letter to Mrs. Arthur Henniker on April 14, he wrote: "I was thinking—the immediate cause of the thought being the disaster to the Titanic, in which I have lost two acquaintances—that we feel it such a blow when friends go off before us."[3] One of these acquaintances was William T. Stead, the editor of the *Review of Reviews*. Two passages in *The Later Years* establish Hardy's acquaintance with Stead: "In December [1895] he replied to Mr. W. T. Stead. . . : 'I am unable to answer your inquiry as to "Hymns that have helped me." But the undermentioned have always been familiar and favourite hymns of mine. . . .' " In 1899, "Mr. W. T. Stead had asked Hardy to express his opinion on 'A Crusade of Peace' in a periodical which he was about to publish under the name of *War against War*. In . . . reply Hardy wrote: 'As a preliminary, all civilized nations might at least show their humanity by covenanting that no horses should be employed in battle except for transport. . . .' "[4] The other acquaintance may have been John Jacob Astor. A sentence in *The Later Years* reads: "At a dinner at the Grand Hotel given by Mr. Astor to his contributors in May [1894], Hardy had a talk with Lord Roberts. . . ."[5] This host, however, may have been William Waldorf Astor.

"The Convergence of the Twain" is not a personal lament; it is a philosophic statement. The proud ship, symbol for "vain-gloriousness," with no mention of perished men, lies on the sea bottom, a victim of the Immanent Will's rebuke. The pride that built the ship is phrased as "human vanity," "the Pride of Life," "the opulent," "Jewels . . . to ravish the sensuous mind," and "gilded gear." The Will's rebuke is phrased as "a sinister mate" and "A Shape of Ice," created and governed by the command of the "Spinner of the Years," who says: "Now!"

The theme seems deterministic. As men built the ship the Will "Prepared a sinister mate / For her." This Will seems a symbol for the processes of natural law. It acts like the Greek concept of Fate that rebukes *hubris*. The personification implies, to feeling at least, that God, working in ways hidden from human sight, will not be mocked.

The technique of the poem is remarkable. The first five stanzas state a thesis. These stanzas that define the "Pride of Life" and picture the sunken ship before the disaster is narrated, describe the rebuke that has been administered. In each stanza the first two lines contrast the items of pride with the nature of the rebuke, as in stanza III: "Over the mirrors meant / To glass the opulent" contrast with "The sea-worm crawls—grotesque, slimed, dumb, indifferent." Then stanzas VI through X state the antithesis, the rebuke in preparation, and stanza XI, the resolution of thesis and antithesis. To picture an arrogance defiant of all simple, natural things, the diction of the thesis is lush: "Steel," "salamandrine," "sensuous," and "gilded." These stanzas present the antithesis and the resolution in the imagery of sexual consummation. The ship, always feminine, is on her maiden voyage, destined to meet a "sinister mate." She is ornamented as if for marriage, "gaily great" to meet a bridegroom, "a vague, menacing 'Shape of Ice.'" They are "to be joined in a lasting union by an 'intimate welding' that is to make them one . . . 'twin halves of one august event.'" When "the Spinner of the Years . . . utters the fatal word 'consummation comes,' . . . a shocking and unexpected end to the maiden voyage of the *Titanic*."[6]

1. Purdy, *Thomas Hardy: A Bibliographical Study*, p. 150.
2. Lord, *A Night to Remember*, p. 38.
3. In the Dorset County Museum.
4. Pp. 45, 81; *Life*, 274-75, 303.
5. P. 30; *Life*, p. 263.
6. Siegel, "Hardy's 'Convergence of the Twain.'"

THE GHOST OF THE PAST expresses Hardy's habit of living much (sometimes painfully) in the experiences of a vivid memory, and at the same time regret that, with advancing age, his remembered visions grow dim. The memories that are fading are not specified, but "up the stair / And down the stair" suggests his boyhood at Higher Bockhampton, where the back stair to Hardy's bedroom was a kind of ladder, and where "the Bygone," including his father and mother, is no longer alive. Perhaps many aging people have felt like Professor H. J. C. Grierson, who wrote Hardy on October 25, 1916, that the " 'Ghost of the Past' laid bare an experience I have often known but never found expressed—the sense of the past which a place revisited awakens & then the dreadful second sense wh. follows of that past growing remote & dead."[1] This musical lament that memory fades uses a refrain-like half-line to make us hear the fading of memory as "echoes faintlier played."

1. In the Dorset County Museum.

AFTER THE VISIT first appeared in the *Spectator* for August 13, 1910, but " ' (To F[lorence] E[mily] D[ugdale]) ' was not added until the poem was collected, when Miss Dugdale had become Hardy's second wife."[1]

The poem was written to Miss Dugdale after she had visited Max Gate some years before her marriage. The occasion may have been in June, 1907, when Hardy "presented her with a copy of *Wessex Poems,* and their friendship had continued and deepened."[2] The poem seems an accurate picture of Miss Dugdale as she looks in her portrait in the Dorset County Museum, with "large luminous living eyes." The details of her walk and her "mute ministrations" picture their impression on Hardy's mind. He liked to be cherished quietly and thoughtfully. Evelyn Hardy says that Miss Dugdale "remembered Mrs. Hardy's birthday, 'the only living soul to do so,' and she did research for Hardy when he was unable to do it himself. With her quiet, unobtrusive sympathy she deftly wove herself into their hearts, into Hardy's more securely than he knew."[3]

The first three stanzas describe Miss Dugdale's graceful physical presence, and the last three picture a spiritual quality, a "phantom's" form of one who seemed to ask of Life the questions Hardy was accustomed to ask. The poem comes to a climax in expressing an affinity of outlook with Hardy himself.

1. Purdy, *Thomas Hardy: A Bibliographical Study,* pp. 160-61.
2. Blunden, *Thomas Hardy,* p. 146.
3. *Thomas Hardy,* p. 298.

TO MEET, OR OTHERWISE was addressed to Florence Emily Dugdale and was first published in the *Sphere* on December 20, 1913.[1] Presumably it was written shortly before publication, or about a year after Mrs. Emma Hardy's death in November, 1912.

It is a love poem, presenting the problem stated in the title. There was no moral barrier to Hardy's meeting the "girl of my dreams." A meeting might be a step toward his remarriage. There was the question of wisdom, for he was seventy-three in 1913, and Miss Dugdale at thirty-four was less than half his age. There was also, perhaps, the question of loyalty to the memory of Emma, for whom his youthful love had revived. He was both lonely and strongly attracted to Miss Dugdale. As the poem argues, a meeting will give them both an opportunity to "scan / Round our frail faltering progress for some path or plan."

Aside from this question, the meeting will be a joy that will have been; almost quoting Milton, Hardy says, "Nor God nor Demon can undo the done."[2] The meeting will yield a moment of "human tenderness" in a universe where "things terrene / Groan in their bondage."

"To Meet, or Otherwise" meant a great deal to Hardy emotionally. He valued it as a revelation of himself and named it together with a love poem of his youth. Edward Thomas had selected some of Hardy's poems for an anthology. In a letter to Thomas on March 3, 1915, he wrote: "If your book is . . . to illustrate the idiosyncrasy of each writer, I am not sure that they [Thomas's selections] are so good as would be, say, 'When I Set Out for Lyonnesse,' or 'To Meet, or Otherwise,' or 'The Ballad Singer.' "[3]

1. Purdy, *Thomas Hardy: A Bibliographical Study*, p. 161.
2. Adam, speaking to Eve after she has eaten the forbidden fruit, says: "But past who can recall, or done undo? / Not God omnipotent, nor Fate." *Paradise Lost*, IX, ll. 925-26. Hardy's "Cimmerian" suggests the "Cimmerian desert" of Milton's "L'Allegro."
3. In the Miriam Lutcher Stark Library, University of Texas.

THE DIFFERENCE seems laid at Max Gate. The "Heartmate" who "will never see this gate" may be Hardy's sweetheart in his youth, Tryphena Sparks, who had died in 1890.

THE SUN ON THE BOOKCASE is both a love song and a self-portrait of young Hardy in love with Emma Gifford, his will to do "great deeds," and his tendency to dream of the "imaged one / Beyond the hills there." Weber relates the poem to Hardy's visit to St. Juliot in August of 1870: "On his return to Bockhampton, he often sat down to his desk to write, but instead found himself mooning about Emma."[1]

The subtitle "Student's Love-song" indicates that Hardy considered himself a student, though not enrolled in any school. The scene is his bedroom at Higher Bockhampton, which faced west and received the light of sunset upon the bookcase on the eastern wall. From the window he could see the "boiling ball" sink and imagine Emma in Cornwall beyond the hills. The date in the subtitle indicates the time of the "action" of the poem, not necessarily that of composition. In 1870, Hardy's great deeds in literature were all in the future. He had completed writing *Desperate Remedies*, but it had not yet been published.

1. *Hardy's Love Poems*, p. 19. See *Early Life*, pp. 103-5; *Life*, pp. 78-79.

"WHEN I SET OUT FOR LYONNESSE" is a lyric record of Hardy's first trip to St. Juliot in Cornwall on March 7, 1870, his falling in love with Emma Lavinia Gifford, and his return to Higher Bockhampton with "magic" in his eyes. *The Early Life* presents an account of this journey and its adventures.[1] Hardy's employer, the architect G. R. Crickmay, sent him to examine the dilapidated St. Juliot Church, near Boscastle on the coast of northern Cornwall, and to make recommendations for its repair. The journey was a tedious one of about a hundred miles, on foot, by a series of trains, and by horse-drawn wagonette. To get to St. Juliot in one day, he had to rise before dawn; he reached its isolated rectory after dark.[2] He associated Cornwall with the legends and poetic romances of King Arthur. He thought of the region as "Lyonnesse," as Swinburne spelled it in "Tristram of Lyonnesse." He took on his journey not only his architect's equipment, but a dream of adventure, a romantic heart, and a poem he had just written.

When he reached St. Juliot Rectory, he was met at the door by Emma Gifford, the sister-in-law of the rector, the Reverend Caddell Holder. Emma was interested to discover that a blue paper sticking out of his pocket was not a blueprint but a poem. During the three days of his stay, he and Emma were much together, investigating the Church, rambling along the picturesque coast, and singing and playing the piano. Hardy, frail, studious, and by no means athletic, was attracted to the opposite in Emma, her vitality. "The riding lessons her father had given her had made her an expert horsewoman, and she loved to gallop a mare she called Fanny over the wind-swept hills and up and down the narrow lanes in the neighborhood of St. Juliot. She could sing and paint, too. Some of her water-color sketches had been sold to help raise money for the restoration of the old Church. . . . King Arthur's ruined castle was not far away, on the rocky, black, northern coast of Cornwall—a coast quite different from the red cliffs and sandy beaches of south Dorset. . . . By night-time on Friday the eleventh he was back in his father's house. His mother noticed that something had happened but said nothing."[3]

Hardy described the form of "When I Set Out for Lyonnesse" in a letter to Mrs. Reginald Gould on May 16, 1924: "The Poem . . . is one of the many varieties of Roundelay, Roundel or Rondel, to which no specific name can be given. The Rondel in its strict form probably came originally from France."[4]

Hardy wrote that the poem "was hailed by a distant voice from the West of America as his sweetest lyric, an opinion from which he himself did not dissent."[5] To Mrs. Arthur Henniker he wrote on December 23, 1914: "I am so glad that you like 'When I set out for Lyonnesse.' It is exactly what happened 44 years ago." When Harriet Monroe proposed an anthology of the "new poetry" to include four poems by Hardy, he sent her a card on February 4, 1916, saying, "Add 'When I Set Out,'"[6] and he made a similar suggestion for Edward Thomas's anthology.

On January 9, 1920, he wrote to John Middleton Murry: "I want some day to get 'When I Set Out for Lyonnesse' set to music—to a pretty country tune that common people can sing. If anybody wants to do it, let me know." He wrote to Murry again on October 26, 1920: "I am awaiting the 'Lyonnesse' setting, which I know nothing of. . . . After all I have not thanked you for getting 'Lyonnesse' done, which however I do now."[7] Musical settings include: Charles Speyer, No. 1 in *Six Selected Lyrics* (London: Schott & Co., 1920); C. Armstrong Gibbs, *Lyonnesse* (London: Boosey & Co., 1933); Rutland Boughton's setting (London: Joseph Williams, 1926); Frederic Austin, in *Three Wessex Songs* (London and New York: Boosey & Co., 1927); Sidney Harrison, *When I Set Out for Lyonnesse* (London: Augener, 1929); Gerald Finzi in *Earth and Air and Rain* (London: Boosey & Hawkes, 1936); Tom M. McCourt, *When I Set Out for Lyonnesse* (York, England: Banks & Son, 1937); Christopher LeFleming, manuscript in the Colby College Library (c. 1938); anonymous music in the Colby College Library (Northampton, June, 1950); John Woods Duke, *When I Set Out for Lyonnesse* (Boston: R. D. Row Music Co., 1953); Harper MacKay, manuscript for *Five Songs* in the Colby College Library (1957); Leslie Walters, *When I Set Out for Lyonnesse* (London: J. B. Cramer & Co., 1957); and Christopher Fleming in *Six Country Songs* (London: Novello & Co., 1963).

1. Pp. 85-87, 98-99; *Life*, 65-66, 74-75.

2. Following maps and railroad schedules, Weber has reconstructed the journey in *Hardy's Love Poems*, pp. 5-7.

3. Weber, *Hardy of Wessex*, 1st ed. pp. 48-50.

4. In the Dorset County Museum. "I Rose and Went to Rou'tor Town" is a companion poem in the same verse form.
5. *Early Life*, p. 99; *Life*, p. 75.
6. In the Dorset County Museum.
7. In the Berg Collection, New York Public Library.

A THUNDERSTORM IN TOWN seems a reminiscence of an experience in which the "She" of the poem was Mrs. Arthur Henniker, whom Hardy met in 1893.

THE TORN LETTER was first published in the *English Review* for December, 1910.[1]

Mayers supposed the narrator of the poem to be a woman: "A woman, in a momentary fit of annoyance, destroys a letter from an unknown admirer. On reflection, she responds positively to the fund of affection it contains, repents, tries to reassemble the pieces, but cannot recover the name and address of the sender."[2] The poem does not say the narrator is a woman, and facts in his correspondence and temperament suggest that the narrator was Hardy and the experience actual. Among the Max Gate papers in the Dorset County Museum hundreds of letters to Hardy express admiration for his novels and poems and speak of the tears and solace they occasioned. Pencil notations on some letters indicate that he was touched by tributes from unknown admirers; other letters are marked "Unanswered." No doubt he destroyed many others.

The Later Years comments that after the publication of *Tess of the D'Urbervilles* Hardy received a large number of letters, many "from wives with a past like that of Tess, but who had *not* told their husbands, and asking for his counsel under the burden of their concealment. . . . However, they did themselves no harm . . . for though he was unable to advise them, he carefully destroyed their letters, and never mentioned their names, or suspected names, to a living soul."[3] Perhaps the torn letter was a poignant one from a woman in Tess's plight, to whom Hardy felt at the moment that he could offer no solace, but whose story made him feel "in darkness on my bed alone" that he should offer some reply. The concluding stanzas reflect his typical regret that an impulse from the Will caused him to miss an opportunity to know a "soul . . . of grain so tender."

1. Purdy, *Thomas Hardy: A Bibliographical Study*, p. 161.
2. "Dialectical Structures in Hardy's Poems," p. 17.
3. P. 5; *Life*, p. 244.

BEYOND THE LAST LAMP was first published with the title "Night in a Suburb" in *Harper's Monthly Magazine* (New York) for December, 1911.[1]

The experience recorded seems to be an actual one that, the poem suggests, occurred thirty years earlier.[2] From March, 1878, until June, 1881, the Hardys lived at 1 Arundel Terrace, Trinity Road, Upper Tooting, London, within walking distance of the scene of the poem "near" Tooting Common, an open parkland of nearly 150 acres six miles southwest of central London. In 1881, it was a somewhat rural area. The "lone lane" may be Church Lane that turns off Tooting Bec (a street beside and through the Common); Church Lane now has houses along one side, but possibly in 1881 the gas lamps on the thoroughfare did not extend down the Lane.

It was characteristic of Hardy to brood upon poignant scenes and recall them years later. The poem does not tell the story of the observed pair, but presents the memory of a scene to which the poet's imagination contributed a tragic meaning. What he imagined is suggested by a parallel scene in *Tess of the D'Urbervilles*. After Angel has turned away from Tess, she follows him out into the night, catches up with him, and appeals in vain for mercy. Then "They wandered on again in silence. It was said afterwards that a cottager of Wellbridge, who went out late that night for a doctor, met two lovers in the pastures, walking very slowly, without converse, one behind the other, as in a funeral procession, and the glimpse that he obtained of their faces seemed to denote that they were anxious and sad. Returning later, he passed them again in the same field, progressing just as slowly, and as regardless of the hour and of the cheerless night as before." He recalled this scene "a long while after." (Chapter XXXV.)

1. Purdy, *Thomas Hardy: A Bibliographical Study*, p. 161.
2. Deacon and Coleman have surmised that the action of the poem took place about 1870, when Hardy was engaged to Tryphena Sparks, and that the loiterers were Hardy and Tryphena, who was then in Stockwell College, three miles from Tooting Common. *Providence and Mr Hardy*, pp. 78-79.

THE FACE AT THE CASEMENT seems to narrate a personal experience. The mention of the garth (churchyard) of "sad Saint Cleather" and "that May eve" indicate the place and time of the action. St. Clether (so spelled) is a village in Cornwall just off the road between Launceston and Camelford, about eight miles east of St. Juliot Rectory, the home of Emma Gifford. In May, 1871, Hardy "enjoyed another visit to Cornwall."[1]

Phelps has supplied facts that tend to relate the poem to Hardy's courtship. He says that the poem "recalls a visit with Emma by pony chaise to the home of her former suitor, then dying from consumption. . . . A headstone in the churchyard marks the grave of Charles Raymond, who died from consumption in December, 1873, aged 38. In

the same grave lies his infant daughter, Emma, who died the pre-
vious August, aged three months. Charles Raymond was a master
miller at Lewannick, a parish 4 miles S.W. of Launceston and Emma
Gifford may well have met him when riding her pony from Bodmin,
her home from 1860 to 1868. In 1864, Raymond married Mary Jen-
kins, daughter of a master mason. . . . If Emma had followed the
career of her old suitor, she would have known of his marriage and
fatal illness. The intriguing fact is that the short-lived infant daughter
must have been conceived towards the end of 1872, a year after Emma's
call with Hardy. . . . Men often choose for their child the name of
their first love." [2]

The last stanza of the poem states the lover's remorse that he
yielded to an impulse prompted by jealous triumph over the dying
former suitor. This theme is expressesd in partial quotations from
two passages in the Bible. "Charity [Love] suffereth long" and other
terms from I Corinthians 13, are rephrased into "brave, / Sweet,
prompt, precious as a jewel," "But jealousy is cruel as the grave" is
from The Song of Solomon 8:6. To the extent that *A Pair of Blue
Eyes* is based upon Hardy's courtship of Emma Gifford, the story
of Felix Jethway, Elfride's dead suitor, may echo that of Charles
Raymond.

1. *Early Life,* p. 111; *Life,* p. 85.
2. *Annotations by Thomas Hardy in His Bibles and Prayer-Book,* p. 9.

LOST LOVE is a soliloquy spoken by a woman, evidently repre-
senting Mrs. Emma Hardy, during the period when relations between
her and Hardy were strained. He was aware of her attempt to recap-
ture his affection by playing for him the songs she had played during
his courtship, but he ignored it. *The Later Years* relates a similar
incident to a similar poem. In the autumn of 1912, shortly before
her death, Emma "one day suddenly sat down to the piano and played
a long series of her favourite old tunes, saying at the end she would
never play any more. The poem called 'The Last Performance' ap-
proximately describes this incident." [1]

1. P. 153; *Life,* p. 359.

"MY SPIRIT WILL NOT HAUNT THE MOUND" was first published in
Poetry and Drama for December, 1913.[1]

The speaker of this monologue may represent Mrs. Emma Hardy
speaking to her husband about plans for her to be buried in Stins-
ford Churchyard. (The poem says "will not," rather than "does not.")
The poem may be a fantasy based upon Hardy's visit to the scenes

of his courtship in Cornwall in 1913, and his sense of communing with Emma's spirit there.

It expresses the folk-belief "that only those who wish to see the dead, will see them, and see them in the old familiar places."[2] Hardy's thought is that in taking Emma out of Cornwall he had robbed her of an environment in which she had found "Life largest, best."

"My Spirit Will Not Haunt the Mound" has been set to music by David Leo Diamond (New York: The Southern Music Co., 1952) and Harper MacKay in *Five Songs* (in manuscript in the Colby College Library).

1. Purdy, *Thomas Hardy: A Bibliographical Study*, p. 162.
2. Firor, *Folkways in Thomas Hardy*, p. 61.

WESSEX HEIGHTS, according to the manuscript, was written in "December, 1896,"[1] the year of Hardy's deepest despair and of the "In Tenebris" poems, to which it is related in mood and in the theme of self-examination. His memories and feelings were engaged with persons poignantly clear in his consciousness, but not intended to be clear to others. That he did not publish "Wessex Heights" in his volumes of 1898, 1902, and 1909 suggests his hesitation to let the public see the poem, even though he had so concealed the persons that they probably would not have recognized themselves.

Two letters that Mrs. Florence Hardy wrote to Alda, Lady Hoare shortly after the poem was published point toward identifications. She wrote on December 6, 1914: "When I read 'Wessex Heights' it wrung my heart. It made me miserable to think that he [Hardy] had ever suffered so much. It was written in '96, before I knew him, but the four people mentioned are actual women. One was dead & three living when it was written—now only one is living." A letter of December 9 adds: " 'Wessex Heights' will *always* wring my heart, for I know when it was written, a little while after the publication of 'Jude,' when he was so cruelly treated."[2] When Hardy's reticence is considered, one may suppose that he asked Florence not to reveal the women's names even to an intimate friend.

The places of the poem are named. The heights are widely separated, each rising toward a corner of Wessex. "Ingpen" (Inkpen) Beacon stands to the northeast, near the junction of Wiltshire, Hampshire, and Berkshire. The peak is a lofty chalk hill with a view over rolling valleys. A line drawn almost due west from Inkpen would reach "Wylls-" (Will's) Neck, a hill 1261 feet high, the highest in the Quantocks. It rises in Somerset seven miles northwest of Taunton. Bulbarrow and Pilsdon "Crest" (Pen) lie to the south. Bulbarrow rises about five miles south of Sturminster Newton. Pilsdon Pen reaches 909 feet (the highest point in Dorset) about four miles west of Beaminster. If the heights are considered the corners of an irregular square, they enclose the heart of Wessex, except that the southern boundary does not extend to Dorchester and the sea. Each of the heights was in ancient times a hill-fort, and each exhibits tumuli and ramparts built by the Britons before the Roman conquest.[3] On these heights Hardy's point of view was concerned with "where I was before my birth, and after death may be."

The identities of the "actual women," one dead and three alive in 1896, but only one alive in 1914, cannot be positively determined. The second stanza as a whole, using the terms "they" and "nobody," seems to refer to people of all kinds in the lowlands who are intolerant of Hardy's ideas, but the word "Her" suggests that the first two lines refer to the first of the four actual women mentioned by Florence Hardy. The lines present a tangle of elliptical phrases in apposition and a Biblical allusion. She is "no comrade, not even the lone man's friend." To make sense of the seemingly contradictory phrases, "not even" must apply also to the phrases in apposition with "the lone man's friend." She is not even "Her who suffereth long and is kind." As this phrase is a partial quotation from I Corinthians, "Charity suffereth long, and is kind" (13:4), she lacks charity. Similarly, she not even "accepts what he [Hardy] is too weak to mend." That is, she is intolerant. What he was too weak to mend may be inferred from "In Tenebris II": his weakness may be that he cannot shut his eyes to injustice and cruelty. He is too weak to mend his vision by affirming that he sees what he does not see.

If this interpretation is right, the woman who is no comrade, no friend, without charity, and without tolerance is Mrs. Emma Hardy in her attitude and behavior in 1896. Aside from a general lack of accord in the 1890's, she had tried to prevent the publication of *Jude the Obscure*, which to Hardy was the most soul-searching of his novels and with which, according to Florence Hardy's letter, "Wessex Heights" was partly concerned. Presumably there was argument at Max Gate behind closed doors, after which Emma took the train for London and pled with Dr. Richard Garnett to prevent the publication of *Jude*. There were other subjects of strife. After *Tess* was published, visitors arrived from around the world to talk with Hardy. When he stated opinions that Emma thought outrageous, she would send apologetic notes to the visitors' hotel, saying that he did not mean what he said.

The second woman, the "figure against the moon" on the "great grey Plain" may represent Hardy's mother, Jemima, as she was in

Hardy's boyhood. The "great grey Plain," which critics have thought to be Salisbury Plain, may stand for Egdon. The sentence structure allows this identification and even suggests Hardy's intention to have the statement misread. He could have placed a period after the word "tune," for the preceding clauses are complete, and the next clause introduces a new place, a town. Though the statements are parallel, there is no necessary apposition. The semicolon would help concealment by *seeming* to link the Plain and Salisbury.

The surmise that the "great grey Plain" is Egdon is supported by the fact that in at least two other places Hardy presented a silhouetted figure on Egdon. The title of the sixth chapter of *The Return of the Native* is "The Figure Against the Sky." This figure is Eustacia on Egdon. In the poem "The Paphian Ball," the exact phrase, a "figure against the moon," describes a tempter who stands "by Rushy-Pond, / Where Egdon-Heath outstretched beyond."

Throughout his poems Hardy presented the moon as a symbol of cold reality. In "Shut Out that Moon," the moon steals away all dreams, fancies, and romances. "A Cathedral Façade at Midnight" presents the moon as opposed to religious dogma. Light from a rising moon creeps across the statues of "prophet, king, queen, cardinal" on a cathedral front. At this the "martyred saints there set" utter a "frail moan." The creeping moonlight is called "Reason's movement, making meaningless / The coded creeds of old-time godliness." The phrase "against the moon" is trivial if it means only silhouetted, but it is significant if it means *opposed* to the moon, or the force of faith opposed to "Reason's movement."

"In Tenebris III" supports the view that this figure may be Jemima. She upheld Hardy's boyhood faith in the lines that read: ". . . on that loneliest of eves when afar and benighted we stood, / She who upheld me and I, in the midmost of Egdon together, / Confident I in her watching and ward through the blackening heather, / Deeming her matchless in might and with measureless scope endued." Many statements indicate that "upheld me" concerns religious faith. When Hardy was a boy he was "kept strictly at church on Sundays . . . till he knew the Morning and Evening services by heart including the rubrics, as well as large portions of the New Version of the Psalms."[4]

That the "figure against the moon . . . makes my breast beat out of tune" also suggests Jemima. In 1896 Hardy could not share with her his views of life and of religious dogma. The poem "Night in the Old Home," presumably written after Jemima's death, pictures the poet sitting alone in his birthplace: "My perished people who housed them here come back to me." The old ones seat themselves in their "mouldy places," Jemima among them. They gaze upon Hardy with "A strange upbraiding smile upon all their faces" and call him "A thinker of crooked thoughts upon Life in the sere." In 1896 Jemima was no longer able to uphold her son in the indifferent universe that Egdon symbolizes.

The phrase "Nobody sees it but I" is significant in the light of Hardy's habits. Whenever he was in Dorchester, he would go each Sunday afternoon or evening to visit his mother. Emma, thinking Hardy's mother socially beneath her, would not go with him. If Jemima upbraided him for his "crooked thoughts," not only his love for his mother but also his religious feeling in conflict with agnostic reasoning would have made his breast beat out of tune.

The third woman seems designated by both the "ghost at Yell'ham Bottom chiding loud" and the "ghost in Froom-side Vale, thin-lipped and vague, in a shroud of white." These ghosts seem to represent Tryphena Sparks. It is possible to read the phrases as referring to two women but, if we rely on Florence Hardy's letter, we would have too many women, five instead of four. Several poems, for instance, "The Voice of the Thorn," suggest that Hardy's courtship of Tryphena took place in the dale below Yellowham Hill and that the lovers had a serious quarrel there, as "chiding loud" suggests. The poem "The Third Kissing-Gate" suggests that he courted Tryphena also in the meadows beside the Frome. That the ghost of Tryphena is "vague" is explained in the only poem that gives even a part of her name, "Thoughts of Phena," which devotes an entire stanza to wondering how she might have changed between his last sight of her in the early 1870's and her death in 1890. The poem says, "Thus I do but the phantom retain / Of the maiden of yore."

The fourth woman, the "one rare fair woman," is identifiable from Florence Hardy's letter of December 9 as Mrs. Arthur Henniker. The letter says: "Again, in 'Wessex Heights' there is one woman 'one rare fair woman' of whom he says 'Now I can let her go.' *She* has always been a sincere & affectionate friend to him, staunch & unaltering—& I am glad to say she is my friend too. There was never any idea of letting her go—for he, too, is true & faithful to his friends but the *poet* wrote that." [5]

These identifications are consistent with the letters. The woman who was dead in 1896 was Tryphena Sparks. Of the three women alive then, Emma died in 1912, and Jemima died in 1904. Mrs. Henniker lived until 1923. Though Hardy calls only one of the women a ghost, he represents each of the three who were alive as, in a sense, a phantom, symbolizing what the woman had been to him, but was no longer. Emma had been a comrade; Jemima, a foundation for his faith; and Mrs. Henniker, more responsive to his feeling.

The four women are not the only persons of the poem. In the towns, Hardy is "tracked by phantoms," some of whom seem friends of his youth in Dorchester, London, and Weymouth, ranging from architectual apprentices to dancing partners. The group must include Horace Moule, who had killed himself in 1873. The phantoms in the towns have "weird detective ways"; the men have a "wintry sneer" and the women "tart disparagings." They must include the journalists and reviewers who, after Hardy published *Tess* and *Jude*, pestered him in London and at Max Gate, prying for material about his private life. Perhaps they include members of Hardy's club, the Savile, who disapproved of these shocking novels, and women who made sharp remarks about them at the dinner tables to which he was invited. They include the reviewer who had called his last novel "Jude the Obscene," Jeanette Gilder who wrote a scathing review in the New York *World* and then, refused an audience with Hardy, eavesdropped, and Rebekah Owen, his ardent admirer who had joined Emma in disparaging *Jude*.

Hardy devotes the fourth stanza to a vision of himself as two phantoms. One is the memory of "my simple self that was," that is, the idealistic youth who composed the Wordsworthian poem "Domicilium" before he was twenty, a little later wrote the rebellious first novel *The Poor Man and the Lady*, and was the starry dreamer of the poem "In the Seventies." The second phantom of himself is the "crass . . . strange continuator" of the earlier "chrysalis," that is, perhaps Hardy the "good hand at a serial," the clubman, and the diner-out in elegant society—a traitor to the earlier self.

The first two lines of the fifth stanza, which may refer to Hardy's mother, are both separated from, and related by a semicolon to the last two lines, which continue a thought associated with religious faith. Lines three and four treat the "forms now passed" in the "tall-spired town," clearly Salisbury. These forms "barred" the poet from something. Possibly he had in mind officials of Salisbury Cathedral who had barred him from preparing to be a clergyman. *The Early Life* says that Hardy, at the age of sixteen, had "wished to enter the Church."[6] Dr. Elsie Smith, Librarian of Salisbury Cathedral, stated to me that she had discovered correspondence indicating Hardy's application to prepare himself for the Church and his rejection by the authorities. This rejection, a turning-point in his career, would in Hardy's "long vision . . . stand there fast." If this surmise is true, the fifth stanza has the unity that it treats his faith when upheld by his mother, and loss of faith when barred from the Church by the now-dead "forms" (authorities) in Salisbury. In *Jude the Obscure*, rejection by Christminster is a turning-point in Jude's career.

In the sixth stanza, the ghost in the railway train is mentioned in the same sentence as the one that may be Tryphena Sparks. This ghost is not certainly identifiable. It suggests "Little Father Time" of *Jude the Obscure* and of the poem "Midnight on the Great Western." Miss Deacon has suggested that this ghost represents "Randy," Hardy's son by Tryphena Sparks, on his way to or from Bristol, where he is alleged to have been brought up by Tryphena's brother, Nathaniel.[7] The evidence that Hardy ever had a son is controversial, but if the ghost is fictional, it seems the only fictional character in the poem.

Like Florence Hardy, Sir George Douglas, Hardy's close friend, related the despair in "Wessex Heights" to the hostile reception of *Jude*. He wrote: "Hardy, most sensitive of men, was grieved to the soul by the brutality and injustice which he saw thus meted out to him. And if anyone desires to judge the depth of his grief, let that person read the poem entitled *Wessex Heights* and dated 1896. . . . To him this persecution meant rejection of his life's work."[8] The total poem suggests that the attacks upon *Jude* were only a part of the forces creating his depression.

Alone on high places he could feel free from crushing pressures, or free to be himself mentally, imaginatively, and spiritually. His memories would be with him on the heights, but the burial mounds of ancient men who had found peace on the hill tops would provide a philosophic perspective in which the ghosts would "keep their distance."

Hardy thus presents, in application to his own life, a thought he had expressed in *Far from the Madding Crowd*: "The poetry of motion is a phrase much in use, and to enjoy the epic form of that gratification it is necessary to stand on a hill at a small hour of the night, and, having first expanded with a sense of difference from the mass of civilized mankind . . . long and quietly watch your stately progress through the stars." (Chapter II.)

1. Purdy, *Thomas Hardy: A Bibliographical Study*, p. 162.
2. In the Stourhead Collection, the County Archives in Trowbridge, Wiltshire.
3. The tumuli are not exactly on each peak. At Bulbarrow, for instance, they are on an eminence about two hundred yards away called Rawlsbury Camp.
4. *Early Life*, p. 23; *Life*, p. 18.
5. Purdy agrees with this identification of Mrs. Henniker. He says that Hardy's "impossible love" for her "had come to an end by December, 1896." *Thomas Hardy: A Bibliographical Study*, p. 346.

IN DEATH DIVIDED is probably a personal poem, in spite of Duffin's statement that the lover is "clearly not Hardy this time."[1] Purdy points to the date "189—" and says that the poem "is perhaps to be associated with Mrs. Henniker."[2] As "The Division," speaking of the "hundred miles between" them, was written to Mrs. Henniker, the word "Divided" suggests her, but Mrs. Henniker lived until 1923, and Hardy in the 1890's would not have known where she might be buried—though certainly it would not be in Stinsford.

Possibly the poem is addressed to his youthful sweetheart, Tryphena Sparks. The date of the poem, "189—," may represent 1890, the year of Tryphena's death. Other suggestions also point to Tryphena. The poet says that he will "rot here" among those whom the beloved never knew, as beside Emma Hardy. The poet speaks of the "simply-cut memorial" in "rustic form" that he expects to have above his grave, in contrast with "that above your bed / A stately make." Tryphena, buried in Topsham Cemetery, had only a Cross as headstone, but ten feet from her grave the tomb of Lieutenant Francis Ross is a somewhat Grecian monument, with the marble effigy of Lieutenant Ross lying upon a couch. In the first edition of *Wessex Poems*, Hardy's illustration for "Thoughts of Phena" is a drawing strikingly similar to the tomb of Lieutenant Ross.[3] If the "divided" burial places are Topsham and Stinsford, the graves are about fifty miles apart.

1. *Thomas Hardy*, p. 290.
2. *Thomas Hardy: A Bibliographical Study*, p. 162.
3. Both Lieutenant Ross's tomb and Hardy's drawing for "Thoughts of Phena" are pictured opposite page 113 in Deacon and Coleman's *Providence and Mr Hardy*. In the first edition of *Satires of Circumstance*, the fourth stanza of "In Death Divided" suggests the "Greek" monument near Tryphena's grave. It reads: "The simply-cut memorial at my head / Perhaps may take / A Gothic form, and that above your bed / Be Greek in make. . . ."

THE PLACE ON THE MAP was first published in the *English Review* for September, 1913, with the subtitle "A Poor Schoolmaster's Story."[1]

Weber believes the poem treats an episode of Hardy's courtship of Emma Gifford. He says that at St. Juliot, in 1873, "Once again, on 'a day of latter summer, hot and dry,' the two paid a visit to the coast. There, near 'a jutting height . . . with a margin of blue sea' —obviously Beeny Cliff again—Emma 'calmly quite . . . unfolded what would happen by and by.' . . . The thing they had to face was the risk of marriage with no more financial security than Hardy's pen was able to provide, and with parental disapproval lowering in the background. Both lovers knew that Mr. Gifford would never forgive them if they married."[2]

Deacon and Coleman believe the poem is concerned with the love of Hardy and Tryphena Sparks in the summer of 1867.[3] In this interpretation the scene of the poem is the "jutting height" of Portland. There, they say, Tryphena told him that she was to bear his child. Their evidence that Hardy and Tryphena had and successfully concealed a child is doubtful.

Interpretations that twist the poem to fit Hardy's life or twist the facts of his life to fit the poem are not necessary. The poem may be what its original subtitle suggests, a fiction about a schoolmaster too poor to marry his pregnant sweetheart, and this man's rebellion against "order-keeping's rigorous control" that would condemn her and himself to an undesired marriage.

1. Purdy, *Thomas Hardy: A Bibliographical Study*, p. 162.
2. *Hardy's Love Poems*, p. 26.
3. *Providence and Mr Hardy*, pp. 184-85.

THE SCHRECKHORN first appeared in F. W. Maitland's *The Life and Letters of Leslie Stephen*, in 1906. The poem was part of a sketch of Stephen that Hardy contributed, but he did not write the poem especially for the biography. He and Stephen had been friends for many years; Stephen was the first man to climb the Schreckhorn (a peak in the Swiss Alps, 13,379 feet high); and when the Hardys toured Europe in 1897, Hardy associated the sight of the mountain with his memory of Stephen. He wrote: "Then and there I suddenly had a vivid sense of him, as if his personality informed the mountain —gaunt and difficult, like himself. . . . As I lay awake that night, the more I thought of the mountain, the more permeated with him it seemed: I could not help remarking to my wife that I felt as if the Schreckhorn were Stephen in person; and I was moved to begin a sonnet to express the fancy."[1]

Leslie Stephen, born in 1832, was about eight years older than Hardy. He did a good deal of mountain climbing and was a member (in 1865-68, president) of the Alpine Club. When Hardy went to London in 1862 to work for the architect Blomfield, the architect's office was at 8 St. Martin's Place; the Alpine Club also had rooms at this address. In that year, Stephen published *Peaks, Passes, and Glaciers*, describing his ascent of the Schreckhorn in 1861. As editor of the *Cornhill* magazine in 1871-82, Stephen read *Under the Greenwood Tree* and asked Hardy for a novel. Hardy sent him *Far from the*

Madding Crowd and later *The Hand of Ethelberta*; however, Stephen rejected *The Return of the Native* (on the basis of early chapters) as not suitable for a "family magazine," not because he was prudish, but because readers of the *Cornhill* were. He said, "I spoke as an editor, not as a man. You have no more consciousness of these things than a child." Stephen had been an Anglican clergyman, but in 1864 gave up his fellowship at Cambridge because of religious scruples. When he wished to withdraw altogether from the ministry, he wrote out a deed relinquishing the rights and privileges of a clergyman and, on March 23, 1875, called in Hardy to witness it. After 1876, Hardy and Stephen continued friendly, exchanged gifts, and corresponded, but met only now and then. Stephen died February 22, 1904.[2]

Hardy's sonnet compares the "spare and desolate" Schreckhorn with Stephen's "personality . . . and rugged trim." Virginia Woolf, Stephen's daughter, wrote Hardy on January 17, 1915: "That poem, and the reminiscences you contributed to Professor Maitland's life of him, remain in my mind as incomparably the truest & most imaginative portrait of him in existence."[3]

1. Maitland, p. 277.
2. Summarized from Maitland; *Early Life*; *Later Years*; and *Life*, all *passim*.
3. In the Dorset County Museum.

A SINGER ASLEEP was published in the *English Review* for April, 1910.[1] Swinburne died on April 10, 1909, and was buried at Bonchurch, on the Isle of Wight near the sea. Hardy did not attend the funeral, but in March of 1910 he "visited Swinburne's grave . . . and composed the poem entitled 'A Singer Asleep.' It is remembered by a friend who accompanied him on this expedition how that windy March day had a poetry of its own, how primroses clustered in the hedges, and noisy rooks wheeled in the air over the little churchyard. Hardy gathered a spray of ivy and laid it on the grave of that brother-poet of whom he never spoke save in words of admiration and affection."[2] He did not complete the poem on the spot. On March 13 he wrote to Frederic Harrison, who had asked for a poem for the *English Review*: "Since receiving your letter I have hunted over my papers for something that might suit. . . . All I can lay hands on is a half-finished monody on Swinburne, which I am completing."[3]

Hardy was both an admirer of Swinburne's poetry and a personal friend. "A Singer Asleep" pictures his reaction to Swinburne's early poetry when he was working as an architect in London. He summed up in a conversation with Ernest Brennecke the substance of the third stanza: "I used to walk from my lodgings near Hyde Park to the draughting office every morning, and never without a copy of the first edition of the *Poems and Ballads* sticking out of my pocket."[4] He met Swinburne about 1887,[5] after which time the poets corresponded. On June 20, 1899, he "visited Swinburne at Putney, of which visit he too briefly speaks; observing, 'Again much inclined to his engaging, fresh, frank, almost childlike manner. Showed me his interesting editions, and talked of a play he was writing. Promised to go again.' " He did so in 1905: "In this June . . . he paid a promised visit to Swinburne. . . . 'Swinburne's grey eyes are extraordinarily bright still —the brightness of stars that do not twinkle—planets namely. . . . He spoke with amusement of a paragraph he had seen in a Scottish paper: "Swinburne planteth, Hardy watereth, and Satan giveth the increase." He has had no honours offered him. . . . We laughed and condoled with each other on having been the two most abused of living writers; he for *Poems and Ballads*, I for *Jude the Obscure.*' " When Hardy heard of the death of Swinburne, he wrote: "No doubt the press will say some good words about him now he is dead and does not care whether it says them or no. Well, I remember what it said in 1866, when he did care."[6]

Swinburne's poetry had some influence upon Hardy.[7] Webster says that "Swinburne's militant anti-theism and his flouting of conventions may have had a definite effect upon Hardy. Reading *Poems and Ballads* Hardy came upon many vigorous denunciations of the Providence against which he himself rebelled. . . . But on the intellectual side Swinburne's influence was negligible. Despite the fact that he wished that he might, Hardy was never able to believe in a 'vengeful God' who wished man's unhappiness and could be defied. Hardy's 'purblind Doomsters' have little in common with Swinburne's God, and Hardy's early philosophy only superficially resembles Swinburne's combination of republicanism and paganism."[8]

"A Singer Asleep" describes where Swinburne "lies in that beautiful orchard-terrace, within an apple-cast of the garden in which his childhood was so happily spent. On loud nights the trumpet of the sea is audible from the spot where he sleeps."[9] It cuts back to tell of Hardy's youthful thrill (the experience of his generation) in reading *Poems and Ballads* and of "the brabble and the roar" occasioned by these unconventional verses.[10] It relates Swinburne as poet to Sappho, a Greek poetess of passion who is said to have drowned herself for unrequited love of Phaon, by leaping from the Leucadian promontory into the sea.[11]

A letter of Katherine Mansfield reports: "Then we [Miss Mansfield and J. Middleton Murry] read Hardy's poem to Swinburne, which J.

adored. I, being an inferior being, was a little troubled by the picture of Sappho and Algernon meeting en plein mer (if one can say such a thing) and he begging her to tell him where her manuscript was. It seemed such a watery rendezvous. But we went on reading Hardy. How exquisite, how marvellous some of those poems are!"[12]

1. Purdy, *Thomas Hardy: A Bibliographical Study*, p. 163.
2. *Later Years*, p. 141; *Life*, p. 349.
3. In the Miriam Lutcher Stark Library, University of Texas.
4. *The Life of Thomas Hardy*, p. 5.
5. Evelyn Hardy, *Thomas Hardy's Notebooks*, p. 73.
6. *Later Years*, pp. 82-83, 111-12, 135; *Life*, pp. 304, 325, 344. The Dorset County Museum has five letters from Swinburne to Hardy, dated from 1887 to 1904, all praising his novels and poems. For some years, a portrait of Swinburne hung over the fireplace in Hardy's study.
7. In the first edition of *Hardy of Wessex*, Weber points out that "in the serial version of *Tess of the D'Urbervilles*, 'The Garden of Proserpine' and 'Behold, When Thy Face Is Made Bare' are quoted. In *Jude* the 'Prelude' to 'Songs Before Sunrise' and the 'Hymn to Proserpine' are quoted. 'Aholibah' is mentioned in *Tess*, and 'Tristram of Lyonnesse' is echoed in poems about Lyonnesse and in Hardy's play *The Queen of Cornwall*." P. 245. Evelyn Hardy says: "The 'Hymn to Proserpine' and 'Atalanta' provided further food for Hardy's tormented thoughts which he transmuted in his own manner." *Thomas Hardy*, p. 73.
8. *On a Darkling Plain*, pp. 60-61.
9. Gosse, *The Life of Algernon Charles Swinburne*, p. 282.
10. For example, the *Saturday Review* for August 4, 1866, said: "And no language is too strong to condemn the mixed vileness and childishness of depicting the spurious passion of a putrescent imagination, the unnamed list of sated wantons, as if they were the crown of character and their enjoyment the great glory of human life."
11. Her poetry remains only in fragments, the "orts" of Hardy's poem.
12. Murry, *The Letters of Katherine Mansfield*, p. 411.

A PLAINT TO MAN in the manuscript was titled "The Plaint of a Puppet."[1] The poem reverses the assumption of *The Dynasts*, in which men are puppets manipulated by impulses from an Immanent Will. In "A Plaint to Man," the anthropomorphic God of traditional religion is the puppet. This puppet speaks to His creator, the human race, to inquire why men created Him and to suggest that it is now time for men to rely upon "the human heart's resource alone," with "visioned help unsought, unknown."

The sources of Hardy's concept that God is a creation of the human mind are complex. One source is probably Shelley's *The Revolt of Islam*, in which the poet asks "What is that Power?" to whom men look for supernatural help, and answers: "Some moon-struck sophist stood / Watching the shade from his own soul upthrown / Fill Heaven and darken Earth, and in such mood / The Form he saw and worshipped was his own."[2] The idea that man seeks in vain for help from an anthropomorphic God is expressed in Swinburne's line on man: "Save his own soul he hath no star."

Hardy quoted this line in his journal for April 15, 1909, and then noted: "But Isaiah had said before him: 'Mine own arm brought salvation unto me.'"[3] Other sources may include J. S. Mill's *Three Essays on Religion*, Matthew Arnolds' *Empedocles on Etna* and *Literature and Dogma*, and the writings of the Positivists.

In relation to *The Dynasts*, "A Plaint to Man" helps define Hardy's meaning in personifying natural forces as an Immanent Will, especially his meaning in the After Scene. The Will is to be understood as a symbol for the aggregate of all individual wills. Then the conclusion, "Consciousness the Will informing, till It fashion all things fair," is not to be read as hope that some manlike Will may become conscious and reform natural law and the impulses by which It guides human action. Instead, human knowledge and compassion may, in evolutionary time, amplify in all men and move them to remedy the ills that flesh has inherited from a subhuman past.

The poem sketches the evolution of man "from the den of Time" through growing "percipience" until man, feeling himself the victim of natural laws and desiring help beyond his powers, day-dreamed of a manlike, all-powerful God to Whose "mercy-seat / Somewhere above the gloomy aisles / Of this wailful world" he could petition for help. Man has so matured intellectually, especially in "the deicide eyes of seers," that he had best depend upon "the human heart's resource alone." These seers are presumably such clergymen as the authors of *Essays and Reviews*, such scientists as Huxley and Haeckel, and such rationalists as Mill and Spencer. Now, according to the poem, only the "showman"—the priest—is able to keep the man-created God "vivified."

The poem is a challenge to man to develop "brotherhood bonded close and graced / With loving-kindness," without any reward beyond the improvement of human life. In this message, "there is here no sneering at the traditional beliefs of mankind. God was needed by earlier generations—a gentle anodyne for the brute facts of life. . . . Yet if there is no sneering at traditional religion, there is no compromise with it either. . . . Man surrenders his hopes of supernatural help. But he is at the same time unloosed from the shackles of supernatural awe and fear."[4] "A Plaint to Man" may be considered a companion-poem to "God's Funeral."

1. Purdy, *Thomas Hardy: A Bibliographical Study*, p. 163.
2. Canto VIII, ix, 1-4. Hardy quotes "the shade from his own soul upthrown" in *The Mayor of Casterbridge*, Chapter XLIV.
3. *Later Years*, p. 137; *Life*, p. 345. The quotations are from line 158 of "Prelude" to *Songs Before Sunrise*, and Isa. 63:5.
4. Wedel, "Our Pagan World," p. 336.

GOD'S FUNERAL is dated 1908-10, denoting when Hardy began and finished the poem. Though *The Later Years* says that he published it toward the end of 1910, it was first published in the *Fortnightly Review* for March, 1912, with the subtitle "An Allegorical Conception of the present state of Theology."[1] He had submitted to the editor an alternative title: " 'The Funeral of Jahveh'—the subject being the gradual decline and extinction in the human race of a belief in an anthropomorphic god of the King of Dahomey type—a fact recognized by all bodies of theologians for many years."[2]

These varied titles help explain what Hardy meant by the shocking suggestion that God is dead. The poem presents in an allegory the fading belief in the God inherited by Christianity from the Hebrew writings of the Old Testament.[3] Though the Bible and Christian creeds include the Old Testament, Hardy supposed that all bodies of theologians had ceased to accept portions of it as literally true, as the Anglican clergymen who published *Essays and Reviews* in 1860 had.

Hardy long pondered the difference between the theology of the Old Testament and religion as a spiritual force within man capable of bringing about human brotherhood. To Frederic Harrison on January 1, 1892, he wrote of *Tess of the D'Urbervilles*: "In the first draft of the story I said much more on religion as apart from theology. But I thought it might do more harm than good, and omitted the arguments, merely retaining the conclusions."[4] On January 17, 1897, he wrote to Edward Clodd: "What seems to me the most striking idea dwelt upon is that of the arrest of light and reason by theology for 1600 years. The older one gets the more deplorable seems the effect of that terrible, dogmatic ecclesiasticism—Christianity so called (but really Paulinism *plus* idolatry) —on morals & true religion: a dogma with which the real teaching of Christ has hardly anything in common." He wrote to Clodd again on February 27, 1902: "If the doctrines of the supernatural were quietly abandoned tomorrow by the Church, & 'reverence & love for an ethical ideal' alone retained, not one in ten thousand would object to the readjustment, while the enormous bulk of thinkers excluded by the old teaching would be brought into the fold, & our venerable old churches & cathedrals would become the centres of emotional life that they once were."[5] In the light of these statements, "God's Funeral" must be interpreted as Hardy's effort to save religion for those who could not accept the ancient superstitions mingled into Christian teachings.

His allegory presents the development of concepts of God from those expressed in early Hebrew writings to those held by modern scholars: the seers of the "slowly-stepping train—/ Lined on the brows, scoop-eyed and bent and hoar" who follow the corpse of the defunct God. In the earliest concepts, God was a monarch of power, "jealous, fierce, at first," as in Exodus 20:5: "for I the Lord thy God am a jealous God." In a later concept, He was a God of justice, but patient and merciful toward His chosen people, as in Ps. 103:6, 8, "The Lord executeth righteousness and judgment for all that are oppressed. . . . The Lord is merciful, slow to anger." In each era men believed that a personal God must possess the attributes they conceived as desirable, but modern "rude reality," for instance, Darwinism, which demonstrates the legendary nature of Genesis, has "Mangled the Monarch" so conceived.[6]

If the God of these anthropomorphic concepts is dead, the question remains: what new, rationally acceptable religion can "fill his place"? The poem suggests "A pale yet positive gleam low down behind, / . . . to lift the general night" of a world without faith. This gleam is partly defined in the companion-poem "A Plaint to Man," and later in Hardy's "Apology" for *Late Lyrics and Earlier*. It is clear (as in stanzas XII and XIV-XVI) that he wished to promote a rationally acceptable religion. It must include "loving-kindness, pale beside the glittering promise of eternal life, but positive in that it promises some discernible movement in the direction of improving man's circumstances."[7] He indicated some details of this concept in a conversation with Frédéric Lefèvre in 1925: "By religion I mean the religious spirit. . . . I believe that we are moving toward the disappearance of dogmas. . . . I dream of an alliance between religions freed from dogmas. The religion which ought to be preserved if the world is not to perish absolutely and which we must achieve if the world is not to perish, an alliance of rationalism and religion, would be created by poetry. . . . Poetry, pure literature, and religion are the visible points of the most authentic mental and emotional life."[8]

Hardy expressed disappointment that reviewers interpreted "God's Funeral" as an attack upon religion rather than an attempt to point toward a faith acceptable to the twentieth century. A deleted passage at the end of *The Later Years* is found in the typescript of the "3rd Rough Copy": "However what happened was that nobody seemed to read more of the poem than the title, the result of this and kindred poems lines [*sic*] of his being that the poet was grotesquely denounced as a blaspheming atheist by a 'phrasemongering literary contortionist' (as Hardy used to call him), and rebuked by dogmatists, because he had turned into verse the view of the age."[9]

1. Purdy, *Thomas Hardy: A Bibliographical Study*, p. 163.

2. *Later Years*, p. 147; *Life*, p. 354.

3. "Jahveh" is a transliteration of the Hebrew for the tribal God called Jehovah. The "King of Dahomey" refers to the monarch of a former African kingdom noted for barbarities and human sacrifices.

4. Bowden, "The Thomas Hardy Collection," p. 10.

5. In the British Museum.

6. The imagery of this description is drawn from the Old Testament. The third and fourth lines of stanza X paraphrase Ps. 130:1, "By the rivers of Babylon, there we sat down, yea, we wept, when we remembered Zion."

7. Tuttleton, "Thomas Hardy and the Christian Religion," p. 336.

8. "An Hour with Thomas Hardy," pp. 101-2.

9. In the Dorset County Museum. The "contortionist" was G. K. Chesterton. See the poem "Epitaph (for G. K. Chesterton)."

SPECTRES THAT GRIEVE was first published in the *Saturday Review* for January 3, 1914, with the title "The Plaint of Certain Spectres."[1] There is no clue to the identity of the spectres, except that they are the ghosts of men misrepresented in "History." The poem rests upon an idea characteristic of Hardy, that the dead have some immortality in the memory of the living. It gives this idea the twist that those remembered falsely and maligned cannot rest in their graves until justice is done to their memory. That they rise on New Year's Eve may owe something to folklore.

1. Purdy, *Thomas Hardy: A Bibliographical Study*, p. 163.

"AH, ARE YOU DIGGING ON MY GRAVE?" appeared in the *Saturday Review* on September 27, 1913.[1]

The similarity in theme and structure between Hardy's poem and A. E. Housman's No. XXVII ("Is My Team Ploughing?") of *A Shropshire Lad*, published in 1896, suggests a source. In a letter of March 28, 1933, Housman wrote to Houston Martin: "I could not say that I have a favourite among my poems. Thomas Hardy's was No. XXVII in *A Shropshire Lad*."[2] *The Later Years* states that Hardy met Housman on June 18, 1899, entertained him at Max Gate and bicycled with him in August, 1900, and was with him at Cambridge in November, 1913, shortly after Hardy's poem was published.[3] Possibly while at Cambridge, Hardy and Housman discussed Hardy's new poem and he told Housman that "Is My Team Ploughing?" was his favorite.

Hardy's poem begins where Housman's ends. Housman's climax is the revelation that the dead man's friend has married his sweetheart; in Hardy's first stanza, the dead woman's lover has just married another woman. Housman's irony concerns a friend and a sweetheart; Hardy's goes farther, to kin, an enemy, and even the dead woman's dog. The structure of questions and answers, each more devastating to the hopes of the dead, is the same in both poems.[4]

Perhaps Housman's poem appealed to Hardy because both the subject (the fading memory of the living for the dead, as in "His Immortality") and the structure that strips away sentimental hopes one by one (as in "Heiress and Architect") are characteristic of Hardy. A difference between the two poems is that Housman's is wryly stark, but Hardy's is humorous. The humor is partly in the surprise that the talking dog is burying a bone, and partly in the imagery and diction, as of the dog on his "daily trot."

1. Purdy, *Thomas Hardy: A Bibliographical Study*, p. 164.
2. Housman, *My Brother, A. E. Housman*, p. 193.
3. Pp. 82, 86, 158; *Life*, pp. 304, 306, 363.
4. For a detailed analysis, see Edgren, "A Hardy-Housman Parallel."

SELF-UNCONSCIOUS describes a scene "Near Bossiney," a village on the coast of Cornwall about two and a half miles southwest of Boscastle, near which Emma Gifford lived. From the "way" between Boscastle and Bossiney, the picturesque coast and the sea are visible across the fields, usually alive with birds. The scene printed itself on Hardy's memory when his mind was too busy with day-dreams either to appreciate its beauty then or to reason objectively about himself.

Weber relates the poem to Hardy's second visit to Cornwall in August of 1870. Concerning that visit, Emma Hardy's *Recollections* says that "Sometimes we all [Hardy, Emma, Mrs. Holder, and perhaps others] drove to . . . Bossiney" among other places along the coast. According to the poem, Hardy was alone at the time recalled, perhaps shortly after a drive with Emma. Weber supposes that "Self-Unconscious" was written in 1913 when he "was revisiting this spot to which he and E. L. G. had driven together."[1] Evelyn Hardy suggests that the poem treats a reverie of the "distressing years" of the 1890's, when Hardy's marriage with Emma was held together by custom rather than affection.[2]

The poem indicates that if Hardy could have seen his own nature clearly and reasoned objectively about Emma he would not have married her. V. H. Collins, puzzled by the poem, asked the meaning of the line "As he was, and should have been shown, that day." Hardy replied, "If he had realized, when young, what he was, he would have acted differently. That is the tragedy of youth: when we know, it is too late to alter things."[3] In the light of this explication, the poem seems to say that Hardy failed realistically to assess himself, Emma, or the facts around him. He did not see the "thing . . . / That loomed with an immortal mien," the distress that, in the 1890's, resulted from his marriage.

[289]

1. *Hardy's Love Poems*, p. 18. See Evelyn Hardy and Gittings, *Some Recollections by Emma Hardy*, pp. 57-58.
2. *Thomas Hardy*, p. 271.
3. Quoted by Weber, *Hardy's Love Poems*, pp. 92-93.

THE DISCOVERY describes the final stage of Hardy's journey to Cornwall on March 7, 1870. *The Early Life* presents the journey as "The dreary yet poetical drive over the hills. Arrived at St. Juliot Rectory between 6 and 7. Received by young lady in brown, (Miss Gifford, the rector's sister-in-law)." The "fires—/ Funeral pyres / Seemingly" were probably the sunset over the Cornish cliffs,[1] but the poem may have fused the recollected sight with another seen the next morning: "Austere grey view of hills from bedroom window. A funeral."[2] The macabre suggestion contrasts with the "Love-nest, / Bowered and candle-lit."

1. They may have been lighthouses along the Cornish coast. "A Man Was Drawing Near to Me," treating the same scene, speaks of "the seaward pharos-fire."
2. P. 98; *Life*, p. 74.

TOLERANCE "dates from the death of Hardy's first wife in November 1912."[1] It states his reflection upon his forbearance toward Emma's eccentricities (including attempts to obstruct his work) in the 1890's. "When a French writer, M. Henri Davray, called at Max Gate, he left with the impression that Hardy was 'timid and resigned to a situation he could not improve.'" What Davray called "timid," Hardy "preferred to call . . . 'tolerant,' and he meant that word in its Latin sense: enduring, forbearing."[2] "Tolerance" suggests how his view that men are ruled by forces and impulses beyond control leads toward pity and love. It is transitional to the "Poems of 1912-13" that recall and idealize Hardy's youthful love for Emma.

"Tolerance" has been set to music by Robin Milford in *Four Hardy Songs* (Oxford University Press, 1939).

1. Purdy, *Thomas Hardy: A Bibliographical Study*, p. 165.
2. Weber, *Hardy's Love Poems*, pp. 49, 58.

BEFORE AND AFTER SUMMER was published in the *New Weekly* for April 4, 1914, which states that it was "Written in 1910."[1] Hardy did not care much for this light but charming comment on the seasons. He wrote to Frederic Harrison on March 23, 1914, about "The Year's Awakening," given to Scott James for publication in the *New Weekly*, and added: "Also another little scrap like it, which I hope he won't print."[2] "Before and After Summer" has been set to music in *Before and After Summer: Ten Songs for Baritone and Piano* (London: Boosey & Hawkes, 1949).

1. Purdy, *Thomas Hardy: A Bibliographical Study*, p. 165.
2. In the Miriam Lutcher Stark Library, University of Texas.

AT DAY-CLOSE IN NOVEMBER in the manuscript was titled "Autumn Evening."[1] Though the poem presents a late afternoon in November, with its "ten hours' light," November in the title and June in the poem seem to refer to old age and youth. The scene is Hardy's home at Max Gate. When the Hardys moved into the new house in June, 1885, it was stark and bare on a hilltop. Then, says *The Early Life,* "Some two or three thousand small trees, mostly Austrian pines, were planted around the house by Hardy himself, and in later years these grew so thickly that the house was almost entirely screened from the road, and finally appeared, in summer, as if at the bottom of a dark green well of trees."[2] The poem has been set to music by Benjamin Britten in a song-cycle called *Winter Words* (London and New York: Boosey and Hawkes, 1954).

1. Purdy, *Thomas Hardy: A Bibliographical Study,* p. 165.
2. Pp. 226-27; *Life,* p. 173.

THE YEAR'S AWAKENING was first published in the *New Weekly* for March 21, 1914.[1] Writing to Frederic Harrison on March 23, Hardy said, "Please don't look at the 'New Weekly'—I mean my contribution to it. Scott James came here one day, and I found that poor pair of stanzas in a drawer and could find nothing else, so I let him have them at his earnest request."[2]

The poem expresses two of Hardy's characteristic ideas. First, he wondered at the knowledge animals and plants have of secrets not comprehensible to the rational mind. Of course he knew the scientific term "ecological adaptation" as the name of a biological process, but he wondered what force impels and guides this process.

Second, regretting that consciousness, with its awareness of pain and its illusion of freedom (and hence responsibility), developed in man as a part of evolution, he saw in the instinctive will-to-live some hope of a purpose in the life-process not yet understood by human reason. The poem states the question "How do you know?" six times. The answer must be an intuition or impulse that springs from the unknowable reality at the core of existence. (This idea is developed in the conclusion of "The Darkling Thrush.")

In defining the seasons with reference to the stars, Hardy makes use of the zodiac. The "Fishes' bounds / And into the Ram" denotes from late February until mid-April.

1. Purdy, *Thomas Hardy: A Bibliographical Study,* p. 165.
2. In the Miriam Lutcher Stark Library, University of Texas.

UNDER THE WATERFALL in the manuscript was titled "The Glass in the Stream."[1]

The poem is based upon an incident of Hardy's trip to Cornwall in August of 1870, to visit Emma Gifford. Shortly before her death, Emma Hardy wrote *Some Recollections* that included the story of Hardy's courtship. *The Early Life*, quoting her description of the lovers' activities, includes the story of "Under the Waterfall": "We sketched and talked of books; often we walked to Boscastle Harbour down the beautiful Vallency Valley where we had to jump over stones and climb over a low wall by rough steps, or get through a narrow pathway, to come out on great wide spaces suddenly, with a sparkling little brook going the same way, in which we once lost a tiny picnic-tumbler, and there it is to this day no doubt between two of the boulders."[2] The date of the incident is given on a pencil-sketch Hardy drew of Emma and inscribed: "E. L. G. by T. H. Aug. 19, 1870. Searching for the glass (water colour sketching in Valency valley)." The picture shows Emma kneeling and reaching for the glass as described in the poem.[3]

The loss of the glass took place in a waterfall of the small, clear Valency River[4] flowing westward between steep, partly wooded hills, through Boscastle Harbour, and into the Atlantic. The waterfall is nearly half a mile east of the harbor at a point where the hills come close together but are separated by a level valley about seventy-five feet wide. Oak, beech, and poplar trees overhang the stream. The fall of the river here is in two stages, a few feet apart, over moss-grown rocks worn or split ("creased," in Hardy's term) into crevices; the fall is about three spans wide (roughly a yard) and two spans high. The banks are higher, and to reach a glass fallen into the lower part of a crevice would be difficult without wading into the stream.

As Hardy found the idea for the poem in Emma's *Some Recol-lections,* he makes her the speaker who recalls the scene whenever she plunges her arm into a basin of water, and himself the questioner who leads her to tell the story. Though Hardy's sketch shows only Emma reaching for the glass, the poem suggests that he laid down his sketch-book and came to her assistance, for "we stooped and plumbed the little abyss / With long bared arms."

He made fictional use of this love-play. In *Under the Greenwood Tree*, when Dick and Fancy get their hands soiled while preparing tea, they wash in the same basin: "Thereupon he plunged in his hands, and they paddled together. It being the first time in his life that he had touched female fingers under water, Dick duly registered the sensation as rather a nice one." (Part the Second, Chapter VII.) Hardy used the incident again in *Tess of the D'Urbervilles.* When

Angel and Tess have just been married: "The place having been rather hastily prepared for them, they washed their hands in one basin. Clare touched hers under the water. 'Which are my fingers and which are yours?' he said, looking up. 'They are very much mixed.' 'They are all yours,' said she, very prettily, and endeavoured to be gayer than she was." (Chapter XXXIV.)

1. Purdy, *Thomas Hardy: A Bibliographical Study*, p. 165.

2. P. 94; *Life*, p. 71. A footnote says: "This incident was versified by Hardy afterwards, and entitled 'Under the Waterfall.'"

3. The sketch is reproduced in Evelyn Hardy and Robert Gittings, *Some Recollections by Emma Hardy*, between pp. 56 and 57.

4. *Sic*, as on ordnance maps. Hardy's erratic spelling of place-names sometimes has Vallency.

POEMS OF 1912-13

Hardy's motto for "Poems of 1912-13," "*Veteris vestigia flammae*," from Virgil's *Aeneid*, IV, line 23, translated as "Relics of the old fire," states the theme of the twenty-one poems in the group. Generally considered among the finest of Hardy's poems for their directness, frankness, and fidelity to fact—somewhat idealized—they form an elegy of great biographical interest. The subjects of the poems are the sudden death of Hardy's first wife, Emma, on November 27, 1912; his sense of bewildered loss; Emma's tastes and habits; a domestic rift that had made them both unhappy for some years; Hardy's visit to scenes of his courtship of Emma in the 1870's and the revival of old emotions; his remorse for his part in the rift of their later married life; and his forgiveness for her part in this division. Other poems in *Satires of Circumstance* and later volumes, a total of more than a hundred, continue and elaborate these themes.

THE GOING properly introduces the "Poems of 1912-13," for it traces Hardy's shocked reaction to the unexpected death of his wife Emma, the realization of the "yawning blankness" of his life without her, and the rebirth of his feelings about his courtship in Cornwall in a long-ago but not forgotten time.

Though the poem is addressed to Emma as a listening spirit, in a sense the poet is talking to himself, wondering "Why . . . Why . . . Why?" At last he does not so much reproach Emma's spirit as the facts of life and death and himself for their failure to renew their early love.

The facts that underlie the opening stanza are stated in *The Later Years*: Hardy had been in London in the early summer of 1912, but "in July he had returned to Max Gate just in time to be at a garden party on July 16—the last his wife ever gave—which it would have much grieved him afterwards to have missed. The afternoon was sunny and the guests numerous on this final one of many occasions of such a gathering on the lawn there, and nobody foresaw the shadow that was so soon to fall on the house, Mrs. Hardy being then, apparently, in her customary health and vigour. . . .

"She went out up to the 22nd November, when, though it was a damp, dark afternoon, she motored to pay a visit six miles off. The next day she was distinctly unwell, and the day after that was her birthday, when she seemed depressed. On the 25th two ladies called;[1] and though she consulted with her husband whether or not to go downstairs to see them, and he suggested that she should not in her weak state, she did go down. The strain obliged her to retire immediately they had left. . . .

"The next day she agreed to see a doctor, who did not think her seriously ill, but weak from want of nourishment through indigestion. . . .

"The next morning the maid told him in answer to his inquiry that when she had as usual entered Mrs. Hardy's room a little earlier she had said she was better, and would probably get up later on; but that she now seemed worse. Hastening to her he was shocked to find her much worse, lying with her eyes closed and unconscious. The doctor came quite quickly, but before he arrived her breathing softened and ceased."[2]

The second stanza emphasizes Hardy's unawareness of Emma's condition up to the moment of death. He gave details in a letter of December 17 to Mrs. Arthur Henniker: "I was with her when she passed away. Half an hour earlier she had told the servant that she felt better. Then her bell rang violently, & when we went up she was gasping. In five minutes all was over."[3]

The third stanza reports his trouble in realizing that Emma was not in her customary haunts. A letter to Pearce Edgcumbe on December 26 says that Emma's death was "so unforeseen that I can scarcely realize it at times even now, my impression having been for many years that she would be with me till I departed."[4] Failing to find Emma at Max Gate, in the fourth stanza he pictures her in a memory of his courtship in Cornwall, when "Life unrolled us its very best." The "red-veined rocks far West" are the Cornish cliffs near St. Juliot and Boscastle. Along these cliffs, among them "beetling Beeny Crest," young, physically vital Emma had galloped on her pony Fanny. The pony "might stop and browse while her mistress gathered wild-flowers, or made water-colour sketches, or clambered down over . . . 'the red-veined rocks' of the west to the haunts of the seals."[5]

The fifth stanza turns to regret and self-reproach that Emma and Hardy had never, after their marriage, gone to Cornwall to renew their youthful love. In the final stanza, he accepts his self-rebuke fatalistically and pictures himself as "a dead man held on end / To sink down soon."

1. "They were the Misses Rebekah and Catharine Owen." Weber, *Hardy's Love Poems*, p. 66.
2. Pp. 153-55; *Life*, pp. 359-60.
3. In the Dorset County Museum.
4. In the Miriam Lutcher Stark Library, University of Texas.
5. Evelyn Hardy, *Thomas Hardy*, p. 120.

YOUR LAST DRIVE treats an incident mentioned in *The Later Years*. Emma Hardy "went out up to the 22nd November, when, though it was a damp, dark afternoon, she motored to pay a visit six miles off."[1] The poem indicates the drive as along the London Road toward Puddletown, and perhaps beyond. On returning to Max Gate after dark, Emma faced the "borough lights" of Dorchester and passed Stinsford Churchyard on her left. Home again, she "told of the charm of that haloed view" of the town seen through the mist. An entry in Hardy's notebook for October 30, 1872, suggests what she had seen: "Returning from Dorchester. Wet night. The town, looking back from South Hill, is circumscribed by a halo like an aurora: up the hill comes a broad band of turnpike road, glazed with moisture, which reflects the lustre of the mist."[2]

Hardy did not sit "at her side that eve." The poem suggests that he had scarcely missed her, a fact for which he reproaches himself in the imaginary words he "read" in "the writing upon your face." The poem hints, remorsefully, that he scolded her for going out, in her weakened condition, on a wet day and that he often censured Emma with "indifference, blame" for her vagaries, when she had need for his "love, praise."

1. P. 154; *Life*, p. 359. The "eight days" of the poem are those from November 22 to Emma's funeral, November 30.
2. Evelyn Hardy, *Thomas Hardy's Notebooks*, p. 39.

THE WALK does not mention Emma Hardy's name, but the poem clearly concerns her. The "hill-top tree" may be Culliford Tree, nearly three miles southwest of Max Gate. The poem excuses Emma, "weak and lame" in her later years, for not going with Hardy on his walk. The principal theme is his regret that he "did not mind," for she would be waiting at home on his return.

RAIN ON A GRAVE in the manuscript was titled "Rain on Her Grave,"[1] the "Her" being Emma. In structure, the poem is unusual, for Hardy's poems often proceed from a pleasant illusion to a realization of fact. "Rain on a Grave" opens with an expression of dismay that the rains Emma dreaded now "spout" upon her grave, but closes with serenity in the feeling that grass and daisies will grow "from her mound . . . Till she form part of them." This theme is characteristic, that nature provides a form of immortality in the life of flowers that spring from the bodies of the dead.

The fancy that the flowers to grow from Emma's grave will be daisies may be due to Hardy's reading Emma's *Some Recollections* shortly after her death. She wrote: "I can quite well remember when I was three years old being taken a little way into the country to see daisies, as children are taken to see the sea; my surprise and joy were very great when I saw a whole field of them, I can never forget the ecstatic state it put me in."[2] Emma loved daisies "With a child's pleasure / All her life's round." In a letter to Rebekah Owen on April 24, 1899, she wrote: "I gather daisies, do you smile? Remember Wordsworth doubtless he gathered some too. I like gathering them as well as I did when a child."[3] At the funeral service held for Hardy in Dorchester, the vicar, Mr. Cowley, "told how Hardy used to gather buttercups and daisies and cowslips and put them on the grave of his wife and other kin in the churchyard."[4]

1. Purdy, *Thomas Hardy: A Bibliographical Study*, p. 166.
2. Evelyn Hardy and Gittings, eds., *Some Recollections*, p. 3.
3. In the Colby College Library.
4. See the London *Daily Mail* for January 16, 1928.

"I FOUND HER OUT THERE" was dated in *Selected Poems* (1916) as written in December, 1912,[1] three months before Hardy revisited Cornwall. The poem, therefore, presents Hardy's memories of Cornwall as visited in the 1870's.[2]

The Early Life mentions Hardy's visit to Tintagel in August of 1870, with Emma Gifford and members of her family. "His hosts drove him to various picturesque points on the wild and rugged coast near the Rectory, among others to King Arthur's Castle, Tintagel, which he now saw for the first time." The poem evidently owes some of its description to Emma's *Some Recollections*, which he nearly quoted in the third stanza: "Scarcely any author and his wife could have had a much more romantic meeting . . . at this very remote spot, with a beautiful sea-coast, and the wild Atlantic Ocean rolling in with its magnificent waves and spray, its white gulls, and black choughs and grey puffins, its cliffs and rocks and gorgeous sunsettings, sparkling redness in a track widening from the horizon to the shore."[3]

The places named have romantic associations. "Dundagel's famed head" (now called Tintagel Head) is the site of the extensive ruins called "King Arthur's Castle," on the coast near the town of Tintagel. According to legend, King Arthur was born there. The "sunk Lyonnesse" of the poem refers to the tradition that the southern coast of Cornwall, toward the Scilly Islands, was formerly Arthur's Lyonnesse.

A theme of the poem seems to be that in marrying Emma and taking her out of her environment, Hardy had robbed her of the joy and vitality which had attracted him to her. He associated her sense of vibrant life with the Atlantic, Cornish cliffs, wild birds, etc. A second theme is that Emma rejoiced in Cornwall because she had "the heart of a child." To the extent that Elfride in *A Pair of Blue Eyes* is based upon Emma, Knight's thoughts of her may reflect an aspect of Hardy's feeling. Knight finds Elfride "childishly full of life and spirits," and when she has fallen asleep by his side muses: "It was pleasant to realize the implicit trust she placed in him, and to think of the charming innocence of one who could sink to sleep in so simple and unceremonious a manner." (Chapter XXIX). This feeling about Emma may account for the playful tone of "I Found Her Out There," especially in the first two stanzas, and for the fantasy of the final stanza.

1. Purdy, *Thomas Hardy: A Bibliographical Study*, p. 166.
2. *Later Years*, p. 156; *Life*, p. 361.
3. *Early Life*, pp. 103 and 90; *Life*, pp. 78 and 69.

WITHOUT CEREMONY may be read as a note upon the opening stanza of "The Going." According to these poems, just as Hardy went his own way when absorbed in some intention, so did Emma, and her death without warning was characteristic. Written as if spoken to Emma, the poem is conversational, with intentional humor (or slang) in its phrasing, as in the word "career." Reviewers have paid obtuse attention to the precise but "unpoetic" phrase "as I inferred." Charles Williams, for instance, wrote in indignation: " 'As I inferred'! the circumlocution! the word bullied into its place for the sake of the rhyme!"[1]

1. "Thomas Hardy," p. 10.

LAMENT presents Hardy's musings upon Emma's tastes and pleasures. The first part of each stanza pictures a characteristic pleasure, and the second, her lack of this pleasure in her grave. The third stanza, in speaking of her "child's eager glance," suggests between her and Hardy a temperamental difference commented upon in the final stanza. Her delight in social "gaying" and "junketings" (entertainments) would "cloy" him.

THE HAUNTER is a monologue by the ghost of Emma Hardy, anxious but powerless to rebuke or console her husband. Weber says truly that Hardy "had *not* always sought Emma's company,"[1] on trips to London, on walks, or to muse in the aisles of old churches.

1. *Hardy's Love Poems*, p. 79.

THE VOICE seems a companion poem to "The Haunter," as it is Hardy's reply to the spirit of his dead wife, saying that he seems to hear her voice, not as she was in her years of division from him, but as she was in August of 1870, when she had awaited his arrival in town (Boscastle, near St. Juliot?). He found her no longer in winter's brown, but "metamorphosed into a young lady in summer blue"; their love throve, and "the visit was a most happy one."[1]

In idealizing Emma of 1870, the poet does not evade their later differences: "neither sentimental nostalgia nor bitterness is allowed to distort the truth. In the third stanza he admits that the woman is gone forever and that the voice he hears cannot be hers; he declines . . . the comforts of a belief in immortality."[2] Upon this admission rests the heart-broken final stanza.

In structure, "The Voice" presents a number of sharp contrasts: two contrasted past times, both leading into a desolate present; a happy moment of life against the fact of death; and wistful hope, an illusion, against despair, the fact. Three stanzas present the illusion in a waltzing meter of dactyllic tetrameter lines with triple rimes: "call to me . . . all to me," "view you then . . . knew you then," and "listlessness . . . wistlessness." The fourth stanza falters forward, as the poet does, in a broken meter. The "Leaves around me falling" and the "Wind . . . from norward" symbolize that the "woman calling" summons toward death.

1. *Early Life*, p. 103; *Life*, p. 78.
2. Hynes, *The Pattern of Hardy's Poetry*, p. 138.

HIS VISITOR is a fantasy stating, in a monologue by Emma's spirit, her reactions to changes at Max Gate since she had died. Emma's spirit leaves her grave in Stinsford Churchyard ("Mellstock") to visit her home for "twenty years and more."[1]

Weber sums up the changes that Emma saw on her visit. In 1913, "Upon his return from his pilgrimage to Cornwall and Devon, Hardy set about making some needed renovations at Max Gate. Some of the rooms were repainted, some pictures were replaced, some new cups and saucers were acquired, and 'a formal-fashioned border' of flowers was constructed in the garden 'where the daisies used to be.' Emma had been very fond of daisies. The removal of her flowers made Hardy imagine that Emma's ghost would not approve of the changes he was making."[2] Weber indicates elsewhere that, in these changes, Miss Florence Dugdale had some part. When the household seemed in a muddle, "In despair Hardy turned to Florence Dugdale for help. Before Christmas 1912 she came to Max Gate and there soon brought order and system into the household arrangements."[3]

"His Visitor" suggests that Emma had run the household, arranged furniture, and laid out the garden to suit herself; the concluding stanza indicates that she liked to have her own way. Hardy's changes were not radical, and probably he made even these changes (or allowed Miss Dugdale to make them) with some deference to Emma's taste. Even after his marriage to Miss Dugdale, he tended to resist change in the house and garden. Mrs. Florence Hardy wrote to Rebekah Owen as late as May 5, 1916, of "an interesting man at Weymouth," an expert on plants and gardens, and said: "I got him to come and look at our garden and he gave me many most valuable hints—but there would be a difficulty in carrying them out unless I had a free hand, which I have not. I may not alter the shape of a garden bed, or cut down or move the smallest bush, any more than I may alter the position of an article of furniture."[4]

1. Emma had lived at Max Gate from June 29, 1885, until her death on November 27, 1912. *Early Life*, p. 229; *Life*, p. 175.
2. *Hardy's Love Poems*, p. 80.
3. *Hardy of Wessex*, 2nd ed., p. 263.
4. In the Colby College Library.

A CIRCULAR probably presents a fact in Hardy's life some time after Emma died. That a "gay-pictured, spring-time shout / Of Fashion" arrived after Emma's death appealed to his feeling for the irony of events.

A DREAM OR NO in the manuscript is titled "A [The] Dream indeed?"[1] Dated February, 1913, the poem was written before Hardy began to revisit, on March 6, the scenes of his courtship of Emma Gifford. He wrote the poem in anticipation of this pilgrimage as he dreamed of it and planned it. The center of the trip should be St. Juliot Rectory, where he had met Emma. The other places are those they visited in March of 1870.

The lines that speak of "a maiden abiding" at St. Juliot "as in hiding" suggest the isolation of the Rectory and Church. The "Bos" of the poem seems to be the village and harbor of Boscastle.[2] The coast northeast and southwest of Boscastle is a line of steep, picturesque cliffs, among them Beeny. These cliffs, to which Emma led Hardy, overhang strips of beach where sea-birds circle and swarm.

"A Dream or No" presents a distant memory so idealized that it seems at first a dream, but as the poem progresses and particulars emerge, becomes a reality. Hardy was by temperament introspective, living, in a sense, two lives, one in the visions of memory and another in actuality. The actual was often less vivid at the moment than the dream, but his memory was curiously photographic in storing up sensations later given added dimensions in dreams. (See Hardy's statements of this fact in such poems as "Self-Unconscious," "Wessex Heights," "In Front of the Landscape," and "The Self-Unseeing.") Because of this characteristic he liked solitude, and one trait in Emma Gifford that may have attracted him is suggested in the line "There lonely I found her." Perhaps she seemed at the time a "soul-mate," yet different in her vitality, one like "The sea-birds around her."

The progress of "A Dream or No" is a "strange necromancy" that brings emotionally laden dream-images into consciousness as realities. The opening stanzas are playful, as Hardy toys with the idea that his "fancy" may be real. Details rise from memory: the "maiden . . . in hiding" has particular eyes, shoulders, brows, and tresses; the poet recalls being "coastward bound on a night long ago." By the final stanza, the vague "West" has taken on identities as Saint-Juliot, Valency Valley, Beeny, and Bos "with its flounce flinging mist." The apparent dream may be a fact, and, though the poem does not say so, the thing to do is go and see.

Hardy did go and see, and the poignancy of the dream made real, but without the maiden there, nearly overcame him. Florence Dugdale wrote to Edward Clodd on March 11, 1913: "Yesterday there arrived—together with your kind letter—one from T. H. in which he writes:—'The visit to this neighbourhood (i.e., Boscastle) has been a very painful one to me, & I have said a dozen times I wish I had not come—What possessed me to do it!' I knew it was an unwise thing to do, & I expect he will come back this afternoon, very miserable. However he meant to go some time & it is over now, & done with, I hope." [3]

1. Purdy, *Thomas Hardy: A Bibliographical Study*, p. 167.
2. "Bos" in Cornish speech means "headland."
3. In the Brotherton Library Collection, Leeds.

AFTER A JOURNEY presents Hardy's meditations at Pentargan Bay during his visit to Cornwall in March of 1913, where "he had not once set foot in the long interval" since he had married Emma Gifford.[1] The title suggests that the poem was written after his return to Max Gate with his mind full of his reflections as he had walked along the cliffs that encircle the Bay. The poem was evidently given shape as a monologue addressed to Emma's "voiceless ghost" by Hardy's reading her diaries and *Some Recollections*. Her account of his visits to Cornwall in 1870 included: "I rode my pretty mare Fanny and he walked by my side, and I showed him . . . the cliffs . . . sometimes gazing down at the solemn small shores below, where the seals lived, coming out of great deep caverns very occasionally."[2]

Pentargan Bay is a small bay surrounded by a semicircle of steep cliffs of black rock, on the coast less than a mile north of Boscastle Harbour. In the northeastern part of the bay, a tiny stream falls from a depression in the cliffs as a waterfall about twenty feet high; at the base of the waterfall sea waves beat into caverns where seals are said to haunt; sea-birds wheel and call below the cliffs. Hardy's phrases "the unseen waters' ejaculations" and "our paths through flowers" are realistic as well as symbolically suggestive. Waves beat against the cliffs on which the observer may stand without being able to see the breakers directly below. The meadows east of the bay are dotted with daisies, buttercups, and other field flowers.[3]

Hardy had previously described this scene as one of dream and mystery. His 1912 Preface for *A Pair of Blue Eyes* said: "The ghostly birds, the pall-like sea, the frothy wind, the eternal soliloquy of the waters . . . lend to the scene an atmosphere like the twilight of a night vision." In the novel, Elfride goes to Pentargan to look for Stephen's passing ship; "the waterfall, above which the mist-bow shone" is pictured: "The small stream here found its death. Running over the precipice it was dispersed in spray before it was half-way down, and falling like rain upon projecting ledges, made minute grassy meadows of them. At the bottom the water-drops soaked away amid the débris of the cliff. This was the inglorious end of the river." (Chapter XXI.)

The intervening years had exhibited, as Hardy says to Emma's ghost, "Time's derision." The second stanza mentions in a series of questions the "division" that had embittered his marriage in the 1890's and afterwards. He seems to refer to Emma's diaries in the phrases "through the dead scenes I have tracked you" and "you tell?" The questions, then, are not so much inquiries as invitations to see, with him, that "all's closed now." The third stanza suggests that Emma's ghost shares his view and is "leading me on" to return to the scene and the emotion of forty years before. The reality to be treasured in the mind is not the dowdy, childish woman, but the vital girl "all aglow." Suggesting remorse for his share in the estrangement of the dark years, he invites Emma to see that now "I am just the same as when / Our days were a joy, and our paths through flowers."

1. *Later Years*, p. 156; *Life*, p. 361.
2. *Early Life*, pp. 93-94; *Life*, p. 71.
3. Lea, *Thomas Hardy's Wessex*, has a picture of Pentargan Bay as Plate 134 on p. 173. The photograph does not show the waterfall clearly or do justice to the grandeur of the scene.

A DEATH-DAY RECALLED presents essentially that conventional portion of a classic elegy in which features or places of nature familiar to the dead are personified as mourners. In Hardy's poem, however, the convention is realistically inverted. After his pilgrimage to Cornwall in March of 1913, he discovered that the places Emma had loved in her maiden years remained just as he remembered them. He rebukes them for exhibiting no reaction to a loss so great to him. The places, all actual, are rather listed than described. "Bos" is evidently the high, clifflike headland that semicircles Boscastle Harbour; "Targan" is Pentargan Bay.

BEENY CLIFF has two dates below the title, March, 1870, and March, 1913. They indicate the fusion of two visions of the cliff as Hardy saw it when he was taken there by Emma Gifford on his first visit and when he returned alone after her death. His journal for March 10, 1870, records: "Went with E. L. G. to Beeny Cliff. She on horseback. . . . On the cliff. . . . 'The tender grace of a day,' etc. The run down to the edge."[1] Then in 1913: "On March 6 . . . he started for St. Juliot, putting up at Boscastle, and visiting . . . Beeny Cliff, on which he had not once set foot in the long interval."[2] The statement overlooks several visits to Beeny Cliff during Hardy's courtship. For instance, "On Monday, August 22 [1870], the pair [Hardy and Emma] visited Beeny Cliff, where Hardy made the sketch now in the Dorset County Museum. The foreground shows, on the right, the hooded figure of Emma (it had begun to rain)."[3]

Beeny Cliff is often covered in mists that give the sea below a slate-blue color; sea-birds circle and call below the crest. In sunlight, underwater rocks color the water with rainbow colors. Hardy's description in the poem is accurate. He gave other details of the scene in a notebook entry in 1872: "*August*: At Beeny Cliff . . . green towards the land, blue-black towards the sea. Every ledge has a little, starved, green grass upon it: all vertical parts bare. Seaward, a dark-grey ocean beneath a pale green sky, upon which lie branches of red cloud. A lather of foam around the base of each rock. The sea is full of motion internally, but still as a whole. Quiet and silent in the distance, noisy and restless close at hand."[4] In reply to the editor of the *Saturday Review* in 1897, asking Hardy to name "The Best Scenery I Know," he listed, among five items, "The coast from Trebarwith Strand to Beeny Cliff, Cornwall."[5]

Beeny Cliff is portrayed in *A Pair of Blue Eyes*. On March 6, 1925, Hardy wrote to Marie Flower that "The Cliff without a Name . . . so far as it is anywhere, is near Beeny [a village near the cliff], about a mile from Boscastle."[6] It seems, therefore, justifiable to associate the scenes on the cliff in the novel with Hardy's experience and with the poem. Ellis wrote that "When Mr. Hardy showed me the portrait of his first wife, with her long, fair hair hanging down over the shoulders, he said she was the prototype in many respects of Elfride in *A Pair of Blue Eyes*, particularly in her physical attributes."[7] Hardy wrote from memory in describing "the woman . . . with bright hair flapping free," and the same memory underlies a passage in *A Pair of Blue Eyes*: " 'See how I can gallop. Now, Pansy, off!' And Elfride started; and Stephen beheld her light figure contracting to the dimensions of a bird as she sank into the distance— her hair flowing." (Chapter VII.)

The phrase "the woman riding high above" suggests that Hardy, on a "run down to the edge," remembered himself on a slope of the cliff, while Emma on her pony was silhouetted at the top. From either place, the breakers seem at a distance; the sea seems a "nether sky," and great chasms in the cliff justify the terms "chasmal" and "wild weird."

1. *Early Life*, p. 99; *Life*, p. 75. The ellipses are Hardy's.

2. *Later Years*, p. 156; *Life*, p. 361.

3. Phelps, *Annotations by Thomas Hardy in His Bibles and Prayer-Book*, p. 8. The drawing is reproduced on p. 82 of Hardy and Gittings, *Some Recollections by Emma Hardy*.

4. Evelyn Hardy, *Thomas Hardy's Notebooks*, p. 38. Lea, *Thomas Hardy's Wessex*, has a picture of Beeny Cliff as Plate 135 on p. 177, though it does not convey the grandeur of the scene.

5. *Later Years*, p. 71; *Life*, p. 295.

6. Pencil-draft of Hardy's reply is in the Dorset County Museum. See also his Preface of 1895 to *A Pair of Blue Eyes*.

7. "Some Personal Recollections of Thomas Hardy," p. 402.

AT CASTLE BOTEREL presents Hardy's memory in March, 1913, of an event that took place there. "Castle Boterel" is Hardy's name for Boscastle, a small town on the Cornish coast a mile or more from St. Juliot Rectory. At the point where the Valency River, flowing down a valley between hills, winds into the sea through cliffs or headlands, the small bay thus formed is Boscastle Harbour. The town is on the crest of a steep hill just south of the harbor. The highway from the harbor to the town winds around the hill to provide an easy ascent for vehicles, but a narrow, steep lane leads directly to the town and the area where Bottreaux Castle had stood. The action of the poem evidently took place on this lane, which is nearly straight

uphill. A "sturdy pony" drawing a chaise up this lane would natural-
ly "sigh and slow," and humane passengers would walk to ease the
load. Slate-colored rocks, stone walls, and a few houses border the
lane. The "Primaeval rocks" exhibit fossil shells that provided Hardy
with his meditation on the "transitory in Earth's long order" and a
background for the ecstatic "minute" of the poem.[1]

Possibly the occasion is that briefly recorded in his journal for
March 9, 1870: "Drove with Mrs. Holder and Miss Gifford to Bos-
castle, and on to Tintagel."[2] Presumably he and Miss Gifford
walked up the hill while Mrs. Holder (Emma's sister) drove the
chaise, and the love-passage that "filled but a minute" took place
when the lovers were out of Mrs. Holder's sight.[3] Hardy's trip to
Boscastle in March of 1913 recalled the scene so poignantly that he
resolved to "traverse old love's domain / Never again."

1. Perhaps these rocks as well as those of Beeny Cliff suggested the scene of the
"imbedded fossil" in *A Pair of Blue Eyes*, Chapter XXII.

2. *Early Life*, p. 98; *Life*, p. 75.

3. Possibly the event took place on some other visit to Boscastle that is not
recorded, when Hardy and Emma were alone and walked up the hill beside the
chaise. The reference to March suggests the visit of March 9, but "benighted"
suggests some other time.

PLACES is noted as written in Plymouth during March of 1913.
From his pilgrimage into Cornwall at that time, Hardy returned home
by way of Plymouth,[1] where Emma had been born and had lived
until she was nineteen. *The Early Life* gives these details: "She was
born at 10 York Street, Plymouth, and baptized at St. Andrew's
Church, being the younger daughter of Mr. J. Attersoll Gifford, a
solicitor. She had grown up in a house close to the Hoe, which she
used to call 'the playground of her childhood.' She would relate how,
to her terror at first, she was daily dipped as a little girl in the pools
under the Hoe; and on its cliffs—very much more rugged than now
—had had her youthful adventures. . . . Her education was carried on
at a school for young ladies also overlooking the Hoe's green slopes,
where, to use her own words, 'military drills took place on frequent
mornings, and then our dear instructress drew down the blinds.' At
nineteen she removed from Plymouth with her parents."[2]

Emma's "own words" are quoted from her *Some Recollections*,
which Hardy read after her death. She wrote of her childhood in
Plymouth: "The Churches of Plymouth were not numerous as now—
I believe five only St. Andrew's being the finest which had a curfew
bell regularly tolled and chimes which played every four hours that
fine old tune [the 'Old 113th'].[3] I have good reason to remember it—
as we lived for five years not far away, and that tune with its haltings

and runs plays up in my head often even now."[4] Perhaps Emma's mention of the "haltings and runs" of St. Andrew's chimes inspired Hardy's "stammering chimes" of the poem.[5]

The third stanza also seems based on *Some Recollections*. Emma wrote of her riding near Boscastle: "An unforgettable experience to me, scampering up and down the hills on my beloved mare alone, wanting no protection, the rain going down my back often and my hair floating on the wind. . . . The Villagers stopped to gaze when I rushed down the hills. A butterman laid down his basket once to exclaim loudly for no one dared except myself to ride in such wild fearless fashion."[6]

The term "beneaped" is used of a ship left aground by a neap tide; the reference is to Hardy himself, desolate after Emma's death.

1. *Later Years*, p. 156; *Life*, p. 361.

2. P. 87; *Life*, p. 66. Hardy did not visit Plymouth with Emma during their married life, though in this period she at least once visited Plymouth alone. In an album called "Sketches," in the Dorset County Museum, she has a water-color painting labelled "Plymouth Hoe 1886." In her girlhood what is the modern city of Plymouth (rebuilt after the devastation of World War II) was the "Three Towns" of the poem, Plymouth, Devonport, and Stonehouse, stretched along Plymouth Sound between the mouths of the Rivers Plym and Tamar. The Hoe is a sea-front park on a terraced hill overlooking the central Sound. The Church of St. Andrew is the "mother church" of Plymouth, situated at "City Center," about a quarter of a mile north of the Hoe. This church was partly destroyed during World War II, but has been restored. "Boterel Hill" is Hardy's name for the steep ascent from Boscastle Harbour to Boscastle, which Hardy visited just before going to Plymouth. See the notes on "At Castle Boterel."

3. Hardy's note in the manuscript.

4. Evelyn Hardy and Gittings, *Some Recollections by Emma Hardy*, pp. 11-12.

5. In *Desperate Remedies*, completed shortly after Hardy became acquainted with Emma, the "bewildered chimes" of a church clock "wandered through the wayward air of the Old Hundred-and-Thirteenth Psalm." Chapter X, 3.

6. Hardy and Gittings, *Some Recollections by Emma Hardy*, pp. 50-51.

THE PHANTOM HORSEWOMAN presents Hardy's state of mind when, in March of 1913, he revisited the scenes of his courtship of Emma Gifford near Boscastle, Pentargan Bay, and Beeny Cliff. The point of view in the first two stanzas is that of an observant gossip picturing the poet as he stands transfixed in the long-remembered places and seems to see Emma on her pony, riding as she rode more than forty years before.

The third and fourth stanzas present what "they," the gossips of Boscastle, might say if they could see into the poet's mind and share his memory. Though he ages, trapped in Time, the girl of his vision, like the maiden on Keats's Grecian urn, cannot fade. In effect the poem is "a splendid taunt hurled at oblivion by the imagination."[1] The technique does much to heighten this effect as the "careworn craze" observed by the gossip leads seaward, so to speak, to the ecstatic vision of the gaily singing "ghost-girl-rider."

1. Stewart, *Eight Modern Writers*, p. 61.

THE SPELL OF THE ROSE is a soliloquy by the ghost of Emma. Its sources include Hardy's remorseful memory of his life with her, probably portions of her *Some Recollections* and the diaries that he destroyed, and his meditations upon a rose bush that Emma planted, but that flourished only after her death. He wrote to Mrs. Florence Henniker on December 28, 1918: "As it is an exceptionally mild afternoon I have been gardening a little, & had to tie up a rosebush planted by Emma a month or two before her death: it has grown luxuriously, & she would be pleased if she could know & that I care for it."[1]

The poem is an allegory in which the rose stands for love. In the opening stanza, Emma's ghost quotes Hardy's statement of his intention in building Max Gate as a permanent home after the Hardys' wanderings for some years.[2] The third and fourth stanzas treat the domestic frictions between Hardy and Emma during her late years and her efforts to recall to him their early love and "end divisions dire and wry."

Hardy's building Max Gate and planting "many trees" around it perhaps displeased Emma, especially as he planted no rose. The poem suggests in Emma's surmise (as in fact) that her efforts to revive his love failed to flower before her death, but flowered abundantly afterward.

1. In the Dorset County Museum.
2. The stanza partly describes Max Gate. For photographs, see *Early Life*, facing p. 226; *Later Years*, facing p. 192; for a description of the house and Hardy's planting trees around it, see *Early Life*, pp. 226-27; *Life*, 173-74.

ST. LAUNCE'S REVISITED was in manuscript dated 1913 and titled "At St. Launce's."[1] "St. Launce's" is Hardy's name for Launceston, Cornwall. The poem presents his first visit to Launceston in 1870 as he recalled it on his visit in 1913. On the first visit, the railway line from Dorchester toward St. Juliot extended only to Launceston. On March 7, 1870, he reached Launceston at four in the afternoon and there "hired a conveyance for the additional sixteen or seventeen miles' distance by the Boscastle road towards the north coast" and St. Juliot.[2] Presumably, as the poem was written in 1913, he paused in Launceston on his way to Boscastle in March of that year and there indulged in the wistful memories of the poem.

Launceston is an ancient market-town in northeastern Cornwall, on a hill about two miles west of the Tamar River. The town is dominated by the ruins of a castle built by Robert of Mortain, Earl of Cornwall, in 1086, on the cone-like peak of the hill. Steps lead to the keep or fortress walls, still towering some fifty feet above the grounds and overlooking the countryside. Hardy's "inn / Smiling nigh" is the White Hart Hotel on Broad Street about two hundred feet south of the castle's outer walls and gateway.[3]

1. Purdy, *Thomas Hardy: A Bibliographical Study*, p. 166.
2. *Early Life*, p. 86; *Life*, p. 65.
3. Lea, *Thomas Hardy's Wessex*, has photographs of Launceston, with the castle ruins in the background, as Plate 129, p. 167, and Plate 137, p. 181; and of the White Hart Hotel as Plate 138, p. 181.

WHERE THE PICNIC WAS seems to have been generally misinterpreted. Weber relates the remembered picnic to Hardy's courtship of Emma Gifford in 1870. He suggests that the site of the outing was Beeny Cliff and the date was August 22. But he does not identify the two extra persons of "we four."[1] They might be surmised as Emma's sister Helen and her husband, Reverend Caddell Holder.

This interpretation overlooks several lines in the poem. If the statement (written after Emma's death in 1912) is literal, "last year" indicates that the picnic took place in the summer of 1912, when the "one" (Emma) who "has shut her eyes / For evermore" was still alive. Though later published with "Poems of 1912-13," the poem first appeared outside this group concerned largely with Hardy's courtship.[2] Lea did not believe that the poem referred to Beeny. In pencil-notes that did not name the poem, he quoted a line of it and conjectured the site: " 'The Hill to the Sea' = Ridgeway?"[3] Ridgeway is a ridge of hills about four miles south of Dorchester and a mile to two miles north of Weymouth Bay; it overlooks the sea, which from Ridgeway appears in the distance as a "strange straight line."

Certainly "last year" is important. It can hardly be read "*as if* last year" to mean forty-three years ago. The poem describes the "burnt circle" and the "stick-ends, charred" that might remain for a year, but not imaginably for nearly half a century.

If the picnic was held in 1912, the two who accompanied Hardy and Emma may be Henry Newbolt and W. B. Yeats. *The Later Years* records of 1912: "On June 1 at Max Gate they had a pleasant weekend visit from Henry Newbolt and W. B. Yeats, who had been deputed by the Royal Society of Literature to present Hardy with the Society's gold medal on his seventy-second birthday. The two eminent men of letters were the only people entertained at Max Gate for the occasion."[4] Possibly Hardy and his wife took Newbolt and Yeats on a sight-seeing tour that included a picnic. The lines stating that "two have wandered far" into the "urban roar" of London support this surmise. The week-end of June 1 sounds right, for Hardy was in London after the middle of June. The poem seems to reflect Hardy's memory of a pleasant outing in a "summer time" before Emma's death; her death is symbolized (realistically enough) in "winter mire" and the details of a "forsaken place."

"Where the Picnic Was" has been set to music by Gerald Finzi in *By Footpath and Stile* (London: J. Curwen & Sons, 1925).

1. *Hardy of Wessex*, 2nd ed., pp. 82-83.
2. On p. 39 of *Satires of Circumstance*. Purdy, *Thomas Hardy: A Bibliographical Study*, p. 162.
3. Cox, ed., *Thomas Hardy through the Camera's Eye*, p. 52.
4. P. 152; *Life*, p. 358.

MISCELLANEOUS PIECES

THE WISTFUL LADY is a dialogue between a wife and a husband about a "plaintive lady pale and passionless"—by suggestion, a ghost —who had appeared to the wife while the husband was away from home. Possibly Hardy had in mind his second wife Florence, as the first speaker, himself as the husband, and the ghost of his first wife Emma, as the lady. If so, the final stanza may reflect some threat Emma had made before her death to haunt any supplanter. As "but she knew me" suggests, Florence Dugdale had been well known to Emma. That the lady had appeared out of doors, presumably in the garden, is suggestive. Emma had planned the garden at Max Gate and tended it. After her marriage in February, 1914, Florence made changes in the flower beds to which Emma probably would have objected.

THE WOMAN IN THE RYE is a dialogue expressing a woman's remorse for hastily spoken words of recrimination that came true. Possibly the poem was suggested by Emma's bitterness expressed in "What I Think of My Husband." (See Emma Hardy in the Key to Persons.) If so, Hardy disguised the fact by imagining himself as dead and Emma still alive and distressed with remorse.

THE CHEVAL-GLASS tells a quasi-ghostly story in which the ghost seems a figment of the grieving lover's fantasy. Hardy characteristically imagined the dead haunting pieces of furniture they had used. (See "Old Furniture" and "The Garden Seat.") The "valley farm" in "ancient England" suggests a location near Dorchester.

THE RE-ENACTMENT is a retrospective narrative of a woman who, while awaiting the arrival of her lover, sees the phantom (?) of another lover who has come to keep a tryst with another woman there. When the lover of the present arrives, the memory and its "emanation" dampen the "fervours" of the pair.

Duffin states the theme as "a present substantial love is recognized as slight and tame beside the mere ghost of a dead romance."[1] This theme and the theme that an old house may be haunted by the passions of former inhabitants are characteristic of Hardy. He wrote of Melbury's house in *The Woodlanders*: "It was a house in whose reverberations queer old personal tales were yet audible if properly listened for." (Chapter IV.) In his notebook for April 19, 1893, he wrote: "The worst of taking a furnished house is that the articles in the rooms are saturated with the thoughts and glances of others."[2]

Some details suggest a relation to Hardy's life. That it may be his dramatization of one of Emma Hardy's hallucinations is suggested by Hermann Lea's note that the scene of the poem is Boscastle.[3] The "boom / Of the ocean" echoing "up the copse-clothed [Valency] valley" suggests the trysting place as St. Juliot Rectory (though it was not "hired"). It seems likely from various poems and parallels in *A Pair of Blue Eyes* that Emma Gifford, twenty-nine years old when she met Hardy, had attracted at least one lover before that time. (See the notes on "The Face at the Casement" and in the novel the story of young Jethway, Chapter VIII.)

1. *Thomas Hardy*, p. 297.
2. *Later Years*, pp. 17-18; *Life*, p. 254. See also "The Two Houses" and "A House with a History." These poems, "The Re-enactment," and others presenting psychic emanations from old rooms may owe something to stories told in Boswell-Stone's *Memories and Traditions*, pp. 10-14.
3. Cox, ed., *Thomas Hardy Through the Camera's Eye*, p. 52.

HER SECRET is a wryly humorous poem that possibly reflects Emma Hardy's accusations in "What I Think of My Husband." (See Emma Hardy in the Key to Persons.) If so, Hardy, to disguise any personal application, reversed the role of man and wife. Emma, prone to jealousy, would not suspect that Hardy still dreamed of his "lost prize," dead Tryphena.

"SHE CHARGED ME" possibly treats a cause of the division between Hardy and Emma in the 1890's and afterward. The poem presents the manner and underlying feeling of the charge as more divisive than the attraction to another woman. It neither identifies the other woman nor denies that the charge may have some basis in fact.[1]

1. The other woman may be Mrs. Arthur Henniker. See the notes on "Alike and Unlike."

THE NEWCOMER'S WIFE is a melodramatic tale with a morbid ending. Hardy used the idea of suicide by drowning "with crabs upon his face" in his novel *The Well-Beloved*. Pierston, on learning that Elsie Targe is engaged to be married, contemplates suicide, but the vision of crabs restrains him: "I had been told that crabs had been found clinging to the dead faces of persons who had fallen in thereabout, leisurely eating them, and the idea of such an unpleasant contingency deterred me." (Part First, Chapter VII.) As the scene in the novel is Weymouth, the poem may rest upon something Hardy heard when working in that city in 1869.

The idea that a naïve young man may be cruelly deceived by a clever "Hack of the Parade" appears in a number of Hardy's poems, as in "At the Altar Rail."

A CONVERSATION AT DAWN dramatizes the essence of a realistic novel or of the "problem play" current on London stages in the 1890's. The place is left vague except that the "white hotel on a white-stoned quay" is in a seaside town, with rooms facing eastward to the sea. A reference to "this isle" and the "packet" from "yonder shore" suggests that the bride and groom are honeymooning in Guernsey or Jersey.

Though, as in the problem play, there are two rights in the story, the right of the heart to love freely opposed to the legal right of a hard and possessive husband, Hardy's sympathies are with the bride. His theme is the inhumanity of the laws then (in 1910) governing marriage and divorce. The bride's lover could not easily be freed of his criminal wife, and the bride, who seeks release from her hardhearted husband, must remain his thrall. The bride expresses the theme: "No God intends / To thwart the yearning He's father to!" She challenges the legal rights of the husband by appeal to the higher law of compassion, but without effect. In this particular the poem contrasts with "The Burghers."

The theme is debated at length in *Jude the Obscure*. When Sue makes clear to her husband Phillotson that she is unhappy with him, he releases her to go to her lover Jude. To Gillingham, who represents the legal point of view, Phillotson defends his action: "I, like other men, profess to hold that if a husband gets such a so-called preposterous request from his wife, the only course that can possibly be regarded as right and proper and honourable in him is to refuse it, and put her virtuously under lock and key, and murder her lover perhaps. But is that essentially right and proper and honourable, or is it contemptibly mean and selfish?" The incident of the poem in which the husband requires his wife to swear fidelity occurs in *Jude*.

After misfortune has brought Sue to the conviction that she had sinned, Phillotson requires her to swear on the New Testament not to see Jude again. (Part IV, Chapter IV, and Part VI, Chapter IX.) Hardy stated in an article published in 1912: "As the present marriage laws are, to the eyes of anybody who looks around, the gratuitous cause of at least half the misery of the community, that they are allowed to remain in force for a day is, to quote the famous last word of the ceremony itself, an 'amazement,' and can only be accounted for by the assumption that we live in a barbaric age, and are the slaves of gross superstition."[1]

In structure, the poem is incremental: the bride reveals in stages the extent of her violation of the marriage contract. The coming of dawn, while realistic, is also symbolic: the husband is gradually enlightened about his bride's behavior and feeling, and the bride, about her husband's character. The indifference of nature is suggested in the sea that "Flung its lazy flounce at the neighbouring quay."

1. Orel, ed., *Thomas Hardy's Personal Writings*, p. 252.

A KING'S SOLILOQUY ON THE NIGHT OF HIS FUNERAL is an imaginary meditation by the spirit of King Edward VII (January 22, 1901–May 6, 1910) on the night of May 20. Hardy had some acquaintance with the King: on June 22, 1907, he and Mrs. Hardy were guests at the King's Garden Party at Windsor Castle. They were in London at the time of the King's death. "Looking out of the window while at breakfast on the morning after their arrival, they beheld placarded in the street an announcement of the death of King Edward. Hardy saw from the Athenaeum the procession of the removal of the King's body to Westminster, and the procession of the funeral from Westminster three days later. On account of the suggestiveness of such events it must have been in these days that he wrote 'A King's Soliloquy on the Night of his Funeral.' "[1] In addition to the "suggestiveness of such events," Frederic Harrison of the *English Review* asked Hardy for a poem about the King. Hardy replied on May 9: "I do not feel, to tell the truth, any impulse, or faintest power, to write anything upon the sudden termination of the late reign. I will not attempt to explain why."[2] Perhaps watching the funeral procession suggested a theme for the poem. Rider Haggard wrote: "I saw King Edward's body lying in state in Westminster Hall and afterwards watched the noble panorama of his funeral from the upper balcony of the Athenaeum. Thomas Hardy and I sat together."[3]

Edward's spirit meditates that his life had been not what he wished, but what it was destined by "That" to be. (For "That," the Immanent Will, see the notes on *The Dynasts*.) Hardy seems to have put his own feeling about worldly glory into the soliloquy of the King. Florence Hardy noted, on November 11, 1927, when he was at the height of his fame, that he said: ". . . if he had his own life over again he would prefer to be a small architect in a country town, like Mr. Hicks at Dorchester, to whom he was articled."⁴

1. *Later Years*, pp. 126, 142; *Life*, pp. 335, 350.
2. In the Miriam Lutcher Stark Library, University of Texas.
3. Haggard, *The Days of My Life*, II, 214.
4. *Later Years*, p. 262; *Life*, p. 443.

THE CORONATION presents a satiric dialogue on preparations for the coronation of George V in Westminster Abbey on June 22, 1911, a ceremony Hardy did not attend. Months before the occasion, Clement Shorter asked him for a poem about it. He replied on December 31, 1910: "On receiving the request for a Coronation ode . . . I felt quite incompetent for the job; & up to now feel just the same. Of course I don't know what may come into my head between now and then, but I cannot promise such an article. In any case my production would not be of the joyful character that people would deem suitable for the occasion."¹

The Later Years says that Hardy "had been compelled to decline . . . an invitation from the Earl-Marshal to the Coronation in Westminster Abbey in the coming June."² His letter, dated March 2, is phrased with politeness and evasion: "Mr. Hardy much regrets that unavoidable circumstances prevent his acceptance of the high honour offered and deny him the pleasure he would have derived from being at the ceremony."³ He expressed his real feeling in a letter to Mrs. Arthur Henniker on March 17: "They have asked me to Westminster Abbey to the Coronation, but I am not going. All that week I am thinking of doing as good men did in the Scriptures, & going away into a desert place."⁴ He chose "a tour with his brother in the Lake Country, including Carlisle Cathedral and Castle, where the dungeons were another reminder to him of how 'evil men out of the evil treasure of their hearts have brought forth evil things.' However, the tour was agreeable . . . and probably Hardy got more pleasure out of Coronation Day by spending it on Windermere than he would have done by spending it in a seat at the Abbey. Of Grasmere Churchyard he says: 'Wordsworth's headstone and grave are looking very trim and new. A group of tourists who have never read a line of him sit near, addressing and sending off picture postcards. . . . Wrote some verses.' "⁵ The verses probably included "The Coronation." Like a truant schoolboy, he felt shamefaced, as he wrote to Mrs. Henniker on August 22: "I felt myself a poor creature, for I went off to the Lakes to be away from the millions."⁶

Hardy's treating the kings and queens buried in Westminster Abbey as talking ghosts may owe something to a visit there in April, 1899, when he "rambled in Westminster Abbey at midnight by the light of a lantern."[7] Perhaps his flippant attitude was suggested by the remarks of tourists visiting Wordsworth's grave "who have never read a line of him." His listing the monarchs in doggerel verse may owe something to a poem pencilled in his handwriting, presumably copied when he was a schoolboy. Labelled "Rhyme to remember the Kings and Queens of England up to Queen Victoria," it reads:

> First William the Norman, then William his son,
> Henry, Stephen, Henry, then Richard & John.
> Next Henry the third, Edwards one two & three
> And again after Richard, three Henrys we see. . . .[8]

And so on to Victoria.

The scene of "The Coronation" is the Chapel of King St. Edward the Confessor, who, as "the Pious," is the first-named. This chapel is just east of the high altar. The monarchs buried there are St. Edward (reigned 1042-66), Edward I (reigned 1272-1307), Edward III (reigned 1327-77), Richard II (reigned 1377-99), Henry III (reigned 1216-72), and Henry V (reigned 1413-22). The others, except Henry VIII, are buried in, or in aisles beside Henry VII's Chantry Chapel, which adjoins that of Edward the Confessor. They are Henry VII (reigned, 1485-1509), James I (James VI of Scotland, reigned in England, 1603-25), Charles II (reigned 1661-85), George II (reigned 1727-60), Mary I (Mary Tudor, "Bloody Mary," reigned 1553-58), Elizabeth I (reigned 1559-1603), Anne (reigned 1702-14), Mary II (reigned jointly with her husband William of Orange, 1689-95), and Mary Queen of Scots (Mary Stuart, reigned Queen of Scotland, 1542-67). Apparently the ghosts were able to move about freely. One king in the poem, Henry VIII (reigned 1509-47), was not buried in Westminster, but in St. George's Chapel, Windsor.[9]

The poem does not state what monarch opens the conversation, but as he objects to activities "Infringing all ecclesiastical laws," he may be St. Edward the Confessor; this devout king is later shocked by Henry VIII's "rare time with those six women!" The comments of the ghosts are consistent with their idiosyncrasies when they inhabited the flesh. Mary Stuart, Queen of Scots, supposes the carpenters are erecting a scaffold, for it was "that way I died." As claimant for the throne of England, she was beheaded in 1587 on a charge of plotting to assassinate Queen Elizabeth. The "many-wived" Henry VIII naturally associates construction work with preparations for a wedding. His "I never would bow down to Rimmon" is suitably a reference to the Bible (II Kings 5:18), for he was the first head of the English Church and "Defender of the Faith." The phrase also fits his wilful character, as he would neither bow to the Pope nor conform to custom. Henry V fittingly remarks that six wives at once "would have been transgression"; though reputed "wild" as "Prince Hal," Henry as a king was noted for his religious principles and inflexible justice. Richard II, musing that the construction may be a "catafalque . . . for some funeral," had been deposed by Henry of Lancaster in 1399 and, imprisoned at Pontefract Castle, was either murdered or starved to death the next year. The same thought occurs to Anne, whose coronation took place only ten days after the funeral of William III. Elizabeth is right in her opinion that the workmen are preparing for a coronation. Her own coronation was noted for its theatrical pageantry. Yet, perhaps reflecting upon the "sound of chisels, augers, planes, and saws," she feared damage to the Cathedral; in her many "progresses" throughout England she admired the "ancient architecture." If she were still in her "gold robes," she would see that no harm was done to the Abbey.[10] Charles II's quip in reply is consistent with his light and witty character. For all of them, the "Clamour" of royal executions, weddings, funerals, and coronations "dogs kingship." The ghosts, like Hardy, would prefer a "desert place." Hardy amused himself with such odd rimes as "third" with "widowered" and "Rimmon" with "women."

1. In the Princeton University Library.
2. P. 148; *Life*, p. 355.
3. Pencil-draft in the Dorset County Museum.
4. In the Dorset County Museum.
5. *Later Years*, pp. 148-49; *Life*, p. 355.
6. In the Dorset County Museum.
7. *Later Years*, p. 83; *Life*, p. 304.
8. In the Dorset County Museum.
9. Possibly Hardy forgot where Henry was buried; or he included Henry VIII either as a joke in this humorous poem or as an echo of the tourists near Wordsworth's grave. For a similar joke, see the notes on "In the British Museum."
10. Her "gold robes" perhaps reflects Hardy's memory of the effigy of Elizabeth in the Abbey Museum, where she is shown in the robes worn at the service of thanksgiving for the defeat of the Spanish Armada.

AQUAE SULIS is set in the ruins of the temple to the goddess Sul-Minerva, beside the Abbey Church of St. Peter and St. Paul in Bath. Hardy was well acquainted with this city. Besides several previous visits, in March, 1911, he "visited Bristol Cathedral and Bath Abbey."[1] The poem was probably inspired by this visit and, being subscribed "Bath," was possibly written then.

The hot springs of Bath were the site of a temple to the British Sul, goddess of waters, before the Romans came. The Romans combined her worship with that of Minerva and erected to Sul-Minerva an altar in a richly ornamented temple. After they departed, the walls and roof of the temple fell in; the elaborate baths constructed by the Romans filled with silt and rubbish. In 1727, a gilded bronze head, presumably Sul-Minerva, was discovered, and in 1755 and afterwards excavations uncovered the Roman baths, the temple, and the altars. Discoveries lagged until 1878, when new excavations laid bare Roman houses lying fifteen to twenty feet below modern structures. These excavations, continuing through Hardy's visit in 1911 as the "daytime parle on the Roman investigations," were close to Bath Abbey. A Saxon monastery, a forerunner of the Abbey Church, had extended over a portion of the baths during the eighth to the tenth centuries. In a sense, the monastery and the Church had usurped the pagan temple.

"Aquae Sulis" presents Hardy's imaginative interpretation of the facts. The time is midnight "just at interlune," when the moon is invisible. In the silence the "husky tune" of the "bubbling waters" in the springs close to the Abbey is heard. Hot waters give off a fog-like steam that in the darkness suggests a "filmy shape unsepulchred," which might be imagined Sul-Minerva rising from her "shrine . . . beneath the pile" of the Abbey. To this classic goddess, the Gothic architecture and statues might well seem "sculptures crude."

The theme of the poem is the "equality of all religions . . . the anthropomorphic tendency in general."[2] It includes the evolution of Christianity and the mortality of its forms and beliefs, especially in the years when Darwinism was calling into question the dogmas considered, when the Abbey was built, to rest on facts. This theme was often expressed in Victorian years, as in Swinburne's "Hymn to Proserpine," where a Roman philosopher meditates that religions come and go "under . . . the wave of the world," and even victorious Christianity "shall die . . . / In the darkness of time, in the deeps of the years, in the changes of things." Hardy expressed this theme in various places, as in "Evening Shadows" and the comment of the Spirit of the Years in *The Dynasts*: the rites in a cathedral represent "A local cult, called Christianity, / Which the wild dramas of the wheeling spheres / Include, with divers other such, in dim / Pathetical and brief parentheses, / Beyond whose span, uninfluenced, unconcerned, / The systems of the suns go sweeping on." (Part First, I, vi.)

In the definitions spoken by Sul-Minerva, "a Jumping-jack you, and myself but a poor Jumping-jill," and in her proposal, "Let us kiss and be friends!" the poem is wryly humorous.

1. See *Early Life*, pp. 95, 123; *Later Years*, pp. 100, 148; *Life*, pp. 72, 93, 317, 355.
2. Stevenson, *Darwin Among the Poets*, p. 248.

SEVENTY-FOUR AND TWENTY is ironic, contrasting the cocksureness of youth with the disillusion of experienced age. Hardy was seventy-four in 1914, and it is possible that the old man in the poem represents him, and the youth, "in years a score," represents memories of himself and his dreams in the 1860's.

THE ELOPEMENT, with "I" as the narrator, suggests an incident in Hardy's life, but no such incident is known. His marriage to Emma Gifford was, in a sense, an elopement, for instead of being married at Emma's home with the approval of her father, the pair were married in London by a sympathetic uncle.[1] There is no evidence that Emma disguised herself and was followed.

The final lines of the poem, suggesting that even the most emancipated woman tends to become conventional in old age, is paralleled in *The Well-Beloved*, where the once-daring, intellectual Mrs. Pine-Avon had "now retrograded to the petty and timid mental position of her mother and grandmother, giving sharp, strict regard to the current literature and art that reached the innocent presence of her long perspective of girls, with the view of hiding every skull and skeleton of life from their dear eyes." (III, iv.)

1. *Early Life*, pp. 132-33; *Life*, p. 101.

"I ROSE UP AS MY CUSTOM IS" presents a retrospective narrative by the ghost of a poet who, on All-Souls' evening, leaves his grave to visit his widow, now remarried to a "man snoring here—/ . . . no romantic chanticleer," but a good provider. Expecting his wife to be desolated, the ghost is dismayed to find her relieved that her second husband "makes no quest into my thoughts," as the poet had done.

The poem may be considered an imaginative reversal of Emma's death and Hardy's remarriage, into his death and her remarriage. She had loved him as "quite the ideal" in her youth, but later had accused him of self-absorption and impracticality.

The humor of the poem lies in its mixture of the ghostly, folk-lore, and homely fact. In folk-lore, it is the custom for ghosts to rise on All-Souls' eve (November 1). The ghost calls upon his "former Love," who receives him matter-of-factly. To express the ghost's dismay, the poem returns in the last stanza to the eerie in folk-lore: the nightmares hags ride, vampires, and harpies. These horrors are presented as they might seem to a ghost familiar with the everyday inhabitants of "Death's inviolate halls."[1]

1. That rural people in Wessex considered nightmares to be actualities is suggested in *The Woodlanders*, Chapter XXVIII. When Fitzpiers rode Grace's mare all night and left her sweating in the stable, the groom (unaware of Fitzpiers's excursion) explains that the mare had been "hag rid."

A WEEK has been interpreted as referring to the five days (March 7-11) of Hardy's first visit to Emma Gifford at St. Juliot in 1870.[1] Both the discrepancy in the number of days and the contents of the poem suggest that the week is after the visit.

Hardy returned from Cornwall on Friday, March 11, presumably in love with Emma as in "When I Set Out for Lyonnesse." The Monday night of "A Week" may be the following Monday, when his flush of feeling had cooled into "I . . . thought you were not as heretofore." Then the week of the poem presents the gradual idealization of Emma, an idealization that he always associated with love.

"A Week" is incremental, as the idealization advances step-by-step. Hardy associated certain moods with days of the week. Elliot Felkin wrote in his diary for July 21, 1919, that Hardy "went on to talk about days of the week and colours and associations. Monday was colourless, and Tuesday a little less colourless, and Wednesday was blue—'this sort of blue' pointing to an imitation Sèvres plate—and Thursday darker blue, and Friday is quite dark blue, and Saturday is yellow, and Sunday is always red."[2] The tone of the poem suggests a humorous intention.

1. See Weber, *Hardy's Love Poems*, pp. 14-15. The "week" of Hardy's first visit is presented in *Early Life*, pp. 98-99; *Life*, pp. 74-75. See "The Change," which seems to treat this visit.
2. "Days with Thomas Hardy," p. 30.

HAD YOU WEPT, biographers and critics agree, is a personal poem, but they do not agree upon the identity of the woman. The key to her identity may lie in the "tidings" that "had slain that day."

Weber relates the poem to Hardy's wife Emma,[1] in which case the occasion of the "deep division" may be jealousy of his attentions to other women, as in "She Charged Me." If the poem concerns Emma, it seems to say: "If you had shown me while alive the pain I found in *Some Recollections*, you would have reached through my irritation to a deeper feeling." Evelyn Hardy, however, says that "This poem was not written to Emma as Carl Weber indicates. The eyes of Hardy's first wife could never have been called either 'large' or 'luminous,' as her portrait shows." She proposes that the poem was written to Florence Hardy, whose eyes were large and luminous "as the drawing of her by William Strang shows."[2] Lois Deacon has a third theory, that the poem concerns a quarrel between Hardy and Tryphena Sparks over the subject of Horace Moule, who had been paying court to Tryphena without knowing fully the relation between her and Hardy. In this theory, Tryphena answers Hardy's charges haughtily and so widens the breach between them.[3]

The poem states a theme that Hardy meditated in his notebook: "Misapprehension. The shrinking soul thinks its weak place is going to be laid bare, and shows its thought by a suddenly clipped manner. The other shrinking soul thinks the clipped manner of the first to be the result of its own weakness in some way, not of its strength, and shows its fear also by its constrained air! So they withdraw from each other and misunderstand."[4] The poem also indicates a feature of Hardy's personality: when resisted, he was quietly stubborn, but when he was conscious of giving pain to others, he was quick to yield.

1. See *Hardy of Wessex*, 1st ed., p. 170, and *Hardy's Love Poems*, p. 47.
2. *Thomas Hardy*, p. 299.
3. *Cross-in-Hand*, unpublished typescript, p. 25.
4. *Early Life*, p. 232; *Life*, p. 177.

BEREFT, SHE THINKS SHE DREAMS in the manuscript was titled "She Thinks She Dreams."[1] The poem, spoken by a woman mourning the death of a husband, seems to have no biographical significance, unless Hardy may have reversed the roles of himself and Emma and imagined that he died first. It was set to music by Russell Boughton and included in his operatic version of *The Queen of Cornwall*.

1. Purdy, *Thomas Hardy: A Bibliographical Study*, p. 168.

IN THE BRITISH MUSEUM is set in the "Elgin Marble Room."[1] The poem presents a miniature drama that includes concealed irony. Hardy knew that the marbles displayed in the Elgin Room came from the Acropolis, not the Areopagus.[2]

The speakers of "In the British Museum" would seem to be a know-it-all man-about-town, eager to display his erudition, and a devout "labouring man," who confesses to "know but little, / Or nothing at all." The laboring man supposes a stone in the Elgin Room is from the Areopagus, and his eager informant confirms this error. Perhaps the poem represents a conversation that Hardy overheard.

The laboring man's reverence is based upon a passage in Acts 17: 19-23, concerned with St. Paul's preaching in Athens. In part, it reads: "And they took him, and brought him unto Areopagus, saying, May we know what this new doctrine, whereof thou speakest, is? . . . Then Paul stood in the midst of Mars' hill, and said, Ye men of

Athens, I perceive that in all things ye are too superstitious. For as I passed by, and beheld your devotions, I found an altar with this inscription, TO THE UNKNOWN GOD. Whom therefore ye ignorantly worship, him declare I unto you." The stone of "In the British Museum" is not an altar with an inscription; it displays "ashen blankness." The laboring man, confusing Areopagus with Acropolis, supposes it "echoed / The voice of Paul."

Both men know something of the Bible, but little of Athens. Hardy satirizes both the informer's ignorance and the laboring man's regard of the stone as something like a talisman. Neither man gives a thought to the magnificent gods of classic Greece, who were in Hardy's view better for life than Paulinism.

1. Purdy, *Thomas Hardy: A Bibliographical Study*, p. 168.
2. See "Christmas in the Elgin Room." No marble or other stone in the Elgin Room or any other room in the British Museum came from the Areopagus. The distance of half a mile or so between the Areopagus and the Acropolis would have prevented words spoken on the Areopagus from being echoed by any stone on the Acropolis. These facts were attested by the Curator of the Elgin Room.

IN THE SERVANTS' QUARTERS was titled in the manuscript "Humour in the Servants' Quarters."[1] The story is based upon the account of Peter's denial of Christ in the four Gospels: Matt. 26:55-75; Mark 14:48-72; Luke 22:52-62; and John 18:12-27, with details selected from their slightly varied accounts and elaborated in the colloquialisms of the poem.

As the story is told in the Gospel of Matthew: The time was early morning just before dawn, and the place was the servants' hall in the palace of the high priest Caiaphas. Jesus had been seized by servants of the high priest, who came against him "with swords and staves." His disciples had fled. "But Peter followed him afar off unto the high priest's palace, and went in, and sat with the servants." (Mark, Luke, and John indicate that the servants' quarters were "beneath in the palace," that the night was cold, and that Peter "warmed himself at the fire.") There a "damsel came unto him, saying, Thou also wast with Jesus of Galilee." When Peter had denied this charge, "another maid saw him and said unto them that were there, This fellow was also with Jesus of Nazareth." (At this time Peter had "gone out into the porch," a detail that Hardy omits. The "constables" of Hardy's poem are the "officers" who, in John's account, stood among the servants.) Peter denied Jesus "with an oath, I do not know the man." Then the constables came to Peter and said that his dialect showed he did not come from afar: "thy speech bewrayeth thee." Peter's dialect was that of Jesus, who, meanwhile, was being questioned upstairs and overheard in the servants' hall. (Apparently Hardy invented the "shudder when his chain clinks" and other details.) Thus accused for the third time, Peter began "to curse and to swear, saying, I know not the man." (Hardy invented the curse, "I'll be damned in hell.") Immediately the cock crew. "And Peter remembered the word of Jesus, which said unto him, Before the cock crow, thou shalt deny me thrice. And he went out, and wept bitterly."

In following the Gospel accounts, the poem hardly "vitiates the magic of the Christian myth intentionally, bringing its legendary characters into disillusioning daylight."[2] Hardy simply treated the episode realistically. Browning, among other Victorian writers, had treated Biblical scenes with similar realism, as in "An Epistle . . . of Karshish," where Christ is called a "learned leech" who "Perished in a tumult many years ago, / Accused . . . of wizardry."

Hardy stated his attitude toward the fictional use of episodes from the Bible, in a comment on "advance sheets" of Odin Gregory's "Jesus," sent to him for criticism by the Colony Press of New York. On March 23, 1927, Hardy wrote this Press: ". . . the tragedy, though an ambitious performance, appears to be laid down on safe and ortho-dox lines, largely based on Scriptural passages. That this limits its possibilities of originality is what the author would doubtless admit, and own himself content to waive a novelty he does not desire."[3] "In the Servants' Quarters" is original and novel in its homely realism of phrasing and in its theme, an instance of the "frailty of human nature" and "the cowardice induced by the imminence of danger."[4]

1. Purdy, *Thomas Hardy: A Bibliographical Study*, p. 168.
2. Hogan, "Structural Design in Thomas Hardy's Poetry," pp. 175-76.
3. In the Dorset County Museum.
4. Vinson, "Diction and Imagery in the Poetry of Thomas Hardy," p. 81.

THE OBLITERATE TOMB treats a haunting remorse and an impulse to right an old wrong, thwarted first by coincidence and later by the passage of time. A secondary theme is the callous attitude of "church-restorers" and the "spruce church-warden" toward memorials of the dead. Hardy treated these themes in other poems and stories, as in "The Enemy's Portrait," "The Levelled Churchyard," and the story "The Grave by the Handpost." The verse has been called faulty for such unpoetic phrases as " 'Ha,' they hollowly hackered [stuttered]."

"REGRET NOT ME" is something like a dramatic monologue, spoken as if by a dead woman to a lover mourning beside her grave. (Presumably the speaker is a woman, as phrases like "my faery flight" suggest.)

The poem may have been suggested by Hardy's reading some

poem with a similar theme, possibly Christina Rossetti's "Song" that begins "When I am dead, my dearest, / Sing no sad songs for me." The dead woman can hardly represent Emma Hardy, who apparently found little pleasure in country "junketings." One critic has associated the poem with *Tess of the D'Urbervilles*.[1] Tess may have been in Hardy's mind in an imaginary scene, suggesting to Angel that he continue to find pleasure in the merrymakings they had enjoyed together at Talbothays. As the police approach Tess at Stonehenge, she says to Angel: "This happiness could not have lasted. It was too much. I have had enough," and when the police arrive, she says, "I am ready." (Chapter LVIII.) Angel's memory of her might have seemed to tell him what the poem says. It mentions activities not pictured in the novel, but so does "Tess's Lament." If Hardy did imagine Tess's spirit as the speaker, the poem is subtly ironic, for Tess recommends to Angel joys that had given him pleasure in the flush of their love at Talbothays, but that were alien to his basic nature. When asked why he did not give *Tess* a happy ending, Hardy said: "Do you not see that under *any* circumstances they were doomed to unhappiness? A sensitive man like Angel Clare could never have been happy with her. After the first few months he would inevitably have thrown her failings in her face."[2]

The speaker need not be a woman. Perhaps, as he did in the poem "Afterwards," Hardy wrote the poem in anticipation of his own death, summarizing what he had enjoyed in life: cider-makings, country dances, and similar "junketings." "Regret Not Me" has been set to music by Gerald Finzi (London: Oxford University Press, not dated).

1. Blyton, *We Are Observed*, p. 219.
2. Blathwayt, "A Chat with the Author of 'Tess,'" p. 238. Tess's failings were presumably her lack of education, social graces, etc., not to mention her family.

THE RECALCITRANTS seems a poetic expression of a long-continued discussion between Jude and Sue in *Jude the Obscure*, for which novel Hardy had suggested the title *The Recalcitrants*.[1] The speaker of the monologue seems to be unconventional Sue, who objects to the binding legality of the marriage contract. The "You" who "would think it strange at first" seems the more conventional Jude. The reference in the poem to the "offence our course has given" and the proposal of flight to "a place / Where yours and mine can be natural lives" reflect Part V of *Jude*, Chapters III-VI, in which Jude and Sue draw back from their intention to marry, are persecuted by the people of Aldbrickham, and leave the town to wander from place to place.

A reference in the Preface of *Jude* to the death of a woman in 1890 suggests that Sue was based in part upon Hardy's sweetheart of the late 1860's, Tryphena Sparks. On this basis, Deacon and Coleman ask: ". . . in 'The Recalcitrants,' is it Hardy who is speaking, and is Tryphena the woman addressed?"[2] Their general discussion, alleging that Tryphena was Hardy's mistress and that the situation had aroused scandal, answers in the affirmative. Miss Deacon says "Hardy hoped, for a time, that the two might flee away together to the other side of the world."[3]

Purdy, however, supposes "The Recalcitrants" was written shortly after 1893 and associates it "possibly" with Mrs. Arthur Henniker.[4] Though Hardy was warmly attracted to Mrs. Henniker in the 1890's, an elopement would have been unthinkable.

The poem expresses Hardy's sympathy with lovers who, finding freedom necessary to their natures, defy the legal contract of marriage and the pressure of public opinion.

1. The first title of *Jude* was *The Simpletons*, changed in the second serial instalment to *Hearts Insurgent*. Then Hardy wrote to the publishers on November 5, 1894, asking them to change the title to *The Recalcitrants*. Purdy, *Thomas Hardy: A Bibliographical Study*, p. 87.
2. *Providence and Mr Hardy*, p. 207.
3. *Hardy's Sweetest Image*, p. 22.
4. *Thomas Hardy: A Bibliographical Study*, pp. 345-46.

STARLINGS ON THE ROOF first appeared in the *Nation* for October 18, 1913, with the subtitle " (Moving House, Michaelmas) ."[1]

Starlings, common in Dorset, nest in the thatch of the thatch-roofed houses still found there. Perhaps Hardy grew up with a fellow-feeling for these tenants of his home in Higher Bockhampton. In Chapter III of *The Woodlanders*, Marty South, awake at five in the morning, "heard the sparrows walking down their long holes in the thatch above her sloping ceiling to their exits at the eaves." One may fancy that birds nesting in a roof year after year know the people of a house and regard themselves as part of the family, and that they might philosophize about the disadvantages of moving from house to house as the seasons change.

Hardy's starlings express an idea he was fond of having his human "philosophers" state. In *A Laodicean*, Sir William De Stancy reflects: "But with a disposition to be happy, it is neither this place nor the other than can render us the reverse. In short, each man's happiness depends upon himself." (Book the First, Chapter V.)

1. Purdy, *Thomas Hardy: A Bibliographical Study*, p. 169.

THE MOON LOOKS IN presents a soliloquy by the moon, personified as a peeping Tom observing a lover and his beloved. To the lover imagining that the woman "dreams of me," the moon, shining upon her also "In her far-off home," suggests romance. Ironically, the moon observes the beloved adorning herself to attract whatever new lover she may meet. To Hardy the moon in this poem and elsewhere is more a goblin than a cupid; it has a "chilly ray" and is a symbol for nature's indifference to human dreams. The lover should have known better than to look at the moon through his window pane. In folk-lore, to do so is a portent of evil.

THE SWEET HUSSY sketches a satiric story to illustrate Hardy's view that the spider is not invariably male and the fly invariably female. In *The Trumpet-Major*, Matilda Johnson, an experienced actress familiar among the "—th Dragoons," would have married Bob Loveday if his brother John had not persuaded her to go away the night before the wedding. (Chapter XIX.)

THE TELEGRAM first appeared in *Harper's Monthly Magazine* of New York in December, 1913.[1] The poem presents a drama of distractedly mixed loyalties acted out before the eyes of a doting, middle-aged bridegroom. The impact of the drama is summed up in the bridegroom's bitter wish that he were "away from this, with friends I knew when young."

The "brief twelve words" of the telegram represent in England the maximum message to be sent for the minimum charge. The place seems Weymouth, with its esplanade and bay where "yachts ride mute at anchor." The bridegroom is a serious man who regards the promenaders as "giddy folk . . . strutting up and down the smooth parade."

1. Purdy, *Thomas Hardy: A Bibliographical Study*, p. 169.

THE MOTH-SIGNAL is a variant of the scene in *The Return of the Native* in which Wildeve uses a moth to lure Eustacia out of her house. (Book IV, Chapter 4.) The episode in the novel differs from that of the poem, as if Hardy meditated two scenes, selected one for the purposes of the novel, and wrote out the other in the poem, or, after writing the novel, imagined how the episode might have been if Diggory had not interfered. In the novel, Diggory watches Wildeve release a moth through a window chink into the room where Eustacia is sitting alone, a signal that he is waiting. She understands the signal, but before she can leave the room, Clym enters. (In the poem, he is in the room reading.) Eustacia then tells a lie similar to that in the poem: she is warm and will go out for air. When Clym proposes to go with her, she says: "O no. I am only going to the gate." Then they hear a rapping at the door, toward which Eustacia starts, but

Clym steps ahead of her. No one is there, for Diggory, to frustrate Wildeve, had knocked and disappeared. The scene of the poem in which Eustacia meets Wildeve near a tumulus is not in the novel.

The poem makes use of Dorset folk-lore. The white miller moth was believed to be a human soul that escapes from the mouth at the moment of death. The moth burned to a cinder may symbolize the burnt-out love between Eustacia and Clym. Other symbols appear in the poem. When Eustacia goes to meet her lover, Clym, buried in "the annals of ages gone," is "little heeding." The tumulus near which the lovers embrace suggests something sinister.[1] Eustacia's reference to her marriage as shattered into potsherds leads into the stanza in which the ghost of an "Ancient Briton" comments upon the timeless universality of "hearts . . . thwartly smitten."[2]

1. In *The Mayor of Casterbridge* Hardy makes the point that lovers seeking a meeting-place seldom choose the Roman Ring. Chapter XI.
2. In view of the relation of the poem to *The Return of the Native*, the Ancient Briton may be a substitute for Diggory, called a "weird" (fateful) character and a "Mephistophelian visitant."

SEEN BY THE WAITS seems to present another adventure of the "Mellstock" choir of "Friends Beyond" and "The Dead Quire." They feel too shocked to talk at seeing their respected manor-lady dance in her thin night-gown to the sacred music of the Christmas carols.

The anecdote may be one that Hardy heard from his grandmother, Mary Head Hardy. If so, he may have made a somewhat different use of the same anecdote in *Two on a Tower*. There the "lonely manor-lady" is Lady Constantine, whose husband is in South Africa. She does not dance upon receiving news of his death, but she soon becomes coquettish toward Swithin St. Cleeve, a fact commented upon by the country people. (See Chapters XI-XIII.) A relationship between the poem and the novel is suggested by the fact that Swithin's maternal grandmother seems a portrait of Mary Head Hardy.

THE TWO SOLDIERS in the manuscript was titled "A Rencounter." Two soldiers meet after many years. Each sees in the other's "fixed face" a "memory-acted scene." The soldiers do not speak to one another.

Their reaction is the only item in the story that is entirely clear. Only hints suggest what had happened in "those years gone by." Perhaps both men had, as rivals, loved "that strange woman." That a "drama" took place "which she / Had dyed incarnadine / For us, and more" suggests that her behavior was wanton or criminal in some way that involved her lovers. The "corner of the wall" suggests a prison. The woman may have been executed for a deed of violence and buried "Tombless and trod" in a prison yard. Lime would have been thrown upon her body to decay it, as suggested by her "poor half-perished residue." Such a background would explain the soldiers' meeting with "fixed face . . . / Lit by a lurid shine," their hostile indifference to each other, and the "tragic shadow" of the scene they recall.

Hardy's interest in stories of violence is evident in his notebooks, his novels, and his poems, as in "The Sacrilege," "The Mock Wife," and "On the Portrait of a Woman about to be Hanged." Perhaps he left vague the underlying "drama" of "The Two Soldiers" because the poem was based upon facts he chose to conceal.

THE DEATH OF REGRET puzzled Alda, Lady Hoare. Mrs. Florence Hardy wrote to her on December 9, 1914: "You mentioned 'The Death of Regret.' As it stands . . . it is a lament for a friend—a man, 'to forget him'—'his last departure,' etc. The poem was, in the first place, written about a cat—a little cat who was strangled in a rabbit wire on the barrow in sight of this house, & she is buried by a sycamore in our garden here. My husband thought the poem too good for a cat, & so made it apply to a person."[1] That Hardy wrote a poem about a cat, so full of feeling that he "made it apply to a person," a "comrade," indicates his fondness for his pets, often photographed in his lap. About another pet lost in 1901, he wrote on April 3 to Sir George Douglas: "A gloom has been cast over us here since yesterday by the loss of a favourite cat, which was mutilated by the mail-train the night before last. The violent death of [a] dumb creature always makes me revile the contingencies of a world in which animals are in the best of cases pitiable for their limitations."[2]

The "hill hard by" where the "comrade . . . wandered up there to die" is Conquer Barrow. The theme of the poem, structured by a pattern of the passage of time, is an expansion of Tennyson's lament in *In Memoriam A. H. H.*: "O last regret, regret can die!" (Lyric LXXVIII.)

1. In the Stourhead Collection, the County Archives in Trowbridge, Wiltshire.
2. In the National Library of Scotland, Edinburgh.

IN THE DAYS OF CRINOLINE was titled in the manuscript "The Vicar's Young Wife" and dated "July: 1911."[1] The poem tells an anecdote of the "high Victorian" period that Hardy in the poem "1967" called a "blinkered time." He suggests blinkers in the "plain tilt-bonnet" the vicar's young wife wore, with its awning-like wings on each side of her face. The poem was perhaps suggested by a painting Hardy treasured. When J. M. Murry visited him in 1921, he recorded: "Hardy showed me a stiff little watercolour of Westminster from the Green Park which he had made when he first came to London. It was done in the faintest of yellows and greens. In the middle distance was a man with a chimney-pot hat and a lady with a crinoline. It brought back the time to him, he said."[2] He told a critic of the poem, "Oh, but it is a true story."[3]

It is also a picture of a vanished time. The vicar is clearly a middle-aged advocate of the patriarchal family, in which the "young person" must be shielded from all that might bring a blush to a maidenly cheek. His comment to himself suggests his suspicion that his young wife does not altogether share his views. His final words to her are like a father's admonition to a daughter, paid for by a fatherly kiss on the cheek.

1. Purdy, *Thomas Hardy: A Bibliographical Study*, p. 169.
2. "Thomas Hardy," p. 223.
3. Hynes, *The Pattern of Hardy's Poetry*, p. 6.

THE ROMAN GRAVEMOUNDS was first published in the *English Review* for December, 1911, with the title "Among the Roman Gravemounds," though the manuscript bore the title "By the Roman Earthworks."[1] The poem treats Hardy's burial of a favorite cat in the garden at Max Gate.

Florence Dugdale, later the second Mrs. Hardy, wrote to Edward Clodd on November 8, 1910: "Mr. T. H. has been in the depths of despair at the death of a pet cat. 'Providence,' he wrote, 'has dealt me an entirely gratuitous & unlooked for blow.' . . . he is also finding a melancholy pleasure in writing an appropriate inscription for 'Kitsey's' headstone, so that Providence has not done all the harm it intended this time." She wrote again to Clodd in a letter dated "Saturday morn": "I went into Mr. Hardy's study yesterday & found him working at a pathetic little poem describing the melancholy burial of the white cat. I looked over his shoulder and read this line: 'That little white cat was his only friend.' That was too much for even my sweet temper, & I romped around the study exclaiming: 'This is hideous ingratitude.' But the culprit seemed highly delighted with himself, & said, smilingly, that he was not exactly writing about himself but about some imaginary man in a similar situation."[2]

The background of Roman mounds is both realistic for Hardy's garden and a device to contrast the meaning of Rome with the present fact that a loved pet is dead. When he was building his house at Max Gate, ". . . before the well-diggers had got deeper than three feet they came upon Romano-British urns and skeletons. Hardy and his wife found the spot was steeped in antiquity, and thought the

omens gloomy; but they did not prove so, the extreme age of the relics
dissipating any sense of gruesomeness. More of the sort were found in
digging the house-foundations."[3] The theme of the poem is expressed
in the observer's concession that the "mourner's mood has a charm
for me."

1. Purdy, *Thomas Hardy: A Bibliographical Study*, p. 169.
2. In the Brotherton Library Collection, Leeds.
3. *Early Life*, pp. 212-13; *Life*, p. 163.

THE WORKBOX is a humorous poem on the ballad-like theme of
the lover who died of grief when his beloved married another. The
lover's ghost does not (as in a ballad) come back to haunt the woman,
but the workbox made from the wood of his coffin has the effect of
a visitation, with the irony that the husband does not know what gift
he gives his "little wife." The poem is like early English ballads also
in its question-and-answer form and "surprise" ending.

THE SACRILEGE first appeared in the *Fortnightly Review* for
November, 1911.[1] This ballad-tragedy of gipsy life is laid in the area
around Dunkery Beacon ("Dunkery Tor") in the wilds of Exmoor
("Exon Moor"), a high plateau topped by wind-swept hills, between
some of which lie forested valleys and ravines. It extends about
twenty-five miles along the northern coast of Somerset and Devon, on
the Bristol Channel, and though irregular in shape is in the center
about fifteen miles wide. Thinly populated, it presents, especially in
misty weather, a lonely, eerie scene. Dunkery Beacon, 1706 feet high,
is the highest hill in Exmoor. Situated about five miles south of the
Bristol Channel (visible from the peak) and seven miles southwest
of Minehead, it is a windy, boggy, sedge-and-heather-covered wilder-
ness.

Priddy Fair, where the gipsy lover "snatched a silk-piece red and
rare," was held at a village high in the Mendip Hills in Somerset,
about four miles northwest of Wells and forty miles northeast of
Dunkery Beacon.[2] The cathedral from which the gipsy sought to steal
treasure for his mistress is presumably Wells. The thief has "gathered
gear / From Marlbury Downs to Dunkery Tor." Marlborough ("Marl-
bury") Downs is about eighty miles northeast of Dunkery Beacon.
Wells lies about halfway between the two, just south of the Mendip
Hills.

As Wells is in Somerset, Taunton ("Toneborough," on the River
Tone) is the county town; there the captured thief was tried and
hanged. Apparently the girl, as well as the thief's brother, witnessed
the hanging, as he "shadowed her / From Toneborough Deane to

Dunkery Tor." ("Toneborough Deane" is the farmland around Taunton.)

The poem does not name the river in which the thief's brother drowned the "wanton woman." Hardy may have had in mind the ancient Tarr Steps across the Barle River. Tarr Steps, about six miles south of Dunkery Beacon, in one of the most rugged areas of Exmoor, is a "clapper" bridge (made of huge stones used as supports for planks). Of prehistoric origin and reputedly the oldest bridge in England, it spans the river at a narrows where, in flood, the torrent has sometimes displaced even the huge stones.[3]

The "Ballad-Tragedy" is written in an eight-line stanza, with re-frain-like incremental repetition (typical of ballads) in the fourth and eighth lines. The structure is in other ways derived from balladry. Part I is a retrospective quotation of the thief as he told his story to his twin-brother and swore this brother to vengeance if his "Love" should yield to "Wrestler Joe." As in balladry, the lover suggests that if this vengeance is not taken "My rafted spirit would not rest." Part II (except the final stanza) is the brother's narrative of the theft, the woman's infidelity, and his pitying but pledged murder of the "wan-ton." The final stanza, a commentary, follows ballad-tradition in suggesting that the avenger is haunted by the dying woman, seen and heard in dreams. (Presumably the thief's "rafted spirit" has found rest because his faithful twin has avenged him.)

Hardy's gipsies are superstitious in pagan ways rather than Chris-tian: the brother does not know whether a "fay" or "one more foul" (some evil spirit) governs the thief's actions. They are pictured as professional thieves, yet the lover is commanded by some inner feeling, "Curbed by a law not of the land," not to rob a church. This law also demands the severest punishment, death, for unfaithfulness in love.

1. Purdy, *Thomas Hardy: A Bibliographical Study*, p. 170.

2. The area around Priddy is dotted with ancient earthworks, caverns, and stone circles, features that probably attracted Hardy.

3. Hutchings, *Inside Somerset*, inset v following p. 88 has pictures of Dunkery and Tarr Steps.

THE ABBEY MASON presents a romantic, apocryphal account of the invention of English Gothic architecture. *The Later Years* states Hardy's inspiration. In December, 1911, "Being interested . . . in the only Gothic style of architecture that can be called especially and exclusively English—the perpendicular style of the fifteenth century—Hardy made a journey to Gloucester to investigate its origin in that cathedral, which he ascertained to be in the screen between the south aisle and the transept. . . . He was so much impressed by the thought that the inventor's name . . . was unknown, that on his return he composed a poem thereon, called 'The Abbey Mason.' "[1] The poem was published in *Harper's Monthly Magazine* in December, 1912, illustrated with five drawings by Harvey Emrich. It did not carry the note " (With Memories of John Hicks, Architect) ," which was added when it was published in *Satires of Circumstance*.[2]

Though Hardy added fiction to explain the origin of the perpendicular style, he believed that it originated at Gloucester. On July 22, 1898, he wrote to Mrs. Arthur Henniker: "I went to the afternoon service . . . at Gloucester—a most interesting building for it was there that the Perpendicular style was *invented*: you can see how it grew in the old masons' minds."[3] Apparently on his visit of December, 1911, he did just what the poem says his abbey mason did: "He closelier looked; then looked again." Perhaps he saw icicles hanging from some part of the cathedral and drew the conclusion that the mason invented the style from a similar sight. That Hardy relied more upon intuition than upon research is suggested by a passage in the typescript of *The Later Years* omitted from the published version: "He was unaware at this time that the new style arose at Gloucester partly in consequence of the money that poured in at the shrine of Edward II."[4]

In the evolution of the Benedictine Monastery of St. Peter into Gloucester Cathedral, the abbey church was "new vamped" a number of times. In the years 1318-20, the south aisle of the nave had buckled. The builders placed straight up-and-down (perpendicular) tracery over the old Norman work and replaced the small Norman windows with lofty ones decorated with tracery. In 1330 and afterwards they altered the roofs by erecting a high clerestory and raising a roof about twenty feet higher than that of the nave, with perpendicular tracery over the Norman arches. These elaborations, which were made possible by the burial of Edward II there in 1327 and consequent large gifts to the abbey, gave rise to the report that the perpendicular style was invented at Gloucester. Dean Evans of Gloucester Cathedral wrote to me on August 11, 1966: "The perpendicular style of architecture was, as far as we know, begun at Gloucester—but there had been previous essays by the King's Master Mason, Willm de Ramsey, at Old St Paul's and St Stephen's Chapel. . . . The Mason's Apprentice story, is sheer romance & has no foundation at all."

John Harvey's *Gothic England* studies the origin and evolution of the perpendicular style. Between 1290 and 1335, the King's chief masons, Masters Michael, Walter, and Thomas of Canterbury, and their associates "laid the foundations of a National style." On the basis of their innovations, about 1330 William of Ramsey, then a King's Mason, in building St. Stephen's Chapel, introduced verticality and straight-line tracery, features that "stood on each side of the frontier of Perpendicular." This mason, in building a new Chapter House and Cloister at old St. Paul's, begun in 1332, made use of "all the elements of the new style: tracery comprising straight lines and vertical members; window mullions extended downwards to form wall-panelling; the four-centered arch; and the broad casement moulding. . . . The Gloucester work . . . built around the tomb of the martyred Edward II, is too closely akin to the design of St. Paul's Chapter House and cloister arcades for this to be a matter of coincidence."[5]

Though Hardy overlooks these developments, he accurately names Abbot Wygmore of the years 1329-37, under whom the work was done, and the succeeding abbots, Adam of Staunton (1337-57) and Thomas Horton (1357-77).

Hardy's reference to John Hicks, Dorchester architect under whom he had served an apprenticeship from July, 1856, until April, 1862, seems merely a memorial. Hicks had died in 1870. Hardy's concepts seem to owe something to the writings of John Ruskin, especially *The Seven Lamps of Architecture* and "The Nature of Gothic" in *Stones of Venice*. The poem is a psychological study of a devout Christian who acted on the principles set forth in Ruskin's "The Lamp of Sacrifice": sacrifice for the love of God and give Him the glory. Ruskin developed at length the ideas that medieval builders "toiled for pleasure more than pay" and invented architectural forms by imitating natural forms.

Hardy's central intention was to comment upon "the thought that the inventor's name . . . was unknown." He wrote to Sir Sydney Cockerell on May 15, 1912: "The point . . . is what has struck me so often in relation to mediaeval art—the anonymity of its creators. They seem in those days to have had no personal ambition: and thinking of this last year I was led to write a poem bearing on it."[6] Hardy "felt a personal indebtedness to those who by words or deed had lit up the general travel of mankind,"[7] and the poem seems an effort to pay a portion of this debt.

The poem contains a number of architectural terms: "parpend ashlars" (squared stones reaching through a wall to bind it together), "ogees" (mouldings with a profile in the form of the letter S), "flexures" (curves), "stalactitic" (like an icicle), "cusping marks" (triangular points extending from leaf-like tracery), "ogive" (pointed arch), "templates" (beams across openings), "mullions" (slender bars in windows), and "spandrels" (spaces between the curves of an arch and an enclosing angle). "Winton" is Hardy's name for Winchester. "Solway Frith" (Firth) is a bay in northwest England, between England and Scotland.

1. Pp. 150-51; *Life*, p. 357.
2. Purdy, *Thomas Hardy: A Bibliographical Study*, p. 170.
3. In the Dorset County Museum.
4. "T. H. Vol. II, 1892 to [end] . . . Mrs. Hardy (Personal Copy)," in the Dorset County Museum.
5. Summarized and quoted as indicated from pp. 42-51.
6. Meynell, ed., *Friends of a Lifetime*, p. 275.
7. Blunden, *Thomas Hardy*, p. 254.

THE JUBILEE OF A MAGAZINE in the manuscript was titled " 'The Cornhill's' Jubilee," but the poem was published in the *Cornhill Magazine* for January, 1910, as "An Impromptu to the Editor."[1] The jubilee was the fiftieth anniversary of the *Cornhill*, founded in 1860 by the publishers Smith and Elder, with W. M. Thackeray as the first editor. In 1871, Leslie Stephen became editor. Having read *Under the Greenwood Tree*, Stephen asked Hardy for a novel, and Hardy supplied *Far from the Madding Crowd*, which ran in the *Cornhill* from January to December, 1874, and was his first popular success. In 1875-76, *The Hand of Ethelberta* appeared in the *Cornhill*, but in 1878 Stephen rejected *The Return of the Native* as not suitable for a family magazine. The rejection did not rupture Hardy's friendship with Stephen or his respect for the magazine. It published also his short-story "Blue Jimmy, the Horse-Stealer," his essay "Memories of Church Restoration," and a number of his poems: "The Souls of the Slain," "The Ballad-Singer," "The Pine-Planters," "The Noble Lady's Tale," "The Spring Call," and "Let Me Enjoy."

Hardy agreed with the policies of the *Cornhill*, especially under Stephen's editorship (1871-82). Treating the magazine as a civilizing force, he comments on the Victorian faith in progress. The *Cornhill*, he says, bears on its cover an emblem of the "sower, reaper, thresher" who work "in ancient style," even though their tasks are nowadays done by machinery. To most men, this "mechanic furtherance" is progress. He asks whether there has been a similar advance in "rightness, candour," and implies that the answer is negative in spite of the *Cornhill's* "gentle aim / To straighten visions wry and wrong."

Hardy expressed this attitude in a letter to the American Red Cross on October 3, 1900: ". . . though, in the past century, material growth has been out of all proportion to moral growth, the existence of such a society as this leaves one not altogether without hope that during the next hundred years the relations between our inward and our outward progress may become less of a reproach to civilization." [2]

1. Purdy, *Thomas Hardy: A Bibliographical Study*, p. 170.
2. Yale University Library, *Thomas Hardy, O. M. Catalogue of a Memorial Exhibition*, p. 22.

THE SATIN SHOES first appeared in *Harper's Monthly Magazine* of New York in January, 1910, where it bore the subtitle "A Quiet Tragedy." Hardy identified the setting as Higher Bockhampton.[1]

One can visualize the dairy beside the lane that leads to Hardy's birthplace, Stinsford Church a little more than a mile away, the drenched meadows between, and water "like a pool" in the path of the wedding-party. The definite locality suggests that "The Satin Shoes" tells a factual story, which Hardy may have heard from his grandmother. This possibility is heightened by a scene in *Under the Greenwood Tree*, where Hardy had his "Mellstock" (Stinsford) folk comment on a woman's vanity on her wedding day. As Fancy is donning her wedding dress, the waiting neighbors talk: " 'Ah!' said grandfather James to grandfather William as they retired, 'I wonder which she thinks most about, Dick or her wedding raiment!'

" 'Well, 'tis their nature,' said grandfather William. 'Remember the words of the prophet Jeremiah: "Can a maid forget her ornaments, or a bride her attire?" ' " [2]

Hardy provides a crisis for "The Satin Shoes" in a frequent fact of Dorset weather, a soaking rain. The incident recalls the rain that helps to wreck Eustacia's elopement with Wildeve in *The Return of the Native*.

1. Purdy, *Thomas Hardy: A Bibliographical Study*, pp. 170-71.
2. Part the Fifth, Chapter I. If the story is based upon fact, Hardy may have simplified it. A dairyman would have had the required "coach," or at least a wagon; getting to the church without wading would not have been a problem, but it was the custom in Dorset for the wedding party and the musicians to parade around the village or town, as in *Under the Greenwood Tree* and in the poem "The Country Wedding." Omission of the parade might cause the bride to brood herself into madness.

EXEUNT OMNES in the manuscript was titled "Epilogue." [1] The date, June 2, 1913, was Hardy's seventy-third birthday.

The poem dramatizes the passing away of friends, Hardy's loneliness, and his approaching death. The phrase "Exeunt Omnes" was a stage direction in old plays before a curtain was used, to call all actors off the stage. In the poem, life is presented as the Dorchester Fair. The "Everybody else" or the "Omnes" who have left the fair must include Hardy's father, who had died in 1892; his mother, in 1904; and his wife Emma, in 1912, besides friends and loved ones of his youth, for instance, Horace Moule (1873) and Tryphena Sparks (1890).

The site of the fair is South Street at its junction with High West and High East Streets; the steeple is on St. Peter's Church, which stands at this corner; the bridge is Grey's Bridge just outside town at the foot of High East Street; and the highway is the road toward Stinsford and London.

The allegory is explained in Fackler's comment: concerning death, "Hardy thinks . . . of an area or atmosphere vast, vague, cold, unwelcoming though engulfing, in which all individual being is swallowed up, and all awareness. . . . This poem is built up with severe economy and plainness on the figure of a closed-up, played-out fair, once so stirring, bright, sociable, so full of attractions, now dull, deserted by all the 'loungers,' except for one solitary stroller, who muses on the passing of the show. . . . In 'clammy and numbing night-fog,' the poem reveals the revulsion of soul with which the writer waits for the inevitable last."[2]

"Exeunt Omnes" has been set to music by Gerald Finzi in *By Footpath and Stile* (London: J. Curwen & Sons, 1925).

1. Purdy, *Thomas Hardy: A Bibliographical Study*, p. 171.
2. "Death: Idea and Image in Some Later Victorian Lyrists," pp. 161-63.

A POET seems Hardy's suggestion for his epitaph. In July, 1914, he had been married to Florence Dugdale only five months, but he knew that, at seventy-four, he might not live much longer, and that *Satires of Circumstance* might be his last volume.

The poem lists the everyday events of his life, his tastes, and his personality, with a suggestion of his annoyance at the lionizing that fame had brought. Preferring a quiet life, he was plagued by "urgent writs to sup or dine" and a stream of callers at Max Gate: reviewers, critics, biographical-sketch writers, and tourists eager for tit-bits of Hardiana.

He would like to be remembered for something flattering to himself as a person, that "Two bright-souled women clave to him." In her later life, Emma and Hardy did not live in harmony, but in 1914, his memories returned to the early years of their marriage.[1]

"A Poet" is written in the long meter of many church hymns. The word "clave" is an archaic past tense of "cleave" used in the sense of "cling," as in Acts 17:34, which says of Paul, "certain men clave unto him." Hardy's "wrinkled gear" suggests the worn-out body that the soul puts off at death.

1. Lois Deacon expressed to me the opinion that, though Hardy wished his readers to identify the women as Emma and Florence, "bright-souled" does not

accurately describe either of them, and that Hardy had in mind his mother
Jemima and his early sweetheart Tryphena Sparks. Tryphena did not "cleave"
to him.

The poems grouped as "Satires of Circumstance in Fifteen
Glimpses" are dated 1910 in the manuscript. Eleven of them were
first published in the *Fortnightly Review* for April, 1911, together
with a twelfth, "On the Doorstep," which was omitted when the group
was published in *Satires of Circumstance.*[1] One, "At the Draper's,"
was first published in the *Saturday Review* for May 16, 1914. In pub-
lishing the poems in book form, Hardy added three not previously
printed: "In the Study," "On the Death-Bed," and "In the Moon-
light."[2]

Hardy used the title phrase in the description of Christopher
Julian in *The Hand of Ethelberta*, saying that he "sometimes had
philosophy enough to appreciate a satire of circumstance, because
nobody intended it." (Chapter XIII.) This statement suggests a
feature of the poems grouped under this title: most of them present
ironic situations that no one intended. The squabble of "In the
Cemetery" and the revelation of "Outside the Window" are rooted in
circumstances of which the persons satirized are not aware. Not even
the dying man of "On the Death-Bed" realizes all that his confession
reveals. Several of the poems are built upon overhearing or seeing
something not intended to be heard or seen: "In Church," "Outside
the Window," and "At the Draper's." Others, like "In the Restau-
rant," are presented as conversations somehow overheard by the poet.

The poems may be considered candid-camera snapshots, each
snapped at some crisis that implies a pathetic, sordid, or tragic story.
"At a Watering Place," for instance, has the bitterness of a naturalistic
novel.

Yet the satires are comic. Some of the victims of circumstance are
simply foolish, like the squabbling women of "In the Cemetery";
others are vain like the widow-to-be of "At the Draper's." Even the
pathetic lady of "In the Study" is amusing in her affectation and
transparent fib. The illicit lovers of "In the Restaurant" and the
murderer of "On the Death-Bed" are trapped in evil, but they have
incautiously set the traps.

Writing to Mrs. Arthur Henniker about the poems published in
the *Fortnightly*, Hardy said on May 3, 1911: "You will remember, I
am sure, that being *satires* they are rather brutal. I express no feeling
or opinion myself at all. They are from notes I made some twenty

years ago, & then found more fit for verse than prose."[3] *The Later Years* comments that the poems "were caustically humorous productions which had been issued with a light heart before the war. So much shadow, domestic and public, had passed over his head since he had written the satires that he was in no mood now to publish humour or irony, and hence he would readily have suppressed them if they had not already gained such currency from magazine publication that he could not do it."[4] The "currency" was partly due to the republication of selected satires in anthologies, presumably because the compilers found them brief and thought they represented Hardy's widely proclaimed cynicism.

1. It is not the poem of the same name published in *Moments of Vision*; see "On the Doorstep" in Part Two.
2. Purdy, *Thomas Hardy: A Bibliographical Study*, pp. 164-65.
3. In the Dorset County Museum.
4. P. 164; *Life*, p. 367.

AT TEA presents a glimpse beneath the surface of social decorum into the emotions of a love-triangle that "the fates ordained."

IN CHURCH resembles an experience described in *The Early Life*, when Hardy was about eleven: "This was at church when listening to the sermon. Some mischievous movement of his mind set him imagining that the vicar was preaching mockingly, and he began trying to trace a humorous twitch in the corners of Mr. S——'s mouth, as if he could hardly keep a serious countenance. . . . Like Sterne in the pulpit, the vicar seemed to be 'always tottering on the verge of laughter,' and hence against his will Thomas could hardly control his merriment."[1]

Hogan discusses the poem, saying: "Its glib mockery obscures the seriousness of the sin of vanity in a preacher, while it is over-serious about his acting, which is after all necessary to his role: he can be pleased with his performance and still be serious with his text. Not knowing the girl parishioner, we cannot actively share her disillusionment, yet it divides our attention."[2] The girl deepens the comedy into a potential tragedy that Hardy leaves the reader to imagine.

His experience may have been in his mind when he wrote *The Return of the Native*. When Mrs. Yeobright arose in church to forbid the banns for Thomasin's marriage to Wildeve, Timothy Fairway was amazed at the parson: " 'I'll speak to you after the service,' said the parson, in quite a homely way—yes, turning all at once into a common man no holier than you or I." In describing old Yeobright's performance on the bass-viol, Fairway expresses astonishment that "Old Pa'son Williams lifted his hands in his great holy surplice as natural as if he'd been in common clothes." Christian Cantle pauses in his account of Eustacia's being pricked by a needle in church to express amazement that the parson is human: "There were the pa'son in his surplice holding up his hand. . . . O, and what d'ye think I found out, Mrs. Yeobright? The pa'son wears a suit of clothes under his surplice!—I could see his black sleeve when he held up his arm." (Book One, Chapters III and V, and Book Three, Chapter II.)

1. P. 28; *Life*, p. 22.
2. "Structural Design in Thomas Hardy's Poetry," p. 178.

BY HER AUNT'S GRAVE resembles an experience recorded in Hardy's journal for November, 1894: "Painful story. Old P—— . . . died at West Stafford, his native village, and was buried there. His widow long after died in Fordington, having saved £5 to be buried with her husband. The rector of the village made no objection, and the grave was dug. Meanwhile the daughter had come home, and said the money was not enough to pay for carrying the body of her mother out there in the country; so the grave was filled in, and the woman buried where she died."[1]

Fordington is a part of Dorchester, and West Stafford is a village two miles to the southeast. Dorchester has no inn called "The Load of Hay," but this is a common name for many inns. The poem dramatizes the "Painful story" by making a lover and a dance the subversive attraction. Though the poem states no condemnation, Hardy felt deeply about callousness toward the poverty-stricken dead. He said of church restoration that uprooted tombstones: "It was more often the stones of the poor inhabitants, purchased and erected in many cases out of scanty means—that suffered most."[2]

He elsewhere observed how the living sometimes rob the dead. The chorus characters in *The Mayor of Casterbridge* comment upon the death of Susan, who had saved her pennies for her burial. She had said to Mother Cuxom: " 'And when you've used 'em, and my eyes don't open no more, bury the pennies, good souls, and don't ye go spending 'em, for I shouldn't like it.' . . . Well, and Martha did it, and buried the ounce pennies in the garden. But if ye'll believe words, that man, Christopher Coney, went and dug 'em up, and spent 'em at the Three Mariners. . . . ' 'Twas a cannibal deed;' deprecated her listeners." (Chapter XVIII.)

1. *Later Years*, p. 34; *Life*, pp. 266-67.
2. Holland, *Thomas Hardy's Wessex Scene*, p. 22.

IN THE ROOM OF THE BRIDE-ELECT condenses into thirteen lines a short-story Hardy planned. In the Dorset County Museum an envelope labelled "M. S. Short Stories" contains a one-page, pencil-written plot-sketch called "Scheme of Short Story" setting forth essentially the story of the poem. The sketch includes: ". . . she [the girl] passionately reproaching them [the parents] for not having insisted on her marrying the one they chose." The conclusion of the sketch reads: "She puts on a dreadful artificial gaiety. The wedding takes place. [What happens afterwards is not told.]"[1]

The sketch contains the sentence: "She suspects that he drinks (?)." The poem, to explain the girl's reluctance to marry the man she had chosen, offers only "here he comes with his button-hole rose." This difference makes the poem more interesting as an observation of perversity in feminine psychology. The rose suggests that the bridegroom was a dashing fancy-man in courtship, but he seems a "dolt" in the prospect of domestic life. The girl's perversity includes her revolt against having her parents choose her husband.

1. The brackets are Hardy's. See Evelyn Hardy, ed., "Plots for Five Unpublished Short Stories," p. 36. It is not known whether the plot-sketch was written before or after the poem.

AT A WATERING-PLACE pictures an "esplanade" with "far chalk cliffs, to the left," which suggests that the watering-place is Swanage, about twenty-five miles southeast of Dorchester, or Weymouth, seven miles south of Dorchester. Both cities have cliffs to the left as one faces the sea.

IN THE CEMETERY is in tone a poem of cynical humor, but Hardy's compassion is implied.

OUTSIDE THE WINDOW presents one of Hardy's many eavesdropping scenes. In line with Strachey's comment that "It is easy to imagine the scene as the turning-point in a realistic psychological novel,"[1] Ketcham surmises that Hardy derived his poem from Thackeray's *Pendennis*. There Lightfoot describes Blanche Amory: "The second season in London, Mr. Soppington was a goin' to propose for her, and actially came one day, and sor her fling a book into the fire, and scold her mother so, that he went down softly by the back droringroom door, which he came in by; and next thing we heard of him was, he was married to Miss Rider."[2]

1. "Mr. Hardy's New Poems," p. 223.
2. " 'A Vixen Voice': Hardy and Thackeray," p. 130.

IN THE STUDY, in its cameo of a "type of decayed gentility," exhibits Hardy as an observer of "small signs" of the kind which reveal that the caller, lightly laughing, is "almost breakfastless." The observer, presumed to be interested in the "works / Of eminent divines," may be Hardy's friend, the Reverend William Barnes, who, as poet and art-collector, would notice such hints.

AT THE ALTAR-RAIL dramatizes a theme Hardy treated in "Rose-Ann" and "The Sweet Hussy."

The scene is Dorchester shortly after a fair, which included a "Cattle-Show." The altar-rail seems to be that of St. Peter's Church, which faces the area of the fair. For their rendezvous the young farmer and the girl walked a few blocks to the shrub-sheltered nook of the Dorchester Borough Gardens where a white-marble fountain "leaps."[1] The lovers reached the Borough Gardens from High West Street by walking along Albert Road, which bends in a quarter-circle as it comes to the park entrance and "sweeps" around the park.

1. The fountain has three bowls, one above the other, given to Dorchester by Charles Hanford in memory of G. J. G. Gregory, the mayor who in 1895 purchased the land for the "pleasure gardens for the health and recreation of the inhabitants."

IN THE NUPTIAL CHAMBER presents a bride who, like Hardy, is moved to ecstasy by music. "For Hardy, music was not only a pleasurable experience in itself, but it could have a grotesque, bewitching effect: it could condition neurotically the behaviour of a sensitive listener. . . . The lives of the young couple of 'In the Nuptial Chamber' are momentarily isolated and a . . . para-psychological bondage to a 'mastering tune' is paraded in gnomish irony."[1]

The music is a wedding serenade like that for Bathsheba and Gabriel in *Far from the Madding Crowd* (Chapter LVII), but in the poem the "townsfolk's cheery compliment" is made ironic by the bridegroom's explanation to "my Innocent," the bride's ecstatic revelation, and the reader's wonder about what follows.

1. Wing, *Hardy*, p. 94.

IN THE RESTAURANT is a study in masculine and feminine fears. The lovers express no remorse for their betrayal of an evidently loving husband. The man states some slight concern for the child they will bring into the world, but the woman (contrary to the usual concept of mother-love) seems callous toward her children at home and her child to be born. The man fears the opinion of the world, "the teeth of scorn," but the woman, brazen toward the world, expresses distaste for her husband and fear that he may discover her deceit.

AT THE DRAPER'S was first published under the title "How He Looked in at the Draper's." The poem is built upon an old jest found, for instance, in Act V of Dion Boucicault's *London Assurance* (1841), in the following dialogue: "*Spanker*: Lady Gay Spanker, are you ambitious of becoming a widow? *Lady Gay*: Why, Dolly, woman is at best but weak, and weeds become me." The jest underlies Lord Henry's *bon mot* in Wilde's *The Picture of Dorian Gray*: when Madame de Ferrol's "third husband died, her hair turned quite gold from grief." (Chapter XV.) In Hardy's treatment, this jest is embittered by the presence of the dying man and his inadvertent eavesdropping.

ON THE DEATH-BED is subtly ironic. The dying man's confession is motivated not so much by a change of heart leading to compassion for his victim, as by loss of the reward he expected, the woman's continued love, and of the reward he ignored, the "hope . . . of Heaven."

OVER THE COFFIN treats a theme Hardy had treated in "A Wife and Another" and later treated in *The Queen of Cornwall*, where Iseult the Whitehanded is willing to forgive Tristram and allow him to live with the other Iseult if only she too may remain with him. (Scene XVI.) It would seem that Hardy agreed with the first wife of "Over the Coffin," that divorce because of wounded pride or public opinion brings greater misery than tolerance. The irony of the first wife's wrong choice is deepened by the suggestion that the dead man is eavesdropping.

IN THE MOONLIGHT expresses the theme of too late realization, a favorite with Hardy. Evidently the "lonely workman" had chosen to follow some romantic dream and to ignore the real worth of the dead woman, who perhaps had loved him. That he preferred illusion to reality but now sees the truth is suggested by "the shine of this corpse-cold moon," in Hardy's works a symbol for disillusioned reality.

One may imagine the situation by reversing the conclusion of *The Woodlanders* and supposing that Marty South is dead and Giles, standing over her grave, has realized the affinity of their natures. The workman's remorse is now as futile as Sergeant Troy's planting flowers on Fanny Robin's grave in *Far from the Madding Crowd*.

MOMENTS OF VISION

Hardy sent the manuscript of *Moments of Vision and Miscellaneous Verses* to Macmillan in August of 1917. Published on November 30, it contained 159 poems, to which one was added when the volume was included in *Collected Poems*. It is his largest volume of poems. Most of them were written after 1914, the date of *Satires of*

Circumstance, but thirteen are dated (at least in an early draft) be-fore 1914. They are: "The Change," "Lines to a Movement in Mo-zart's E-Flat Symphony," "Something Tapped," "Love the Monopo-list," "The Last Performance," "It Never Looks Like Summer," "He Wonders About Himself," "Old Excursions," "Paths of Former Time," "The Shadow on the Stone," "The Young Glass-Stainer," "Looking at a Picture on an Anniversary," and "His Country." A few other poems, not so dated, are described as "Taken from an old note."

Poems on Hardy's experiences with his first wife Emma run through the volume, continuing the memories of "Poems of 1912-13." Seventeen poems dealing with World War I are grouped as "Poems of War and Patriotism."

The phrase "moments of vision" refers to incidents of observation, feeling, or insight. Many poems treat personal experiences, and rel-atively few the philosophical questions prominent in earlier volumes. Perhaps because he realized the personal nature of the volume, Hardy wrote in his journal: "I do not expect much notice will be taken of these poems: they mortify the human sense of self-importance by showing, or suggesting, that human beings are of no matter or ap-preciable value in this nonchalant universe."[1]

1. *Later Years*, p. 179; *Life*, p. 378.

MOMENTS OF VISION presents times of flash-like insight when men, as Wordsworth phrases it in "Tintern Abbey," "see into the life of things." The poem suggests that such glimpses come when the mind is relaxed, drawing more from memory in "night hours of ache" than from the senses "When the world is awake." The "mirror" seems to symbolize memory, introspection, and conscience penetrating the gloss of everyday self-justification and revealing the "tincts" (stains) of the soul.

Hardy may have drawn the imagery and the philosophy of the poem from a passage in Eduard Von Hartmann's *Philosophy of the Unconscious*, which he used extensively in writing *The Dynasts*. Dis-cussing the relation between the consciousness of individual men and the Unconscious Mind (Hardy's "Immanent Will"), Von Hartmann wrote: "The light radiating from the unconscious central sun strikes upon the concave mirror of organisms, and is reflected and united in the focus of the self-conscious mind. In this way arise the separate centres of the individual conscious minds, but with these the absolute centre does not communicate directly, but only by means of the un-conscious rays (functions) affecting the organism (the brain), which are reflected from this to the focus of consciousness."[1]

Hardy was seventy-seven when the volume that this poem intro-
duces was published. World War I was in progress. The poem fitting-
ly leads into poems that treat soul-searching.

1. II, 232-33.

THE VOICE OF THINGS may be dated from "Hardy's journey to
Cornwall in March 1913 or, better, his last visit to these scenes in
September 1916."[1] If the September date is right, the first stanza
refers to his courtship of Emma Gifford in August of 1870.[2] The
second stanza, concerning a "double decade after" (1890), seems to
symbolize some return to Cornwall in memory at a time "When
thwarts had flung their toils in front of me," that is, in the years of
"division" between Hardy and Emma.[3] The third stanza treats the
journey of Hardy and his wife Florence to this area in 1916. They
received so little welcome in Tintagel Church that they walked out,
a fact paralleled in the concluding lines of the poem. The record
reads: "*September* 10. Sunday. To Tintagel Church. We sat down
in a seat bordering the passage to the transept, but the vicar appalled
us by . . . saying we were in the way of the choir who would have to
pass there. He banished us to the back of the transept. However,
when he began his sermon we walked out. He thought it was done to
be even with him, and looked his indignation: but it was really be-
cause we could not see the nave lengthwise, which my wife, Emma,
had sketched in watercolours when she was a young woman before it
was 'restored,' so that I was interested in noting the changes, as also was
F., who was familiar with the sketch. It was saddening . . . that we
were inhospitably received in a church so much visited and appreci-
ated by one we both had known so well."[4]

The poem makes use of Hardy's version of the pathetic fallacy
as stated in his notebook for August 23, 1865: "The poetry of a scene
varies with the minds of the perceivers. Indeed, it does not lie in the
scene at all."[5] The poem presents the voices of the waves in three
moods, when they "huzza'd," in "long ironic laughter," and in suppli-
cation "like a congregation" he could not join. In the concluding
metaphor, he yearned to believe that he might meet Emma again,
but realized that he could not.

1. Purdy, *Thomas Hardy: A Bibliographical Study*, p. 194.
2. See *Early Life*, p. 103; *Life*, p. 78.
3. Hardy did not revisit Cornwall after his marriage to Emma in 1874 until 1913.
4. *Later Years*, pp. 172-73; *Life*, p. 373.
5. *Early Life*, p. 66; *Life*, p. 50.

"WHY BE AT PAINS?" presents a seaman wooing a girl who,
though reluctant, has blushed. The lover pleads his loneliness and

will return to the sea unless they may "join hands" for an uncertain future.

"WE SAT AT THE WINDOW," with its headnote of *"Bournemouth, 1875,"* is a personal poem. Hardy and Emma Gifford were married in August of 1874. After a honeymoon at Rouen and Paris, they lived a roving life in England, in Surbiton, London, and Childe-Okeford in Dorset, but they wished to settle down. *The Early Life* says: "In July [1875] the couple went to Bournemouth, and then by steamer to Swanage, where they found lodgings at the house of an invalided captain of smacks and ketches; and Hardy, suspending his house-hunting, settled down there for the autumn and winter."[1] As nothing more is known of the Hardys' apparently transient stay in Bourne-mouth (a seaside resort-city about twenty-five miles east of Dor-chester), "We Sat at the Window" has biographical significance in describing a crisis in the young couple's relations.

In the poem, it was raining on St. Swithin's day, July 15. Folklore holds that rain on this day promises rain for the next forty days. Rain and the promise of rain symbolize Hardy's meaning, suggested in the first line, where they are "looking out" at a "witless" scene. They are not only bored, but are "irked by the scene, by our own selves; yes." As he looks back upon the scene after half a lifetime with Emma, he intends the poem to mark a "moment of vision," an early realization that he had nothing to say to Emma, and she had nothing to say to him.

He seems to blame himself for dwelling in his own thoughts, that caused him not to invent conversation to interest Emma. It may be an afterthought of remorse after her death, that there was much "to see and crown / By me in her." In this perspective, on that July day of rain, presaging more of the same, "great was the waste."

1. P. 141; *Life,* p. 107.

AFTERNOON SERVICE AT MELLSTOCK presents a personal reminis-cence of Hardy's boyhood when, as the date *"Circa 1850"* indicates, he was about ten years old. As "Mellstock" is his name for Stinsford, the scene is Stinsford Church on an afternoon in summer or autumn.

When a child, he so enjoyed the services of the Church that "on wet Sunday mornings" he would "wrap himself in a tablecloth, and read the Morning Prayer standing in a chair, his cousin playing the clerk with loud Amens, and his grandmother representing the con-gregation. The sermon which followed was simply a patchwork of the sentences used by the vicar." At a slightly later period, "Thomas was kept strictly at church on Sundays as usual, till he knew the

Morning and Evening Services by heart including the rubrics, as well as large portions of the New Version of the Psalms. The aspect of that time is clearly indicated in the verses 'Afternoon Service at Mellstock.' "[1] The imagery of the poem appears in a notebook entry for April, 1871: "In church. The sibilants in the responses of the congregation, who bend their heads like pine-trees in the wind."[2]

The "Tate-and-Brady psalm / To the tune of 'Cambridge New' " was from the *New Version of the Psalms*, published in 1696. The singers are pictured as watching outdoor scenes while they sang. Though the windows of Stinsford Church are now nearly all of stained glass (including the Hardy Memorial Window), the church had little stained glass when Hardy was a boy.[3]

"Afternoon Service at Mellstock" is a sad poem. It is not likely that the boy Hardy thought of the "outpourings" as "mindless." The final stanza is his mature judgment of the uncritical faith that he had once held, but lost. He had bartered faith and hope for the rationalist's "truth," because he could not do otherwise.

He made use of his memory of the scene in many places. The opening paragraph of *An Indiscretion in the Life of an Heiress* reads: "The congregation in Tollamore Church were singing the evening hymn, the people gently swaying backwards and forwards like trees in a soft breeze. The heads of the village children . . . were inclined to one side as they uttered their shrill notes, their eyes listlessly tracing some crack in the old walls, or following the movement of a distant bough or bird, with features rapt almost to painfulness." The scene appears again in Chapter XII, 8, of *Desperate Remedies*. It seems to underlie the stage-direction in the Preface of *The Dynasts*: the speeches of the characters should take the shape "of a monotonic delivery . . . with dreamy conventional gestures, something in the manner traditionally maintained by the old Christmas mummers."

1. *Early Life*, pp. 19, 23; *Life*, 15, 18.
2. Evelyn Hardy, *Thomas Hardy's Notebooks*, p. 36.
3. Moule, *Stinsford Church and Parish*, p. 25.

AT THE WICKET-GATE presents a concealed drama enacted before church-time on a Sunday morning, with the major action in the "still meadows" and the crisis at a wicket-gate through which church-going neighbors passed. The gate may be at the foot of Church Lane leading downhill from Stinsford Church; a gate there separates the Lane from the meadows.[1]

The characters may be Hardy, Tryphena Sparks, and Tryphena's father, James Sparks. It may be supposed from what is known about Hardy's engagement to Tryphena that at this time her father revealed some information sufficient to endanger their engagement. The father's words must have stated more than his disapproval, for when Hardy married Emma Gifford it was against her father's wishes, and in Hardy's fiction and poetry a parent's disapproval strengthens the lover's will to wed. In *The Return of the Native,* Mrs. Yeobright's disapproval of Eustacia causes Clym to argue heatedly in her defense. (Book Three, Chapter 3.)

As Hardy and Tryphena were cousins, the father's remarks may have concerned the dangers in the marriage of close relatives, especially if hereditary weaknesses should be duplicated.[2] That something of this kind was revealed is suggested in the appearance of the subject in Hardy's novels. In *Two on a Tower,* when Lady Constantine insists that Swithin leave her, Swithin wonders why. He supposes that "There might be family reasons—mysterious blood-necessities which are said to rule members of old musty-mansioned families, and are unknown to other classes of society—and they may have been just now brought before her by her brother Louis on the condition that they were religiously concealed." (Chapter XXXVII.) From Hardy's statement in the Preface of *Jude the Obscure* that some of the circumstances of the novel were "suggested by the death of a woman" in 1890, it is generally accepted that Sue Bridehead was based upon Tryphena, and that Jude has many traits of Hardy himself.[3] Jude and Sue are cousins, and the novel is shot through with warnings that, for this reason, they should not marry. In Part II, Chapter VI, Jude's aunt warns him against any fondness for Sue: "Don't you be a fool about her! . . . If your cousin is civil to you, take her civility for what it is worth. But anything more than a relation's good wishes it is stark madness for ye to give her." And in Part III, Chapter VI, Sue tells Jude that they should not marry: "And then we are cousins, and it is bad for cousins to marry." Sue has pointed out that marriages in her family have been unlucky, and Jude, a cousin in the same family, admits that ". . . it was always impressed upon me that I ought not to marry—that I belonged to an odd and peculiar family— the wrong breed for marriage." Sue says, "Ah—who used to say that to you?" "My great-aunt. She said it always ended badly with us Fawleys." "That's strange! My father used to say the same to me!" Hardy comments: "They stood possessed by the same thought, ugly enough, even as an assumption; that a union between them, had such been possible, would have meant a terrible intensification of unfitness —two bitters in one dish."

1. These meadows are the scene of "The Third Kissing-Gate."
2. According to Deacon and Coleman, the relationship was closer than that of first cousins. Unknown to Hardy, the theory states, Tryphena was his niece.

It is alleged that Tryphena's mother was not Maria Sparks, Hardy's maternal aunt, but Rebecca Sparks, brought up as the daughter of Maria, but in fact the illegitimate daughter of Jemima Hand (later Hardy), Hardy's mother. See Chapter 15 of *Providence and Mr Hardy* for the surmises supporting this theory.
3. See, for instance, Weber, *Hardy of Wessex*, 2nd ed., pp. 199-204.

IN A MUSEUM, written at Exeter, was conceived when Hardy visited the Albert Memorial Museum on Queen Street, a few hundred yards from the Cathedral of St. Peter. *The Later Years* records that on June 10, 1915, he "Motored with F[lorence] to Bridport, Lyme, Exeter, and Torquay. . . . Then back to Teignmouth, Dawlish, and Exeter, putting up at the 'Clarence' opposite the Cathedral."[1]

The "ancient bird" that he saw in this Museum is the cast of a skeleton labelled "Archaeopteryx macrura. The oldest fossil bird. Upper Jurassic Lithographic Stone, Solenhafen, Bavaria."[2] The skeleton is large, the length of the body and tail being fifteen inches, with the possibility that plumes, traces of which are evident, made the bird even longer. An official assured me that this bird had no song, but at best a primitive kind of croak, by no means the "coo" Hardy imagined.

The poem presents a meditation upon Time as an illusion of the senses. Lowes's statement of this theme conveys Hardy's view of the universe as haunted by the still-existing past: "And in that universe in a sense that one deeply feels, whatever the cold intellect may think, nothing ever truly dies. The upper air—and this was never more intelligible than now, when over seas and continents the encircling atmosphere is a pulsing thoroughfare of disembodied voices—the upper air holds everlastingly all that through endless time has been committed to it."[3]

Hardy's idea includes some echo of Keats's "Ode to a Nightingale," as in Keats's lines, "The voice I hear this passing night was heard / In ancient days."

1. P. 169; *Life*, p. 370.
2. An official of the Museum stated that this was "Hardy's bird," inquired after by many visitors.
3. "Two Readings of Earth," p. 520.

APOSTROPHE TO AN OLD PSALM TUNE is dated Sunday, August 13, 1916, and the first stanza indicates the evening service. The poem concerns Psalm 69, the evening psalm for the thirteenth of the month. This psalm begins: "Save me, O God; for the waters are come in, even unto my soul." As it is a psalm of thirty-six verses, a service may include only a part of the psalm. In the Psalm Book now in use, music for parts of Psalm 69 is by J. Barnby, verses 1-12, and J. Turle, verses 13-22, 23-30, and 31-end; with the alternative of Teesdale, verses

1-30, and Hawes, 31-end. It is not clear whether Hardy's apostrophe is to a tune for the entire psalm or only a part of it.

The poem apostrophizes the *old* tune sung in Stinsford Church when Hardy was a boy. The second and third stanzas treat a new arrangement in which the tune was so "stripped" by "Monk, or another" that it startled him as a young man.[1] He first "met" this new tune "in a temple / Where summer sunset streamed upon our shapes," possibly in St. Juliot Church, Cornwall, on Sunday, August 13, 1870. He had left London on August 8 to visit Emma Gifford, who played the harmonium in this church on Sundays.[2] The fourth stanza evidently refers to Emma as "the one who evoked you often." She, during her married life, was fond of playing and singing her "sweet old airs."[3] When Emma died in 1912, Hardy mourned that the tune she had played had passed from his life, though in memory it still "waylaid" him.

The "new stirrer of tones" in the sixth stanza would seem to be his second wife Florence, who played and sang the psalm in the "old attire," to the tune he had heard in boyhood. He valued this tune because it "wakes your speech," or presents the words of the psalm in music that gives them added power. These words are a prayer in time of trouble, as in "these turmoiled years of belligerent fire." World War I moved Hardy to a despair about the human race that he felt was a permanent view stated in the words and reinforced in the old tune of Psalm 69. The old tune may live until the end of the world.

The compelling power of this tune to wake the words is suggested in the reference to the Witch of Endor, who called up for King Saul the spirit of the aged prophet Samuel. Though prophesying doom to Israel, Samuel recalled Saul to worship of the Lord. (See I Samuel 28.)

Chapter I of *A Laodicean* nearly parallels an idea of the poem. The action is set in August. Somerset is in some despair about his future, but is revived by hearing an old hymn, the "New Sabbath," sung to a tune "anterior to the great choral reformation and the rule of Monk." The song is sung "with all the emotional swells and cadences that had of old characterized the tune," as the psalm tune may have been sung before it was stripped of the "minim's waver, / And the dotted quaver."

1. William Henry Monk (1823-89) was the musical editor of *Hymns Ancient and Modern* (1861) and the composer of the tune for the well-known "Abide with Me."
2. *Early Life*, p. 103; *Life*, p. 78.

3. The phrase is quoted from "Lost Love"; see the notes on this poem and on "The Last Performance."

AT THE WORD "FAREWELL," Hardy wrote, is "literally true." In a letter to Mrs. Arthur Henniker on February 7, 1918, he said of his poems: "I myself (naturally I suppose) like those best which are literally true—such as 'At Lanivet,'—'At the Word Farewell,'—'Why Did I Sketch' &c, &c."[1]

On March 11, 1870, Hardy ended his first visit to Cornwall, where he had met Emma Gifford. *The Early Life* records from his journal for that date: "Dawn. Adieu. E. L. G. had struck a light six times in her anxiety to call the servants early enough for me. The journey home." The biography then adds: "The poem entitled 'At the Word "Farewell" ' seems to refer either to this or the following visit" in August.[2]

Evelyn Hardy suggests that the fatalism of the second stanza reflects Emma's feeling: "Emma Lavinia's religious convictions made her feel that each step in her life had led her forward with singular intention to this provident meeting. Hardy on the other hand felt no such conviction."[3] It may be doubted that he "felt no such conviction"; he acted "as if quicked by a spur / I was bound to obey," that is, an impulse from the Immanent Will.

He made use of this incident in *A Pair of Blue Eyes*. Stephen has to leave Elfride "in the gray light of dawn. . . . Elfride had fidgeted all night in her little bed lest none of the household should be awake soon enough to start him, and also lest she might miss seeing again the bright eyes and curly hair" of Stephen. "Elfride wandered desultorily to the summer house. Stephen followed her thither." Elfride invited Stephen to come again; there was some shy lover's talk, but no kiss. Stephen promised to return in August. (Chapter VI.)

1. In the Dorset County Museum.
2. P. 99; *Life*, p. 75. The visit in March was perhaps too brief to encourage a parting kiss, even on one cheek, especially as Hardy at the time was engaged to Tryphena Sparks. If the poem is "literally true" a "clammy lawn" and "bare-browed" suggest August. On the other hand, "bare boughs" suggest March. "The Frozen Greenhouse" seems to refer to the parting in March.
3. *Thomas Hardy*, p. 118.

FIRST SIGHT OF HER AND AFTER was first published in *Selected Poems* in October, 1916, with the title "The Return from First Beholding Her." It was published in *Moments of Vision* as "The Day of First Sight."[1] The position of the poem immediately following "At the Word 'Farewell' " suggests that "First Sight of Her and After" presents Hardy's thoughts on his way back to Higher Bockhampton after visiting Emma Gifford.

1. Purdy, *Thomas Hardy: A Bibliographical Study*, p. 194.

THE RIVAL was intended to be read as humor. A review titled "Mr. Hardy's Poetry" in the *Westminster Gazette* for December 8, 1917, called the poem a "grim and characteristic fancy." Hardy commented in pencil beside his copy of the review: "The reviewer, having no sense of humour, misses the point."[1] The woman, in realizing her folly, is justly punished for her petty jealousy.

The incident of the poem cannot apply literally to his wife Emma, who died before he did. It may have been suggested by his awareness (if he was aware) that Emma, forbidden to rummage through his desk, sometimes did so in his absence. He may have kept in his desk a picture of the quite different Emma he had loved in the 1870's.

1. In Hardy's scrapbook "Reviews of T. H.'s Books (Poetry)" in the Dorset County Museum.

HEREDITY is based upon an entry in Hardy's journal for February 19, 1889: " 'The story of a face which goes through three generations or more, would make a fine novel or poem of the passage of Time. The differences in personality to be ignored.' [This idea was to some extent carried out in the novel *The Well-Beloved*, the poem entitled 'Heredity,' etc.]"[1] In the latter part of 1890, Hardy read August Weismann's *Essays on Heredity*,[2] which sets forth a theory of the immortality of the germ plasm, the theme of Hardy's poem.

Hardy's concept that not only the "family face" but also traits of character and temperament continue from generation to generation appears in his novels and many poems. In *Tess of the D'Urbervilles*, Angel observed Tess's "fine features . . . unquestionably traceable" in the paintings of the D'Urberville ladies on the wall at Wellbridge, and their look of "merciless treachery" and "arrogance to the point of ferocity" shaped his mood for rejecting Tess. That Tess in sudden anger stabbed Alec suggests that her inheritance was not in features alone. *Jude the Obscure* discusses throughout the novel the continuance of hereditary traits. *The Well-Beloved*, as Hardy's journal mentions, traces Pierston's idealization of the same features through three generations. Concern with heredity appears notably in the poems "The Pedigree," "The Rover Come Home," and "Family Portraits."

1. *Early Life*, p. 284; *Life*, p. 217. The brackets are in the biography.
2. *Early Life*, p. 301; *Life*, p. 230. The book was translated from the German by Edward B. Poulton, Oxford: The Clarendon Press, 1889.

"YOU WERE THE SORT THAT MEN FORGET" may be Hardy's analysis of his first wife Emma, as she was in the 1890's. Weber says: "As a rule Hardy did not retaliate on his wife: he preferred to 'ache deep, but make no moans; smile out, but stilly suffer.' But in 'You Were the Sort that Men Forget' he speaks out. Here he does strike back. He speaks of Emma's lack of social 'art,' of her 'words inept' that offended everybody, of her failure to understand 'friends whose mode was crude,' and of her over-valuation of 'the courtesies of the bland.' Of all the personal characteristics put on record in this poem by the sorrowing but critical husband, none received more frequent corroboration from other observers than Emma Hardy's addiction to 'words inept.' . . . Desmond MacCarthy remembered her saying to him sharply at tea one day: 'If you listen to what *I* am saying, you will find it as well worth hearing as Mr. Hardy's remarks.' Rebecca West once heard her say: 'Try to remember, Thomas Hardy, that you married a lady!' "[1]

If the poem is about Emma, it is more a defense of her than a retaliation. It admits her tactlessness, but affirms qualities that Hardy valued highly: her good intentions, eagerness to please, loyalty, and "warm devotion."

1. *Hardy's Love Poems*, pp. 48-49.

SHE, I, AND THEY in the manuscript has "August 1" added to the date.[1] The poem seems a personal one that may picture Hardy and his first wife Emma (or possibly his second wife Florence), on a quiet evening at home. He uses a ghostly sigh from portraits to dramatize the rebuke of his ancestors for the couple's failure to continue a "sturdy line." In the early years of his marriage, he was saddened by his and Emma's childlessness. He wrote in his journal for August 13, 1877: "We hear that Jane, our late servant, is soon to have a baby. Yet never a sign of one is there for us."[2]

1. Purdy, *Thomas Hardy: A Bibliographical Study*, p. 194.
2. *Early Life*, p. 153; *Life*, p. 116.

NEAR LANIVET, 1872 shows in the manuscript, deleted, "From an old note." Purdy says, "The scene, an actual one, occurred between Hardy and his first wife before their marriage."[1] The event of the poem was important in Hardy's life, especially in view of Emma's pretensions in the 1890's and later to social superiority. *The Early Life* says that his courtship of Emma "ran, in fact, without a hitch from beginning to end, and with encouragement from all parties concerned."[2] This statement overlooks the harsh opposition of Emma's father to their engagement and the event described in the poem.[3]

In 1872, Hardy and Emma Gifford went to Bodmin, in Cornwall, to talk with her father about their engagement. Florence Dugdale (later Mrs. Hardy) wrote sarcastically to Edward Clodd on July 3, 1913, that Hardy had just "started for Plymouth to find the grave of

Mrs. H.'s father (that amiable gentleman who wrote to him as a 'low-born churl who has presumed to marry into my family.') " [4]

Concerning "Near Lanivet," Hardy wrote to Edmund Gosse on January 18, 1918: "You knew my late wife, and the scene occurred between us before our marriage." [5] In a letter to Mrs. Arthur Henniker on February 7, 1918, he declared the poem "literally true." [6] He was fond of it, perhaps because it was a record of Emma's loyalty. When Harold Child reviewed *Moments of Vision* without commenting on "Near Lanivet," Hardy on February 11, 1919, wrote to him: "One poem that I thought critics might select (not for its supposed excellence but for the strange incident which produced it, and really happened) was 'Near Lanivet,' but *nobody* did." [7]

He identified the handpost of the poem on the end-papers of Hermann Lea's copy of *Thomas Hardy's Wessex* as "Handpost on the St. Austell Road." [8] Lanivet is a little more than two miles southwest of Bodmin, where Hardy and Emma were rebuffed by Gifford. A road leading southeast from Lanivet after three-quarters of a mile crosses two other roads at a place called Reperry Cross. There on a raised bank (Hardy's "just on the crest"), I found the "stunted handpost." [9] It is an ancient stone monument or marker about three feet high and six inches thick. The lower part (nearly two feet above ground) is a supporting pillar for a circular disk carved from the same stone. The disk is about eighteen inches in diameter. On the face of the disk toward the crossroads is a Greek cross with arms extending nearly to the rim.

It is possible to read the poem as saying that Emma rested on the stone pillar; "against its stem" seems to refer to the "stunted handpost," but in the preceding clause Emma stopped "for her rest / At the crossways close thereby" and did not climb "the crest." She could not have thrown her arms upon the cross of the stone, which is only carved into the face of the disk. Opposite the stone, across the roads meeting there, a multiple cross of directional signs points six ways. This cross is of a height to furnish arm-rests. It would seem that Emma rested upon the directional signs, in which situation she would have seen the ancient stone directly in front of her. This sight, more than feeling a cross under her arms, might have suggested to her the "Something strange" of the poem.

The poem presents a premonition prompted by her weariness after a tramp from Bodmin, and her tendency to feel omens in signs. The poem says that Hardy remarked of her premonition: "There's nothing in it. For *you*, anyhow!" She had not been called a "base churl." The final stanza indicates that her premonitions came true. She was "crucified." The reference is, no doubt, to Emma's mental eccentricities in her later years, partly foreseen at this time. (See the notes on "The Interloper.") In the light of the final "Alas, alas!" the poem is one of Hardy's most poignant personal statements.

Gifford's rejection of Hardy seems reflected in *A Pair of Blue Eyes* in the scene where Parson Swancourt rejects Stephen Smith as a suitor for Elfride: "He, a villager's son; and we, Swancourts, connections of the Luxellians. We have been coming to nothing for centuries, and now I believe we have got there . . . . the son of one of my village peasants,—but now I am to make him my son-in-law! Heavens above us, are you mad, Elfride?" (Chapter IX.)

1. Purdy, *Thomas Hardy: A Bibliographical Study*, p. 195.
2. P. 97; *Life*, p. 74.
3. A marginal notation in Mrs. Florence Hardy's copy of *The Early Life*, opposite the passage quoted above, reads: "No. Miss Gifford's father was very contemptuous of Hardy's social position." In the Dorset County Museum.
4. In the Brotherton Library Collection, Leeds.
5. Weber, *Hardy's Love Poems*, p. 93.
6. In the Dorset County Museum.
7. Typewritten copy in the Dorset County Museum.
8. Cox, ed., *Thomas Hardy Through the Camera's Eye*, p. 50.
9. The roads crossing at that point are from Lanivet to Trebell, from Lower Woon to Trebyan, and from Bodmin, via Treliggon, southward to St. Austell. Possibly Hardy and Emma had wandered down this road from Bodmin, without going through Lanivet.

JOYS OF MEMORY seems to treat March 7, the "certain day" on which Hardy met Emma Gifford in 1870. His memory was vivid enough that he could indeed, when he wished to take a holiday from labor, forget the world about him and live in a recreated past.

TO THE MOON has in the manuscript, deleted, "Questions" as either a title or an addition to the title.[1] The poem presents the moon as a symbol for a cold, aloof observer of human history, to whom this history seems a sorry show.

1. Purdy, *Thomas Hardy: A Bibliographical Study*, p. 195.

COPYING ARCHITECTURE IN AN OLD MINSTER pictures Hardy as he pauses in drawing features of architecture in Wimborne Minster, lets his drawing slip from his hand, loses his pencil in a cranny, and looks around in a "moment's forgetfulness." The time is apparently dusk, indicated by his imagination of shadowy ghosts, just after the quarter-jack has struck the hour perhaps selected for quitting his labors—or his pastime, for he had given up the practice of architecture as a profession.[1]

The Hardys moved from London to Wimborne on June 25, 1881, and lived there until June, 1883.[2] The Minster Church of St. Cuthburga exhibits architectural features in all styles from the time of its founding about the year 713 to the present. It was established as a nunnery by Cuthburga, the sister of Ina, King of the West Saxons. Alfred the Great in 871 buried there his brother Ethelred (not the Unready). In 1318 Edward II declared the Minster his free chapel or a "Royal Peculiar." The church has been subject to numerous social, ecclesiastical, and architectural changes, ravages, and rebuildings. It interested Hardy both for its historical associations and for its varieties of architecture.

The "jack-o'-clock" or quarter-jack that called him to pause is the carved statue of a sentinel perched outside a window of the church high on the north wall. Animated by the mechanism of a clock, the jack raises a hammer in each hand and strikes two bells to mark the quarter hours. Carved in 1613, the jack was originally clothed as a monk, but during the Napoleonic wars was repainted in the colorful dress of a British grenadier.

As Hardy pauses in the growing dimness to ponder the passage of time, he imagines the quarter-jack as calling up the ghosts of the dead in the minster and seems to see them emerging from their tombs. In spite of the pronoun "his," the Courtenay tomb in the chancel is a memorial to Gertrude, Marchioness of Exeter, who was found guilty of treason against Henry VIII and imprisoned in the Tower of London, but pardoned. She died in 1558. The "Duke and his Duchess near" emerge (in Hardy's vision) from a carved tomb surmounted by the reclining alabaster effigies of John Beaufort, Duke of Somerset and grandson of John of Gaunt, who died in 1444, with his lady, Margaret, by his side; they were the grandparents of Henry VII. Sir Edmund "in columned gloom" is Sir Edmund Evedale, whose tomb is in St. George's Chapel (a part of the church). When he died in 1606, his widow built his memorial in Renaissance style; his effigy has the head raised and the eyes open as if waking to the resurrection. The Saxon king arises from a marble slab in the floor near the sanctuary; the slab commemorates "St. Ethelred, King of the West Saxons, Martyr, Who in the Year of Our Lord 873 [in fact, 871] . . . Fell by the Hand of the Pagan Danes."

The poem may be associated with Hardy's attitude toward World War I, during which it may have been written, instead of with the occasion of the drawing, presumably in 1881-83. The ghosts arise to discuss "some plan / To better ail-stricken mankind" in a world "ancient and trouble-torn." He does not seem to catch their words, but substitutes his own remedies, "lovingkindness" and "ardours." This meeting in an ancient church of the living, the dead, and the thought of the unborn is presented in a grotesquely humorous tone.

In *Far from the Madding Crowd* Hardy apparently made use of the quarter-jack of Wimborne Minster in describing the jack of "All Saints'" Church, where Sergeant Troy waits to marry Fanny Robin. There the jack dramatizes Troy's impatience.

The poem uses a number of technical words in architecture: cusp (a point projecting from an inner curve of tracery), ogee (a moulding shaped like S), and quatre-foiled (an opening in tracery divided by cusps into four leaves or "cusp's eyes"). A "passager" is a bird of passage.

1. See Beatty, ed., *The Architectural Notebook of Thomas Hardy*, for Hardy's drawings.
2. *Early Life*, pp. 193, 210; *Life*, pp. 149, 161.

TO SHAKESPEARE AFTER THREE HUNDRED YEARS was written as a contribution to a tercentenary celebration. On February 2, 1916, Professor Israel Gollancz of King's College, London, wrote to ask Hardy to contribute, "if only with a few lines," to a *Book of Homage to Shakespeare*. On this letter Hardy wrote in pencil: "Ansd. Will send it in a week or 10 days from the 11th Feb." His date on the manuscript is "February 14, 1916." Gollancz wrote on February 18: "I am overjoyed at receiving the noble poem." It was published in the *Book of Homage* in April.[1]

"To Shakespeare" has four parts. The first two stanzas present a conventional tribute to Shakespeare's "Bright baffling Soul, least capturable of themes," echoing in "thou-thee" language the idea of Matthew Arnold's sonnet "Shakespeare," which begins: "Others abide our question. Thou art free." The third stanza, on Shakespeare's death "like other dwellers' deaths," leads into the fourth and fifth stanzas, which present Shakespeare as his neighbors of Stratford spoke of him. These stanzas are Hardy's characteristic contribution: a comment on Shakespeare as man and neighbor, with the implication that the great man is not always evident in the everyday world. The concluding stanza draws the two previous themes together: the "Bright baffling Soul," known to his neighbors as a "worthy man and well-to-do," was for a while on earth a "radiant guest."

For Shakespeare's neighbors, to create typical townspeople, Hardy turned to Dorchester. Mrs. Florence Hardy wrote to Alda, Lady Hoare on April 2, 1918: "T. had certain Dorchester folk in mind when he wrote—many of whom would say, if Shakespeare had lived here to-day, 'We did not know him.' "[2] He did locate his characters in a particular setting. On the end-papers of Hermann Lea's copy of

[353]

Thomas Hardy's Wessex, Hardy wrote: "To Shakespeare: Stratford-on-Avon Church, from the other side of the river."[3] He had his townspeople aware of everyday facts about Shakespeare. He was "well-to-do," for his income in his later life was nearly four hundred pounds a year, at that time relative wealth. New Place, Shakespeare's home, was the largest mansion in Stratford. That "he left his wife with us" reflects the view that about 1596 Shakespeare sent his wife and children to live in Stratford. In Stratford he would be known not as a poet and playwright, but as "one of the tradesmen's sons," for his father, John Shakespeare, had been a glover, tanner, and dealer in wood, grain, malt, and farm products.

1. Purdy, *Thomas Hardy: A Bibliographical Study,* p. 177, and letters in the Dorset County Museum.
2. In the Stourhead Collection, the County Archives, Trowbridge.
3. Cox, ed., *Thomas Hardy Through the Camera's Eye,* p. 50.

QUID HIC AGIS? was first published in the *Spectator* for August 19, 1916, with the title "In Time of Slaughter." It was then revised and, in October, published for Mrs. Florence Hardy in a pamphlet titled "When I Weekly Knew." Purdy says, "The poem recalls St. Juliot Church in the 70's and Hardy's first wife. The 'chapter from Kings' (I Kings xix) was a special favourite of the poet's and was appropriately chosen for his memorial window in Stinsford Church."[1]

In I Kings 19 after the prophet Elijah had overcome and slain the prophets of Baal, Queen Jezebel threatened to have him killed. Elijah then fled into the wilderness and lodged in a cave. There the word of the Lord came to him and asked, "What doest thou here?" ("Quid Hic Agis?") When Elijah replied that "they seek my life," the voice said: "Go forth, and stand upon the mount before the Lord. And, behold, the Lord passed by, and a great and strong wind rent the mountains, and brake in pieces the rocks before the Lord; but the Lord was not in the wind: and after the wind an earthquake; but the Lord was not in the earthquake: and after the earthquake a fire; but the Lord was not in the fire: and after the fire a still small voice." The Lord commanded Elijah to return to Damascus and anoint kings and prophets, and Elijah did so.

"Quid Hic Agis?" is autobiographical.[2] The first stanza presents Hardy as a boy in weekly attendance at Stinsford Church. There he listened to "That chapter from Kings," but "did not apprehend" all that it meant or make any application of it to his own life. Instead he obediently "sat to the end" of the reading and looked across the "sunned aisle" for the approving smile of his mother.[3] His fondness for this passage as a young man is expressed in a letter from London to his sister Mary on August 17, 1862: " 'After the fire a still small voice'—I have just come from the evening service at St. Mary's Kilburn and this verse, which I always notice, was in the 1st Lesson."[4]

The second stanza refers to Emma Gifford, later Mrs. Hardy. In his courtship, Hardy became friendly with Emma's brother-in-law, the Reverend Caddell Holder, rector of St. Juliot Church. Commenting on Mr. Holder's death in 1882, *The Early Life* says: "Hardy regretted the loss of his relative, and was reminded sadly of the pleasure he used to find in reading the lessons in the ancient church when his brother-in-law was not in vigour. The poem 'Quid hic agis?' . . . is in part apparently a reminiscence of these readings."[5] As the "chapter from Kings" is a reading for the tenth Sunday after Trinity, and in 1870 this Sunday fell on August 21, it seems probable that he read the lesson during his visit to St. Juliot in August of 1870. The probability of this date is heightened by his use of the fact in *A Pair of Blue Eyes*. In August, toward the end of Knight's visit to Endelstow Vicarage: "Mr. Swancourt had undertaken the whole of the evening service, and Knight read the lessons for him. The sun streamed across from the dilapidated west window, and lighted all the assembled worshippers with a golden glow, Knight as he read being illuminated by the same mellow lustre . . . . he went deliberately through the chapter appointed—a portion of the history of Elijah— and ascended that magnificent climax of the wind, the earthquake, the fire, and the still small voice." (Chapter XIX.)

A theme of the poem is that Hardy, like others in the church, did not feel "overmuch / Concerned" about Elijah's despair, but that "at last," when both his mother and Emma are dead, he does identify himself with Elijah and "spiritless / In the wilderness / . . . shrink from sight." As the original title, "In Time of Slaughter," suggests, his despair is deepened by World War I. Like Elijah, he feels some divine command to "Go forth, and stand / And prophesy in the land."

The "marble, men say" of the third stanza refers to a memorial tablet to Emma that he had had erected in St. Juliot Church, but had not seen at the time he wrote the poem. Because of his fondness for I Kings 19, the memorial window to Hardy in Stinsford Church pictures the prophet Elijah in the storm described in the Bible, with the inscription cited above, beginning "Behold, the Lord passed by" and continuing through "the Lord was not in the fire."

1. *Thomas Hardy: A Bibliographical Study*, pp. 188-89.
2. Mrs. Florence Hardy wrote to Rebekah Owen on August 15, 1916: "There is a poem I like immensely in last week's Spectator which is autobiographical and would interest you." In Colby College Library.

3. This interpretation is supported by Rutland, *Thomas Hardy*, p. 5, and Moule, *Stinsford Church and Parish*, p. 2.
4. *Early Life*, p. 50; *Life*, p. 38.
5. P. 203; *Life*, p. 157.

ON A MIDSUMMER EVE makes fanciful use of several items of folklore. As presented in Chapter XX of *The Woodlanders*, midsummer eve is a time of magic. The Hintock village girls "attempt some spell or enchantment which would afford them a glimpse [a phantom] of their future partners for life." According to Firor, ghosts of dead lovers also appear at this time.[1] "The cutting of parsley is a sign that the person so occupied will sooner or later be crossed in love. . . . Among the Greeks . . . the plant was used to strew the tombs of the dead."[2] Ignoring this lore, the poet idly cut a parsley stalk. Then he "blew therein towards the moon," which in Hardy's symbolism forebodes something sinister. The triple spell summons the phantom of a dead beloved. To the extent that the poem symbolizes a personal experience, the phantom may be either Tryphena Sparks or Emma Hardy. The final stanza presents the poetic process as "rhymes of chance" that come to the mind unsought, but are shaped into tenderness by a phantom voice.

1. *Folkways in Thomas Hardy*, p. 51.
2. Copps, "The Poetry of Thomas Hardy," p. 597.

TIMING HER seems to treat a personal experience that Hardy embroidered from his reading in the Latin poet Horace and wrote to the "old folk-tune" mentioned in the headnote. The poem presents him eagerly awaiting the arrival of Lalage, who is coming across fields and hills like those near Max Gate. Lalage may be Lalage Acland, the daughter of John Acland of Wollaston House, Dorchester, the Curator of the Dorset County Museum from 1905 until 1932 and a close friend of Hardy's. In the summer of 1966, Miss Verena Acland, sister of Lalage, told me that when Lalage was a young girl her father would send her to Max Gate with messages or documents from the Museum. Though the landscape of the poem suggests the open country east of Max Gate, rather than a journey from the center of Dorchester to Hardy's home, it seems probable that he had in mind Lalage Acland, but that he adorned the poem with features more suitable to his "old folk-tune" than a journey from town would provide.

The fact that a Lalage is celebrated in the odes of the Latin poet Horace suggests a second bit of embroidery. The last lines of Horace's "Integer Vitae," Carmen I, xxii, read in translation: "I love Lalage and her sweet laughter, Lalage and her sweet prattle."[1] The tone of the poem, with its antique ornaments ("gilt chair," "slippers of vair," etc.), was perhaps echoed from Horace. Certainly such items cannot be realistic for welcoming a girl of perhaps fifteen or sixteen.[2]

In stanza-form, the poem bears some resemblance to "Remember Adam's Fall" as quoted in *Under the Greenwood Tree* (Part First, Chapter IV) or to the variant "Remember, O Thou Man," by Thomas Ravenscroft, 1611.[3] The lilting folk-measure, the country landscape, and English rural customs combine with suggestions from Horace to form a charming picture of a pretended lover's anticipation of Lalage's arrival with "her sweet laughter" and "her sweet prattle."

1. As translated by E. C. Wickham, *Horace for English Readers*, Oxford: The Clarendon Press, 1903, p. 47. Hardy quoted from the same ode in *Tess of the D'Urbervilles*, Chapter XXXIV.

2. The poem, though published in 1917, must recall an earlier time. Lalage Acland was married on August 21, 1915, to her second cousin, Captain H. G. D. Acland of the British Royal Navy. She died on May 6, 1961. A letter to me from Captain Acland, on September 6, 1966, says: "I would be very happy to have my Lalage's name linked with one of Hardy's poems if you could make it clear that it was linked with a young girl," as it seems to be.

3. See Erik Routley, *University Carol Book*. Evidently Hardy made use of the same tune in "Meditations on a Holiday."

BEFORE KNOWLEDGE echoes a note in Hardy's journal for June 2, 1865: "Walked about by moonlight in the evening. Wondered what woman, if any, I should be thinking about in five years' time."[1] The idea is characteristic of Hardy that love is foreordained and that foreknowledge would brighten the loneliness before the lovers' meeting.

1. *Early Life*, p. 65; *Life*, p. 50.

THE BLINDED BIRD rests on a basis deeper than sentimental pity. *The Origin of Species* convinced Hardy that beneath the Christian tenet of the brotherhood of man lies a fact in nature, the kinship of all life.

The bird of the poem has been blinded so that when placed in a cage it will sing. As Sanders and Nelson state it, "Long before science knew anything about the localization of the various nerve-centers in the human brain, the devil had revealed to his disciple man his ghastly discovery that by stinging out the eyes of a bird with a red-hot needle the bird would sing automatically."[1] According to the poem, that a bird would reply to cruelty by singing sweetly and continually was less an instinctive response of the crippled brain than an epitome of the Christian virtues.

The final stanza of the poem is a paraphrase of St. Paul's statement of these virtues; Hardy's irony indicts a society that calls itself Christian but practices cruelty. The passage paraphrased is I Cor. 13:4-7, "Charity suffereth long, and is kind; charity envieth not; charity vaunteth not itself, is not puffed up, doth not behave itself unseemly, seeketh not her own, is not easily provoked, thinketh no evil; rejoiceth not in iniquity, but rejoiceth in the truth; beareth all things, believeth all things, hopeth all things, endureth all things."

An analysis of *Tess of the D'Urbervilles* has shown that Hardy, in symbols and direct comparisons, viewed Tess as like a bird caught in a trap or otherwise cruelly treated.[2] In presenting Tess's discussion with Angel just after her confession, he makes use of the same chapter from I Corinthians to say of Tess: "The firmness of her devotion to him was indeed almost pitiful; . . . nothing that he could say made her unseemly; she sought not her own; was not provoked; thought no evil of his treatment of her. She might just now have been Apostolic Charity herself returned to a self-seeking modern world." (Chapter XXXVI.)

1. *Chief Modern Poets of England and America*, p. 23.
2. Griffith, "The Image of the Trapped Animal in Hardy's *Tess of the D'Urbervilles*."

"THE WIND BLEW WORDS" expresses the thought that Hardy (or any man) is kin to all living nature, a doctrine he derived from Darwin's *The Origin of Species* and that he illustrates in the sufferings of trees, dumb animals, and men of the "black, dwarfed, and browned" races. In ethical meaning, this doctrine leads to realization that all suffering lies within the "pathetic Me" and to universal compassion. The poem is hopeful that this compassion may grow and destroy the "law" (manifest in the evolutionary struggle for survival) "To kill, break, or suppress." A meditation, during World War I, upon the fact of cruelty, the poem presents Hardy's philosophic animism that sees even trees as alive and suffering in the "huge distress" of the universe.

THE FADED FACE is a lament that the poet, observing the remains of youthful beauty in an aging woman, did not know her when her charms were "rich and choice." The last lines mourn the law of Time, that her face had to fade.

THE RIDDLE expresses Hardy's wonder about an apparent change of personality in his first wife. As young Emma Gifford of Cornwall, she had zest for life, freshness of view, spontaneity of emotion, and delight in the sea; but as the older Mrs. Hardy of Max Gate, she was conventional in view, fond of the social life of cities, and limited in emotional range, symbolized in her always facing eastward.

THE DUEL was drawn from Hardy's notebook called "Facts" in the Dorset County Museum. The note reads: "'*My Recollections,*' By the Countess of Cardigan. Lady Anne Brudenell, dau. of the 2d E. of Cardigan, was one of the most lovely of the beauties associated with the Court of Charles II. She married the Earl of Shrewsbury, & the story is well known of how she, dressed as a page, held the Duke of Buckingham's horse whilst he fought with & slew her husband. . . . The wicked Countess & her lover lived at Cliveden—'the bower of wanton Shrewsbury & of love'—& her spirit is supposed to haunt the beautiful riverside retreat."

Other facts apparently known to Hardy are: Lord Shrewsbury "was too polite . . . to venture on reproaches to his wife, but being resolved on some redress to his injured honor, he, very much to his friends' surprise, finally sent a challenge to Buckingham. . . . The meeting was fixed for Thursday, 21 January 1668 in a close near Barn Elms." As in the poem the Earl of Shrewsbury dies immediately, possibly Hardy did not consult Pepys's *Diary*, which recalls that the Earl was "run through the body, from the right breast through the shoulder," but did not die on the spot; he lived until March 16. One story about the Countess was that she had concealed pistols about her person, to shoot both herself and her husband if the Duke should be defeated. "The Duke, however, when arraigned before his peers in 1674, stated that she was at the time of the duel in a 'French monastery', and it does not appear that the story was controverted even by an assembly eager to convict him of infamy."[1]

1. This paragraph is partly quoted and partly summarized from Copps, "The Poetry of Thomas Hardy," pp. 598-600, which cites Lady Burghclere's *George Villiers Second Duke of Buckingham* and Pepys's *Diary* (VII, 265-66).

AT MAYFAIR LODGINGS in the manuscript is titled "At Lodgings in London."[1] The background is recorded in *The Later Years*. In December of 1894, Hardy "ran up to London alone on publishing business, and stayed at a temporary room off Piccadilly, to be near his club. It was then that there seems to have occurred . . . some incident of the kind possibly adumbrated in the verses called 'At Mayfair Lodgings'. . . . He watched during a sleepless night a lighted window close by, wondering who might be lying ill there. Afterwards he discovered that a woman had lain there dying, and that she was one whom he had cared for in his youth, when she was a girl in a neighbouring village."[2]

The identity of the woman is not discoverable. The *Dorset County Chronicle* for January 17, 1895, lists among "Deaths": "At Poplar,

London, Mrs. J. Sprackland, wife of Mr. John Sprackland (and daughter of the late Mr. Thomas Turnbull, Dorchester), aged 48." The newspaper states no day of death, but lists several deaths in December, 1894. The area called Poplar is some three miles east of Mayfair, where Hardy's club, the Savile, was located. The phrasing of both the poem and *The Later Years* suggests some concealment.

Conversing with Hardy about this poem on December 27, 1920, Vere H. Collins asked: "Why and how, 'need not the tragedy have come due'? Because she would have married him, and there would not now have been the tragedy of her dying apart from him?" Hardy replied: "Yes."[3]

1. Purdy, *Thomas Hardy: A Bibliographical Study*, p. 195.
2. P. 35; *Life*, p. 267.
3. *Talks with Thomas Hardy*, p. 24.

TO MY FATHER'S VIOLIN in the manuscript was titled "To my Father's Fiddle."[1] Violin-playing was important in the life of Thomas Hardy the Second. In a sense, his skill as a musician was hereditary. Thomas Hardy the First, on moving to Higher Bockhampton in 1801, found the music in Stinsford Church "in a deplorable condition. . . . He immediately set himself . . . to improve it, and got together some instrumentalists, himself taking the bass-viol . . . which he played in the gallery of Stinsford Church at two services every Sunday from 1801 or 1802 till his death in 1837, being joined later by his two sons, who, with other reinforcement, continued playing till about 1842." Until the choir was disbanded then, Hardy's father took a leading part in the playing and singing of Christmas carols as described in *Under the Greenwood Tree*. In addition he, and Hardy himself as a boy, played "endless jigs, hornpipes, reels, waltzes, and country-dances" for merrymakings in the neighborhood.[2]

When Hardy's father died in 1892, the printed program Hardy prepared for his burial service on July 25 stated that he had been for twenty years a musician for Stinsford Church. A memorial brass on the west wall of the Church, in Latin, was prepared by Hardy, who translated it as: "A sacred monument to the memory of Thomas Hardy the father, of James and of Thomas the sons, who formerly in this church for forty years (from 1802 to 1841) performed the office of violinist. Thomas, Henry, Mary, Katherine, the sons and daughters of the junior Thomas, caused this to be placed here 1903."[3]

Hardy treasured his father's violin in his study during his life. After his death the violin passed into the possession of his sister Kate. Elna Sherman described it as "a beautiful instrument; its tail-piece is decorated with inlaid ivory or mother-of-pearl in a trefoil design."[4] It is now in the Dorset County Museum with two others that belonged to Hardy, but it is not known which of the three belonged to his father. The "Ten worm-wounds in your neck," mentioned in the poem, do not identify it, as the violins have been repaired and a new head has replaced the worm-eaten one.[5]

The poem is a tribute to Hardy's father in terms of a central passion of his life. Some years after the poem was published, certainly in all reverence for his father's memory, Hardy was scolded for employing in the poem the fantasy of a pagan underworld. *The Later Years* quotes his amazed reaction: "This week [in December, 1920] I have had sent me a review which quotes a poem entitled 'To my Father's Violin,' containing a Virgilian reminiscence of mine of Acheron and the Shades. The writer comments: 'Truly this pessimism is insupportable. . . . One marvels that Hardy is not in a madhouse.' Such is English criticism, and I repeat, why did I ever write a line!"[6]

1. Purdy, *Thomas Hardy: A Bibliographical Study*, p. 196.
2. Summarized and quoted from *Early Life*, pp. 10-18; *Life*, pp. 8-15.
3. Hardy's translation is in the Dorset County Museum.
4. "Thomas Hardy: Lyricist, Symphonist," p. 150.
5. Neither Mr. Francis Dalton, former Curator of the Museum, nor Mr. Roger Peers, the present Curator, could state certainly which violin had belonged to Hardy's father. The violin that now stands in the reconstructed "Hardy's study" may be Hardy's, his father's, or his uncle's. The other two are stored elsewhere in the Museum. See Evelyn Hardy, *Thomas Hardy*, p. 13.
6. *Later Years*, p. 218; *Life*, pp. 409-10.

THE STATUE OF LIBERTY is a dialogue of question-and-answer with an ironic revelation in the conclusion. So far as I could find out, no city or town in England has a statue of liberty. (The American Statue of Liberty is not in a "city square.") The statue seems invented to support the theme that zeal for liberty may decay into license. The poem may have grown from Hardy's reflection on a passage in his notebook for September 10, 1888: "Destitution sometimes reaches the point of grandeur in its pathetic grimness: *e.g.*, as shown in the statement of the lodging-house keeper in the Whitechapel murder: 'He had seen her in the lodging-house as late as half-past one o'clock or two that morning. He knew her as an unfortunate, and that she generally frequented Stratford for a living. He asked her for her lodging-money, when she said, "I have not got it. I am weak and ill, and have been in the infirmary." He told her that she knew the rules, whereupon she went out to get some money.' (*Times* report.) O richest City in the world! 'She knew the rules.' "[1] Mentioning the harshness of this poem and others, Chew comments that "these are transcripts from life."[2] Hardy often defended an ugly story by saying that it was true.

1. *Early Life*, p. 280; *Life*, p. 214.
2. *Thomas Hardy: Poet and Novelist* (1921 ed.), p. 206.

THE BACKGROUND AND THE FIGURE may present Hardy's memory of a site where he met a sweetheart in his youth, but the site, the girl, and the incident are not identifiable.

THE CHANGE presents "a recollection of Hardy's courtship and first marriage" to Emma Gifford.[1]

The "week" of the first three stanzas seems to indicate his first visit to St. Juliot rectory, from March 7 to 11, 1870. In his journal for March 9, he speaks of "Music in the evening. The two ladies [Emma Gifford and her sister, Mrs. Caddell Holder] sang duets, including 'The Elfin Call,' 'Let us dance on the sands,' etc."[2] Reference to "a mocking note" in the singing suggests that one of the songs may have been "The Mocking-Bird," named in the poem "The Prophetess," which seems to refer to the same occasion. Hardy's journal makes no mention of "the white owl" that wondered about the singing, but in speaking of the removal of her family from Plymouth to Bodmin in 1860, Emma wrote: "Owls of every kind and voice assailed our ears the whole night long."[3] He may have taken the owl from Emma's statement.[4]

The fourth and fifth stanzas recall his meeting Emma at a railroad station. Weber assumes that this meeting took place in London in 1873, when, Emma wrote in her *Some Recollections*, "I went as country cousin to my brother in London, and was duly astonished, which gave him even more pleasure that it did me."[5] Emma's statement does not mention Hardy, and his account of his courtship does not mention this meeting, but it seems probable. He speaks of a visit to London at some time in the winter of 1873.[6] Phelps, examining Hardy's Bibles, says: "The date was probably Friday, 28th October, for we find the initials 'E. L. G.' and the date, pencilled alongside certain verses from the Song of Solomon."[7] The stanzas may recall Hardy's meeting Emma in London "Mid murks of night" on September 16, 1874, before they were married the next day.

"The Change" contrasts the happy courtship, when every "mocking note" went unheeded, and the destined "doom" and unforeseen "bale" of later married years. "The Change" resembles in verse-form and theme the poem "During Wind and Rain." Especially the refrain

"Who shall read the years O!" is echoed in "Ah, no; the years O!" of the latter poem.

1. Purdy, *Thomas Hardy: A Bibliographical Study*, p. 196.
2. *Early Life*, p. 99; *Life*, p. 75.
3. Evelyn Hardy and Gittings, *Some Recollections by Emma Hardy*, p. 35.
4. Some of the mockery perhaps symbolized by the owl had its origin in Bodmin, where Emma's father denounced Hardy. See the notes on "Near Lanivet, 1872."
5. *Early Life*, p. 95; *Life*, p. 72. See Weber, *Hardy's Love Poems*, p. 25.
6. *Early Life*, p. 132; *Life*, p. 100.
7. *Annotations by Thomas Hardy in His Bibles and Prayer-Book*, p. 8. The verses thus annotated are Chapters 4:2, 3, and 5:2, 9, in passionate praise of a beloved one.

SITTING ON THE BRIDGE echoes an "old song," evidently the Irish melody "Take Me Paddy, Will You Now?" The poem suggests that the "lancer" with a "Royal Irish" eye belonged to "The Fifth" regiment. Irish soldiers were stationed in Dorchester from time to time, but the Fifth Regiment was made up of Northumberland Fusiliers.[1] The girls sitting on the stone parapet of Grey's Bridge just east of Dorchester evidently came from some farm or village to the west, for they had come "Past the barracks, town and ridge." The military barracks are on the "Top o' Town" west of central Dorchester; the ridge may be either that of the barracks or the slight ridge between branches of the River Frome. The "curfew-ringing" before sunset suggests a summer evening in the nineteenth century, when the bells of St. Peter's Church rang curfew at 8:00 P.M.

"Sitting on the Bridge" has been set to music by Arnold Bax in *On the Bridge* (London: Murdoch, 1926).

1. Information supplied by Lt.-Col. D. V. Wakely, Curator of the Military Museum in Dorchester.

THE YOUNG CHURCHWARDEN in the manuscript bore the note "At an Evening Service [Sunday] August 14, 1870." Purdy says that "The poem is a reminiscence of St. Juliot Church and Hardy's courtship."[1]

Evidently the poem presents an incident of Hardy's courtship of Emma Gifford, but the scene does not seem to be St. Juliot Church. Examining Hardy's Prayer Book, Phelps found a notation beside the 73rd Psalm that reads: "Lesnewth, Evening Prayer, Aug. 14, 1870." Phelps concludes that "Hardy and Emma crossed the Valency Valley for Evensong at the neighbouring church of Lesnewth, an occasion that prompted, in later days of disillusion, the poem *The Young Churchwarden*."[2]

The poem suggests that the young warden was an admirer of Emma Gifford who understood, when Hardy and Emma came in together, that "his dream was done." This episode and others seem to underlie Hardy's creation of young Jethway, Elfride's unsuccessful suitor in *A Pair of Blue Eyes.* (See the notes on "The Face at the Casement.")

The second stanza concerns Hardy's recall of the episode, perhaps in the 1890's "When Love's viol was unstrung," and his wish then that the churchwarden had won Emma. The third stanza is confusing. Emma was not buried at either St. Juliot or Lesnewth, but in Stinsford Churchyard. Perhaps Hardy intended to lead the reader away from interpretation of the poem as personal.

1. *Thomas Hardy: A Bibliographical Study,* p. 196.
2. *Annotations by Thomas Hardy in His Bibles and Prayer-Book,* p. 8. Figure 3, p. 4, presents a photograph of "Lesnewth Church choir stalls."

"I TRAVEL AS A PHANTOM NOW" echoes an entry in Hardy's journal for June, 1888. Speaking of "the value of life," he wrote "whimsically": "I have attempted many modes [of finding it]. For my part, if there is any way of getting a melancholy satisfaction out of life it lies in dying, so to speak, before one is out of the flesh; by which I mean putting on the manners of ghosts, wandering in their haunts, and taking their views of surrounding things. . . . Hence even when I enter a room to pay a simple morning call I have unconsciously the habit of regarding the scene as if I were a spectre not solid enough to influence my environment."[1] Hardy's "wonder if Man's consciousness / Was a mistake of God's" springs from compassionate participation in the pain of others.

The third stanza, however, suggests that the ecstasy of love makes life worth its cost in pain. This idea is characteristic of Hardy, and he was annoyed that it was misunderstood. He wrote to Sir Henry Newbolt on April 8, 1924: "A d——d good-natured reviewer who was bent on proving me a pessimist—blessed word—at all costs, cooked up my little love-poem called 'I Travel as a Phantom Now' into one of irreligious despair by leaving out the last verse, a bit of ingenuity which did him credit if you leave honesty out of the argument."[2]

1. *Early Life,* p. 275; *Life,* pp. 209-10.
2. In the Miriam Lutcher Stark Library, University of Texas.

LINES TO A MOVEMENT IN MOZART'S E-FLAT SYMPHONY in the manuscript has "Minuet" for "Movement."[1]

Weber has related the episodes of the poem to Hardy's first visit to St. Juliot Rectory and Emma Gifford.[2] The poem does seem to treat his courtship of Emma, but on later occasions than the first visit in March of 1870. The opening stanza speaks of "Junetide's prime" and of a trip "by meads and mountains northerly!" The occasion would seem to be his meeting Emma in Bath in June of 1873. The second stanza recalls a "sandy bay" and a "pestered sea," and may refer to any one or more of his visits to Cornwall "two or three times a year" in 1870-74, mentioned in Emma's *Some Recollections,* on which occasions they explored the coast near Boscastle. The "pinnacled tower" of the third stanza may refer to "King Arthur's Castle," Tintagel, which the couple visited several times. The line "We eyed each other and feared futurity!" may refer to their being locked in the ruins in August of 1870.[3] Though the kiss by the strawberry tree is not identifiable, the poem seems a synopsis of happy moments in Hardy's courtship. That the poem is dated as begun in November of 1898 suggests that long before Emma's death Hardy was making some effort to revive his love for his wife by recalling episodes of their courtship, an effort perhaps stimulated by Mozart's music.

Critics have admired the technique of the poem: the parallel stanzas, each beginning "Show me again" and continuing like a movement in a minuet, the alliteration in each fourth line, and the repeated theme, "Love lures life on."

1. Purdy, *Thomas Hardy: A Bibliographical Study,* p. 196.
2. *Hardy's Love Poems,* p. 16.
3. *Early Life,* pp. 123, 93, 103; *Life,* pp. 93, 71, 78.

"IN THE SEVENTIES" has a motto from the Vulgate Bible that is translated in the King James version (Job 12:4) as "I am as one mocked of his neighbour."

The poem expressses Hardy's memory of himself, his dreams, his aspirations, and his disappointments in the years 1869-72. In 1869, he was still an architect, but with an ardent desire to succeed in literature. He had written *The Poor Man and the Lady,* but it had been rejected by Chapman and Hall unless he would guarantee the firm against loss. He meditated whether to follow "the course he loved, and which was his natural instinct, that of letters, or the course all practical wisdom dictated, that of architecture." In March, the Messrs. Chapman invited him to talk with their reader, George Meredith, who found the story too ardent in its zeal for social reform: "a sweeping dramatic satire of the squirearchy and nobility, London society, the vulgarity of the middle class, modern Christianity, church-restoration, and political and domestic morals in general, the author's views, in fact, being obviously those of a young man with a passion for reforming the world." Meredith advised him to lay the novel aside and write another with more plot. (The "friend" of the second stanza *may* be Meredith, but is more probably Horace Moule.) Following Meredith's counsel, Hardy wrote *Desperate Remedies.* Though declined by Macmillan, it was brought out by Tinsley Brothers in 1871. It was scornfully reviewed in the *Spectator* and did not sell. In June, he "received a fresh buffet from circumstance in seeing at Exeter Station *Desperate Remedies* in Messrs. Smith and Son's surplus catalogue for sale at 2s. 6d. the three volumes, and thought the *Spectator* had snuffed out the book, as it probably had done."

Meanwhile, he had fallen in love with Emma Gifford, a fact that sharpened the question of whether he should continue architecture or follow his "vision" of literary achievement. At one time he decided against the dream. He wrote to Emma "declaring that he had banished novel-writing for ever, and was going on with architecture henceforward." She, "with that rapid instinct which serves women in such good stead, and may almost be called preternatural vision, wrote back instantly her desire that he should adhere to authorship, which she felt sure would be his true vocation." Needing money to marry, he resisted her advice and "applied himself to architectural work during the winter 1871-72 more steadily than he had ever done in his life before, and in the spring of the latter year again set out for London, determined to stifle his constitutional tendency to care for life only as an emotion and not as a scientific game, and fully bent on sticking to the profession which had been the choice of his parents for him rather than his own; but with a faint dream at the back of his mind that he might perhaps write verses as an occasional hobby."[1]

The crisis came to an end in favor of his dream when *Under the Greenwood Tree*, published in May of 1872, was a success.

1. *Early Iife*, pp. 79, 81, 112, 114; *Life*, pp, 60, 61, 85, 86, 87.

THE PEDIGREE expresses Hardy's absorbed interest in his ancestry. Consulting parish registers, he worked out several pedigrees, now in the Dorset County Museum; one of them is reproduced by Evelyn Hardy, facing page 224 of *Thomas Hardy*.

That Hardy, examining the record of his ancestors "in the deep of night," found there troublesome "tangles" and unpleasant facts is symbolized in his image of a cynical "moon in his old age." Here as elsewhere, he presents the moon as a goblin of the sky, throwing upon the facts a nightmarish light.

He was interested in the natural laws governing heredity. (See the notes on "Heredity.") Seeing himself as the end of a line, he expressed the conviction that "every heave and coil and move I made / Within my brain and in my mood and speech" was "forestalled" by his ancestors' "so making it." This reasoning leads to the conclusion that, in spite of feeling "I am I," he enjoys no freedom of the will.

HIS HEART A WOMAN'S DREAM is a fantasy of a widow's realization, through reading the "quaint vermiculations" inscribed on her dead husband's heart, of the husband's love and loyalty through their "long sit-out of years" of misunderstanding. It has been suggested that "If we invert the poem, and imagine a man examining the graven lines and 'quaint vermiculations' of his wife's heart when she is dead, we get a reflection of what the poet felt when his wife died."[1] The poem may represent his feelings about Emma when, after her death, he read her *Some Recollections* of their life together and realized that many of her actions, though done in "blindness," were none the less in "good faith."

1. Evelyn Hardy, *Thomas Hardy*, p. 274.

WHERE THEY LIVED in the manuscript is dated "[March, *deleted*] Oct. 1913." As March, 1913, is the date when Hardy revisited Cornwall after his wife Emma's death, the poem "refers, therefore, to St. Juliot Rectory."[1] "He found the Rectory and the other scenes with which he had been so familiar changed a little, but not greatly."[2] The change in the date reconciles it with the autumnal scene of falling leaves, more symbolizing the poet's mood than picturing facts. The voice that had called "Come in, Dears" in the 1870's was that of Emma's sister, Mrs. Caddell Holder.

1. Purdy, *Thomas Hardy: A Bibliographical Study*, p. 196.
2. *Later Years*, p. 156; *Life*, p. 361.

THE OCCULTATION cannot refer to a physical death, as the "I" of the poem speaks. It refers to the loss of ardor in an "irradiate soul." Hardy asks whether his ardor still exists in his nature, though hidden as the sun may be hidden by a cloud.

LIFE LAUGHS ONWARD portrays Hardy's tendency to live much in his memories. He regrets that an "old abode" has been replaced by a new. The second stanza seems to refer to his wife Emma's grave in Stinsford Churchyard. Emma had especially loved daisies, associated with her in a number of poems, as in "Rain on a Grave." The "figure" that had once sat on a terrace may be Emma's. Hardy meditates that the new and young forever replace the old. "Life Laughs Onward" has been set to music by Gerald Finzi in *Till Earth Outwears* (London and New York: Boosey and Hawkes, 1958).

THE PEACE-OFFERING seems to express Hardy's remorse after his wife Emma's death that, irritated or absorbed in his own thoughts, he had rejected an effort she had made to revive his old affection. The peace-offering may be her playing on the piano the old tunes she had played during Hardy's courtship. (See "The Last Performance.")

"SOMETHING TAPPED" pictures Hardy's illusion that he was visited by the ghost of his wife Emma in August after her death in the preceding November. Her spirit had come to ask him to join her in Stinsford Churchyard. The illusion is rationalized: the tapping was that of a "pallid moth." In folklore a white miller moth is said to be the soul of a dead person.[1] It is also a belief that a tapping on the window pane is an omen of death.

1. In *Jude the Obscure*, when Sue returns to Phillotson on the occasion of his illness, "She was in light spring clothing, and her advent seemed ghostly—like the flitting in of a moth." Part IV, Chapter VI.

THE WOUND is cited by Hardy's biographers (except Mrs. Florence Hardy) in relation to the discord between Hardy and his first wife in the 1890's. Evelyn Hardy says: "During these distressing years, although the Hardys continued to live side by side, to travel abroad together, to visit in manor houses, to examine cathedrals, castles and churches in each other's company, and to appear in public as one, bitter things were said, wounds were given, and unhealed scars remained." To define the wound, she says: "Hardy perceived, or thought that he perceived, that his wife sometimes suffered from delusions."[1] (See Emma Hardy in the Key to Persons.)

King points out that Hardy used the image of the setting sun as a wound in *Tess of the D'Urbervilles*: "When Tess at Talbothays Farm, is 'touched in the tender place in her experience' by hearing the farcical tale of Jack Dollop the deceiver who was forced by the girl's mother to promise marriage, she goes out of doors and the evening sun now seems 'ugly to her, like a great inflamed wound in the sky.' (Chapter 21.) . . . . Tess . . . gave and had given 'no sign' that the wound, 'of which none knew,' had pierced her through."[2]

1. *Thomas Hardy*, pp. 271-72. See also Weber, *Hardy of Wessex*, 1st ed., p. 170; 2nd ed., p. 255.
2. "Verse and Prose Parallels in the Work of Thomas Hardy," pp. 59-60.

A MERRYMAKING IN QUESTION seems an exercise in contrasted imagery. Hynes says: "The first stanza is an arrangement of joyous images as uncomplicated as a C major chord. The second stanza makes that simplicity complex and dissonant by 'mismarrying' the imagery of dancing and singing to images of death."[1] The "oddest of answers" to the meaning of life is a realization that death mocks life, that men dance through life to the inevitable grave.

1. *The Pattern of Hardy's Poetry*, p. 128.

"I SAID AND SANG HER EXCELLENCE" may be a personal poem, as suggested by the footnote, "By Rushy-Pond." A number of poems, including "Neutral Tones" and "At Rushy-Pond," indicate that this pond was a trysting place for Hardy and Tryphena Sparks in the days before he met Emma Gifford. Hardy is the fickle lover of the subtitle. The song seems to say that he idealized Tryphena in terms that he later discovered best suited the "very She," Emma.

A JANUARY NIGHT suggests a mysterious crisis in the lives of Hardy and his wife, Emma. In 1879 the Hardys were living at "The Larches," 1 Arundel Terrace, Trinity Road, Upper Tooting, London. *The Early Life,* under the date of January 1, says: "The poem 'A January Night. 1879' . . . relates to an incident of this new year (1879) which occurred here at Tooting, where they seemed to begin to feel that 'there had passed away a glory from the earth.' And it was in this house that their troubles began."[1]

The poem does not define the "troubles," but the imagery of the weather, the term "hid dread," and the question whether the ghost of a dead neighbor is "astray" hint that Hardy then discovered, or rediscovered, a tendency toward delusions (or mild madness) in Emma. (See the notes on "The Interloper.")

This surmise rests upon Hardy's grotesque imagery, which critics called unpoetical, but he defended because it pictured truth. That the rain "smites," the wind "snarls and sneezes," and the water "wheezes" may not be "naive animism,"[2] but symbolism to represent a delusion. The delusion includes suggestions that these effects are the work of a "spirit astray."

1. P. 163; *Life,* p. 124.
2. So called by Vinson, "Diction and Imagery in the Poetry of Thomas Hardy," p. 166.

A KISS may treat the kiss of "At the Word 'Farewell' " or of "Lines to a Movement in Mozart's E-Flat Symphony." Suggesting its continuing consequences, the poem presents a metaphysical speculation on its immortality. Like Tennyson's echoes that "roll from soul to soul" or the improvisations of Browning's Abt Vogler, it still exists somewhere in the universe.

THE ANNOUNCEMENT in the manuscript has " (January 1879) " under the title. Purdy comments that this fact "suggests the poem is to be associated with 'A January Night, 1879' above. Elsewhere, however, Hardy identifies the scene as Higher Bockhampton."[1] In January, 1879, the Hardys were living at 1 Arundel Terrace, Trinity Road, Upper Tooting, London, and if the announcement was made there, the man whose death was announced may be "the man at the house below" of "A January Night." (See the notes on this poem.)

If the scene is Higher Bockhampton, the "we" of the poem *may* be Hardy's father and mother. On January 1, 1879, Thomas Newman of Dorchester, member of the Town Council and Quartermaster of the Dorset Rifle Battalion, died "after a short illness." The account of the funeral names as chief mourners two brothers, Mr. G. Newman and Mr. W. Newman.[2]

1. *Thomas Hardy: A Bibliographical Study*, p. 197.
2. *Dorset County Chronicle*, January 2, 1879, p. 11, and January 9, p. 3.

THE OXEN was first published in the *Times* (London) on December 24, 1915.[1] Mrs. Florence Hardy wrote to Alda, Lady Hoare on January 7, 1917: "It was, of course, his [Hardy's] mother who told him the legend of the oxen kneeling in their stables at midnight on Christmas Eve."[2] He may have heard the legend from many sources. "The belief that the animal creation worships at the season of Christ's birth is . . . widespread; only those who can see ghosts at Christmas have the power of hearing the cattle, sheep, and horses talk, as they do talk at this holy season."[3] Blunden quotes from *Kilvert's Diary*: " 'James, tell me the truth, did you ever see the oxen kneel on old Christmas Eve at the Weston?' And he said, 'No, I never saw them kneel at the Weston, but when I was at Hinton at Staunton-on-Wye I saw them. I was watching them on old Christmas Eve and at 12 o'clock the oxen that were standing knelt down upon their knees and those that were lying down rose up on their knees, and there they stayed kneeling and moaning, the tears running down their faces.' "[4]

The last two stanzas of "The Oxen" are set in Stinsford Parish near Higher Bockhampton. The poem "refers to the 'lonely barton' under the wood on the right, as one turns into the lane leading to Higher Bockhampton."[5] These stanzas express Hardy's feeling about the legend of the first two. The old people sitting "in hearthside ease" are a Christian "flock" who do not doubt that the oxen kneel. "In these years" of World War I, he cannot believe with the flock.

Suitably, the poem is written in common-meter ballad stanzas. It uses rustic words with religious connotations: elder, flock, barton (farmyard), and coomb (valley).

Hardy made use of similar legends in "The Lost Pyx" and in *Tess of the D'Urbervilles*. In *Tess*, Dairyman Crick tells the story of William Dewy, who, coming from a wedding where he had played his fiddle, was crossing a pasture on a moonlit night. A bull took after him. Dewy, remembering that cattle kneel on Christmas Eve, played the Nativity Hymn on his fiddle. The bull went down on bended knees, and Dewy got across a hedge. He reported "that he'd seen a man look a fool a good many times, but never such a fool as that bull looked when he found his pious feelings had been played upon, and 'twas not Christmas Eve." (Chapter XVII.) Rebekah Owen commented in her copy of *Tess*: "Mr. Hardy said, 'There was something like this once.' William Dewy and the 'Tivity Hymn played to the bull are founded on fact."[6]

"The Oxen" has been frequently set to music. The manuscript of a setting by Edward Dent (January, 1919) is in the Dorset County Museum. Other settings are by Graham Peel, *The Oxen* (London: Chappell & Co., 1919); Gerald Finzi in *By Footpath and Stile* (London: J. Curwen & Sons, 1925); Leslie Cochran, *The Oxen* (London: Augener, 1927); Robert Fleming, *The Oxen* (London: Oxford University Press, 1945); C. Armstrong Gibbs, *The Oxen* (London: Boosey & Hawkes, 1953); and Harper MacKay in *Five Songs* (1957, in manuscript in the Colby College Library).

1. Purdy, *Thomas Hardy: A Bibliographical Study*, p. 175.
2. In the Stourhead Collection, The County Archives, Trowbridge, Wiltshire.
3. Firor, *Folkways in Thomas Hardy*, p. 151.
4. *Thomas Hardy*, p. 153.
5. Moule, *Stinsford Church and Parish*, p. 2.
6. In the Colby College Library.

THE TRESSES is a soliloquy in which Emma Hardy reflects upon her hair. Perhaps Hardy drew upon her *Some Recollections*, imagining what she thought as she recalled ". . . scampering up and down the hills on my beloved mare alone . . . my hair floating in the wind."[1]

1. *Early Life*, p. 91; *Life*, p. 69.

THE PHOTOGRAPH tells a story that Hardy said took place at Max Gate.[1] Possibly the photograph was that of Tryphena Sparks, which Hardy destroyed in some year between the completion of Max Gate in 1884 and the writing of "Thoughts of Phena" in March, 1890.

"Thoughts of Phena," the only poem that gives even a part of Tryphena's name,[2] says twice "Not a line of her writing have I, / Not a thread of her hair." That Hardy was engaged to Tryphena suggests that he had had letters from her and a lock of her hair, but had destroyed them, perhaps from a sense of loyalty to his wife Emma. Lines in "The Photograph" point to Tryphena. Destruction of the photograph elicits "a cry of hurt," for "The spectacle was one that I could not bear." The picture is one "unsheathed from the past." Hardy did not see Tryphena after his marriage, which would include the "packs of years" from 1874 until the destruction of all that would

remind Hardy of his "lost prize" (so called in "Thoughts of Phena"),
or Emma of her rival. The photograph was burned in "a casual
clearance of life's arrears," though the pain expressed in the poem
brings "casual" into question.

The last stanza suggests that at the time the photograph was
burned Hardy did not know whether Tryphena was alive or dead.
His statement concerning "Thoughts of Phena" supports this identifi-
cation: "In the train on the way to London. . . . The woman whom I
was thinking of—a cousin—was dying at the time, and I quite in ig-
norance of it."[3] No photograph of Tryphena has been found among
Hardy's effects.

1. Purdy, *Thomas Hardy: A Bibliographical Study*, p. 197.
2. *Early Life* and *Later Years* do not mention Tryphena by name.
3. *Early Life*, p. 293; *Life*, p. 224.

ON A HEATH seems a personal poem, with a setting on Puddle-
town ("Egdon") Heath near Hardy's birthplace. The site of the
lovers' tryst may be near Rushy-Pond. The "town-shine in the dis-
tance" would be the lights of Dorchester about three and a half miles
away as reflected on the clouds. Since Hardy, before meeting Emma
Gifford, was engaged to Tryphena Sparks of Puddletown, across the
heath, the girl of the poem may be Tryphena.

The third stanza is puzzling. In a conversation with Hardy on
December 27, 1920, V. H. Collins asked: "C: Who or what is it that
is referred to in the last stanza?—H: There is a third person.—C:
'Another looming,' 'one still blooming,' 'a shade entombing'—are
not there three different things?—H: No, only one."[1]

One interpretation of Hardy's evasive "third person" is that, at
the time of the tryst on the heath, Hardy had met Emma Gifford and
fallen in love with her. Since she is in far-away Cornwall, her life
can not be seen; she is "blooming" in Hardy's affection; but she is a
shadow clouding or "entombing" his love for Tryphena.

Deacon and Coleman, however, suggest that Hardy and Tryphena
had an illegitimate son and that the "third person" of the poem is
Tryphena's unborn child.[2]

1. Collins, *Talks with Thomas Hardy*, pp. 24-25.
2. The evidence that Hardy had a son is too complex for full discussion here
and is controversial. See Deacon and Coleman, *Providence and Mr Hardy*, especial-
ly Chapter 14, "The Child."

AN ANNIVERSARY is a meditation upon Hardy's memories of
Kingston-Maurward ewelease in relation to an anniversary not speci-
fied. In walking to and from Dorchester during his youth, Hardy
crossed this ewelease. The "garth" of the poem is the nearby cemetery

of Stinsford Church. Some of the "white stones" of the garth mark the graves of members of his family.

He made use of the Kingston-Maurward estate in his poems ("The Harvest-Supper," "In Her Precincts," etc.) and his novels. Kingston-Maurward House (given fictional names) is the principal setting for *An Indiscretion in the Life of an Heiress*[1] and *Desperate Remedies*.

The event memorialized in "An Anniversary" may be any one of many. Aside from Hardy's affection for Mrs. Martin (see the notes on "Amabel"), *The Early Life* associates many facts of his youth with Kingston-Maurward. In his study of the Greek New Testament when he was about nineteen, Hardy and his fellow-apprentices in architecture would "take out their Testaments into the fields and sit on a gate reading them. The gate of the enclosure in Kingston-Maurward eweleaze [*sic*] . . . was the scene of some of the readings." When *Desperate Remedies* was savagely reviewed in the *Spectator* for April 22, 1871, Hardy "remembered, for long years after, how he had read this review as he sat on a stile leading to the eweleaze he had to cross on his way home to Bockhampton.[2] "An Anniversary" may concern this bitterness.

Hardy remembered especially sad anniversaries. He wrote to A. C. Benson on December 26, 1924: "We have been as cheerful as may be this Christmas. . . . But I long ago entered the region in a lifetime in which anniversaries are the saddest days of the year."[3] The poem pictures the features of the eweleaze and compares them with Hardy's own as both were when he "pilgrimed" there in his youth and as they are half a century later.

1. Composed from portions of Hardy's first, unpublished novel, *The Poor Man and the Lady*.
2. *Early Life*, pp. 40, 111; *Life*, pp. 31, 84.
3. In the Miriam Lutcher Stark Library, the University of Texas.

"BY THE RUNIC STONE" may, as usually assumed, or may not treat Hardy's courtship of Emma Gifford. Purdy comments that " *'Two who became a story'* was added at the head of the poem in subsequent editions [after *Moments of Vision*], presumably a reference to Hardy's courtship in Cornwall and its reflection in *A Pair of Blue Eyes*."[1] The phrase "she in brown" suggests Emma Gifford, and the last two lines may refer to Hardy's life with Emma after their marriage. *The Early Life*, in presenting his courtship of Emma in the spring of 1870, states: "He kept up a regular correspondence with 'the young lady in brown' who had attracted him at St. Juliot Rectory." Again on August 8, he visited St. Juliot and "Here . . . he found the 'young lady in brown' of the previous winter."[2]

The identification could be considered certain if a runic stone on a grassy slope at or near St. Juliot Rectory could be found. Mrs. Gwendolen Bax, who has occupied the Old Rectory at St. Juliot for many years, wrote on July 12, 1966, that many people have visited the Rectory in search of the runic stone "but have not discovered anything like it." Possibly, the poem may represent Hardy's courtship of someone else by a runic stone in some other place than St. Juliot. Perhaps the girl was Tryphena Sparks, to whom he was engaged before he met Emma. She, as well as Emma, could have worn brown. Possibly he wrote "she in brown" to conceal Tryphena, who is not even named in *The Early Life* and *The Later Years*. It is as true of Tryphena as of Emma that Hardy had seen "Time toss their history / From zone to zone." Then the story referred to is *Jude the Obscure*.

A stone within a few yards of a trysting place of Hardy and Tryphena supports this theory. It is a large fragment of mysterious origin lying on its side (partly underground, but with enough projecting to form a seat) beneath a clump of holly trees beside the course of the old Roman Road across Puddletown ("Egdon") Heath. It is on the slope of a hill about a hundred yards south of Rushy-Pond, about half a mile from Hardy's birthplace. Apparently he and Tryphena frequently met at Rushy-Pond, between Puddletown (Tryphena's home) and Higher Bockhampton. Before the present growth of young trees planted on the heath, the view from the stone was probably down a grassy slope.

In *The Old Stone Crosses of Dorset* Pope says that the stone ". . . is of Ham Hill [mined near Yeovil], and may, at one time, have formed a portion of a late fourteenth or early fifteenth-century cross. On the west side is a rudely sculptured figure standing on a corbel in a canopied and cusped niche, with right hand uplifted to the head, and the left crossing the body. . . . It is a rectangular oblong measuring one foot six inches by twelve inches, and was formerly, including the part in the ground, about four feet six inches high; but some three feet of the upper portion, *Mr. Hardy informs me*, was broken off and carried away well within his recollection, leaving the stump only . . . in the ground."[3] Thus the stone is not runic in the strict sense of marked with Germanic runes. Perhaps Hardy used the term commonly used in Dorset for such stones.

A third possibility is that Hardy did have Emma in mind as "she in brown" but, intending to bring the poem to a climax with a suggestion of fatalism, used poetic license to move the stone to Cornwall in support of this suggestion.

1. *Thomas Hardy: A Bibliographical Study*, p. 197.
2. Pp. 102, 103; *Life*, pp. 77, 78.
3. Pp. 116-17. The italics are mine.

THE PINK FROCK is based on an incident narrated in *The Later Years*. In May, 1894, Hardy and his wife Emma were paying calls. "At the Countess of ——'s 'a woman very rich and very pretty' [Marcia, Lady Yarborough], informed him mournfully in *tête-à-tête* that people snubbed her, which so surprised him that he could hardly believe it, and frankly told her it was her own imagination. She was the lady of the 'Pretty pink frock' poem, though it should be stated that the deceased was not her husband but an uncle." [1]

"The Pink Frock" exhibits Hardy's amused observation of woman's vanity, evident in his work since the portrayal of Bathsheba in the opening chapter of *Far from the Madding Crowd*. The poem has been set to music by Robin Milford in *A Book of Songs* (Oxford University Press, 1940).

1. P. 31; *Life*, p. 264. The brackets are Hardy's.

TRANSFORMATIONS in the manuscript shows " 'In a Churchyard' as an earlier title (or perhaps subtitle). Hardy identified the scene as Stinsford Churchyard." [1]

The concept of the poem is imaginatively a very old one. It appears in FitzGerald's "Rubáiyát of Omar Khayyám": "I sometimes think that never blooms so red / The Rose as where some buried Caesar bled." (Stanza XIX.) Besides this imaginative concept, Hardy had read such scientific essays as T. H. Huxley's "The Physical Basis of Life," which says that animal life may live in other forms only by feeding upon protoplasm that has lived, but died. In this scientific law, "There is a sort of continuance of life after death in the change of the vital animal principle, where the body feeds the tree or the flower that grows from the mound." [2]

Hardy's meditation is in Stinsford Churchyard. The "fair girl long ago / Whom I often tried to know" is evidently Louisa Harding, the daughter of a rich farmer in Stinsford, about a year younger than Hardy and, when he was a boy, socially superior.

"Transformations" has been set to music by Gerald Finzi in *A Young Man's Exhortations* (Oxford University Press, 1933).

1. Purdy, *Thomas Hardy: A Bibliographical Study*, p. 198.
2. Ransome, "Thomas Hardy's Poems and the Religious Difficulties of a Naturalist," p. 187.

IN HER PRECINCTS, Hardy stated, describes "an experience." [1] Kingston-Maurward House was the home of Mrs. Julia Augusta

Martin, the lady of the manor of Stinsford from 1845 to 1853. A sentimental romance grew up in young Tommy Hardy's feeling for Mrs. Martin. (See the notes on "Amabel.") "In Her Precincts" seems to picture Hardy as a boy of about thirteen haunting Kingston-Maurward Park, love-sick for Mrs. Martin's caresses, dismayed that she had felt he had deserted her, and the distressed when he found the "gloom of severance" his alone.[2]

Purdy, briefly considering Mrs. Martin, suggests that the poem is concerned "more probably with one of the daughters of James Fellowes, who bought the estate in 1853." I have seen no evidence to relate the poem to a Miss Fellowes.

1. Purdy, *Thomas Hardy: A Bibliographical Study*, p. 198.
2. Evelyn Hardy, *Thomas Hardy*, pp. 31-32, offers this interpretation.

THE LAST SIGNAL is one of Hardy's several tributes to the Reverend William Barnes. From his youth until Barnes's death, they were close friends. Barnes's school in Dorchester was next door to John Hicks's offices, where Hardy was an architectural apprentice from 1856 to 1862. Ardently studying the classics and knowing Barnes "to be an authority upon grammar, Hardy would often run in to ask Barnes to decide some knotty point in dispute between him and his fellow-pupil," Hicks. When Edmund Gosse visited Hardy in 1883, Hardy took him "To Winterborne-Came Church . . . to hear and see the poet Barnes. Stayed for sermon. Barnes, knowing we should be on the watch for a prepared sermon, addressed it entirely to his own flock, almost pointedly excluding us. Afterwards walked to the rectory and looked at his pictures." By moving into Max Gate in 1885, Hardy became a near neighbor of Barnes, for Winterborne-Came Rectory was only a few hundred yards away. He often dropped in to chat with Barnes. His record for October 17, 1885, describes a conversation with Barnes about "old families," Louis Napoleon's residence in England and visits to Dorchester, and amusing incidents in the town.[1] Shortly afterward, on November 23, 1885, he wrote to Gosse that "Barnes is growing weaker every day. . . . I go to sit by his bed whenever he is able to talk."[2] Barnes lived on for nearly a year, dying on October 7, 1886. Hardy wrote an obituary essay, "The Rev. William Barnes, B.D.," published in the *Athenaeum* for October 16.[3]

The Early Life states that "Hardy's walk across the fields to attend the poet's funeral was marked by the singular incident to which he alludes in the poem entitled 'The Last Signal.' "[4] When he was on his way from Max Gate to Winterborne-Came Church, a flash of sunlight was reflected from Barnes's coffin, "As with the wave of his hand." In front of Max Gate, "Winterborne-Came Path" descends southward into a valley and rises to cross a low hill. Barnes's rectory was on the eastern side of the Wareham Road a few hundred yards east of this path. The coffin being borne from the rectory turned from the rectory gate into the road for a short distance before veering westward into a lane leading to the church. The afternoon sun[5] reflected from the brass of the coffin as it turned into the road.

As an additional tribute to Barnes, Hardy used in "The Last Signal" "Welsh techniques introduced into English poetry by Barnes. . . . The internal rhyme scheme ('road-abode') is called in Welsh poetry *union*; Barnes used it in 'Times o' Year.' There is also in Hardy's poem the repetitive consonantal pattern called in Welsh *cynghanedd*; in the third line, for example, the pattern is LLSNSLLNS (compare Barnes's use of the device in 'My orcha'd in Linden Lea') ."[6]

1. See *Early Life*, pp. 37, 160, 200, 210, 229-30; *Life*, pp. 28, 122, 154, 161, 175-76.

2. In the British Museum.

3. See Orel, *Thomas Hardy's Personal Writings*, pp. 100-106.

4. P. 240; *Life*, p. 183.

5. "The funeral procession left the rectory shortly before three, the coffin being carried on a bier. It was of polished elm with brass mountings." Apparently Hardy, having crossed the hill, waited at the lane for the bier; he was listed among those following it to the church. *Dorset County Chronicle*, October 14, 1886, p. 8.

6. Hynes, *The Pattern of Hardy's Poetry*, p. 29. Hynes refers to: "Ye*ll*owly the sun *sl*oped *l*ow down to westward." See also Zietlow, "Thomas Hardy and William Barnes: Two Dorset Poets."

THE HOUSE OF SILENCE is set on "The Lawn, Max Gate,"[1] from the outer edges of which trees that Hardy had planted nearly hid the house.[2] Evidently the "phantom" is Hardy. That in his later years he lived much within himself is suggested in a letter from Mrs. Florence Hardy to John Cowper Powys on October 26, 1930: "It is late at night . . . in this silent house—a clock ticking near me—in the room we have so often sat together with T. H. & it is rather like a grave. Do you know his poem 'The House of Silence,' which begins 'This is a quiet place'? It described Max Gate then, & even more aptly describes it now—when I am the phantom left alone."[3]

In describing himself as a "phantom . . . the last of its race," Hardy was evidently thinking of his childlessness and that of his brother Henry and two sisters, Mary and Kate. Otherwise the poem is a self-portrait of Hardy as poet-and-dreamer. His having "powers . . . To pierce the material screen" means, perhaps, that he lives more in memories of youth, gayety and sorrows, than in present awareness. His dreams of "mankind in its ages seven" is an allusion to Jaques's speech in Shakespeare's *As You Like It*, II, vii, defining man's life in the ages of infant, school-boy, lover, soldier, judge, old man, and dotard.

1. Cox, ed., *Thomas Hardy Through the Camera's Eye*, p. 50.
2. See *Early Life*, pp. 226-27; *Life*, p. 173.
3. In the Miriam Lutcher Stark Library, University of Texas.

GREAT THINGS, placed next to "The House of Silence," concerned with Hardy's dreams of "funereal shades," presents a complementary side of his temperament. Perhaps "the same sensibility that made him so acutely susceptible to life's sorrows made him also exquisitely responsive to its joys," here listed as the light-hearted gayeties of "drinking, dancing, and light love."[1] Only in the final stanza does the poet meditate the ultimate values of these pleasures, and even there he would seem to prefer "impassioned flings" to Paradise. That the sentiment is more than a passing mood is clear in Robert Graves's record of a visit to Max Gate in 1920: "At dinner that night he [Hardy] grew enthusiastic in praise of cider, which he had drunk since a boy, and which, he said, was the finest medicine he knew."[2] Hardy's novels (not to mention his poems) are sprinkled with his "great things": the cider-making scenes in *The Woodlanders*, the dancing in *Under the Greenwood Tree*, and the love-making everywhere.

The first three stanzas rest on memories. Hardy was a bicyclist and doubtless had often gone "Spinning down to Weymouth town" seven miles from Dorchester, and stopped about halfway at the Ship Inn on Ridgeway.[3] As a boy, he and his father fiddled for "nightlong" country dances, and as a young man in London and in Weymouth, he was a "dancing man."

"Great Things" has been set to music by John Ireland (London: Augener, 1935).

1. Cecil, *Hardy the Novelist*, p. 105.
2. *Good-Bye to All That*, p. 363.
3. The Inn is on the main highway, A354. There, in Part the Third, Chapter 2, of *Under the Greenwood Tree*, Dick Dewy proposed to Fancy Day.

THE CHIMES presents the eight bells of St. Peter's Church in Dorchester during Hardy's youth when they still played the "sweet Sicilian sailors' tune" and caused him to dream of a loved one far away,[1] Emma Gifford of Cornwall. Later these bells ceased to ring except for church purposes.

The third stanza presents the "hard utilitarian times" after the chimes had ceased to play secular tunes and after Hardy had the "one desired" by his side as his wife, but found her no longer desirable there. As early as January, 1879, "there had passed away a glory from the earth" in his relations with Emma.[2] The reference to "bale," however, suggests a later time, perhaps in the 1890's.

1. In Chapter IV of *The Mayor of Casterbridge*, the clocks in Casterbridge struck at eight o'clock, and "then chimes were heard stammering out the Sicilian Mariners' Hymn."
2. *Early Life*, p. 163; *Life*, p. 124.

THE FIGURE IN THE SCENE describes an incident in Hardy's courtship of Emma Gifford. During his second visit to Cornwall, he and Emma made a trip to Beeny Cliff. While they were sketching the scene, rain began to fall. Emma wrapped herself in a cape and sat down, but Hardy kept on sketching in pencil and included the "hooded" figure of Emma in his picture. This sketch is now in the Dorset County Museum; on it he wrote in pencil: "Beeny Cliff, in the rain—Aug. 22, 1870. 'It never looks like summer.' E. L. G. (on Beeny)." The Museum also has a copy of this drawing in ink. Below the copy, in Hardy's handwriting, are the title "The Figure in the Scene" and lines 3, 4, and 5 of the poem. The picture, showing the cliff edge, the ocean beyond, and rain slanting down, is somewhat dark; Emma's figure is only an outline in a corner, where she seems almost a part of the landscape, as suggested in the second stanza of the poem.[1]

The line saying that Emma has not visited Beeny Cliff "Ever since that day" is an exaggeration. Hardy did not marry Emma until 1874, and she certainly visited the cliff between August of 1870 and September of 1874.

1. The drawing in ink is reproduced on p. 82 of Evelyn Hardy and Gittings, *Some Recollections by Emma Hardy*.

"WHY DID I SKETCH" has the same background as "The Figure in the Scene." Writing to Mrs. Arthur Henniker on February 7, 1918, Hardy said of his poems: "I . . . like best those which are literally true" and named "Why Did I Sketch."[1] Perhaps "literally true" refers not only to the background of the poem, but also to its theme, the pain of recalling a happy scene and realizing that the loved one is dead.

1. In the Dorset County Museum.

CONJECTURE treats the influence upon Hardy's life of his two wives, Emma and Florence, and his favorite sister, Mary. If "Conjecture" was written shortly before it was published in *Moments of Vision*, 1917, Emma and Mary were dead; Florence outlived him.

The theme of the poem is Hardy's wonder at how his life had been shaped by these women, and at what a "strange aspect" it would have if he had not known them. This thought is curiously related to his note dated June 10, 1923, as reproduced in *The Later Years*: "Relativity. That things and events always were, are, and will be (*e.g.* Emma, Mother and Father are living still in the past) ."[1]

1. P. 231; *Life*, p. 419. Evelyn Hardy points out that in Hardy's notebook the parenthesis read: " (e.g. E. M. F. etc. are living still in the past.)" Her note on this entry says: "The initials stand for Emma, Mary, Florence, named in 'Conjecture.' " *Thomas Hardy's Notebooks*, pp. 99-100. In view of the phrase "still living in the past," as in memory, and the fact that Florence was alive, this identification seems an error.

THE BLOW concerns a disaster that seems the work of a fatal force, variously named as "That Which some enthrone," "the Inscrutable, the Hid," the "Immanent Doer," and "It." The force resembles the Immanent Will of *The Dynasts*. In ethical quality, the blow is "Below the lowest" of human actions; it is also below the lowest that can be imagined of any conscious "aimful" Will. It must be the work of a force "That doth not know." Yet, because the force is immanent in man, and thus may be brought to consciousness "in some age unguessed of us," It may grieve for having done what It will then recognize as evil.

Critics have supposed that the poem alludes to the alleged madness of Hardy's first wife, Emma.[1] (See the notes on "The Interloper.") Other critics and the date of publication in *Moments of Vision*, 1917, suggest that the blow was World War I.[2] In either case, the term "blow" for a disaster caused by a higher power seems to echo Ps. 39:10, "I am consumed by the blow of thine hand."

1. For instance, Lewis, "The Lyrical Poetry of Thomas Hardy," p. 170.
2. See Blunden, *Thomas Hardy*, p. 157.

LOVE THE MONOPOLIST "refers to a train departure from Launceston in Cornwall, an episode of Hardy's courtship"[1] of Emma Gifford. In 1871, the railway-station nearest to St. Juliot Rectory was at Launceston. The poem expresses the "Young Lover's" somewhat petulant egoism, or at least a feeling that Emma should be unhappy at his departure and think only of him.

1. Purdy, *Thomas Hardy: A Bibliographical Study*, p. 199.

AT MIDDLE-FIELD GATE IN FEBRUARY in the manuscript had "Middle-Hill" for "Middle-Field," either term referring to fields along Bockhampton Lane.[1] Several gates open into fields lying between Lower and Higher Bockhampton, but the gate of the poem is probably that opening into "Second Middle Field," a few yards south of the course of the old Roman Road that runs near Hardy's birthplace.

The gate is now an iron gate wide enough to admit tractors, but at the time the poem was written it may have been of wooden bars. Hedgerows separate the Second Middle Field from the North and South fields. The meadow at this point is level enough to invite picnicking and merrymaking.

Following comments about December, 1889, *The Early Life* says: "Among other poems written about this time was the one called 'At Middle-Field Gate in February,' describing the field-women of the author's childhood. On the present writer's once asking Hardy the names of those he calls the 'bevy now underground,' he said they were Unity Sargent, Susan Chamberlain, Esther Oliver, Emma Shipton, Anna Barrett, Ann West, Elizabeth Hurden, Eliza Trevis, and others, who had been young women about twenty when he was a child."[2] In 1889 Hardy was working on *Tess of the D'Urbervilles*, and it seems likely that he created the May-Day dance or "club-walking" scene of Chapter II partly from memory of the "amorous play" mentioned in the last stanza.

1. Purdy, *Thomas Hardy: A Bibliographical Study*, p. 199.
2. P. 292; *Life*, p. 223.

THE YOUTH WHO CARRIED A LIGHT was first published in the *Aberdeen University Review* for February, 1916. Aberdeen University had awarded Hardy the honorary degree of LL.D. in 1905. In a letter of October 19, 1907, to a Mr. Pantin, he wrote that he thought Aberdeen "a University which can claim . . . to an exceptional degree that breadth of view & openness of mind that all Universities profess to cultivate, but many stifle."[1] Perhaps he sent "The Youth Who Carried a Light" to the University magazine because he regarded his degree as, in a sense, an answer to the questions of the final stanza.

The poem presents Hardy's recollection of himself, his ambitions, and his youthful visions of the period 1856-62, when, working as architectural apprentice for John Hicks of Dorchester, he was also rising early each morning to study French, Latin, and Greek. This memory is dramatized as the wondering observation of a neighbor who saw young Hardy on his way from Higher Bockhampton and his labors over Latin odes, perhaps, to Hicks's office.

1. In the Colby College Library.

THE HEAD ABOVE THE FOG has the intensity of a personal poem. It presents Hardy's vision in a fog that recalls a girl, presumably now dead, "Tripping along to me for love." The girl may be Tryphena Sparks.

Hardy made use of fog in a number of lovers' scenes, as in Chapter

XX of *Tess of the D'Urbervilles*. There, as Tess and Angel walked together at dawn: "She looked ghostly, as if she were merely a soul at large. . . . Or perhaps the summer fog was more general, and the meadows lay like a white sea, out of which the scattered trees rose like dangerous rocks."

OVERLOOKING THE RIVER STOUR in the manuscript adds "(1877)" to the title, indicating the time of the incident.[1]

Hardy and his wife Emma settled in Sturminster-Newton, about fifteen miles northeast of Dorchester, in 1876. *The Early Life* says: "A pretty cottage overlooking the Dorset Stour—called 'Riverside Villa'—offered itself at Sturminster Newton, and this they took at mid-summer, hastily furnished it in part by going to Bristol and buying £100 worth of mid-Victorian furniture in two hours; entering on July 3. It was their first house and, though small, probably that in which they spent their happiest days."

Riverside Villa, on the southwestern edge of Sturminster, sits on a high bluff a few hundred feet east of the Stour River. The Stour, across a meadow below the bluff, is split into two channels by an island; the current at this point is tranquil enough to give the river the look of a pond. Beyond the river lies a low, flat meadow, in spring sprinkled with such flowers as the kingcups (marsh marigolds) mentioned in the poem. Trees along the river banks and on the island are usually alive with birds.

The Hardys' enjoyment of this setting is described in *The Early Life*: "Rowed on the Stour in the evening, the sun setting up the river. Just afterwards a faint exhalation visible on surface of water as we stirred it with the oars. . . . Mowers salute us. Rowed among the water-lilies to gather them. Their long ropy stems. Passing the island drove out a flock of swallows from the bushes and sedge, which had gone there to roost. Gathered meadow-sweet. . . . A cloud in the sky like a huge quill-pen." Hardy, though busy writing *The Return of the Native*, enjoyed the "Country life at Sturminster. Vegetables pass from growing to boiling, fruit from the bushes to the pudding, without a moment's halt, and the gooseberries that were ripening on the twigs at noon are in the tart an hour later." He recorded on March 18, 1878: "End of the Sturminster Newton idyll. . . . Our happiest time."[2] They moved to London.

On page 157 of *The Early Life* that belonged to Mrs. Florence Hardy, in the handwriting of her friend Irene Cooper Willis, the following note explains the move: "Mrs. Hardy told me that T. H.'s married happiness with his first wife ended here. They left Sturminster Newton because the first Mrs. Hardy's brother came one day and exclaimed at their living in such an out of the way place where, he remarked, the sight of a strange bird on the lawn was an event. This incited Mrs. H. to long for London where she thought she would be someone; and their unhappiness came from her social snobbishness." [3]

The Later Years, treating the year 1916, states the occasion for Hardy's writing the poem: "In the same month of June he paid a visit with his wife [Florence] and remaining sister [Kate] to a house he had never entered for forty years. This was Riverside Villa, Sturminster Newton. . . . He found it much as it had been in the former years; and it was possibly this visit which suggested the poems about Sturminster that were published in Moments of Vision." [4]

The first three stanzas describe the idyllic scenes that gave Hardy pleasure in his Sturminster home, and the final stanza expresses remorse that he had not turned from the scenery "To see the more behind my back." The "less things" seen from the window held his gaze away from Emma's need for attention and laid a basis for later misunderstandings. For some details of Hardy's neglect of Emma at this time see "The Musical Box."

"Overlooking the River Stour" has been set to music in Before and After Summer: Ten Songs for Baritone and Piano (London: Boosey & Hawkes, 1949).

1. Purdy, Thomas Hardy: A Bibliographical Study, p. 199.
2. Pp. 147, 152-53, 156; Life, pp. 111-12, 116, 118. A photograph of Riverside Villa as seen from the river and one of the river as seen from the house are in Evans, The Homes of Thomas Hardy, pp. 13-14.
3. In the Dorset County Museum.
4. P. 172; Life, p. 373.

THE MUSICAL BOX is a coda to "Overlooking the River Stour." It suggests that, while living at Sturminster, Hardy was accustomed to go walking alone. (Perhaps, of course, Emma did not wish to go walking as often as he did.) It also suggests, in some remorse, that he, dreaming over the scenes of his outings, paid little attention to Emma's lonely waiting. Her eager welcome as he came home was both a pleasure and a matter-of-course, "Lifelong to be." Introspective, living in his dreams (writing The Return of the Native at this time), he "did not see" Emma's loneliness.

The musical box, the "mindless lyre" that plays a "thin mechanic air," was presumably among the "£100 worth of mid-Victorian furniture" Hardy and Emma had purchased for Riverside Villa. In the poem it seems also a symbol for the perfunctory nature of his expressions of interest in her.

ON STURMINSTER FOOT-BRIDGE in the manuscript was titled "On Stourcastle Foot-Bridge (1877)."[1] It is related to "Overlooking the River Stour" and "The Musical Box." The foot-bridge is a narrow, railed bridge across the Stour River a few hundred yards from Hardy's home in Riverside Villa in 1876-78. It is supported by two stone pillars.[2]

"On Sturminster Foot-Bridge" suggests that Hardy's meditative walks alone (as in "The Musical Box") sometimes involved his neglect of Emma even until "midnight moans."

His accurate reproduction of sounds on Sturminster Foot-Bridge at midnight brought forth scornful remarks from critics. One of them declared with "merry conviction" that such poetry as Hardy's "does not make for immortality." Hardy, defending his fidelity to fact, said: "One case of the kind, in which the poem 'On Sturminster Foot-Bridge' was quoted with the remark that one could make as good music as that out of a milk-cart, betrayed the reviewer's ignorance of any perception that the metre was intended to be onomatopoeic, plainly as it was shown; and another in the same tone disclosed that the reviewer had tried to scan the author's sapphics as heroics." He wrote that his lines "were intended to convey by their rhythm the impression of a clucking in ripples into riverside holes when blown upon by an up-stream wind; so that when his reviewer jested on the syllables of the verse sounding like milk in a cart he was simply stating that the author had succeeded in what he had tried to do—the sounds being similar."[3] The poem includes two unusual phrases: "scrabbled" (scratched, scrawled) and "eyot withies" (willows on the island).

1. Purdy, *Thomas Hardy: A Bibliographical Study*, p. 199.
2. For a photograph of the Stour meadows and the footbridge, see Evelyn Hardy, *Thomas Hardy*, facing p. 156.
3. *Later Years*, pp. 79, 193; *Life*, pp. 301, 390.

ROYAL SPONSORS sounds like a tale that Hardy may have heard from his grandmother, retold with wry amusement. J. C. Squire wrote that "the hopelessness of the subject has drawn Mr. Hardy into worse writing than he usually perpetrates. The first two lines are thoroughly comic."[1] In his scrapbook containing this review, Hardy wrote in pencil opposite this sentence: "As intended to be."[2]

The poem satirizes baptism that is rendered meaningless through pride. Though agnostic, Hardy thought of the rites of the Church as having meaning, especially those that involved promises and obligations.

1. "Mr. Hardy's Old Age," p. 146.
2. In the Dorset County Museum.

OLD FURNITURE presents Hardy's meditation in what is evidently his boyhood home, surrounded by "relics of householdry" that bring into memory visions of their long-dead users. He seems to see his mother's hands setting the clock, his father's fingers "dancing" on his "old viol," his grandmother's face in the chimney corner, and beyond them "images" of ancestors he had known only in old tales.

Ghostliness is suggested in such phrases as "Hands behind hands" and the "tentative touches" of a "foggy finger . . . In the wont of a moth." This tendency to see a ghostly life in old houses is characteristic of Hardy. Melbury's house in *The Woodlanders*, for instance, "was a house in whose reverberations queer old personal tales were yet audible if properly listened for." (Chapter IV.)

A THOUGHT IN TWO MOODS seems to present Hardy's memory of an incident in his courtship of Emma Gifford. During his early married life, he called his wife "Em" and occasionally "Emleen," for which "Ethleen" seems a substitute. Ethleen is presented on a "daisied field," and Emma was especially fond of daisies. She had a tendency to see omens like that suggested in the last stanza.

The second stanza suggests an idea characteristic of Hardy, the essential identity of mankind and the rest of nature, as in "The Wind Blew Words" and "Voices from Things Growing in a Churchyard."

THE LAST PERFORMANCE dramatizes an event at Max Gate shortly before the death of Emma Hardy in the autumn of 1912. *The Later Years* says: "Strangely enough, she one day suddenly sat down to the piano and played a long series of her favourite old tunes, saying at the end she would never play any more. The poem called 'The Last Performance' approximately describes this incident."[1] In discussing the estrangement between Hardy and Emma, Weber suggests that her playing was a final effort, futile at the time, to recapture his love: "There had once been a time when the sound of the piano would catch his attention and keep him at home. But that time was past."[2]

That he understood her playing to be a peace-offering is suggested by his use of a similar device in *Tess of the D'Urbervilles*. At lonely Flintcomb-Ash farm, Tess practices singing all the old ballads she knows in order to charm Angel when he may return: "It would have melted the heart of a stone to hear her singing these ditties, whenever she worked apart from the rest of the girls in this cold dry time; the tears running down her cheeks all the while at the thought that perhaps he would not, after all, come to hear her." (Chapter XLIX.) Hardy interprets Emma's playing as evidence of her mysterious premonition of death.

[385]

"The Last Performance," retitled "The Old Tunes," has been set
to music by Barbara Rawling (London: J. Curwen and Sons, and
New York: G. Schirmer, 1965).

1. P. 153; *Life*, p. 359.
2. *Hardy's Love Poems*, p. 63.

"YOU ON THE TOWER" seems an allegorical conversation in which
the questioner stands for Hardy immersed in his writing and dream-
ing of "Enjoyment" (fame, fortune, leisure?) when his work may be
"full-finished." The answering figure on the tower of the "factory"
may represent a publisher who promises that Enjoyment is "with
wide wings / Advancing." The questioner, unable to leave his "mill"
(the habits of years?), was only "brushed" as Enjoyment flew past him.

THE INTERLOPER in the manuscript was titled "One Who Ought
Not to be There." " 'The interloper' was the threat of madness which
hung over Hardy's first wife, at St. Juliot, Sturminster Newton, &c."[1]
That Emma Hardy was threatened with madness has been so hinted,
implied, and openly stated in various studies of Hardy,[2] that it seems
justifiable in connection with "The Interloper" to examine the avail-
able evidence.

Hardy's implication that Emma suffered from periods of in-
sanity is reported in V. H. Collins's *Talks with Thomas Hardy*. On
December 27, 1920, Collins talked with Hardy and his wife Florence
about "The Interloper," as follows:

"C: What is 'that under which best lives corrode'?—H: Madness.
—C: In each case?—H: Yes. I knew the family.— Mrs. H: I always
thought the poem was obscure.—H [*reads it*]: Certainly it is not clear.
No one could possibly guess.—C: I asked several people, and they were
all puzzled. One of my colleagues, Mr. Williams—himself a poet—
suggested that it was no definite thing, but a sort of undermining rot
which destroys everything.—H: That was a remarkably good guess. He
got as near it as one possibly could. [*He reads the poem again, over
C's shoulder.*] Write down 'Insanity'; that is a better word than 'Mad-
ness.' I wonder how I could make it clear." (P. 25.) A little later
Collins had a conversation with Mrs. Florence Hardy, of which he
wrote: "She [Florence] then told me that . . . She [Emma] came from
a tainted stock. More than one of her relatives had been in a lunatic
asylum. She herself was subject at times to delusions. She would then
make the wildest accusations against anyone, including her husband.
'As his secretary I had, of course, experience of these fits. Life with
her at such times was almost unbearable. Yet she kept to the end
a strange lovableness,——a gay, inconsequent, childlike charm.' "[3] Mrs.

Florence Hardy had written similarly to Rebekah Owen. A letter of October 24, 1915, says that at the time of Hardy's courtship of Emma "Her [Emma's] father . . . was a bankrupt . . . another brother had shown signs of insanity—and another was bringing the whole family into disgrace."[4] Emma's mental instability was known to members of the Gifford family. In a letter to Hardy on November 25, 1914, Kate Gifford wrote: "Cousin Emma and I met at my Brother's at Black-heath not long before her death, & I was so glad to see her again. . . . It must have been very sad for you that her mind became so un-balanced latterly."[5] Subsequent to these statements, in the 1923 edi-tion of *Collected Poems* Hardy added the motto: "And I saw the figure and visage of Madness seeking for a home."

On the other hand, Emma Hardy did not seem insane to most acquaintances. The "figure and visage of Madness" was apparently more a threat manifested in occasional delusions than recognizable in-sanity. A memorandum book labelled "Some Words on the Hardys by Irene Cooper Willis" contains the statement: "ELG was not a stupid woman, but H said: She was quaint, in her inconsequence & had a certain charm from that."[6] Later Miss Willis examined the letters in the Dorset County Museum, to and from Emma Hardy, and appended to them a note dated February, 1938. It says: "These letters appear to me to dispose of the idea that Mrs. Hardy No. 1 was 'mad' —as Mrs. Hardy No. 2 so often declared. The truth was, I think, that Miss Dugdale, afterwards the second Mrs. Hardy, got to know T. H. through the first Mrs. Hardy, & evidently, as these letters show, flat-tered her powers of writing, & was grateful for her friendship. When T. H. became fond of Miss Dugdale, Mrs. Hardy No. 1 probably be-came very jealous & may have shown her jealousy by unusual be-haviour. . . . This *can* be the only explanation of the 'madness'. . . . Apart from one or two 'bees in her bonnet,' on cruelty to animals and Romish practices in the Church of England, the whole correspondence of the first Mrs. H., of which this file is a selection, goes to disprove the notion."[7] Since Hardy and his executors destroyed many papers, no more definite evidence is available.

The first stanza of "The Interloper" seems to describe an incident during Hardy's courtship of Emma in Cornwall. The occasion may be that stated in his journal for March 9, 1870: "Drove with Mrs. Holder and Miss Gifford to Boscastle, and on to Tintagel and Penpethy slate-quarries, with a view to the church roofing."[8] (Perhaps the poem "The Man with a Past" refers to this incident.) Then the "I" of the stanza is Hardy in two aspects, as one of the "three folk" in the chaise and as his memory looking back on the scene. Another possibility is that Hardy was not one of the three in the chaise. Evelyn Hardy and Gittings quote from Emma's *Some Recollections*: "In the intervals of his [Hardy's] visits we corresponded, and I . . . drove my brother-in-law and my sister in the basket-carriage to the nearest market town Camelford nine miles off, or to Launceston to see my cousins." On this basis, they surmise that "it is at least likely that Emma's companions were her sister and brother-in-law." (Pp. 58 and 79.) In either case, the stanza suggests that Hardy, before he married Emma, had some intimations of her tendency toward delusions, but at that time possibly considered them merely an odd, interesting way of looking at things.

The second stanza seems to treat an otherwise unrecorded scene at Sturminster Newton in 1876-78. (See the notes on "Overlooking the River Stour.") The third stanza evidently treats a scene described in "At a Fashionable Dinner." This poem, picturing a gruesome fancy, comes close to defining the nature of Emma's delusions.[9] The fourth stanza seems to describe the scene of a tea on the lawn at Max Gate, where Emma was "mirthless" among her guests.[10] Her odd behavior may be that suggested in the poem "You Were the Sort that Men Forget." The fifth stanza adds no new scene, but rules out Death as the interloper, and by an allusion to "the Fourth Figure the Furnace showed," rules out Christ.[11]

Besides the poems mentioned above, "The Division," "Near Lanivet, 1872," and "The Change" seem to refer to Emma's delusions.

1. Purdy, *Thomas Hardy: A Bibliographical Study*, p. 200.
2. See, for instance, Evelyn Hardy, *Thomas Hardy*, pp. 272-73.
3. In a letter to Carl Weber, September 13, 1943, now in the Colby College Library.
4. In the Colby College Library. Some jealousy is possible in this outpouring. The "Poems of 1912-13" may not have been pleasant to Florence Hardy as the young second wife of a somewhat exacting husband who, seventy-five years old in 1915, persisted in idealizing his first wife.
5. In the Dorset County Museum.
6. In the Dorset County Museum.
7. In the Dorset County Museum.
8. *Early Life*, p. 98; *Life*, p. 75.
9. That "At a Fashionable Dinner" was published next to "Green Slates," which treats a trip to Penpethy, suggests that the first stanza of "The Interloper" treats the trip to Penpethy on March 9, 1870, as mentioned above.
10. Hardy may have seemed to her overly attentive to feminine guests.
11. Dan. 4:25, reads: "Lo, I see four men loose, walking in the midst of the fire, and they have no hurt; and the form of the fourth is like the Son of God."

LOGS ON THE HEARTH, written in December of 1915, presents a memory of Hardy's sister Mary, who had died on November 24. Mary, born on December 23, 1841, was only a year and a half younger than Hardy. According to the poem, it was a memory precious to him that as children they had climbed the Bockhampton apple trees together. In the symbolism of logs slowly burning, he meditates the slowly devouring fires of life that have taken her first.

THE SUNSHADE is set at Swanage Cliffs, just north of the seaside town of Swanage, about twenty-five miles southeast of Dorchester. It is on a semicircular bay, built up on the southern and western sides along a road, esplanade, and sandy beach, but on the northern side the beach rises into steep cliffs. Perhaps the sunshade was found near the cliff called Ballard Point. Lovers might stray up the slopes of the cliff and forget a sunshade left in "the hard rock's chink."

In July of 1875, Hardy and his bride Emma "went . . . by steamer to Swanage, where they found lodgings at the house of an invalided captain of smacks and ketches; and Hardy . . . settled down there for the autumn and winter to finish *The Hand of Ethelberta*. . . . While here at Swanage they walked daily on the cliffs and shore."[1] In June of 1916, Hardy motored to Swanage,[2] and possibly at this time found the sunshade someone lost there perhaps twenty years before.

1. *Early Life*, pp. 141, 142; *Life*, pp. 107, 108. In Swanage the Hardys' lodging was at West End Cottage.
2. *Later Years*, p. 172; *Life*, p. 373.

THE AGEING HOUSE describes Hardy's home, Max Gate, which he had built of red brick in 1884-85, and around which he had planted thousands of small trees. As the years passed, the walls were hidden in ivy and other climbing vegetation.

THE CAGED GOLDFINCH as originally published in *Moments of Vision* had a third stanza that explained the bird as placed on the grave of a false lover by a woman who then killed herself. In Hynes's opinion, the first version was "simply another of Hardy's dreary little tragedies of false lovers," greatly improved when the explanatory stanza was omitted.[1] As it stands, the poem suggests a theme Hardy deeply felt, compassion for caged birds. At his death, Hardy left a hundred pounds to be used for "condemnatory action against the caging of wild birds."[2]

The poem is ironic. The goldfinch is left to starve in a churchyard, with no thought that Christianity is a religion of compassion. Perhaps the person who left the bird there thought the act one of devotion to the dead who loved the bird; in Hardy's view, it was heartless. The poem recalls the caged goldfinch of *The Mayor of Casterbridge* that Henchard thoughtlessly left to starve. (Chapter XLV.)

1. *The Pattern of Hardy's Poetry*, p. 144.
2. Cox, ed., *Thomas Hardy's Will*, p. 2.

[389]

AT MADAME TUSSAUD'S IN VICTORIAN YEARS was in the manuscript titled "At Madame Tussaud's and Later."[1] The poem may have been suggested to Hardy by a booklet in his library, W. Wheeler's illustrated *Catalogue of Napoleonic Relics Pictures and Other Works of Art & Curiosities: Madame Tussaud & Sons' Exhibition*. The Booklet is dated by an inserted notice that reads: "Her Gracious Majesty Queen Victoria, to the grief of all her subjects, passed away just as the pages of this Catalogue were printed." Possibly Hardy, working on *The Dynasts*, acquired the *Catalogue* to examine its pictures of Napoleonic relics. It may have recalled an early visit to Madame Tussaud's waxworks and a curious legend he had heard.

Madame Marie Tussaud (1760-1850), after modelling a number of important people in France, was invited to Versailles in the 1780's as art tutor for Madame Elizabeth. In 1792, during the Revolution, she was imprisoned on a charge of Royalist sympathies. In 1802 she secured permission from Napoleon to bring her collection of wax figures from the Palais Royal to England. She toured England, Scotland, and Ireland for thirty-three years before, in 1835, she established her waxworks in Baker Street, London. Visitors to the waxworks were entertained by an orchestra, replaced before the end of the century by an electric organ.

Madame Tussaud believed that the Dauphin of France, "Louis XVII," son of Louis XVI, had not died in May of 1795 as reported, but had escaped to live in obscurity, and that the "first fiddler" of her orchestra, who was called Mèves, was the dauphin in disguise. A letter to Mrs. Hutton of Bennetts Hill, near Birmingham, England, on August 8, 1839, written by J. Tussaud but also signed by Madame Tussaud, says of a book sent to her about the Duc De Normandie (the dauphin's title) that it came "we have every reason to think from the Dauphin himself. She is of opinion he may still be in existence, for although there was a report of his death . . . still it was strongly suspected it was not the real Dauphin, but she never saw him after having left the Palace of Versailles previous to the Revolution breaking out, but it was said he was poisoned in the Temple, but whether it was true or not, is quite a mystery up to the present time."[2]

Other evidence of Madame Tussaud's belief is found in "The Secrets of London: Queer Facts about Madame Tussaud's," in *Answers*, December 1, 1888. Speaking of Mèves, the article says: "Madame Tussaud . . . testified repeatedly to the fact that the pretender had on his body identical physical marks with those on the person of the Dauphin," whom she had nursed in France.

In Victorian years, visitors were taken through "the greater galleries under the kindly guidance of Mr. John Tussaud." Possibly Hardy took this tour in the 1860's or later, remembered it when he read the illustrated *Catalogue* and then wrote the poem.

In the poem the fiddler is "watched by kings, councillors, and queens," who are waxen figures, but the phrasing suggests the story of the dauphin. The final stanza is Hardy's reminiscent comment.

Fittingly, a waxen figure of Hardy has been, since the spring of 1928, one of the exhibits at Madame Tussaud's.

1. Purdy, *Thomas Hardy: A Bibliographical Study*, p. 201.
2. A photostat of this letter, together with other information given here, was sent to me by Mrs. P. F. Chapman, Records and Archives, Madame Tussaud's Ltd. The letter is evasive, as it would be if Mèves did not wish to be identified.

THE BALLET presents Hardy's reflection upon the identity of the individual "underneath" the action of a group; even in the ensemble action of a ballet, each girl in a "one-pulsed chain" lives essentially within her own mind and heart. This thought appears often in *The Dynasts*, where distant armies seen as crawling worms are then shown close-up as separate struggling individuals.

THE FIVE STUDENTS presents a problem in the identities of the students, about which scholars and commentators are not agreed. I propose that the five, in the order of the first stanza, may be Horace Moule ("dark He," died 1873), T. W. Hooper Tolbort ("fair He," died 1883), Tryphena Sparks ("dark She," died 1890), Mrs. Emma Hardy ("fair She," died 1912), and Hardy.

The five were not students enrolled in a university; the four others were simply friends of Hardy's youthtime, eager to understand life and its experiences, and hopeful of the future. One by one in the course of the poem, all except Hardy die without realizing their hopes.

It is clear from *The Later Years* that the "dark He" is Horace Moule. In May of 1920, C. W. Moule, writing about some verses he had sent to Hardy, spoke of a letter from him "in which you told me that dear Horace was one of 'The Five Students.'"[1] In the poem, Moule, authentically a student and Hardy's friend and mentor, is the first to die.

The second to die, according to the third stanza, is the "dark She," Tryphena Sparks, the "lost prize" of Hardy's youth. She was a student at Stockwell Training College and later a schoolmistress, and she had dark eyes and hair. In "The Wind's Prophecy," Hardy contrasts her "ebon loops" with Emma Gifford's "tresses flashing fair."[2] If the identifications above are right, Tryphena was not the second but the third to die, in 1890, later than "fair He," Tolbort, in 1883. Possibly

Hardy considered Tryphena as if dead after his last sight of her in the early 1870's, or after he had married Emma Gifford and she had married Charles Gale.[3]

The third to die, according to the fourth stanza, is the "fair He," who may be T. W. Hooper Tolbort. *The Early Life* says of him: "During the years of architectural pupillage Hardy had two other literary friends in Dorchester. One was Hooper Tolbort . . . who had an extraordinary facility in the acquisition of languages. He was a pupil of the Rev. W. Barnes, and was preparing for the Indian Civil Service. The other was Horace Moule."[4] Tolbort went to India and achieved distinction as Commissioner of Umballa in the Bengal Civil Service. When he died in 1883, Hardy wrote an obituary notice in the *Dorset County Chronicle*. He said that Tolbort's circumstances "left him much spare time, which he devoted entirely to study. I distinctly remember . . . his marvellous passion for the acquisition of languages, and how he was to be discovered poring over grammars at all hours and seasons."[5] Hardy repeated this idea in his journal for August 13, 1883: "Tolbort lived and studied as if everything in the world were so very much worth while. But what a bright mind has gone out at one-and-forty."[6]

Commentators are generally agreed that the "fair She" who dies to leave the poet alone is Emma Hardy, to be considered a "student" with Hardy in the days of his courtship when she encouraged his literary ambitions and loyally copied his manuscripts. After her death in 1912, Hardy's memory went back to these years.

The theme of the poem, that the conditions of life and the fact of death defeat the students one by one, is developed in a pattern of downward steps, from high hope to hopelessness. Their effort weakens stanza by stanza, from "strenuously," to "urgent," to "forward still," to "on the beat," to the mechanical "stalk." The seasons follow one another from spring, through summer, through autumn, to winter. Even the time of day follows the pattern of dawn, noon, evening, and night.[7]

1. Pp. 211-12; *Life*, p. 405.

2. See the portrait of Tryphena in Deacon, *Tryphena and Thomas Hardy*, frontispiece.

3. Scholars are not agreed that the "dark She" is Tryphena. Frank Pinion considers Mrs. Helen Gifford Holder, Emma Hardy's sister, as the "dark She," on the basis that in *Some Recollections* Emma wrote "My sister and I were very noticeable, she dark and I fair." *A Hardy Companion*, p. 370. Evelyn Hardy and Gittings agree with this identification; see their edition of *Some Recollections*, p. 36. I have seen no evidence that Hardy considered Mrs. Holder a "student." She was simply the friendly sister of his betrothed. Also, as far as dates are guides, Mrs. Holder died in 1900, ten years later than Tryphena.

4. Pp. 42-43; *Life*, p. 32.
5. Issue of August 16, 1883; see Orel, *Thomas Hardy's Personal Writings*, p. 255.
6. *Early Life*, p. 211; *Life*, p. 162.
7. The manuscript has two additional stanzas that take the action into the "Pale Land" of the next world. These stanzas are printed by Purdy, *Thomas Hardy: A Bibliographical Study*, p. 201. For analyses of imagery and rhythm, see Hynes, *The Pattern of Hardy's Poetry*, p. 53; Kennedy, *An Introduction to Poetry*, pp. 155-56; and Lewis, "The Lyrical Poetry of Thomas Hardy," p. 169.

THE WIND'S PROPHECY treats Hardy's "first journey into Cornwall and the drive from Launceston to St. Juliot (7 March 1870)."[1] The railroad into Cornwall ended at Launceston, and Hardy had to proceed to St. Juliot in a horse-drawn vehicle, a "dreary yet poetical drive over the hills."[2]

At this time Hardy was engaged to Tryphena Sparks, then a student at Stockwell Training College in London, and he was on his way to his first meeting with Emma Gifford. Within the poem, the first four lines of each stanza describe the landscape of Cornwall in his gradual approach to St. Juliot; the stanzas proceed from the "barren farms" toward "lofty coastlands" and to the "headland" near Emma's home. The last four lines of each stanza present a debate between the poet, preoccupied with visions of Tryphena, and the prophecy of the wind. Though the poem was completed after Hardy had married Emma, the prophecy need not be considered entirely imaginary. On his first journey into the picturesque land that he later called Lyonnesse, Hardy may have felt some anticipation of romantic adventure. In contrast with both dreams of Tryphena and his memory (at the time he completed the poem) of his life with Emma, the wind's prophecy is one of ironic foreboding; the wind "outshrieks" and at last "laughs . . . as if it grinned." The suggestion is one of fatality. A companion poem, "A Man Was Drawing Near to Me," presents Emma's similar premonitions as Hardy approaches.

1. Purdy, *Thomas Hardy: A Bibliographical Study*, p. 201.
2. *Early Life*, p. 98; *Life*, p. 74.

DURING WIND AND RAIN, Evelyn Hardy and Gittings have shown, presents Hardy's imaginative development of scenes in Emma Gifford's girlhood as they are described in Mrs. Hardy's *Some Recollections*.[1]

The poem is laid in Plymouth, where the Gifford family lived during Emma's girlhood. The scenes of the first three stanzas are at "number nine [?] Sussex Street, very near the Hoe."[2] The first stanza is drawn from Emma's memory of family singing: "My Father played the violin and my mother could play beautifully on the piano and sing like a professional. Her musical abilities were much enjoyed by us all as we stood round her piano to hear the Battle of Prague—

Mary Queen of My Soul, and pieces and songs then in vogue. They taught us to sing harmony and our four voices went well together. . . . We sang rounds, such as 'See our Oars with feathered Spray' and 'Wisdom is better than silver or gold,' etc."

The second and third stanzas are laid in the garden. Such details as the "Elders," the "shady seat," the "summer tree," the "glimpse of the bay," and the "pet fowl" are drawn from the following passages: "This garden had fine fruit trees in full bearing, besides a large kitchen garden and many flower beds. An unusual possession for a house in a street was a magnificent Elm tree of great age and girth showing itself high above the houses. . . . Underneath the tree were on each side of it long garden seats with long tables and a circular seat encircling it, nothing could have been better arranged by our elders, a most delightful spot it was for happy childhood. . . . At one end of our garden we had a poultry-house put up, and a choice selection of poultry was bought, for there was a mania at that time for keeping handsome fowls . . . we loved and admired them all . . . at the top of the large garden . . . rose trees had used to flourish named by me Rosewood . . . often as my sister and I lay in bed with the blinds up moonlight nights we could see the fishing-boats." Hardy's "white storm-birds" were perhaps suggested by Emma's mention of a much later scene in Tintagel, of "the winter waves and foam reaching hundreds of feet up the stern, strong dark rocks with the fantastic revellings of the gulls, puffins and rooks, jackdaws, in attendance, 'black souls and white,' sometimes called." The "rotten rose" was "ript from the wall" in after years when, Emma reported, a street was run through "our old garden."

The "high new house" of the fourth stanza is "Bedford Terrace, North Road [Tavistock Road] . . . our next pleasant home. It was a fine Terrace with handsome houses and flights of steps, a stone front parade with the houses all standing high above the wide terrace." The rain may have been suggested by frequent mentions of bad weather in *Some Recollections*, as when the family moved to Bodmin: "The heavens poured down a steady torrent on our farewells, and never did so watery an omen portend such dullness, and sadnesses and sorrows as this did for us." The furniture on the lawn all day seems imaginatively developed from mention of the move to Bodmin: the family's "brightest things" would have been spoiled in the rain. That, when years have passed, the rain-drop "ploughs" down the "carved names" on tombstones may represent a fact in Hardy's experience. Though Emma evidently visited Plymouth in 1886 (an album labelled "Sketches" contains her water-color dated "Plymouth

Hoe 1886"),[3] Hardy did not go with her. After her death, when he had read *Some Recollections,* he made the trip. Hermann Lea recorded, without a date: "Another memorable outing was when we went to Plymouth. Mr. Hardy's motive in going was to renew his recollection of Plymouth and its surroundings, to visit some relatives of the late Mrs. Hardy's and to identify the tombs of some of those of the family buried there."[4] Perhaps Hardy viewed the Gifford tombstones during a rain. The poem is not dated, but in theme and verbal echoes it is a companion poem to "The Change," which is dated *"Jan.-Feb.* 1913."

"During Wind and Rain" develops the theme of mutability, of happiness and hope that pass away. Each stanza presents a double vision, of Emma's happy girlhood and of the poet's meditation upon the wreckage the years have brought. Each meditation is sharply symbolized in the images of "sick leaves," "storm-birds," "rotten rose," and rain. The stanzas are arranged in a seasonal structure: an indoor scene in winter, a gardening scene in spring, an outdoor breakfast in summer, and perhaps two moves, to a "high new house" and to Bodmin in the rain.[5]

1. See especially pp. 66-68. The notes here are indebted to this analysis.
2. Ibid., p. 5. Brackets enclose Hardy's insertions. The following passages are from pp. 14, 15, 30, 31, 32, 34, 42.
3. In the Dorset County Museum.
4. In Cox, ed., *Thomas Hardy Through the Camera's Eye,* p. 36.
5. The poem has been repeatedly analyzed. See Hynes, *The Pattern of Hardy's Poetry,* pp. 121-23; Gross, *Sound and Form in Modern Poetry,* pp. 46-48; Brown, *Thomas Hardy,* pp. 147-52; and Kreuzer, *Elements of Poetry,* pp. 162-64.

HE PREFERS HER EARTHLY was titled in the manuscript "He Prefers the Earthly."[1] The poem seems to be Hardy's meditation about his dead wife Emma in the light of her theories of immortality.[2] The "chasm of splendour" suggests some romantic concept of the soul as absorbed into an Oversoul, as pictured in Lyric CXXX of *In Memoriam,* in which Tennyson says of his dead friend: "Thy voice is on the rolling air; / I hear thee where the waters run; / Thou standest in the rising sun, / And in the setting thou art fair." Hardy finds it unsatisfactory to imagine Emma (if the "fond and fragile creature" of the poem is the physically vigorous girl he had courted in Cornwall) as "a firmament-riding earthless essence."

1. Purdy, *Thomas Hardy: A Bibliographical Study,* p. 201.
2. See her "Spaces" in *Poems and Religious Effusions,* pp. 15-17.

THE DOLLS presents an amused reflection upon the gallantries of the soldiers stationed in the military barracks in Dorchester. The poem suggests a soldier like Sergeant Troy of *Far from the Madding Crowd*.

MOLLY GONE seems a reminiscence of Hardy's companionship with his sister Mary when he was a boy. Toward the end of her life in 1915 Mary had lived at Talbothays[1] with her brother Henry and her sister Kate.

The plantings "Where the beds used to be" may refer to flower-gardening at Hardy's birthplace. The places to which he and "Molly" went on their jauntings are within strenuous walking or bicycling distance from Dorchester. The "town by the sea" is Weymouth, about seven miles to the south. Whitesheet and Winyard's ("Wynyard's") gap lie to the northwest. From these places one may see Montacute Crest, about eight miles north of Winyard's Gap. It is a conical hilltop near Montacute, a village about four miles west of Yeovil. Sedgmoor is far to the north. "Corton's far-distant cap" is Corton Beacon, 645 feet high, about five miles north of Sherborne. Pilsdon and Lewsdon are hills near Beaminster, to the west and slightly north of Dorchester.

1. The phrase "her home" in the last stanza suggests a memory of Molly at Talbothays. This farm about three miles southwest of Dorchester on the road past West Stafford is not to be confused with the dairy of this name in *Tess of the D'Urbervilles*.

A BACKWARD SPRING presents Hardy's observation of trees and flowers. He attributes to some of them emotions like fear and timidity in the face of hostile weather, though the aggressive snowdrop and primrose blossom promptly with no apparent "gloom."

LOOKING ACROSS expressed Hardy's feeling after the death of his sister Mary. He wrote in his journal for November 29, 1915: "Buried her under the yew-tree where the rest of us lie. As Mr. Cowley read the words of the psalm 'Dixi Custodiam' they reminded me strongly of her nature, particularly when she was young: 'I held my tongue and spake nothing: I kept silence, yea, even from good words.' That was my poor Mary exactly. She never defended herself; and that not from timidity, but indifference to opinion." Writing again on December 31, 1917, he related Mary's death to the poem: "Went to bed at eleven. East wind. No bells heard. Slept in the New Year, as did also those 'out there.'" The biography comments: "This refers to the poem 'Looking Across' . . . Stinsford Churchyard lying across the mead from Max Gate."[1] The mead is the valley of the River Frome.

Mary was buried near Hardy's father, who died in 1892; his

mother, who died in 1904; and his first wife, Emma, who died in 1912, the One, Two, and Three of the poem. Mary is Four, and Hardy himself is Five. References to a dark sky, a dawn "not nigh," silence in which one hears the Frome waters "sigh," and the dropping wind suggest that "Looking Across" is the fruit of a sleepless night.

1. *The Later Years*, pp. 170, 179-80; *Life*, pp. 371, 379.

AT A SEASIDE TOWN IN 1869 is set in Weymouth during the time Hardy (the "young lover" of the poem) was employed by the architect G. R. Crickmay. At this time he had begun work on his first novel to be published, *Desperate Remedies*. *The Early Life* says: "Hardy considered this brief occupation would afford . . . breathing time while he should ruminate on what it was best to do about the writing of the novels. . . . He used to remember that after coming away from the interview with Crickmay . . . he stood opposite the Burdon Hotel on the Esplanade, facing the beautiful sun-lit bay, and listened to the Town band's performance of a set of charming new waltzes by Johann Strauss. He inquired their name, and found that it was the 'Morgenblätter.' The verses 'At a Seaside Town' must refer in their background to this place at this time and a little onward. . . . He now became regularly resident at Weymouth, and took lodgings there, rowing in the Bay almost every evening of this summer, and bathing at seven in the morning either on the pebble-beach towards Preston, or diving off from a boat."[1] He also enlisted in a dancing class "where a good deal of flirtation went on."

Hardy was engaged to Tryphena Sparks, who was then a student at Stockwell Training College in London. "At a Seaside Town" and other poems suggest that he was not entirely whole-hearted in his love for her.[2]

The poem treats Hardy's inner struggle whether to yield himself to the distractions of the town or to withdraw into a dream-world in which his vision of a well-beloved would satisfy all emotional needs. The distractions listed in the poem are alluring. Weymouth Bay is colorfully alive with boats; a sandy beach stretching for more than a mile along the Esplanade is thronged with bathers and sightseers; the chalk cliffs gleam in the evening sunlight; picturesque sea-salts offer adventurous tales. The conclusion suggests that the dream of a distant well-beloved was not enough.

The well-beloved may be simply Tryphena Sparks. Possibly she is wholly or in part a symbol for Hardy's resolve to write his novel, temporarily defeated by the distractions of the town. In February, 1870, "Hardy gave up his rooms at Weymouth and returned to his rural home to be able to concentrate more particularly on the MS. than he could do in a lively town."[3]

1. P. 84; *Life*, pp. 63-64.
2. See Deacon and Coleman, *Providence and Mr Hardy*, pp. 76-78.
3. *Early Life*, p. 85; *Life*, p. 64.

THE GLIMPSE tells of the narrator's falling in love with the ghost of a "maid with red hair," buying the house she haunts, and waiting vainly for her to come again. She may be Sarah Fletcher, who hanged herself in 1799 in the village of Clifton Hampden, about two miles from Dorchester, Oxfordshire, and was buried in Dorchester Abbey. This Dorchester is about seven miles southeast of Oxford.

Hardy was in Oxford in 1893[1] and at various later times. Possibly he visited this Dorchester and its Abbey and read on a slab in the south aisle a lengthy tribute to Sarah's "artless Beauty, Innocence of Mind," gentle manners, youth, and soul denied peace on earth. He could have learned more of this red-haired beauty whose ghost is said to appear in black velvet and to lure all men who see her to fall in love with her.[2]

1. *Later Years*, p. 22; *Life*, p. 257.
2. Mrs. Barbara Denness of Ipswich, Suffolk, sent me this suggestion of Hardy's possible inspiration for "The Glimpse." The full story is told in Christina Hole's *Haunted England*, Batsford, 1940 and 1950.

THE PEDESTRIAN describes an incident that took place on "Coll-Hill near Wimborne."[1] Wimborne is an ancient ecclesiastical center and market town about twenty-five miles northeast of Dorchester. Hardy lived in Wimborne from June 25, 1881, until he moved to Dorchester in June of 1883. Presumably the incident of the poem occurred during an evening drive he took across the heath in his phaeton, whose lamps shone down upon the pedestrian's face, whose language and learning suggest that he may have been a master or a lecturer in the school connected with the Minster in Wimborne.

The date of publication in *Moments of Vision*, 1917, suggests that the poem was not written at the date given for the incident. A letter of Mrs. Florence Hardy to Alda, Lady Hoare on November 27, 1915, says: "We are reading some extraordinary letters lent to us by my husband's great friend Sydney Cockerell . . . written by a man dying of consumption, madly in love with a horrible wife who is unfaithful to him."[2] Though these letters may have nothing to do with Hardy's pedestrian, the "man dying of consumption" may have recalled an incident of 1883 to his mind.

1. Purdy, *Thomas Hardy: A Bibliographical Study*, p. 202. "Coll-Hill," about a mile northeast of Wimborne, is variously spelled as "Colehill" and "Colt Hill" on maps.
2. In the Stourhead Collection, County Archives in Trowbridge, Wiltshire.

"WHO'S IN THE NEXT ROOM?" was identified by Hardy as a scene at Max Gate.[1] It is not likely that the speakers are Hardy and his wife Florence, who would hardly assure him that the "figure wan" (presumably death) is nearby. The poem seems an eerie dialogue between Hardy's feeling of dread and his reason.

1. Purdy, *Thomas Hardy: A Bibliographical Study*, p. 202.

AT A COUNTRY FAIR was based on a fact. Hardy's notebook labelled "Facts" (items from newspapers) contains this note: "*Blind Giant.*—His dimensions had attracted cupidity of an exhibitor, who had barely allowed him necessaries & kept him a sort of prisoner. Age 19."[1]

The poem suggests a significance deeper than the observed fact: the "dominance of cunning over helpless innocence."[2] *The Dynasts* echoes this idea: "The pale pathetic peoples still plod on / Through hoodwinkings to light" (Part III, IV, iv), in which the peoples, like the giant, are "unaware" that they hold all power. Hardy's "The Pity of It" finds the "kin folk kin tongued" of World War I blindly led to mutual slaughter by "gangs whose glory threats and slaughters are."

1. In the Dorset County Museum. No particular fair is named.
2. Bowra, "The Lyrical Poetry of Thomas Hardy," p. 235.

THE MEMORIAL BRASS: 186— reflects Hardy's architectural experience. The "mere student sketching the mediaeval" may be Hardy. In the 1860's he was an architectural assistant for John Hicks of Dorchester, Arthur Blomfield of London, and G. R. Crickmay of Weymouth, all engaged in repairing churches. He sketched architectural features of churches in scattered parts of the country. (See his sketches of "the mediaeval" in Beatty, ed., *The Architectural Notebook of Thomas Hardy*.) The story told in the poem may be a fiction based upon facts similar to those underlying "The Inscription."

HER LOVE-BIRDS is a retrospective narrative that seems to be spoken by Tryphena Sparks and to treat a crisis in Hardy's life. Deacon and Coleman, citing a letter from Tryphena's daughter, Mrs. Nellie Bromell, to Lois Deacon, dated January 18, 1960, say that Tryphena had a cage of love-birds. After her marriage to Charles Gale, the birds were the source of a quarrel with Charles's sister Minnie, who disliked the birds and "threw the cage across the room." Deacon and Coleman interpret "Her Love-Birds" as the story of Hardy's breaking his engagement to Tryphena in order to marry Emma Gifford. Inferences from the poem itself (and other poems) are reasonably convincing.[1]

Though the poem does not say that the "speech that chilled the love-birds" is a broken engagement, the phrase "broken words" is suggestive. Presumably, the meeting took place in Plymouth, where after Christmas of 1871 Tryphena was headmistress of the Public Free School. In speaking of the "long journey citywards," the poem suggests the journey from St. Juliot to Plymouth. It is relevant that Sue Bridehead in *Jude the Obscure* kept a pair of pet pigeons.[2]

1. See *Providence and Mr Hardy*, pp. 47, 82-83.
2. Hardy's preface to *Jude* makes it clear that Sue is partly based on Tryphena. Emma Gifford had no love-birds; like Hardy, she disliked the idea of caging birds. As Miss Deacon said to me, "Emma's specialty was cats."

PAYING CALLS was first published in *Selected Poems* in October, 1916. In "called upon some friends" the poem exhibits Hardy's attitude toward the dead. At his funeral service, the vicar at Stinsford, Mr. Cowley, told "how Hardy used to gather buttercups and daisies and cowslips and put them on the grave of his wife and other kin in the churchyard,"[1] more as a pleasure than as a formal tribute. He would sometimes lead guests to Stinsford Churchyard and tell them stories of the people buried there.

The ballad-like meter of "Paying Calls" helps to domesticate death. Its tone is convivial rather than macabre; it is even humorous in the surprise of the last line. The poem has been set to music by Gerald Finzi in *By Footpath and Stile* (London: Curwen, 1925).

1. *Daily Mail*, January 16, 1928.

THE UPPER BIRCH-LEAVES in the manuscript was titled "The Upper Leaves."[1] This poem presents a thought typical of Hardy, the unity of all life in that all life dies. He felt himself in 1917 to be in his "November."

1. Purdy, *Thomas Hardy: A Bibliographical Study*, p. 202.

"IT NEVER LOOKS LIKE SUMMER" was written when Hardy journeyed to Cornwall to revisit the scenes of his courtship of Emma Gifford. The quoted lines that open the poem were spoken by Emma when she and Hardy were on Beeny Cliff in the rain on August 22, 1870. (See the notes on "The Figure in the Scene.") The poem has been set to music by Gerald Finzi in *Till Earth Outwears* (London and New York: Boosey and Hawkes, 1958).

EVERYTHING COMES depicts Hardy's home, Max Gate.[1] The Hardys moved into this house on June 29, 1885. It was a square-turreted house of red brick, more substantial than handsome.[2] It stood on an elevation surrounded by bare fields, with a clump of trees on Conquer Barrow in the distance. Hardy built the house for his wife Emma, but she found it bleak, cold, windy, and open to peering eyes, and so he immediately labored to provide privacy. *The Early Life* says: "Some two or three thousand small trees, mostly Austrian pines, were planted around the house by Hardy himself, and in later years these grew so thickly that the house was almost entirely screened from the road."[3]

According to the poem, Emma was both pleased with his effort and unhappy that the "grove" was slow in growing.[4] The title suggests the proverb "Everything comes to him who waits," but death did not allow Emma to wait.

1. Purdy, *Thomas Hardy: A Bibliographical Study*, p. 202.
2. See a photograph facing p. 226 of *Early Life*.
3. Pp. 226-27; *Life*, p. 173.
4. The grown trees displeased his second wife. " 'This place,' wrote Florence Hardy in 1920, 'is too depressing for words in the winter, when the dead leaves stick on the window-pane and the wind moans and the sky is grey and you can't even see as far as the high road.' " Weber, *Hardy of Wessex*, 2nd ed., p. 143.

THE MAN WITH A PAST offers Hardy's explanation of "why and how / Two lives were so," apparently his life and that of his first wife Emma. The first of the "blows" of the poem seems to be Emma's mental instability, observed as early as in the "merry-making" of Hardy's courtship, then discounted, but later "fully bared." (See the notes on "The Interloper.") The second may be their drift into discord, each innocent of any intention, until it became "wry" in the 1890's. The third was Emma's death in 1912. For the blow that fell on the poet, Hardy may have had in mind either the discord of their later years together or, none the less, Emma's death.[1]

1. Deacon and Coleman relate the poem to Hardy's love for Tryphena Sparks. In this interpretation, the first blow was discovery of a relationship too close to permit a marriage; the second would be the birth of an unwanted child; and the third, their separation. See *Providence and Mr Hardy*, pp. 206-7.

HE FEARS HIS GOOD FORTUNE is Hardy's self-analysis as, now an old man, he looks back over his life. The "glorious time" may be that of the poem "In the Seventies," the years of joyful creation in *Under the Greenwood Tree*, mounting fame with *Far from the Madding Crowd*, and marriage to Emma of "Lyonnesse." Even then, the poem says, the feeling that had engendered the "Crass Casualty" and "dicing Time" of "Hap" whispered to be wary. At some time not specified, certainly by the time of *Jude the Obscure*, the turn came. His powers were as great as ever, but he lost zest and developed the resignation that he calls "serene." The poem does not specify the "end foreseen" that had come; it perhaps included the death of Emma, World War I, and Hardy's sense that he was manipulated by forces that negated will or effort.

The poem analyzes a particular mood. To the end of his days, Hardy preserved a good deal of gaiety; whether or not for fame, he wrote long past the usual age for retirement.

HE WONDERS ABOUT HIMSELF is one of Hardy's statements about freedom of the will. The date 1893 suggests his growing sense that man is a puppet in the hands of the Immanent Will. The first two stanzas develop this idea with concreteness and humor. The third stanza rebels against automatism on a basis he stated in a letter to Edward Wright: "Whenever it happens that all the rest of the Great Will is in equilibrium the minute portion called one person's will is free."[1] The individual, by exercising his "minute portion" of the Will to fulfil a "fair desire," may influence the Will. Though the individual may be relatively less than a grain of sand on the seashore, he is that much within the great Will, and the beach is made of grains of sand. This reasoning is the basis for Hardy's evolutionary meliorism in *The Dynasts*.

He debated the question all through *The Dynasts*, beginning with the Fore Scene. There the Spirit of the Pities echoes "He Wonders About Himself" in saying of men: "And each has parcel in the total Will." The Spirit of the Years denies that the individual may influence the Will. In the end of the epic-drama (though, as Hardy says, it proves nothing) the Pities have won some concessions: human awareness, hope, and effort may inform the Will "till It fashion all things fair!" The common sense of this concept is that the "general Will" is a symbol for the total of human desires, impulses, and strivings. Men cannot change the external conditions of life, but they can, within the limits of natural law, change the human lot.

Purdy suggests some association of the poem with Mrs. Arthur Henniker: "No poem bears Mrs. Henniker's name, but a date in the 90's, particularly 1893, is often a key." He then includes "He Wonders About Himself" in a list of poems that may refer to Mrs. Henniker.[2] If this surmise is correct, "thee" of the second stanza may be Mrs. Henniker, and the "fair desire" of the third stanza may express some wish for a closer union with her.

1. *Later Years*, p. 125; *Life*, p. 335.
2. Purdy, *Thomas Hardy: A Bibliographical Study*, p. 345.

JUBILATE presents the tale of a vaguely recognized wanderer, apparently told in a "pub," where the man is slightly tipsy. The scene of the tale seems Stinsford Churchyard, where the musicians of "The Dead Quire" are buried, along with a "great company" whose antique musical instruments suggest the medieval ages.

The tale presents a vision of eerie magnificence, something like a mid-Victorian extravaganza seen "As you see the stage from the gallery." Before the curtain rises, so to speak, the world of the living, though glistening in the icy snow, is grim: "The yew-tree arms, glued hard to the stiff stark air." The orchestra of the dead heralds a transparency of the snow-curtain. Through it, as "through a crystal roof," the wanderer sees "the dead minueting in stately step," making "a joyful noise unto God."[1] They are joyful that they are "out of it all!—yea, in Little-Ease cramped no more!"—Little-Ease being the vexed world of the living. The sorriness of the living world is suggested in the closing lines, where the wanderer "in the ashes . . . emptied the dregs of his cup" and departed into the darkness.

The breastplate of the second stanza is that of Exod. 28:15-30. It is "of gold, of blue, of purple, and of scarlet," set with four rows of stones, "a sardius, a topaz, and a carbuncle . . . an emerald, a sapphire, and a diamond . . . a ligure, an agate, and an amethyst . . . a beryl, and an onyx, and a jasper." In the breastplate shall be placed "the Urim and the Thummim," objects with power to enable Aaron the priest to see into the will of God.

1. The words "Jubilate Deo" open Psalm 65 in the Latin Bible, which is Psalm 66 in the King James version, which reads: "Make a joyful noise unto God."

HE REVISITS HIS FIRST SCHOOL describes Hardy's visit to a school which he had attended only one year.[1] It was established in 1848 at Lower Bockhampton by Mrs. Julia Augusta Martin. Hardy's career there is described in *The Early Life*: "Until his fifth or sixth year his parents hardly supposed he would survive to grow up, but at eight he was thought strong enough to go to the village school . . . and by a curious coincidence he was the first pupil to enter the new schoolbuilding. . . . Here he worked at Walkingame's Arithmetic and at geography, in both of which he excelled, though his handwriting was indifferent."[2] According to both the biography and the poem, he worked at "Walkingame" with bee-like industry. This textbook was Francis Walkingame's *The Tutor's Assistant . . . A Compendium of Arithmetic*, published in 1751 and a standard through most of the nineteenth century.[3] The "Rule of Three" that evidently seemed magic to young Hardy is a method for finding the fourth term of a proportion when three terms are given. Sydney Cockerell records that in 1926 Hardy pointed out his first school: "We passed the school at Lower Bockhampton . . . T. H. was the first pupil and it still looks much the same as when he went there at eight years old, still in a frock."[4]

The poem reflects upon the differences between Tommy Hardy at eight, "Pink, tiny, crisp-curled," and the self-conscious old man who appeared at the school one day "when none wished to see me come there."

1. Cox, ed., *Thomas Hardy Through the Camera's Eye*, p. 50.
2. P. 20; *Life*, p. 16.
3. Among the few books Gabriel Oak of *Far from the Madding Crowd* brought to Bathsheba's farm is Walkingame's *Arithmetic*. Chapter VIII.
4. "A Memorial to Thomas Hardy," London *Times*, Oct. 27, 1928.

"I THOUGHT, MY HEART" seems to concern the rift between Hardy and his first wife Emma, from the 1890's until her death. The first stanza seems to blame Emma, but the second to exonerate her, or to suggest that she forgives him for blaming her. In thought, the poem reflects Browning's "A Woman's Last Word": the differences and the scars are there, but a deeper love covers them.

FRAGMENT is an eerie dramatization of a philosophic problem. In the first three stanzas the poet encounters corpses "nevertheless not dead," for their souls linger in their bodies, "waiting" for God to become conscious of them and of human pain. They are not certain of the nature of God and whether He may be called "the Will, or Force, or Laws" or the "Ultimate Cause."[1] Their waiting resembles the waiting for a revelation in Rom. 8:19-22, "For the earnest expectation of the creature waiteth for the manifestation of the sons of God" when "the creature itself shall be delivered from the bondage of corruption into the glorious liberty of the children of God. For we know that the whole creation groaneth and travaileth in pain together until now."

The reasoning in reply to the poet's final question is that "Life's tears," reacting upon the Creator, will cause Him to know pain and (it is implied) to amend injustices that cause it. Hardy developed this concept in many places, as in "God's Education," "Xenophanes, the Monist of Colophon," and *The Dynasts*, especially the After Scene. Perhaps the poem is called "Fragment" because it does not completely develop the thought of these pieces.

1. See the various names for the Immanent Will in *The Dynasts*, listed in Bailey, *Thomas Hardy and the Cosmic Mind*, pp. 92-95.

MIDNIGHT ON THE GREAT WESTERN, Purdy says, presents "undoubtedly a figure Hardy had seen and recorded."[1] The description of the boy follows that of Little Father Time in *Jude the Obscure*. In this novel, the boy is the son of Jude and Arabella, whom Arabella sends to Jude from London to Aldbrickham on the Great Western Railway: "In the down train that was timed to reach Aldbrickham station about ten o'clock the next evening, a small, pale child's face could be seen in the gloom of a third-class carriage. He had large, frightened eyes, and wore a white woollen cravat, over which a key was suspended round his neck by a piece of common string, the key attracting attention by its occasional shine in the lamplight. In the band of his hat his half-ticket was stuck. His eyes remained mostly fixed on the back of the seat opposite, and never turned to the window, even when a station was reached and called. On the other seat were two or three passengers, one of them a working-woman, who held a basket on her lap, in which was a tabby kitten. The woman opened the cover now and then, whereupon the kitten would put out its head, and indulge in playful antics. At these the fellow-passengers laughed, except the solitary boy bearing the key and ticket, who, regarding the kitten with his saucer eyes, seemed mutely to say: 'All laughing comes from misapprehension. Rightly looked at, there is no laughable thing under the sun.' "

As the boy walks from the station toward Jude's home, Hardy says of him: "To him the houses, the willows, the obscure fields beyond, were apparently regarded not as brick residences, pollards, meadows, but as human dwellings in the abstract, vegetation, and the wide, dark world." When later Father Time has hanged himself, Jude says to Sue: "It was in his nature to do it. The doctor says there are such boys springing up amongst us . . . the outcome of new views of life. They seem to see all its terrors before they are old enough to have staying power to resist them. He says it is the beginning of the coming universal wish not to live."[2]

Dr. Emma Clifford suggests that the boy is a self-portrait of Hardy as a child. She writes: "Indeed, all we know about Hardy as a child is slightly fantastic. He is a dreamy, precocious boy who does not like the company of other children; his mother is proud of his forwardness and he prefers to be with adults, he may even have fallen in love. He does not like intrusions into his private world. He hates to be touched, he dislikes receiving presents, and he is very shy and does not want to be noticed in any way by others. And, like Peter Pan, he has a feeling that childhood itself may well encompass all that he will want to know. . . . More than one child in Hardy's novels has this characteristic of satiety, of having already seen enough of life."[3]

Another theory is advanced by Deacon and Coleman in *Providence and Mr Hardy*. They suggest that the boy was the son of Hardy and Tryphena Sparks. It is alleged that the boy's name was Randal, called "Randy," that he passed as the son of Mrs. Rebecca Sparks Payne while Rebecca lived with Tryphena in Plymouth, and that he was later sent to live with Tryphena's brother Nathaniel in Bristol. "To travel from Plymouth to Bristol, the boy would have had to go by the Great Western line." Even after Tryphena's marriage to Charles Gale, the boy visited Tryphena in Topsham, near Exeter. Presumably the boy, said to have been feeble, died in early manhood.[4]

The evidence that Hardy had a son lies chiefly in the identification of two photographs by Tryphena's daughter, Eleanor Tryphena Bromell, who was eleven years old when her mother died. On February 10, 1965, before she died on February 24, Mrs. Bromell reluctantly told Miss Lois Deacon that the photographs of a boy about eight and of a young man about twenty-one were those of Randy, Hardy's son.[5] That these photographs present Hardy's son is denied in a letter signed "J. H.," by John Antell of Puddletown, in the *Dorset Evening Echo* for July 7, 1967, a relative of both Hardy and Tryphena. The letter asserts that the so-called "Tryphena's Portrait Album" "is not and never was known in the family as Tryphena's album," but is an album that "belonged to the Gale family into which Tryphena married," though it does include photographs of Tryphena. The photograph alleged to be that of Randy as a boy is asserted to be a portrait of Charles Gale, and that of Randy at twenty-one, that of a member of the Sparks family. If Hardy had a son, such evidence as baptismal records was effectively concealed.

Aside from these questionable identifications, "Midnight on the Great Western" presents a portrait of an introspective boy remarkably like Hardy in moods of idealistic dreaming when the actual world by contrast seemed a "region of sin" and sordidness. The poem has been set to music by Benjamin Britten in *Winter Words* (London and New York: Boosey and Hawkes, 1954).

1. *Thomas Hardy: A Bibliographical Study*, p. 203.
2. Part V, Chapter III, and Part VI, Chapter II.
3. "The Child; the Circus; and *Jude the Obscure*," p. 532.
4. Pp. 188-96.
5. The photographs are reproduced in Deacon, *Tryphena's Portrait Album*, pp. 9, 11.

HONEYMOON TIME AT AN INN is a poem of foreboding on the theme that romantic love rapidly decays. The theme is illustrated in the disillusion a newly married couple feel, and is then stated by the Spirits Ironic to be a law that "fits all mortal mould."

The foreboding is given an eerie quality through Hardy's use of symbols and folklore. The word "honeymoon" suggests the sentimental idea of the moon as a symbol of romance. In Hardy's symbolism the moon stands for a cold, somewhat cynical observer of human vanities. That the moon "conned" the lovers before dawn (the disillusioning light of day?) seems to bring about their sadness. The broken mirror is, in folklore, a portent of evil to follow, usually seven years' bad luck or a death.[1] It is even suggested that the bride may die soon, for to pick up pieces of the mirror she "like a moth skimmed forth." Hardy frequently uses a moth to symbolize a spirit of the dead. The Spirits Ironic, who comment upon the situation, are those of *The Dynasts*, where they stand for a realistic view of the human lot. The Spirits of Pity, also from *The Dynasts*, helplessly protest the realistic view of life.

The diction and imagery of the poem avoid the sentimental, as in "Deedily" (actually, realistically) and "as by an adze." Guerard calls the poem "ruthlessly experimental" in technique. It proves "on close examination to be very queer indeed. The fifth line of the first stanza repeats the first line. This occurs again, with a slight change in wording, in the seventh stanza. This leaves us with a theoretical possibility, for a forty-eight line poem, of forty-six different types of metrical line. *And this is precisely what we have!* Except for the lines noted above, no two are rhythmically alike. Granted the principle of monotony implicit in perpetual variety, such extreme variation is no mean *tour de force*."[2]

1. Firor, *Folkways in Thomas Hardy*, p. 15. A somewhat similar portent appears in *The Dynasts*. When Maria Louisa agrees to marry Napoleon, a portrait of Marie Antoinette falls on its face. Part Second, V, iii.

2. "The Illusion of Simplicity," p. 382.

THE ROBIN expresses Hardy's fellow-feeling for birds. The "Feathery ball!" of the final line recalls an episode in Hardy's boyhood. About 1844 Hardy was in the garden with his father: "They noticed a field-fare, half-frozen, and the father took up a stone idly and threw it at the bird. . . . The field-fare fell dead, and the child Thomas picked it up and it was . . . all skin and bone, practically starved."[1]

1. *Later Years*, p. 263; *Life*, p. 444.

"I ROSE AND WENT TO ROU'TOR TOWN," Purdy says, is a "pendant to 'When I Set Out for Lyonnesse' . . . closely reproducing its metrical pattern in particular."[1] A better term than "pendant" would be "contrasting companion." "When I Set Out for Lyonnesse" expresses Hardy's ecstasy when he realized his love for Emma Gifford. The *"She, alone"* beneath the title of "I Rose and Went to Rou'tor Town" is Emma Gifford; the poem expresses her love for Hardy, tells the story of her action when she realized it, and the result of that action.

"Rou'tor Town" is Hardy's fictional name for Bodmin, Cornwall, and, like all his concealments, it contains a hint. There is no town called Rou'tor in England, but one of the highest points on Bodmin

Moor is Rough Tor, about nine and a half miles north and slightly east of Bodmin. Emma's father lived at Bodmin, about sixteen miles south of Emma's home, St. Juliot. According to the poem, when Emma realized her love for Hardy (or perhaps soon after he proposed marriage, about 1872), she went "With gaiety and good heart" to tell her father. (Hardy may have gone with her at this time; the occasion may be that of "Near Lanivet, 1872.") Mr. Gifford disapproved of her proposed marriage on the ground that Hardy was a penniless churl socially beneath her. When Vere H. Collins asked Hardy in 1920, "What is 'The evil wrought at Rou'tor Town'?" he answered guardedly, "Slander, or something of that sort."[2] He and Emma were married in London, and Mr. Gifford was not present.

1. *Thomas Hardy: A Bibliographical Study*, p. 203.
2. *Talks with Thomas Hardy*, p. 26.

THE NETTLES may be associated with Mrs. Jethway's sorrow for her son in *A Pair of Blue Eyes*, though in the novel the son died without marrying Elfride.

IN A WAITING-ROOM is made drab by a "bagman's counts of cost" scribbled over the Gospel of John. Blunden comments upon the "stuffed-owl simplicities" of the diction,[1] but Hardy sought to portray the fact, in tone as well as statement. The diction is suddenly elevated when arrive "Like the eastern flame / Of some high altar, children." Perkins, theorizing that the children symbolize poetic vision, expresses disappointment that "the child's comments are insufficient to dispel . . . the harshness of the scene."[2] Perhaps the child's vision, though it "spread a glory through the room," is naïve. The ugly station is the substantial fact.

1. *Thomas Hardy*, p. 264.
2. "Hardy and the Poetry of Isolation," p. 156.

THE CLOCK-WINDER does not have in the manuscript the last sixteen lines, they "apparently having been added when the poem was in proof."[1] Without these lines, the poem presents simply two scenes, of a burial under the church floor and of the parish-clerk winding the clock. Possibly on reading the poem in proof, Hardy invented a story to unite the scenes. If so, the burial may be that of the woman the clock-winder laments. The final stanza suggests that he had loved in secret and in silence.

1. Purdy, *Thomas Hardy: A Bibliographical Study*, p. 203.

OLD EXCURSIONS, dated five months after Emma Hardy's death, recalls Hardy's outings with her in days gone by. He wonders whether it may be futile to go to the customary places without her.

The places are within walking or bicycling distance from Max Gate, in various directions. Ridgeway Hill, overlooking both Dorchester and Weymouth, is a little more than three miles to the south. Cerne Abbas is about seven miles north of Dorchester. Sydling Mill, at Sydling St. Nicholas, was (for the old mill no longer exists) [1] about the same distance to the northwest. The village lies in the valley of "Sydling Water," a tributary of the Frome River. Yell'ham (Yellowham) Hill is about three miles northeast of Max Gate.

The poem concludes that it will be a pleasure to visit the old haunts where the poet may meet Emma's "phasm." This conclusion contrasts with that of "Paths of Former Time."

1. The mill was operated by Robert Spriggs. When he died, milling ended in Sydling. His millstone, set up in the churchyard as a headstone for the Spriggs family, is engraved: "In Memory of Robert Spriggs, the Last Miller of Sydling Died Feb. 19th 1919."

THE MASKED FACE presents in allegory the theme that efforts to understand Life are useless. The "great surging space" is Life; its doors are birth and death. The infirm floor represents basic uncertainties. The "mask-clad face" seems the incomprehensible Supreme Power. The "light and air" that are not clear may represent natural laws. That the doors are "fast-locked" suggests human ignorance of what precedes life and follows death. Man is a "vassal-wight" of forces beyond his comprehension.

Stevenson comments that "despite this recognition of man's limitations, Hardy is bound to obey the instinct which has always driven men to seek a system explaining their place in the world."[1] Neiman suggests that the poem states the basis upon which existentialism rests: recognition that the universe does not declare its meaning or the meaning of human life. Then a man may give meaning to life in his thought and behavior.[2]

1. *Darwin Among the Poets*, p. 260.
2. "Thomas Hardy, Existentialist," p. 213.

IN A WHISPERING GALLERY is set in St. Paul's Cathedral. The whispering gallery encircles the great dome at its base, 100 feet above the floor of the cathedral. The diameter of the gallery is 107 feet. Because the voice of a speaker is rebounded from all parts of the dome in focus upon the opposite side of the gallery, a softly spoken word may be heard across the wide space.

The poem expresses Hardy's feeling of awe at a whisper heard across the "gaunt gray gallery" on an afternoon of such haze that he could hardly see the speaker. Under the dome, with its scenes from the life of St. Paul, the poet believes "for a moment" that the whisper may be "a soul's voice," though he knows that it belongs to "fleshed humanity." The "lacune" (lacuna) is the space between opposite sides of the gallery.

THE SOMETHING THAT SAVED HIM is a sketchy allegory that seems to echo both Bunyan's *Pilgrim's Progress* and Browning's "Childe Roland to the Dark Tower Came." The "hand to deliver" is not clearly either Bunyan's Christian faith or Browning's courage to endure.

The second and third stanzas may refer to Hardy's despair in the 1890's set forth in the "In Tenebris" poems, and the saving hand may be that defined in "Wessex Heights," when he could rise above the opinions and pressures of others and "know some liberty." It may be his turning from novels, written to please a public, to poetry, written to please himself. He may have had in mind his despair after the death of his first wife Emma, and the "hand" may be that of his second wife Florence. More generally, it may be a faith in man that developed after he had lost his faith in the orthodox Christian God. This faith in the human spirit is defined in "A Plaint to Man." The poem seems a companion to "For Life I Had Never Cared Greatly."

THE ENEMY'S PORTRAIT seems fiction, with an ironic point similar to that of "The Obliterate Tomb." In contrast with "The Obliterate Tomb," where the passage of time and the tendency to postpone weaken a good impulse to right an old wrong, in "The Enemy's Portrait" time and postponement weaken the evil impulse for vengeance. Compare also the short story "The Grave by the Handpost" in *A Changed Man.*

IMAGININGS presents a vain and socially ambitious woman who married a "striver" unable to satisfy her daydreams. Anschutz suggested that the woman may represent Emma Hardy, who "saw herself a lady" and was unhappy in her life with Hardy.[1]

1. "The Road to Nirvana," p. 183.

ON THE DOORSTEP in the manuscript had the title "Staying and Going." The poem refers to the singing of Hardy's first wife Emma, who died in November, 1912.[1] In contrast with other poems (for instance, "The Last Performance") that present Hardy as ignoring Emma's efforts to revive his love, "On the Doorstep" shows his giving up an errand in order to "abide" with her and her "song's sweet note." The rain helped to hinder the poet, but after Emma's death the rain is no hindrance.[2]

1. Purdy, *Thomas Hardy: A Bibliographical Study,* p. 204.
2. This poem is not to be confused with "On the Doorstep" published as num-

ber X of the "Satires of Circumstance." The latter is treated in Part II of these notes.

SIGNS AND TOKENS presents folk-signs that forecast death. The first three speakers are crones like the witches in *Macbeth*, but the "black-craped fourth" represents Death. The signs of the poem are authentic superstitions. The "limp corpse, or the corpse which will not keep its eyes decently closed" is a "token of another death before the year is out." Flies that wear crape scarves and trotting does in a deserted park are ghostly tokens that the master is to die.[1] The personified Death offers no tokens, but explains that "hints . . . / Of more takings away" cannot appal the man who is to die.

1. Firor, *Folkways in Thomas Hardy*, pp. 17, 24.

PATHS OF FORMER TIME in the manuscript had the title "The Old Paths." "Hardy identified the scene as the meadows behind Max Gate."[1] Dated in the year after the death of his first wife Emma, the poem expresses his reluctance to ramble through the meadows where they had wandered, for the associated memories would renew the pain of her death. The questioner of the sixth stanza may be any companion. The poem contrasts with "Old Excursions," which reaches an opposite conclusion.

1. Purdy, *Thomas Hardy: A Bibliographical Study*, p. 204.

THE CLOCK OF THE YEARS in the manuscript had the title "The Clock of Time."[1] The motto for the poem is a quotation from Job 4:15.

The poem plays with the mystery of time. It dramatizes Hardy's memory of his first wife Emma, in a sequence of years that reach back to his courtship in Cornwall, and then back through Emma's *Some Recollections* into her childhood. Then she vanishes. The meaning is that of Tennyson's *In Memoriam*, lyric LXXXV: " 'Tis better to have loved and lost, / Than never to have loved at all." "The Clock of the Years" has been set to music by Gerald Finzi in *Earth and Air and Rain* (London: Boosey & Hawkes, 1936).

1. Purdy, *Thomas Hardy: A Bibliographical Study*, p. 204.

AT THE PIANO, Purdy says, is, "perhaps, to be associated with 'The Interloper' or with 'The Last Performance.' "[1] If associated with "The Interloper," the scene would be St. Juliot Rectory during Hardy's courtship of Emma Gifford. She is playing the piano, and Hardy is daydreaming. The "Apparition" that appears is a suggestion of madness in Emma. The poem, symbolizing rather than defining, does not say what evidence of delusion Hardy observed. Emma, perhaps, was not aware of anything unusual, and he apparently brushed aside the warning. In the symbols, personified Time "laughed awry," the meaning of this laugh to become apparent years later.

If associated with "The Last Performance," the "Apparition" is Emma's death that, "The Last Performance" suggests, she somehow felt approaching. In this interpretation, she did not dread death; she "saw no bale." Hardy did not receive the warning, and thought of it only later.

1. *Thomas Hardy: A Bibliographical Study*, p. 204.

THE SHADOW ON THE STONE concerns the five-foot stone called "Druid" that, in March, 1891, Hardy erected on the lawn at Max Gate. "This was a large block they discovered about three feet underground in the garden, and the labour of getting it from the hole where it had lain for perhaps two thousand years was a heavy one even for seven men with levers and other appliances. . . . Round the stone, which had been lying flat, they had found a quantity of ashes and half charred bones."[1] As the years passed, the stone became lichen-stained, and the Hardys would take visitors to see it. Paul Jordan Smith wrote to Vincent Starrett on September 21 [192–?]: "When I left the house Mrs. Hardy took me out into the garden where besides the beautiful shrubbery . . . was an old Druid altar—a place to dream by."[2]

Besides its archaeological interest, Hardy regarded it with awe for its mysterious origin. He inquired of his antiquarian friend, Rev. Henry J. Moule, about it. Moule wrote to him on September 20, 1900: "As to the great stone, found with a burial, it is noteworthy that . . . Mr. Cunnington found a similar combination quite near. . . . It struck me as just possible that the Max Gate great stone may have at first been set up as a Menhir. Then in after ages it was found a hindrance to the plough and was buried out of the way. This might account for the relics of the burial being round it & (perhaps) under it."[3] Regarding the name "Druid," Firor says, "The peasant calls any great upstanding stones 'Druidical'; they cannot be proved to have any historical connection with the mysterious religion . . . which we call Druidism."[4] Clive Holland visited Hardy in 1898 and wrote: "After lunch he asked me whether I would like to go out to see the garden; there it was I took the photo of him standing talking near the great upright stone, which he always believed was of Druidical origin, and possibly a sacrificial one. . . . 'Do you believe in ghosts?' he asked with a smile. 'If you do you ought to see such manifestations here, on a moonlight night.' And he laughed."[5] The stone is associated with Emma Hardy in a note on page 306 of the copy of *The Early Life* that had belonged to Mrs. Florence Hardy, apparently in the handwriting of Miss Irene Cooper Willis: "Mrs. Hardy, the second, walking round the garden with me, the first time I stayed at Max Gate (1933) on coming to the erected stone, remarked: 'Hardy found his first wife burning all his love-letters to her behind that stone, one day.' "[6]

In folklore "ghosts tend to return to the places they knew in life."[7] The poem suggests that Hardy had some belief in this superstition. Wishing to believe that Emma's spirit haunts about the stone, he refuses to destroy the feeling that she is there.

1. *Early Life*, p. 306; *Life*, pp. 233-34.
2. In the Yale University Library.
3. In the Dorset County Museum.
4. *Folkways in Thomas Hardy*, p. 268.
5. "My Walks and Talks in Wessex with Thomas Hardy," p. 170.
6. In the Dorset County Museum.
7. Firor, *Folkways in Thomas Hardy*, p. 75.

IN THE GARDEN treats Hardy's sister Mary, who died on November 24, 1915. The sun-dial is evidently in the garden at their birthplace in Higher Bockhampton, for there was none at Max Gate. (The sun-dial Hardy planned to have there was installed only after his death.) Perhaps the scene is a memory of his childhood, and "We" in the poem are the four Hardy children. Thomas, Henry, and Kate all outlived Mary. The poem makes use of the superstition that when the sun throws a shadow toward one of a group, that one will be first to die.[1]

1. Firor, *Folkways in Thomas Hardy*, p. 23.

THE TREE AND THE LADY suggests Hardy's feeling that all nature may be sentient. That the life of the tree is linked with that of the lady who found pleasure under its shade echoes the story of Old South in *The Woodlanders*, who felt a fatal bond between a tree and himself and died when the tree was cut down. (Chapter XIV.)

AN UPBRAIDING is a speech by the ghost of Hardy's first wife Emma, who died in 1912. To try to revive their love in her later years, she had played and sung her songs that had attracted Hardy during his courtship, but he had sometimes ignored them. The poem expresses his remorse.

THE YOUNG GLASS-STAINER rests upon notes Hardy made as a young man. In discussing George Meredith's comments upon his first, unpublished novel, *The Poor Man and the Lady*, *The Early Life* says: "The satire was obviously pushed too far. . . . One instance he could remember was a chapter in which . . . he described in the first person his introduction to the kept mistress of an architect . . . the said mistress adding to her lover's income by designing for him the

[413]

pulpits, altars, reredoses, texts, holy vessels, crucifixes, and other ecclesiastical furniture which were handed on to him by the nominal architects who employed her protector." Hardy copied into his notebook on November 3, 1883, a passage from the *Athenaeum*: "The glass-stainer maintains his existence at the sacrifice of everything the painter holds dear. In place of the freedom and sweet abandonment which is Nature's own charm and which the painter can achieve, the glass-stainer gives us splendour as luminous as that of the rainbow . . . in patches, and stripes, and bars." He recorded the composition of "The Young Glass-Stainer" on November 23, 1893.[1]

In 1893 Hardy was working on *Jude the Obscure*, and perhaps his poem is a comment upon Sue Bridehead of that novel. Employed in something like ecclasiastical glass-staining, she designs and illuminates scrolls in church texts. She is bored with "those everlasting church fal-lals," and when on an outing purchases for her private pleasure statues of Venus and Apollo. (Part II, Chapters II and III.)

1. *Early Life*, pp. 81-82, 213, and *Later Years*, p. 26; *Life*, pp. 61-62, 163, 260.

LOOKING AT A PICTURE ON AN ANNIVERSARY in the manuscript shows "March" deleted from the date of composition. "The anniversary was 7 March, the day on which Hardy met his first wife,"[1] who died on November 27, 1912. *The Later Years* states that "On March 6—almost to a day, forty-three years after his first journey to Cornwall—he started for St. Juliot."[2] Hardy may have taken the picture (or a photograph) with him to Cornwall or may have looked at the painting of Emma at Max Gate just before leaving.

1. Purdy, *Thomas Hardy: A Bibliographical Study*, p. 205.
2. P. 156; *Life*, p. 361.

THE CHOIRMASTER'S BURIAL in the manuscript was titled "The Choirmaster's Funeral."[1] The poem presents the burial of Thomas Hardy the First, Hardy's grandfather. He had organized the choir of Stinsford Church, "himself taking the bass-viol . . . which he played in the gallery . . . at two services every Sunday from 1801 or 1802 till his death in 1837." He had also conducted the music for funeral services. When he died on January 8, 1837, there was no music for his burial. "The First Thomas's death having been quite unexpected, inasmuch as he was playing in the church one Sunday, and brought in for burial on the next, there could be no such quiring over his grave as he had performed over the graves of so many, owing to the remaining players being chief mourners."[2] These players were his sons, Thomas Hardy the Second, playing the tenor violin, and James Hardy, playing the treble violin. The "tenor man" of the poem, who told the story, was evidently Hardy's father.

The biography and the poem do not agree upon why the customary music was omitted. Possibly, as the burial took place in January, the reason given in the poem was a factor in the vicar's decision: the "frosts and hoars" may have made it difficult to find substitute musicians. Presumably ("'twas said that") the coda the angels sang at the graveside is part of the story Hardy's father told "When he had grown old."

The choirmaster had requested "The psalm he liked best— / The one whose sense suits / 'Mount Ephraim.' " This psalm is "The Lord God Jehovah Reigns," which was sung at the memorial services for Hardy at Stinsford Church on June 2, 1940. The words were copied from an old music book belonging to his father.[3] "The Choirmaster's Burial" has been set to music by Benjamin Britten in *Winter Words* (London and New York: Boosey and Hawkes, 1954).

1. Purdy, *Thomas Hardy: A Bibliographical Study*, p. 205.
2. *Early Life*, pp. 10-11, 15-16; *Life*, pp. 9, 13.
3. "The Bishop Analyzes Hardy's Religion," *Dorset County Chronicle*, June 6, 1940.

THE MAN WHO FORGOT is set at a crossing of lanes near St. Juliot Rectory, which Hardy revisited in March, 1913. In the poem, he is evidently daydreaming of the time, forty years earlier, when he had courted Emma Gifford in a summer-house so close to the Rectory that the couple could hear Helen Holder call, "Come in, Dears." (See the notes on "Where They Lived.") Though evidence suggests that Hardy's daydreams were so vivid they sometimes obscured reality, it is likely that, having reached the area and not found the summer-house, he asked a boy where it was, and then made the poem dramatic with the question about the lady waiting there.

WHILE DRAWING IN A CHURCHYARD combines several of Hardy's characteristic fantasies, that a yew tree is sentient and, in "soughing," speaks words that can be overheard, that the dead likewise are sentient and are content, and that it is better to be dead than alive, and to remain so than that "God trumpet us to rise." (See these ideas in "Friends Beyond," "Jubilate," and "Voices from Things Growing in a Churchyard.") The poem has been set to music by Gerald Finzi (London: Boosey & Co., 1936).

"FOR LIFE I HAD NEVER CARED GREATLY" presents Hardy's analysis of his temperament. As a child, he had questions about the value of life (see "Childhood Among the Ferns"), but the "Conditions of doubt, / . . . that leaked slowly out" were probably those that undermined his religious faith in the 1860's. The third stanza suggests the discovery of love and the idealism of the poem "In the Seventies." Then disillusion set in again until life "uncloaked a star." Looking toward this star, the poet has "no humour for letting / My pilgrimage fail." Speaking of this star, Weber says that in "For Life I Had Never Cared Greatly" Hardy "wrote his companion to Browning's 'Epilogue to Asolando.' "[1]

He did not define the star. It may be, as in Matthew Arnold's "Stanzas from the Grande Chartreuse," "the high white star of Truth," as opposed to pleasure or love. Zachrisson offers Hardy's "artistic purpose, the message he had delivered to the world, especially in his late lyrics."[2] Weber surmises that the star may be a symbol for Hardy's second wife Florence, who "now beams so brightly upon him that he is able to forget 'the rough highway' of the past."[3] The star may resemble the hope that kept Clym Yeobright, in *The Return of the Native*, to his futile task of preaching the "eleventh commandment" of loving-kindness. Clym's conclusion resembles that of the poem: "He did sometimes think he had been ill-used by fortune, so far as to say that to be born is a palpable dilemma, and that instead of men aiming to advance in life with glory they should calculate how to retreat out of it without shame." (Book Sixth, Chapter I.)

1. *Hardy of Wessex*, 1st ed., p. 208.
2. *Thomas Hardy as Man, Writer, and Philosopher*, p. 19.
3. *Hardy of Wessex*, 2nd ed., p. 265.

POEMS OF WAR AND PATRIOTISM

Hardy developed two major themes in "Poems of War and Patriotism," compassionate regret and protest that such "kin folk kin tongued" as the Germans and the English were engaged in mutual slaughter, and a bitter curse upon the war-lords who drove the peoples into battle to satisfy ambitions for power. The poems are roughly arranged to develop these themes. They are stern in Biblical curses upon those who "flung the flame." It was England's duty to stand firm against their arrogance and brutal evil.

"MEN WHO MARCH AWAY" was published in the London *Times* on September 9, 1914, under the title "Song of the Soldiers." As copyright was not reserved, the poem was widely reprinted. In November, Hardy included it, under the present title, in *Satires of Circumstance*, from which it was transferred to *Moments of Vision*.[1]

He was distressed by World War I but, convinced of the justice of the English cause, he took part in the efforts of British authors to arouse patriotic sentiment. On September 3, a conference of authors was held at Wellington House to discuss how they might state Britain's case to neutrals. Blunden prints Arnold Bennett's notes of this occasion: " 'Zangwill talked a great deal too much. The sense was talked by Wells and Chesterton. . . . Thomas Hardy was all right.' To Hardy it was a memorable afternoon, 'the yellow sun shining in upon our confused deliberations in a melancholy manner that I shall never forget.' "[2] Presumably the occasion prompted "Men Who March Away," dated two days later.

In meter as in sentiment the poem is a marching song for soldiers full of "faith and fire" in the belief that their cause is just and in their readiness to march away from their rural homes to death if necessary. Hardy wrote to Arthur Symons on September 13: "I am glad to hear that you liked the verses, though I fear they were not free from some banalities which it is difficult to keep out of lines which are meant to appeal to the man in the street, & not to 'a few friends' only."[3] Edgar Lane set the poem to music immediately,[4] and Hardy offered it to H. Granville-Barker for use in a production of *The Dynasts*. He wrote: ". . . if you like I can send the music of 'Men Who March Away!'—the Song of the Soldiers that appeared in 'The Times' the other day."[5]

Besides the setting by Lane (London: Edwin Ashdown, 1914), other musicians set the poem to music. On November 10, 1914, Mrs. Alfred Sutro wrote to Hardy for permission for her nephew to publish the poem with music he had written; permission was granted.[6] F. Wilson Parish set it to music under the title "Song of the Soldiers" (New York: H. W. Gray Co., 1916; London: Novello & Co., 1917). On November 28, 1918, James D. Barber sent Hardy music he had composed for the poem.[7]

1. Purdy, *Thomas Hardy: A Bibliographical Study*, p. 157.
2. *Thomas Hardy*, p. 147.
3. In the Dorset County Museum.
4. In a letter to Clement Shorter on September 22, Hardy wrote: "The song of the soldiers—'Men who march away'—has been set to music by a composer—Mr. Edgar Lane—who has a school of music in this town [Dorchester]. . . . I think the tune a very catching one, which may possibly be popular if known. Soldiers' songs are badly wanted in the army, and I should like this to be published." In the British Museum.
5. In the Dorset County Museum.
6. Ibid.
7. Ibid.

HIS COUNTRY was written before World War I broke out. *The Later Years* says: "A long study of the European wars of a century earlier had made it appear to him [Hardy] that common sense had taken the place of bluster in men's minds; and he felt this so strongly that in the very year before war burst on Europe he wrote some verses called 'His Country,' bearing on the decline of antagonism between peoples."[1]

The "I" of "His Country" is a travelling English patriot who discovers "how patriotism of the genuine kind admits the right to similar sentiment in other people, and thus makes for that real international understanding which is based on the recognition of common rights and a unity of aspiration. Such a patriotism . . . finds in the war-spirit a direct contradiction to love and loyalty to one's motherland."[2] As originally published, the poem had a final stanza: " 'Ah, you deceive with such pleas!' / Said one with pitying eye. / 'Foreigners—not like us—are these; / Stretch country-love beyond the seas?—/ Too Christian.' 'Strange,' said I."

When Leonard Rees of the London *Sunday Times* wrote Hardy on October 19, 1923, for a poem on "War and Patriotism," Mrs. Hardy replied that Rees might reprint any of Hardy's poems on this subject, but "He thinks the one entitled 'His Country' . . . might suit the peaceable views we have, or say we have, nowadays."[3]

1. P. 162; *Life*, p. 365.
2. Chakravarty, *"The Dynasts" and the Post-War Age in Poetry*, p. 171.
3. In the Dorset County Museum.

ENGLAND TO GERMANY IN 1914 was composed in October[1] and was first published in a pamphlet in February, 1917, for Mrs. Florence Hardy, together with "The Pity of It," "I Met a Man," and "A New Year's Eve in War Time." Opening with the slogan by which the German war lords justified their attack upon England, the poem presents an appeal by the English people to the German people, for they are racially brothers. It warns that the war may "foul" the "ancient name" of Germany in future judgments.

1. *Later Years*, p. 164; *Life*, p. 367.

ON THE BELGIAN EXPATRIATION was first published as "Sonnet on the Belgian Expatriation" in *King Albert's Book* (London, 1914) for the benefit of the Belgian Fund of the *Daily Telegraph*.[1]

The octave reflects Hardy's appreciation of Belgian chimes he had heard. The *Dorset Evening Echo* for February 18, 1967, records Mrs. Ann Gillespie's memories of Hardy in the years before World War I: "I used to meet him at garden parties that were given annually at Cattistock Rectory when a Belgian came over from Malines to play on the carillon for the benefit of the guests." The bells were in the church tower at Cattistock, a village about eight miles northwest of Dorchester. The sestet refers to the German destruction of Belgian cities and the flight of Belgians to England in the early months of the war.

1. Purdy, *Thomas Hardy: A Bibliographical Study*, p. 205.

AN APPEAL TO AMERICA ON BEHALF OF THE BELGIAN DESTITUTE was first published in the *New York Times* on January 4, 1915, and in other American papers, with the following introduction: "This poem, written as an appeal to the American people on behalf of the destitute people of Belgium by Thomas Hardy, the English writer, was given out by the American Commission for Relief in Belgium yesterday."[1] He wrote the poem in response to a letter of December 9, 1914, from W. A. M. Goode of the Commission for Relief in Belgium. The letter asked for " 'something else' which would be of such incalculable value in helping us to get food and money from America which are so much needed by the Belgian people." Hardy noted on this letter: "Two eight-line stanzas called 'An Appeal to America on Behalf of the Belgian Destitute' also sent."[2]

1. Purdy, *Thomas Hardy: A Bibliographical Study*, p. 191.
2. In the Dorset County Museum.

THE PITY OF IT, Purdy says, in spite of the date at the end of the poem, "was written in February 1915 and first printed in the *Fortnightly Review*, April 1915. . . . The sonnet was suggested by a contemporary article by Dr. Caleb Williams Saleeby on 'Eugenics.' "[1] The poem bases its assertion that the German and the English peoples are "kin folk kin tongued" also on Hardy's observation "in loamy Wessex lanes." In *The Woodlanders* of 1887, Grammer Oliver, native of the "Hintocks" (the area around Minterne Magna, some eight miles north of Dorchester), uses such German words as " 'ch woll" and "er woll." (Chapter XVII.) Hardy explained to Edmund Gosse on October 26, 1888, that these words were heard in Dorset: " 'Ich,' this & kindred words—e.g.—'Ich woll,' 'er woll,' 'er war,' &c. are still used by old people in N. W. Dorset & Somerset (*vide* Grammer Oliver's conversation in *The Woodlanders* which is an attempted reproduction). I heard 'Ich' only last Sunday; but it is dying rapidly."[2]

Other items in the background include a letter Hardy wrote to Mrs. Arthur Henniker on March 23, 1915: "I, too, like you, think the Germans happy as a people: but the group of oligarchs and munition-makers whose interest is war, have stirred them up to their purposes —at least so it seems. I have expressed the thought in a sonnet that is coming out in the Fortnightly."[3]

Later Hardy became friends with German prisoners of war in Dorchester. Writing to Sir Sydney Cockerell on November 10, 1916,

Mrs. Florence Hardy said: "Yesterday my husband paid a visit to the Commandant of the Prison Camp here who took him to see the German prisoners. T. H.'s kind heart melted at the sight of the wounded and he expressed his sympathy with them by eloquent gestures to which they responded in a most friendly manner . . . and now he is sending them some of his books in German—for their library."[4] Phelps reports Hardy's interest in the German prisoners, some of whom worked at Max Gate: "Mr. Hardy took a personal interest in every prisoner who worked on his place. He gave food and medicines, treating them not only with solicitude for their welfare, but with respect for them as individuals. . . . It is pleasant to know that these Germans were grateful, that they wrote to their families in Germany about him, and that a letter came back saying that as a result of his consideration, the English prisoners in that part of Germany were receiving better treatment."[5]

The publication of "The Pity of It" stimulated a large number of "Letters to the Editor." In a scrapbook labelled "T. H. Personal," Mrs. Florence Hardy (presumably) pasted a number of these protests, and wrote: "Apropos of T. H.'s poem 'The Pity of It'—in which he said we were 'kin folk' to the Germans—a statement denied by the Jingo papers." In a pencilled note to Mrs. Hardy about *The Later Years,* Hardy wrote: "Insert at mention of the poem on the Wessex dialect, & our relations to the Germans: 'Fussy jingoes, who were hoping for knighthoods, attacked H for his assumptions & asserted that we had no sort of blood relationship with Germany. But the Germans themselves, with far more commonsense, translated the poem, approved of it, & remarked that when relations did fall out they fought more bitterly than any."[6] Mrs. Hardy did not follow these instructions.

The theme of "The Pity of It" is that the *peoples* of Germany and England were not responsible for the war; the common soldiers were puppets of the war-lords. Upon these war-lords, "Whoever they be / At root and bottom of this," Hardy launched the most terrible curse his decorous language could command. This curse resembles his similar attitude toward Napoleon. In *The Dynasts,* the "pale pathetic peoples" are driven to destruction to satisfy the ambitions of a callous egoist.

1. *Thomas Hardy: A Bibliographical Study,* p. 189.
2. In the Dorset County Museum. A part of this letter is reproduced in *The Early Life,* p. 290; *Life,* p. 221.
3. In the Dorset County Museum.
4. Meynell, ed., *Friends of a Lifetime,* p. 294.
5. *Autobiography with Letters,* pp. 396-97.
6. In the Dorset County Museum.

IN TIME OF WARS AND TUMULTS was first printed as "In the Time of War and Tumults" in the *Sphere* on November 24, 1917.[1] This sonnet is a fantasy about someone who wished he had not been born to see World War I. It would have come anyway through "Empery's insatiable lust of power."

1. Purdy, *Thomas Hardy: A Bibliographical Study*, pp. 205-6.

IN TIME OF "THE BREAKING OF NATIONS" was first published in the *Saturday Review* for January 29, 1916.[1]

Hardy commented upon the mystery of his memory: "I believe it would be said by people who knew me well that I have a faculty . . . for burying an emotion in my heart or brain for forty years, and exhuming it at the end of that time as fresh as when interred. For instance, the poem entitled 'The Breaking of Nations' contains a feeling that moved me in 1870, during the Franco-Prussian war, when I chanced to be looking at such an agricultural incident in Cornwall. But I did not write the verses till during the war with Germany of 1914, and onwards."[2]

The idea underlying the poem came to Hardy during his courtship of Emma Gifford in Cornwall: "On the day that the bloody battle of Gravelotte was fought[3] they were reading Tennyson in the grounds of the rectory. It was at this time and spot that Hardy was struck by the incident of the old horse harrowing the arable field in the valley below, which, when in far later years it was recalled to him by a still bloodier war, he made into the little poem of three verses entitled 'In Time of "The Breaking of Nations."' "[4] The stimulus to put the observation of 1870 into a poem came from a letter George A. B. Dewar, editor of the *Saturday Review*, wrote to Hardy on December 31, 1915, saying: "I hope you will send me a few lines for the 'Saturday'—a verse, a letter, anything. We try—against disheartening influences—still to keep the torch alight in the black." Hardy wrote on the bottom of this letter: " 'In Time of "The Breaking of Nations"' sent Jan. 18."[5]

He had frequently meditated the idea that man's basic life of labor and love goes "onward the same" in spite of the devastations of war. In describing the shearing barn in *Far from the Madding Crowd*, he discusses the decay of the church and the castle, but remarks of the barn: "The defence and salvation of the body by daily bread is still a study, a religion, and a desire." (Chapter XXII.) The title of the poem, paraphrasing "break in pieces the nations," refers to God's judgment against Babylon. Its theme is like God's promise to Noah after the flood: "While the earth remaineth, seedtime and harvest, and cold and heat, and summer and winter, and day and night shall not cease." [6]

"In Time of 'The Breaking of Nations' " has been set to music by Gordon Slater (Oxford University Press, 1926), Frederic Austin in *Wessex Songs* (London and New York: Boosey & Co., 1927), and Harper MacKay in *Five Songs* (in manuscript in the Colby College Library, dated 1957).

1. Purdy, *Thomas Hardy: A Bibliographical Study*, p. 176.
2. *Later Years*, p. 178; *Life*, p. 378.
3. August 18, 1870, between the Germans under King William of Prussia and the French under Marshal Bazaine.
4. *Early Life*, p. 104; *Life*, pp. 78-79.
5. In the Dorset County Museum.
6. Jer. 51:20, and Gen. 8:22.

CRY OF THE HOMELESS was Hardy's reply to an appeal by Edith Wharton, sent to him by Henry James, who wrote on July 21, 1915: "Mrs. Wharton has written me from Paris a request that I will appeal to your generosity and your genius in the interest of the beneficent volume of which the enclosed is a prospectus." Hardy presumably promised a poem. James wrote again on July 28, asking that he "distil the liquor of your poetic genius, in no matter how mild a form, into three or four blest versicles, on Mrs. Wharton's behalf, by August 10th." Hardy noted on the letter, " 'Cry of the Homeless' sent—Aug. 8, 1915." On August 12, Mrs. Wharton wrote thanks for "Your splendid Cry of the Homeless." [1] The poem was published in Edith Wharton, ed., *The Book of the Homeless* (New York and London, 1916).[2]

Speaking for the homeless of Belgium, the poem presents a grim curse upon the war lords behind the Prussian invasion, and then "a richer malediction," that they come to feel compassion for their victims and endless remorse for their deeds.

1. In the Dorset County Museum.
2. Purdy, *Thomas Hardy: A Bibliographical Study*, p. 192.

BEFORE MARCHING AND AFTER was first published in the *Fortnightly Review* for October, 1915.[1] It is a memorial to Second Lieutenant Frank William George of the Fifth Dorset Regiment, killed in action in Gallipoli on August 22, 1915. He was the oldest son of the deceased William George of Bere Regis, Dorset, and through his mother was Hardy's cousin.

Frank George, his favorite among relatives outside his immediate family, was a frequent visitor at Max Gate. On May 19, 1913, he wrote from Bristol to ask Hardy to recommend him to "the Benchers of Gray's Inn generally" in connection with an application for a "call to the bar," and presumably Hardy recommended him. He received his commission in the army in March of 1915. *The Later Years* says that George called at Max Gate shortly before leaving for the front: "In April a distant cousin of promising ability—a lieutenant in the 5th Batt. Dorset Regiment—came to see him [Hardy] before going abroad, never to be seen by him again."[2]

The poem as printed in a pamphlet for Mrs. Florence Hardy in December, 1915, is accompanied by a photograph of George in uniform. A foreword says of George: "A few days before his death he performed a fine act of gallantry of which news was sent home by his colonel and by a brother officer, in consequence of which his name was forwarded for reward. He describes the incident himself, as follows, in a letter to a friend: '. . . The night before last the regiment received orders to take a house and two small sections of a trench in our front. . . . I was given orders at dusk, and had to start at one o'clock. Well, I did start with two platoons, about 60 men, but very soon lost direction in the dark. However, we carried on, and seeing the flashes of rifles straight to our front, I gave the order to charge, and myself and twelve men got into the trenches. We bayonetted and shot seven or eight of the defenders, and the rest either escaped in the darkness or were taken prisoners. We held the trench for some time, but . . . retired on our own trenches with 14 prisoners. The 9th Army Corps Commander sent me a message, "Well done, Dorsets." ' His last recorded action by a sergeant in his company was one which fitly closed an unselfish life. Before leaving his trenches Lieutenant George divided the contents of his water-bottle among those nearest to him. He then advanced a few yards, but was killed instantly by a shell bursting over his head."

Hardy heard of George's death in a telegram from George's mother, Bertha George: "Frank was killed on 22nd." A letter from Brigadier General Cathcart Hannay of the Thirty-Fourth Infantry Brigade told Hardy how George had died "just as his Company was leaving the trenches to attack." The letter adds that "I sent his name forward for reward & it was forwarded by the Brigade."

Correspondence exhibits the parental affection both Hardy and his wife Florence felt for George. In a letter to Rebekah Owen on June 23, 1915, Florence wrote: "Our one promising relative . . . on either side—is off to the Dardanelles this week. He is the only one we felt we could be at all proud of."[3] On August 30, Florence wrote to Alda, Lady Hoare: "We had hoped that when we were gone he [George] would live here [at Max Gate] after us, & that in my husband's last days he (T. H.) would have had that strong arm to lean upon. . . . He was, as my husband says, *'Our one.'* "[4] She wrote to Rebekah Owen on September 1: "We had decided, T. and I . . . to look upon him as a sort of son—although he was exactly my own age, —and to leave him Max Gate, and all sorts of family possessions belonging to T. He was quite handsome—tall and well-mannered."[5] To the end of his life, Hardy mourned George's death. *The Later Years* says that on November 11, Armistice Day, 1927: "T. came downstairs from his study and listened to the broadcasting of a service at Canterbury Cathedral. . . . He said afterwards that he had been thinking of Frank George, his cousin, who was killed at Gallipoli."[6]

The first two stanzas of "Before Marching and After" present Frank George's meditations on a visit to his mother's home just before going overseas. The third stanza presents the arrival of the telegram (the "quick comer") announcing his death. (See the notes on "Outside the Casement.")

1. Purdy, *Thomas Hardy: A Bibliographical Study*, p. 174.
2. P. 168; *Life*, p. 370.
3. In the Colby College Library.
4. In the Stourhead Collection, the County Archives, Trowbridge.
5. In the Colby College Library.
6. P. 261; *Life*, p. 443.

"OFTEN WHEN WARRING," first published in the *Sphere*, November 10, 1917,[1] may rest upon some story told to Hardy by German prisoners of war in Dorchester. Actions similar to that of the poem are described in *The Dynasts*, as at the battle of Talavera. (Part Second, IV, v.)

1. Purdy, *Thomas Hardy: A Bibliographical Study*, p. 206.

THEN AND NOW, first published in the *Times* on July 11, 1917,[1] attacks the methods of modern warfare that include the slaughter of civilian populations, especially children, by comparing this "total war" with the chivalric warfare alleged of earlier times. Modern warfare is like Herod's killing of the children in the Gospels: "Then Herod . . . sent forth, and slew all the children that were in Bethlehem, and in all the coasts thereof, from two years old and under. . . . In Rama was there a voice heard, lamentation, and weeping, and great mourning, Rachel weeping for her children."[2]

1. Purdy, *Thomas Hardy: A Bibliographical Study*, p. 206.
2. Matt. 2:16-18.

A CALL TO NATIONAL SERVICE was published in the *Times*, the *Morning Post*, and other papers on March 12, 1917. Hardy wrote to Sydney Cockerell on March 31 that the poem was "written in a great hurry at the request of the N. S. Depart^t."[1]

The octave of this sonnet is a public appeal to "Up and be doing" at a time when England was showing signs of exhaustion. That England must not be left a "land / Untended as a wild of weeds and sand" recalls Shakespeare's description of England in *Richard II*. The servant to the gardener asks whether it is worth while in wartime to tend "our sea-walled garden" when "the whole land, / Is full of weeds." (III, iv.) In the sestet Hardy, then nearly seventy-seven, regrets his own inability to "stir as once I stirred" in early-rising years.

1. Purdy, *Thomas Hardy: A Bibliographical Study*, p. 191.

THE DEAD AND THE LIVING ONE was first printed in the *Sphere* on December 25, 1915, and in the New York *World* on January 2, 1916.[1] Hardy called the poem a "war-ballad of some weirdness . . . written several months before."[2] This ghostly tale treats a wartime dislocation that ends in a complex of ironies.

1. Purdy, *Thomas Hardy: A Bibliographical Study*, p. 206.
2. *Later Years*, p. 171; *Life*, p. 372.

A NEW YEAR'S EVE IN WAR TIME, Hardy wrote to Mrs. Arthur Henniker on December 22, 1916, treats "an incident that happened here [at Max Gate] on a New Year's Eve not so long ago."[1] In a letter to Sir Sydney Cockerell on January 15, he gave more details: "I am rather surprised at people liking the *Sphere* poem . . . for I thought it was of a middling sort. The incident of the horse galloping past precisely at the stroke of midnight between the old and new year is, by the way, true; it happened here, and we never learnt what horse it was. It is strange that you should have lighted on the Blake picture[2] which in some respects almost matches the verses."[3]

This horse that clattered past while Hardy sat brooding upon the New Year and the war apparently suggested not only the "pale horse: and his name that sat on him was Death," but the three other horses of Revelation 8, bringing (in Hardy's interpretation) "Tears," "Famine and Flame," and "Severance and Shock."[4] The theme of "A New Year's Eve in War Time" seems to be that Fate has decreed the war, and mankind must endure it.

Vinson has pointed out that, in the technique of the poem, "every line is rhymed with the corresponding line in every other stanza. The first and last stanzas have an extra line and longer line at the end, rhyming with the preceding one, and these two are almost alike. . . . The form seems to have been original with Hardy."[5]

1. In the Dorset County Museum.
2. Blake's color-print "Pity."
3. Meynell, ed., *Friends of a Lifetime*, p. 284.

4. Ibáñez's *The Four Horsemen of the Apocalypse* was not published in English until 1918.

5. "Diction and Imagery in the Poetry of Thomas Hardy," pp. 175-76.

"I MET A MAN" was first published in the *Fortnightly Review* for February, 1917.[1] Wishing to speak about the horror of World War I in tones of the prophets of Israel, Hardy invented the mask of a prophet who had seen and heard "the Moulder of Monarchies." The poem is an imaginary conversation with this man, who has the "shining face and eye" of "Moses' after Sinai," as in Exod. 34:29, ". . . when Moses came down from mount Sinai with the two tables of testimony . . . Moses wist not that the skin of his face shone while he talked." The Moulder of Monarchies laments "that old mistake of mine / I made with Saul," as in I Sam. 15:11, "It repenteth me that I have set up Saul to be king: for he is turned back from following me, and hath not performed my commandments."

Mingled with these Biblical references that define the man as prophet and the Moulder of Monarchies as the Lord, Hardy's phrases describe the war-makers, their game, and their victims in medieval images. The nations are "gambling clans" of cock-fighters that "pit liege men" in "death-mains." The "Lords of War . . . enshrine / Liberticide," so that "With violence the lands are spread / Even as in Israel's day."

The poem suggests that the Lord is becoming conscious of the evil of the "armipotents lust-led" that He unwittingly "bred," but has not yet decided to destroy.

1. Purdy, *Thomas Hardy: A Bibliographical Study*, p. 189.

"I LOOKED UP FROM MY WRITING" states Hardy's feeling that it was futile to combat the madness of World War I by writing idealistic poems (*e.g.*, "The Pity of It" and "I Met a Man"). While he is dreaming, "rapt in my inditing," he observes the moon gazing at him. Here, as elsewhere, the moon is a symbol for realistic fact. The moon's story of a father's "frenzied tattle" and suicide when his innocent son was brutally slain suggests that only a man with "blinkered mind" would wish to write or even to live in such a world.

FINALE

THE COMING OF THE END is a suitable penultimate poem for *Moments of Vision*. It surveys Hardy's life with his first wife Emma, especially in relation to the poems about her in this volume. The poem refers in chronological sequence to incidents presented in other poems.[1]

The incidents begin with "the meeting afar from the crowd," as in "The Wind's Prophecy," "First Sight of Her and After," "It Never Looks Like Summer," "The Figure in the Scene," and "Why Did I Sketch." The "parting when much was avowed" is treated in "At the Word 'Farewell' " and "Love the Monopolist." The second stanza sums up the substance of "Overlooking the River Stour." The "house-building, furnishing, planting" of the third stanza are treated in "Everything Comes." The "welcoming, feasting" at Max Gate are recalled in "You Were the Sort that Men Forget," and the "jaunting," in "Old Excursions." In the fourth stanza "That journey of one day a week" possibly refers to Hardy's weekly visit to his parents. In their first years at Max Gate, Emma would go with him on these visits; she later refused to go. "Paths of Former Time" may refer guardedly to these visits.[2] The final stanza describes how his life with Emma "stopped without jerk." The rift between them had existed for some years, and he had ignored Emma's efforts to revive their affection, as in "The Peace-Offering." When she died unexpectedly "it came to an end."

1. I am naming only poems in *Moments of Vision*, though some of the incidents mentioned are treated also in *Satires of Circumstance* and elsewhere.
2. Purdy associates this stanza with Hardy's visits to Mrs. Arthur Henniker in Winchester when they were collaborating on "The Spectre of the Real." *Thomas Hardy: A Bibliographical Study*, p. 344. In *Hardy's Love Poems*, Weber agrees. P. 45. "The Coming of the End," however, is about Hardy's life with Emma.

AFTERWARDS, closing *Moments of Vision*, was sent to the publisher in the summer of 1917, when Hardy was seventy-seven years old. The opening line of the poem suggests his "tremulous stay" in a world then at war. Aware that he might not live to publish another volume, he wrote the poem to tell his neighbors how he wished them to remember him. It says nothing of literary fame. Striking no note of pessimism or even regret, it presents his sensitivity to the beauty and mystery of the world and his compassion for all innocent, helpless creatures.[1]

The "May month" is alive: it "flaps its glad green leaves." The hawk is no predator, but a visitor at dewfall to the lonely "wind-warped upland thorn." The "nocturnal blackness" is not forbidding, for it is "mothy and warm," suggesting in his use of folklore some friendly spirits near. The hedgehog is no threat to the gardener, but one of many "innocent creatures" to be shielded from harm.[2]

In structure, the poem touches upon each of the seasons, May, summer dusk, autumn's "nocturnal blackness," and the "full-starred heavens that winter sees." "A sense of time runs through the poem —the 'when' of each stanza is set up in the first line, and the rest of the stanza develops an action appropriate to that moment."[3] Each stanza ends with a statement almost prose: "He was a man who used to notice such things," the point of the poem. "Afterwards" has been set to music by Christopher LeFleming in *Six Country Songs* (London: Novello & Co., 1963).

1. Hardy's will left legacies to the Royal Society for the Prevention of Cruelty to Animals and to the Council of Justice to Animals to be "applied so far as practicable to the investigation of the means by which Animals are conveyed from their Homes to the Slaughter-houses with a view to the lessening of their sufferings in such transit and to condemnatory action against the caging of wild birds and the captivity of rabbits and other animals." Cox, ed., *Thomas Hardy's Will*, p. 2.

2. Hardy once said that he thought the hedgehog "a piece of Divine creation which God for some reason or other had put under spikes." Evelyn Hardy, *Thomas Hardy*, p. 290.

3. Hynes, *The Pattern of Hardy's Poetry*, p. 126.

LATE LYRICS AND EARLIER

When *Late Lyrics and Earlier* was published on May 23, 1922, Hardy lacked only ten days of being eighty years old. He stated his mature view of the world, what was wrong with it and what must be done to right it, in a preface called "Apology," but for the most part laid philosophy aside in the 151 poems of the volume. They are chiefly lyric voicings of impressions. Many reflect a mulling over of memories, the fruit of notebooks (at a time when he was making notes toward his biography), and the rediscovery of old poems rejected for previous volumes. Perhaps a third of the poems treat long-past incidents, like "The Maid of Keinton Mandeville," which recalls a concert he had heard in 1878, or "The West-of-Wessex Girl," which recalls *Some Recollections* of his first wife Emma. Old notebooks provide poems like "On Stinsford Hill at Midnight" and "The Beauty." A number of the poems were written in the nineteenth century: "Dream of the City Shopwoman," 1866; "A Young Man's Exhortation," 1867; "After Reading Psalms XXXIX., XL., Etc.," 187—; "Rake-Hell Muses," 189—; and "Murmurs in the Gloom," 1899. Other poems treat events between *Moments of Vision*, 1917, and 1922: World War I in "Jezreel," its end in "And There Was a Great Calm," and domestic matters, as in "A Jog-Trot Pair" and "Evelyn G. of Christminster." In tone, most of the recently written poems are serene.

APOLOGY.—Except in prefaces, letters, and scattered comments on individual pieces, Hardy wrote little literary criticism. That little is concentrated in "Apology," his preface for *Late Lyrics and Earlier*. Hardy hesitated to enter the arena of criticism, either in self-defense or as a prose-protagonist for ideas in his poems. He wrote to Edmund

Gosse on February 14, 1922, concerning "Apology": "I don't alto-
gether jump at the chance of appearing on the literary stage again.
. . . I have now been able to put in among the short prefatory words
that 'some illustrious men of letters' have asked for the poems."[1] On
February 15, before sending "Apology" to the publisher, Hardy asked
Sir Sydney Cockerell for his advice: "I am sending it to ask your
opinion whether I shall prefix it to the new volume or not. I don't
wish to, and should not at all mind destroying it. It came into my
mind mostly while lying in bed during the late weeks, and seemed
then almost necessary. Is it uncalled for, or, if not altogether so, is it
too cantankerous in respect of reviewers, &c., for a writer whose books
are fairly well received nowadays?" When Cockerell replied favorably,
Hardy wrote again on February 18: "I am abridging the whole some-
what, in spite of your saying you would not omit a word; for I fancy
it is a little long and iterative."[2] The revised "Apology" was sent
to the publisher on February 21.[3]

It develops two themes. One is Hardy's defense of his poetry and
his point of view against the attacks of critics, some of whom had
spoken of his opinions in shocked horror, and others, in pontifical
condescension. He quoted Frederic Harrison's "This view of life is
not mine." Speaking with assumed superiority, Harrison had written
of Hardy's poems: "My philosophy of life is more cheerful and hope-
ful than that of these lyrics."[4] In reply, Hardy asserts that his poems
in *Late Lyrics* "contain little or nothing in technic or teaching that
can be considered . . . so much as agitating to a ladies' school." He
defends his "alleged . . . 'pessimism' " with the argument that a real-
istic view of life is necessary to bring about any "evolutionary
meliorism," or gradual betterment in human nature. It is the func-
tion of poetry, he argues, to apply ideas to life.[5]

With this transition, he turns to commentary on the state of the
post-war world, saying that "we seem threatened with a new Dark
Age."[6]

He was not content to let the Dark Age come without a word of
protest. His positive message in the rest of "Apology," his "forlorn
hope," is for an "alliance between religion . . . and complete ration-
ality," through the "interfusing effect of poetry." By "religion" in
this statement, he does not mean theology or creeds expressing belief
in an anthropomorphic God. Himself "churchy; not in an intellectual
sense, but in so far as instincts and emotions ruled,"[7] Hardy had long
ceased to believe in a theology of the supernatural. He believed that
religion could regain its hold upon human life if the Church "could
be made to modulate by degrees . . . into an undogmatic, non-theologi-

cal establishment for the promotion of that virtuous living on which all honest men are agreed."[8] He wrote to Edward Clodd on February 27, 1902: "If the doctrines of the supernatural were quietly abandoned tomorrow by the Church, & 'reverence & love for an ethical ideal' alone retained, not one in ten thousand would object to the readjustment, while the enormous bulk of thinkers excluded by the old teaching would be brought into the fold, & our venerable old churches & cathedrals would become the centres of emotional life that they once were."[9] In his notebook for 1907, he jotted a synopsis for an article on religion that would include: "The days of creeds are as dead and done with as the days of Pterodactyls. Required: services at which there are no affirmations and no supplications. . . . *Religious, religion*, is to be used in the article in its modern sense entirely, as being expressive of nobler feelings toward humanity and emotional goodness and greatness, the old meaning of the word—ceremony, or ritual— having perished, or nearly."[10]

His "complete rationality" to be interfused with religion by means of poetry owes a great deal to Matthew Arnold. In *Literature and Dogma*, Arnold sought to defend Christianity for the modern world by separating it from "the theology of the Fathers or Protestant theology," which "do not reach the aim" of Christian teaching. They substitute "Catholic dogma or Lutheran justification by faith . . . for the method and secret of Jesus." The method and secret of Jesus are "conscience and self-renouncement"; "they *are* righteousness, bring about the kingdom of God or the reign of righteousness." To the method and secret, Arnold would add Jesus's "sweet reasonableness."[11] Simply, without reference to an afterlife of rewards and punishments, he would have the Church teach such doctrines as those of the Sermon on the Mount. He would preserve the Church for its power to add poetry (emotion) to truth: "Our religion has materialized itself in the fact, in the supposed fact; it has attached its emotion to the fact, and now the fact is failing it. But for poetry the idea is everything; the rest is a world of illusion, of divine illusion. Poetry attaches its emotion to the idea; the idea *is* the fact. The strongest part of our religion today is its unconscious poetry."[12] Hardy was even more rationalistic than Arnold, who had tried to support some elements of dogma by tracing the hardening of Hebrew concepts of eternal principle, righteousness, etc. into terms for a personal God. He defined God as a Power not ourselves that makes for righteousness. Regarding these efforts and perhaps rejecting "not ourselves" (see "A Plaint to Man"), Hardy wrote in his notebook for October 7, 1888: "When dogma has to be balanced on its feet by such hair-splitting as the late

Mr. M. Arnold's it must be in a very bad way."[13] In a letter to the *Times* on January 17, 1928, J. H. Morgan quoted Hardy in support of the Church if it might be reformed and become "more rationalist": "I believe in going to church. It is a moral drill, and people must have something. If there is no church in a country village, there is nothing. . . . I believe in reformation coming from *within* the Church. The clergy are growing more rationalist, and that is the best way of changing."

1. In the British Museum.
2. Meynell, ed., *Friends of a Lifetime*, pp. 288-89.
3. Purdy, *Thomas Hardy: A Bibliographical Study*, p. 227.
4. "Novissima Verba," p. 183.
5. He quotes Matthew Arnold's "familiar phrase" on this subject. It is found in Arnold's "On Translating Homer," "Wordsworth," and elsewhere.
6. A letter he wrote to General John Hartman Morgan on April 5, 1921, states his source for this phrase: "A friend of mine, a Professor at Cambridge, in spite of being quite a Radical, says he thinks we are at the beginning of a New Dark Ages centuries long." In the Berg Collection, New York Public Library.
7. *Later Years*, p. 176; *Life*, p. 376.
8. Letter to Lord Morley, Nov. 20, 1885; copy in the Dorset County Museum.
9. In the British Museum: "reverence and love for an ethical ideal" is quoted from T. H. Huxley.
10. *Later Years*, p. 121; *Life*, p. 332.
11. Chapter XII. Hardy's "Commonplace Book I" in the Dorset County Museum quotes passages from Arnold's *Literature and Dogma*.
12. "The Study of Poetry." Hardy copied this passage in his "Literary Notes I," p. 225, in the Dorset County Museum.
13. *Early Life*, p. 281; *Life*, p. 215.

WEATHERS was first published in *Good Housekeeping* (London) for May, 1922.[1] Perhaps Hardy selected this poem to open *Late Lyrics and Earlier* to symbolize two moods running through the volume. Both spring and autumn have rain, but the showers of spring only "betumble," while the steady drip of autumn floods the meadows; one revives, the other depresses. The scenes are near Dorchester. Several inns in Dorset are named "The Travellers' Rest," as one on the Bridport Road about twelve miles west of Dorchester and one in Sherborne.[2]

The movement of the poem is that of a folk-dance or country jig, lively with anapests in the first stanza, tired with spondees ("hill-hid tides throb") in the second. Many composers have set "Weathers" to music: John Ireland (London: J. B. Cramer & Co., 1925), Thomas Wood (London: Stainer & Bell, 1927), Michael Head (London: Boosey & Co., 1933), Phyllis Tate (London: Oxford University Press, 1935), Roger Fiske (London: Oxford University Press, 1951), Celius Dougherty (New York: G. Schirmer, 1954), William Lovelock (London: Chappel & Co., 1958), Christopher LeFleming in *Six Country Songs* (London: Novello & Co., 1963), James Butt (London: Novello

& Co., 1965), Eric H. Thiman (London: Elkin and Co., undated), Eric Smith (London: Joseph Williams, undated), and Edgar Proudman (in manuscript in the Dorset County Museum). E. L. Wright wrote to Hardy on May 26, 1922, saying that he had set the poem to music. I have not seen a record of publication.[3]

1. Purdy, *Thomas Hardy: A Bibliographical Study*, p. 215.
2. I was told that the "Quiet Woman" of *The Return of the Native* represented the Duck Inn, which had been called "The Travellers' Rest." It no longer exists as an inn, but was located about three miles east of Dorchester on the Tincleton Road.
3. In the Dorset County Museum.

THE MAID OF KEINTON MANDEVILLE was first published in the *Athenaeum* for April 30, 1920. The parenthesis under the title then read: "(A tribute to Sir Henry Bishop on the sixty-fifth anniversary of his death: April 30, 1855)."[1] Sir Henry Bishop (1786-1855) was a composer for Covent Garden Theatre, where he turned out operas, burlettas, cantatas, and incidental music for plays; for *Clari*, he composed the music for "Home, Sweet Home." In 1830, he became musical director at Vauxhall, and in 1841 Reid Professor of Music at the University of Edinburgh; he was knighted in 1842. Hardy's interest in Bishop seems motivated by his fondness for the song "Should He Upbraid." "The song is a paraphrase of Petruchio's speech just before the entrance of Katharina (*Taming of the Shrew*, II, i). It was composed by Sir Henry Bishop for a revival of *The Two Gentlemen of Verona* at the Covent Garden Theatre in 1821, and was first sung by Miss Ellen Tree in that play."[2]

Hardy was enchanted by a rendition of this song on March 5, 1878. *The Early Life* says: " 'Concert at Sturminster. A Miss Marsh of Sutton [Keinton?] Mandeville sang "Should he upbraid," to Bishop's old tune. She is the sweetest of singers—thrush-like in the descending scale, and lark-like in the ascending. . . .' Many years after Hardy was accustomed to say that this was the most marvellous old song in English music in its power of touching an audience."[3]

Apparently Hardy was stimulated to write "The Maid of Keinton Mandeville" by his memory of her singing, and he also wished to pay a tribute to the composer by publishing the poem on his birthday. When J. M. Murry, editor of the *Athenaeum*, asked for a poem, Hardy wrote: "I have found some verses which at first I thought would only suit publication in a *daily* paper dated April 30th. But I find by accident there will be an Athenaeum on April 30th next, and therefore I shall have pleasure in sending you the verses for . . . that number . . . . the aforesaid poem would lose some of whatever point it may have if it were published at another date."[4]

1. Purdy, *Thomas Hardy: A Bibliographical Study,* p. 215.
2. Copps, "The Poetry of Thomas Hardy," p. 632.
3. P. 156; *Life,* p. 118. *The Early Life* says "Sturminster," whereas the poem says "Stower Town" (normally Stourton, twelve miles north of Sturminster Newton). Sturminster, on the Stour River, must be right; it is where the Hardys lived. The brackets and question mark are Hardy's. Sutton Mandeville is about fifteen miles northeast of Sturminster Newton, near Salisbury; Keinton Mandeville is about fifteen miles northwest, north of Yeovil.
4. In the Berg Collection, the New York Public Library.

SUMMER SCHEMES seems the song of a lover planning summer outings with his sweetheart, but with doubt about fulfilment in the last line of each stanza. The moon in the final line, in Hardy's poetry a symbol of cold reality, is ominous. The poem has been set to music by John Ireland (London: J. B. Cramer & Co., 1925) and Gerald Finzi in *Earth and Air and Rain* (London: Boosey & Hawkes, 1936).

EPEISODIA seems a swift summary of Hardy's courtship of Emma Gifford in the Valency Valley in Cornwall, their meeting in London for marriage, and Emma's burial (and Hardy's expected burial) in Stinsford Churchyard, a few hundred feet above the bywaters of the "random river," the Frome.

"Epeisodia" has a curious rime-scheme: "Each stanza . . . ends with a double rhyme . . . with two syllables rhyming with the last line of the other stanzas parallel with it, making a chain-rhyme: 'There caressed we,' 'There pressed we,' and 'There shall rest we.' "[1] The poem has been set to music in *Before and After Summer* (London: Boosey & Hawkes, 1949).

1. Vinson, "Diction and Imagery in the Poetry of Thomas Hardy," p. 250.

FAINTHEART IN A RAILWAY TRAIN first appeared in the *London Mercury* for January, 1920, with the title "A Glimpse from the Train." The poem is light and mocking, but even if Hardy laughed at himself, he had a tendency to build day-dreams on the sight of a pretty face. He described this trait in Pierston of *The Well-Beloved,* who says: "I was standing on the kerbstone of the pavement in Budmouth-Regis . . . when a middle-aged gentleman on horseback, and beside him a young lady, also mounted, passed down the street. The girl turned her head, and . . . smiled at me. Having ridden a few paces, she looked round again and smiled. It was enough, more than enough, to set me on fire. I understood in a moment the information conveyed to me by my emotion." (Part First, Chapter VII.) Pierston had never seen the girl before and never saw her again.

AT MOONRISE AND ONWARDS is a meditation addressed to the moon, personified as "Wan Woman of the waste." The poet is viewing the rising moon from Max Gate, for "Heath-Plantation Hill" is

Hardy's name for Frome Hill, topped by a tumulus, about half a mile east of Max Gate.[1] A "vill" to be seen from this eminence is Higher Bockhampton. The poem symbolizes the moon as a "furtive feminine," cynical view of reality.

1. See the notes on "Seeing the Moon Rise" and Evelyn Hardy, *Thomas Hardy*, p. 165.

THE GARDEN SEAT Hardy identified as treating a seat at Max Gate.[1] A letter from Mrs. Florence Hardy to Lady Grogan, dated September 14 (no year is stated), says that the garden seats at Max Gate are decaying and the wooden legs are sinking into the ground.[2]

Observing a rotting seat, Hardy sees a double vision: the seat and the memory-ghosts of friends who had sat on it. "But here the ghosts of the dead persons are subordinate . . . to another instance of mortality: the imminent mortality of the rotting bench. . . . The parenthetic remark that the ghost-people are indifferent to winter and flood sounds as if it might be comfortable to have the ghosts' order of existence."[3] "The Garden Seat" has been set to music by Michael Head (London: Boosey & Co., 1933).

1. Purdy, *Thomas Hardy: A Bibliographical Study*, p. 215.
2. In the possession of Mrs. Vera Mardon of Dorchester.
3. Ransom, "Honey and Gall," pp. 8-9.

BARTHÉLÉMON AT VAUXHALL dramatizes the imaginary scene when Barthélémon was inspired to write his music for Bishop Ken's "Awake My Soul." This hymn had been one of Hardy's boyhood favorites. At Stinsford Church " 'Barthélémon' and 'Tallis' were played to Ken's Morning and Evening Hymns respectively every Sunday throughout the year."[1] In 1895, when W. T. Stead, editor of the *Review of Reviews*, asked Hardy to name "Hymns that have helped me," he replied: "I am unable to answer your inquiry. . . . But the undermentioned have always been familiar and favourite hymns of mine as poetry: 1. 'Thou turnest man, O Lord, to dust.' . . . 2. 'Awake, my soul, and with the sun.' (Morning Hymn, Ken.). 3. 'Lead, kindly Light.' " "Awake My Soul" continued a favorite all his life. On March 8, 1928, H. F. Whitley wrote to Howard Bliss about Hardy's attendance at St. Peter's Church in Dorchester, saying that "when Thomas Hardy was seen to be in the church before the service commenced, word was sent into the vestry & whatever first hymn had been chosen, it was altered to 'Awake my soul & with the sun.' "[2]

This interest caused him to summarize in his notebook labelled "Facts" the life-story of François Hippolite Barthélémon (1741-1808), including: "In 1770 B. became leader at Vauxhall Gardens. . . . An acquaintce. with the Revd. Jacob Duché, chaplain of the French

Orphan Asym. led to his composing, about 1780, the well-known tune for the Morng Hymn 'Awake my Soul.' . . . As a player he was distingd. by the firmness of his hand, the purity of his tone, & the admble. manner of executing an adagio."[3]

"Barthélémon at Vauxhall" was first published in the London *Times* on July 23, 1921. There Hardy's note preceding the poem says: "To-day is the anniversary of his death in 1808. The circumstances of the following lines have no claim to be more than suppositious."[4] *The Later Years* indicates the occasion for Hardy's composition of the poem in July, 1921: "About this time he went to St. Peter's Church, to a morning service, for the purpose of hearing sung by the choir the morning hymn, 'Awake my Soul,' to Barthélémon's setting. This had been arranged for him by Dr. Niven, the Rector of St. Peter's. . . . He had often imagined the weary musician, returning from his nightly occupation of making music for a riotous throng, lingering on Westminster Bridge to see the rising sun and being thence inspired to the composition of music to be heard hereafter in places very different from Vauxhall."[5] The memorial services for Hardy held in Stinsford Church on June 2, 1940, opened with "Awake My Soul."[6]

1. *Early Life*, p. 14; *Life*, p. 10.
2. In the Berg Collection, New York Public Library.
3. In the Dorset County Museum. Besides the poem, Hardy sketched three plots for a short-story to be called "The Vauxhall Fiddler." Each of the plots presents a different way of telling the story of Barthélémon's composition of music for "Awake My Soul." See Evelyn Hardy, ed., "Plots for Five Unpublished Short Stories,'" pp. 37-39.
4. Purdy, *Thomas Hardy: A Bibliographical Study*, p. 215. Hardy's note says nothing about Bishop Thomas Ken (1637-1711), author of the words of the hymn, which he wrote about 1674.
5. Pp. 223-24; *Life*, p. 414. Vauxhall Gardens in Lambeth, London, were opened for suppers, fireworks, music, and entertainments about 1661. The entertainments degenerated, and the Gardens were closed in 1859.
6. "The Bishop Analyzes Hardy's Religion," *Dorset County Chronicle*, June 6, 1940.

"I SOMETIMES THINK" Hardy wrote as a tribute to his second wife Florence. His meditation of "things I have done" may be related to his preparation of notes for his biography, issued by Mrs. Hardy after his death as *The Early Life* and *The Later Years of Thomas Hardy*.

The second stanza points to some of his achievements that he valued, but that few people "cared to heed." The "press / To sow good seed" may refer to his ideas toward social reform, as in *Jude the Obscure*. The "saving from distress / In the nick of need" may refer to his efforts to aid Belgian refugees during World War I. The "words in the wilderness" may refer to his internationalism, unheeded in the years after the war. (See "His Country.")

The tribute to Florence indicates that she is like a guardian angel "spiriting into the house." That she "heeds all" suggests her efforts in matters like those of the second stanza. Her obituary notice names some of these efforts. She was "Patron of Dorset County Hospital and member of its Committee of Management and House Committee, contributing generously toward facilities for treating children. Justice of the Peace for Dorchester after March 7, 1924, noted for merciful judgments. First President of Mill-street Housing Society, concerned with housing for the poor at reasonable, low rents, erection of model dwellings, etc. Secretary of the Dorchester and District Branch of the Royal Society for Prevention of Cruelty to Animals, active in Society for Protection of Birds and Trees and the Society for Promotion of Christian Knowledge." [1]

1. "Death of Mrs. Thomas Hardy," *Dorset County Chronicle*, October 21, 1937.

JEZREEL was first published in the *Times* on September 27, 1918.[1]

Jezreel, an ancient city of Palestine, is the modern village of Zerin (or Zirin) in northern Israel. It was a part of the Turkish Empire, an ally of Germany in World War I. It was taken in September, 1918, as part of the conquest of the Turks by the British under General Edmund Allenby. Hardy's imagination was caught by the fact that the British occupied ancient Jezreel, of renown in the wars of the Old Testament. His poem concerns whether the British troops in Zerin realized that they were in Jezreel and saw there visions of ancient slaughter, especially phantom-scenes of Queen Jezebel. He does not mention biblical events in chronological order, but they may be cited as they occur in his lines:

Line 2: "the ancient Esdraelon Plain."—Jezreel was the capital of the Plain. There the idolatrous King Ahab and Queen Jezebel ruled over a portion of Israel in 919-896 B.C. (I and II Kings, *passim*.)

Line 3: "they crossed where the Tishbite stood forth in his enemy's way."—The Tishbite was the prophet Elijah, sent by the Lord to denounce Ahab and Jezebel for their sins and to prophesy their destruction. (I Kings 21:17-24.)

Line 4: "he bade the King haste off amain."—In a time of drought that the priests of Baal could not break, Elijah challenged Ahab to summon his priests to Mount Carmel, to test whether Baal or Jehovah were the true God. Elijah faced four hundred and fifty prophets of Baal, who prepared a bullock for burning, while Elijah soaked a bullock in water. Jehovah sent a fire to consume Elijah's offering

[436]

and show that He was God. Elijah, prophesying that God would send abundance of rain, told Ahab: "Prepare thy chariot, and get thee down, that the rain stop thee not. . . . And Ahab rode, and went to Jezreel." (I Kings 18.)

Line 7: "he who drove furiously."—At the command of the prophet Elisha, Jehu was anointed King of Israel that he might smite the sinful King Ahab. When Jehu approached Jezreel, the watchman on the tower reported: ". . . the driving is like the driving of Jehu the son of Nimshi; for he driveth furiously." (II Kings 9:1-20.)

Line 8: "that queen . . . that proud Tyrian woman who painted her face."—"And when Jehu was come to Jezreel, Jezebel heard of it; and she painted her face . . . and looked out at a window." (II Kings 9:30.)

Lines 9-10: " 'Throw her down!' from the Night eerily, / Spectre spots of the blood of her body on some rotten wall."—Conquering Jezreel, Jehu called to Jezebel's eunuchs, "And he said, Throw her down. So they threw her down: and some of her blood was sprinkled on the wall." (II Kings 9:33.) [2]

Line 11: "A King's daughter is she."—Ahab "took to wife Jezebel the daughter of Ethbaal king of the Zidonians." (I Kings 16:31.)

Line 12: "where she trodden was once by the chargers' footfall."—Jezebel's blood "was sprinkled . . . on the horses: and he trode her under foot." (II Kings 9:33.)

Line 15: "one on horseback who asked Is it peace?"—When Jehu rode toward Jezreel, "So there went one on horseback to meet him, and said, Thus saith the king, Is it peace?" (II Kings 9:18.)

Apparently Mrs. Arthur Henniker teased Hardy for being fond of Jezebel, for he wrote to her on October 27: "I was much gratified to hear that you liked 'Jezreel,' . . . It was written very rapidly, & was published the day after. . . . I thought people did not seem to realize that Esdraelon & Jezreel were the same. Well, as to my having any affection for Jezebel, I don't think I can admit that: I have the same sort of admiration for her that I have for Lady Macbeth, Clytaemnestra, & such. Her courage was splendid." [3]

1. Purdy, *Thomas Hardy: A Bibliographical Study*, p. 210.
2. When Hardy was in Paris in 1888, he went on June 4 and 7 to a Salon, and wrote in his journal: "Was arrested by the sensational picture called 'The Death of Jezebel' by Gabriel Guays, a horrible tragedy, and justly so, telling its story in a flash." *Early Life*, p. 273; *Life*, p. 208.
3. In the Dorset County Museum.

A JOG-TROT PAIR presents Hardy and his second wife, Florence. When he married Florence Dugdale on February 9, 1914, he was almost seventy-four, and she was thirty-five. The couple avoided a formal wedding: the only guests were Mr. Edward Dugdale and Hardy's brother Henry. There was no honeymoon. On February 12, three days after the marriage, Mrs. Hardy wrote from Max Gate to Edward Clodd: "T. & I have settled down & become a very humdrum married couple."[1]

"The Jog-Trot Pair" says that the couple were "happier than the cleverest, smartest, rarest." Their happiness realized an ideal that Hardy had expressed as early as *Far from the Madding Crowd* (1874) in describing the marriage of Bathsheba and Gabriel Oak: "Theirs was that substantial affection which arises . . . when the two who are thrown together begin first by knowing the rougher sides of each other's character, and not the best till further on, the romance growing up in the interstices of a mass of hard prosaic reality. This good-fellowship—*camaraderie*—usually occurring through similarity of pursuits . . . proves itself to be the only love which is strong as death."[2] Hardy speaks with humor in applying this ideal to himself, as in "Trite usages in tamest style." The phrase "just worth while" recalls the question "Is it worth while, dear?" of "Long Plighted."

1. In the Brotherton Library Collection, Leeds.
2. Chapter LVI.

"THE CURTAINS NOW ARE DRAWN" in the manuscript has " (Song: Major and Minor) ," to mark the tones of the first and second stanzas.[1] The first presents a scene during Hardy's courtship of Emma Gifford, set in the St. Juliot Rectory, Cornwall; the second, a scene in Stinsford Churchyard, where Emma was buried. "A song . . . is incorporated into each stanza, where it is both part of the dramatic action and a gloss upon the meaning of that action. The move . . . is a transition from the protected and secure world of love to the exposed and defenseless condition of bereavement."[2] "The Curtains Now Are Drawn" has been set to music by Rob H. Paterson (Edinburgh: R. W. Pentland, 1927) .

1. Purdy, *Thomas Hardy: A Bibliographical Study*, p. 216.
2. Hogan, "Structural Design in Thomas Hardy's Poetry," p. 53.

"ACCORDING TO THE MIGHTY WORKING" was first published in the *Athenaeum* on April 4, 1919.[1] John Middleton Murry, on becoming editor of the revived *Athenaeum* in 1919, asked Hardy for some poems, suggesting that they treat a new start or something topical. He replied on March 2: "The only verses I can light upon do not relate to a new start, & are not what is called topical." On March 9, he sent Murry a card: "Have found two verses which can be sent when required."[2]

"According to the Mighty Working" may seem more philosophical than topical, but *The Later Years* indicates its relation to current events: "In February he signed a declaration of sympathy with the Jews in support of a movement for 'the reconstitution of Palestine as a National Home for the Jewish People.' . . . about the same time there appeared a relevant poem by Hardy in *The Athenaeum* . . . entitled in words from the Burial Service, 'According to the Mighty Working.' "[3] World War I is over, and peace has come, but the peace has brought "this hid riot, Change," specifically, agitation about the British mandate over Palestine.[4]

The theme includes both the Heraclitean concept of constant flux and concepts derived from science. The "Mighty Working" is "the creative activity . . . constantly at work, sustaining matter through atomic motion and remodelling its forms through evolution."[5] This theme forms a part of Elizabeth-Jane's meditation in *The Mayor of Casterbridge* as she sits by the bedside of her dying mother: ". . . all this while the subtle-souled girl asking herself why she was born . . . why things around her had taken the shape they wore in preference to every other possible shape . . . what that chaos called consciousness, which spun in her at this moment like a top, tended to, and began in." (Chapter XVIII.)

The poem has been analyzed for its technical excellencies, as by Hynes: "One is immediately conscious of certain favorite Hardy effects: vastness in 'wide roomage stormless'; determinism in 'mumming' and the 'spinner's wheel'; semi-darkness; a turmoil of verbals. The language is abstract—one is conscious of words-as-words rather than as images (especially in *Peace, Change, being,* and *becoming* . . .) —but it is not heavy . . . in fact monosyllables predominate. . . . The impression the poem gives is . . . of language used to its full potential, yet with ease and control. The verse form, with its short lines, regular meter, and framing rhymes *(cease-peace, change-range)* contributes considerably to this effect."[6]

1. Purdy, *Thomas Hardy: A Bibliographical Study,* p. 216.
2. In the Berg Collection, New York Public Library.
3. P. 190; *Life,* p. 388. The words from the Burial Service are those of Eph. 1:19, "And what is the exceeding greatness of his power to us-ward who believe, according to the working of his mighty power."
4. This topic interested Hardy, perhaps because of its relation to Old Testament history; see "Jezreel."
5. Stevenson, *Darwin Among the Poets,* p. 285.
6. *The Pattern of Hardy's Poetry,* pp. 103-4. See also Vinson, "Diction and Imagery in the Poetry of Thomas Hardy," pp. 356-57; Ransom, "Honey and Gall," pp. 10-11; and Squire, "Mr. Hardy's Old Age," pp. 149-50.

"I WAS NOT HE" seems a love song by a lover who was not his sweetheart's choice. Though there is nothing clearly personal in the poem, Anshutz associates it with Hardy and Emma Gifford; it "implies that Emma had had an earlier lover,"[1] as she may well have had before the age of thirty when she met Hardy.

1. "The Road to Nirvana," p. 184.

THE WEST-OF-WESSEX GIRL treats Emma Gifford, who became the first Mrs. Hardy. Purdy says: "Plymouth was Mrs. Hardy's birthplace, and the poet paused in the city on his return from Cornwall and the scenes of their courtship. He gave the Plymouth Free Public Library a MS. of the poem in 1923."[1] When A. J. Rhodes of the *Western Weekly News*, Plymouth, asked permission to reprint the poem Hardy replied on June 17, 1922, that "it would be advisable not to publish it alone, but to include for the sake of clearness the supplemental poem on Plymouth entitled 'The Marble-Streeted Town.' "[2]

The poem reflects not only his visit to Plymouth in March of 1913, but also his reading of Emma's *Some Recollections* after her death, which describes her girlhood there. (See the notes on "Places," "During Wind and Rain," and "The Marble-Streeted Town.")

As the last line of the poem says, he did not go with Emma to her beloved Plymouth, "as planned." It is not clear that he refused to go. When Emma wrote to him about joining him in London during some bad weather, he replied on July 6, 1908: "I had rather take you to Cornwall [including Plymouth on the way?] than about London."[3] Perhaps the willingness and the time when both felt free to go never coincided.

In theme, the poem belongs with the "Poems of 1912-13," written in Hardy's first flood of remorse after Emma's death. "The West-of-Wessex Girl," begun in 1913 and completed later, indicates his tendency to regret the good deed intended, but neglected.

1. Purdy, *Thomas Hardy: A Bibliographical Study*, p. 216.
2. In the Dorset County Museum.
3. Weber, *"Dearest Emmie,"* p. 70.

WELCOME HOME may be read as Hardy's experience. Between his marriage in 1874 and his return to Dorchester to build Max Gate in 1883, he and his wife had travelled on the Continent and lived in London, Swanage, Sturminster, Weymouth, and Wimborne, with little time for Dorchester except on visits to his parents in nearby Higher Bockhampton. The word "Plans" (to build Max Gate) suggests this period. Perhaps some citizens whom he remembered had, by 1883, nearly forgotten the young man they had known as an architect, not yet as a famous writer.[1]

1. Zietlow, "Thomas Hardy and William Barnes: Two Dorset Poets," p. 293, suggests that "Welcome Home" was influenced by Barnes's contrasting "Went Hwome."

GOING AND STAYING had its first two stanzas published in the *London Mercury* for November, 1919.[1] In this publication, the poem presents images of youth, joy, and love that vanish away, and by contrast the distresses of World War I that persisted after the armistice. The third stanza was added in *Late Lyrics and Earlier* to reflect upon Time as a phantom-like broom that sweeps away both "sinister" and "sublime." To a "closelier" view, all things vanish away.[2]

Responding to a request that he send data about himself for a reference book, *Men of Today and Their Work*, Hardy jotted on the letter: "11 March '24—biogrl data being sent, a portrait, & 'Going & Staying.' "[3] Perhaps Hardy considered the poem a summary of his view of life at this time.

1. Purdy, *Thomas Hardy: A Bibliographical Study*, p. 216.
2. Hardy's image of Time as "ghostly arms revolving" recalls his phrase "the whirligig of time . . . having again set Viviette free" in *Two on a Tower*, Chapter XLI. He found the latter phrase in Shakespeare's *Twelfth Night*, V, i.
3. In the Dorset County Museum.

READ BY MOONLIGHT was written when Hardy was going through old papers for his biography. If the poem may be taken literally, the first stanza presents his coming upon an early love-letter that he recalls reading tenderly, and the second his reading the same writer's last letter "By the moon's cold shine," but without "Eyeing it in the tenderest way." In his symbolism, the moon stands for a realistic view of life, expressed in the memory of "pain and pine" between the time of the first and the last letter.

AT A HOUSE IN HAMPSTEAD was first published in *The John Keats Memorial Volume* (London, February 23, 1921).[1] On March 25, 1920, Hardy "Joined National Committee for acquiring Wentworth Place—the house once occupied by John Keats."[2] His notes for *The Later Years* included a further statement: "July 28 [1920]. Hardy sent the poem on Keats at Hampstead as a contribution to the book proposed to be published on the Centenary of Keats's death."[3]

Wentworth Place in Hampstead, London, was a house with two apartments at the foot of John Street: it stood in a garden with trees. "After the death of his brother Tom in December 1818 Keats went to live at Wentworth Place with Charles Brown." Each had an apartment with two bedrooms; they shared the garden. Keats had a front parlor; Brown, a back. "Keats's commanded a view of Hampstead Heath across the road."[4] The house is on a street now named Keats Grove, a residential area with many trees and birds, so that Hardy's fourth line may be unjustified. The "ancient tree" that he mentions is said to be an old, gnarled, now-propped-up mulberry in the front, near Keats's parlor, presumably the tree in which the nightingale of Keats's "Ode to a Nightingale" sang. The house is a national shrine, well kept and open to the public.

Hardy's interest in Keats included some local pride based on the theory that Keats came of Dorset stock. He "considered it possible that John Keats on the occasion of landing at Lulworth, at the time he composed his last sonnet . . . may have gone to visit relatives at a village called Broadmayne which lies between Dorchester and Winfrith. . . . He himself, he said, remembered people of the same name who lived in this village and were stablemen like Keats's own father; one of them, so he asserted, born about 1800, being remarkably like John Keats in appearance."[5] Mrs. Florence Hardy wrote to Amy Lowell that "there was a family named Keats living two or three miles from here [Max Gate] who Mr. Hardy was told by his father, was a branch of the family of the name living in the direction of Lulworth. . . . They kept horses, being what is called 'hauliers,' and did also a little farming. They were in feature singularly like the poet, and were quick-tempered, as he is said to have been. . . . All this is very vague, and may mean nothing, the only arresting point in it, considering that they were of the same name, being the facial likeness, which my husband says was very strong. He knew two or three of these Keatses."[6]

References in "At a House in Hampstead" to "the Seven famed Hills," to Rome, and to a pyramid concern Hardy's visit to Keats's grave in Rome in the spring of 1887. (See the notes on "Rome: At the Pyramid of Cestius.") "Where the Piazza steps incline" refers to Keats's lodgings in Rome in the house on the right as one climbs the stairway from the Piazza di Spagna to the Trinita de' Monti.

The theme of the poem is Hardy's characteristic one of change. The first four stanzas question whether Keats's ghost will haunt this familiar house, yet changed in all its neighborhood, with houses instead of heath in the view from the parlor. Perhaps more of Keats's spirit remains in the house in Hampstead than in his grave in Rome.

1. Purdy, *Thomas Hardy: A Bibliographical Study*, p. 216.
2. *Later Years*, p. 210; *Life*, p. 404.
3. In an early draft of *The Later Years* labelled "T. H. Memoranda and Notes towards completing the remainder of Vol. II," to be included on p. 214; *Life*, p. 406. In the Dorset County Museum.
4. Lowell, *John Keats*, II, 120.
5. Blunden, *Thomas Hardy*, p. 162.
6. Quoted in "Hardys and Keatses" in *Dorset Year-Book*, 1928, p. 136.

A WOMAN'S FANCY exhibits Hardy's interest in both love as an idealization and the importance of burial among loved ones. The poem is something like a companion to "A Gentleman's Epitaph on Himself and a Lady."

HER SONG seems a soliloquy by the ghost of Hardy's first wife. Then the Monday when the song was chosen "as fittest to beguile" would be the evening of Monday, March 7, 1870, when Hardy first met Emma Gifford at St. Juliot Rectory. The summer would be August of that year, when he paid his second visit to Cornwall. The "afteryears" would refer to the period of "The Last Performance." (See the notes on this poem.) In the final stanza, Emma's ghost wonders whether Hardy, yet alive in "some dim land afar," sings the song, perhaps in memory of her.

"Her Song" has been set to music by John Ireland (London: J. B. Cramer & Co., 1925) and Christopher LeFleming in *Six Country Songs* (London: Novello & Co., 1963).

A WET AUGUST refers to Hardy's second visit to Emma Gifford in August of 1870.[1] The answer to the questions of the second stanza is that there was rain in Cornwall in August of 1870, as described in "The Figure in the Scene," "Why Did I Sketch," and "It Never Looks Like Summer."

1. Purdy, *Thomas Hardy: A Bibliographical Study*, p. 217.

THE DISSEMBLERS in the manuscript had the title "The Evaders."[1] The reference to daisies suggests that the dead woman was Hardy's first wife, who delighted in daisies. The first stanza seems his memory of a scene (perhaps in Stinsford Churchyard) when Emma had teased him; and the second stanza, his evasive remark about her after her death when, perhaps, someone had asked about her influence upon his "ways . . . works, or thoughts."

1. Purdy, *Thomas Hardy: A Bibliographical Study*, p. 217.

TO A LADY PLAYING AND SINGING IN THE MORNING seems to treat Hardy and his first wife. The poem suggests that he felt some sense that he was neglecting his work to listen to her playing and singing, and that she even teased him about doing so. The poem offers a contrast to "The Last Performance."

"A MAN WAS DRAWING NEAR TO ME" in the manuscript adds " (Woman's Song) ."[1] The poem, written as if by Emma Gifford, presents her feeling about Hardy's arrival at St. Juliot Rectory on the evening of March 7, 1870. The background for the poem is stated in *The Early Life*, quoted from her *Some Recollections*: "It was a lovely Monday evening in March [1870] . . . that we were on the *qui-vive* for the stranger, who would have a tedious journey, his home being two counties off by the route necessitated changing trains many times . . . a sort of cross-jump journey like a chess-knight's move. The only damp to our gladness was the sudden laying up of my brother-in-law by gout. . . . The dinner-cloth was laid; my sister had gone to her husband who required her constant attention. At that very moment the front-door bell rang, and the architect was ushered in. I had to receive him alone, and felt a curious uneasy embarrassment at receiving anyone. . . . I was immediately arrested by his familiar appearance, as if I had seen him in a dream."

The passage is followed by a footnote: "The verses entitled 'A Man was drawing near to Me' obviously relate to this arrival. But in them Hardy assumes that she was not thinking about his coming, though from this diary one gathers that she was; which seems to show that when writing them he had either not read her reminiscence of the evening as printed above, or had forgotten it." The footnote was probably written by Mrs. Florence Hardy, for correspondences between the passage quoted, other passages in *Some Recollections*, and the poem are hardly accidental.

In the poem, Emma is thinking "only of trifles—legends, ghosts." An earlier passage in *Some Recollections* reads: "St. Juliot is a romantic spot indeed of North Cornwall. It was sixteen miles away from a station then, [and a place] where the belief in witchcraft was carried out in actual practice among the primitive inhabitants. Traditions and strange gossipings [were] the common talk."[2] Evidently her interest in these matters was concerned with literary ambitions. In a passage omitted from *The Early Life, Some Recollections* says: "Sometimes I visited a favourite in the scattered parish—an amusing woman, pleasant-mannered and lively—who told me fine old tales and strange byegone [*sic*] experiences of her own young life and hardships endured in service, which I took down afterwards in my pocket book for matter with which to begin writing country stories, having come to the conclusion that I was hearing from one [and] other of these country-folk a good deal that was fresh, peculiar, and not yet written about. . . . I liked much to visit this kind of person and had various queer tales and information from them, and many oddities of ways under observation."[3]

These passages form a background for the suggestions in the poem that Emma felt premonitions about a man she had never seen, but whom she immediately recognized as "My destiny." Though the poem says that she did not think of the man who was on his way to her, the suggestion in the series of Halworthy, Otterham, Tresparret Posts, and

Hennett Byre is that in some scarcely conscious way, she thought of the villages along his route.[4]

The poem is a companion to "The Wind's Prophecy," which describes the journey from Hardy's point of view. Upon both poems a parable of fate is erected.

1. Purdy, *Thomas Hardy: A Bibliographical Study*, p. 217.
2. Pp. 92 and 89; *Life*, pp. 70 and 68. The brackets are Hardy's additions.
3. Evelyn Hardy and Gittings, eds., pp. 51-52.
4. Hardy was coming in a horse-drawn conveyance from Launceston, about sixteen miles southeast of St. Juliot. The list of villages may indicate his route, but if modern roads and lanes are considered, he came in a zigzag course several miles longer than necessary. Hallworthy (so spelled on maps) is about eleven miles northwest of Launceston on Road 395; Otterham is on a lane northwest of Hallworthy; Tresparrett (so spelled) Posts is still farther northwest; and Hennett, less than a mile from St. Juliot, is south of Tresparrett Posts. It would have been shorter to go from Otterham to Hennett, without going north to Tresparrett Posts. Perhaps Hardy's driver lost his way. Perhaps, though the poem says "Tresparret Posts," Hardy confused this village with Tresparrett, a village on the nearly direct road from Otterham to Hennett.

THE STRANGE HOUSE imagines the conversation of people who may live in Max Gate in the year 2000. One of the speakers is "psychic" and senses the presence of Hardy and his first wife; the other is a rationalist, who senses nothing, but remembers tales of a queer couple who once lived there. (The rationalist sees by the light of the moon, Hardy's symbol for realistic vision.)

That Hardy thinks of Emma, rather than his second wife Florence as haunting the house with him is suggested by the reference to the piano playing (see the notes on "The Last Performance") and to "love-thralls." That Max Gate could seem haunted is suggested in a letter from Florence to W. L. Phelps on November 3, 1928: "Max Gate seems very desolate & empty tonight, & full of ghosts."[1] Hardy often fancied old houses to emanate the presence of people who had lived in them. In *Jude the Obscure*, Sue and Phillotson move into an old house. Sue says to Jude: "We don't live at the school, you know, but in that ancient dwelling across the way called Old-Grove's Place. It is so antique and dismal that it depresses me dreadfully. . . . I feel crushed into the earth by the weight of so many previous lives there spent." (Part IV, Chapter I.)

The final stanza indicates Hardy's awareness that he and his wife were considered a little "Queer in their works and ways."

1. In the Yale University Library.

"AS 'TWERE TO-NIGHT" presents Hardy's memory of the end of the first week of his courtship of Emma Gifford, on Friday, March 11, 1870. That the song concerns Emma is indicated in the phrase "girl of grace," which is used of her in "Places," and which appears as "words of grace" in "On a Discovered Curl of Hair."

THE CONTRETEMPS, footnoted "Weymouth," treats an incident (perhaps fictional) of 1869 or early 1870, when Hardy was employed in Weymouth by the architect Crickmay. The last stanza, with its reference to "this late day," indicates that the poem was written (or rewritten) much later. The action takes place at the harbor bridge, a stone bridge built in the 1820's in downtown Weymouth, a few hundred feet from the dock for the Jersey boat.

A GENTLEMAN'S EPITAPH ON HIMSELF AND A LADY, WHO WERE BURIED TOGETHER is spoken by the ghost of a dead man with an urbane sense of humor. The poem may be compared with "A Woman's Fancy," also about strangers buried together. "A Gentleman's Epitaph on Himself" offers no explanation. Perhaps the gentleman and the lady were placed together during some church restoration.

THE OLD GOWN expresses the sentiment of Thomas Haynes Bayly's "She Wore a Wreath of Roses." In Hardy's "memoried passion" the final stanza seems a picture of Emma Gifford's singing after dinner on Thursday evening, March 10, 1870, at the close of his first visit to St. Juliot Rectory. He was to leave for Bockhampton early the next morning.[1]

He made use of the incident in *A Pair of Blue Eyes*; he comments upon the impression such a scene makes upon a young lover and possibly describes Emma's "gown of fading fashion." "Every woman who makes a permanent impression on a man is usually recalled to his mind's eye as she appeared in one particular scene, which seems ordained to be her special form of manifestation throughout the pages of his memory." Elfride is singing to Stephen Smith: "The profile is seen of a young woman in a pale gray silk dress with trimmings of swan's-down, and opening up from a point in front, like a waistcoat without a shirt; the cool colour contrasting admirably with the warm bloom of her neck and face." (Chapter III.)

The poem surveys Hardy's life with Emma in terms of her gowns. The first stanza, in "walking, riding" and "the foam-fingered sea," suggests episodes of courtship in Cornwall.[2] The "rain-reek" of the second stanza recalls the episode of "The Figure in the Scene" and "Why Did I Sketch." The picture of Emma as "Court-clad" seems a reference to an incident of June 2, 1907, Hardy's birthday, when they were invited to a Royal Garden Party at Windsor Castle. A crowd arrived "so great that there were not nearly enough conveyances to carry everybody from the station up the steep hill to the Castle. Mrs.

Hardy, wearing a long green veil, promptly took a place in one of the royal carriages and invited Madame Blanche to come and sit beside her. The latter declined, urging Hardy to take the seat. . . . He was so obviously frail that other guests who were headed for Windsor Castle followed Mme Blanche's example in urging Hardy to ride. Mrs. Hardy, however, settled the matter in emphatic words which Blanche never forgot. . . . 'Mr. Hardy ride? Why, that walk up the hill in the sun will do him a lot of good!' So up the stony hill to Windsor Castle Thomas Hardy . . . trudged on foot, following the open carriage with its driver in King Edward's scarlet livery and its Devonshire lady in a green veil, seated under a bright silk parasol."[3]

1. Weber, *Hardy's Love Poems*, p. 13.
2. Much later, perhaps in an effort to appear young, Emma affected gay muslins that somewhat embarrassed Hardy.
3. Weber, *Hardy of Wessex*, 2nd ed., pp. 253-54. Emma Hardy was born in Plymouth, Devonshire.

A NIGHT IN NOVEMBER seems to treat the night of the anniversary of Mrs. Emma Hardy's death on November 27, 1912. The poem is built upon the symbols of dead leaves and a mourning tree, one leaf of which, touching Hardy's hand, seems to be Emma. He is consoled by the fancy that her spirit at last understands his abiding love.

A DUETTIST TO HER PIANOFORTE is spoken by Mrs. Emma Hardy. Her partner in the remembered duets was Mrs. Helen C. Holder, her sister, who died in December, 1900. The scene is recorded in Hardy's diary of his courtship of Emma in Cornwall under the date of March 9, 1870: "Music in the evening. The two ladies sang duets, including 'The Elfin Call,' 'Let us dance on the sands,' etc."[1] Though Emma may have expressed some such sentiment as that of the poem, she did not give up playing her piano after her sister's death.

1. *Early Life*, p. 99; *Life*, p. 75.

"WHERE THREE ROADS JOINED" in the manuscript identifies the place as " (Near Tresparrett Posts, Cornwall) ,"[1] less than three miles north of St. Juliot Rectory and a little more than two miles east of Beeny Cliff. The scene is probably on a hill near some tumuli, less than half a mile east of the Cliff and the sea. Three country lanes join at this point, and across a gate to a pasture one may look out to "the sun-glazed sea."[2]

The poem concerns Hardy's courtship of Emma Gifford in Cornwall. The occasion remembered in the first stanza may be that recorded in Hardy's journal for March 10, 1870: "Went with E. L. G. to Beeny Cliff. She on horseback. . . . On the cliff. . . . 'The tender

grace of a day,' etc. The run down to the edge. The coming home."[3]
The "pair" of the third stanza seem to be Emma, who died in 1912,
and her sister, Mrs. Helen Holder, who died in 1900. The "phasm of
him who fared" seems Hardy on his return to Cornwall in March
of 1913: he speaks of visiting Beeny Cliff.[4] The last line refers to
his distress at the revival of his memories.

It is possible to read the three roads as symbols for three lives once
joined in bliss, but now "rutted and bare" through the death of two
and the sorrow of the third.

1. Purdy, *Thomas Hardy: A Bibliographical Study*, p. 217.
2. Phelps, in *Annotations by Thomas Hardy in His Bibles and Prayer-Book*,
p. 4, presents a photograph of this junction and the gate.
3. *Early Life*, p. 99; *Life*, p. 75.
4. *Later Years*, p. 156; *Life*, p. 361.

"AND THERE WAS A GREAT CALM" was first published in a special
Armistice Day Section of the *Times* on November 11, 1920.[1] *The
Later Years* says: "The request to write this poem had been brought
to him from London by one of the editorial staff. At first Hardy was
disinclined, and all but refused. . . . In the middle of the night, how-
ever, an idea seized him, and he was heard moving about the house
looking things up."[2] He took the title from a phrase found in both
Matt. 8:26 and Mark 4:39, "And he arose, and rebuked the wind, and
said unto the sea, Peace, be still. And the wind ceased, and there was
a great calm."

To give the poem dramatic conflict and philosophic perspective,
Hardy made use of the Spirits he had created to comment upon the
Napoleonic wars of *The Dynasts*.[3] The question that the Spirit of
Pity asks, "Why" the war had to be, is Hardy's question, with the
suggestion that something sinister in human nature brought it about.

Besides the quasi-supernatural, philosophic comment, he expresses
a number of his characteristic attitudes. The "bereft, and meek, and
lowly" used to dream that Lovingkindness might come to rule the
world, but it is implied that (as in *The Dynasts*) power-hungry
leaders inflamed common men, and " 'Hell!' and 'Shell!' were yapped
at Lovingkindness." His compassion includes the helpless animals
maimed or slaughtered by the war. When the armistice came, men
who had acted like automata were dazed, unable to realize the long-
forgotten calm and become men again.

Hardy supported these attitudes with realism of detail. He phrased
the opening stanza and the final one in abstractions, but in the body
of the poem presented war in slangy, crass, factual images. He knew
the war from reading the newspapers, talking with German prisoners
stationed in Dorchester, and talking with returned soldiers, but he had

not experienced it in the front lines. Perhaps when "moving about the house" he was looking for letters from men who wrote to him while shells were bursting around them. For instance, a letter to him from Captain Stair A. Gillon on November 21, 1915, says: "There was a perfect tornado of fire on the Turkish trenches 'to make them keep their heads down' as the cant phrase has it. Monitors with marvellous accuracy made vast craters, High Explosive Shells & Shrapnel yelled over our heads, machine guns tapped out a hail of small stuff & then crack crack came the answering machine-gun and rifle fire."[4] Such letters helped Hardy give his pictures the firmness and tone of actuality.

1. Purdy, *Thomas Hardy: A Bibliographical Study*, p. 211.
2. Pp. 214-15; *Life*, p. 407.
3. As the Spirits are characterized in *The Dynasts*, the speech of Irony in the seventh stanza should be that of the Sinister Spirit, and that of Sinister in the ninth should be that of Years. Perhaps the pointless evil of World War I moved Hardy to let Sinister express the determinism of Years' point of view. See the definitions of these Spirits and their roles in Bailey, *Thomas Hardy and the Cosmic Mind*, Chapter II.
4. In the Dorset County Museum.

HAUNTING FINGERS first appeared in the *New Republic,* New York, for December 21, 1921. The editor, Ridgely Torrence, had written Hardy on August 24, 1920, to ask for a poem. Receiving no reply, Torrence wrote again. Hardy's pencil-notation on the letter says: " 'The Haunting Fingers.' Sent Nov. 7, 1921 'for use' in New Republic."[1] The poem was one that he valued highly. Writing Paul Lemperly on June 14, 1922, about her pamphlet that contained "Haunting Fingers" and "Voices from Things Growing," Mrs. Florence Hardy said: "With regard to the literary value my husband thinks the poems of greater merit than any others I have published in my private series."[2]

The "Museum of Musical Intruments" is not named, but Hardy may have had in mind the Horniman Museum on London Road, Forest Hill, London. The collection of musical instruments there, said to be the finest in Europe, includes strange instruments from Asia, Africa, and South America, and ancient and medieval instruments, as well as all the ones mentioned in "Haunting Fingers."[3]

The poem presents Hardy's characteristic "Phantasy" that the instruments had a kind of life given them by the long-dead people whose fingers had drawn music from them, and that at night the instruments conversed, expressing their memories of the days when they were in joyful or solemn use.

"Haunting Fingers" is interesting for its verse-forms. It "has a virtuosity in that two different kinds of stanza are employed systemati-

cally. Five separate times there are two stanzas spoken by the in-
struments in the one form, followed by a stanza of narrative in the
other form."[4] The poem contains a number of learned references
as well as the names of unusual instruments, for instance, Phosphor
(the morning star), Amphion (in Greek myth, a musician so skilled
that the walls of Thebes rose to the music of his lyre), contra-basso
(a double-bass violin), harpsichord (an early form of piano), clavier
(keyboard), shawm (a medieval predecessor of the oboe), Cecilian
(concerning St. Cecilia, the patron saint of music), and "faced the
sock" (played for actors in Greek comedy).

1. In the Dorset County Museum.
2. In the Colby College Library.
3. In 1966, no harpsichord was on display in the crowded rooms; the guide said
that several were in storage.
4. Ransom, "Hardy—Old Poet," p. 31.

THE WOMAN I MET was first published in the *London Mercury*
for April, 1921.[1] The poem tells a ballad-like story of Hardy's con-
versation with the ghost of a prostitute, who tells him that she had
seen him in his "far-off youthful years," and, unable otherwise to lure
him, had sought to attract him with a "costly flower." This item
seems based on an incident of April, 1891, recorded in *The Early Life*:
"Piccadilly at night. 'A girl held a long-stemmed narcissus to my nose
as we went by each other.' "[2]

The story told by the ghost seems fiction in the pattern of the
moralizing melodrama of Victorian years. It was almost a convention
(as often a fact) that the "fallen woman" should contract a venereal
disease and die in the Lock.[3] In his copy of *Collected Poems*, edition
of 1923, Hardy struck through the word "Forms" in the final stanza,
and in the margin wrote "Flesh," perhaps to make explicit that the
ghost was that of a prostitute.[4]

1. Purdy, *Thomas Hardy: A Bibliographical Study*, p. 218.
2. P. 308; *Life*, p. 235.
3. The Lock-hospital, a lazar-house in Southwark, London, for the treatment
of venereal disease.
4. In the Dorset County Museum.

"IF IT'S EVER SPRING AGAIN" has been treated harshly by the
critics. One of them begins an analysis of the poem by saying: "One
can immediately point to a number of technical flaws in this poem:
the multiple and awkward inversions and the comic *flounder-around
her* rhyme in the first stanza, the padding in the second (there is no
point to the parenthetical *two* in the thirteenth line or in the last
three words of the fourteenth, and the final line is entirely filler).
Cuckoos rhyme and bees chime to make the rhyme scheme, not be-

cause rhyming and chiming are natural to them. The device of repetition is overworked and ineffective; the last lines of the stanzas in particular are feeble as refrains."[1]

Musicians have not agreed. "If It's Ever Spring Again" has been set to music by Robin Milford in *Four Hardy Songs* (Oxford University Press, 1939) and Christopher LeFleming (London: J. & W. Chester, 1943). When Russell Boughton prepared an operatic version of *The Queen of Cornwall,* he included the poem as one of six lyrics to be inserted into the opera.

1. Hynes, *The Pattern of Hardy's Poetry,* pp. 69-70.

THE TWO HOUSES was first published in the *Dial* of New York for August, 1921. On November 13, 1920, Ezra Pound had asked Hardy for a poem for this magazine. Hardy replied that he had nothing that would "exactly suit," but would "hunt again." On June 8, 1921, Scofield Thayer, editor of the *Dial,* acknowledged receipt of "The Two Houses," forwarded by Pound.

The poem purports to be a conversation between an old house and a new one, though it is mostly a lecture by the old house in support of one of Hardy's characteristic ideas. He wrote in his notebook for April 28, 1893: "The worst of taking a furnished house is that the articles in the rooms are saturated with the thoughts and glances of others."[1] The idea appears in a number of poems, as in "The Strange House."

1. *Later Years,* pp. 17-18; *Life,* p. 254.

ON STINSFORD HILL AT MIDNIGHT is based upon an incident Hardy recorded in his notebook for February 4, 1894: "Curious scene encountered this (Sunday) evening as I was walking back to Dorchester from Bockhampton very late—nearly 12 o'clock. A girl almost in white on the top of Stinsford Hill, beating a tambourine and dancing. She looked like one of the 'angelic quire,' who had tumbled down out of the sky, and I could hardly believe my eyes. Not a soul there or near but her and myself. Was told she belonged to the Salvation Army, who beat tambourines devotionally."[1]

It is doubtful whether Hardy, usually shy, addressed the singing woman. To make a poem of the incident, he dramatized it with the material of his thought to express a theme. Hogan's analysis states the theme: "Hardy's questions are couched in spatial terms: 'Come nearer,' 'What home is yours now?' and 'This world is dark, and where you are . . . I cannot be.' The woman is (perhaps literally) in another sphere, a spiritual one about which Hardy is curious and envious. 'Are you so happy now?' 'You seem to have no care.' He cannot leave his 'dark' world and share the spirit of her song: 'much that kind of note I need!' Each stanza (excluding the second and third) is a small drama of rejection, the speaker advancing verbally, the singer intently not hearing. This repetitive structure gives the sense of a bird beating wings against cage walls—but it is a cage which the speaker would like to enter, not escape from."[2]

1. *Later Years*, p. 28; *Life*, p. 262.
2. "Structural Design in Thomas Hardy's Poetry," p. 179.

THE FALLOW DEER AT THE LONELY HOUSE may be set at Max Gate, and the pair inside may be Hardy and his wife, Florence, but deer are not known to inhabit the farmlands nearby, and the snow would hardly look like a "sheet of glistening white" under the thickly planted trees.

The scene may be Hardy's birthplace in Higher Bockhampton, and his companion, his mother. James Skilling, caretaker of the birthplace, reports that deer from the heath behind the house still appear and eat the roses in the garden: "The small sika deer come in from the Heath at night and scarcely a budding rose survives."[1] On the other hand, the birthplace also is surrounded by trees and bushes.

A third possibility is Riverside Villa, where Hardy and his first wife lived from midsummer of 1876 until March of 1878. This villa is on the western edge of Sturminster Newton, just a little over three miles east of Stock Park. "Fallow deer can be seen to advantage in the grounds of Stock Park . . . often obliging by coming right up to the railings beside the main Sherborne-Sturminster Road."[2] Possibly, in the 1870's, deer sometimes roamed outside this park. Items in the poem that suggest Riverside Villa are the "sheet of glistening white" as in the meadows below the house and across the river, and the fact that the couple who "sit and think / By the fender-brink" seem as isolated in their "lonely house" as the deer. "Overlooking the River Stour" indicates that a period of introspective loneliness for Hardy and Emma began at Riverside Villa.

"The Fallow Deer at the Lonely House" has been set to music by Arthur Bliss (London: J. Curwen and Sons, 1925).

1. "Hardy's Birthplace—That's Our Home," p. 9.
2. Hutchings, *Inside Dorset*, p. 23.

THE SELFSAME SONG seems a comment upon stanza VII of Keats's "Ode to a Nightingale." This stanza uses the phrase "the self-same song," though Hardy's poem in saying "But it's not the selfsame bird" contradicts the opening line of Keats's stanza: "Thou wast not born for death, immortal Bird!"[1]

In "The Selfsame Song," the "we" who listen and the bird are not named, just as the nightingale is not named in Keats's "Ode" except in the title. The bird is presumably a nightingale, perhaps in the copse near Hardy's birthplace or in the grove at Max Gate. In 1903, when the Hardys were in London, H. J. Moule lived at Max Gate for a while. He wrote to Hardy on May 30: "It is a real satisfaction to me that you, coming from a nightingale-besung native home, should also have the glorious song here in this home, and that within the borough of Dorchester!! Margie heard a nightingale the night before last."[2]

Rejecting the immortality of the bird, "perished to dust," Hardy marvels at the instinct that teaches the bird the "selfsame song / With never a fault in its flow." The poem expresses one of his characteristic themes, the mortality of the individual, but the persistence of inherited traits. In *The Mayor of Casterbridge*, Henchard and Susan hear "the voice of a weak bird singing a trite old evening song that might doubtless have been heard on the hill at the same hour, and with the self-same trills, quavers, and breves, at any sunset of that season for centuries untold." (Chapter I.)

1. Hardy sometimes inverted the thought of a romantic poet. In *Tess of the D'Urbervilles*, Chapter XXXVII, Angel quotes from Pippa's morning song "with peculiar emendations of his own—God's *not* in his heaven: all's *wrong* with the world!"

2. In the Dorset County Museum. See Moule, *A Revised List of the Birds of Dorset*, p. 14, for the frequency of nightingales, "locally common."

THE WANDERER in the manuscript shows the deleted title, "The Benighted Traveller."[1] The original title suggests an ordinary workman overtaken by darkness, like Gabriel Oak in Chapter VI of *Far from the Madding Crowd*. The final title, however, and the phrase "witch-drawn" indicate that the poem is the philosophic soliloquy of a man temperamentally a tramp. For a possible identification, see the notes on "Vagrant's Song."

1. Purdy, *Thomas Hardy: A Bibliographical Study*, p. 218.

A WIFE COMES BACK seems what the opening lines say it is: a story Hardy heard of a man's delusion. It touches upon several of Hardy's characteristic themes: the inconstancy of love aroused in "pleasures merely,"[1] the idealizations of memory, and the corrosions of time.

1. See *Far from the Madding Crowd*, Chapter LVI.

A YOUNG MAN'S EXHORTATION in the manuscript was titled simply "An Exhortation."[1] Presumably Hardy in 1867 exhorted himself on the basis of ideas from the classics, art galleries, the theater, and poetry, much of it romantic. He "had been accustomed to shut himself up in his rooms at Westbourne Park Villas every evening from six to twelve, reading incessantly."[2] Under these circumstances he exhorted himself to seek ecstasy by living in "the passing preciousness of dreams."

His dreams seem his attempt to escape the materialism of London in the 1860's. *The Early Life* adds weakening health, editors' rejection of his poems, and revulsion against "stage realities" as reasons for Hardy's returning to Dorset in the summer of 1867. There he found his proper area for creative dreaming, in the legends and the land of *Under the Greenwood Tree.* "A Young Man's Exhortation" has been set to music by Gerald Finzi (Oxford University Press, 1933; London and New York: Boosey and Hawkes, 1957).

1. Purdy, *Thomas Hardy: A Bibliographical Study*, p. 218.
2. *Early Life*, p. 70; *Life*, p. 53.

AT LULWORTH COVE A CENTURY BACK has a footnote that states the belief upon which the poem rests. Because he had consumption, Keats was advised to go to Italy. On September 17, 1820, he and his friend Joseph Severn boarded the *Maria Crowther* in London. The ship was delayed by storms and then a calm. On September 28, somewhere on the Dorset coast, passengers were allowed to go ashore. Severn's record says of this landing that Keats "was in a part that he already knew, and showed me the splendid caverns and grottoes with a poet's pride, as though they had been his birthright." Severn did not name the caverns and grottoes, but Colvin identified them as Lulworth Cove, Stair Hole, and Durdle Door. On board ship that night, Keats wrote out for Severn the sonnet "Bright star, would I were stedfast as thou art." Colvin remarks that this sonnet "was work of an earlier date, and the autograph given to Severn is on the face of it no draught but a fair copy."[1]

To identify the caverns and grottoes, Colvin wrote Hardy on June 13, 1914: "Most biographers have assumed that Lulworth Cove was the place of 'splendid caverns & grottoes. . . .' Could it possibly fit, say, Worbarrow Bay? . . . I thought perhaps your minute local knowledge might be able to suggest the likeliest spot."[2] Hardy replied in a letter not dated: "We . . . have come to the conclusion that he must mean 'Durdle Door,' close to Lulworth Cove. . . . To see it from the inside . . . they would have landed in the Cove, & have walked over the Cliff to the west, & down behind the 'Door.'"[3] Colvin wrote again on July 28 that Severn "speaks of 'the shores, with the beautiful grottoes which open to fine verdure and cottages.' Would you say that these words tended to confirm the identification of the scene with Durdle Door and the neighbourhood, or otherwise?"[4] Hardy replied the next day: " 'Beautiful grottoes' is certainly rather an exaggerated description. . . . The 'Door' is an archway in the cliff, as you know; Stair Hole has caves & fissures into which the sea flows, & there is another cave at Bat's Corner, also close at hand. . . . 'Cottages' would be those of the adjoining Lulworth Cove & village."[5]

This Cove is a placid almost circular bay about a quarter of a mile in diameter, surrounded by cliffs and hills. It is, as the crow flies, a little more than ten miles southeast of Dorchester. The village of Lulworth lies inland from the Cove.[6] Worbarrow Bay is a larger, semi-cirular bay about a mile east of Lulworth Cove. Stair Hole and Durdle Door lie about a mile and a quarter west of Lulworth Cove. Bat's Corner (or Bat's Head) is a rocky promontory about three quarters of a mile west of Durdle Door.

In the poem, Hardy takes an imaginary trip to Lulworth Cove at the time Keats landed there. He goes from Dorchester by way of Warmwell Cross, four and a half miles southeast of Dorchester, where the Dorchester-Wareham Road (A352) crosses the Warmwell-Weymouth Road (A353).[7] He imagines Keats's ship as having sailed "round Saint Alban's Head," a promontory on the Channel about eight miles east of Lulworth Cove.

The person who points out Keats—"*You see that man?*"—represents Joseph Severn. Characteristically (as in "To Shakespeare"), Hardy imagines Keats as a "commonplace" looking youth, and is surprised when Severn predicts that Keats will die in Rome and that the fame of his poetry will draw all the world to his grave.

1. *John Keats*, pp. 492-93. The statement that Keats was "in a part that he already knew" concerns his relationship to the Keatses of Dorset. See the notes on "At a House in Hampstead."
2. In the Dorset County Museum.
3. In the Fitzwilliam Museum, Cambridge, England.
4. In the Dorset County Museum.
5. In the Harvard University Library. See also Lucas, *The Colvins and Their Friends*, pp. 318-20.
6. The Cove is described as "Lulwind Cove" in *Far from the Madding Crowd*, Chapters XLVII and XLVIII.
7. Hardy made a pen-and-ink drawing of Lulworth Cove in 1868, and Mrs. Emma Hardy made a water-color painting on September 26, 1881. In the Dorset County Museum. A photograph of the cove and surrounding cliffs is presented opposite p. 142 of Pinion, *A Hardy Companion*.

A BYGONE OCCASION may treat the occasion of "The Curtains Now are Drawn" or of "The Old Gown."

TWO SERENADES seems to be fiction. "From an old copy" suggests that it may be a symbolic treatment of Hardy's shifting his loyalty from Tryphena Sparks to Emma Gifford. The poem personifies Cas-

[455]

siopeia (a northern constellation) and the "Seven of the Wain" (Charles's Wain, the Dipper), perhaps to suggest the influence of the stars on human destiny.

THE WEDDING MORNING seems a piece of versified, ironic fiction.[1] The poem may be considered a part of Hardy's protest, as in *Jude the Obscure*, against conventions that would in effect force a pregnant woman to marry her child's father even though she has discovered that he loves another woman.

1. Copps, "The Poetry of Thomas Hardy," p. 653, asks about Carry in the poem: "Is this perhaps the same person as Carrey Clavel in 'To Carrey Clavel'?"

END OF THE YEAR 1912 was titled in the manuscript "End of the Old Year."[1] Hardy added the date to identify the "You" of the poem as his first wife Emma, who died in November, 1912. The "we" of the poem may include Florence Dugdale, who became the second Mrs. Hardy. She was a friend of Emma. The "star-lit avenue" is the Dorchester-Wareham Road that runs past Max Gate. The poem indicates that Emma celebrated New Year's Eve by singing as the six bells of a nearby church, St. George's, Fordington, "swung thereto."[2]

1. Purdy, *Thomas Hardy: A Bibliographical Study*, p. 219.
2. Fordington is now a part of Dorchester; the Church of St. George has a peal of six bells.

THE CHIMES PLAY "LIFE'S A BUMPER!" may express Hardy's memory of his ecstasy as he departed for London to marry Emma Gifford. The journey townward in which the "sun arose behind me ruby-red" would be his early-morning walk westward from Higher Bockhampton to Dorchester to take the train. The "chiming bells" would be those of St. Peter's in Dorchester, which in 1874 often played secular tunes. The third stanza may represent him walking from Max Gate to Stinsford Churchyard, where Emma had been buried in 1912. Ironically, the chimes play the same cheery tune.

"I WORKED NO WILE TO MEET YOU" presents the accidental meeting of two who became lovers. It is characteristic of Hardy to wonder about events brought by the "flux of flustering hours."

AT THE RAILWAY STATION, UPWAY spells "Upway" for Upwey, a village on the River Wey about three and a half miles south of Dorchester. The railway from Dorchester to Weymouth, and then on to the Isle of Portland, runs by Upwey, but the station is the Upwey and Broadwey Station to serve also Broadwey, about a mile to the south. The prisoner is probably being taken to Portland Prison on the Isle. The poem has been set to music by Benjamin Britten in *Winter Words* (New York: Boosey and Hawkes, 1954).

SIDE BY SIDE presents an ironic situation that Hardy may have observed.

DREAM OF THE CITY SHOPWOMAN, written in 1866, the year before Hardy left London for Dorset, suggests his disillusionment with city life. Aside from idealizing life in the country, the poem is notable for its early statement of a philosophic idea developed in *The Dynasts*. When the shopwoman protests "O God, that creatures framed to feel / . . . Should writhe on this eternal wheel," she anticipates the protest of the Pities, "O, the intolerable antilogy / Of making figments feel!" (Part First, IV, v.)

The poem seems a contrasting companion to "From Her in the Country." Though published in separate volumes, both are dated 1866; both are written as if spoken by a woman. The woman in the country thinks she ought to feel about the "crass clanging town" as the shopwoman does, but she longs for "city din and sin." The shopwoman dreams an idyll of country life, which the country woman finds boring.

A MAIDEN'S PLEDGE presents the views of a girl who values love more than respectability if she may feel certain of her lover's faithfulness. The theme echoes much of the argument in *Jude the Obscure*.

THE CHILD AND THE SAGE presents one side of a conversation between a sensitive child and a wise man. The questions are those of Hardy's childhood opposed to his mature experience. The child's view suggests that of Little Father Time in *Jude the Obscure*.

MISMET treats an ingredient in the frequent mismatings of Hardy's novels. The immediate emotions obscure the young man's reflection upon the right mate for him, and the woman's reflection upon her right mate.

AN AUTUMN RAIN-SCENE was first published as "A December Rain-Scene" in the *Fortnightly Review* for December, 1921.[1] In a letter of December 19, 1921, to Mrs. Arthur Henniker, Hardy called the poem "trifling."[2] It presents his observation of the activities of the people of Dorchester in the rainy season, most of the winter.

1. Purdy, *Thomas Hardy: A Bibliographical Study*, p. 219.
2. In the Dorset County Museum.

MEDITATIONS ON A HOLIDAY, dated as written in May, was dated in the manuscript "April 21, 1921."[1] Though the poem opens " 'Tis a May morning," Hardy possibly wrote it as dated in the manuscript. Steeped in the classics, he may have had in mind April 21 as the

Vinalia urbana, the birthday of Rome when the wine of the previous autumn was first tasted. If so, the poem looks back to shrines of Hardy's past, now rejected as points of pilgrimage. The "old folk-measure" of the poem is not identified, but the meter resembles that of "Timing Her," written to an "old folk-tune."

The Later Years mentions no holiday-trip in April or May of 1921. Perhaps a trip was contemplated and, as in the poem, rejected. The first stanza suggests a trip to "Lyonnesse," or Cornwall, but, under the names of Tristram and Isolt, young Hardy and Emma Gifford are no longer there. The third speaks of Stratford, but Shakespeare is not living by the Avon; the same is true of "Lakeland" and Wordsworth, and of Scotland and Burns and Scott. The poem pauses upon the thought of Percy Shelley, Mary Godwin, and Claire Clairmont. The "town street" was the home of William Godwin on Skinner Street, London, and Mary Godwin, his daughter, who eloped with Shelley in 1814, accompanied by Claire Clairmont, who became Byron's mistress. Hardy rejects a pilgrimage to this shrine in a now "mud-bespat city."

1. Purdy, *Thomas Hardy: A Bibliographical Study,* p. 219.

AN EXPERIENCE speaks of the effects of an experience without saying what it was. Mention of the hills and the breeze suggest an incident during a picnic. The poem records the poet's emotional reaction to a personality.

THE BEAUTY is footnoted as from a "London paper, October 1828," but Hardy's notebook labelled "Facts"[1] gives the *Dorset County Chronicle* for October 16, 1828, as the source. The note in "Facts" continues: "Only 17. Buried at St. George's burying-ground, Bayswater—body attempted by resurrectionists." The conclusion in the *Chronicle* reads: "Since her death, a number of unfeeling wretches have assembled round the house, and amused themselves in a manner which can only be accounted for by supposing that they are destitute of a particle of the common feelings of humanity." The paragraph is among "fillers" headed: "London, Monday, October 13, 1828."

Regent Street, in central London, runs from north of Oxford Circus, through Piccadilly, to Waterloo Place. Near Piccadilly it is a center of London night life. The meaning of Regent Street to Hardy is indicated in his diary for April 28, 1888: "In Regent Street, which commemorates the Prince Regent. It is in the fitness of things that The Promenade of Prostitutes should be here."[2] The beauty's soliloquy seems his fictional presentation of a girl's protest against her life in an environment where only the external values of beauty were understood.

1. In the Dorset County Museum, p. 90.
2. *Early Life*, p. 273; *Life*, p. 208.

THE COLLECTOR CLEANS HIS PICTURE portrays the Reverend William Barnes of Came Rectory, Hardy's friend and neighbor. Barnes's role as art-collector is described by his daughter, Mrs. Lucy Baxter: "The antiquarian shops knew him well, for if a dark old painting were hung at the door William Barnes might be seen stopping to examine it, and many a time he returned with a dusty picture under his arm, in which nothing but blackened varnish could be seen. With this he would retire to his den, and subject the dark canvas to a mysterious process of restoration known only to himself; it . . . filled the house with the smell of oils and varnish. After some days he would come down stairs with a beaming face, and display the astonishing results of his labour."[1]

The retrospective monologue may be a story Barnes told Hardy. The poem represents Barnes's diction. As linguist he rejected words of Latin origin in favor of Anglo-Saxon equivalents, as in phrases like "delve at whiles for easel-lumber" and words like "artfeat," "brushcraft," and "grimefilms."

The Latin of the motto is translated in the King James Bible as: "Son of man, behold, I take away from thee the desire of thine eyes with a stroke." (Ezek. 24:16.)

1. *The Life of William Barnes*, pp. 151-52.

THE WOOD FIRE narrates what may have happened to the wood of the Cross on which Christ was crucified. Blunden says of the inspiration for the poem, public reaction to it, and Hardy's attitude: " 'The Wood Fire,' outwardly referring to the crucifixion but in reality inspired by the news of the clearance of the wooden crosses on the old Western Front, brought down on Hardy the allegation of blasphemy, which he very keenly resented."[1] Hardy's inspiration may have included his memory of Browning's imaginative realism in treating the popular interpretation of the crucifixion in "An Epistle . . . of Karshish." "The Wood Fire" is (except for the opening line) a dramatic monologue, spoken to a guest by a man who may be an innkeeper. (For Hardy's attitude toward the fictional use of Biblical materials, see the notes on "Panthera" and "An Evening in Galilee.")

The poem looks through the haloed view of the crucifixion (the view that in the Middle Ages attributed miraculous powers to a fragment of the Cross) into the possible attitudes of the "average man" of the time. Hardy labelled his poem "A Fragment," meaning, perhaps, a snapshot of an isolated incident, related to larger events only in the mind of the reader. The time of the action is early spring, just after Easter, when the town must be cleaned up for the Jewish Passover. He has his speaker use the Greek word "Kranion," meaning "Golgotha . . . a place of a skull" (Matt. 27:33), perhaps to suggest that he is a Greek and was therefore outside the "political" disturbance of the crucifixion. He says, "I heard the noise from my garden." His word "shroff" is dialectal for "waste."

1. *Thomas Hardy*, p. 167.

SAYING GOOD-BYE expresses a common human sentiment concerning friends who go away to unforeseen destinies.

ON THE TUNE CALLED THE OLD-HUNDRED-AND-FOURTH concerns Ravenscroft's musical setting for Psalm 104. Thomas Ravenscroft (1592?-1635?) was a musician who in 1621 published his most famous work, *The Whole Book of Psalms*, which contained this setting. The book was reprinted many times, in one printing as late as 1844. In the poem Hardy wonders why he and his first wife did not sing together this tune they both loved, with the implication that Hardy in his study (on an upper floor of Max Gate) sometimes heard her sing it in the distance. For neglecting it, perhaps they will be doomed to sing it together in Sheol, the afterworld, a wryly humorous touch in an otherwise serious poem. In 1921 (before the poem was published) Rebekah Owen visited the Hardys, read the poem, and wrote to Mrs. Florence Hardy that she liked it. On August 7, Mrs. Hardy replied that "I did like it very much myself. That old hymn has a peculiar fascination for my husband."[1]

1. Weber, *Hardy and the Lady from Madison Square*, p. 205.

THE OPPORTUNITY treats Helen Paterson, whom Hardy met in 1874. Their acquaintance is set forth with reticence in *The Early Life*. Returning from a visit to Emma Gifford on December 31, 1873, he purchased a copy of the *Cornhill* magazine at the railway station, and on opening it "to his surprise saw his story placed at the beginning of the magazine, with a striking illustration, the artist being—also to his surprise—not a man but a woman, Miss Helen Paterson." He met Miss Paterson when he visited G. Murray Smith, the publisher, in May of 1874, "and gave her a few points." The only other entry that mentions her says: "In the November following *Far from the Madding Crowd* was published in two volumes, with the illustrations by Miss Helen Paterson, who by an odd coincidence had also thought fit to marry William Allingham during the progress of the story."[1] The "odd coincidence" is Miss Paterson's marriage in August just before Hardy's in September.

Purdy quotes a letter from Hardy to Edmund Gosse dated July 25, 1906: "The illustrator of Far from the Madding Crowd began as a charming young lady, Miss Helen Paterson, and ended as a married woman,—charms unknown—wife of Allingham the poet. I have never set eyes on her since she was the former and I met her and corresponded with her about the pictures of the story. She was the best illustrator I ever had. She and I were married about the same time in the progress of our mutual work, but not to each other. . . . Though I have never thought of her for the last 20 years your inquiry makes me feel 'quite romantical' about her (as they say here), and as she is a London artist, well known as Mrs. A. you might hunt her up, and tell me what she looks like as an elderly widow woman. If you do, please give her my kind regards, but you must not add that those two almost simultaneous weddings would have been one but for a stupid blunder of God Almighty."[2]

The "Forty springs back" of the poem suggests that it was written in 1914, but the concluding stanza so echoes the final sentence of Hardy's letter that one may suppose the poem written before Emma had died. It could have been revised to conceal the identity of "H. P." If, as *The Early Life* implies, Hardy's acquaintance with Miss Paterson was brief, then the poem illustrates his characteristic idealization of a woman on the basis of little more than a conversation.

1. Pp. 128, 132, 133; *Life*, pp. 97, 100, 101.
2. Purdy, *Thomas Hardy: A Bibliographical Study*, p. 220.

EVELYN G. OF CHRISTMINSTER is a memorial to Evelyn Gifford of Oxford, a cousin of Emma. ("Christminster" is Hardy's name for Oxford, as in *Jude the Obscure*.) When Emma Gifford married Hardy against her father's wishes, the marriage was performed by her uncle, Dr. E. Hamilton Gifford, Canon of Worcester and afterwards Archdeacon of London.[1] Evelyn Gifford was Dr. Gifford's daughter.[2] When Hardy went to Oxford on February 9, 1920, to receive the degree of Doctor of Letters, among these present at the ceremony were "His wife, Evelyn Gifford, and her sister. . . . Evelyn . . . was his bright and affectionate cousin by marriage, whom Hardy was never to see again." On September 6, he wrote in his notebook: "Death of Evelyn Gifford, at Arlington House, Oxford. Dear Evelyn! whom I last parted from in apparently perfect health."[3]

On September 13, Margaret Gifford wrote to Hardy: "My mother and I were much touched by your letter. Evelyn was so proud of the affectionate kindness you showed her, and it pleases us much to know you loved her." At this time, she had not seen the poem. She wrote again on July 22, 1922: "My mother and I have only just seen your poem to our Evelyn. She was very proud of your friendship and it has pleased and touched us *very* much that you should show, in this beautiful way, your affectionate remembrance of her."[4]

1. *Early Life*, p. 133; *Life*, p. 101.

2. It is not clear when Hardy first met Evelyn. Two letters from her to Hardy, November 30, 1916, and "Xmas Eve," 1919, commenting on Hardy's poems, are in the Dorset County Museum.

3. *Later Years*, pp. 202-3; *Life*, p. 398. These relationships and Hardy's reaction to Miss Gifford's death are detailed by Henry Gifford: "Francis Jeune, afterwards Lord St. Helier, was an eminent judge. . . . Edwin Hamilton Gifford, the uncle who married Emma and Hardy, wedded as his second wife Jeune's sister. . . . On 11 December, 1920, he [Hardy] wrote to my grandfather: 'We were so grieved to hear of the death of Dr. Gifford's daughter Evelyn. When we were at Oxford early this year she went about with us, & seemed so cheerful, & yet she was going to undergo an operation the very next day, which she would not tell us of lest it might be depressing.'" "Thomas Hardy and Emma," p. 112.

4. In the Dorset County Museum.

THE RIFT, Weber surmises, treats the almost unnoticed (but later remembered) beginning of the emotional cleavage between Hardy and his first wife about 1875.[1] To the extent that the poem is autobiographical, Hardy says: "never I knew or guessed my crime." After Emma's death, however, he several times indicted himself for neglect due to introspective self-absorption, as described in "We Sat at the Window" and "Overlooking the River Stour."

1. *Hardy's Love Poems*, p. 29.

VOICES FROM THINGS GROWING IN A CHURCHYARD was written about June, 1921, and first published in the *London Mercury* for December, with the title "Voices from Things Growing."[1] The churchyard is that of Stinsford Church, and the voices are those of people buried there symbolized in the plants that grow from their bodies. Each plant expresses the character of the person it names.

On June 17, 1921, Hardy took Walter de la Mare on a walk to Stinsford; there, as they read the poem, Hardy talked of the various graves. Treating this occasion, *The Later Years* comments: "Fanny Hurd's real name was Fanny Hurden, and Hardy remembered her as a delicate child who went to school with him. She died when she was about eighteen, and her grave and a headstone with her name are to be seen in Stinsford Churchyard. The others mentioned in this poem were known to him by name and repute."[2] The English daisy is both a common flower and a lovely one, suggesting a shy country girl. Perhaps Elizabeth Hurden, whom Hardy remembered as dancing in Middle-Field meadow, was a sister of Fanny. (See the notes on "At Middle-Field Gate in February.")

A tablet in Stinsford Church reads: "In Memory of Benjamin Bowring, gent. late of Kingston Who Departed this life at Dorchester Feb. 17, 1837, Aged 68 years." Hardy's emphasis upon "Gent" suggests that it took this formal fellow "In shingled oak" a long time to learn to dance in green leaves on a wall.

Fittingly Thomas Voss is transformed into red berries on a yew tree. Voss appears in *Under the Greenwood Tree* as the man to bring their post-midnight refreshments to the Mellstock "Quire" on their rounds. Reuben says to him: "And, Voss . . . you keep house here till about half-past two; then heat the metheglin and cider in the warmer you'll find turned up upon the copper; and bring it wi' the victuals to church-hatch, as th'st know." (Part the First, Chapter IV.) Using fictional names for most of the characters, Hardy said, "The only real name in the story is that of 'Voss,' who brought the hot mead and viands to the choir on their rounds. It can still be read on a headstone, also quite near to where the Hardys lie."[3]

Lady Gertrude is not identifiable. Hardy may have let Gertrude stand for a number of ladies of the "proud, high-bred" Grey family, fittingly alive in laurel. She is contrasted with "poor Fanny Hurd" and jolly Eve Greensleeves.

Hardy's footnote explains Eve Greensleeves, transformed into an "innocent withwind," a clematis called the "virgin's bower." In a typescript of *The Later Years*, a passage not published says that Hardy "had discovered the story of Eve Greensleeves, of the poem, during his researches in the copy of Stinsford Register in January of this year [1921]. She was Eve Trevelyan."[4]

Squire Audeley Grey is memorialized on a marble monument in the north aisle of Stinsford Church. The inscription reads in part as "Near this place are interred Audley Grey, esq. and Margaret his wife. He was the second son of Angel Grey, of Kingston Marleward and Bridport," and so on through family connections to a maternal grandfather named George Trevelyan, probably related to Eve Trevelyan.

"Voices from Things Growing in a Churchyard" is a serene poem. Though the voices sound to human ears "All night eerily!" by day they are cheerful. Insofar as the voices represent the dead, they are content; they have no interest in rank, station, or the strain and fret of human life, a theme of "Friends Beyond." The poem fuses into imagery a number of Hardy's ideas taken from science, fantasy, and perhaps balladry. As T. H. Huxley pointed out, life lives on death: the dead humus of buried bodies lives again in plants. That the life thus continued has some memory of its source is suggested in such ballads as "Lord Lovel," in which out of the bosom of Lady Nancy grew a rose, and out of her lover's a briar, which entwined in a love-knot.

Mrs. Florence Hardy wrote to Paul Lemperly on June 14, 1922: "With regard to the literary value, my husband thinks the poems ["Haunting Fingers" and "Voices from Things Growing"] of greater merit than any others I have published in my private series."[5]

"Voices from Things Growing in a Churchyard" has been set to music by Gerald Finzi in *By Footpath and Stile* (London: J. Curwen & Sons, 1925) and *Earth and Air and Rain* (London: Boosey & Hawkes, 1936). It has been recorded as a dramatic reading with six voices acting out the characters and a seventh to sum up. A twelve-year-old child spoke for Fanny Hurd, with the result "something which could not have been produced by any other method."[6]

1. Purdy, *Thomas Hardy: A Bibliographical Study*, p. 213.
2. P. 223; *Life*, pp. 413-14.
3. *Early Life*, p. 122; *Life*, p. 92.
4. In the Dorset County Museum. The passage is cut from material printed on p. 223; *Life*, p. 414.
5. In the Colby College Library.
6. Clinton-Baddeley, "The Written and the Spoken Word," pp. 73-82.

ON THE WAY presents joyful lovers about to keep a tryst. To them the world seems cheerful in spite of dismal weather, for the inner dream is bright.

"SHE DID NOT TURN" may concern, Phelps says, Hardy's broken engagement to Tryphena Sparks: "Tryphena was, almost certainly, the girl who passed the gate of Hardy's Bockhampton home 'foot-faint with averted head'. . . ."[1]

1. *Annotations by Thomas Hardy in His Bibles and Prayer-Book*, p. 7.

GROWTH IN MAY is set near Chard, a town in Somerset about twenty-eight miles northwest of Dorchester. The woman of the final line may seem irrelevant in a poem concerned with the lushness of meadows in May. Hardy associated love with the upsurge of vegetable saps in spring, as in Chapter XX of *Tess of the D'Urbervilles*. It opens with "The season developed and matured," and portrays the growth of Tess's passion as an irresistible result of natural forces. The waiting girl in the poem is not Tess, for Talbothays Dairy is many miles east of Chard.

THE CHILDREN AND SIR NAMELESS in the manuscript had the title "The Children versus Sir Nameless." The poem was first published in *Nash's and Pall Mall Magazine* for May, 1922, though the publisher had distributed a broadside preprint in early April.[1]

That Sir Nameless was "once of Athelhall" identifies the effigy. "Athelhall" is Hardy's name for Athelhampton Hall, a short distance east of Puddletown. It was the ancient seat of the Martyn family, whose tombs, with effigies and fragments of effigies, are in the Athelhampton Aisle (or small chapel) of St. Mary's Church in Puddletown.[2]

Several effigies are broken or marred and are not identifiable. Sir Nameless seems to be an alabaster effigy about seven feet long with toes, nose, and fingers broken. It represents a knight in armor, with his feet resting upon a small, grinning ape.[3] Sir Nameless is not now on the floor, as some of the effigies are, but lies on a tomb. A guide to St. Mary's Church says that the effigy, "although it bears no inscription, is almost certainly that of Sir William Martyn, Knight Bachelor," builder of Athelhampton in the fifteenth century.[4] The account says that "if the date 1471-1475, which is assigned to the effigy by the late Viscount Dillon, is correct, it must have been made thirty years before he died. It will be noticed that he wears a Collar of Suns and Roses, the Yorkist badge." As the effigy is fixed with modern cement, it was possibly once on the floor. Formerly, during the sermon, children were seated in the Athelhampton Aisle, where they may have kicked off projecting parts of statuary under their feet.

Hardy, for the sake of his ironic theme (a fable on vanity), made some alterations in treating the facts. He chose to call the alabaster effigy Sir Nameless, and interpreted "Knight Bachelor" (a knight not a member of a chivalric order) to mean that Sir Nameless was unmarried, or at least had no children. He omitted mention of the "Collar of Suns and Roses," which would have dated the effigy in the fifteenth century. He referred to a church restoration, presumably that of 1634-35, as occurring three hundred years after Sir Nameless had died. This would date Sir Nameless in the fourteenth century, a hundred years earlier than Sir William Martyn.

Hardy wrote to Sir Sydney Cockerell on March 10, 1922: "The effigy of Sir Nameless I have dated back a hundred years further, to get rid of the doubt about the ruff. I *fancy* it was worn when real armour had ceased and dress-armour was in fashion; but I am not sure —though I studied and copied Strutt's plates many years ago when an architect's pupil."[5] Possibly he mingled folk-tradition with his knowledge of fact. The legend may be represented in *The Return of the Native* when Timothy Fairway describes Mrs. Yeobright's face as she forbade the banns for the marriage of Thomasin: "Ah, her face was pale! Maybe you can call to mind that monument in Weatherbury church—the cross-legged soldier that have had his arm knocked away by the school-children? Well, he would about have matched that woman's face, when she said, 'I forbid the banns.' " (Book First, Chapter III.) In this version, the "cross-legged" indicates that the soldier was a crusader, as Sir Nameless was not.

1. Purdy, *Thomas Hardy: A Bibliographical Study*, p. 221.
2. This is the church that Sergeant Troy pretended to attend in *Far from the Madding Crowd*, Chapter XXIX. Hardy's name for Puddletown was "Weatherbury."
3. Effigies of knights often had their feet resting upon a dog; the Martyn effigies rest their feet upon the ape of the family crest. The ape has its head turned to look at its master, with the effect of mockery. The family motto is: "He who looks at Martyn's ape, Martyn's ape shall look at him."
4. Helps, *St. Mary's Church, Puddletown*, p. 16.
5. Meynell, ed., *Friends of a Lifetime*, p. 291.

AT THE ROYAL ACADEMY seems a versification of notes later used in Hardy's biography. In April of 1891, he visited the Royal Academy of Arts, looked at the landscapes, and wrote: "They were not pictures of *this* spring and summer, although they seem to be so. All this green grass and fresh leafage perished yesterday; after withering and falling, it is gone like a dream."[1]

1. *Early Life*, p. 308; *Life*, 235.

HER TEMPLE echoes the thought of Shakespeare's sonnet XVIII: "So long as men can breathe, or eyes can see, / So long lives this, and this gives life to thee." The woman of the poem may be Hardy's first wife, and the "temple," the "Poems of 1912-13." "Her Temple" has been set to music by John Ireland in *Five Poems by Thomas Hardy* (Oxford University Press, 1927) and Gerald Finzi in *A Young Man's Exhortation* (Oxford University Press, 1933).

A TWO-YEARS' IDYLL presents Hardy's judgment of his nearly two years with his first wife Emma at Riverside Villa, Sturminster Newton, which Hardy described as "Our happiest time."[1] According to the poem, they regarded their shared, simple joys as "Nought." They were looking for something "larger, life-fraught," perhaps Hardy for greater success or fame,[2] and Emma for life in London, to which they moved from Sturminster. For details see the notes on "Overlooking the River Stour" and "The Musical Box."

1. *Early Life*, p. 156; *Life*, p. 118. The period was from midsummer, 1876, to March 18, 1878.
2. He wrote *The Return of the Native* in this period.

BY HENSTRIDGE CROSS AT THE YEAR'S END was first published in the *Fortnightly Review* for December, 1919, as "By Mellstock Cross at the Year's End." The headnote about Henstridge Cross was added when the poem was collected. "The scene was moved from Mellstock (Stinsford) to Henstridge in Somerset perhaps a little to obscure the personal implications of the first 4 stanzas."[1]

Though Henstridge (east of Sherborne) is situated on the major crossroads of the note, the poem presents Hardy's home at Stinsford as a crossroads from which he had departed in four directions and reached some disaster on each road. The east road seems to refer to his venture in London in 1862-67, seeking "mirth," from which he returned disillusioned, disheartened, and in poor health. The north road seems to refer to his search for his ancestors (his "forefolk yeomen"), who had owned broad lands in areas near Melbury Bubb, Up Sydling, and Melbury Osmund, only to discover unpleasant facts about their decline. The west road refers to Emma Gifford of Cornwall, who became Hardy's first wife, but caused him much unhappiness in the period 1890-1912, and more, of another kind, in her death. The south road leads to Weymouth, where Hardy had not been entirely happy in 1869; southward too, in the emphasis of the poem, soldiers had departed for World War I, among them his favorite relative, Frank George, killed in the Dardanelles. (See the notes on "Before Marching and After.")

The last two stanzas express a personal conclusion. As every road he had tried brought unforeseen disappointment, Hardy asks, what is the use of action? He was an old man who lived in memories. Life offered no new hope in any direction.

1. Purdy, *Thomas Hardy: A Bibliographical Study*, p. 221.

PENANCE offers a dialogue between a questioner (perhaps Mrs. Florence Hardy, or perhaps the practical side of Hardy's nature) and his dreaming, remorseful self. This self is brooding over memories that he had ignored his first wife Emma, who had sought to renew his love by playing for him the tunes they had once played together. (See "The Last Performance.")

"I LOOK IN HER FACE" seems a companion-poem to "Penance," with emphasis upon Emma's singing rather than piano-playing. The face may be Emma's portrait, now in the Dorset County Museum.

AFTER THE WAR presents the irony of a soldier who returned unscathed from World War I to find his sweetheart dead. Presumably the bugle sounded from the barracks at Dorchester to the soldier's home across a meadow.

"IF YOU HAD KNOWN" in the manuscript was titled "If I Had Known" and was written in the first person.[1] The first person of the manuscript indicates that the first stanza refers to Hardy's courtship of Emma Gifford in Cornwall, with details (the "far down moan" of the sea, and the rain) that point to their outing on Beeny Cliff on August 22, 1870. (See "The Figure in the Scene.")

The second stanza refers to his laying roses on Emma's grave "Fifty years thence to an hour," on August 22, 1920. For Hardy, roses symbolized love. Emma's grave was not, as the poem seems to imply, upon a "luxuriant green" in Cornwall, but was in Stinsford Church-yard. Guerard remarks that the theme of "If You Had Known" was of "almost obsessive importance for Hardy: failure to anticipate the loved one's death and so failure to act appropriately while she was still alive . . . and his subsequent feelings of guilt."[2]

1. Purdy, *Thomas Hardy: A Bibliographical Study*, p. 221.
2. "The Illusion of Simplicity," p. 369.

THE CHAPEL-ORGANIST is a soliloquy by the organist at Dorford Baptist Church, Dorchester, just before she takes poison. Treating the fact that a soliloquy by a woman now dead would have to be inferred, Hardy wrote to Sir Sydney Cockerell on March 10, 1922: "I have altered a word or two in the first verse of 'The Chapel Organist,' to make it clear that she is indulging in those reflections on the *last* night—immediately before her suicide—not, as it seemed to you, on a later occasion. Of course, it is all inferential since nobody could *know* the final thoughts of a woman who was dead when they found her: but this is a recognized licence in narrative art, though it should be veiled as much as possible."[1]

The date "185—" suggests that the poem is based upon fact. References in the poem to deacons and a pastor indicate the chapel as Baptist. It seems likely that Hardy heard the story from Baptist friends when he was working as architectural apprentice for John Hicks in 1856-62. *The Early Life* says of Hardy's acquaintance with Baptists in this period: "Bastow, the other pupil (who, strangely enough for an architect mostly occupied with church-work, had been bred a Baptist), became very doctrinal during this time; he said he was going to be baptized, and in fact was baptized shortly after." He and Hardy engaged in heated doctrinal controversies. "To add to the heat, two of the Dorchester Baptist minister's sons, friends of Bastow, hard-headed Scotch youths fresh from Aberdeen University, good classics . . . joined in the controversy." Hardy agreed to attend the Baptist Chapel with these young men.[2] It was the Dorford Church, of which the Reverend Frederick Perkins was pastor in the years 1858-60,[3] dates that fit Hardy's "185—," though the organist's suicide may have occurred before Perkins became pastor.

Aside from the dramatic nature of the story told in "The Chapel-Organist," Hardy would have remembered it because of his interest in music and his dream of being an organist. The idea of a poem to tell the story possibly sprang from an incident of May 14, 1920: "Motored with F. and K. to Exeter. . . . Cathedral service: the beautiful anthem, 'God is gone up' (Croft). Well sung. Psalms to Walker in E flat. Felt I should prefer to be a cathedral organist to anything in the world. 'Bidding my organ obey, calling its keys to their work, claiming each slave of the sound.' "[4] The quotation from Browning's "Abt Vogler" suggests a model for the meter of "The Chapel-Organist."

Hardy told the story with great realism of detail. The Dorford Baptist Church was so called because it stood near the boundaries of Dorchester and Fordington. Writing in 1886, Young said of it: "The Baptists have a small chapel at the extreme end of this street [High East], facing the hill leading to Fordington. . . . The chapel they now occupy was built in 1830."[5] The "Havenpool" of the poem is Hardy's name for Poole, a seaport town twenty miles east of Dorchester, far enough from Dorford Church that the organist might hope to conceal her indiscretions, yet close enough to permit her weekly trip and to make ultimate discovery inevitable. The organist's self-characterization presents a dramatic conflict between her inherited passionate sexuality ("too much sex in her build . . . / A bosom too full for her age," etc.) and her equally passionate love of organ music.[6] Regretting her sensuality, she is philosophic about what she cannot help: "But who put it there? Assuredly it was not I." Her love of music is "far beyond every lower delight." Her characterization of the deacon and the congregation is without rancor: the deacon was "a worthy man." She does not resent their prying piety and gossip; she understands why she must be dismissed for "the good name of the chapel."

1. Meynell, ed., *Friends of a Lifetime*, pp. 290-91.
2. *Early Life*, pp. 37-39; *Life*, pp. 29-30.
3. Jackman, *300 Years of Baptist Witness*, p. 16.
4. *Later Years*, p. 211; *Life*, p. 404.
5. *Dorchester*, p. 66. The old chapel was replaced in 1914 by a Baptist Church at the "Top o' Town" on High West Street.
6. The hymns she loved included Hardy's favorites. "New Sabbath" is mentioned in "A Church Romance"; Ken of the "Evening Hymn" is mentiond in "Barthélémon at Vauxhall."

FETCHING HER seems to summarize Hardy's discovery of Emma Gifford in Cornwall, his courtship, his bringing her to Max Gate, and her apparent change there. The poem is written as a friend's explanation of why Emma seemed to change. The friend is uninformed about some details. Hardy did not, as suggested in the first stanza, go to Cornwall on horseback. He did not, as in the second stanza, bring Emma immediately to a "new-builded door." The theme and imagery suggest that the friend may personify an idea Hardy perhaps found in Emerson's poem "Each and All." Emerson writes of finding "delicate shells" on the seashore, where "The bubbles of the latest wave / Fresh pearls to their enamel gave, / And the bellowing of the savage sea." When the poet brought the shells home they "Had left their beauty on the shore / With the sun and the sand and the wild uproar." Similarly, Hardy found Emma on her "surfy shore" and thought that in bringing her to Max Gate he was bringing with her "The pure brine breeze, the sea." When she was taken from the environment that had formed part of his "magic-minted conjurings," she was out of the setting that had created the magic.

"COULD I BUT WILL" seems a fantasy of a timeless earthly Paradise. The second stanza may refer to Emma when young or to Tryphena Sparks (or to both, for the first stanza says "sweethearts"), both now dead for many years.

SHE REVISITS ALONE THE CHURCH OF HER MARRIAGE in the manuscript was titled "A Lady Revisits Alone the Church of Her Marriage."[1] The lady may be Emma, Hardy's first wife, who often went on jaunts alone. On a trip to London she may well have visited St. Peter's Church, Elgin Avenue, Paddington, where she and Hardy were married; she may have told him of doing so, and the poem may reflect what she said.

1. Purdy, *Thomas Hardy: A Bibliographical Study*, p. 222.

AT THE ENTERING OF THE NEW YEAR was first published on December 31, 1920, in the *Athenaeum*,[1] though it is dated as written "During the War." In sending the poem to John Middleton Murry, the editor, who had requested a poem, Hardy was aware of continued disturbances and felt that some of the wartime threat still shadowed the world. He wrote on September 12, 1920: "Will this do? If the second part shd. seem too 'pessimistic' (word beloved of the paragraph gents) please leave it out and print the first part only."[2]

Perhaps with some memory of Tennyson's "Northern Farmer, Old Style" and "New Style," Hardy broke his poem into the same parts. "Old Style" presents New Year's Eve as he had known it in the rural society of his boyhood, when the New Year was a "Youth of Promise."

"New Style" presents "bereaved Humanity" in dread of what the New Year may bring.

1. Purdy, *Thomas Hardy: A Bibliographical Study*, p. 222.
2. In the Berg Collection, New York Public Library.

THEY WOULD NOT COME seems Hardy's meditation upon his visit in March of 1913 to the scenes of his courtship of Emma Gifford. The first stanza treats a visit to St. Juliot Church, where pious Emma's spirit might have appeared to him, but did not. The second stanza, also in the Church, treats the Reverend Caddell Holder, Emma's brother-in-law, Rector of St. Juliot. He and the prophets of whom he had "lectioned" were not there, perhaps forbidden by "gear of the Present," modern thought. The third stanza recalls the scene of a picnic with Emma, perhaps on Beeny Cliff, but the memory would not bring back the scene as fully as Hardy could "vision" it in his study at home. The scenes he saw, thus empty, seemed "wisps of bogland" that "bruised the heart of me!"

AFTER A ROMANTIC DAY in the manuscript adds to the title "Your young men shall see visions,"[1] a quotation from Acts 2:17. Hardy may have had in mind his return from a visit to Emma Gifford in Cornwall. On a casual reading, the moon seems the typical song-writer's aid to romance. The moon to Hardy symbolized a realistic, often cynical, illumination. So read, the moon's "weathered face" is only a "convenient sheet" on which "The visions of his mind were drawn." Then the visions are those of young Hardy, seen by the aging poet as illusions. Norman, commenting upon the modernity of Hardy's poetry, says that these "verses on a railway cutting, harsh-lined and angled as a cubist picture" are named "slyly 'After a Romantic Day.'"[2]

1. Purdy, *Thomas Hardy: A Bibliographical Study*, p. 222.
2. "Thomas Hardy," p. 216.

THE TWO WIVES dramatizes a grimly humorous story that Hardy may have heard at his club, the Savile, in London. He treated a similar perversity of chance in the short-story "Fellow Townsmen" (1880).

"I KNEW A LADY" has the subtitle, "Club Song," though why this cynical story should be a song is not clear, except as melodrama and cynical humor were popular in Victorian England. *Punch* of the Victorian time has many a quip similar to the poem.

A HOUSE WITH A HISTORY expresses one of Hardy's frequent themes, that houses retain "memories" of their occupants or are haunted by dramatic events that have taken place there.

A PROCESSION OF DEAD DAYS presents Hardy's memories of his life with his first wife Emma in a series of scenes, each visualized as the ghost of a day. In this fantasy, he characteristically presents nature as living and sentient: in the final stanza the sleeping trees turn upon their "windy pillows" as the dawn comes.

The day of the first stanza seems March 7, 1870, when Hardy journeyed to St. Juliot and met Emma Gifford. The day of the second stanza, whose "features are not cold or white," may be a day in August of 1870, when he paid his second visit to Emma. The "mumbling river" in the third stanza identifies the picnic spot beside the Valency River, and the day as August 19, 1870. (See the notes on "Under the Waterfall.") The fourth stanza treats the unknown date of the "promise made to me," when Emma became engaged to Hardy. The day in morning clothes of the fifth stanza seems to be that of their wedding. The day of the sixth stanza may mark Hardy's realization of Emma's jealousy or tendency to domineer. The day of the seventh and eighth stanzas seems to be that of Emma's death, November 27, 1912. The "third hour" of the day was nine o'clock, approximately the time she died.

HE FOLLOWS HIMSELF is Hardy's dramatization of two forces in conflict within himself. In the drama, the "leading self" of impulses and desires may be called Feeling. The critical, restraining "following self" may be called Reason. Feeling resents being restrained by Reason, but Reason explains that he has often seen Feeling go astray. When Feeling asks, "What do you see?" Reason replies that he sees an aged man whom he must protect. This man is the physical Hardy in his eighties, still susceptible to impulses that lead to "dree" (sorrow). Feeling wishes to join his old friend (perhaps Horace Moule). Reason, pointing out that the friend is dead, says that Feeling "should fight free" of the death-wish. They pause at the friend's grave, where Feeling still says, "I bend a knee." Feeling and Reason, in stalemate, remain by the graveside.

In his copy of the 1923 *Collected Poems* Hardy underscored "friend's" in the first line of the fifth stanza and wrote in the margin "Qy love's?" underscored "friend" in the first line of the sixth stanza and wrote "Qy love?" and in the third line of the stanza underscored "his" and wrote "Qy her?" These changes suggest Hardy's first wife Emma.[1] Whatever the identities, the poem portrays the conflicts within Hardy between the side of his nature that felt, dreamed, and perhaps longed for death, and the side that saw through illusion, distrusted feeling, and labored onward.

1. In the Dorset County Museum.

THE SINGING WOMAN seems a general meditation upon a woman's growing old, but "riding" in the first stanza suggests that Hardy may have had in mind his first wife Emma, proud of her youthful horsemanship in Cornwall.[1] The woman "crooning" also suggests Emma, alone and neglected as in "The Last Performance." "The Singing Woman" has been set to music by Mary Sheldon (in manuscript in the Dorset County Museum).

1. See *Early Life*, p. 91; *Life*, p. 69.

WITHOUT, NOT WITHIN HER seems to treat Hardy's first wife Emma. The poet was attracted to the woman's "strange freshness." All descriptions of Emma Gifford during Hardy's courtship indicate her vitality. *The Early Life* offers a one-word summary of what attracted Hardy: "She was so *living*, he used to say."[1] The poem suggests that he placed little value upon her mind: "no thought of yours tarried / Two moments."[2] The final stanza suggests that at last Hardy hurt Emma through scorning her. Remorse and self-accusation seem implied. The poem has been set to music by John Ireland in *Five Poems by Thomas Hardy* (Oxford University Press, 1927).

1. P. 96; *Life*, p. 73.
2. Hardy may have had in mind Emma's unpublished novels, one of which remains in the Dorset County Museum. It is a sentimental romance titled "The Maid on the Shore." Evelyn Hardy and Gittings, eds., *Some Recollections*, evaluate it on pp. 90-91. No doubt he was embarrassed by the poems Emma published in the *Dorset County Chronicle*. See Cox, ed., *Poems and Religious Effusions by Emma Lavinia Hardy*.

"O I WON'T LEAD A HOMELY LIFE" is a song to "an old air." Purdy said: "There is a separate MS. of the poem, with the music of the 'old air,' in the possession of Sir Sydney Cockerell. They were copied out by Hardy in pencil on the back of a circular dated 23 August 1922."[1] The poem is something like a versification of the theme of Hardy's short-story "The Fiddler of the Reels" in *Life's Little Ironies*. F. H. Brown has set the poem to music with the title "The Fiddler's Dear" (in manuscript in the Dorset County Museum).

1. *Thomas Hardy: A Bibliographical Study*, p. 222.

IN THE SMALL HOURS presents Hardy's dream of the fiddle-playing days of his youth. As a boy "little Thomas played sometimes at village weddings, at one of which the bride . . . kissed him in her intense pleasure at the dance; once at a New Year's Eve party in the house of the tailor who had breeched him; also in farmers' parlours; and on another occasion at a homestead where he was stopped by his hostess clutching his bow-arm at the end of a three-quarter-hour's unbroken footing to his notes by twelve tireless couples."[1] "Haste to the Wedding" was played at the wedding-party of Fancy Day and Dick Dewy in the final chapter of *Under the Greenwood Tree*.[2]

1. *Early Life*, p. 29; *Life*, p. 23.
2. Music for this dance has been published by Elna Sherman in *Wessex Tune Book* (London: Schott & Co., 1963) from "a manuscript book belonging to the family of Thomas Hardy."

THE LITTLE OLD TABLE is the small, oblong table of pine that now stands in a corner of the reconstructed "Hardy's Study" in the Dorset County Museum. A tag on the table identifies it as "Thomas Hardy's Work Table—On Which Were Written His Earlier Works." The tag then quotes the poem. *The Later Years* seems to refer to this table in a paragraph about Sir Frederick Treves: ". . . it was from the shop of Treves's father that Hardy as a boy purchased his first writing desk. The care which he took of all his possessions during his whole life is shown by the fact that this desk was in his study without a mark or scratch upon it at the time of his death."[1]

The poem, which speaks of "one who gave you to me," contradicts the statement that Hardy purchased the table. Lois Deacon says: "It is highly probable that Tryphena [Sparks] gave this table to Hardy 'with her own hand.' "[2] Perhaps, in preparing notes for his biography, Hardy concealed the origin of the gift, as he concealed other facts about Tryphena.

"The Little Old Table" has been set to music by Benjamin Britten in *Winter Words* (London and New York: Boosey and Hawkes, 1954).

1. P. 236; *Life*, p. 423.
2. *Tryphena and Thomas Hardy*, p. 19.

VAGG HOLLOW was drawn from a note in Hardy's journal for April 20, 1902, a part of which he used as a headnote for the poem. "Vagg Hollow, on the way to Load Bridge (Somerset) is a place where 'things' used to be seen—usually taking the form of a wool-pack in the middle of the road. Teams and other horses always stopped on the brow of the hollow, and could only be made to go on by whipping. A waggoner once cut at the pack with his whip: it opened in two, and smoke and a hoofed figure rose out of it."[1] In the poem, Hardy ignored the wool-pack and the hoofed figure and told a story of a little boy who was "not afraid at all!" He may have been inspired by the Dorset motto: "Who's afeär'd?"

Perhaps the boy who goes through Vagg Hollow with a wagoner at five o'clock each morning is helping deliver milk to Ilchester or Yeovil. Vagg Hollow, scrubbily wooded as well as marshy, is on a lane about two miles northwest of Yeovil and four miles south of Ilchester; Load Bridge is a bridge over the Yeo River north of the village of Long Load. Tintinhull is a village between Long Load and Vagg Hollow.

1. *Later Years*, p. 96; *Life*, p. 314.

THE DREAM IS—WHICH? in the manuscript had the title "As if Not There."[1] The date, March, 1913, is that of Hardy's journey into Cornwall to revisit the scenes of his courtship of Emma Gifford. The "haggard rooms" and a "lonely stair" suggest Max Gate, and the "mounded green" may be in Stinsford Churchyard, where Emma was buried. Perhaps the poem was written after Hardy's return home, with the scenes of the old romance so revived that the realities of Max Gate and Stinsford seemed the dream.

The scene by the brook seems to be that of "Under the Waterfall," beside the little Valency River. The scene of the second stanza may be the summer-house of "The Man Who Forgot."

The technique of the poem supports the question of the title. Hogan says of it: "The partitioning of each stanza implies the equal validity of both aspects of the experience. Furthermore, past actions are set in the present tense. . . . The present condition is asserted only conditionally."[2]

1. Purdy, *Thomas Hardy: A Bibliographical Study*, p. 223.
2. "Structural Design in Thomas Hardy's Poetry," p. 72.

THE COUNTRY WEDDING, with the title "The Fiddler's Story," was first published in a pamphlet for Mrs. Florence Hardy in October, 1917.[1] The poem tells a ballad-like story of a country wedding in the nineteenth century. Michael and Reub are among the musicians of *Under the Greenwood Tree*. In that novel, "Old William Dewy, with the violincello, played the bass; his grandson Dick the treble violin; and Reuben [Dewy] and Michael Mail the tenor and second violins respectively." Then the narrator, who "bowed the treble," must be Dick Dewy. The time of the wedding may be a little later than that of the novel, for Reuben, rather than "Old William Dewy," plays the bass-viol. The musicians for the wedding include Jim, who plays the serpent. Jim is not one of the musicians of *Under the Greenwood Tree*, who were divided in opinion about the serpent. An unnamed speaker says that choirs should have "done away with serpents. If you'd thrive in musical religion, stick to strings, says I." But Mr. Penny defends the serpent as a "good old note: a deep rich note was the serpent."[2] Jim does not appear in other poems about the Mellstock (Stinsford) choir. As the wedding is in Puddletown (Hardy's

"Weatherbury"), he may be a musician of that village, perhaps the Jim of "In Weatherbury Stocks."

The scene is Puddletown, about five miles northeast of Dorchester on the London Road, but only a little over three miles from Stinsford. The players from Stinsford "marched . . . over the heather" by way of Beacon Corner and Coombe Lane (locally called "Lovers' Lane," overshadowed by great trees). The wedding party gathered at Mill-tail-Shallow, on the River Piddle in the northern part of the village, at a corner called Sparks Corner. To march from there to St. Mary's Church, the wedding party did not need to go up Styles-Lane, but by doing so the party would proceed from the Town Square (close to the Church) to Salisbury Road and enter Front Street at a distance from the Church. The party would thus parade down Front Street and back to the Square en route to the Church. This parade through the village is important in the poem, related to the musicians' break with tradition in taking the lead and the bride's "Too gay!" as premonitions of sorrow.[3] The bride's home near Sparks Corner suggests a member of the Sparks family.

There is no causal relationship between the irregularities of the wedding and the deaths of the final stanzas, but the ending is characteristic of Hardy. Ransom says: "So the weather was equivocal, and was designed no better for the wedding than for the funeral. A special and very characteristic pointedness in the irony is provided in the circumstance that the lovers must be buried, as they were married, on the same day."[4] The versification is more complex than the apparent simplicity of the poem suggests. Vinson points out "four-line stanzas linked by interstanza rhyme of both first with first and last with last lines in slightly irregular pattern, the two middle lines of each stanza rhyming. The first four stanzas have matching first and last line rhymes; the next three are similarly linked, while the last two match the first group in first-line rhyme but are coupled by a different fourth-line sound."[5]

1. Purdy, *Thomas Hardy: A Bibliographical Study*, p. 192.
2. Part the First, Chapter IV. The serpent was an obsolete bass wind instrument of the trumpet type, but with a semi-coiled tube.
3. The "Front-Street houses" are pictured in "Plate 26, Puddletown Village" of Lea's *Thomas Hardy's Wessex*, p. 33.
4. "Honey and Gall," pp. 5-6.
5. "Diction and Imagery in the Poetry of Thomas Hardy," p. 177.

FIRST OR LAST is a ditty on the theme of "Gather ye rosebuds while ye may." It has been set to music by Mary Sheldon in *The Colour* (London: Swan & Co., 1924) and C. A. Speyer (manuscript in the Dorset County Museum).

LONELY DAYS is footnoted as "Versified from a Diary." As the poem treats the feelings of Hardy's first wife Emma, the diary was probably Emma's, which apparently Hardy destroyed, as well as portions of *Some Recollections*[1] and "What I Think of My Husband," which it is stated that Hardy burned. The portions of *Some Recollections* that remain do not contain much that is directly echoed in the poem.[2]

The first stanza presents Emma's declining years at Max Gate.[3] There Emma was "Environed from sight" by the growth of trees that Hardy had planted in 1886 to secure her privacy. Often he was away, as in London, and when at home he was absorbed in literary labors and did not give her much attention. Perhaps the second stanza refers to Emma's life at St. Juliot, where she had been an isolated spinster nearly thirty years old before Hardy arrived in 1870. The third stanza seems to refer to her visit to Plymouth, her girlhood home, on the occasion of her father's funeral in 1890. Then, fifty years old, she found things she had known different from her memory of them. The poem implies Hardy's sense of remorse that he had neglected Emma.

1. In a footnote, Hardy calls Emma's *Some Recollections* a "diary." *Early Life*, p. 92; *Life*, p. 70.
2. Evelyn Hardy and Gittings, eds., *Some Recollections*, pp. 72-73, examine some details in relation to Emma's memories and Hardy's poem.
3. The "house were the gate was" refers, apparently, to the old site of Mack's Gate, or toll-station, selected for Hardy's home, not to the gate to the yard.

"WHAT DID IT MEAN?" may be a personal poem with the occasion and persons concealed. The "I" of the poem seems a woman. The poem may treat in symbols the triangle of Hardy, Tryphena Sparks, and Emma Gifford. If so, it suggests that Hardy's memory of Tryphena helped to darken his marriage to Emma.

AT THE DINNER-TABLE, a soliloquy by an aging woman, has the tone of an actual incident. Perhaps the poem is a fantasy to express a thought in many of Hardy's poems, that beneath the bloom of youth lurks old age and at last the skull. (See "Amabel" and "The Revisitation.") Possibly the poem dramatizes a thought in Hardy's mind about his first wife Emma. The phrase "in my prime" suggests the 1890's. As observers commented and photographs show, aging Emma continued to dress in the styles of her youth, in muslins and ribbons. Perhaps Hardy suggested she ought to dress her age, and observed her reaction. If so, the "sideboard glass" dramatizes his view. The poem, though published after Emma's death, presents the woman as outliving her husband.

THE MARBLE TABLET in the manuscript was titled "The Marble Monument."[1] When Mrs. Emma Hardy died in 1912, Hardy did not bury her in Cornwall, where she had lived before her marriage, but in Stinsford Churchyard. He erected to her memory in St. Juliot Church in Cornwall, the marble tablet of the poem. The story is told in *The Later Years*. In March of 1913, Hardy revisited the scenes of his courtship of Emma Gifford in Cornwall. In St. Juliot, "He found the rectory . . . changed a little, but not greatly, and returning by way of Plymouth arranged for a memorial tablet to Mrs. Hardy in the church with which she had been so closely associated as organist before her marriage. . . . The tablet was afterwards erected to his own design." In September, 1916, he revisited St. Juliot to see if his "design and inscription for the tablet in the church had been properly carried out and erected."[2]

The tablet, erected in the north aisle of the church, reads: "To the Dear Memory of / EMMA LAVINIA HARDY born Gifford / Wife of Thomas Hardy Author & Sister / In Law of the Rev. C. Holder Formerly / Incumbent of this Parish: Before Her / Marriage She Lived at the Rectory / 1868-1873 Conducted the Church Music / & Laid the First Stone of the Rebuilt / Aisle & Tower: She Died at Dorchester / 1912 & Is Buried at Stinsford Dorset. / Erected By Her Husband 1913." Hardy's drawings for this tablet are in the Dorset County Museum.[3]

Besides Hardy's tablet for Emma, St. Juliot has a tablet for Hardy, similar in design to Emma's and set in the wall beside hers, though with a window separating them. It reads: "Thomas Hardy: O. M. Litt. D. / Author of Many Works in Verse / & Prose & in Early Life Architect / Made Drawings in March 1870 of / This Church In Its Ancient State & / Later for the Alterations & Re- / pairs Executed 1871-2 Which He as- / sisted to Supervise: He Died 1928 / & Is Buried in Westminster Abbey: / Erected 1928 As a Record of His Associa- / tion with the Church & Neighborhood." Hardy designed this tablet for himself, and in his will left the following instructions: "I request my Literary Executors to cause to be erected in the Church of St. Juliot near Boscastle Cornwall a Tablet memorising my connection with the restoration of the said Church a design for which tablet will be found among my papers."[4]

1. Purdy, *Thomas Hardy: A Bibliographical Study*, p. 223.

2. *Later Years*, pp. 156, 172; *Life*, pp. 361, 372.

3. A letter from Joseph Geach of Plymouth on April 1, 1913, restates Hardy's specifications: "Wall Tablet for St. Juliot Church: To supply & fix same at the above church, namely 'Carnsew Granite' slab 2'-7" × 2'-1" × 2½" with square edges, polished where seen with two corbels (which are required) 4½" × 4" × 8"

polished where seen; with Sicilian marble polished tablet 2'-0" × 1'-6" × 1", with the lettering sent me deeply cut & painted the cost would be £16.12.0. All fees extra." In the Dorset County Museum.

4. Cox, ed., *Thomas Hardy's Will*, pp. 3-4.

THE MASTER AND THE LEAVES was first published in the *Owl* in May, 1919.[1] Robert Graves, in a letter of January 4 [1919?] asked Hardy for "a contribution, prose or verse on any subject . . . to a miscellany called the Owl." Hardy replied, "I think I can send a short poem—I fear a very trifling one."[2]

The speaker of the first three stanzas is the "Master's" favorite tree. "March drought and April flooding" seems to echo the opening lines of Chaucer's Prologue to *The Canterbury Tales* as well as reflect Hardy's observation that springtime arouses all things in nature. Perhaps "treen" for trees also echoes Chaucer as well as rimes with "green." "The Master and the Leaves" has been set to music by Gerald Finzi in *By Footpath and Stile* (London: J. Curwen & Sons, 1925).

1. Purdy, *Thomas Hardy: A Bibliographical Study*, p. 210.
2. Letter and pencil-note of Hardy's reply are in the Dorset County Museum.

LAST WORDS TO A DUMB FRIEND is Hardy's tribute to a cat that strayed from Max Gate to a "tragic end." Perhaps this cat is the one about which Hardy wrote Sir George Douglas on April 3, 1901: "A gloom has been cast over us here since yesterday by the loss of a favourite cat which was mutilated by the mail train the night before last."[1] Hardy wrote more feelingly to Mrs. Arthur Henniker on April 4: "A gloom has been thrown over the house by the tragic death of a favourite cat—*my* cat—the first I had ever had 'for my very own.' He was run over by the train on Monday night; & I blame myself for letting him stay out, after taking the trouble to shut him up myself every night all this winter."[2] In her copy of *Late Lyrics*, Hardy's friend Rebekah Owen wrote in the margin opposite "Last Words to a Dumb Friend," "This was Peachblossom or Marco. Marco I remember was the white one."[3] Miss Owen may have been mistaken. S. M. Ellis, describing a visit to Max Gate in 1913, said that in the shrubbery of Hardy's garden "little inscribed tombstones, partly covered with ivy, mark the resting places of the former pets of Max Gate, a dog and five cats—among the latter 'Comfy,' 'Moss,' and white 'Snowdove,' who inspired that beautiful tribute in verse, *Last Words to a Dumb Friend*. . . . This was written in 1904, and though it was nine years after when he sadly pointed out the little grave to me, I think his sense of pain and loss was as sharp as on the first day."[4]

"Last Words to a Dumb Friend" echoes the feeling of Hardy's

letter to Mrs. Henniker, whether or not the letter and the poem treat the same cat. The cat is remembered in pictures that include his imaginative identification with the cat's point of view: the cat "humoured" the "queer ways" of the Hardy household. The sorrow so upsets the poet that he vows "Never another pet for me!"[5] and seeks to escape the memory and the pain. It is characteristic that he felt the loss to outweigh (for the moment, at least) the pleasure and that he should try to "Selfishly escape distress."

1. Parker, "Hardy's Letters to Sir George Douglas," p. 221. The railway from Dorchester to Weymouth runs through a cutting near Max Gate. That Hardy did not write the poem until 1904 is his way with subjects of remorse.

2. In the Dorset County Museum.

3. In the Colby College Library.

4. "Some Personal Recollections of Thomas Hardy," p. 401.

5. Hardy did have, love, and mourn later pets. See "A Popular Personage at Home."

A DRIZZLING EASTER MORNING in the manuscript had the title "A Wet Easter Morning."[1] The scene of the poem is a churchyard (perhaps Stinsford, with its yew tree overhanging the Hardy graves), where Hardy, standing "amid" the dead, wonders about the resurrection, which he questions in the opening line and seems to reject in the closing line. Schwartz's analysis points out his mixture of emotional wish to believe and disbelief: "It is the belief and disbelief in Christ's resurrection which not only make this poem possible, but make its details so moving . . . . the weary wain which plods forward heavily and the dead men in the graveyard . . . become significant of the whole experience of suffering and evil just because the belief exists for Hardy and provides a light which makes these particular things symbols. *Without the belief, it is only another rainy morning in March or April.*"[2]

For Hardy, belief in the Easter promise of resurrection would not be satisfactory. Perhaps the dead would not wish to "pass again their sheltering door." Men's experience of life, its labors and aches, makes them "fain / For endless rest."

1. Purdy, *Thomas Hardy: A Bibliographical Study*, p. 223.

2. "Poetry and Belief," p. 74.

ON ONE WHO LIVED AND DIED WHERE HE WAS BORN, Purdy says, "in spite of one or two discrepancies, seems to refer to Hardy's father (who had died in 1892)."[1] The discrepancies are in dates. Hardy's father was born in Higher Bockhampton on November 15, 1811,[2] and died there on July 20, 1892. He last ascended the stairs in his birthplace, not in November as the poem says, but, *The Later Years* says, in April, 1892: "On the 27th of the month, his [Hardy's] father . . .

'went upstairs for the last time.' "[3] At this time, he was eighty years and five months old, instead of exactly eighty as the poem implies.

Hardy's memories of his boyhood present his father as a lover of life, music, and merriment. He was "Wealth-wantless." "Thomas Hardy the Second had not the tradesman's soul. Instead of way-laying possible needers of brick and stone in the market-place or elsewhere, he liked going alone into the woods or on the heath, where, with a telescope . . . he would stay peering into the distance by the half-hour; or, in hot weather, lying on a bank of thyme or camomile with the grasshoppers leaping over him."[4] He viewed life with a sane, amused "philosophy": "Hardy frequently stated in after years that the character of Horatio in *Hamlet* was his father's to a nicety, and in Hardy's copy of that play his father's name and the date of his death are written opposite the following lines: 'Thou hast been / As one in suffering all that suffers nothing; / A man that fortune's buffets and rewards / Hast ta'en with equal thanks.' "[5] Toward the end of his life, he became the "frail aged figure" of the poem. Hardy wrote to Sir George Douglas on October 8, 1892, that his father "had been an invalid for many years, & was seen of nobody but ourselves in the secluded spot near here in which he lived and was born about 81 years ago."[6] He loved his home: "Almost the last thing his father had asked for was water fresh drawn from the well—which was brought and given him; he tasted it and said, 'Yes—that's our well-water. Now I know I am at home.' "[7]

The title of this tribute to his father reflects Hardy's thought about country life. On March 6, 1902, H. Rider Haggard asked him for "your opinions as to the past, present & future of the agricultural labourer, ditto as regards the tenant farmer, & what you think will be the result of the exodus from the country side to the towns." Hardy replied: "For one thing, village tradition—a vast mass of un-written folk lore, local chronicle, local topography and nomenclature —is absolutely sinking, has really sunk, into eternal oblivion. I cannot recall a single instance of a labourer who still lives on the farm on which he was born, & I can only recall a few who have been five years on their present farm. Thus, you see, there being no continuity of environment in their lives, there is no continuity of information, the names, stories, & relics of one place being speedily forgotten under the incoming facts of the next."[8]

1. *Thomas Hardy: A Bibliographical Study*, p. 223.

2. See "The Hardy Pedigree" prepared by Hardy himself, reproduced facing p. 224 of Evelyn Hardy, *Thomas Hardy*.

3. P. 8; *Life*, p. 247.

4. *Early Life*, pp. 26-27; *Life*, p. 21.

5. *Later Years*, p. 10; *Life*, p. 248.
6. Parker, "Hardy's Letters to Sir George Douglas," p. 219.
7. *Later Years*, p. 10; *Life*, p. 248.
8. Letter and pencil-draft of Hardy's reply are in the Dorset County Museum. See also "The Dorsetshire Labourer," in Orel, *Thomas Hardy's Personal Writings*, pp. 168-89.

THE SECOND NIGHT tells an eerie tale of an unfaithful lover who missed a rendezvous with his "old Love" one night, appeared at the appointed place the second night, was greeted by her ghost, who vanished, and then learned that she had killed herself the night before.

The city is Plymouth. The rendezvous takes place "at Cremyll side," across the Hamoaze River from downtown Plymouth. The lover has come to Cremyll by boat from West-Hoe Pier, about a mile southwest of the central city. The girl is from Mount Edgcumbe, a high hill just south of Devil's Point and Cremyll. She had hurled herself from a height to the Cremyll shore.

Possibly the poem reflects a meeting between Hardy and Tryphena Sparks in Plymouth. The lover speaks of seeing his "new Fair" the night before. He had come to bring news of her to his "old Love"; he had "travelled all day," and he is in a hurry to get away to "a differing scene / Before the dark has died." Hardy was in Plymouth on December 31, 1873, returning from a visit to Emma Gifford in Cornwall.[1] No reason is stated why he returned to Higher Bockhampton or London on a roundabout way by Plymouth. At this time, Tryphena Sparks, to whom Hardy had been engaged before he met Emma Gifford, was headmistress of a school there. These facts suggest some relation between Hardy's detour to Plymouth and "The Second Night." Certainly the suicide of the poem is fiction.

Hickson points out that in the poem Hardy "used the Pantoum rime-scheme: The rime-word (not the entire line) of the second and fourth line of each stanza is repeated in the first and third of the following stanza. The closing stanza gets the rime for its second and fourth lines from the first and third of the opening stanza, thus completing the circle."[2]

1. *Early Life*, p. 128; *Life*, p. 97.
2. *The Versification of Thomas Hardy*, p. 50.

SHE WHO SAW NOT presents a conversation between a Sage and a Lady. The Sage points to a man, whom the Lady sees as only "average head to feet." After the man's death, the Lady sees as a vision what the Sage was unable to show her. The poem may be a parable to suggest that the wife of a genius is likely to see in her husband only a common man. The Sage may stand for insight that the Lady rejects. The roses and the garden seat suggest Max Gate, and Hardy may have intended the Lady to represent his first wife Emma. She could not share his thoughts, as in *Jude the Obscure*, or his dreams. That she understood after his death must be fiction.

The reference to the "face of Moses" echoes Exod. 34:29. When Moses returned from talking with God on Sinai, "the skin of his face shone."

THE OLD WORKMAN in the manuscript had the title "The Old Mason."[1] The poem is a tribute to the pride of an aging mason in a house well built, even though building it sprained his back for life. The poem has the tone and meaning of Wordsworth's "Resolution and Independence." As Hardy's father was a builder, the story may be true of a workman he employed. (Compare Hardy's similar tribute to a workman in "A Man.")

1. Purdy, *Thomas Hardy: A Bibliographical Study*, p. 223.

THE SAILOR'S MOTHER was first published in the *Anglo-Italian Review* for September, 1918. "The poem is a versification of the closing lines of 'To Please His Wife.'" This short-story was published in *Black and White* for June 27, 1891, and in *Life's Little Ironies* in 1894.[1]

In the story, laid in "Havenpool" (Poole), Joanna Jolliffe, jealous of the wealth of her neighbor, Emily Lester, sent her unwilling husband and two sons to sea to make a fortune. When they did not return, Joanna, now penniless, was taken to live with Emily Lester, where she became crazed in constantly looking for the return of her husband and sons. As the story ends, Joanna has heard a noise that she imagines signals their return. She rushed out into the night to her old home. The last lines read: " 'Has anybody come?' asked the form. —'O, Mrs. Jolliffe, I didn't know it was you,' said the young man kindly, for he was aware how her baseless expectations moved her. 'No; nobody has come.' "

The poem, in versifying this ending, reduces the three sailors to one, a son.

1. Purdy, *Thomas Hardy: A Bibliographical Study*, pp. 223, 82, and 81.

OUTSIDE THE CASEMENT in the manuscript was titled "After the Battle."[1] It seems probable that the "message" of the poem was a telegram announcing the death of Second Lieutenant Frank William George, killed in action at Gallipoli on August 22, 1915. (See the notes on "Before Marching and After.") If so, the people in the room were probably Hardy and Mrs. Florence Hardy, and the girl "in the portico-shade outside" was George's fiancée, or at least someone dear to him.

1. Purdy, *Thomas Hardy: A Bibliographical Study*, p. 224.

THE PASSER-BY in the manuscript adds to the title "In Memoriam L—— H———. (She speaks)."[1] The "L. H." of the poem was Louisa Harding. Both *The Early Life* and "To Louisa in the Lane" describe Hardy's shy "courtship" of her that scarcely reached an exchange of greetings. Insofar as "The Passer-By" is a memorial poem, it was perhaps prompted by Miss Harding's death on September 12, 1913,[2] at the age of seventy-two, and her burial in an extension of Stinsford Churchyard.

The statement about her in *The Early Life* includes the belief that she shyly returned Hardy's admiration. "He believed that his attachment to this damsel was reciprocated, for on one occasion when he was walking home from Dorchester he beheld her sauntering down the lane as if to meet him. He longed to speak to her, but bashfulness overcame him, and he passed on with a murmured 'Good evening,' while poor Louisa had no word to say."[3] The poem, her reminiscent soliloquy, rests on this assumption. Whatever Hardy meant, her words "he became . . . my fate" suggest that she did not marry because of him.

1. Purdy, *Thomas Hardy: A Bibliographical Study*, p. 224.
2. *Dorset County Chronicle*, September 18, 1913, p. 16.
3. P. 33; *Life*, p. 26.

"I WAS THE MIDMOST" seems a lyric statement of Hardy's view of himself in three ages, boyhood, the years of youth and courtship, and old age. Though the biographies indicate that he was a pensive boy, they also describe his merrymaking. He was the center of a small company: fond parents, beloved sister Mary, admiring teachers, and boyhood friends. The second stanza refers to years of youth, ambition, and love, with its "Polestar" Emma Gifford in Cornwall. The third stanza, abandoning a focus on self, treats his old age and his compassion for all the sufferers from World War I and "everywhere / On Earth's bewildering ball!"

A SOUND IN THE NIGHT is a ballad-like tale of murder at Woodsford Castle in the eighteenth century. Woodsford Castle, four miles east of Dorchester on the road toward Moreton, is the oldest inhabited building in Dorset. It was built during the reign of Edward III (1312-77) as a fortified castle with massive greystone walls, towers with arrow-slits, and turrets with loopholes. The Frome River runs in a serpentine course through a moorland a few hundred yards north of the Castle. The Castle was originally called "Wyrdesford" for the nearby "weird" or fateful ford of Rocky Shallow across the Frome. (It is a deep "shallow," suitable only for men on horseback and dangerous even then.) In the eighteenth century, the Castle was converted into a large farmhouse, four stories high: the great halls have been made into modern rooms, and, in many alterations, the Castle has been roofed with thatch, as it still is. The original dungeons are now filled in.[1]

Woodsford is an authentic haunted castle, if "authentic" means an actual medieval castle "known" in local traditions to be haunted. The tales of the hauntings vary, some of them concerning a monk or nun who was tortured there. The old kitchen was once a "priest's hole," or hide-out for persecuted priests.[2]

The poem exhibits Hardy's knowledge of Woodsford Castle and the moorland around it. The bridegroom of the poem identifies an eerie sound as "the eaves dripping down upon the plinth-slopes." These are downward-sloping stone slabs that, about halfway down the walls, take the drip from the eaves away from the lower walls. The wife speaks of the Castle as a "lonely place." Even today, the nearest house is a quarter of a mile away. The bridegroom explains that the noise may be made by a tree that "rubs his arms acrosswise." A number of trees are behind the Castle. The sound may be "the river at the bend, where it whirls about the hatches." A quarter of a mile northeast of the Castle, weirs dam the Frome, which swirls noisily over the hatches. To satisfy his bride, the groom will throw his lantern-light over the moor, now a cattle-pasture often ankle-deep in muck. The bridegroom "vanished down the turret," in which the narrow, circling stairs are still in use. He went out by the "postern," the original guard-gate at the southern end of the Castle, now the gate to the road. On his return, the bridegroom speaks of a "tree that taps the gargoyle-head." No present tree is close enough to tap a gargoyle on the Castle, but an old tree may have been there in Hardy's time. Later "They" found a woman's body at Rocky Shallow, mentioned above.

Perhaps Hardy heard the tale from workmen when as a boy he assisted his father in a "restoration" of Woodsford Castle. *The Early Life* mentions the incident in speaking of John Hicks's observation: "Having seen Thomas Hardy junior when his father conjointly with another builder was executing Mr. Hicks's restoration of, it is believed, Woodsford Castle, and tested him by inviting him to assist at a survey, Hicks wished to have him as a pupil."[3] The tale may be fiction suggested by an entry in Hardy's notebook for August, 1902:

"A Squire in a remote part of Wessex brings home his bride. She finds in the manor-house a woman who has had children by him."[4] If this is the source, Hardy invented the murder and set the action in "haunted" Woodsford Castle to heighten the effect.[5]

The poem is an eerie melodrama of a farmer's fascination by a new love whom he calls a witch, a murder, and the suggestion of hauntings. That the murder occurs on the wedding night heightens the horror.

1. Based upon a visit and conversations with the present tenant.

2. Ernest Hardy of Dorchester, who lived in the Castle for some years, told of a haunted stairway leading up from a room called the "Queen's bedchamber"; on the halfway-landing of the stairs, formerly the entrance to a chapel (now a bathroom), "things" were supposed to be seen, though he had not seen any. The occupant in 1966, Mr. Gell, had heard tales of hauntings, but had seen no ghosts.

3. P. 35; *Life*, p. 27.

4. Evelyn Hardy, *Thomas Hardy's Notebooks*, pp. 70-71.

5. Other possible sources come to mind. John Hardy and Mary Knight, the parents of Hardy's grandfather, Thomas Hardy the First, were married at Woodsford on December 1, 1777. Tales of Woodsford may have come down to Hardy from his grandmother, wife of Thomas Hardy the First. (See "One We Knew.") Hardy may have found the story in Heath's typescript history of the families of Dorset. (See the notes on "The Dame of Athelhall.")

ON A DISCOVERED CURL OF HAIR describes a lock of hair contained in a green leather locket with a miniature of Hardy's first wife Emma. The miniature, prominently showing young Emma's curls, is reproduced in *The Early Life*, facing page 96.[1] The portrait of Emma as she was about 1870 and the curl of hair were not (as the poem implies) entirely forgotten. Rebekah Owen, annotating the poem in her copy of *Late Lyrics*, wrote opposite the poem: "Mr. Hardy showed me this curl once in his wife's presence. Also a miniature of her. I should call the colour more golden than brown—not red-golden."[2]

The poem is a soliloquy addressed to Emma's spirit three months after her death when Hardy had "discovered" the curl of hair and returned in memory to his courtship. The particulars of this courtship are much concerned with Emma's curls. (See the poems that picture Emma's hair, "A Dream or No," "After a Journey," "Beeny Cliff," and "The Tresses.") The "discovered" curl is related to the "forgotten" miniature. (See "A Forgotten Miniature.")

Hardy made dramatic use of a coil of hair in his novels. In *Far from the Madding Crowd*, the coil of Fanny Robin's hair in Sergeant Troy's watch is the fuse that exploded his marriage to Bathsheba. (Chapter XLI.) In *The Mayor of Casterbridge*, exiled Henchard carries with him a curl of Elizabeth-Jane's hair. (Chapter XLIV.)

1. *Life*, facing p. 66.

2. Weber, "From Belmount Hall to Colby," p. 89.

AN OLD LIKENESS in the manuscript was called "The Old Portrait." Possibly "Recalling R. T." refers to some sweetheart of Hardy's youth whose portrait he kept in some nearly forgotten place and rediscovered as, in the 1920's, he was going over his past. The poem presents her as witty, jolly, and sentimental, engaged in riming and painting, and now dead. The term "blight-time," when Hardy rediscovered her long-forgotten portrait, suggests his old age.

HER APOTHEOSIS has a Latin motto that may be translated as "My secret to myself." The phrase occurs in the Latin Bible in Isa. 24:16, and is translated in the King James version as "My leanness, my leanness, woe unto me!" Hardy, in his copy of the 1923 *Collected Poems*, underscored "them" in lines one and three of the second stanza and in the margin wrote "? me," and underscored "their" in the fourth line and wrote "? my." These emendations suggest that he applied the poem to some particular faded woman who had lived "Ringed" by an "iris" in her memory of being loved.

"SACRED TO THE MEMORY" is a tribute to Hardy's beloved sister Mary. When she died, he phrased the inscription for her tomb in Stinsford Churchyard as: "Sacred to the Memory of Mary Elder Daughter of Thomas and Jemima Hardy born at Bockhampton Dec. 23, 1841. Died at Talbothays Nov. 24, 1915."[1] The poem says that the simple, conventional phrasing cannot represent his memories of Mary.

1. Hardy's design for the tombstone with this phrasing is in the Dorset County Museum.

TO A WELL-NAMED DWELLING does not name the "old house of lichened stonework" with the "fair title." Clues suggest that Hardy meant the older of the two manor houses called Kingston Maurward. The full name is hardly a "fair title," but "Kingston" may be so considered in sound, general suggestion, and associations for Hardy. The estate was often called in his time, as today, simply "Kingston." Hardy's interest in Kingston is clear not only in several poems ("Amabel," "An Anniversary," "In Her Precincts," and "The Harvest Supper") but also in his full-page, handwritten "Chronicle of Kingston Maurward House & Estate" inserted into his copy of Hutchins's *History* (II, 565) opposite a full-page drawing of "Kingston House."[1] A guidebook to Dorchester dated 1886 calls the manor "Kingston House," with no mention of Maurward during two pages of discussion.[2] Hardy drew a plan of Kingston Maurward House, but labelled it simply "Kingston House."[3]

Hardy knew the answer to the question of the poem, "How by that fair title came you?" He had read the account of the house in Hutchins's *History of Dorset* and even corrected errors in pencil. Hutchins says that the house "takes its first name from its being anciently, probably, part of the demesnes of the crown; its latter from the Maurwards, its ancient lords."[4] Hardy's question seems intended to make a reader think of "Kingston" as "King's Town."

His tribute is concerned with what Kingston meant to him in lifelong associations. Stinsford Church contains prominent memorials to the families at Kingston whose lives had been, in a sense, the history of Stinsford Parish, among them the Greys and the Pitts. In Hardy's boyhood (1845-53) the house was the dwelling of Julia Augusta Martin, who founded the school that he first attended, taught him to read, and was a subject of his worshipful dreams. In the arduous self-education of his later youth, his "lone work, / Noon and night," Hardy trudged daily past Kingston on his way to and from school in Dorchester. As architectural apprentice to Hicks, studying Greek with the Baptist minister's sons, he would go into the fields to pore over his Testament: "The gate of the enclosure in Kingston Maurward eweleaze . . . was the scene of some of the readings."[5] The "Knapwater House" of Hardy's first published novel, *Desperate Remedies*, is based upon Kingston. In later life, Hardy was friendly with the families who lived there: his notebook of September 21, 1923, for instance, reads: "Lunched at Kingston and met Augustus John."[6]

1. The "Chronicle" lists the ownership of the estate from about 1400 to the twentieth century; a note indicates that Hardy prepared it in 1916 for Mrs. Cecil Hanbury, then living in the manor.

2. Young, *Dorchester: Its Ancient and Modern History*, p. 108.

3. Beatty, ed., *The Architectural Notebook of Thomas Hardy*, p. 45. Lea, in *Thomas Hardy's Wessex*, presents two photographs, one of the newer "Kingston Maurward House" and the other of "The Old Manor-House, Kingston Park." Plates 180, 182, pp. 235, 237.

4. II, 561. Relying on more recent investigation, Hutchings says in *Inside Dorset* about the two houses: "The first is the old manor built in Kingston Park in 1591. . . . The 'new' manor house was built in 1717 and finished in 1720." P. 97.

5. *Early Life*, p. 40; *Life*, p. 31.

6. Evelyn Hardy, *Thomas Hardy's Notebooks*, p. 101.

THE WHIPPER-IN presents a grimly humorous anecdote. A whipper-in is a caretaker of hunting dogs, with the duty of whipping them in during a hunt. In traditional English fox-hunting, the hunters wore red coats.

A MILITARY APPOINTMENT has the stage-direction "Scherzando," referring to music to be played in a joking style.

THE MILESTONE BY THE RABBIT-BURROW concerns the third milestone from Dorchester on the road toward Puddletown. The old milestone is no longer there. During World War II, markers that might guide invaders were taken down.[1] Hardy must have seen it many times in his youth, for it was less than half a mile from his birthplace by a woodland path called Snail's Creep. In *Under the Greenwood Tree*, Dick Dewy follows this path when he goes nutting in Grey's Wood, just west of Yellowham; he "entered a hazel copse by a hole like a rabbit's burrow." (Part the Fourth, Chapter I.)   In the poem, Hardy presents a rabbit's wonder at the meaning of a milepost and people's behavior when they look at it.

1. Mr. Cutler, caretaker for Yellowham Wood, told me that the milestone had stood about halfway up Yellowham Hill, that a rabbit-burrow had been nearby, and that when the stone was removed it was buried somewhere. The first time I entered Yellowham Wood a rabbit scurried across the path.

THE LAMENT OF THE LOOKING-GLASS is a soliloquy by a personified mirror, presumably one at Max Gate. The woman whose image the mirror no longer beholds may be Emma, Hardy's first wife, who died in 1912.

CROSS-CURRENTS tells an ironic tale of the interference of a young man's friends (in the second stanza) or kinsfolk (in the fifth) to prevent a wedding that the girl admits she did not desire. She is none the less grieved for her lover's pain.

THE OLD NEIGHBOUR AND THE NEW is set at "Came Rectory, and the reference is presumably to William Barnes (who was 'carried out' in October, however) and his successor."[1] Barnes, Dorset poet and Hardy's intimate friend and near neighbor, was buried on October 11, 1886. Perhaps Hardy said "September" in the poem in memory of the last time he had talked with Barnes (the facts are not known), or perhaps simply to rime with "remember."

The new neighbor was the Reverend William Ernest Evill, who had "been presented by the patron, Captain Dawson-Damer, to the livings of Winterborne-Came *cum* Farringdon and Whitcombe. The revd. gentleman will probably be instituted about the 20th inst.," that is, in December.[2] It was characteristic of Hardy that in calling at Came Rectory he should remember his old friend there so vividly that the present seemed an illusion and the "olden face" of his friend the reality.

1. Purdy, *Thomas Hardy: A Bibliographical Study*, p. 224.
2. *Dorset County Chronicle*, December 9, 1886, p. 6, and December 30, p. 50.

THE CHOSEN has a motto from Gal. 4:24, translated in the King James Bible as "Which things are an allegory." Read as an allegory, the poem develops the theme that the lover idealizes woman in a way not realized in any actual person. The "I" of the poem is temperamentally a man who throughout his life has sought to find his ideal in five women. He has been unsuccessful. Though each he loved was a "passable maid," he has found in each that "charms outwear." The sixth, a composite of the five and a symbol for the ideal, flees from him, is caught, and is placed in an "arbour small" to be adored till the narrator's life ends. This theme is essentially that of the poem "The Well-Beloved" and of the novel *The Well-Beloved*. In this novel, Ann Avice Caro explains to Pierston why she rejected him as her lover: " ' 'Tis because I get tired of my lovers as soon as I get to know them well. What I see in one young man for a while soon leaves him and goes into another yonder, and I follow, and then what I admire fades out of him and springs up somewhere else; and so I follow on, and never fix to one. I have loved *fifteen* a'ready! Yes, fifteen, I am almost ashamed to say,' she repeated, laughing. 'I can't help it, I assure you. Of course it is really, to *me*, the same one all through, only I can't catch him! . . .'

"Pierston was surprised into stillness. Here was this obscure and almost illiterate girl engaged in the pursuit of the impossible ideal, just as he had been himself doing for the last twenty years. She was doing it quite involuntarily, by sheer necessity of her organization, puzzled all the while at her own instinct."[1]

The thought is so characteristic of much throughout his works that we may suppose the "I" of the poem is in some measure Hardy. Lois Deacon, reasoning from hints and parallels, has published identifications that, at least, do not distort the meaning of the poem. She states that, at one time or another, Hardy was in love with each of the women and that he "indicated the five women in the reverse order of the extent of his love or passion for each of them." She identifies "the first with her eating eyes" as Hardy's second wife Florence, whose portraits and photographs, as well as references in Hardy's poems, show the prominence of her eyes. (See "After the Visit," which speaks of Florence's "large luminous living eyes.") She says that the second with "green-gray" eyes "may well have been . . . Elizabeth Browne, of the 'beautiful bay-red hair,' for red-headed folk often have greenish eyes." Hardy's poem "To Lizbie Brown" speaks of her as a boyhood sweetheart whom he let "slip." On the basis that the third is called "experienced, wise," Miss Deacon identifies her as Mary Waight, to whom Hardy is said to have proposed marriage in 1862, when she was twenty-nine and he was only twenty-two. She rejected him and shortly afterward married another man.[2] Miss Deacon says that the " 'fourth who sang all day' could only refer to Emma Lavinia, Hardy's first wife." She identifies the "fifth, whom I'd called a jade" as Tryphena Sparks, called a jade in various references, especially the poem "She, to Him II."[3]

The places mentioned in "The Chosen" may be identified. The "bark of a beech" may refer to the large, old beech in Yellowham Wood near the cottage of Fancy Day in *Under the Greenwood Tree.* In flight the sixth, composite woman leads the narrator to a "Christ-cross stone," which may be the stone of many legends, "Cross-in-Hand," of "The Lost Pyx" and *Tess of the D'Urbervilles.* If so, the woman's flight is through central Wessex, along the road between Minterne Magna and Evershot. The obscurity of the action suggests that even the real places are private symbols.

1. Part Second, Chapter VIII.

2. Mary Waight is not mentioned in *The Early Life* or *The Later Years,* but the story of Hardy's proposal in told by Constance Oliver in *Thomas Hardy Proposes to Mary Waight.*

3. *The Chosen,* throughout. Miss Deacon considers other women for whom Hardy had shown affection, but rules them out. Taking literally Hardy's phrase "a passable maid," she rules out the married women, Mrs. Julia Augusta Martin and Mrs. Florence Henniker, and Louisa Harding on the ground that Hardy barely spoke to her.

THE INSCRIPTION in the manuscript is titled "The Words on the Brass."[1] Hardy locates the brass in "the aged Estminster aisle." "Estminster" is the medieval name for the village of Yetminster, about fourteen miles north of Dorchester. The brass is now set in a modern grey granite slab on the wall of the south aisle of the thirteenth-century Church of St. Andrew in Yetminster. The inscription, in the Old English script represented in the poem, reads: "Of yor charyte pray for ye soules of John Horsey Esquyer for ye body to our sov'aigne lord Kyng Henry ye VIII and su'tyme lord of Clyfton in ye Countie of dorssett and Elizabeth his wyfe, sometyme lady of Turges Melcombe in the said Countie, syster and heyre of Robert Turges, Esquyer, sone and heire of Richard Turges, Esquyer, su'tyme lord of the seid Turges Melcombe, which John dep'tid ye VIII day of July, ye yer of or Lord MVcXXXI and Elizabeth dep'tid ye   day of   ye yer of or Lord MVc   : on whose soules Jh'u have mercy. Amen." Above the brass are effigies of Sir John Horsey and his wife Elizabeth, with the notation: "Restored by Major Edward Ralph Horsey, 1890."[2]

The poem concerns the folly of the wife's idealizing her grief as permanent. Characteristically, Hardy rested his tale upon fact and even invited the reader to "Estminster" to "read even now" the evidence, and included in the penultimate stanza, the suggestion of mystery and a moaning "wraith."

"The Inscription," dated as written on October 30, 1907, may be the basis for "The Memorial Brass: 186—," which was not published until 1917. "The Memorial Brass: 186—" may represent an experience of the 1860's that, when Hardy visited Yetminster, gave him the idea for the tale of "The Inscription."[3]

1. Purdy, *Thomas Hardy: A Bibliographical Study*, p. 225.
2. Similar inscriptions with the date of the death of the spouse omitted are to be found in other churches in Wessex. The omitted death-date is not always that of the wife. In St. John's Church, Yeovil, for instance, an inscription gives the date of the death of the wife, Isabell Penne, but leaves blank the date for the death of her husband, "Giles Penne, Gentilman."
3. The inscription on the brass is reproduced in Hutchins, *History of Dorset*, IV, 365, where undoubtedly Hardy saw it, but Yetminster is so close to Dorchester that probably he also saw it in St. Andrew's Church.

THE MARBLE-STREETED TOWN in the manuscript is dated "(1913?)."[1] Hardy visited Plymouth in March of 1913 on his return from a trip to Cornwall to the scenes of his courtship of Emma Gifford.

"The Marble-Streeted Town" seems a companion to "The West-of-Wessex Girl." Both poems recall phrases in Mrs. Emma Hardy's *Some Recollections*, especially her girlhood memory that the streets of Plymouth were "paved with marble at that time." The phrase is not accurate. Evelyn Hardy and Gittings quote a Plymouth City Engineer who said that "the paving slabs of the footpaths were in the greater majority of cases made of limestone. The surface wears smooth after a while and looks very much like marble especially in wet weather. This stone was most likely taken from the Quarries of West Hoe or Dead Man's Quarry, Cattedown."[2]

1. Purdy, *Thomas Hardy: A Bibliographical Study*, p. 225.
2. Eds., *Some Recollections*, p. 70.

A WOMAN DRIVING seems a memory of Hardy's courtship of Emma Gifford in Cornwall driving a pair of horses down a steep road, perhaps near Boscastle. (See the notes on "At Castle Boterel.") The closing vision of her as a phantom driver "in a chariot of the air" resembles the similar vision of "The Phantom Horsewoman."

A WOMAN'S TRUST is a tribute to a woman's faith in a man's capacities and ultimate success in spite of the defeats and delays of "cruel years." The poem may be read as Hardy's tribute to Emma Gifford's faith in him in the years between 1870 and 1874, when *Far from the Madding Crowd* brought literary fame. On December 15, 1870, Hardy, working on *Desperate Remedies*, "was far from being in bright spirits about his book and his future." He marked and dated a passage in his copy of *Hamlet*: "Thou wouldst not think how ill all's here about my heart." He had to use nearly all the money he had saved to subsidize *Desperate Remedies,* and "received a fresh buffet from circumstance" when the novel was almost immediately offered as "surplus" at two shillings, six pence. Throughout this time Emma had been faithfully laboring to make a "fair copy" for the printer of his "interlined and altered" manuscripts. When he sent *Under the Greenwood Tree* to Macmillan's and misread the letter from the publishers as a rejection, "he got it back, threw the MS. into a box with his old poems, being quite sick of all such, and began to think about other ways and means. He consulted Miss Gifford by letter, declaring that he had banished novel-writing for ever, and was going on with architecture henceforward. But she . . . wrote back instantly her desire that he should adhere to authorship, which she felt sure would be his true vocation."[1]

1. *Early Life,* pp. 109-14; *Life,* pp. 83-87.

BEST TIMES in the manuscript is titled "Not Again."[1] The poem presents three scenes in Hardy's courtship of Emma Gifford, with a final stanza about her death. The picnic of the first stanza is that beside the Valency River described in "Under the Waterfall." Records offer no clue to details of the second stanza. If the visit follows that of the first stanza (in August, 1870), it may be an undated visit in late May of 1871. (See the notes on "The Seven Times.") I have found no clue to the arrival of the third stanza. The fourth stanza presents the prelude to Emma's death. The "calm eve" is that of November 25, 1912. Misses Rebekah and Catharine Owen had called, and Emma and Hardy had entertained them. As he walked to the gate to see these American ladies off, she went slowly upstairs, and was brought down only as a corpse.[2]

1. Purdy, *Thomas Hardy: A Bibliographical Study,* p. 225.
2. Weber, *Hardy's Love Poems,* p. 66.

THE CASUAL ACQUAINTANCE offers no clue to the acquaintance or his service. If the phrase "casual jot" refers to writing, the service may have been an encouraging review at a time when Hardy was despondent. Agnes, Lady Grove, who wrote to Hardy on October 13, 1922, thought of the service in general terms: "I loved 'The Casual Acquaintance.' The 'cup of cold water' and 'bread cast upon the waters' rolled into one!"[1]

1. In the Dorset County Museum.

INTRA SEPULCHRUM is a fantasy in which the spirit of one dead person speaks to another, perhaps his wife, buried within talking distance. In the calm unworldliness of the grave, the spirit is amused at the curious, self-centered things the two of them had done while living, their feeling then that they were unique, and their perception now that none among the living hold that view.

THE WHITEWASHED WALL was first printed in *Reveille* in November, 1918.[1] Presumably Hardy wrote the poem in response to a letter from John Galsworthy dated August 30, 1918, which said: "I'm sending you a copy of the first number of 'Reveille' the Government's official Quarterly devoted to the disabled sailors and soldiers of which I am now editor. . . . Will you give me a poem for the second number which comes out on Nov. 1?"[2] In view of the purpose of the magazine and the theme of the poem, it seems likely that the poem is fiction to remind disabled sailors and soldiers that they were loved.

The poem has been much admired. Gorman says of it: "The secret of great poetry, beyond all analysis, is in these verses. The verses are simple enough and so is the phrasing, yet something transforms them into a magic that is Hardy's own."[3]

He had expressed the idea of the poem in various places. In *Two on a Tower*, when Swithin has gone to the Cape, his grandmother refuses to clean his room: " 'Here's all his equinoctial lines, and his topics of Capricorn, and I don't know what besides,' Mrs. Martin continued, pointing to some charcoal scratches on the wall. 'I shall never rub 'em out; no, though 'tis such untidiness as I was never brought up to, I shall never rub 'em out.' " (Chapter XXXVIII.) In *The Woodlanders*, when Grace has gone away to school, Melbury covers the track of her shoe in the garden with a tile to preserve it. (Chapter III.)

1. Purdy, *Thomas Hardy: A Bibliographical Study*, p. 225.
2. In the Dorset County Museum.
3. "Hardy and Housman," p. 181.

JUST THE SAME is a meditation that, in spite of personal bereavement or disaster, the world goes on just the same.

THE LAST TIME Weber relates to Hardy's last kiss for his first wife, Emma, before her sudden, unexpected death.[1]

1. *Hardy's Love Poems*, p. 70.

THE SEVEN TIMES frames Hardy's personal story in the narrative of a stranger who encounters an eighty-year-old man who, in the dark, seems a boy. The stranger presents the story the old man tells, clearly

Hardy's courtship of Emma Gifford and his visit to Cornwall after her death.

Though the seven journeys are more indicated than described, the poem offers enough details that a comparison with Hardy's biography seems to identify each. The "first time" was Hardy's trip to St. Juliot, Cornwall, on March 7-11, 1870, when he unexpectedly met the "eyesome maiden" he was to marry. The second visit seems that of August 8, 1870, lasting some weeks of "adventure fit and fresh and fair." The third seems the visit of late May to early June of 1871; the fourth that of August 7, 1872, for an unrecorded period; and the fifth a "flying visit" early in 1873, at which time (the poem suggests) Hardy proposed marriage. Apparently the sixth visit was not to St. Juliot. He "reached a tryst before my journey's end came." The tryst seems that of his visit to meet Emma in Bath on June 21 or 22 to July 2, 1873.[1] The seventh journey was to Cornwall after Emma's death. He revisited the scenes of his courtship from March 6 to about March 12, 1913.[2] The last three stanzas of "The Seven Times" present Hardy as he may have seemed to a stranger in his old age.

1. See *Early Life*, pp. 98-99, 103-5, 111-12, 120, 121, 123-24; *Life*, pp. 74-75, 78-79, 85, 91, 92, 93-94.
2. *Later Years*, p. 156; *Life*, p. 361.

THE SUN'S LAST LOOK ON THE COUNTRY GIRL treats Hardy's beloved sister Mary, who died on November 24, 1915. The theme is the sun's blessing upon her. Whereas for Hardy the moon was a symbol of sinister forces, the sun was a symbol of benevolence. In *The Return of the Native* the sun seems to bless the country girl Thomasin. As she climbs to a loft for apples to celebrate Clym's return, "the sun shone in a bright yellow patch upon the figure of the maiden as she knelt and plunged her naked arms into the soft brown fern." When Thomasin, after her marriage, visits her aunt, "The oblique band of sunlight which followed her through the door became the young wife well. It illuminated her as her presence illuminated the heath." (Book Second, Chapter II, and Book Third, Chapter VI.)

IN A LONDON FLAT in the manuscript had the title "In a London Lodging."[1] Possibly the joking woman was Hardy's first wife Emma, and the man who was reading "late on a night of gloom" and looked to his wife "like a widower" was Hardy. The Hardys were in London in the spring of 1912, before Emma's death in November. They "did not take a house, putting up at a hotel with which Hardy had long been familiar, the 'West Central' in Southampton Row." He was in London in July of 1913, approximately the "next year" of the poem, though whether he stopped at the West Central this time is not stated.[2] The Spirits who add eeriness and a sense of fatalism to the poem are those of *The Dynasts*.

1. Purdy, *Thomas Hardy: A Bibliographical Study*, p. 225.
2. *Later Years*, pp. 152, 157; *Life*, pp. 358, 362.

DRAWING DETAILS IN AN OLD CHURCH represents Hardy's repeated experiences during his architectural work. His *Architectural Notebook* exhibits hundreds of carefully drawn details that "some Gothic brain designed." The old church of the poem may be any one.

RAKE-HELL MUSES in the manuscript was titled "The Seducer Muses."[1] Weber states that the date "189—" stands for 1893,[2] at which time Hardy was working on *Jude the Obscure*.

The poem is the soliloquy of a seducer who is aware of the "moody madness" of his temperament and who reasons that it is ultimately an act of kindness toward the girl he seduced to reject the convention that he marry her and make her life miserable. The question of the fourteenth stanza, "For, is one moonlight dance, / One midnight passion, / A rock whereon to fashion / Life's citadel?" seems to represent Hardy's reasoning as set forth in *Jude*. There he presents a number of marriages contracted to make an indiscreet or a scheming girl into an "honest woman," including the revolting picture of a soldier and his bride that causes Sue to draw back from marrying Jude: "The soldier was sullen and reluctant, the bride sad and timid; she was soon, obviously, to become a mother, and she had a black eye. Their little business was soon done, and the twain and their friends straggled out, one of the witnesses saying casually to Jude and Sue in passing. . . : 'See the couple just come in? Ha, ha! That fellow is just out of jail this morning. She met him at the jail gates, and brought him straight here. She's paying for everything.'" (Part V, Chapter IV.)

The Rake-Hell's reasoning that in spite of the girl's present shame "Our unborn, first her moan, / Will grow her guerdon" states a theme of "The Dark-Eyed Gentleman."

1. Purdy, *Thomas Hardy: A Bibliographical Study*, p. 225.
2. *Hardy of Wessex*, 2nd ed., p. 229.

THE COLOUR is Hardy's version of "Jinny Jones," a long question-and-answer poem, with children enquiring and Jinny's mother answering. It opens:

Enquirers.

> Please can I see Jinny Jones, Jones, Jones, Please can I see Jinny Jones; how is she now?

Jinny's Mother.

Jinny Jones is washing, washing, washing, Jinny Jones is wash-
ing; you can't see her now.

The poem continues with such refusals (while Jinny is ironing, ill,
and worse) until Jinny is dead in the fourteenth stanza, and the
children ask what they can wear. It then proceeds:

Enquirers.

Please will red do, red do, red do? Please will red do? Will
that do?

Jinny's Mother.

Red is for soldiers, soldiers, soldiers, Red is for soldiers; that
won't do.

The song goes on through blue for sailors and white for weddings
to black:

Enquirers.

Please will black do, black do, black do? Please will black do?
Will that do?

Jinny's Mother.

Black is for mourning, mourning, mourning, Black is for
mourning; that *will* do.[1]

"The Colour" has been set to music by Christopher LeFleming in
The Echoing Green (London: J. and W. Chester, 1923), Mary Shel-
don (London: Swan & Co., 1924), Robin Milford in *Four Hardy
Songs* (Oxford University Press, 1939), and Winifred E. Houghton
(in manuscript in the Dorset County Museum).

1. Pentin, "Dorset Children's Doggerel Rhymes," pp. 113-14; the tune is given.

MURMURS IN THE GLOOM is significantly dated September 22,
1899. Hardy was still suffering from the onslaughts of reviewers of
Jude the Obscure who had labelled his examination of sexual ques-
tions "Jude the Obscene." England was waging a war in South
Africa that Hardy thought an imperialistic adventure. In general
review of prevailing opinions at the close of the nineteenth century,
he was despondent. Perhaps the poem was not published at the time
it was written because it attacked too frankly those whom Hardy
called "the many and strong."[1] Perhaps he published it after World
War I because the post-war confusions made him feel gloomy about
material progress at the expense of integrity.

The "I" of the poem seems to represent Hardy as an observer who
hears, interprets, and reports the sighs of the suffering peoples, misled

by false or bigoted seers, leaders, teachers, writers, and rulers. The poem protests the promulgation of outworn dogmas, creeds, conventions, and irrational doctrines. The final stanza, stating Hardy's positive message, calls for teachers and leaders of "searching sight" to "lead the nations . . . / From gloom to light." One may suppose he had in mind humane, wise, disinterested leaders who would seek above all "To make reason and the will of God prevail."[2]

In the fourth stanza, the description of dynasts as "breathing threats and slaughters" paraphrases Acts 9:1, in which Saul is described as "breathing out threatenings and slaughter." The poem makes unusual use of triple rimes. The third, fourth, and fifth lines of each stanza exhibit a triplet of triple rimes, with the last one or two syllables in a triplet identical, as "sigh around . . . nigh around . . . cry around."

1. See "In Tenebris II." "Murmurs in the Gloom" has much in common with this poem.
2. From Matthew Arnold's "Sweetness and Light." See Hardy's echo of Arnold's ideas in the closing paragraph of the "Apology" of *Late Lyrics and Earlier.*

EPITAPH was published when Hardy was nearly eighty-two, sufficiently aware of death that he thought it could be his final statement. In the opening "I never cared for Life," he overlooks his reasonably happy childhood, his youthful ambitions, and his ecstasies in love. Perhaps he counted his arduous labors as a debt to Life that "cared for me." He is right, that he asked "no ill-advised reward," in spite of much sensitivity to criticism.

AN ANCIENT TO ANCIENTS was first published in the *Century Magazine* of New York for May, 1922.[1] The poem is an address that an "ancient" might deliver at a club dinner to the seniors, with the juniors waiting in the background. It is both a regretful farewell to an age that in 1922 was passing away and a humorous commentary on Victorian culture.

The poem is flecked with Hardy's memories. The opening stanza suggests his pleasures of the 1860's as described in "Reminiscences of a Dancing Man." The second stanza recalls his life in Weymouth in 1869, his "rowing in the Bay almost every evening of this summer."[2] In the third stanza he had in mind the passing of many a friend from the "ranks" in which he had stood: Meredith, Swinburne, etc. The fourth stanza returns to the dance and mentions some of his favorites, among them the old-fashioned country dance, "Sir Roger de Coverley." It is not certain that he attended some revival of Balfe's *The Bohemian Girl*, first produced in 1843, or of Verdi's *Il Trovatore* of 1853. Stanza five names genre painters (William Etty, William Mulready, and Daniel Maclise) and novelists (Edward Bulwer-Lytton, Walter Scott, Alexandre Dumas, and George Sand) who were admired in the mid-century. As not all these artists and writers were among his favorites, perhaps the stanza treats with sly humor the sentimental tastes of the age.

The sixth stanza, though about Tennyson's falling reputation generally, makes a personal reference to Hardy's experience. The "she who voiced those rhymes" was Emma Gifford, his first wife. "On the day that the bloody battle of Gravelotte was fought [August 18, 1870] they [Hardy and Emma] were reading Tennyson in the grounds of the rectory."[3] The imagery used to symbolize the decay of Tennyson's reputation suggests "Mariana" and perhaps the old garden of St. Juliot Rectory as Hardy had seen it in 1913.[4]

Though the first line of the seventh stanza, "We who met sunrise sanguine-souled,"[5] includes Hardy of the 1870's, most of the stanza is general. The term "Aïdes' den" refers to Hades, the Greek underworld, that is, approaching death. The ninth stanza can be read as something like Hardy's defense of his writing poetry when nearly eighty-two. Whatever critics may say in comparing his novels with the poetry of his old age, he regarded his later years as artistically the greatest period of his life. In defense of his recent labors he listed ten "ancients" whose lights "Burned brightlier towards their setting day": the Greek tragic poet Sophocles, active until his death at eighty-nine; Plato, whose wisdom ripened in his later seventies; Socrates, put to death at seventy for his unconventional views; the Greek philosopher-mathematician Pythagoras, who lived to about seventy-five; Thucydides, Greek historian, who lived to about seventy; Herodotus, the "father of history," active at sixty; Homer, reputedly aged and blind; Clement of Alexandria, a Father of the Church and Christian leader to the age of seventy; Saint Augustine, active till his death at seventy-six; and Origen, prolific theological writer till his death at sixty-nine.

In the final stanza, Hardy turns to the junior men, described in a mixture of wistfulness and some bitterness as "red-lipped and smooth-browed." They need not rush; their time will come; there is much to do; and "we are going, / Gentlemen."

1. Purdy, *Thomas Hardy: A Bibliographical Study*, p. 226.
2. *Early Life*, p. 84; *Life*, p. 64.
3. *Early Life*, p. 104; *Life*, pp. 78-79.
4. Except in relation to Emma, Hardy had not "shrined" Tennyson. In a letter to Sir George Douglas on December 19, 1897, he wrote: "We have been reading 'The Life of Tennyson'; a great artist, but a mere Philistine of a thinker." In the National Library of Scotland, Edinburgh.
5. Perhaps a reference to Swinburne's *Songs Before Sunrise*.

AFTER READING PSALMS XXXIX., XL., ETC., Vinson says, "has the ring of a recessional hymn."[1] and Blunden says that Hardy is exploring "life and spiritual performance gravely,"[2] but the diction, the twisted syntax, and the mixture of English and Latin all suggest a whimsical point of view. In relation to the date, "187—," the poem sums up Hardy's boyhood naiveté, his studies, his effort to write poetry, his failures, and perhaps even his despairing prayers "at dead of night."

The Latin phrases from the Vulgate Bible, all from the Psalms, occur in the King James Bible in a slightly different arrangement of chapter and verse. "Quoniam Tu fecisti" (38:10) is translated as "because thou didst it" (39:9); "me deduxisti" is Hardy's transposition of "Deduxisti me" (60:3), translated as "lead me" (61:2); "Me suscepisti" ("Me . . . suscepisti," 40:13), translated as "me . . . in mine integrity" (41:12); "Dies . . . Meos posuisti" ("posuisti dies meos," 38:6), translated as "thou hast made my days" (39:5); "Domine, Tu scisti" (39:10), translated as "O Lord, thou knowest" (40:9); and "Quem elegisti" (64:5), translated as "whom thou choosest" (65:4). In each Latin phrase, Hardy submits himself to the will of God.

The "start by Helicon" (Hardy's first effort to write poetry) may refer to "Domicilium," a "Wordsworthian" description of his birthplace, written when he was seventeen to twenty years old. The later "fervid rhymes" are poems sent to publishers but rejected, in the 1860's.[3]

Of the verse Vinson says, "Lines 1 and 3 rhyme, and lines 2 and 4 of each quatrain are double rhymes, the fourth being in Latin, these *b* rhymes being the same in all six stanzas."[4] The poem has been set to music by Gerald Finzi (London: Boosey & Co., 1936).

1. "Diction and Imagery in the Poetry of Thomas Hardy," p. 95.
2. *Thomas Hardy*, p. 261.
3. *Early Life*, pp. 4-5, 64; *Life*, pp. 4, 48.
4. "Diction and Imagery in the Poetry of Thomas Hardy," pp. 168-69.

SURVIEW has a motto from the Vulgate Bible, Ps. 68:59, translated in the King James Bible, Ps. 69:59, as "I thought on my ways." The fantasy that the poet heard a voice speaking from the fire is from Ps. 39:3, "My heart was hot within me; while I was musing the fire burned: then spake I with my tongue." The words of the voice, or the poet's conscience, are from the New Testament. Lines 1, 3, and 4 of the second stanza paraphrase Phil. 4:8, "Finally, brethren, whatsoever things are true . . . whatsoever things are just, whatsoever things are pure, whatsoever things are lovely . . . think on these things." Lines 1, 3, and 4 of the third stanza and lines 1 and 3 of the fourth

stanza echo I Cor. 13:4, 7, 13, "Charity suffereth long, and is kind
. . . vaunteth not itself . . . hopeth all things, endureth all things. . . .
And now abideth faith, hope, charity, these three; but the greatest of
these is charity."

"Surview," concluding a volume Hardy published when he was
nearly eighty-two, is his meditation upon his failure in perfect charity
throughout his life. Though not a Christian in theology, he applies to
his life the test of Christian ethics and finds that he has fallen short.
The "her that endureth all," it would seem, is his first wife Emma, who
exasperated him in his later years beyond endurance. The word
"taught" in the final stanza seems to mean "practised," and "set
about," "set as an ideal."

HUMAN SHOWS

"At the end of July [1925] Hardy sent off the manuscript of
his volume of poems, *Human Shows*, to the publisher."[1] The last
of his volumes published during his life, it contains 152 poems, only
25 of which had been previously printed. The manuscript was titled
"Poems Imaginative and Incidental; with Songs and Trifles." On
August 25, Hardy suggested to the publishers *Human Shows* to which
was added *Far Phantasies / Songs, and Trifles*. The volume appeared
on November 20, 1925.[2]

The several phrases of the title suggest the varied contents. It con-
tains a few old poems omitted from previous volumes; many poems
based on old letters and diaries Hardy was examining while working
on *The Early Life*, and on memories stimulated by this work; others
based on reading; and many treating experiences and events of the
years 1922-25. The poems include humorous pieces, love lyrics, philo-
sophical meditations, and narrative and dramatic pieces.

Two poems are dated as written in the 1860's, "Discouragement"
(1863-67) and "Retty's Phases" (1868), but others are marked as
revised from an old draft, "Lover to Mistress" and "The Pair He saw
Pass." Five are dated as written in the 1890's: "The Caricature"
(about 1890, dated in the manuscript), "A Beauty's Soliloquy During
Her Honeymoon" (1892), "A Cathedral Façade at Midnight" (1897,
in the manuscript), "On Martock Moor" (1899), and "Last Love-
Word" (189—). Others bear dates through the first two decades of the
twentieth century.

In addition to poems written before 1900, many treat events during
the nineteenth century. For example, "Life and Death at Sunrise,"
treating an event of 1867, may be drawn from a note made in that

year; "Coming Up Oxford Street: Evening," marked "As seen July 4, 1872," must rest upon a notation made at the time; and "At a Fashionable Dinner" presents a scene in the life of Hardy and his first wife Emma, presumably soon after their marriage. Other poems seem to rest on memories and family traditions. "A Bird-Scene at a Rural Dwelling" seems a memory of boyhood; "At Rushy-Pond" recalls an early love affair; and "On the Esplanade" recreates a scene from Hardy's work in Weymouth in 1869. "At Wynyard's Gap" may rest on a tradition or a tale told by his grandmother, as do presumably "In Sherborne Abbey" and "The Fight on Durnover Moor."

Other poems reflect his reading in history, biography, philosophy, or otherwise. Examples include "Xenophanes, the Monist of Colophon," "Queen Caroline to Her Guests," and "The Absolute Explains." Some treat such events from the newspapers as "On the Portrait of a Woman About to Be Hanged" and "The Sea Fight." A number of poems concern such personal matters as Hardy's dog "Wessex" in "A Popular Personage at Home"; a visit to Salisbury, as in "The High-School Lawn"; or the christening of a goddaughter, "To C. F. H." A few poems are memorials, as "Before My Friend Arrived," "Nothing Matters Much," and "In the Evening." "Bags of Meat" makes a satirically humorous attack upon cruelty to animals, and "Compassion" is a nobly serious plea for mercy to them.

1. *Later Years*, p. 242; *Life*, p. 428.
2. Purdy, *Thomas Hardy: A Bibliographical Study*, pp. 234, 247.

WAITING BOTH was first published in the *London Mercury* for November, 1924.[1] The poem was sent in response to a letter from J. C. Squire asking for a poem to celebrate the completion of the fifth year of this magazine.[2] *The Later Years*, printing a letter Hardy wrote to the Reverend Handley Moule on June 29, 1919, suggests the source of the poem. The Hardys "were reading a chapter in Job, and on coming to the verse, 'All the days of my appointed time will I wait, till my change come,' I interrupted and said: 'That was the text of the Vicar of Fordington one Sunday evening about 1860.' And I can hear his voice repeating the text as the sermon went on."[3]

The poem suitably introduces *Human Shows*, published when Hardy was nearly eighty-six. It is an imaginary conversation between a star and the poet. Both accept in patience the processes that will merge time into eternity and fulfil the purpose toward which creation moves. This theme is not new in Hardy's thought. He expressed it of Egdon Heath in *The Return of the Native*: "Every night its Titanic form seemed to await something; but it had waited thus, unmoved, during so many centuries, through the crises of so many things, that it could only be imagined to await one last crisis—the final over-throw."

"Waiting Both" has been set to music by Gerald Finzi in *Earth and Air and Rain* (London: Boosey & Hawkes, 1936), Harper Mac-Kay in *Five Songs* (in manuscript in the Colby College Library, dated 1957), and Christopher LeFleming in *Six Country Songs* (London: Novello & Co., 1963).

1. Purdy, *Thomas Hardy: A Bibliographical Study*, p. 234.
2. In the Dorset County Museum.
3. P. 194; *Life*, pp. 390-91.

A BIRD-SCENE AT A RURAL DWELLING was first published in *Chambers's Journal* for January, 1925.[1] Hardy's first publication, "How I Built Myself a House," had appeared in this journal for March 18, 1865. When, responding to a request for a contribution to celebrate the sixtieth anniversary of this event, Hardy sent the poem, Chambers replied that it was "most appropriate," and republished also his essay.

The "domicile of brown and green" is his thatch-roofed birth-place at Higher Bockhampton. There in his strenuous youth, rising before daybreak to work on his Latin or Greek, he would hear the "enactments" of the poem. His memory of them appears in his novels. In *Two on a Tower*, Swithin, rising early on the day of his departure, hears "the house-martins scratching the back of the ceiling over his head as they scrambled out from the roof for their day's gnat-chasing, the thrushes cracking snails on the garden stones outside with the noisiness of little smiths at work on little anvils." (Chapter XXXVII.) In *The Woodlanders*, Marty, "Having tossed about till five o'clock . . . heard the sparrows walking down their long holes in the thatch above her sloping ceiling to their exits at the eaves; where-upon she also arose and descended to the ground floor." (Chapter III.) Perhaps Hardy drew upon his memories almost unconsciously; he forgot where in his novels he had described these scenes. Edmund Gosse wrote on February 21, 1903, asking where a bird-scene had ap-peared: "It is this—a note of the curious sound made in the very early morning by the feet of birds—sparrows or swifts (?)—on the rafters under the thatch, heard by some one lying awake in a garret." Hardy replied: "A passage about the sparrows over the rafters does occur in some page of mine, but for my life I cannot tell where. . . . As you probably know, sparrows, starlings, etc., pull out the straw from the eaves of roofs till they have made a sort of tunnel in the thatch, and it is their creeping down from the further end at dawn that makes the tiny trampling."[2]

1. Purdy, *Thomas Hardy: A Bibliographical Study*, p. 235.
2. Gosse's letter is in the Dorset County Museum; a copy of Hardy's reply is in the Colby College Library.

"ANY LITTLE OLD SONG" expresses Hardy's feeling about his poems drawn from memories of past joys and old friends. The poem has been set to music by D. Chamier (in manuscript in the Dorset County Museum).

IN A FORMER RESORT AFTER MANY YEARS was titled in the manuscript "In an Old Place of Resort after Many Years."[1] The resort would hardly be the seaside resort of Weymouth, close enough to Dorchester that Hardy would have visited it often.

He stated the theme of the poem in his journal for March 28, 1888: "On returning to London after an absence I find the people of my acquaintance abraded, their hair disappearing, also their flesh, by degrees."[2] This note seems to refer to some of his acquaintances he had not seen since he had lived in London in the 1860's, after a relatively short lapse of time. The poem presents his acquaintances known in their youth, but scarcely recognized in their decrepit old age. They reminded him of his own accumulation of years and of friends now "underground." The reference to El Greco (the Greek-Spanish painter Dominico Theotocopuli, c. 1542-1614) is apt. El Greco painted emaciated figures in cold tones and grey shades.

1. Purdy, *Thomas Hardy: A Bibliographical Study*, p. 235.
2. *Early Life*, p. 271; *Life*, p. 206.

A CATHEDRAL FAÇADE AT MIDNIGHT in the manuscript is dated 1897.[1] The poem reflects an experience recorded in Hardy's journal for August 10, 1897: "*Salisbury*. Went into the Close late at night. The moon was visible through both the north and south clerestory windows to me standing on the turf on the north side. . . . Walked to the west front, and watched the moonlight creep round upon the statuary of the façade—stroking tentatively and then more and more firmly the prophets, the martyrs, the bishops, the kings, and the queens."[2]

The moonlight of the poem, as in Hardy's journal, is a fact, but the "lunar look," as it moves across the sculptures, symbolizes "Reason's movement," a rationalistic view of the "coded creeds of old-time godliness." The poem reaches its climax in the martyred saints' "sighings of regret" for the passing of the medieval faith; these sighings reflect Hardy's feeling. The poem may be compared with Matthew Arnold's "Dover Beach," in which the "Sea of Faith" retreats "down the vast edges drear / And naked shingles of the world." Arnold's image is literary, drawn from Sophocles's *Antigone*; Hardy's poem records an experience.

1. Purdy, *Thomas Hardy: A Bibliographical Study*, p. 235.
2. *Later Years*, p. 71; *Life*, p. 296.

THE TURNIP-HOER was first published in *Cassell's Magazine* for August, 1925, with three illustrations and a fourth on the cover.[1] It tells a ballad-like tale of country life in Wessex. The reference to the Duke and Duchess of "Southernshire" does not identify them; they are only visiting in Wessex.

A theme is partly stated in the first stanza, which paraphrases Shakespeare's "There is a tide in the affairs of men / Which, taken at the flood, leads on to fortune."[2] It is accident that the turnip-hoer for a little while held the Duchess of Southernshire in his arms. A second theme is the turnip-hoer's idealization of the Duchess that causes him to day-dream himself into folly, drink, and death. "Terminus" in the sixth stanza is a reference to the Roman god of boundaries, represented as without feet or arms to indicate that he never moved.

1. Purdy, *Thomas Hardy: A Bibliographical Study*, p. 235.
2. *Julius Caesar*, IV, iii, 216-17.

THE CARRIER tells the story of the driver of a van for passengers. In the opening paragraph of the stories collected as "A Few Crusted Characters," Hardy describes carriers' vans: "These vans, so numerous hereabout, are a respectable, if somewhat lumbering, class of conveyance, much resorted to by decent travellers not overstocked with money, the better among them roughly corresponding to the old French *diligences*." The van of the poem begins its journey in the city of Exeter near St. Sidwell's Parish Church. Around the churchyard, near the center of the city, walls set it off from Sidwell Street and from streets and alleys on the sides and at the rear of the Church.[1] The present coach station, from which roads lead in all directions, is within two blocks of this church. The "Exon Towers" are those of Exeter Cathedral.

Hardy's naming places suggests that the story of "The Carrier" may rest on fact. Perhaps he did not mean Jane to be considered a ghost or the carrier to be deluded. The widower may comfort himself by pretending that Jane is there beside him.

1. Though old St. Sidwell's Church was destroyed in the "blitz" of World War II, the old walls around the churchyard remain. The Church has been rebuilt.

LOVER TO MISTRESS seems a song for any lover to any mistress. The facts that the poem is noted as "From an old copy" and that it specifies "Two fields, a wood, a tree" between the lover and his mistress have prompted attempts at identification. Miss Deacon has suggested that the lover was Hardy and the mistress was Tryphena Sparks of Puddletown. She says that "forecasts . . . rough" and "Parents more bleak than bland" refer to the opposition of Hardy's parents to his involvement with his cousin Tryphena. Hardy and Tryphena

[505]

"first met and laughed and danced together in Coomb Eweleaze, where Puddletown folk held their open-air festivities."[1] Coomb (or Coombe) Eweleaze lies just southwest of Puddletown, less than two miles from Hardy's boyhood home at Higher Bockhampton. Between the two places are a wood, two fields, and several lone trees, one near the spot for dancing. (See "In a Eweleaze Near Weatherbury.")

Miss O'Rourke, Hardy's secretary from 1923 to his death, believes that the poem concerns Hardy and Louisa Harding, daughter of a wealthy farmer of Stinsford. The line "Parents more bleak than bland" may refer to Louisa's parents. "It has been well known in the Harding family that Thomas Hardy when he was 15 years old had been in love with Louisa, but her parents would not permit her to have anything to do with him. Louisa never once spoke to Hardy."[2] Her girlhood home was separated from his birthplace by two fields, a number of trees, and a lone tree.

"Lover to Mistress" has been set to music by John Ireland in *Five Poems by Thomas Hardy* (Oxford University Press, 1927).

1. *Hardy's Sweetest Image*, p. 8.
2. O'Rourke, *Thomas Hardy: His Secretary Remembers*, p. 50.

THE MONUMENT-MAKER was suggested by Hardy's visit in September of 1916 to St. Juliot Church to "inspect the tablet he had designed and erected in memory of his first wife," Emma.[1] (See the notes on "The Marble Tablet.")

The poem presents the comments of Emma's ghost as she and Hardy together look at the tablet. Emma's ghost is right, that the tablet "Tells nothing about my beauty, wit, or gay time." The memorial is formal in phrasing and contains no words describing her personality or words of endearment besides the phrase "Dear Memory." Perhaps Hardy thought reticence fitting, but then imagined how the inscription might read to Emma. The ghost's playful but none the less accusatory pique leads the poet to "a tear" that he had "not been truly known by her, / And never prized!"—suggesting some memory that Emma had made little of his writings.

The poem is not literal in such details as that Hardy "chiselled her monument," took it to the church by night, and set it up himself; he designed the tablet, but ordered it from Joseph Geach of Plymouth, who carved it and set it up. The reference to "her planet" seems to concern Emma's birthday in terms of the Zodiac. She was born on November 24 and died on November 27, but Hardy's visit to see the tablet was in September.

1. Purdy, *Thomas Hardy: A Bibliographical Study*, p. 235.

[506]

CIRCUS-RIDER TO RINGMASTER was first published in *Harper's Monthly Magazine* of New York for June, 1925. The manuscript added below the title "(Casterbridge Fair, 188–)."[1] *The Early Life* under the date of June, 1884, records: "Hardy seems to have had something of a craze for circuses in these years, and went to all that came to Dorchester. In one performance the equestrienne who leapt through hoops on her circuit missed her footing and fell with a thud on the turf. He followed her into the dressing-tent and became deeply interested in her recovery. The incident seems to have some bearing on the verses of many years after entitled 'Circus-Rider to Ringmaster.'"[2] Perhaps the injury, concern on the part of the ringmaster, and (or) some remark by the circus-rider led Hardy to imagine her soliloquy. Holland has identified the circus as Tayleure's, which performed in a field at Fordington (a part of Dorchester or "Casterbridge").[3]

1. Purdy, *Thomas Hardy: A Bibliographical Study*, p. 235.
2. P. 217; *Life*, p. 166.
3. *Thomas Hardy, O. M.*, p. 105.

LAST WEEK IN OCTOBER exhibits colorful gaiety in the first stanza. Trees are personified as a disrobing woman who flings her ribbons and laces here and there. The second stanza pictures the disrobing as a form of death, toward which all youth and gaiety lead.

COME NOT; YET COME! Purdy says, may be addressed to Mrs. Arthur Henniker. If so, the poem may have been written much earlier than 1925, when published. (Mrs. Henniker died on April 4, 1923.) The phrase "foreign regions" suggests Dublin, Ireland, where the Hardys visited her in 1893. The suggestion of emotional disturbance if she should come suggests a date in the 1890's. The third stanza indicates a previous visit to Max Gate. Hardy and Mrs. Henniker "exchanged occasional visits."[1]

"Come Not; Yet Come!" has been set to music by John Ireland in *Five Poems by Thomas Hardy* (Oxford University Press, 1927).

1. *Thomas Hardy: A Bibliographical Study*, pp. 345-46.

THE LATER AUTUMN was first published in the *Saturday Review* for October 28, 1922. The manuscript dates the poem as written in 1921.[1] Sending the poem to Filson Young of this magazine on October 18, 1922, Hardy wrote: "I have found the little thing I enclose, 'The Later Autumn,' whose only merit is, by chance, its appositeness to the time of year."[2]

The poem uses a number of terms peculiar to Wessex. "Toads-meat" seems to be toads-cheese, a poisonous fungus. The "men who make cyder" recall such itinerant cider-makers as Giles Winterborne in *The Woodlanders.* (Chapter XXV.) "Couch-fires" are fires for burning couch-grass, a tough grass troublesome to farmers. "The Later Autumn" has been set to music by Norman Porteous (in manuscript in the Dorset County Museum).

1. Purdy, *Thomas Hardy: A Bibliographical Study,* p. 235.
2. Pencil-draft in the Dorset County Museum.

"LET ME BELIEVE" was published in *Human Shows* as "Let Me."[1] The passage of the seasons "through green and gray times" echoes a phrase in *The Trumpet-Major*: "The year changed from green to gold, and from gold to grey." (Chapter XXXVIII.)

1. Purdy, *Thomas Hardy: A Bibliographical Study,* p. 236.

AT A FASHIONABLE DINNER in the manuscript read "Emleen" instead of "Lavine."[1] Each name suggests Emma Lavinia, Hardy's first wife. The poem presents a delusion of the kind that gripped her from time to time and that, according to the poem, threw her into gloom. (See the notes on "The Interloper.") Weber says that the dinner of the poem took place within three or four months after Hardy married her on September 17, 1874, while the couple were living at Surbiton in London.[2]

Hardy's question seems a casual remark, and "Lavine's" answer a macabre fancy. His cheerful parry, using the term "satin sheen," suggests to her that he is already thinking of a "new bride" in a "satin dress," and her fancy seems to become a conviction that wrecks the gaiety of the dinner. The last long line indicates that there were thirteen at the table, an unlucky number.

1. Purdy, *Thomas Hardy: A Bibliographical Study,* p. 236.
2. *Hardy's Love Poems,* p. 28.

GREEN SLATES recalls an incident of Hardy's first visit to Cornwall. His journal for March 9, 1870, the second day after he met Emma Gifford, says: "Drove with Mrs. Holder and Miss Gifford to Boscastle, and on to Tintagel and Penpethy slate-quarries, with a view to the church roofing."[1] Penpethy Slate Mines are just north of Camelford Station on Road B3266, or about three and a half miles south of Boscastle. The mines are no longer in operation, though slates of a greenish color are seen on roofs in the vicinity. The "form . . . / Of fairness eye-commanding" is Emma.

1. *Early Life,* p. 98; *Life,* p. 75.

AN EAST-END CURATE was first published in the *London Mercury* for November, 1924.[1] J. C. Squire on September 25 wrote Hardy

for a poem to celebrate the completion of the fifth year of the maga-
zine. Hardy sent "An East-End Curate" and "Waiting Both."[2]

The scene of the poem is "off East Commercial Road," which runs
from Algate, through the somewhat slummy district of Stepney, to
Poplar, in London. The poem may represent Hardy's observation of
a curate of this district. It may be fiction, possibly suggested by an
incident recorded in *The Early Life*. When, in 1862, Hardy was work-
ing for the architect Blomfield at 8 Adelphi Terrace, the rooms under-
neath Blomfield's offices were occupied by a Reform League. Blom-
field's young men, "Tory and Churchy . . . indulged in satire at the
League's expense, letting down ironical bits of paper on the heads of
members, and once coming nearly to loggerheads with the worthy
resident secretary, Mr. George Howell."[3] The similarity of the name
Dowle and Howell, and the possible similarity of the satire "at the
League's expense" and the children's mockery of "Mister Dow-well"
suggest some connection. The curate's "Novello's Anthems" were
popular collections of sacred music published by Vincent Novello.

The poem is both a portrait of a saintly clergyman doing his best
to serve God in the slums, and a satiric comment upon the impotence
of a clergyman, no matter how dedicated, to solve the problems of this
area.

1. Purdy, *Thomas Hardy: A Bibliographical Study*, p. 236.
2. In the Dorset County Museum.
3. P. 49; *Life*, p. 37.

AT RUSHY-POND presents Hardy beside a small pond on a high
part of Puddletown Heath (a part of "Egdon"), about half a mile
southeast of his boyhood home at Higher Bockhampton. The poet
sees the moon as a symbol. It usually stands for a cold or realistic
view of life, but its image in the pond is so "corkscrewed . . . like a
wriggling worm" that it suggests something grotesque and sinister.

His memories of what happened there "once, in a secret year" seem
consistent with this image. The events of the fifth stanza bring the
story that underlies the poem to a climax in a lovers' quarrel and a
separation blighting to the woman. On the basis that Rushy Pond
lies just south of a path from young Hardy's home toward Puddle-
town, Deacon and Coleman surmise that this pond was a trysting
place for Hardy and Tryphena Sparks.[1] If so, the grotesque moon-
image and all the rest of the poem indicate a painful stage in Hardy's
separation from Tryphena.[2]

1. *Providence and Mr Hardy*, pp. 74-75.
2. To the extent that Deacon and Coleman's contention that Hardy had a child
by Tryphena may be credited, the phrase "ended was her time" could refer to
a late stage of her pregnancy. See their evidence in ibid., Chapter 14. The quarrel

could be that of "Neutral Tones" (dated 1867) if we assume that Hardy antedated this poem to conceal the "secret year" of the event.

FOUR IN THE MORNING presents Hardy's memory of himself in his studious youth at Higher Bockhampton, rising before dawn (while the stars, "the Great Nebula, / Or . . . the Pleiads," are still shining), to pore over Latin and Greek before departing for work in Hicks's architectural office.

ON THE ESPLANADE is set at Weymouth in 1869, when Hardy was working there for the architect Crickmay. The Esplanade, facing eastward to Weymouth Bay, is a mile-long curving avenue beside a sandy beach. Behind it is a continuous line of fine houses and hotels. Lights in "a pearl-strung row" follow the avenue.

Hardy, standing on the Esplanade, would see the moon rise over the Bay, "Mild, mellow-faced," apparently a stimulus to romantic dreaming, but as usual in his poetry, the moon symbolizes something ominous. By the end of the poem, it has shone upon "Fate's masked face" behind the poet. This Fate is evidently his later meeting Emma Gifford. It was the architect Crickmay of Weymouth who sent Hardy to St. Juliot and Emma.

In his year at Weymouth he often mused and dreamed along the Esplanade. In *Desperate Remedies*, he describes Cytherea as dreaming there in a scene like that of the poem: "She surveyed the long line of lamps on the sea-wall of the town, now looking small and yellow, and seeming to send long tap-roots of fire quivering down deep into the sea. . . . She heard, without heeding, the notes of pianos and singing voices from the fashionable houses at her back, from the open windows of which the lamp-light streamed to join that of the orange-hued full moon, newly risen over the Bay in front." (III, ii.)

IN ST. PAUL'S A WHILE AGO in the manuscript is titled "In St. Paul's: 1869."[1] St. Paul's, in bustling central London, is "chilly" in July because of its "chasmal classic walls." When it was rebuilt after the Great Fire of 1666, Sir Christopher Wren designed it in a classic style and built it largely of grey stone. Hardy's "lofty fenestration" refers to the high windows under the dome; sunlight through this circle of windows spreads fan-like. Some of the statues in stone or marble are "cadaverous, wan"; others are impressively toga-wrapped. Tourists and loiterers wander through the Cathedral, watched by vergers who seem to have little to do besides fiddle with the red ropes that set off areas not to be entered. "Hebe," "Artemisia," and "Beatrice Benedick" characterize visitors to the Cathedral who have little in common with the "strange Jew" for whom it is named.[2] This "strange Jew" is Saul, as Paul was called before he was converted to Christianity: "And Saul, yet breathing out threatenings and slaughter against the disciples of the Lord, went unto the high priest, And desired of him letters to Damascus to the synagogues, that if he found any of this way, whether they were men or women, he might bring them bound unto Jerusalem." (Acts 9: 1-2.) That St. Paul's Cathedral is "writ his throughout the ages" recalls the series of churches on Ludgate Hill, London, all called St. Paul's, the first of which was consecrated in 604. Paul's "vision-seeing mind" refers to the vision that brought about his conversion: "At midday, O king, I saw in the way a light from heaven, above the brightness of the sun, shining round about me and them which journeyed with me. And when we were all fallen to the earth, I heard a voice speaking unto me, and saying in the Hebrew tongue, Saul, Saul, why persecutest thou me?" (Acts 26: 13-14.) That Paul had no silver or gold may be an inference from Peter's speech to a lame beggar: "Then Peter said, Silver and gold have I none; but such as I have give I thee." (Acts 3:6.) Hardy's suggestion that Paul, if he were to appear at his Cathedral and address its "haunters," would be called an "epilept enthusiast" may owe something to Browning's "Cleon." On hearing of Paul's doctrine, Cleon said it "could be held by no sane man."

The poem subtly satirizes the prevalence of classic-pagan features in a Christian church; it contrasts the doctrines of the church named for Paul with the marketplace around the building. To some extent, no doubt, Hardy regarded Paul as an "epilept enthusiast." He deplored Paul's additions to Christian doctrine, with more emphasis upon sin and penance than upon Christ's "sweet reasonableness."[3] He implied his attitude in describing the good-hearted but doctrinaire old Mr. Clare in *Tess of the D'Urbervilles*: "He loved Paul of Tarsus, liked St. John, hated St. James as much as he dared, and regarded with mixed feelings Timothy, Titus, and Philemon. The New Testament was less a Christiad than a Pauliad to his intelligence—less an argument than an intoxication." (Chapter XXV.) Hardy wrote to Edward Clodd on January 17, 1897: "The older one gets the more deplorable seems the effect of that terrible, dogmatic ecclesiasticism—Christianity so called (but really Paulinism *plus* idolatry) —on morals & true religion: a dogma with which the real teaching of Christ has hardly anything in common."[4]

1. Purdy, *Thomas Hardy: A Bibliographical Study*, p. 236.
2. Some rosy girl, perhaps, suggested Hebe, cupbearer to the gods of Greece. Artemisia, Queen of Caria, built for her husband Mausolus a great tomb called Mausoleum; perhaps Hardy meant some woman who mourned too grandly. "Beatrice Benedick," witty lovers in Shakespeare's *Much Ado about Nothing*, may represent a teasing pair frolicking in a corner.

3. The term is Matthew Arnold's. Perhaps Hardy's ideas were influenced by Arnold's *St. Paul and Protestantism*.
4. In the British Museum.

COMING UP OXFORD STREET: EVENING was first published in the *Nation and Athenaeum* for June 13, 1925. In the manuscript the second stanza is in the first person.[1] Oxford Street, in central London, runs from the Marble Arch at Hyde Park eastward to Tottenham Court Road. The point of view of the first stanza is that of the descending sun, personified as a "warm god" looking eastward along Oxford Street and observing reflections from all that he brightens. He looks into the eyes of a "city-clerk" walking west. According to the manuscript, the clerk represents Hardy himself, feeling walled in by the city and the prospect of spending his life plodding along the "rut" of the street, that is, in architectural drawing.

In the imagery of the poem, the sun is, as usual in Hardy's poetry, benevolent, but, whatever problems it may solve in its reflections from chemists' bottles, it only dazzles the dejected clerk—Hardy. At the date of the poem, he had put his best into *Under the Greenwood Tree*, published anonymously in June. Reviews had been favorable, but sale was very slow.[2] Meeting his friend and advisor, Horace Moule, in Trafalgar Square at this time, "Hardy seems to have declared that he had thrown up authorship at last and for all. Moule . . . advised him not to give up writing altogether, since, supposing anything were to happen to his eyes from the fine architectural drawing, literature would be a resource for him."[3]

1. Purdy, *Thomas Hardy: A Bibliographical Study*, p. 236.
2. Ibid., p. 8.
3. *Early Life*, p. 115; *Life*, p. 87.

A LAST JOURNEY pictures a dying invalid's dream of a journey into scenes of his past. He travels backward from a merrymaking of sturdy manhood into childhood and sees his father shaking down overripe apples with a strange smile, perhaps symbolizing that the dreamer is soon to fall and join his father. His hearing the "watchmen cry the hours" in London seems a dream-symbol of the passing of the years.

As the dreamer journeys first to "Weatherb'ry" (Hardy's name for Puddletown), his home is somewhere near Dorchester. From there he goes to "King's-Stag," presumably the old inn of that name, no longer existing, near Kingstag, a village about ten miles north of Puddletown. At this inn, he joins a group bound for "Weydon-Priors Fair," Hardy's name for a famous fair at Weyhill, about forty-five

miles northeast of Kingstag. The merrymaking is typical of any coun-
try fair.[1]

1. It was at "Weydon-Priors Fair" that Henchard sold his wife in *The Mayor
of Casterbridge*. The mention of gingerbreads recalls Sue's selling gingerbreads at
Kennetbridge Fair in *Jude the Obscure*.

SINGING LOVERS in the manuscript adds " (in 1869) " to the title.[1]
At this time Hardy was working for the architect Crickmay in Wey-
mouth. He and the singing lovers of the poem are boating in
Weymouth Bay. His sweetheart who had gone away is presumably
Tryphena Sparks, to whom he was engaged before he met Emma
Gifford. She had gone to Stockwell College in Clapham, London.[2]
That Hardy "shunned to say" where she had gone perhaps means that
he kept secret everything about Tryphena. The phrase "mirth and
moonlight" need not suggest any more than romance, but Hardy's
constant use of the moon as a sinister symbol suggests his meaning as
the mirth of the lovers and his own sorrow.

1. Purdy, *Thomas Hardy: A Bibliographical Study*, p. 236.
2. Deacon and Coleman, *Providence and Mr Hardy*, p. 34.

THE MONTH'S CALENDAR seems a personal poem. Purdy suggests
in "A Note on the Hon. Mrs. Arthur Henniker" that the poem is
"significant" in relation to Mrs. Henniker, whom Hardy met on May
19, 1893. This "Note" says that, though many letters from Hardy to
Mrs. Henniker are in the Dorset County Museum, "She had destroyed
some of the earlier letters, and we can hardly assume that the corre-
spondence . . . is intact today. The letters range from 3 June 1893
to 29 May 1922 and are particularly frequent in the year 1893."[1]
Possibly the poem treats Hardy and Mrs. Henniker between May 19
and June 1, 1893.

The opening stanza perhaps describes his action on June 1 in
tearing off the calendar sheet for May, and his feeling in doing so.
The Later Years presents extracts from his diary for May 19 through
25, when he and his wife Emma visited Lord Houghton and his
sister, Mrs. Henniker, in Dublin, Ireland. The diary, under the date
of May 19, calls her "A charming, *intuitive* woman apparently." The
second stanza seems to refer to this day, apparently painful to recall
because it marked an emotional disturbance. The third stanza sug-
gests May 20, on which Hardy went sightseeing apart from Mrs. Hen-
niker: "To Dublin Castle, Christ Church, etc., conducted by Mr.
Trevelyan, Em having gone with Mrs. Henniker . . . to a Bazaar."[2]
The rest of this stanza and the fourth mention May 31, when ap-
parently he had written her some expression of affection and had been

offered friendship, but no more. (For details see Mrs. Arthur Henniker in the Key to Persons.)

1. *Thomas Hardy: A Bibliographical Study*, pp. 342-48.
2. Pp. 18-20; *Life*, pp. 254-55.

A SPELLBOUND PALACE had in the manuscript the title "A Sleeping Palace."[1] Hardy's visit to Hampton Court is not mentioned in his biography. Possibly it was early in 1925 with his wife Florence, as suggested by "Our footsteps," though probably he had visited the palace earlier. After his marriage on September 17, 1874, and a brief honeymoon trip to the Continent, he and his first wife Emma returned to London to live in Surbiton until March, 1875. This area is just across the Thames from Hampton Court.

Hampton Court Palace was built by Cardinal Wolsey in 1514-16. When Wolsey entertained King Henry VIII and his wife, Katherine of Aragon, Henry so admired the palace that in 1526 Wolsey presented it to him. It thereafter became Henry's honeymoon-home for his marriages with Anne Boleyn, Katherine Howard, and Katherine Parr. It is now a museum haunted by its portraits, fading tapestries, and, it is said, the ghosts of its past. In the "Cartoon Gallery" hangs a portrait of Henry VIII and his family, with the ghost of Alice Peyton hovering in the doorway of the painting; the ghost of Katherine Howard is said to be seen in a corridor called the " Haunted Gallery." Hardy's poem expresses the mood of these features of the palace.

Hardy and his wife, perhaps, visited Hampton Court in late winter, entering from the grounds overlooked by the Queen's Chambers. There rows of bluish-green yew trees trimmed into cones cast "spires" of shadow across the paths. The building is of dull-rose brick that is "fired vermilion" by the sinking sun. In an inner Fountain Court the thin streams of a fountain seem listless. He evidently visited the Great Hall, where a window exhibits a portrait of Henry VIII, "plumed, / sworded" and "straddling," his feet wide apart below gleaming calves. He saw no portrait there of Cardinal Wolsey. The Cardinal's opposition to Henry's policies in relation to the Roman Catholic Church caused him to fall from favor, after which Henry did his utmost to obliterate the memory of the Cardinal. In the poem, Hardy's knowledge of Wolsey's fate created the ghost that holds the palace somberly "spellbound."

1. Purdy, *Thomas Hardy: A Bibliographical Study*, p. 236.

WHEN DEAD, Weber surmises, is Hardy's imaginative vision of his first wife Emma, speaking to him before she died without the "querulousness" and "stress" of their later married life.[1] Weber speaks of the "technical perfection" of this poem, but Hogan, partly on the basis of the word "infallibly," conceives the poem to be humorous.[2]

1. *Hardy's Love Poems*, p. 75.
2. "Structural Design in Thomas Hardy's Poetry," p. 229.

SINE PROLE is a Latin title that means "without offspring." The fact that *The Early Life* traces Hardy's ancestry from "the Jersey le Hardys who sailed across to Dorset for centuries" suggests that he took a good deal of pride, or wished to do so, in his ancestors as far back as he could discover them. During his later years he explored parish registers in the areas where his family had lived and made several genealogical tables.[1] The poem suggests that Hardy considered his ancestors to be in a sense himself, the moulders of his nature.

He wished to have a child. His diary for August 13, 1877, records: "We hear that Jane, our late servant, is soon to have a baby. Yet never a sign of one is there for us."[2] His distress at being the last of his line was doubtless deepened because his brother Henry and his sisters Mary and Kate had no children. The resignation of the final stanza includes a charge that "Moderns" see no calamity in "their line's cessation." Though from middle age onward Hardy tended to "View Life's lottery with misprision," he was more than ever pessimistic about the future after World War I, and at last, perhaps, was quite content not to have a child.

The headnote for "Sine Prole" calls attention to the "Mediaeval Latin Sequence-Metre" of the poem. *The Later Years* says that Hardy in 1900 "spent time . . . in hunting up Latin hymns at the British Museum . . . of dates ranging from the thirteenth to the seventeenth century, by Thomas of Celano, Adam of S. Victor, John Mombaer, Jacob Balde, etc. That English prosody might be enriched by adapting some of the verse-forms of these is not unlikely to have been his view."[3] Purdy says that Hardy's transcripts "dated 'B. M. 28 Apl.,' are inserted in his copy of *Sequences from the Sarum Missal*, trans. C. B. Pearson (London, 1871)," and that "Sine Prole" "was suggested, in form, by the sequences of Adam of S. Victor."[4]

1. In the Dorset County Museum. See the table reproduced in Evelyn Hardy, *Thomas Hardy*, facing p. 224.
2. *Early Life*, p. 153; *Life*, p. 116.
3. Pp. 85-86; *Life*, p. 306.
4. *Thomas Hardy: A Bibliographical Study*, p. 237.

TEN YEARS SINCE refers to the death of Hardy's first wife Emma on November 27, 1912, and the aging of everything about Max Gate since that time. Hardy's diary for November 27, 1922, records: "E's death-day, ten years ago. Went with F. and tidied her tomb and carried flowers for her and the other two tombs,"[1] those of Hardy's parents (buried together) and his sister Mary.

1. *Later Years*, p. 229; *Life*, p. 418.

EVERY ARTEMISIA comments upon any woman who, like Artemisia, mourns the death of a husband in a grand style. Artemisia was the wife of King Mausolus of Caria, in Asia Minor, who died in 350 B.C. She erected in Halicarnassus a magnificent tomb, the Mausoleum, one of the seven wonders of the ancient world. The poem presents a dialogue between an elderly woman and a somewhat critical sage. The woman had cared little for her husband while he lived, but in a combination of remorse and self-glorification made a show of mourning after his death.

THE BEST SHE COULD in the manuscript had the title "The Fall of the Leaf."[1] The poem personifies a falling leaf, a day that speaks, and "Dame Summer" dressed "the best / She could" in her brief life. The poem has been set to music with the title "The Too Short Time" in *Before and After Summer* (London: Boosey & Hawkes, 1949).

1. Purdy, *Thomas Hardy: A Bibliographical Study*, p. 237.

THE GRAVEYARD OF DEAD CREEDS dramatizes in verse a note Hardy made in 1907 toward an article on religion and included in *The Later Years*. The note reads: "The days of creeds are as dead and done with as the days of Pterodactyls. Required: services at which there are no affirmations and no supplications."[1] Though he did not write the article, the note suggests the discussion of religion in the closing portion of the "Apology" for *Late Lyrics and Earlier*.

Hardy's poem does not define the new creed that shall be the heir of the dead ones, but it is evidently the "pale yet positive gleam" of "God's Funeral," and the "alliance between religion . . . and complete rationality" of the "Apology." In general message, the religious impulse created, in ages of ignorance and superstition, various gods and creeds, now dead because incredible as facts and inadequate as moral guides. The coming "'heir" shall inherit whatever was vital in the old beliefs, embody man's spiritual aspirations, and, allied with rationality, define the goals of human life and attract men toward them. The term "Catholicons" means universal remedies or panaceas.

1. P. 121; *Life*, p. 332.

"THERE SEEMED A STRANGENESS" had in the manuscript the deleted title "The Great Adjustment."[1] The vision is based upon a prayer in the Old Testament and a

prophecy in the New. The first three lines of the third stanza paraphrase a verse in Isaiah. Chapter 64 opens with a prayer that God
will "rend the heavens" and show Himself to man. Verse 4 reads: "For
since the beginning of the world men have not heard . . . neither hath
the eye seen, O God . . . what he hath prepared for him that waiteth
for him." St. Paul, in I Cor. 2:9, says: "But as it is written, Eye hath
not seen, nor ear heard, neither have entered into the heart of man,
the things which God hath prepared for them that love him." He
prophesies in 13:12, "For now we see through a glass, darkly; but
then face to face: now I know in part; but then shall I know even
as also I am known." The first two lines of Hardy's fourth stanza
paraphrase St. Paul. The poem may be read as Hardy's vision of
Isaiah's prayer answered and St. Paul's prophecy fulfilled. The
"Voice" is the voice of God.

In terms of Hardy's philosophy of the unconscious Immanent Will
as developed in *The Dynasts,* the Biblical prophecy is fulfilled when
the Will wakens to consciousness of injustice and needless pain and
decrees that "Right shall disestablish Wrong." The first two lines
of the poem, mentioning a "strangeness in the air" and a "Vermilion
light on the land's lean face" suggest that the "Great Adjustment" is
in the operations of natural law. The third line of the poem and the
second stanza suggest that the adjustment lies in God's making Himself and His purposes clear to human intuition.

1. Purdy, *Thomas Hardy: A Bibliographical Study,* p. 237.

A NIGHT OF QUESTIONINGS presents the poet as overhearing conversations between dead men and the personified wind. It is the
evening before All Souls' Day (November 2); on this evening, according to folk-lore, the souls of the dead come from their graves.
They all ask, "What of the world now?" and the wind as oracle
answers them in variations of: it is "just as in your time." This reply
may represent Hardy's meditation that human history shows no sign
of the amelioration for which he had hoped.

Each of the five stanzas presents a different group. The dead of
the first stanza are those buried by a "tottering tower," perhaps
Stinsford Church. The wind in answer to their question quotes Joel
2:25, to refer to old age as the "years that the locust hath eaten." The
dead of the second stanza are those buried in "old cathedral piles,"
as in Salisbury, all alike in death. Those of the third stanza are men
who "Go down to the sea in ships" and "See the wonders of the deep,"
phrases partly quoted from Ps. 107:23, 24. They are scattered around
the world, from Cape Comorin (the southernmost tip of India), to
Cape Horn (in Chile, the southernmost tip of South America), to

Cape Wrath (the northwestern tip of Scotland). The dead of the fourth stanza are those left in "the flats of France" during World War I; the wind, blowing from Ardennes (in northern France) across the Channel to Dover, brings their question and the wind's reply. The phrasing reflects Hardy's opposition to the "periodic spasms" of war. The wind calls soldiers men so "fooled by foul phantasms"—the dynasts and the war-makers—that instead of evolutionary progress toward brotherhood, they revert "Backward to type," that is, to savagery. Even men executed for their crimes question, in the fifth stanza, how the world goes now. The wind cannot see that their deaths served any purpose: the world remains evil.

XENOPHANES, THE MONIST OF COLOPHON was first published in the *Nineteenth Century* for March, 1924.[1] The Latin note may be read as "In the ninety-second year of his age, at about the year 480," B.C.

Xenophanes was a philosopher-poet, born shortly before 570 B.C. in Colophon, Ionia. He wandered a good deal, and settled at last in Elea in southern Italy, where he lived to be about ninety-two. He contributed to the founding of the Eleatic philosophy, which attacked the anthropomorphic concepts of earlier Greek religions and suggested a monistic theory that God is One.

The poem presents an imaginary address by Xenophanes to the non-personal First Cause and the reply of the "listening Years," the Spirit of the Years from Hardy's *The Dynasts*, that to call upon "It" is useless. Man may muse upon It, but it is dangerous to let word of this heresy get back to Colophon. Years prophesies that even three thousand years in the future men who "hazard a clue" to the riddle of the universe will be "scowled at." Years describes It as asleep, but snoring that some day It may awake and amend Its "doings."

Xenophanes is only a dramatic spokesman for a number of Hardy's concepts of the Immanent Will as set forth in *The Dynasts*. The terms that Xenophanes used in addressing It, the "Mover," the "Great Dumb," and the "close Thing," resemble those the Spirits of *The Dynasts* use to name or describe the Immanent Will, among them the "Prime Mover," the "dumb Thing," the "Unconscious," and the "dominant Thing."[2]

In the reply of Years, Hardy expresses his feeling at being reviled by reviewers of his epic-drama; and he also expresses, in the two closing stanzas, the "evolutionary meliorism" in the "After Scene" of *The Dynasts*, with its climax in "Consciousness the Will informing, till It fashion all things fair!"

1. Purdy, *Thomas Hardy: A Bibliographical Study*, p. 237.

LIFE AND DEATH AT SUNRISE in the manuscript was titled "A Long-Ago Sunrise at Dogbury Gate."[1] That Hardy's headnote names Dogbury Gate and the date 1867 suggests that the anecdote may rest on fact. Dogbury Gate is the name of the point at which a secondary road to Evershot runs west from Road A352, about half a mile north of Minterne Magna, and about ten miles north of Dorchester. There is a wooded "dip" at Dogbury Gate; Blackmoor Vale lies to the north, and the road to Evershot climbs to the ridge that overlooks this valley. The wagon creaking uphill through the fog is evidently climbing from Minterne Magna; the horseman is coming from Dogbury Hill, just northeast of the "Gate."

I have not discovered the identities of the newborn "Jack" or the recently deceased "John Thinn." The Burial Register of Minterne Magna does not record the death of a John Thinn in 1867 or a nearby year. Reverend C. V. Taylor, vicar of this parish, surmised that "T. H. must have concocted the name for rhyming purposes."[2] Even if so, the anecdote has the ring of the kind of fact Hardy liked to record.[3]

Hardy's theme seems the sun's blessing upon a long life well ended and the birth of a fine boy. (In Hardy's poetry, the sun is used as a symbol of a benevolent force, a "warm god.") Since "Jack" is a form of John, as old John passes, another John is born. The poem thus suggests the cycle of life. "We'll go and put him in," suggestive of tucking someone into a restful bed, is a Dorset euphemism for burial.

1. Purdy, *Thomas Hardy: A Bibliographical Study*, p. 237.
2. A note in my possession.
3. If the name is fictional, we may surmise a reason for Hardy's choosing "John Thinn." The Thynne family, with the Marquess of Bath at its head, lived at the mansion of Longleat, about twenty-five miles northeast of Dogbury Gate. Longleat was built by Sir John Thynne. A John Thinn among the common people might be a distant, socially decayed and forgotten relative of the Thynnes. *Tess of the D'Urbervilles* offers an analogy. John Durbeyfield is discovered to be a decayed D'Urberville, a name based upon the knightly Turbervilles. It is interesting, whether or not significant, that Lady Caroline Thynne died in London on October 12, 1867, the year Hardy gave for the anecdote. Her death was reported in the *Dorset County Chronicle*.

NIGHT-TIME IN MID-FALL in the manuscript was titled "Autumn Night-time."[1] The poem pictures a stormy night, perhaps on Hallowe'en, when "witches ride abroad." The term "storm-strid" employs an obsolete past participle of "stride": the storm and the wind are personified as striding through the night. The stanzas offer a report both accurate in naming natural occurrences and yet suggestive of menace. The final line suggests that when nature's violence cracks church-timbers, superstition appears. The suggestion that the poet knows from sounds more than he can see is characteristic of Hardy, who often listened to nature's sounds as voices. The eels, emboldened to cross a road for shelter, echo Gabriel Oak's observation of animal behavior at the approach of a storm in *Far from the Madding Crowd*. (Chapter XXXVI.)

1. Purdy, *Thomas Hardy: A Bibliographical Study*, p. 237.

A SHEEP FAIR is set at "Pummery" (Poundbury), a hill just northwest of Dorchester. A sheep fair, though it may include merry-making, is chiefly concerned with auctioning sheep brought into the fair grounds and penned in "hurdles" (movable wooden fences to group and separate the flocks). The scene is presented with photographic realism. Because their livelihoods depend upon buying and selling, farmers and traders at a fair often endure daylong rain in the frequently wet weather of Dorset.

Perhaps the rain soaking everything at the fair partly inspired Chapter XVI of *The Mayor of Casterbridge*, in which Henchard's public entertainment on "an elevated green spot surrounded by an ancient square earthwork" (Pummery) was rained out, with disastrous results.

SNOW IN THE SUBURBS in the manuscript shows an erased title, "Snow at Upper Tooting."[1] The scene is at "The Larches," No. 1 Arundel Terrace, Trinity Road, London, where the Hardys lived from March 22, 1878, until June of 1881. Evidently looking from a window there, Hardy observed the behavior of snowflakes, soft snow, and a sparrow engaged in inadvertent comedy. In the final stanza, the Hardys, with characteristic compassion, take in a stray cat suffering from cold and hunger.

1. Purdy, *Thomas Hardy: A Bibliographical Study*, p. 237.

A LIGHT SNOW-FALL AFTER FROST presents a scene probably in the winter of 1874-75, when Hardy and his bride Emma were living in Surbiton, London. The pictures of the poem are four scenes apparently observed from a window. The manuscript shows that the second stanza was added late.[1] This addition suggests that the poet was observing a frosty scene before the snow began to fall and the first man appeared.

1. Purdy, *Thomas Hardy: A Bibliographical Study*, p. 238.

WINTER NIGHT IN WOODLAND was first published in *Country Life* on December 6, 1924.[1]

Hardy's headnote "Old Time" and the names of the quire (choir) in the final stanza indicate some Christmas before his birth in 1840, when the quire of *Under the Greenwood Tree* was still making its "yearly rounds." The poem presents, therefore, his memories of what his grandmother and others had told him in his boyhood. As the persons are those of *Under the Greenwood Tree*, the woodland is that of "Mellstock" (Stinsford), near Hardy's boyhood home.

The first two stanzas exhibit Hardy's compassion for animals and birds and his scorn for men who cruelly trick, trap, and kill them for sport, expressed in his imaginative identification with the fox, who "knows not,—will never know" why he is hunted to death. The second stanza, after presenting the bird-baiters who trap the birds to be driven out for their masters to shoot, pictures the "awaiters" boozing themselves into insensibility in preparation for the coming slaughter. The poachers might have the excuse of poverty and hunger for their attack upon sleeping pheasants.

The third stanza turns to a midnight activity common in Dorset in the old days, smuggling. In his notebook for March 22, 1871, Hardy wrote: "Smuggling. While superintending the church music (from 1801 onwards to about 1805) my grandfather used to do a little smuggling, his house being a lonely one. . . . He sometimes had as many as eighty tubs in a dark closet . . . each tub containing four gallons. . . . A whiplash across the window-pane would wake my grandfather at two or three in the morning, and he would dress and go down. Not a soul was there, but a heap of tubs loomed up in front of the door. He would set to work and stow them away in the dark closet aforesaid . . . till dusk the following evening, when groups of dark, long-bearded fellows would arrive, and carry off the tubs in twos and fours slung over their shoulders."[2]

In ironic contrast with the first three stanzas, the fourth stanza presents the message of Christ's birth carried from house to house by the carol-singers of the Mellstock quire.

"Winter Night in Woodland" makes use of several obsolete words: "swingel" (a flail used by poachers), "matches of brimstone" (sulphur matches), and "thrid" (thread or weave through).

1. Purdy, *Thomas Hardy: A Bibliographical Study*, p. 233.
2. Evelyn Hardy, *Thomas Hardy's Notebooks*, p. 35. In his short story "The Distracted Preacher" Hardy gives a detailed account of the smuggling of strong drink along the Dorset coast and inland.

ICE ON THE HIGHWAY presents the amusing picture of seven country women going to market in Dorchester on a day when the road is iced. The "London Road" down Yellowham Hill is steep enough to be dangerous when iced.

MUSIC IN A SNOWY STREET reflects an event of April 26, 1884, which Hardy recorded in his journal as: "Curious scene. A fine poem in it: Four girls—itinerant musicians—sisters, have been playing opposite Parmiter's in the High Street [Dorchester]. The eldest had a fixed, old, hard face, and wore white roses in her hat. Her eyes remained on one close object, such as the buttons of her sister's dress; she played the violin. The next sister, with red roses in her hat, had rather bold dark eyes, and a coquettish smirk. She too played a violin. The next, with her hair in ringlets, beat the tambourine. The youngest, a mere child, dinged the triangle. She wore a bead necklace. All wore brass earrings like Jews'-harps, which dangled to the time of the jig. I saw them again in the evening, the silvery gleams from Saunders's [silver-smith's] shop shining out upon them. They were now sublimed to a wondrous charm. The hard face of the eldest was flooded with soft solicitous thought; the coquettish one was no longer bold but archly tender; her dirty white roses were pure as snow; her sister's red ones a fine crimson; the brass earrings were golden; the iron triangle silver; the tambourine Miriam's own; the third child's face that of an angel; the fourth that of a cherub. The pretty one smiled on the second, and began to play 'In the gloaming,' the little voices singing it. *Now* they were what Nature made them, before the smear of 'civilization' had sullied their existences."[1]

The poem portrays the four girls as playing listlessly, but Hardy's memories of their old tunes, which he had danced to in his youth, give the scene color and life. The tunes are named in the poem only as airs popular in the Napoleonic era and earlier, perhaps in Hardy's memory something like folk-tunes.

1. *Early Life*, pp. 215-16; *Life*, p. 165.

THE FROZEN GREENHOUSE, Hardy's biographers have assumed, is autobiographical. In describing Emma Gifford, who became the first Mrs. Hardy, Evelyn Hardy says: "She loved animals and growing things and once, when the greenhouse stove at the Rectory had been neglected and all the plants had died, her face became 'the very symbol of tragedy.' "[1] Weber dates the event as the day of Hardy's departure after his first visit to St. Juliot, Friday, March 11, 1870. He says that on the morning of Hardy's departure, Emma "struck a light six times in her anxiety to call the servants early enough to get the architect off on time for his return journey. Hardy's poem 'The Frozen Greenhouse' tells us something about that morning."[2] The greenhouse is still standing. Mrs. Gwendolen Bax, who lives in the Old St. Juliot Rectory, wrote me on July 12, 1966, that "It was in a poor state when we came here just over ten years ago, but we had it made serviceable again."

Echoes of the early morning departure appear in *A Pair of Blue Eyes*. When Stephen Smith has to leave Endelstow parsonage after his first visit, "They breakfasted before daylight; Mr. Swancourt, being more and more taken with his guest's ingenuous appearance, having determined to rise early and bid him a friendly farewell. It was, however, rather to the vicar's astonishment that he saw Elfride walk in to the breakfast-table, candle in hand." (Chapter VI.) The last stanza refers to the fact that Emma is dead.

1. *Thomas Hardy*, p. 120.
2. *Hardy's Love Poems*, p. 14. A photograph of the greenhouse faces this page.

TWO LIPS in the manuscript had the title "Two Red Lips."[1] Presumably, the lips are those of Emma, Hardy's first wife. The first two lines seem to refer to the morning of "The Frozen Greenhouse."

1. Purdy, *Thomas Hardy: A Bibliographical Study*, p. 238.

NO BUYERS might be set in almost any city, but Edmund Gosse, calling the poem a "melancholy and thrilling vignette," wrote that it is "a street scene in London, described photographically, with no other emotional intention than to emphasize that gnawing sense of disappointment which haunts the poet."[1]

1. Review of *Human Shows* in *Living Age*, p. 337.

ONE WHO MARRIED ABOVE HIM presents the crisis of a drama, with a narrative conclusion. The names Steve and Farmer Bollen may be fiction. The reference to a "Ham-Hill door" suggests that the scene is in Dorset, for Ham Hill stone is quarried near Yeovil. Many fine old houses are built of this orange-tinted stone. This fact, together with the mullioned windows, suggests that Steve's house was an old one with pretensions to grandeur beyond his means, and was thus a factor in his leaving a wife who demanded more than he could provide. As the conclusion indicates that he left home many years ago, possibly the story is one Hardy heard from his mother or grandmother. The theme is a conflict of the wife's pride in social rank and accompanying comforts, and Steve's pride in sturdy character, together with a demand that his wife respect and care for him.

Characteristically, Hardy described the passage of time in the colors of the seasons, "graytime to green to sere."

THE NEW TOY observes with amusement the pride in her first-born of a mother who looks young enough to play with dolls.

QUEEN CAROLINE TO HER GUESTS portrays the near-neurosis of a pleasure-mad, saddened queen who fears to remain alone with her frustrations. Queen Caroline was the officially recognized wife of King George IV. While still Prince of Wales, George was morganatically married to Mrs. Maria Fitzherbert. In spite of this connection, he was in 1795 forced into marriage with Princess Caroline of Brunswick, a flippant and pleasure-loving girl whom he did not love. Shortly after a child was born, George and Caroline parted. Caroline attempted, with much popular support, to assert her rights, but the Prince denied them. Caroline went to live in Italy, but when George III died she returned to England, where she was allowed the title of queen, but was not allowed to attend the coronation in Westminster Abbey. She attempted to force her way in, but was prevented. She died within a month of George IV's coronation.

Probably Hardy took much of his information about Queen Caroline from *The Journal of Mary Frampton*, which offers many gossipy details. It quotes a letter of May, 1814, that reads: "At home the fêtes, the balls, the Prince's quarrels occupy us. He really wrote to the Queen [of George III] to request her to forbid the Princess of Wales [Caroline] appearing in the Drawing-room. The Queen wrote a civil letter to her, and enclosed this pretty request. The Princess, of course, gives up going, but wishes to know why she is forbid, and talks, as usual, of appealing to the public. White's [where a ball was held on June 22, 1814] have given their tickets for the Royal Family to the Regent [the Prince], and he excludes the Princess, of course." Another letter of March 23, 1821, reads: "So all this [a variety of social activities] went off well, as did the opera the night before, and I believe the Drawing-room yesterday, without the Queen, though she certainly wrote to Lord Liverpool to declare her intention of going, and preparations were made to receive her. She was not to be stopped in her way to Buckingham House . . . but when there was to be received by the Ministers, who were to show her into an apartment below stairs, and tell her that she could not see the King in the Drawing-room above."[1]

Three scenes in *The Dynasts* present, as ironic social comedy, the frustrations of Caroline, while she was still Princess of Wales. (Part Second, VI, vi and vii, and Part Third, IV, viii.)

1. Mundy, *The Journal of Mary Frampton*, pp. 198-99, 322.

PLENA TIMORIS may be translated as "Full of Fear." The moon that, in the second line, seems to bless the lovers, none the less has, in the full story of the poem, its usual symbolic meaning of sinister portent. This symbol suggests that the girl's fear expressed in the final stanza will be realized.

THE WEARY WALKER in the manuscript had the title, deleted, of "The Pedestrian."[1] The poem, apparently a description of the poet's weariness in walking a road across a rolling plain, may be read to symbolize the journey of life into old age.

1. Purdy, *Thomas Hardy: A Bibliographical Study*, p. 238.

LAST LOVE-WORD with the date "189–" tempts one to relate the poem to Hardy's emotional life in the 1890's. Purdy has suggested that the poem may be associated with Mrs. Florence Henniker, to whom Hardy was strongly attracted in 1893 and afterward.[1] Miss Deacon, however, has proposed that the poem concerns Mrs. Tryphena Sparks Gale, who died in 1890.[2]

1. *Thomas Hardy: A Bibliographical Study*, p. 345.
2. *Hardy's Sweetest Image*, p. 24.

NOBODY COMES seems set at Hardy's home, Max Gate. The poem expresses a mood unusual for Hardy, who liked to have time to himself and was often annoyed when strangers came. An atmosphere of expectation, disappointment, and loneliness is suggested in the "crawl of night," the silence in which a humming telegraph wire seems a "spectral lyre," and the passing car "in a world of its own," leaving the poet "mute" in his lonely world.

IN THE STREET Blunden lists among "specimens of the uninspired Hardy."[1] The poem may have meant more to Hardy than it can to a reader with no clue to the identity of the girl. The poem exhibits his tendency to day-dream after seeing a pretty face.

1. *Thomas Hardy*, p. 245.

THE LAST LEAF was first published in *Nash's and Pall Mall Magazine* for November, 1924.[1] The poem presents the common situation in which an absent lover forgets his promise to return to an anxiously waiting sweetheart. It is interesting technically for stanzas of a rimed couplet followed by a short line, with the short lines rimed in pairs of stanzas.

1. Purdy, *Thomas Hardy: A Bibliographical Study*, p. 238.

AT WYNYARD'S GAP is a one-act play in verse that Hardy intended to be acted. In the 1920's the Hardy Players of Dorchester were acting dramatized versions of Hardy's stories and novels, his play *The Queen of Cornwall*, etc. In the margin of the "second proof" of *Human Shows*, on the bottom of page 98, Hardy drew in pencil the scene of "At Wynyard's Gap" as it might be shown on a stage and wrote beside the drawing: "If acted, the world 'top' next page [in the speech that begins 'HE. Go home again.'] to be changed to field, so that they come to front of stage."[1] The dialogue is rimed in couplets and trip-lets, with an occasional quatrain.

Wynyard's (Winyard's) Gap is a high point on the road between Dorchester and Crewkerne, about sixteen miles northwest of Dor-chester. An old stone inn there is called Winyard's Gap Inn; in the nineteenth century it was a coach stop and a gathering place for hunters. Behind the inn a steep hill rises from which "half South Wessex" is visible.

The places of the poem are located accurately, though Hardy's spelling of place-names is not that of Ordnance Survey maps. In the opening, the hounds have gone in full cry toward "Pen's Wood" (Penny's Hill Coppice), about four tenths of a mile south of the Gap. There they may kill, and then turn northeast toward the Yeo River seven or eight miles away. Uncertainty about their location accounts for the woman's "How vexing!" The man's lure to see the view in-cludes an invitation to look far over "combe [valley], and glen." Lewsdon Hill and Pilsdon Pen rise impressively some six miles to the southwest. The woman is amazed, for, though she lives "out there" near Crewkerne, only four miles away, she has never seen the view. (Crewkerne is the "Crookhorn" of the Carrier's speech.) The closing line of the play refers to Marshwood Vale, a broad valley south of Pilsdon Pen. From Marshwood (and the sea beyond) a wind often blows against the great hill, with no effect upon it. The line, there-fore, means "Never."

The characters belong to the fox-hunting country gentry. Win-yard's Gap is within horseback-riding distance from the extensive park of the Earls of Ilchester, who are reputed to have been rovingly amorous. Possibly the story and the reputation of the Earls came to Hardy from his mother or grandmother.

1. In the Dorset County Museum.

AT SHAG'S HEATH, as the headnote says, is "Traditional." The tradition treats an important historical person. The Duke of Mon-mouth, illegitimate son of King Charles II, was a Protestant leader of the factions that would exclude James (later James II) from the king-ship because he was a Roman Catholic. Monmouth, after the death of Charles II, gathered an "army" of miscellaneous Protestants in the west of England and entered Taunton. Parliament had declared it treason to support Monmouth's claim to the crown and offered a re-ward of 5,000 pounds for his capture. Troops sent to take Monmouth met him and his army at Sedgemoor on July 5, 1685. Monmouth, defeated, fled in disguise, but was captured at Shag's Heath on July 8. He was executed on July 15.

Shag's Heath is an area of farm-and-grazing land near the village of Horton. From Horton, one goes southeast on the Ringwood Road for about three miles and turns off northward on a gravel lane to "Monmouth Ash Farm." The tree under which Monmouth hid was an ash in a hedgerow beside a ditch, about a quarter of a mile behind a farmhouse. The shell of the original tree is still standing, but a new tree has sprung from the lower part of its stem. A placard reads: "Monmouth's Ash / After the Battle of Sedgemoor / The Duke of Monmouth lay hidden beneath / This Tree & was found & taken prisoner by / Sir William Portman & his Militia / A.D. 1685."

Hutchins's *History of Dorset* is among the historical sources Hardy consulted. The account of the manor of Woodlands in the parish of Horton includes: "In this manor, in the midst of a heath called Shags [*sic*] Heath, about a mile and a half from this [manor] house . . . between the roads leading to Ringwood and Fordingbridge, is an inclosure of several fields, in one of which, in a ditch . . . was taken the unfortunate Duke of Monmouth, after his flight from the battle of Sedgmoor [*sic*], in Somersetshire. . . . The tradition of the neighborhood is, that . . . the Duke and Lord Lumley quitted their horses at Woodyates, whence the former, disguised as a peasant, wandered hither. . . . The duke went on to the island . . . a cluster of small farms in the middle of the heath, and there concealed himself in a deep ditch under the ash. When the pursuers came up, a woman[1] living in a neighbouring cot gave information of his being somewhere in the island, which was immediately surrounded by soldiers. . . . As they were going away next morning, one of them espied the brown skirt of the Duke's coat, and seized him. . . . The family of the woman who first gave the information are said to have fallen into decay, and never thriven afterwards. The Duke was carried before Anthony Etterick, esq. of Holt, a justice of the peace, who ordered him to London."[2]

Hardy may have consulted Fea's *King Monmouth*, which suggests the remorse in Hardy's refrain. Fea says: "Among the secret service expenses of James II is the following: 'To Amy Farant, bounty for giving notice to the Lord Lumley where the Duke of Monmouth lay concealed, whereby he was apprehended, 50 pounds.'" After Monmouth was taken, Amy Farant's cottage "stood shunned and deserted as all ill-omened dwellings would be in a rural spot such as this." (P. 309.) Another possible source suggesting both remorse and the variety of versions is a letter dated April 23 [1893?], written by Eustace

Cecil to H. J. Moule, a friend of Hardy's. It reads: "Mr. Bennett of Bennett's Farm told me that the late Archdeacon Onslow, after careful investigation, was of opinion that the D. of Monmouth was never found in a ditch at all, but . . . was arrested under the old Elm trees, close to the Farm, early in the morning, by the soldiers . . . who ascertained his whereabouts from an old woman who had seen him hiding in a ditch under the ash tree, or thereabouts. The poor old woman, who apparently was a supporter of the Protestant succession, never forgave herself for artlessly giving information to the soldiers."[3]

Hardy's "traditional" source for the poem includes stories that came to him from his mother. His maternal grandmother was born Elizabeth Swetman, and her mother was born Maria Childs. *The Early Life* says: "The Swetmans and the Childses seem to have been involved in the Monmouth rising, and one of the former to have been brought before Jeffreys, 'for being absent from home att the tyme of the Rebellion.' . . . Several traditions survive in the Swetman family concerning the Rebellion. An indubitably true one was that after the Battle of Sedgemoor two of the Swetman daughters—Grace and Leonarde—were beset in their house by some of the victorious soldiery, and only escaped violation by slipping from the upper rooms down the back stairs into the orchard. . . . Another tradition, of more doubtful authenticity, is that to which the short story by Hardy called *The Duke's Reappearance* approximates. Certainly a mysterious man did come to Swetman after the battle, but it was generally understood that he was one of Monmouth's defeated officers."[4]

The poem seems partly fiction from a medley of sources. The reappearance of Monmouth as a ghost echoes "The Duke's Reappearance." In both the poem and the story, the Duke's tendency to kiss a pretty woman proves fatal.

1. Hardy underscored "woman" and in the margin wrote "(Amy Farrant)."

2. III, 156. In the Dorset County Museum. Opposite this story, Hardy interleaved essentially the same story clipped from the London *Times* of August 4, 1927, after the poem was published. In this account, Amy Farant is named as the woman who betrayed Monmouth. In other accounts, the name is spelled Farrant.

3. Letter in scrapbook VIII of H. J. Moule, pp. 194a-95a, in the Dorset County Museum.

4. Pp. 7-8; *Life*, p. 6. "The Duke's Reappearance" uses the names Swetman and Childs. Monmouth hides in the Swetman home, attempts to kiss a Swetman daughter, and is asked to go for this reason. On going, he disguises himself and leaves with Swetman a gold snuff box, a purse with fifty gold pieces, and his sword. Two nights after the execution of Monmouth his ghost returns and is seen to collect his possessions.

A SECOND ATTEMPT in the manuscript adds "About 1900" as the date of composition.[1] The first line, speaking of thirty years in the past, indicates 1870, the year Hardy met Emma Gifford. The poem may meditate his attempt about 1900 to revive the emotional *rapport* with his wife Emma that had existed during their courtship. The effort is not successful, for the events of life had closed off the receptive emotions.

Hardy's method was "mutely" to "waft her" his "Dreams much dwelt upon." The terms suggest telepathy. He had some interest in telepathy. In his diary for March 5, 1890, he said: "Wrote the first four or six lines of 'Not a line of her writing have I.' It was a curious instance of sympathetic telepathy. The woman whom I was thinking of—a cousin—was dying at the time, and I quite in ignorance of it."[2] William Archer quotes Hardy as saying to him in 1901: "My mother believed that she once saw an apparition. A relative of hers, who had a young child, was ill and told my mother that she thought she was dying. My mother laughed at the idea. . . . Then one night—lying broad awake as she declared—my mother saw this lady enter her room and hold out the child to her imploring. It afterwards appeared . . . that she died at that very time; but the odd thing was that, while she was sinking, she continually expressed a wish that my mother should take charge of the child.'"[3]

1. Purdy, *Thomas Hardy: A Bibliographical Study*, p. 239.
2. *Early Life*, p. 293; *Life*, p. 224. The poem is "Thoughts of Phena."
3. "Real Conversations. Conversations I.—With Mr. Thomas Hardy," p. 313. For details of Hardy's interest in extra-sensory perception, see Bailey, *Thomas Hardy and the Cosmic Mind, passim.*

"FREED THE FRET OF THINKING" was first published in the *Adelphi* for May, 1925.[1] It is a philosophical protest against the fact that man is endowed with introspective consciousness, reason that causes him to question the purpose of life, and judgment that weighs its pain. The "we" of the opening stanza may be mankind, or it may recall Hardy as a boy among his friends, "Song with service linking," before he questioned his childhood faith. The term "bee" recalls Hardy's ardent, happy labor "With the bent of a bee" in his first school. (See "He Revisits His First School.") The second and third stanzas reflect that the human lot might be always happy if men could live with the unthinking acceptance of birds or the unconscious fulfilment of flowers.

1. Purdy, *Thomas Hardy: A Bibliographical Study*, p. 239.

THE ABSOLUTE EXPLAINS was first published in the *Nineteenth Century* for February, 1925.[1] The day of composition, New Year's Eve, suggests that the thought was prompted by the passing years. Though it is light and even humorous (in the fantasy of the Absolute explaining Itself to the poet), the poem is a meditation upon the mystery of Time. In addition to the Absolute's analogy of a man "Plodding by lantern-light," one may picture the theme in the analogy that events are like the images on a motion-picture film. Events are still on the film after they have been projected; or, as the human memory holds the past as idea, the Absolute Mind holds the past as still-existent reality, not observable to human senses.

The Absolute seems to be a personification of the Will of *The Dynasts*, a dreaming Mind. The poet has asked a question of the Absolute concerning "her" (presumably Emma, Hardy's first wife, who had died in 1912), and the poem opens with the Absolute's answer, largely an explanation of Time as an illusion of human perception: the reality is an eternal present. Thus Time is a "mock"; it does not have, as in Shakespeare's *Measure for Measure* (V, i, 12), a "tooth" that gnaws reality into oblivion, but is "toothless." All that was, is, and shall be "are shaped to be / Eternally," and exist so in the Absolute consciousness. To support this concept, Hardy refers to theories of relativity (or Time as a "Fourth Dimension") recently set forth by Einstein.

The surmise that Hardy's question to the Absolute concerns the continued existence of Emma is supported by items he meditates in stanzas VII through IX. Calling upon his memory of past events that, the Absolute says, still exist, he seems to refer in stanzas VII and VIII to his courtship in Cornwall, naming the singing and merry-making, the flowers, the bowers, and the "irised bow" more fully portrayed in "After a Journey," "Beeny Cliff" (with its "irised rain"), "A Duettist to Her Pianoforte," and "The Man Who Forgot." Stanza IX may refer to Hardy's "pilgrimage" to Cornwall or with Emma to Italy in 1887. (See "Poems of Pilgrimage.") In stanza XI the Absolute seems to assure Hardy that Emma still exists alive, in spite of the illusion that she is in Stinsford Churchyard. Stanza XII, especially in the use of "prize," seems to include Tryphena Sparks among "others" yet living. (See the phrase "lost prize" in "Thoughts of Phena.")

1. Purdy, *Thomas Hardy: A Bibliographical Study*, p. 239.

"so, TIME" is a coda for "The Absolute Explains." Where the Absolute had said that "Time is a mock," "So, Time" concludes the thought by mocking Time as an illusion and rejoicing that "my Love's adornings" remain "Firm in the Vast." The opening lines of the poem echo John Donne's "Death, be not proud, though some have called thee / Mighty and dreadful, for thou art not so."

AN INQUIRY has a motto from Ps. 17:5, in the Vulgate Bible, translated in the King James Bible, Ps. 18: 4, as "The sorrows of death compassed me." The poem challenges "It," evidently the Will of *The Dynasts,* to explain why all life leads to death, or why It crowned "Death the King of the Firmament." It is, among other things, a personification of unconscious process; It had no intention. The poem plays with the relativity of time by having It view many years in the human consciousness as "a moment or so" and "an instant."

THE FAITHFUL SWALLOW was sent in March, 1923, for a proposed Queen's College, Oxford, *Miscellany,* apparently not published.[1] Swallows are summer residents in Dorset, but migrate southward in autumn, though now and then a swallow remains all winter.[2] Perhaps Hardy observed one distressed by "Frost, hunger, snow." In various poems he personifies a bird as reasoning and speaking. When the swallow decides to follow a reasoned conclusion, instead of instinct, it suffers.

1. Purdy, *Thomas Hardy: A Bibliographical Study,* p. 239.
2. Moule, *A Revised List of the Birds of Dorset,* p. 12.

IN SHERBORNE ABBEY, Purdy says, is "possibly associated with the clandestine marriage of Hardy's maternal grandparents."[1] They were George Hand and Elizabeth Swetman, who married without the approval of John Swetman, the bride's father, on December 27, 1804. If the poem refers to this marriage, Hardy's date, "17——," is possibly intended to conceal the identities.

John Swetman was a well-to-do yeoman of Melbury Osmund, a village about fifteen miles northwest of Dorchester. *The Early Life* says that his daughter Elizabeth "clandestinely married a young man of whom her father strongly disapproved. The sturdy yeoman, apparently a severe and unyielding parent, never forgave her, and never would see her again."[2] The marriage was not clandestine. The banns were published in the parish church of Melbury Osmund on December 9, 16, and 23, 1804, by the rector, J. Jenkins. Swetman certainly knew of the coming marriage and did not forbid it. Hardy's statement must mean only that he disapproved of his daughter's marriage to George Hand, described in the church registers as a "Servant," apparently a hired shepherd. The source of his disapproval may have been partly moral indignation. Elizabeth Swetman Hand gave birth to a daughter eight days after her marriage.[3]

One may surmise that "In Sherborne Abbey" refers to an earlier attempted elopement, rather than the marriage. Possibly George

Hand and Elizabeth Swetman ran away together some months or even years[4] before their marriage, returned home unmarried, and were wed only when Elizabeth's pregnancy both demanded that her father not oppose the banns and caused him to disown his daughter. The elopement was at least an escape for the time being.

Sherborne Abbey seems a likely hiding place for lovers running away from Melbury Osmund. Instead of going north to Yeovil or southeast to Dorchester, George Hand and Elizabeth Swetman might well have taken secondary roads or lanes northeastward for some seven to ten miles (depending on the route) to Sherborne. The poem indicates that they were on horseback. It suggests that the woman was an "heiress," as the daughter of a well-to-do yeoman might seem to a "servant."

They hid in the Abbey Church of St. Mary the Virgin, Sherborne, a magnificent church dating from Saxon times. Many tombs in stone fill the aisles and chapels. The couple are presented as "recumbent" in a pew in the south aisle (matching the effigies on tombs nearby, some of husbands and wives).

The final stanza suggests in imagery and tone some unhappy outcome of their elopement. Even the moon, usually symbolizing a sinister force, is blacked out by a cloud. Commenting upon the technique of the poem, Hynes points to its asymmetrical forms, or "Gothicness," suitable for the subject and the setting.[5]

1. *Thomas Hardy: A Bibliographical Study*, p. 239.
2. Pp. 8-9; *Life*, p. 7.
3. Deacon, *Hardy's Grandmother, Betsy, and Her Family*, records the facts stated above from the parish registers.
4. Perhaps in the "17——" of the headnote.
5. *The Pattern of Hardy's Poetry*, p. 77.

THE PAIR HE SAW PASS in the manuscript had the deleted title "The Bridegroom."[1] The footnote "From an old draft" suggests that the story was sketched in an earlier period of Hardy's life.

1. Purdy, *Thomas Hardy: A Bibliographical Study*, p. 239.

THE MOCK WIFE treats a fictional incident associated with the execution of Mary Channing in Maumbury Ring, Dorchester, on March 21, 1705. Hardy describes the Ring in Chapter XI of *The Mayor of Casterbridge* and refers to the execution of Mary Channing: ". . . in 1705 a woman who had murdered her husband was half-strangled and then burnt there in the presence of ten thousand spectators. Tradition reports that at a certain stage of the burning her heart burst and leapt out of her body, to the terror of them all."

When archeological excavations at Maumbury Ring were undertaken in 1908, Moberly Bell of the *Times* asked Hardy for an article about it. Hardy replied with "Maumbury Ring," published on October 9, and in this article told the story of Mary Channing: "This was the death suffered there on March 21, 1705-06, of a girl who had not yet reached her nineteenth year. . . . This girl was the wife of a grocer in the town, a handsome young woman 'of good natural parts,' and educated 'to a proficiency suitable enough to one of her sex, to which likewise was added dancing.' She was tried and condemned for poisoning her husband, a Mr. Thomas Channing, to whom she had been married against her wish by the compulsion of her parents."[1]

The article does not mention the incident of "The Mock Wife." The poem names the grocer *John* Channing instead of Thomas. The court records state Mary Channing's conviction for "murdering Thomas Channing . . . by poisoning him."[2] Hardy certainly knew, as his article indicates, that the name was Thomas. In his copy of Hutchins's *History of Dorset,* the name is given as Richard Channing; Hardy in pencil crossed out "Richard" and above it wrote "Thomas."[3] Confusion regarding the name is found in popular broadsides and other accounts of this notorious execution. For example, *The Lives and Adventures of the Most Famous Highwaymen, Pirates &c.* tells the story as "The Life of Mary Channel," gives the wrong date (1703) for the execution, and names the murdered man as "Mr. Channel, a wealthy Grocer of Dorchester," without a first name.[4]

"The Mock Wife," giving the name as John, may rest upon oral tradition. The story is told as by one who heard it (he says, "as they tell") and who verifies it by knowing "the house, the date." In addition to whatever he found in print, Hardy listened to local tales. His notebook for January 25, 1919, records: "Mr. Prideaux tells me more details of the death of Mary Channing, burnt for the poisoning of her husband— (not proven) —in Maumbury Rings, Dorchester, in 1705. They were told him by old M——, a direct descendant of one who was a witness of the execution. He said that after she had been strangled and the burning had commenced she recovered consciousness (probably owing to the pain from the flames) and writhed and shrieked. . . .[5] The above account, with other details— (such as the smell of roast meat, etc.) —was handed down from my respected ancestor who was present and gives a sufficiently horrible picture."[6] Mr. Prideaux may have given Channing's name as John and included the story of Hardy's poem. "The Mock Wife" has the general form of a traditional ballad.

Hardy's "not proven" in his notebook and the sympathy for the accused wife suggested in the poem ("Guilty she may not be" and "truly judged, or false") may reflect an attitude noted in *The Early Life* for August, 1889: "When a married woman who has a lover kills her husband, she does not really wish to kill the husband; she wishes to kill the situation."[7]

1. See Orel, *Thomas Hardy's Personal Writings*, pp. 228-30.

2. Assizes 23/4, for 1697-1712, in the Public Records Office, London.

3. II, 796, in the Dorset County Museum. The name appears as Richard in various other places, as in Windle, *The Wessex of Thomas Hardy*, p. 35.

4. Clipped out and inserted into Charles Warner's scrapbook for the revision (third edition) of Hutchins's *History of Dorset*, in the Dorset County Museum. I have seen references to other such accounts, as to *Serious Admonitions to Youth, in a Short Account of the Life, Trial, Condemnation, and Execution of Mrs. Mary Channing* (London: Benjamin Bragg, at the Black Raven, 1706). This account is not in the British Museum.

5. Some shocking details are here omitted.

6. Evelyn Hardy, *Thomas Hardy's Notebooks*, pp. 82-83.

7. P. 289; *Life*, p. 221.

THE FIGHT ON DURNOVER MOOR may represent an actual event. The date "183—" and the names that refer to places near Dorchester suggest that the fight took place before Hardy's birth and may have been related to the poet by his mother or grandmother.

"Durnover" is Hardy's name for Fordington, now included in Dorchester, and Moor indicates the water-meadows lying between branches of the Frome River just east of Dorchester. Grey's Bridge, on the parapet of which the narrator "pitched" her box, is the second bridge on the London Road leading eastward from Dorchester. "Pummery Ridge" is Poundbury, a hill northwest of the town. Botany Bay was a British penal colony in Australia. The theme of the poem, in which circumstances cause a compassionate action to end in tragedy, is characteristic of Hardy.

LAST LOOK ROUND ST. MARTIN'S FAIR presents the images that came to Hardy's mind at the close of a day at the fair. St. Martin's Fair was formerly held at Martinstown (originally called St. Martin), a village about two and a half miles southwest of Dorchester. The "Great Forest" from which the "heathcroppers" (wild ponies) came is New Forest, an extensive, partly wooded area that was formerly a royal hunting preserve; it lies along the borders of Hampshire, Dorset, and Wiltshire.

The theme of the poem is stated in the images, especially if the sun and the moon are read as having the symbolic significance Hardy usually gave them: the sun as a warm god and the moon as a realistic view of the world. In the poem, the sun is called a "hot idol," and the moon is likened to a "brass dial gone green" and called "cold." As the sun sinks and the moon rises, the aspect of the fair changes. Its marketing and its bright pleasures struggle vainly against everyday reality, as the "woman in red" resolutely "talks ribaldry . . . as natural gaiety." By moonlight, it is seen as "a weary work she'd readily stay," that is, give up.

THE CARICATURE in the manuscript had, deleted, the date of composition, "About 1890."[1] The date, when Hardy was working on *Tess of the D'Urbervilles*, suggests some connection with the novel. When Tess and Angel begin their honeymoon at Wellbridge, they see painted on the wall two "horrid women." "The long pointed features, narrow eye, and smirk of the one, so suggestive of merciless treachery; the bill-hook nose, large teeth, and bold eye of the other, suggesting arrogance to the point of ferocity, haunt the beholder afterwards in his dreams." When Tess explains that these are portraits of "ladies of the d'Urberville family, the ancient lords of this manor," Angel observes that Tess's fine features are traceable in these exaggerated forms. The observation subtly prepares him to reject her after her confession. He cannot dismiss the vision of the cruel faces that seem to caricature Tess's. When irresolute whether to go to Tess or not, Angel again catches sight of one of the "d'Urberville dames. . . . In the candlelight the painting was more than unpleasant. Sinister design lurked in the woman's features. . . . The check was sufficient. He resumed his retreat and descended." (Chapters XXXIV and XXXV.) Possibly Hardy, in meditating this section of *Tess*, invented the story of "The Caricature," with its similar effect upon the lover's emotions. (See the notes on "Amabel.")

1. Purdy, *Thomas Hardy: A Bibliographical Study*, p. 239.

A LEADER OF FASHION was first published in the *Adelphi* for November, 1925. The manuscript shows a deleted title, "The Fine Lady."[1] Hardy's leader of fashion is perhaps derived from reflections like that in his journal for March 15, 1890: "With E. to a crush at the Jeunes'. Met Mrs. T. and her great eyes in a corner of the rooms, as if washed up by the surging crowd. . . . But these women! If put into rough wrappers in a turnip-field, where would their beauty be? . . . Society, *collectively*, has neither seen what any ordinary person can see, read what every ordinary person has read, nor thought what every ordinary person has thought."[2] Yet the poem is more compassionate than satirical. Hardy liked many fashionable women and perhaps pitied them because they missed, in their social whirl, the depth that close contact with nature and the simplicities of toil may give.

1. Purdy, *Thomas Hardy: A Bibliographical Study*, p. 239.
2. *The Early Life*, pp. 293-94; *Life*, p. 224.

MIDNIGHT ON BEECHEN, 187— presents an incident in Hardy's courtship of Emma Gifford in June of 1873. She was visiting a friend in Bath, and he went to see her there. The visit is recorded in *The Early Life*: "From London Hardy travelled on to Bath, arriving late at night and putting up at 8 Great Stanhope Street. . . . June 23. Excursions about Bath and Bristol with the ladies. June 28. To Clifton with Miss Gifford. . . . June 30. About Bath alone. . . . July 1. A day's trip with Miss G. to Chepstow, the Wye, the Wynd Cliff, which we climbed, and Tintern, where we repeated some of Wordsworth's lines thereon. . . . July 2. Bath to Dorchester."[1]

In the poem, Hardy is alone on Beechen Cliff after midnight, where his view takes in the sleeping city, and his mind dwells upon the girl from whom he has just parted. Beechen Cliff rises just south of Bath and overlooks it.[2] The "dim concave" of the poem is the Royal Crescent along which "lamps as glow-worms lie," the towers those of Bath Abbey, and the spire that of St. Michael's Church. The scene to the lover Hardy seemed ecstatic. Though the poem was not published until 1925, the tone of the last stanza suggests that it may have been written near the time of the experience.

1. Pp. 123-24; *Life*, pp. 93-94.
2. Hutchings, *Inside Somerset*, has on p. iv, following p. 88, a photographic "View from Beechen Cliff."

THE AËROLITE seems a fanciful development of a note Hardy made on April 7, 1889: "A woeful fact—that the human race is too extremely developed for its corporeal conditions, the nerves being evolved to an activity abnormal in such an environment. . . . It may be questioned if Nature . . . so far back as when she crossed the line from invertebrates to vertebrates, did not exceed her mission. This planet does not supply the materials for happiness to higher existences."[1]

The poem pictures two groups of "seers," one who would "Oust" this awareness and return now-sentient life to the "Normal unawareness" of, one might say, flowers, and one who would limit awareness to good and conceal "all anguishment."

The fantasy that "a germ of Consciousness" came, by means of an aërolite (meteor) from some happy world, suggests science fiction. Records of Hardy's reading do not show much interest in this genre, though his biography twice mentions meeting H. G. Wells, in 1907 and 1914.[2] The "far globe, where no distress / Had means to mar supreme delight" sounds like a Shelleyan dream. Elliott says that Hardy's "paradisiac tendency derives particularly from the kind of romanticism that found its extreme expression in Shelley: the yearning for a comfortable harmony, social and spiritual, which wears the guise of human happiness but in which the essential conditions of human happiness are slurred or submerged." Elsewhere, as in the conclusion of *The Dynasts*, he would cherish consciousness "as the seed of a new sympathy which may possibly grow, and renovate human life." [3]

1. *Early Life*, pp. 285-86; *Life*, p. 218.
2. *Later Years*, pp. 124, 163; *Life*, pp. 334, 366.
3. "Spectral Etching by Thomas Hardy in the Shorter Poems," pp. 94-95.

THE PROSPECT, dated December, 1912, within a month after the death of Hardy's first wife Emma, treats her garden party of July 16, mentioned in *The Later Years*. Hardy, who had been in London, "returned to Max Gate just in time to be at a garden party on July 16—the last his wife ever gave—which it would have grieved him afterwards to have missed . . . Mrs. Hardy being then, apparently, in her customary health and vigour." [1] The poem contrasts then-and-now. The imagery that describes the "December sky," the aging poet, and the "skeletoned hedge," leads past the "merry boys" to the conclusion: he wishes to join Emma in death.

1. P. 153; *Life*, p. 359.

GENITRIX LAESA is written in the meter of a twelfth-century Latin poem, "Officium Beatae Mariae," by Adam of S. Victor, published in *Sequences from the Sarum Missal*, pages 152-54.[1] (See the notes on "Sine Prole.") The title means "The Wounded Mother." The "concordia discors" of the second stanza means "discordant harmony." "Among the marked passages in his [Hardy's] 1859 Bohn edition of Horace is 'the jarring harmony of things,' which phrase or its Latin original—*concordia discors*—Hardy altered in the After Scene [of *The Dynasts*] to 'the chordless chime of Things.' "[2] Hardy addresses Mother Nature, commenting upon the processes of evolutionary development, which the Mother carries out painstakingly in the effort to fulfill a dreamed ideal, but which are marred by imperfections visible to human reason. Why should man seek to amend Nature's flaws when "all is sinking / To dissolubility?"

1. Purdy, *Thomas Hardy: A Bibliographical Study*, p. 240.
2. Wright, *The Shaping of "The Dynasts,"* p. 10, citing *Epistles* I. 12, *The Works of Horace*, trans. C. Smart. Hardy's copy is in the Colby College Library. The phrase is also found in Lucan I, 98.

THE FADING ROSE personifies a rose that inquires of the gardeners where she has gone who "used to come and muse on me." In relation to "The Spell of the Rose," the dead woman is Hardy's first wife Emma, who had died in 1912.

WHEN OATS WHERE REAPED portrays Hardy in the summer after the death of his first wife Emma in 1912, on his way to her grave in Stinsford Churchyard. He meditates upon the lack of harmony between them in the years before her death and expresses remorse for his share in it. The word "now" suggests that he was not at the time aware how much he wounded her. He discovered the fact when he read her *Some Recollections* after her death. The title and the opening line may be read as suggesting that what is sown in anger must be reaped in remorse.

LOUIE is set in Stinsford Churchyard, where Hardy, visiting the grave of his first wife Emma, the "elect one," thinks also of "Louie the buoyant." She was Louisa Harding, whom Hardy had shyly courted for a while when he was a boy. Miss Harding (for she never married) died on September 12, 1913, and was buried in an unmarked grave not far from Emma's. The poem says "Long two strangers they and far apart" because, though Miss Harding lived in Dorchester, apparently she and Emma were not known to one another.

"SHE OPENED THE DOOR" belongs in theme with the "Poems of 1912-13." It is a summary of Hardy's courtship of Emma Gifford in Cornwall in 1870-74. Emma opened five doors for him, one in fact and four in the metaphors of the poem. When he arrived at St. Juliot Rectory on the evening of March 7, 1870, Emma met him at the door.[1]

Hardy's memories of his courtship were stimulated by his reading her *Some Recollections* after her death in 1912. Evelyn Hardy and Gittings have pointed out that the first stanza echoes a passage in Emma's manuscript: "Tintagel was a very remote place then, and the inhabitants expected few visitors, moreover of those who came few remained long enough to see the winter waves and foam reaching hundreds of feet up the stern, strong dark rocks with the fantastic revellings of the gulls, puffins and rooks, jackdaws, in attendance, 'black souls and white,' sometimes called." They add: "The unusual descriptive word in *Some Recollections*, 'revellings,' applied to the sea-birds in the storm, is echoed closely by Hardy's line 'Of waters rife with revelry,' which is obscure unless one follows . . . its meaning in this passage of *Some Recollections*."[2]

The "cell" of the second stanza seems a reference to the humdrum realities of Hardy's work as an architect, from which he was "fain to flee" into literature, in which flight Emma encouraged him. The fourth stanza, in the present tense, seems a direct reference to *Some Recollections*.

[538]

1. *Early Life*, p. 98; *Life*, p. 74.
2. Eds., *Some Recollections by Emma Hardy*, pp. 76-77.

"WHAT'S THERE TO TELL?" seems a development from the poet's humming the tune suggested in the refrain. The theme is that life is a kind of aimless tune.

THE HARBOUR BRIDGE presents a scene at Weymouth, where a bridge crosses the River Wey at a point where the Wey turns eastward toward the sea. The bridge runs north and south. It separates the outer harbor to the east, in which ocean-going ferries and other ships dock, from the inner basin for small craft. Hardy observed the scene from the quay east of the bridge, so that the bridge and figures on it were silhouetted against the sky at sunset and after. He had one or more companions, as he says "we," apparently watching the traffic described in the poem.

The poem may portray an evening's observation in 1869 or early 1870, when he was working as architect and lived in Weymouth, or it may present a later occurrence. (He was in Weymouth often.) The poem sketches a melodrama perhaps common in sailors' families. A number of unusual words appear in the poem: "cutwater" (V-pointed pier under the bridge), "painters" (ropes for tying up boats), "bollards" (standards to which ropes are tied), "leans and stops" (leans on the parapet), and "stars ghost forth" (appear dimly in the darkening sky).

VAGRANT'S SONG was first published in *Nash's and Pall Mall Magazine* for January, 1925.[1] Miss Deacon, in her researches into Hardy's ancestral background, discovered Hardy's relationship to a "tramp" who may be the vagrant of the poem. Speaking of Melbury Osmund, the birthplace of Hardy's mother, she writes: "Halfway down the hill was the Glebe [tithe] Barn, which, we are told by old people in the neighbourhood, was once the haunt and sleeping place of William Hand, a cousin of Hardy's, a tramp whom Hardy used to visit."[2]

I have not discovered the song in which the "old Wessex refrain" occurs, but Bernard Jones, the poet, of Fifehead Neville, suggests that the phrase "Che-hane, mother" might mean "I am safe, mother." The "Che" seems a corruption of the Germanic "Ich" (I), and "hane" could be a form of the dialect word for "to enclose" (as used of a field) or save from harm. "Burns" are brooks or small streams.

1. Purdy, *Thomas Hardy: A Bibliographical Study*, p. 240.
2. *Hardy's Grandmother, Besty, and Her Family*, p. 4.

FARMER DUNMAN'S FUNERAL presents a characteristic that Hardy attributed to Wessex country-folk: the enjoyment of a jolly funeral. In *The Return of the Native*, he had Timothy Fairway say: "For my part I like a good hearty funeral as well as anything. You've as splendid victuals and drink as at other parties, and even better." (Book First, Chapter III.) With more pathos, but similar humor, the chorus characters in *The Mayor of Casterbridge* discuss the death of Susan. (Chapter XVIII.)

In the "second proof" of the page-proofs for *Human Shows*, Hardy wrote a stanza to be inserted between the second and third stanzas as published: "And that no one should forget them / In boldest scrawls he inked / On the shelf where he had set them / 'Mind that this rum is drinked.' "

THE SEXTON AT LONGPUDDLE may reflect Hardy's hearing some sexton in this vicinity express self-satisfaction at the neatness of the graves he tended. "Longpuddle" is Hardy's name for a string of villages in the valley of the Piddle River that runs south-eastward five to ten miles northeast of Dorchester. The villages include Piddletrenthide, Piddlehinton, and Puddletown.

THE HARVEST-SUPPER was first published in the *New Magazine* for December, 1925.[1] The headnote "*Circa* 1850" identifies the occasion as one described in *The Early Life*. When Hardy was about ten years old, he "jumped at the offer of a young woman of the village to take him to a harvest-supper. . . . The 'Supper,' an early meal at that date, probably about four o'clock, was over by the time they reached the barn,[2] and tea was going on, after which there was singing and dancing, some non-commissioned officers having been invited from the barracks by the Squire as partners for the girls." Hardy, "being wildly fond of dancing, she [Mrs. Julia Augusta Martin, lady of the manor] gave him for a partner a little niece of hers about his own age staying at her house, who had come with her . . . . It was the only harvest-supper and dance that he ever saw, save one that he dropped into by chance years after . . . . this harvest-home was among the last at which the old traditional ballads were sung. . . . The particular ballad which he remembered hearing that night from the lips of the farm-women was that one variously called 'The Outlandish Knight,' 'May Colvine,' 'The Western Tragedy,' etc. He could recall to old age the scene of the young women in their light gowns . . . leaning against each other as they warbled the Dorset version of the ballad. . . :

'Lie there, lie there, thou false-hearted man,
    Lie there instead o' me;
For six pretty maidens thou hast a-drown'd here,
    But the seventh hath drown-ed thee!'

. . . .

'O tell no more, my pretty par-rot,
    Lay not the blame on me;
And your cage shall be made o' the glittering gold,
    Wi' a door o' the white ivo-rie!' "[3]

Hardy was probably stimulated to write the poem by a visit in 1924 to the site of the supper: "On the 22nd of October Hardy with his wife visited for the first time since his childhood the old barn at the back of Kingston Maurward. Here, as a small boy, he had listened to village girls singing old ballads."[4]

The "non-commissioned officers" of *The Early Life* are identified in the poem as the "Scotch-Greys," a cavalry unit (now a tank unit), from time to time housed in the military barracks at Dorchester.[5] The story of Nell and the ghost is ballad-like in substance, in a poem ballad-like in meter, and about ballad-singing.

1. Purdy, *Thomas Hardy: A Bibliographical Study*, p. 241.
2. At Kingston Maurward.
3. *Early Life*, pp. 24-26; *Life*, pp. 19-20.
4. *Later Years*, p. 240; *Life*, p. 426.
5. Information from Colonel Wakeley, Dorset Military Museum, Dorchester.

AT A PAUSE IN A COUNTRY DANCE, with its headnote of "Middle of Last Century," may rest on an incident Hardy observed as a boy, when he went often with his father to fiddle at country dances.[1] The tune that the couple "loved so," "The Dashing White Sergeant," was composed by Sir Henry Rowley Bishop (1786-1855), the first English composer to be knighted for his music. As composer for Covent Garden and Drury Lane Theatres, he was the author of numerous operas and cantatas; he wrote the music for "Home, Sweet Home" in the opera *Clari*.

As often in Hardy's treatment of the effects of music, the tune has an ecstatic effect upon the mother, moving her to neglect her child. The "frozen moon" lighting up "frozen snow" symbolizes the sinister meaning of her behavior.

1. *Early Life*, pp. 29-30; *Life*, p. 23.

ON THE PORTRAIT OF A WOMAN ABOUT TO BE HANGED was first published in the *London Mercury* for February, 1923.[1] The woman was Mrs. Edith Thompson of Ilford, convicted of murdering her husband, Percy Thompson, in complicity with her lover, Frederick Bywaters. A photograph in the *Illustrated London News* for December 16, 1922, shows Mrs. Thompson seated, a slender, handsome woman, demurely dressed in what seems to be a dark silk, with eyes upon a paper in her lap. She looks "comely and capable," more like an attractive housewife than a murderess.

The trial of Mrs. Thompson and Bywaters aroused extraordinary interest. The story is fully told in the *Manchester Guardian* in articles from "Accused Widow and Friend" on November 24, 1922, through "The Ilford Executions" on January 10, 1923. Bywaters was a twenty-year-old ship's storekeeper; Mrs. Thompson, twenty-eight, was a milliner; and her husband was a shipping clerk. Thompson, though aware that his wife and Bywaters were lovers, was unwilling to give his wife a divorce; he had ordered Bywaters to stay away from his home. Mrs. Thompson and Bywaters were convicted of murdering Thompson between June 1, 1921, and October 4, 1922, by Mrs. Thompson's administering poisons during this period, and Bywaters's stabbing Thompson on the night of October 4. Evidence included passionate correspondence between the lovers, with mentions of the efforts to poison. Yet protest marchers paraded at Holloway Prison with posters reading "If these two are hanged, the judge and jury are murderers."

Hardy's poem suggests that he believed Mrs. Thompson guilty, though the theme of the poem is that the deeper guilt lay with her "Causer" that "implanted . . . / The Clytaemnestra spirit" in her.[2] The philosophic question is why the Creator made her "Sound in the germ," but "sent a worm / To madden Its handiwork."

1. Purdy, *Thomas Hardy: A Bibliographical Study*, p. 241.
2. The phrase refers to the story of Clytemnestra and her lover Aegisthus, who murdered her husband Agamemnon, in the dramas of Sophocles and Aeschylus. Madame Tussaud's waxworks has effigies of Mrs. Thompson and Bywaters in the Chamber of Horrors.

THE CHURCH AND THE WEDDING was first published in the *Chapbook* for March, 1923.[1] Harold Monro of this magazine had asked Hardy for a poem, but a letter from Monro on January 20 indicates that both he and Hardy were unhappy about "The Church and the Wedding." Monro wrote: "You describe it as 'a very poor thing.' Is it, I wonder, the 2nd stanza that causes you to be so unflattering to it? That stanza (I feel sure you won't mind my saying so) seems to pull it down. But the three succeeding ones bring it up again. . . . You are kind enough to suggest that if I don't like this poem you will look for another. The idea of sending a M.S. back to you is truly a laughable one. But if by chance you did come across, or write, something be-

fore the end of the month that you yourself thought better, then per-
haps you would add to your kindness by sending it instead."[2]

Possibly Hardy heard the story when employed by Hicks or Crick-
may in restoring old churches. That the lover offered his bride a re-
built church, with the bishop to officiate, and that the quarrel took
place in the church suggest that the would-be bridegroom was a vicar.

1. Purdy, *Thomas Hardy: A Bibliographical Study*, p. 241.
2. In the Dorset County Museum.

THE SHIVER seems a fiction built upon the folk-saying that "If
you shiver, some one is walking on your future grave."[1] Miss Deacon,
however, has surmised that the speaker of the poem may represent
Tryphena Sparks. She writes: "Hardy in extreme old age published
his poem *The Shiver*, as written by Tryphena, on the occasion of one
of his later settings-forth to Lyonnesse."[2] The departure of the poem
does suggest Hardy's first trip to Cornwall on March 7, 1870, when
he left Higher Bockhampton at dawn, and on his return he might
have described Emma Gifford, living near the coast, as a "sea-goddess."
Miss Deacon offers no evidence. Presumably Tryphena at this time
was attending Stockwell College in London. The circumstances of
Hardy's "later settings-forth" differ from those of the poem. Possibly
the poem is in some way based upon the triangle of Tryphena, Hardy,
and Emma, but if so it seems to mingle factual incidents and fiction.

1. Firor, *Folkways in Thomas Hardy*, p. 23.
2. *Hardy's Sweetest Image*, p. 19.

"NOT ONLY I," as the last stanza indicates, is spoken by a dead
woman. She took with her to the grave all the memories, joys, and
secrets of her life. Parallels between these memories and incidents in
the life of Hardy's first wife Emma suggest that he may have had her
and her *Some Recollections* in mind.

SHE SAW HIM, SHE SAID presents an eerie dialogue between a
husband and a wife about a premonitory wraith and the sound of a
tolling bell that had not tolled. That the wraith of the husband was
seen talking with the sexton (the grave-digger) suggests that he is
soon to die. The husband's sight of the moon makes the same sug-
gestion; in Hardy's poems the moon symbolizes something sinister.

Possibly the poem was suggested by a story Hardy's friend Edmund
Gosse may have told him. On July 14, 1923, Gosse wrote to T. J.
Wise: "Last Tuesday . . . I had a hallucination. From the balcony
here I saw you (I could have sworn) arrive in a taxi, and descend
with a large yellow paper parcel. I awaited you with joy, but nobody
came, and the servants declared they had not seen you! A mystery."[1]

Hardy had previously written "The Superstitious Man's Story" in *A Few Crusted Characters*, on a similar theme: William Privett's wraith is seen by his wife to leave the house while in fact William lies upstairs asleep; the wraith is seen by others in the church porch at this time, on Old Midsummer Eve. These apparitions of the still-living man foretell his death shortly after.

1. In the British Museum.

ONCE AT SWANAGE seems to picture a moment in the life of Hardy and his wife Emma during the time they lived at Swanage, from July, 1875, to March, 1876. The couple are watching the sea beat upon the cliffs at Swanage on a moonlit night. They observe nature in turmoil, with weird imagery and sinister suggestions.

The phrase "Roaring high and roaring low" suggests the occasion as one described in *The Early Life*: "Evening. Just after sunset. Sitting with E. on a stone under the wall before the Refreshment Cottage. . . . On the left Durlstone Head roaring high and low, like a giant asleep. On the right a thrush. Above the bird hangs the new moon, and a steady planet." [1]

In Hardy's poetry the moon is a sinister symbol. The moon of the poem is made doubly sinister by the light like "a witch-flame's weird-some sheen" that "greened our gaze," while the roar of the sea "symboled the slamming of doors." The final line suggests that Hardy and Emma stand united against some threat to their newly married happiness, the threat of an alien and frightening force in nature. The poem may be read in the light of later fulfillment of such a threat in Emma's delusions. (See the notes on "To a Sea-Cliff," apparently a companion poem.)

1. Pp. 141-42; *Life*, pp. 107-8.

THE FLOWER'S TRAGEDY treats a flower cherished by a woman, neglected after her death, and discovered as "a mummied thing." Purdy states that the manuscript adds as the date of composition, "About 1910." [1] As Hardy's wife Emma died in 1912, the poem cannot refer to her. It may refer to the death of his mother in 1904, or it may be fiction, perhaps suggested to Hardy by a scene in *The Return of the Native*. When Clym goes to straighten up his mother's home after her death, "He noticed that the flowers in the window had died for want of water, and he placed them out upon the ledge, that they might be taken away." (Book Fifth, Chapter II.)

1. *Thomas Hardy: A Bibliographical Study*, p. 241.

AT THE AQUATIC SPORTS may be set at Weymouth, seven miles from Dorchester and sufficiently rural for the sport of crab-catching.

The theme is Hardy's observation of professional entertainers so jaded by their business that they have no interest in merrymaking.

A WATCHER'S REGRET, subtitled "J. E.'s Story," may be a factual anecdote, but I have not discovered the identity of J. E.

HORSES ABOARD expresses a compassion for animals that runs all through Hardy's poetry. Horses were among the more sensitive animals for whose suffering he suffered. He wrote in his notebook for July 13, 1888: "After being in the street: What was it on the faces of those horses?—Resignation. Their eyes looked at me, haunted me. When afterwards I heard their tramp as I lay in bed, the ghosts of their eyes came in to me, saying, 'Where is your justice, O man and ruler?' "[1] Hardy was outraged that horses were used in battle during the Boer War. In January, 1899, "Mr. W. T. Stead had asked him to express his opinion on 'A Crusade of Peace' in a periodical he was about to publish under the name of *War against War*. In . . . reply Hardy wrote: 'As a preliminary, all civilized nations might at least show their humanity by convenanting that no horses should be employed in battle except for transport.' "[2]

The fact that the scene is an embarcation like that of the poems "Embarcation" and "Departure" suggests that "Horses Aboard" (not dated) either was written at the time of the Boer War (1899-1902) or represents a memory of it. Indignation at the use of horses in war runs through *The Dynasts*, as in the observation of the Pities at the Battle of Borodino: "Those shady shapes / Are horses, maimed in myriads, tearing round / In maddening pangs, the harnessings they wear / Clanking discordant jingles as they tear!" (Part Third, I, v.)

1. *Early Life*, p. 278; *Life*, p. 211.
2. *Later Years*, p. 81; *Life*, p. 303.

THE HISTORY OF AN HOUR celebrates a happy hour of love. Hardy used the rose as a symbol for love.

THE MISSED TRAIN seems to relate an actual experience. In an undated letter, Robert Graves, an editor of the *Owl*, asked Hardy for a poem for the issue "we are getting out this Christmas." On a card marked "Received Oct. 2, 1922," Graves wrote to Mrs. Hardy: "Please thank Mr. Hardy for his exquisite poem which we are all delighted with."[1] The poem appeared in the *Owl* a year later, in November, 1923.[2] It may treat one of Hardy's homeward journeys from Cornwall during his courtship of Emma Gifford in the early 1870's.

1. In the Dorset County Museum.
2. Purdy, *Thomas Hardy: A Bibliographical Study*, p. 241.

UNDER HIGH-STOY HILL seems to present Hardy's memory of a hill-climbing expedition in his youth. (Surely Hardy is the "he brow-lined" still alive of the four who climbed.) High Stoy is a hill about half a mile northwest of Minterne Magna, or nine miles north and slightly west of Dorchester. A group climbing the hill from "Ivel-wards" (Hardy's term for "toward Yeovil") would clamber up steep, difficult paths from Blackmoor Vale.

The tone of the poem, with its "Chattering like birds" and laughter in the moonlight, suggests that his companions were a young man and two girls. Possibly one of the girls was his sister Mary; various poems, for instance, "Molly Gone," speak of his pleasure in outings with her.

The repeated "what lay behind" must mean the realities of the future that the merry young people did not foresee. In the first stanza, the phrase could refer to the valley, but serve also as a symbol for coming experience in the valleys of life. The moon that blinks upon them is a symbol for the cold reality that "since that night / We have well learnt."

In his notebook for August 11, 1922, he wrote: "Motored to Sturminster Newton, and back by Dogbury Gate. Walked to top of High Stoy with [Newman?] Flower (probably for the last time), thence back home."[1] Possibly this walk up High Stoy brought to Hardy's memory the climb described in the poem.

1. *Later Years*, p. 227; *Life*, p. 417.

AT THE MILL is set in Puddletown, five miles northeast of Dorchester on the London Road. The setting is indicated in the term "Yalbury Brow," a local name for Yellowham Hill, less than two miles from Puddletown. The market to which Miller Knox had gone when the murders and suicide took place is Dorchester. The mill may be identified in the ruins of an old mill-and-pond at "Mill-Tail-Shallow" in the River Piddle as it runs through Puddletown.

As Hardy's cousin Tryphena Sparks lived in Puddletown near Mill-Tail-Shallow, the story may rest upon oral tradition that she related to him. If so, the "we" of the opening line may mean "my family." Though the situations are different, the hanging of two children and a suicide recall the similar incident in *Jude the Obscure*. (Part VI, Chapter II.)

ALIKE AND UNLIKE in the manuscript added to the title "*She speaks.*"[1] The subtitle "Great-Orme's Head" relates the poem to an incident recorded in Hardy's diary for May 18, 1893. Hardy and his first wife Emma were on their way to Dublin in response to an invitation to visit Lord Houghton, the Lord-Lieutenant of Ireland, and his sister, Mrs. Arthur Henniker. The entry in the diary reads: "Left Euston by 9 o'-clock morning train with E. for Llandudno, *en route* for Dublin. After arrival at Llandudno drove around Great Orme's Head. Magnificent deep purple-grey mountains, the fine colour being on account of an approaching storm."[2]

The "she" who speaks the poem is Emma. In the first stanza, she and Hardy observed the same sights and stored them up for "joint recallings." On that same day, says the second stanza, something was superimposed upon their similar "eye-records" in a way to blot them out. This new sight made a deep impression, "tragic, gruesome, gray," upon Hardy's mind, but only a slight, "commonplace" impression upon Emma's. As the view at Great-Orme's Head might have drawn the couple together, the superimposed vision tended "to sever us thenceforth alway."

In his list of Hardy's poems to be associated with Mrs. Henniker, Purdy includes, without explanation, "Alike and Unlike."[3] This hint suggests an interpretation. It was not on "the very day" of the trip to Great-Orme's Head, May 18, that Hardy and Emma arrived in Dublin and met Mrs. Henniker, but on the next day, May 19. Hardy wrote: "We were received by Mrs. Henniker, the Lord-Lieutenant's sister. A charming, *intuitive* woman apparently."[4] As Emma, speaking the poem, interprets what happened, Hardy fell in love with Mrs. Henniker; this fact and Emma's jealously tended to "sever" them thenceforth.

Phelps relates "Alike and Unlike" to the poem "That Moment," which may be considered a picture of the moment when Emma spoke out her jealously.[5]

Possibly Hardy based "Alike and Unlike" on observations of Emma's attitude and made use of her manuscript that he destroyed, "What I Think of My Husband," just as in other poems presenting her point of view he used her *Some Recollections*.

1. Purdy, *Thomas Hardy: A Bibliographical Study*, p. 242.
2. *Later Years*, p. 18; *Life*, p. 254.
3. *Thomas Hardy: A Bibliographical Study*, p. 345.
4. *Later Years*, p. 18; *Life*, p. 254.
5. *Annotations by Thomas Hardy in His Bibles and Prayer-Book*, p. 11.

THE THING UNPLANNED is evidently about a crisis in Hardy's life. The "thatched post-office" is that at Lower Bockhampton, where Hardy received his mail as long as he lived at his birthplace. The post office was in a thatched house on Bockhampton Lane a hundred yards or so north of the bridge across a by-water of the Frome River; beyond the bridge, the water-meadows are filled with rills during the winter rains.

As the poem does not name the "thing unplanned" and the "thing better," one can only surmise a crisis when Hardy was moved by a "long tender letter" to give up one plan in favor of another. Possibly the letter was from Emma Gifford about 1871, when he was still engaged to Tryphena Sparks. Then the relationship that "must be snapped!" may be that with Emma, and the thing better is his breaking the engagement to Tryphena and marriage to Emma.

Phelps suggests that the time was in the 1890's, and the tender letter was from Mrs. Arthur Henniker. He says: "One letter that Hardy received from Mrs. Henniker at a time when his feelings were reciprocated is remembered in *The Thing Unplanned.* . . . This letter must have been collected by Hardy 'poste restante' at Bockhampton."[1] If so, the thing better was the decision to continue his friendship with Mrs. Henniker, but not on an emotional basis.

1. *Annotations by Thomas Hardy in His Bibles and Prayer-Book*, p. 11.

THE SHEEP-BOY pictures the coming of a heavy fog to Rainbarrows on Puddletown ("Egdon") Heath. The "yawning, sunned concave / Of purple" seems the valley of rhododendron south of Rainbarrows, along the so-called "Rhododendron Mile" between Stinsford and Tincleton. (In the poem, this valley is called "Draäts'-Hollow," the word "draäts" being Dorset dialect for "drafts" or moist winds.) The sheep-boy sees the fog swirl across the hills and valleys of the Heath from the sea about seven miles to the south. He sees it roll over and blot out the distant "Pokeswell" (Poxwell) Hills five miles away, like the pillar of cloud that guided the Israelites in the wilderness. (Exod. 13:21.) Quickly it blots out "Kite-Hill" (Castle Hill, about a mile northeast of Rainbarrows) and the lonely shepherd boy.

The poem seems a portrait of a mood of the Egdon described in the opening chapter of *The Return of the Native*. Besides the picture of Egdon in its somber moods, the novel presents it in glowing sunlight like that of the poem: "The July sun shone over Egdon and fired its crimson heather to scarlet. It was the one season of the year, and the one weather of the season, in which the heath was gorgeous." (Book Fourth, Chapter I.) The coming of the fog is paralleled in *Far from the Madding Crowd*: "Poorgrass saw strange clouds and scrolls of mist rolling over the long ridges which girt the landscape in that quarter [toward the Heath]. They came in yet greater volumes, and indolently crept across the intervening valleys, and around the withered papery flags of the moor and river brinks. Then their dank spongy forms closed in upon the sky. It was a sudden overgrowth of atmospheric fungi which had their roots in the neighbouring sea, and

by the time that horse, man, and corpse entered Yalbury Great Wood
. . . they were completely enveloped." (Chapter XLII.)

RETTY'S PHASES is "From an old draft of 1868." Purdy points
out that "This 'old draft,' called simply 'Song,' is now in the Dorset
County Museum, the earliest MS. of a poem by Hardy that survives.
It is . . . torn from a diary or note-book and headed 'June 22. 1868.' "[1]
In the manuscript "Retty" was originally "Hetty." This change need
not indicate that Hetty was a real person whose identity Hardy wished
to conceal. In her copy of *Tess of the D'Urbervilles*, Rebekah Owen
commented on the name of the character Retty Priddle: "Retty . . .
Sir William Jones says means affection. It is the name of the Hindoo
Goddess of Pleasure."[2] As Miss Owen talked often with Hardy, she
may have mentioned this fact to him, and he may have changed Hetty
to Retty to suggest the theme of the poem. The "Vale" of the third
stanza may mean the valley of the Frome, but it seems to symbolize
death.

1. *Thomas Hardy: A Bibliographical Study*, p. 242. The manuscript is repro-
duced facing this page.
2. In the Colby College Library.

A POOR MAN AND A LADY was intended to preserve an episode in
Hardy's unpublished novel, *The Poor Man and the Lady*. Fragments
from it were adapted for portions of *Desperate Remedies*, *Under the
Greenwood Tree*, *A Pair of Blue Eyes*, and *The Hand of Ethelberta*.
Hardy considerably altered what was left and published it in the *New
Quarterly Magazine* for July, 1878, under the title *An Indiscretion in
the Life of an Heiress*.[1] The original manuscript was destroyed.

On the basis of available evidence, Rutland traced the piecemeal
changes in the novel. Enough is clear to suggest that the Poor Man
of the poem represents Egbert Mayne of the novel, the son of Dorset
peasants, who went to London and became an architect. The Lady
represents Geraldine, daughter of the local squire. Romantically at-
tracted, but forbidden to meet by Geraldine's parents, they had be-
trothed themselves in "Tollamore" (Hardy's early name for Stinsford)
Church. Geraldine was persuaded by her parents to marry a squire.[2]
The scene in the poem of their meeting in a fashionable church in
Mayfair (in central London) was possibly in the original novel.

In theme, the poem represents Hardy's youthful protest against
the stratification of English rural life into distinct social classes. His
statement about the novel indicates the social radicalism of his youth.[3]
Though he is less radical in later novels, the theme of lovers separated
by a social gulf runs through them: Gabriel and Bathsheba in *Far*

from the Madding Crowd, Giles and Grace in *The Woodlanders,*
Swithin and Viviette in *Two on a Tower,* and Tess and Angel in *Tess
of the D'Urbervilles.*

1.Weber, ed., republished *An Indiscretion in the Life of an Heiress,* Baltimore:
The Johns Hopkins Press, 1935.
2. Rutland, *Thomas Hardy,* pp. 111-33.
3. For this statement, see *Early Life,* p. 81; *Life,* p. 61.

AN EXPOSTULATION seems Hardy's protest against a country girl's
desire to go to the city and there adopt fashions and cosmetics that
would spoil her "born grace."

TO A SEA-CLIFF concerns Durlston Head, a high hill south of
Swanage, where Hardy and his first wife Emma lived in the autumn
and winter of 1875-76. *The Early Life* says: "While here at Swanage
they walked daily on the cliffs and shore, Hardy noting thereon:
'Evening. Just after sunset. Sitting with E. on a stone under the wall
before the Refreshment Cottage. . . . On the left Durlstone [*sic*]
Head roaring high and low, like a giant asleep."[1]

Perhaps the poem tells a true story of this evening. The couple
are a "silent listless pair." Possibly Emma wished to spur Hardy by
arousing jealousy. She had helped him with the recently published
A Pair of Blue Eyes by making fair copies for the publisher, and
surely she thought of herself as the model for Elfride. In the novel,
when Elfride and Knight are on a cliff together, they watch the
steamer *Puffin* pass bearing Stephen Smith, Elfride's former lover.
(Chapter XXI.) Remembering the scene, Emma, in jest, self-dramati-
zation, or delusion, may have made the remark of the poem, with an
unexpected result upon Hardy's feelings.

"To a Sea-Cliff" is related to the same passage in *The Early Life*
as "Once at Swanage." The event of "To a Sea-Cliff" may explain the
sinister symbolism of its companion poem.

1. P. 142; *Life,* p. 108.

THE ECHO-ELF ANSWERS in the manuscript adds " (Impromptu) "
to the title.[1] Though the questioning poet guides the Echo-Elf by
placing the undesirable alternative last in each question, so that its
echo alone is heard, one feels in the cumulative effect that the Elf
answers with prophetic knowledge. As Olivero says, Echo shows the
poet "the anxious faces of his illusions in black aureoles of despair,
pointing out to him inevitable . . . mistakes . . . beyond the power of
wisdom, revealing to him . . . the future veiled from his sight, and
thus stirring up a fear and horror of love."[2]

The poem can be considered a retrospective statement of Hardy's youthful dreams set against the realities of his life. The loved one of the first two stanzas may be any one of various dream-girls, from Louisa Harding to Tryphena Sparks. The right bride of the fifth stanza may be Tryphena or Helen Paterson, and the wrong, Emma Gifford. (See the notes on "The Opportunity.") According to the final stanza, the only escape from the consequences of impulsive wrong decisions is in the grave.

1. Purdy, *Thomas Hardy: A Bibliographical Study*, p. 243.
2. "The Poetry of Hardy," p. 9.

CYNIC'S EPITAPH was first published as a companion to "Epitaph on a Pessimist" in the *London Mercury* for September, 1925.[1] As frequently in Hardy's poetry, the sun may be a symbol for an optimistic view of life.

1. Purdy, *Thomas Hardy: A Bibliographical Study*, p. 243.

A BEAUTY'S SOLILOQUY DURING HER HONEYMOON is apparently Hardy's interpretation of a bride's disdainful and even resentful attitude toward her "plain" but attentive husband, as observed in the Grand Hotel in 1892. This hotel in central London is at 126 Southampton Row, near Russell Square. *The Later Years* mentions Hardy's dining there in May, 1894.[1] The bride is a country girl, "dwelling much alone," whose vanity is stimulated by men's eyes upon her in luxurious surroundings.

1. P. 30; *Life*, p. 263.

DONAGHADEE celebrates a town Hardy had never seen. Donaghadee is a market town of County Down, Ireland, on the coast south of Belfast Lough; it is some twenty miles east of Belfast. The poem was inspired by a letter from a woman who lived there. The poem implies that Hardy had destroyed the letter and forgotten the woman's name, but remembered the "tender" tone and the name of the town.

Various people have speculated upon the identity of Hardy's correspondent. Marjorie Spencer, in a letter to the *Belfast Telegraph* on July 13, 1953, wrote that ". . . these lines were written by Thomas Hardy in reply to a letter from a teenager named Frances Elizabeth Clarke, who belonged to that 'vague far townlet' of the poem." She was the daughter of Edward Clarke, R.N. Hardy was misled regarding her age, as "she could have been no more than fourteen or fifteen at the time." She was later well known as Sarah Grand, novelist, social reformer, and author of *The Heavenly Twins*.[1] St. John Ervine, in the same newspaper on July 16, questioned Marjorie Spencer's assertion that Hardy did not realize the youth of Miss Clarke. He questioned whether the poem was written to Miss Clarke, as it would have had to be written about 1878.[2] Janet Brown wrote in the *Belfast Telegraph* for July 25 that the letter "was written by a Mrs. Harwood, whose maiden name was Hardy. She asked were they in any way related. Her daughter started the Girl Guides movement in Donaghadee about 1925 or 1926, which should date the letter, as the Harwoods did not stay long in Donaghadee."[3]

The woman's identity is unimportant; her letter brought to Hardy's memory romantic Irish songs he had known and loved. Of the songs mentioned, "Kitty of Colrain" [*sic*] was in a music book that had belonged to Hardy's father and grandfather. "Irish Molly O" was a lilting street-ballad. "Nancy Dawson," sometimes called "Miss Dawson's Hornpipe," was an English song, rather than Irish, about a popular stage-dancer at Sadler's Wells Theatre in the eighteenth century.[4]

On August 21, 1924, St. John Ervine wrote to Hardy from Donaghadee: "My wife has a letter from Mrs. Hardy a few days ago, in which she mentioned that you had just written a poem on the name of this village. I have been trying to find out for you the meaning of Donaghadee, and have only this evening succeeded in doing so. There are two suggestions. . . . The first is that the word is derived from a Gaelic phrase, meaning 'The Hill of the Two.' The dun in the village . . . is an unusually large one. It is called the Moat. Donaghadee is a four-syllabled word, pronounced 'Dun-ach-a-dee,' with the second syllable gutteral."[5] On August 25, Hardy replied to Ervine: "It is very good of you to tell me all about Donaghadee, and very strange that you happened to be there when I wrote the few lines of verse. The fact is that some stranger sent me a letter therefrom about some book of mine, & knowing nothing of the town I scribbled down an impromptu suggested by the letter." On September 13, he sent a copy of the poem to Ervine and wrote: "Here it is, if you will accept it—though it is only a thin jingle, which may go very well with a lot of other poems that I am bringing out in a volume in a month or two."[6]

1. "A Maid from the County Down."
2. "Thomas Hardy and the Maid from Donaghadee." Possibly Hardy kept the letter, came upon it in preparing notes for *The Early Life*, destroyed it then, and wrote the poem when he had forgotten the writer's name.
3. "Thomas Hardy's poem on Donaghadee."
4. The words of these songs are given in Copps, "The Poetry of Thomas Hardy," pp. 722-26. Presumably the songs not here identified are of the same kind.
5. In the Dorset County Museum.
6. In the Miriam Lutcher Stark Library, University of Texas. The dates of the letters suggest approximately when Hardy composed the poem.

HE INADVERTENTLY CURES HIS LOVE-PAINS echoes the cavalier verse of the seventeenth century, treating the lover who would not endure the pangs of love, sublimates them in art, and yet, when the smarts are eased, longs for the "old sweet agonies again!"

THE PEACE PEAL in the manuscript added the date 1918.[1] As often, Hardy adopts a bird's point of view to present an irony. The "wistful daw" that speaks in the poem found a nesting-place in St. Peter's Tower in the center of Dorchester ("Casterbridge") during World War I, when the church bells were silenced. Peace for men meant for the daw exile to a "damp dark ditch."

1. Purdy, *Thomas Hardy: A Bibliographical Study*, p. 243.

LADY VI in the manuscript was titled "Lady Clo."[1] Possibly Hardy changed "Clo" to "Vi" to hinder identification. The opening stanza presents his point of view as a spectator sitting on one of the seats beside Rotten Row, an avenue through Hyde Park in London, traditionally reserved for horse-drawn carriages or horseback riding. Hardy's interest in the parade runs through *The Early Life*. He included a scene in the Row in his first novel, *The Poor Man and the Lady*, of which Alexander Macmillan said: "The scene in Rotten Row is full of power and insight." Speaking of himself and his wife Emma in London on May 21, 1880, he wrote that "they were sitting in the chairs by Rotten Row and the Park Drive." He wrote in his notebook for July 11, 1886: "In Rotten Row. Every now and then each woman . . . puts on her *battle face*."[2]

The last three stanzas present Lady Vi's soliloquy as he perhaps surmised it from her "battle face." Besides a mocking exhibit of her mind as occupied by the "wheeling show" of fashionable pleasures, the third and fourth stanzas denounce two aristocratic attitudes that angered Hardy, the cruel pastime of fox-hunting and fashionable lip-service to religion. Fairchild says of Hardy's attitude toward religion in this poem: "As everyone knows, he rejected . . . the Christian creed and its institutional embodiments. And yet an angrily orthodox Christian satirist might be speaking through the lips of Lady Vi."[3]

1. Purdy, *Thomas Hardy: A Bibliographical Study*, p. 243.
2. Pp. 77, 180, 239; *Life*, pp. 58, 137, 182.
3. *Gods of a Changing Poetry*, p. 245.

A POPULAR PERSONAGE AT HOME was first published in the *Flying Carpet*, edited by Lady Cynthia Asquith, in September, 1925.[1] In a letter of October 14, 1924, she asked Hardy for a poem for her "children's annual" and suggested: "One about that uncommon dog 'Wessex' would be ideal." He wrote the poem and mailed it at once; a letter of October 17 says, "It is good of you to let me have it so promptly."[2]

The poem is a soliloquy by Wessex, with Hardy's comment in the final stanza. Wessex belonged to Mrs. Florence Hardy, who "introduced the dog to Max Gate as a companion for herself."[3] He was a pedigreed, wire-haired terrier, so petted by the Hardys and allowed so much freedom that dozens of visitors commented on his behavior. When J. M. Barrie dined at Max Gate, the dog "proved a slight strain to the guests at dinner, by walking about on the table and taking their food."[4] According to Mrs. Hardy's testimony, Wessex was troublesome. She wrote to Rebekah Owen on October 24, 1915: "Wessex does not improve much. He is really the most quarrelsome dog I have ever had—I have had three. He is intelligent and affectionate but sometimes disobedient—sometimes he is most obedient—and of course he is not well-trained for the house. He *will* sleep on the sofa, and he has appropriated a chair to himself in the drawing-room." On May 21, 1916, she wrote again: "Wessex has been *so* wicked; I dare not tell you what he did the other day. T. does not know about it." Wessex bit the postman, about which Mrs. Hardy wrote to Miss Owen on August 1, 1920, adding: "A postman kicked out two of his teeth which was distinctly cruel."[5] Lady Cynthia Asquith wrote of a visit to Max Gate in 1921: "The moment we arrived I was formally introduced to the most despotic dog guests had ever suffered under. This notorious dog . . . had, I am sure, the longest biting list of any domestic pet. The proud master lost no time in telling us that the postman, who had been bitten three times, now refused to deliver any more letters at the door. . . . Wessex was specially uninhibited at dinner-time, most of which he spent not under, but *on*, the table, walking about unchecked, and contesting every single forkful of food on its way from my plate to my mouth."[6] Sir Newman Flower reported that Wessex "bit John Galsworthy, who was always a friend of animals. He tried to bite me."[7]

Hardy regarded Wessex as extraordinarily intelligent and even psychic. He told Flower of Wessex's prescience on an occasion when William Watkins was visiting: "Suddenly, and without warning, 'Wessex' . . . began to bark violently and scratch at the front door, then dashed wildly up and down the hall. . . . It was such an uncommon behavior on the part of 'Wessex' that Hardy and Watkins got up quickly and flung open the front door. . . . They took a lantern and began to search the grounds. . . . Meanwhile the dog was tearing through the bushes. But they found nothing. Shortly afterwards Watkins returned to his hotel in Dorchester and died in the night."[8]

J. M. Barrie told of going with Hardy and Wessex to a rehearsal of a dramatization of *Tess of the D'Urbervilles*. There "the dog who was with us behaved beautifully until the time came when he knew the wireless would be putting on the 'children's hour.' It was *his* favorite item. He howled for it so that even Tess's champion had to desert her and hurry home with him."[9] Siegfried Sassoon, describing Hardy's affection for Wessex, wrote: "when he gazed down at 'Wessie.' . . . The face of the wizard became suffused with gentle compassion for all living creatures whom he longed to defend against the chanceful injustice and calamity of earthly existence."[10] Hardy pondered the nature of Wessex's intelligence. The final stanza of the poem reflects an observation by Lady Cynthia Asquith. On a walk, Wessex "had a habit of pelting on ahead, and then, as if in sudden misgiving, stopping at intervals to look back at his master with an anxious, questioning expression. Hardy said he had often noticed this enquiring, apprehensive look in the eyes of dogs."[11]

1. Purdy, *Thomas Hardy: A Bibliographical Study*, p. 243.
2. In the Dorset County Museum.
3. Scudamore, *Florence and Thomas Hardy*, p. 10.
4. Mackail, *Barrie*, p. 558.
5. In the Colby College Library.
6. "Thomas Hardy at Max Gate," p. 753.
7. "Walks and Talks with Hardy," p. 194.
8. "Our First President," p. 18.
9. *New York Times* story from London on Barrie's speech at the Society of Authors, November 29, 1928.
10. *Siegfried's Journey*, p. 138.
11. "Thomas Hardy at Max Gate," p. 754.

INSCRIPTIONS FOR A PEAL OF EIGHT BELLS seems to concern the bells of St. Peter's in Dorchester. In *The Trumpet-Major* John Loveday says to Anne Garland: " 'The finest tenor bell about here is the bell of Peter's, Casterbridge [Dorchester]—in E flat. Tum-m-m-m— that's the note—tum-m-m-m.' The trumpet-major sounded from far down his throat what he considered to be E flat." (Chapter XI.) Hardy mentions the same bell in his diary for December 31, 1884: "To St. Peter's belfry to the New-Year's-Eve ringing. The night-wind whiffed in through the louvres as the men prepared the mufflers with tar-twine and pieces of horse-cloth. Climbed over the bells to fix the mufflers. I climbed with them and looked into the tenor bell: it is worn into a bright pit where the clapper has struck it so many years, and the clapper is battered with its many blows. . . . Old John . . . says, 'Tenor out?' One of the two tenor men gently eases the bell forward—that fine old E flat (probably D in modern sharpened pitch), my father's admiration, unsurpassed in metal all the world over."[1]

The inscriptions on the eight bells of St. Peter's are recorded by Metcalfe as follows: "1st Bell or Treble, Mr. John King and Mr. Thomas Jones, Churchwardens, 1750, T. Bilbie, fecit.—2nd Bell. This bell was re-cast in the year 1808, George Frampton and John Cooper, Churchwardens, T. Bilbie, Collumpton, fecit.—3rd Bell, the gift of Robert Brown, Esq. 'Altho' my sound it is but small / I will be heard amongst you all.'—4th Bell, Mr. Daniel Arden and Mr. Joseph Gigger, ch. w., 1734, T. Bilbie, fecit.—Bells 4, 6, and 7 were re-cast and the whole Peal re-hung by public subscription at a cost of £300, A.D. 1889. A. H. Lock, Mayor. T. Warner and Sons. —5th Bell, Mr. Daniel Arden and Mr. Joseph Gigger, ch. w., 1734, George Richards, Esq., Mr. Renaldo Knapton, Mr. Thomas Loader, Mr. Thomas Cooper, Mr. Wm. Bryer, Bilbie, fecit.—6th Bell, recast by John Warner and Sons, London, 1889, J. Marvin Lock, Robert Holland, Churchwardens. 'God send us good luck.'—7th Bell, Re-cast by John Warner and Sons, London, 1889, Rev. Thomas Kingdon Allen, Rector. 'Come let us go up to the house of the Lord.'—8th Bell, Mr. Renaldo Knapton saw me cast the 21st Sept 1734, Mr. Daniel Arden, Mr. Joseph Gigger, Ch. w. Thomas Bilbie cast all these six bells. 'Ring to the Glory of God.' "[2]

The poem has been set to music by Nicholas Marshall (London: Augener, and New York: Galaxy Music Corporation, 1963).

1. *Early Life*, p. 221; *Life*, p. 169.
2. *A Popular and Illustrated Guide to St. Peter's Church*, pp. 49-50. This book was in Hardy's library and is now in the Colby College Library.

A REFUSAL is Hardy's mocking reply, in the form of an imaginary monologue by the Dean of Westminster, to the refusal of the Dean to place a memorial tablet to Lord Byron in the Poet's Corner of the Abbey on the centenary of Byron's death.

When Byron's remains were brought to England from Greece, burial in Westminster Abbey was proposed and refused. In 1924, a proposal was circulated to place a tablet to Byron in the Abbey. Hardy received a letter from Sir Rennell Rodd asking for his signature to a letter in the *Times* in support of the proposal. He replied on June 27, 1924: "I give my name and support to the proposed letter to the Times with pleasure. Whatever Byron's bad qualities he was a poet, & a hater of cant, & I have often thought some memorial of him should be at Westminster."[1] Under the title of "Byron and the Abbey," a letter to the editor of the *Times* was published on July 14. The letter said: "Bryon, the product of certain influences of heredity and environment, like other over-sensitive temperaments, displayed weakness in matters of conduct in contrast with his conspicuous courage in matters of opinion . . . . he became a trumpet voice for inarticulate people stifled by reaction and repression." The letter was signed with fifteen prominent names, among them Edmund Gosse, G. M. Trevelyan, Thomas Hardy, and Rudyard Kipling.

Replying in the *Times* for July 19, Herbert E. Ryle, Dean of Westminster, refused. His letter included: "(1) The available room for memorials in the Abbey is distressingly small; in Poet's Corner more especially so. . . . (2) The Abbey is not a mere literary Walhalla. . . . Byron was a great poet. . . . Unfortunately, Byron, partly by his own openly dissolute life and partly by the influence of the licentious verse, earned a world-wide reputation for immorality among English-speaking people."

Hardy's poem mocking this refusal, perhaps taking its cue from the implied sneer in "mere literary Walhalla," reduces the remarks of the "grave Dean" to intentional doggerel.

1. Letter and pencil-draft of Hardy's reply are in the Dorset County Museum.

EPITAPH ON A PESSIMIST was first published in the *London Mercury* for September, 1925, where it was noted as "From the French." Hardy stated on September 29, 1925, in a letter to J. C. Squire, that he "imitated" the epigram from a French version, not named.[1] He soon received letters from scholars pointing out its Greek source. In Mackail's *Select Epigrams from the Greek Anthology* (in Hardy's library) the Greek, author unknown, reads: Ἐξηκοντούτης Διονύσιος ἐνθάδε κεῖμαι / Ταρσεύς, μή γήμας· αἴθε δὲ μήδ' ὁ πατήρ. Mackail translated it as "I Dionysius of Tarsus lie here at sixty, having never married; and I would that my father had not." Like Smith, Stoke is a common name derived from Old English, with the meaning of "a place." Many towns in southern England include Stoke as part of the name. The poem is in the common meter ballad stanza.

1. Weber, *The Letters of Thomas Hardy*, pp. 113-14.

THE PROTEAN MAIDEN was in the manuscript titled "The Protean Lady."[1] It comments on the changefulness of a girl, baffling to her lover.

1. Purdy, *Thomas Hardy: A Bibliographical Study*, p. 244.

A WATERING-PLACE LADY INVENTORIED presents Hardy's view of a woman observed at some such seaside resort as Weymouth or Bournemouth. She is conventionally charming and ladylike, but so sweetly agreeable that she lacks personality. The poem quietly mocks the lady in multiple rimes on words she might use: "unforgettable" and "regrettable," and "charitable" and "unnarratable." Her "hints" of the final stanza suggest some loneliness willing to be comforted.

THE SEA FIGHT is a memorial to Captain Cecil Irby Prowse of the *Queen Mary*, who went down with his ship in the battle of Jutland on May 31, 1916. This battle was fought in the North Sea between the British Grand Fleet under Admiral Sir J. R. Jellico and the German High Seas Fleet under Admiral Reinhard Scheer. Shortly after 4:00 in the afternoon the *Queen Mary* engaged the German *Derfflinger* and *Seydlitz*. At 4:26 a salvo crashed into the *Queen Mary* and an explosion so tore the ship apart that she sank with 57 officers and 1,209 men. Shortly afterward the German fleet fled through a fog to its bases.

Members of the Prowse family, living in the area of Yeovil, about twenty-one miles northwest of Dorchester, were noted for heroism in England's wars. In St. John's Church, Yeovil, a large stained-glass window is dedicated to heroes of this family. It is in four panels, one of which is dedicated "In Memoriam Cecil Irby Prowse." Below the window, a brass plaque is devoted "To the Glorious and Immortal Memory" of Charles Bertie Prowse, D.S.O., and his brother Cecil Irby Prowse, Captain, R.N., with the inscription for Captain Prowse: "Served in the Egyptian War 1882, and in E. Africa 1895-96. Commanded H.M.S. *Queen Mary*, sunk in action at the battle of JUTLAND, withstanding with the battle cruiser squadron the full strength of the German fleet. May 31, 1916. Aged 49."

Hardy's poem may be explained as simply his celebration of a Wessex hero. The statement ". . . we knew him / As our fellow" suggests a personal relationship. In a letter to Edward Clodd on June 3, 1916, Hardy wrote that ". . . the news has just reached us here . . . of the naval battle on Wednesday, & we are anxious about the fate of friends."[1] He knew well Mrs. Henry G. B. Cowley, wife of the Vicar of Stinsford Church from 1911 to 1936, who was a sister of Captain Prowse. When the broken pieces of an old Norman font were found in Stinsford Churchyard, Hardy suggested that the font be repaired. In 1920, Mrs. Cowley had this font restored and set up in Stinsford Church as a memorial to her brothers, Charles and Cecil Prowse. Hardy "almost certainly" designed the stem and the base for the font.[2]

1. In the British Museum.
2. Beatty, *Stinsford—A Hardy Church*, p. 5.

PARADOX treats Hardy's sister Mary, who had died on November 24, 1915. Though the poem was published first, a note in Hardy's journal for December 23, 1925, expresses a theme suggested in the poem: "Mary's birthday. She came into the world . . . and went out . . . and the world is just the same . . . not a ripple on the surface left."[1]

The paradox seems to be that this country girl (as Hardy calls her in "The Sun's Last Look on the Country Girl") may still live in the spirit-world, where with now "largened sight," she may look with deepened compassion upon human life "as one bringing peace to us."

1. *Later Years*, p. 245; *Life*, p. 430.

THE ROVER COME HOME suggests the rover's rambling over the world. Canso Cape is a headland in northeastern Nova Scotia; Horn is Cape Horn on the southern extremity of South America; East Indian Comorin is the southern tip of India; and Behring Strait is the narrow sea between Alaska and Russia.

The last four lines suggest that places and circumstances do not alter character; the rover is still his mother's son in basic features. Hardy had stated this theme in his description of Bob Loveday in *The Trumpet-Major*. When Bob returns home, though he "had been all over the world from Cape Horn to Pekin, and from India's coral strand to the White Sea, the most conspicuous of all the marks that he had brought back with him was an increased resemblance to his mother, who had lain all the time beneath Overcombe church wall." (Chapter XV.)

"KNOWN HAD I" has, in Hardy's handwriting on the "second proof" of the page-proofs for *Human Shows*, after "Song," "[Tune 'Jeanette & Jeanot']."[1] The poem suggests his remorse that he had failed to understand his first wife Emma until, after her death, he read her *Some Recollections*.

1. In the Dorset County Museum.

THE PAT OF BUTTER is set at an Agricultural Fair at Yeovil, about twenty-one miles northwest of Dorchester. The samples of butter come from areas near Yeovil. Netherhay is farmland about ten miles southwest and Kingcomb Hill about ten miles south of the town; Coker Rill is a stream running through the Coker villages (West Coker, East Coker, etc.) two to four miles southwest of Yeovil. Yeo-Lea is the valley of the Yeo River and its tributaries in this area.

BAGS OF MEAT in the manuscript identifies the scene as Wimborne,[1] where the Hardys lived from June 25, 1881, to June, 1883. Traditionally a cattle-market was held in Wimborne on the Friday preceding Good Friday and continued for some weeks.[2] The size of the market is suggested by the facts that the steer came from the Vale, presumably distant Blackmoor, and a buyer had "dragged here from Taunton Town!" more than fifty miles to the northwest.

The title rests on the auctioneer's calling the "quivering steer" a "fine bag of meat." The phrase is both part of the humor in Hardy's pictures of the auctioneer and a protest against viewing living animals only as meat.

The poem is a part of Hardy's protest against the inhumane practices of butchers, realistically set forth in *Jude the Obscure* when Jude and Arabella quarrel over Jude's attempt to be humane in slaughtering their pig. (Part I, Chapter X.) *The Later Years* defines his attitude: "The sight of animals being taken to market or driven to slaughter always aroused in Hardy feelings of intense pity, as he well knew . . . how much needless suffering is inflicted. In his notebook at this time he writes: '. . . Walking with F. by railway, saw bullocks and cows going to Islington (?) for slaughter.' Under this he drew a little pencil sketch of the rows of trucks as they were seen by him, with animals' heads at every opening, looking out at the green countryside they were leaving for scenes of horror in a far-off city."[3] He had been active for some years in efforts to promote humane methods of slaughter. In 1911, he was the principal witness in a prosecution for cruelty to a cow in Dorchester.[4] *Who's Who, 1918* stated that he had written "against bird-catching, performing animals, careless butchering, and the chaining of dogs." He was pleased to be elected the first honorary member of the Wessex Saddleback Pig Society, and on August 23, 1919, wrote to its chairman, W. J. Malden: "I do not know much about breeding such stock. I am more bent on humane methods of slaughtering, than on anything else in relation to it. So that in accepting with appreciation Honorary Membership of the Society I add a suggestion that the question of slaughtering, & transit before slaughtering, should be among the matters that the society takes up, with a view to causing as little suffering as possible to an animal so intelligent [as a pig]." An early draft of *The Later Years* contained this letter, followed by the comment: "It is satisfactory to know that Hardy's suggestions were acted upon by the Society."[5] Hermann Lea wrote: "Many times he congratulated me on my being a vegetarian, simply and entirely on account of the misery and suffering caused through eating meat. . . . He often told me in later years that meat-eating held a certain aesthetic repugnance in his mind, and that had he been younger in years he would assuredly have given vegetarianism a protracted personal trial."[6]

1. Purdy, *Thomas Hardy: A Bibliographical Study*, p. 244.
2. Hutchins, *The History of Dorset*, III, 180.
3. P. 250; *Life*, p. 434.
4. Sherman, "Thomas Hardy and the Lower Animals," p. 304.
5. Hardy's draft of the letter and the biographical comment are in the Dorset County Museum. The item omitted from the published biography would have been on p. 194 (*Life*, p. 391).
6. Lea, *Thomas Hardy Through the Camera's Eye*, p. 23.

THE SUNDIAL ON A WET DAY, with the footnote "St. Juliot," suggests that the sundial was at St. Juliot Rectory, as it may have been during Hardy's courtship of Emma Gifford in the early 1870's. The Old Rectory now has no sundial, and Mrs. Gwendolen Bax, living there, wrote me that there "has not been one during the last 30 years."[1] The poem may present a memory of a sundial elsewhere in the neighborhood.

Though Hardy planned to erect a sundial at Max Gate, he died before the plan was carried out. Dr. Richard Garnett wrote to him about 1901: "Mrs. Hardy and you were speaking of getting a sun-dial, and I observe some second hand dials (unmounted) at C. Brown's, 21 Oxford Street."[2] The sundial now at Max Gate was "one alteration (and that a fulfilment, rather) made since the poet's death—a bright sun-dial affixed to the easternmost turret . . . the sun-dial was actually being made in Dorchester at the time of his death."[3]

The poem, a soliloquy by the sundial, may be read as symbolizing Hardy's feeling. Consistently he presented the sun as a benevolent force, a "warm god." The poem suggests his yearning for faith in a benevolent God that, "though unseen," rules the world and that he would like to "declare."

1. Letter of July 12, 1966.
2. In the Dorset County Museum.
3. H. R., in "Max Gate: Memories of Thomas Hardy's Home," *Birmingham Post*, June 15, 1938.

HER HAUNTING-GROUND, Purdy says, "seems to refer to St. Juliot and Hardy's first wife."[1] Weber follows Purdy, saying that, "Whether the ghost was scornful or appreciative, one thing was certain: the church at St. Juliot was the appropriate place for the erection of a memorial to Emma Lavinia Gifford. For there, as Hardy pointed out, '. . . she flourished sorrow-free, / And, save for others, knew no gloom.'"[2] As the poem offers no direct reference to anything in St. Juliot, Miss Deacon challenges this interpretation, pointing out that Emma Hardy's tomb in Stinsford Churchyard was by no means "slighted." Hardy visited it often, brought flowers, and planted there daisies, Emma's favorite. She suggests that the poem concerns Tryphena Sparks, to whom Hardy was engaged before he met Emma Gifford. Her grave at Topsham was indeed like that of the poem, slighted. Miss Deacon says that "Her shadow swept this slope and mound" is clearly a reference to Tryphena, as in the poem "The Mound."[3]

1. *Thomas Hardy: A Bibliographical Study*, p. 244.
2. *Hardy's Love Poems*, p. 85.
3. *Hardy's Sweetest Image*, p. 10. See also Deacon and Coleman, *Providence and Mr Hardy*, pp. 134-36.

A PARTING-SCENE presumably treats an occurrence in the military barracks in Dorchester.

SHORTENING DAYS AT THE HOMESTEAD in the manuscript is titled "Autumn [October] at the Homestead."[1] The homestead is Hardy's birthplace in Higher Bockhampton, with its living-room windows opening westward so that the sun-rays "thread . . . through" the smoke rejected by the chimney. His reference to the astonishment of sparrows when cold weather returns is characteristic.

The poem reverses Hardy's typical pattern of a gloomy final stanza. The coming of the cider-maker is a happy event, suggesting the portrait of Giles Winterborne as "Autumn's very brother" in *The Woodlanders*. (Chapter XXVIII.) The poem has been set to music by Gerald Finzi in *A Young Man's Exhortation* (Oxford University Press, 1933).

1. Purdy, *Thomas Hardy: A Bibliographical Study*, p. 244.

DAYS TO RECOLLECT presents an autumn day of 1875, when newly married Hardy and Emma were living in Swanage and walked toward St. Alban's Head, and November 27, 1912, the day of Emma's death. The poem contrasts a day of happiness and a day of sorrow.

Hardy's image of thistle-seeds that rise like ghosts and float on the breeze like a "comet's tail" echoes a passage in *The Hand of Ethelberta*, largely written at Swanage in 1875. Ethelberta goes from "Knollsea" (Hardy's name for Swanage) to "Corvsgate Castle" (Corfe Castle), about five miles to the northwest. There the ladies, after hearing a lecture on the ruins, wander over the area, their dresses "sweeping over the hot grass and brushing up thistledown . . . so that it rose in a flight from the skirts of each like a comet's tail." (Chapter XXXI.)

TO C. F. H. was Hardy's christening present to Caroline Fox Hanbury, daughter of Mr. (later, Sir) Cecil Hanbury of Kingston Maurward House. Hardy and the Hanburys were close friends during his old age. *The Later Years*, speaking of the opening of a club-room in Lower Bockhampton, says that in December, 1919, Hardy "danced, for the last time in his life, with the then lady of the manor," Mrs. Hanbury.[1] Often he would walk from Max Gate to Kingston Maurward House to chat with the Hanburys.[2] "Dodo" (Mrs. Cecil) Hanbury, wrote to him on August 5, 1921: "My father will have told you of the arrival of my small & very plain daughter last week! Will you be a dear, & be Godfather?" She wrote on August 18 that "The Christening is to be on Thursday September 1st at 12:30. . . . My father will probably have told you we are calling her 'Caroline Fox' after a great grandmother of mine, the first Lady Holland."[3] *The Later Years* says that Hardy's "gift to his little godchild was the manuscript of a short poem contained in a silver box."[4] On December 17, 1925, little Caroline wrote: "My dear Godfather / Thank you very much for the book you sent me. My mother is in a Nursing Home in London, so I opened the parcel my self / Love from / Your little god child / Caroline Fox Hanbury / I am always called Sammy."[5]

1. P. 198; *Life*, p. 394. This statement contradicts a birthday greeting to Agnes, Lady Grove, in which Mrs. Hardy wrote on June 2, 1924, that Hardy "Says I am to tell you he often thinks of you & does not forget that you are the last person he ever danced with (if his memory serves) at the Larmer Tree." See the notes on "Concerning Agnes."
2. Voss, *Motoring with Thomas Hardy*, p. 7.
3. In the Dorset County Museum.
4. P. 224; *Life*, p. 414.
5. In the Dorset County Museum. A pencil notation says, "Written with governess holding her hand." A letter from Mrs. "Dodo" Hanbury on December 22 reveals that the book was a volume of poems. Mrs Hanbury was in a nursing home recovering from an operation.

THE HIGH-SCHOOL LAWN does not concern a high school in the usual sense. The "high school" is the Training College for teachers at No. 65, The Cathedral Close, in Salisbury, which Hardy and his wife Florence visited on June 25, 1923. *The Later Years* says: "At Salisbury they stopped for a little while to look at the Cathedral . . . and at various old buildings, including the Training College which he had visited more than fifty years before when his two sisters were students there, and which is faithfully described in *Jude the Obscure*.[1] The "lawn" of the Training College is across the road from the College, beyond a low hedge and trees through which the field is visible.

The bell of the final stanza, with the suggestion that it is like a passing bell, seems to relate the poem to Mary Hardy, who had once romped on that lawn and had died in 1915.

1. P. 231; *Life*, p. 420. I am indebted for this identification to R. F. Dalton, former curator of the Dorset County Museum. In *Jude*, the Training College is called a "Training-School" at "Melchester" or the "Melchester Normal School." See Part III, Chapters I-III.

THE FORBIDDEN BANNS may tell a story that Hardy heard from his mother or grandmother. It may rest upon an item Hardy found in an old newspaper. His notes record facts taken from newspapers published before his birth, but unfortunately he destroyed many pages from his notebooks.

The poem is related to his interest in the transmission of hereditary traits. *Jude the Obscure* is shot through with discussions of tragic heredity, as in Jude's reasoning that he should not marry Sue because they both belonged to a family in which "marriage usually meant a tragic sadness" and "marriage with a blood-relation would duplicate the adverse conditions, and a tragic sadness might be intensified to a tragic horror." (Part II, Chapter II.)

THE PAPHIAN BALL was first published with the title "The Midnight Revel" in *McCall's Magazine* of New York, for December, 1924. The manuscript adds: "The foregoing was composed several years ago; but being cast in a familiar mediaeval mould was not printed till now, when it has been considered to have some qualities worth preserving."[1] "Paphian" means "of Paphos," a city of Cyprus sacred to Aphrodite (or Venus), suggestive of the pagan revel where "Half-naked women tripped" and their partners swore "strange oaths," perhaps swearing by pagan gods. As Hardy's note suggests, the tale seems more medieval than Greek or Roman. The "figure against the moon" is apparently the Devil.

"The Paphian Ball" inverts Hardy's short story "Absent-Mindedness in a Parish Choir."[2] There a church choir, after carousing all night, becomes drowsy and, when called upon to play a hymn, strikes up "The Devil Among the Tailors." In the poem, the choir when drowsy inadvertently plays the Christmas hymn "While Shepherds Watched."[3]

The "Mellstock Quire" of "The Paphian Ball" is the choir of *Under the Greenwood Tree*, "The Rash Bride," and "The Dead Quire," though only "the tenor-viol, Michael Mail," narrator of the story, is named.[4] The places of the poem are those mentioned in other experiences of the choir: Rushy Pond on Egdon Heath, nearby Rainbarrow, distant Clyffe-Clump, and "Mellstock" (Stinsford) Church. The songs "While Shepherds Watched" and "Rejoice, Ye Tenants of the Earth" are standard Christmas carols of the choir.

The miracle that while the choir revelled their neighbors seemed to hear them play as never before suggests a parallel with medieval legends: a choir of angels took the place of the musicians.

1. Purdy, *Thomas Hardy: A Bibliographical Study*, p. 245.
2. In *Life's Little Ironies*.
3. The disappearance of the Satanic crew at this point may owe something to Hawthorne's "Young Goodman Brown."
4. In *Under the Greenwood Tree*, and elsewhere Michael Mail plays the second violin and Reuben Dewy, the tenor.

ON MARTOCK MOOR in the manuscript had the title "On Durnover Moor."[1] As "Durnover" is Hardy's name for Fordington, possibly the story of the poem is based on fact. In the change he kept "Weirwater," the name of the pools at Ten Hatches on the Frome just east of Dorchester. Near Martock, Hardy found a moor similar to that of

Fordington. Martock is a village about eight miles northwest of Yeovil; north of the village the Yeo River runs through meadows usually called King's Moor, but sometimes Martock Moor. Near a bridge across the Yeo at the village of Long Load, a canal enters the river; there a weir of two hatches roughly corresponds to Ten Hatches Weir near Dorchester. The woman who speaks the poem is apparently a person of some wealth.

1. Purdy, *Thomas Hardy: A Bibliographical Study*, p. 245.

THAT MOMENT in the manuscript had the title "The Misery of that Moment."[1] Critics have surmised that the poem presents a sudden and deep breach between Hardy and his first wife Emma, though Collins says that beyond this "a mystery must remain."[2] Phelps, relating the poem to "Alike and Unlike," suggests that it treats Emma's expression of jealousy of Hardy's feeling for Mrs. Arthur Henniker.[3] (See the notes on "Alike and Unlike.")

"That Moment" has been set to music by John Ireland, with the title "The Tragedy of That Moment" in *Five Poems by Thomas Hardy* (Oxford University Press, 1927).

1. Purdy, *Thomas Hardy: A Bibliographical Study*, p. 245.
2. "The Love Poetry of Thomas Hardy," p. 83.
3. *Annotations by Thomas Hardy in His Bibles and Prayer-Book*, p. 11.

PREMONITIONS in the manuscript has the title "Forebodings" deleted.[1] The poem is primarily a list of omens that someone is soon to die.[2] It seems related to Hardy's "The Superstitious Man's Story" in *Life's Little Ironies*. In this story, omens foretell to Betty Privett the death of her husband William. They include Betty's seeing William's wraith go out of the house to the church on Old Midsummer Eve, while William in fact is asleep in his bed. Among the premonitions, one Sunday "at a time that William was in very good health to all appearance, the bell that was ringing for church went very heavy all of a sudden." This item, matching the first premonition of the poem, and the name Betty in both the story and the poem suggest that Hardy wrote the poem from the story, listing additional items of folk-lore. If so, the narrator of "Premonitions" is the Superstitious Man.

1. Purdy, *Thomas Hardy: A Bibliographical Study*, p. 245.
2. Firor, *Folkways in Thomas Hardy*, pp. 18-19, 22-23.

THIS SUMMER AND LAST with the conjectured date "1913?" concerns Hardy's first wife Emma, who died in November, 1912. In a literal interpretation, the poem contrasts the summer of 1912 with that of 1913. Some phrases suggest that Hardy had in mind the summer of 1870, when he was courting Emma Gifford in Cornwall. The "breezes," the "humourous wit / Of fancy," and the "corn-brown curls" suggest the often-described scenes of Cornwall and Emma as she was at this time.

Perhaps the poem was suggested by Hardy's contemplation of a curl of hair that Emma had given him in a locket in 1870. This incident is described in "On a Discovered Curl of Hair," in which the first stanza contains phrases referring to 1870 like those in the second stanza of "This Summer and Last." The "corn-brown curls" are, in "On a Discovered Curl of Hair," pictured as originally "brightest brown" and "live brown," but in 1912 they had "donned a gray." The "alert brook" of "This Summer and Last" may refer to the Valency River of "Under the Waterfall."

Emma's hair may have recalled to Hardy's mind an item in his revision of *Desperate Remedies*. He had completed the novel before he met Emma, but it had been rejected. He revised it in the autumn of 1870; Emma made a fair copy of it; and the novel was accepted for publication.[1] Evelyn Hardy has conjectured that among the revisions Hardy "made the image of the imagined Cytherea tally with that of the living woman," Emma.[2] The revised description of Cytherea's hair reads: "Her hair rested gaily upon her shoulders in curls, and was of a shining corn yellow in the high lights, deepening to a definite nut-brown as each curl wound round into the shade." (Chapter I, 3.)

1. Purdy, *Thomas Hardy: A Bibliographical Study*, p. 4.
2. *Thomas Hardy*, p. 118.

"NOTHING MATTERS MUCH" presents a memory of Judge Benjamin Fossett Lock, who had been born in Dorchester on December 13, 1847. He was a friend of Hardy's youth, a "younger brother of the Warden of Keble College, Secretary of the Positivist Society, and one of Leslie Stephen's 'Sunday Tramps.' "[1] He had been a vice-president of the Dorset Men of London, of which group Hardy was at one time president. Judge Lock died at Bridlington on August 11, 1922, and was buried there. Bridlington is a North Sea port in Yorkshire, about five miles from the promontory Flamborough Head. The woman who listened to him patiently and, according to the poem, was saddened by his pessimism, was his wife, who died two years before his death.

Judge Lock's phrase that gives the poem its title echoes an attitude frequent in Hardy's writing. In *The Dynasts* Marie Louise, on Napoleon's return from Elba, says: "Nothing matters much!"[2] Hardy's attitude as expressed in the final stanza is based upon his reflection that "Time . . . shatters" all things. Fittingly for a memorial poem, the fourth stanza has the imagery of religious ceremony.

1. Purdy, *Thomas Hardy: A Bibliographical Study*, p. 245.
2. Part Third, V, iv. T. E. Lawrence, a close friend of the Hardys and a frequent guest, inscribed over the doorway of his cottage, "Cloud's Hill" near Moreton, the Greek for "Nothing matters."

IN THE EVENING is Hardy's memorial to his friend Sir Frederick Treves, written in the form of a graveside dialogue between Treves's spirit and a "spirit attending," spokesman for Hardy.

The Later Years comments: "On December 10 [1923] the death was announced of Sir Frederick Treves, Hardy's fellow townsman, the eminent surgeon. Frederick Treves as a child had attended the same school as Hardy's elder sister Mary, and it was from the shop of Treves's father that Hardy as a boy purchased his first writing desk.[1] . . . Because of the early association and the love which they both bore to the county there was a strong link between these two Dorset men. . . . '*January* 2. Attended Frederick Treves's funeral at St. Peter's. Very wet day. Sad procession to the cemetery. Casket in a little white grave.' . . . On January 5 a poem by Hardy, 'In Memoriam, F. T.,' appeared in the *Times*, a last tribute to an old friend."[2] The last three lines of the version published in the *Times* are quoted on Treves's monument in Dorchester Cemetery: "A marvelous Deftness called you forth—to do / Much that was due. / Good. You have returned. And all is well."

When the poem appeared, Sir Newman Flower praised it, and Hardy wrote to him: "I am so glad you liked my hasty tribute to our friend in Saturday's *Times*. Longer reflection would have made a better thing of it."[3] He revised the poem for publication in *Human Shows*.

Sir Frederick Treves, the most famous surgeon of his time, had been Surgeon in Extraordinary to Queen Victoria; in 1902, he performed an appendectomy on King Edward VII shortly before his coronation and was chosen as his Sergeant Surgeon, a post he held also under George V; he was Surgeon in Ordinary for Queen Alexandra. He died in Lausanne and was cremated; his ashes were brought to Dorchester for burial.

Besides the acquaintance mentioned in *The Later Years*, other ties united Treves and Hardy. Fond, like Hardy, of bicycling through his native countryside, Treves wrote *Highways and Byways of Dorset*, not to mention books of surgical reminiscence and other books of travel; Hardy's library contained a presentation copy of his *The Cradle of the Deep*. Treves became the first President (1904-7) of the Society of Dorset Men in London, in which post Hardy followed him (1907-9). The Dorset County Museum has six letters from Treves to Hardy, written in the period 1900-1911, on topics that vary from the treatment of the wounded in the South African War to the poems of William Barnes. Hardy expressed his feeling for Treves in a letter to Sir George Douglas on January 4, 1924: "A shadow has been cast over the opening of the year for me by the funeral of Frederick Treves, . . . a friend of many years' standing."[4]

The funeral services were held on Wednesday, January 2, in St. Peter's Church. Hardy, asked to choose the hymns, chose Psalm 40, "Thou turnest man, O Lord, to dust," which had been sung for his father's funeral, and Archbishop Maclagan's "The Saints of God." The urn containing Treves's ashes was then taken to Dorchester Cemetery. The soil there is chiefly chalk, a fact mentioned in the poem. Though the urn was lowered to its bed during rain and wind, Hardy was sturdily there. Newman Flower records that he telephoned "to say that, in view of the weather, I thought he would be well advised to stay at home. His reply was, 'I have known Treves since he was young, and I am going through with it.' I stood beside Hardy in the driving rain at the open grave. . . . The rain pouring on to his bare head, ran in little rivulets down the grey hair about his neck and under his collar. I saw him shivering in the cold, as his blue-veined, ageing hands held aloft his hat."[5]

The poem is written as if overheard at the graveside. Treves's spirit seems to ask why he was called into life from the chalk of his native land, and the answering spirit, to reply that he was "beckoned . . . forth" by the phantoms of Aesculapius, Greek god of medicine, Galen (c. 130 A.D.-c. 200), philosopher-physician of Rome and founder of experimental physiology, and Hippocrates of Cos (460 B.C.-c. 370?), Greek "father of medicine."

1. The poem "The Little Old Table" says that it was a gift.
2. Pp. 236-37; *Life*, pp. 423-24.
3. Flower, *Just As It Happened*, p. 126.
4. In the National Library of Scotland.
5. *Just As It Happened*, pp. 125-26.

THE SIX BOARDS exhibits Hardy's characteristic concern with images of death and the idea of lying through all the future in a strange place. He was not buried in six boards. His ashes were placed in Westminster Abbey, and his heart in Stinsford Churchyard.

BEFORE MY FRIEND ARRIVED presents Hardy's memory (presumably about 1925) of his awaiting in Dorchester the arrival of the body of his friend, Horace M. Moule. Moule killed himself at Cambridge on Sunday evening, September 21, 1873, and on late Thursday afternoon was being brought home for burial on Friday in the churchyard of Fordington St. George, where his father was vicar.

The Early Life says that on September 24 Hardy (then in Bockhampton) "was shocked at hearing of the tragic death of his friend Horace Moule. . . . The body was brought to be buried at Fordington, Dorchester, and Hardy attended the funeral."[1] Presumably, he had visited the churchyard, where the grave had been dug in the chalky ground and then retired to meditate alone on the "evelit weir," Ten Hatches, just east of Dorchester, from which he could look across the meadows of the Frome to the tower of St. George's Church less than half a mile away on a hill.[2]

His meaning in "Overmuch cause had my look!" and his answer to the question "Why did I pencil that chalk?" are not entirely clear. Possibly in despair at the loss of his friend, he momentarily contemplated suicide and drew the "white chalk mound" to picture the consequences. It was in Ten Hatches Weir that Henchard, in *The Mayor of Casterbridge*, intended to drown himself, but was restrained by seeing his effigy in the pool. (Chapter XLI.)

1. P. 126; *Life*, p. 96.
2. Lea, *Thomas Hardy's Wessex*, has a photograph of "Fordington Church" on its hilltop as Plate 219 on p. 291.

COMPASSION was first published by Edward G. Fairholme and Wellesley Pain in *A Century of Work for Animals*, London, June 16, 1924, the centenary volume of the Royal Society for the Prevention of Cruelty to Animals, and in the *Times* for the same day, the centenary day.[1] *The Later Years* says that the poem "was written in answer to a request. . . . Although not one of his most successful efforts . . . it served to demonstrate the poet's passionate hatred of injustice and barbarity."[2]

On January 5, 1924, Captain Fairholme of the Royal Society for the Prevention of Cruelty to Animals wrote to Mrs. Hardy that he had asked whether Hardy "could possibly write us an Ode in celebration of the Centenary of the Society's foundation. . . . For that purpose . . . if such an Ode were suitable for setting to music, I would try and get some well-known composer to do this and then possibly have a well-known singer to sing it at our Congress, and elsewhere." On January 18, she replied that Hardy "is already beginning something that might suit, & that can be set to music for singing at your Congress & elsewhere." On January 23, the poem was sent, with the statement that "we both hope it will suit the Society & the occasion & that a composer will not find it difficult for music.

Glad to do this in the cause of animals." Captain Fairholme on April 4 wrote that he had "not been able to find a suitable composer," but he asked whether the Ode might be published in the *Times* on June 16. Mrs. Hardy replied: "My husband will be pleased for you to send the verses to the Times for publication on the Centenary day, June 16. . . . He suggests . . . that you should put 'No Copyright' under the poem . . . in order that other newspapers may be able to reprint the Ode in the interest of animals."[3]

Hardy's feeling for the suffering of animals was one of the deepest of his life, manifested in many poems ("The Puzzled Game-Birds," "Bags of Meat," etc.) and throughout his prose. He based it upon a combination of Darwinian evolution and Christian ethics. As Blunden says: "Hardy also marked the twentieth anniversary of the Humanitarian League . . . with a published letter. . . : 'Few people seem to perceive fully as yet that the most far-reaching consequence of the establishment of the common origin of all species is ethical; that it logically involved a readjustment of altruistic morals, by enlarging, as a necessity of rightness, the application of what has been called "The Golden Rule" from the area of mere mankind to that of the whole animal kingdom.' "[4] In a "Letter to the Editor" published in the *Times* on December 19, 1913, he wrote in protest against the use of performing dogs in fairs, the use of drugs on animals, and the caging of birds, saying: "As to the caging of birds, the assertion that a caged skylark experiences none of the misery of a caged man makes demands upon our credulity. Anyhow, a caged skylark usually dies soon, while an imprisoned man will live out his natural years."[5]

Admitting that in human nature "from Columbia Cape to Ind" helplessness still invites cruelty, Hardy points out that great teachers of both Greek and Christian ethics call for mercy. He quotes "Ailinon! . . . But may the good prevail!" from the Agamemnon of Aeschylus,[6] and matches this with Christ's words in the Sermon on the Mount, "Blessed are the merciful!"

1. Purdy, *Thomas Hardy: A Bibliographical Study*, pp. 231-32.
2. P. 238; *Life*, p. 425.
3. In the Dorset County Museum, Mrs. Hardy's letters in the form of Hardy's pencil-drafts.
4. *Thomas Hardy*, pp. 128-29.
5. "Performing Animals" in the Dorset County Museum; see Orel, *Thomas Hardy's Personal Writings*, p. 252.
6. Rutland, *Thomas Hardy*, p. 36, gives the Greek with Gilbert Murray's translation: "Sorrow, sing sorrow, But good prevail, prevail."

"WHY SHE MOVED HOUSE" seems to portray one of Hardy's visits to the grave of his first wife in Stinsford Churchyard accompanied by the dog Wessex. (See "A Popular Personage at Home.") If so, the humorous musings of the dog are not realistic. Wessex was Mrs. Florence Hardy's dog, not Emma's.

TRAGEDIAN TO TRAGEDIENNE is spoken by an elderly lover of a young actress with whom he has played many tragic roles that have been paralleled in their "days of stress." On the day of the conversation, they have played together "in mock" a drama that included the tragedian's death. He meditates his actual death, expected soon. The poem may bear some relation to Hardy's observations during his brief experience on the stage. (See "A Victorian Rehearsal.") It can be read as an allegory of Hardy's anticipation, at the age of eighty-five, that he would die before his much younger wife Florence.

THE LADY OF FOREBODINGS is set in a restaurant in which a lady and her lover are happy together until the lady has a premonition that the "dearness" of the moment will not last.

THE BIRD-CATCHER'S BOY was first published in the *Sphere* for January 4, 1913.[1] The poem voices Hardy's characteristic protest against caging birds. Freddy's flight when told that he must make his living by catching larks and nightingales recalls Jude's rebellion against driving birds away from Farmer Troutham's field: " 'Poor little dears!' said Jude aloud. 'You *shall* have some dinner—you shall. There is enough for us all. Farmer Troutham can afford to let you have some. Eat, then, my dear little birdies, and make a good meal!' "[2] The feeling is expressed by Tess when she tells Angel of her girlhood: "I never could bear to hurt a fly or a worm, and the sight of a bird in a cage used often to make me cry."[3] Like *Tess* and *Jude*, "The Bird-Catcher's Boy" suggests that sensitivity in a callous world leads to tragedy.

In ironic suggestion, the poem employs Christian symbolism. The birds are "caged choirs"; the boy sweeps his fingers over the cages as upon a harp. The birds sing like the captives in Babylon: "By the rivers of Babylon, there we sat down, yea, we wept, when we remembered Zion. . . . For there they that carried us away captive required of us a song." (Ps. 137:1-3.) The boy dies at Christmastide. The supernatural appears in the parents' feeling that Freddy returned, though the white moon, as usual a symbol for reality, showed only an empty bed. Freddy apparently had found work on a hoy (a barge) that was wrecked at Durdle Door, near Lulworth Cove. (See the notes on "At Lulworth Cove a Century Back.")

1. Purdy, *Thomas Hardy: A Bibliographical Study*, p. 246.
2. *Jude the Obscure*, Part I, Chapter II.
3. *Tess of the D'Urbervilles*, Chapter LVIII.

A HURRIED MEETING seems to present a scene Hardy developed from his early, lost novel *The Poor Man and the Lady*, though the lady's bearing the poor man's child seems not to have been in the novel. (See the notes on "A Poor Man and a Lady.")

The poem protests the convention that an unmarried woman bearing a child must be made respectable by marriage and the social stratification that makes the "haughty-hearted" woman scorn to marry her lover. Hardy's attitude toward marriage for respectability is explicit in *The Early Life*. In December, 1882, "Hardy was told a story by a Mrs. Cross . . . of a girl she had known who had been betrayed and deserted by a lover. She kept her child by her own exertions, and lived bravely and throve. After a time the man returned poorer than she, and wanted to marry her; but she refused. . . . The young woman's conduct in not caring to be 'made respectable' won the novelist-poet's admiration."[1] His protest against social stratification runs throughout his work, as in Parson Swancourt's remark, in *A Pair of Blue Eyes*, that the marriage of Elfride and Stephen would be a "preposterous thing" (Chapter X) and in Melbury's demand, in *The Woodlanders*, that Grace marry Fitzpiers instead of Giles. (Chapter XXIV.)

The "August moonlight" throws a cold, realistic light upon the lovers' meeting and leads to the cynical statement of the night-jar (a bird) that closes the poem.

1. Pp. 203-4; *Life*, p. 157.

DISCOURAGEMENT in the manuscript is dated "1865-7."[1] The poem seems to reflect Hardy's reading *The Origin of Species* and his early view of evolution as purposive, the process by which "the Mother, naturing Nature" intends to develop mankind toward what Tennyson, offering a similar interpretation of evolution, called a "higher race." (Lyric CXVIII of *In Memoriam*.) Hardy's term "naturing Nature" is his translation of "Natura Naturans," used in medieval philosophy to describe nature as a creative principle, the agent of God as Creator.[2] The Mother operates in the processes of birth.

Mother Nature's plan for perfecting the human race is "racked and wrung," frustrated, by "her unfaithful lord," man. Hardy's statement of how man thwarts Nature's purpose protests man's attention, in mating, to traits that have nothing to do with ethical or intellectual advancement: "loves" are dependent upon "a feature's trim," good looks and possibly fashion; life-development may be hampered by "hap of birth," or social appetites, the "body's whim."

The title suggests at least a personal feeling. Lines 9-11 may be read as stating a theme developed in "A Hurried Meeting." Both poems may have some relation to Hardy's *The Poor Man and the Lady*. Evelyn Hardy says that "the line 'A whole life's circumstance on hap of birth' implies unhappiness connected with love for some aristocratic girl (which Hardy's first novel also suggests) for in his work he was advancing swiftly and had no cause for dissatisfaction with his birth as a barrier to progress."[3]

Critics have found fault with the technique of this early poem. Rutland says of it: "Here we have a strange combination of power and clumsiness. The poem is full of faults; the striving after alliteration is very bad; 'genial hour' suggests a club; 'divinest hues' and 'flower of heroism and worth' come from the cheapest magazines; 'visions ghast and grim' is a lame ending in a forced rhyme. Yet there is a certain undeniable passion about the thing; and 'Eternal Heaven upon a day of Earth' is the work, not of a poetaster, but of a poet."[4]

1. Purdy, *Thomas Hardy: A Bibliographical Study*, p. 246.
2. On p. 273 of the "second proof" of the page-proofs of *Human Shows*, Hardy wrote *"Natura Naturans"* under the title of the poem. In the Dorset County Museum.
3. *Thomas Hardy*, p. 64.
4. *Thomas Hardy*, pp. 266-67.

A LEAVING exists in a separate manuscript titled "A Last Leaving." The poem treats the last time Hardy's first wife went for a drive.[1] *The Later Years* says of this drive: "She went out up to the 22nd November [1912], when though it was a damp, dark afternoon, she motored to pay a visit six miles off."[2] She died five days later, on November 27. ("Your Last Drive" describes her return to Max Gate.)

Certain phrases in the poem may suggest that it treats Emma's funeral. The phrase "a journey afar" suggests more than "six miles off," and "Knowing what it bore!" suggests the corpse in the hearse. Such is Weber's interpretation in *Hardy's Love Poems*. (P. 70.) The phrase "rain-smitten car" identifies the drive of November 22 on a "damp, dark afternoon." On the day of Emma's funeral, November 30, "the sun shone blandly on the sward and sombre evergreens of 'Mellstock' [Stinsford] churchyard, when on Saturday afternoon the body of Mrs. Thomas Hardy . . . was gently lowered into the grave."[3]

1. Purdy, *Thomas Hardy: A Bibliographical Study*, pp. 246-47.
2. P. 154; *Life*, p. 359.
3. *Dorset County Chronicle*, December 5, 1912, p. 6.

SONG TO AN OLD BURDEN has the movement of various dance-tunes. Hardy recalls scenes of a happy boyhood, with reflections that those who made it happy are dead. The fiddler for the country dancing is his father, who now, in Stinsford Churchyard, "Sleeps by the gray-grassed 'cello player,' " Hardy's paternal grandfather. The voice that "trilled, none sweetlier" must be that of Jemima, his mother. *The Early Life* says of her: "She sang songs of the date, such as the then popular Haynes Bayly's 'Isle of Beauty,' and 'Gaily the Troubadour'; also 'Why are you wandering here, I pray?' and 'Jeannette and Jeannot.' "[1] Perhaps, as the poem is about Hardy's boyhood, the "eyes" of the third stanza are those of his sister Mary.

1. Pp. 17-18; the fiddler and the 'cello player are identified on p. 13 and *passim*; *Life*, pp. 14 and 11.

"WHY DO I?" seems to present the questioning "I" as Hardy's mind, and the "you" as his emotional self. The phrase "doing these things" seems to mean writing and publishing poems. The final line suggests that, even at eighty-five, not mere habit ("mechanic repetitions"), but the pain (or at least the sensations) of life prompt the poems. In view of the contents of *Human Shows*, he might have added "the memories."

WINTER WORDS

Winter Words in Various Moods and Metres was published on October 2, 1928, after Hardy's death on January 11. In the meantime, serial rights to 50 of the 105 poems had been sold by the executors, Mrs. Hardy and Sydney Cockerell, to the *Daily Telegraph*, and the poems had appeared there between March 19 and September 26. Before his death, Hardy had been assembling the poems for publication. He hoped to bring it out on a birthday, presumably his eighty-eighth, June 2, 1928. His "Introductory Note" expresses some pique at being called "wholly gloomy and pessimistic by reviewers" of previous volumes, states that the volume is "probably my last appearance on the literary stage," and concludes that "no harmonious philosophy is attempted in these pages—or in any bygone pages of mine, for that matter."

Winter Words is made up chiefly of poems written after the publication of *Human Shows* in 1925, but it includes poems dated as written (wholly or in part) in earlier decades: two poems of the 1860's, "The Musing Maiden" and "Gallant's Song"; one of the 1880's, "A Countenance"; two of the 1890's, "Liddell and Scott" and "June Leaves and Autumn"; three of the 1900's, "Thoughts at Midnight," "A Daughter Returns," and "Christmas in the Elgin Room"; and one of the following decade, "The Catching Ballet of the Wedding Clothes." Hardy probably sought out poems omitted from earlier volumes and selected all that he wished published. As most of the poems are not dated, possibly others than those named above were written earlier. For instance, "Standing by the Mantelpiece," with no date of composition stated, may have been written shortly after the event it commemorates, the death of Horace Moule in 1873, held back to conceal for a time a privately known incident, and published at last when it would do no harm.

Winter Words as a whole presents a wide range of moods and topics. A few poems may be praised as highly as any Hardy ever wrote; others suggest that his fountains of inspiration were drying up. Though the volume contains some satiric pieces and some that must be judged pessimistic, as a whole the poems indicate a good deal of reflective serenity (and sometimes hilarious humor) in his old age. Some philosophic poems are more amused than bitter, for instance, "A Philosophical Fantasy" and "Drinking Song."

In the period 1925-28, he was continuing work on notes for *The Early Life* and *The Later Years*. Many poems seem based on events recalled to him in diaries and notebooks consulted for the biography, for instance, "Childhood Among the Ferns," "To Louisa in the Lane," "The Mound," "I Watched a Blackbird," "To a Tree in London," "In the Marquee," "Concerning Agnes," "The Second Visit," "In Weatherbury Stocks," "No Bell Ringing," and "Family Portraits." Others poems rest upon his miscellaneous reading, for instance, "The Bad Example," "Aristodemus the Messinian," "Squire Hooper," and "The Gap in the White." A few poems are commemorative: "Liddell and Scott," "How She Went to Ireland," and "Dead 'Wessex.'" Others concern experiences or observations of the time: "Concerning His Old Home" and "Lorna the Second." Some are reflectively satiric: "The Lady in the Furs," "So Various," and "Christmas in the Elgin Room." Many present amusing or catchy anecdotes, bits of gossip: "The New Boots," "The Three Tall Men," "The Son's Portrait," and "The Mongrel." The poems include jolly ditties, songs, and epigrams. Only a few express philosophic bitterness and despair: "We Are Getting to the End" and "He Resolves to Say No More."

THE NEW DAWN'S BUSINESS was first published in the *Daily Telegraph* on March 20, 1928.[1] Rutland remarks that the poem was "suggested by the Book of Job."[2] Perhaps it was, though the colloquial tone exhibits a wryly humorous view of death. The humor is supported by the insertion of a birth between a killing and the burial of "a corpse or two" and "other such odd jobs." In the poem, Time is the killer, and the Dawn a subaltern. Ironic Time leaves alone the jesting poet and "takes those loth instead."

1. Purdy, *Thomas Hardy: A Bibliographical Study*, p. 252.
2. *Thomas Hardy*, p. 2.

PROUD SONGSTERS was first published in the *Daily Telegraph* on April 9, 1928.[1] Aside from expressing Hardy's feeling for birds, the poem reaches into his philosophy. Dorothy Hoare says: "Behind its apparent simplicity is a complex attitude—stoic acceptance of the inanimate origin and return of animate life; a feeling of pity and tenderness for the creatures momentarily so vital, as if all time were theirs, when the irony is both the fact that they have so little of it, and that they are unconscious of the dusty end which awaits them; and, surprisingly, a hint, since earth and air and rain are integral elements for life, of the miraculous re-birth from nothingness."[2]

"Proud Songsters" has been set to music by Gerald Finzi in *Earth and Air and Rain* (London: Boosey and Hawkes, 1936) and Benjamin Britten in *Winter Words* (London: Boosey and Hawkes, 1954).

1. Purdy, *Thomas Hardy: A Bibliographical Study*, p. 252.
2. "The Tragic in Hardy and Conrad," p. 119.

THOUGHTS AT MIDNIGHT, dated May 25, 1906, suggests Hardy's reflections upon *The Dynasts*, on which he was working at that time. The "Mankind" to whom the poem is addressed may be the puppets of the Immanent Will, and "Time's buffets," the erratic impulses that move the characters in the epic-drama and in the history from which it was drawn. The "madnesses" are illustrated in the behavior of Napoleon, from his suicidal drive into Russia to his defeat at Waterloo. The poem protests not the evil that men choose to do, but their reckless follies that defeat their own ends.

"I AM THE ONE" was first published in the *Daily Telegraph* on April 2, 1928.[1] The modesty running through the poem partly hides Hardy's pride that ringdoves, hares, and mourners find him harmless. The poem expresses his conviction held at least since reading *The Origin of Species* that all living beings are kin. The final stanza even suggests human kinship with the stars, earlier expressed in "Waiting Both."

1. Purdy, *Thomas Hardy: A Bibliographical Study*, p. 253.

THE PROPHETESS, Weber suggests, concerns Hardy's first wife Emma.[1] The first stanza may picture an evening at St. Juliot during his courtship, perhaps March 9, 1870, when "The two ladies sang duets, including 'The Elfin Call,' 'Let us dance on the sands,' etc."[2] The final stanza reflects, with some hint of derision, upon the "hopes and fears" in his life with Emma. The phrasing suggests some relation to the third stanza of "The Change."

1. *Hardy's Love Poems*, p. 64.
2. *Early Life*, p. 99; *Life*, p. 75.

A WISH FOR UNCONSCIOUSNESS was first published in the *Daily Telegraph* for July 5, 1928.[1] Hardy enjoyed many pleasures, but he was so sensitive to pain, including the pain of others, that in some moods he entertained the fancy of being without consciousness. The thought of being "a picture in a hall" contains some playful humor.

1. Purdy, *Thomas Hardy: A Bibliographical Study*, p. 253.

THE BAD EXAMPLE, noted as "Partly from Meleager" (a Greek poet of the first century B.C.), is based on an epigram that Hardy annotated in his copy of *Select Epigrams from the Greek Anthology*, edited by J. W. Mackail. It reads:

> Ἀρνεῖται τὸν Ἔρωτα τεκεῖν ἡ Κύπρις ἰδοῦσα
> ἄλλον ἐν ἠϊθέοις Ἵμερον Ἀντίοχὸν.
> Ἀλλά, νέοι, στέργοιτε νέον Πόθον. ἦ γὰρ ὁ κοῦρος
> εὕρηται κρείσσων οὗτος Ἔρωτος Ἔρως.

Mackail translates it as: "The Cyprian denies that she bore Love, seeing Antiochus among the youths, another desire; then O you who are young, cherish the new Longing; for assuredly this boy is found a Love stronger than Love." Hardy's poem is more colloquial and humorous than the Greek.

TO LOUISA IN THE LANE was first published in the *Daily Telegraph* for April 26, 1928.[1] The poem presents Hardy's fantasy of summoning back to life and love a long-remembered, now-dead sweetheart. In adolescence, he was attracted in a shy, idealizing way to a variety of maidens living near his home. Among them was Louisa Harding. *The Early Life* says of her: "Yet another attachment . . . which went deeper, was to a farmer's daughter named Louisa. . . . He believed that his attachment to this damsel was reciprocated, for on one occasion when he was walking home from Dorchester he beheld her sauntering down the lane as if to meet him. He longed to speak to her, but bashfulness overcame him, and he passed on with a murmured 'Good evening,' while poor Louisa had no word to say. Later he heard that she had gone to Weymouth to a boarding school for young ladies, and thither he went, Sunday after Sunday, until he discovered the church which the maiden of his affections attended with her fellow scholars. But, alas, all that resulted from these efforts was a shy smile from Louisa. . . . Louisa lies under a nameless mound in 'Mellstock' churchyard. That 'Good evening' was the only word that passed between them."[2]

A notation in Hardy's Bible suggests one of the Sundays when he journeyed to Weymouth for a "shy smile" from Louisa. He noted in the margin opposite I Kings 19: "Ninth Sunday after Trinity, St. Johns, Weymouth. Evensong, August 21st, 1859."[3] *The Early Life* as published tells the story more guardedly than Hardy originally wrote it. The typescript marked "Mrs. Hardy (Personal Copy)" says that his fondness for Louisa "may have lasted a year or longer, since he used to meet her down to his 23rd or 24th year on his visits to Dorset from London."[4] Omission of this passage suggests Hardy's (or Mrs. Hardy's) attempt to make his feeling for Louisa seem more a passing daydream than it was.

Though Louisa lived most of her mature life at No. 4 Maumbury Road, Dorchester, and never married, Hardy did not renew his acquaintance with her. When she died on September 12, 1913, she was buried in Stinsford Churchyard. Apparently he did not attend her funeral or seek out her grave until some time later. On May 29, 1916, Mrs. Ethel Inglis visited Hardy and went to the Churchyard with him. The next day she wrote to her sister: "We first of all hunted for the grave of a Miss Harding, & Mr. Hardy is very agitated at the family not erecting a tombside [*sic*]. He said he would like to do it himself but the family would not like it."[5]

The biographical facts suggest that Hardy's feeling for Louisa was more a sentiment than a passion.

1. Purdy, *Thomas Hardy: A Bibliographical Study*, p. 253.
2. Pp. 33-34; *Life*, p. 26.
3. Phelps, *Annotations by Thomas Hardy in His Bibles and Prayer-Book*, p. 2.
4. In the Dorset County Museum.
5. In the Dorset County Museum.

LOVE WATCHES A WINDOW presents a woman's dream of love for a man who "had quite forsaken her / And followed another." She kept her dream alive by watching and even worshipping in a stained-glass window the image of a saint that resembled her lover.

THE LOVE-LETTERS, Purdy says, exists in "A fragment of an early draft on ruled paper, all but the title and first stanza cut away . . . now in my possession. It suggests that this is a late reworking of a discarded poem."[1] The initials "H. R." suggest that the poem treats a real person. Copps says: "The initials H. R. are the same as those of Henry Reeve (1813-1895), English man of letters with whom Hardy was acquainted, but whether it was to him that this poem was dedicated I do not know."[2] *The Early Life* says: "It was during this summer [1886] that the Hardys either began or renewed their acquaintance with Mrs. Henry Reeve and her sister Miss Gallop, whose family was an old Dorset one; and with Reeve himself, the well-known editor of the *Edinburgh Review* and of the famous *Greville Memoirs*."[3]

1. *Thomas Hardy:A Bibliographical Study*, p. 253.
2. "The Poetry of Thomas Hardy," p. 737.
3. P. 238; *Life*, p. 181.

AN UNKINDLY MAY was first published in the *Daily Telegraph* for April 23, 1928. The manuscript adds to the title "(1877)."[1] Under the heading of "Notes by F[lorence] E. H[ardy]" and the date of November 27, 1927,[2] *The Later Years* records: "'T. H. has been writing almost all the day, revising poems. When he came down to tea he brought one to show me, about a desolate spring morning, and a shepherd counting his sheep and not noticing the weather.' This is the poem in *Winter Words* called 'An Unkindly May.'"[3] A typescript of *The Later Years* adds: "Since writing the above I have been up to T. H.'s study and read the poem again and told him how much I liked it."[4]

Perhaps the poet observed the boisterous weather from the window of his home in Sturminster Newton in 1877. Two notes for November of this year describe the weather in imagery like that of the poem: "*November* 12. A flooded river after the incessant rains of yesterday. Lumps of froth float down like swans in front of our house. At the arches of the large stone bridge the froth has accumulated and lies like hillocks of salt against the bridge; then the arch chokes, and after a silence coughs out the air and froth, and gurgles on. *End of November.* This evening the west is like some vast foundry where new worlds are being cast."[5]

The phrase "still stands" in the penultimate line suggests that possibly the poem was at first only the central description of the weather, which Hardy in revision framed (for ironic contrast) by adding the picture of the stolid shepherd. The shepherd may have been suggested by a painting in his bedroom. Llewellyn Powys wrote: "Once when I was at Max Gate I had admired very much a small oil-painting of just such a weather-beaten shepherd. Mrs. Hardy told me that Mr. Hardy was so fond of it that he had always had it hanging near his bed."[6] The poem is both factual in its diary-like reporting and vivid in its imagery. Vinson comments that in its "homely and unpoetic diction . . . the imagery is more complex and 'modern' than is to be expected in a late Victorian."[7]

1. Purdy, *Thomas Hardy: A Bibliographical Study*, p. 253.
2. This date is the fifteenth anniversary of the death of Hardy's first wife Emma, though this fact seems to have no bearing on the poem.
3. P. 263; *Life*, p. 444.
4. In the Dorset County Museum.
5. *Early Life*, p. 155; *Life*, pp. 117-18. The poem speaks of May, the "spring wind," and buds that have tried to open, items that support the poet's "Better to-morrow!" Perhaps the poem fuses items of boisterous weather from several seasons.

6. "Stinsford Churchyard," p. 186.
7. "Diction and Imagery in the Poetry of Thomas Hardy," p. 88.

UNKEPT GOOD FRIDAYS was first published in the *Daily Telegraph* for April 5, 1928.[1] Possibly the idea for the poem came to Hardy when, reading his Bible, he came upon a note written many years before at the head of the Book of Ezekiel: "Mar. 25, 1864. Good Friday." Citing this note, Phelps says, "There is no clue to the association here, unless it was Hardy's growing sense of the betrayal of Christ's message by the idolatry and materialism of the age, at least equal in degree, if not in kind, to the targets of Ezekiel's anger."[2] Ezekiel's targets include idolatry, false prophecy, sensual sins, pride, tyranny, and hypocrisy.

The poem memorializes the many nameless "men whom rulers slew / For their goodwill." Perhaps Hardy had in mind not only the "heretics" of the medieval inquisitions but also the men of Dorchester condemned to death for non-conformity in Judge Jeffreys's "bloody assizes." (See George Jeffreys, 1648-89, in any reference book.)

1. Purdy, *Thomas Hardy: A Bibliographical Study*, p. 253.
2. *Annotations by Thomas Hardy in His Bibles and Prayer-Book*, p. 5.

THE MOUND seems to treat the lovers' quarrel suggested in the third stanza of "The Voice of the Thorn." If so, the thorn of the earlier poem is the "thin thorn hedge" of the later one, and the mound may be, as Miss Deacon suggests, in Yellowham Wood. She also suggests that the mound, the tree, and the thorn may be those of Hardy's drawing to illustrate "In a Eweleaze Near Weatherbury." If so, the scene is Coombe Eweleaze near Puddletown.

The poem seems to concern a quarrel between Hardy and Tryphena Sparks, to whom he was engaged before he met Emma Gifford. This surmise is supported by the statement in the Preface of *Jude the Obscure* that Sue Bridehead of the novel was partly based on a woman who died in 1890, as Tryphena did. Sue at eighteen had formed "a friendly intimacy with an undergraduate at Christminster" for a while (Part III, Chapter IV), and Hardy's first title for the novel was "The Simpletons," which seems echoed in the "innocent simpleton" of the poem. Miss Deacon suggests that the "comradeship" of the poem was Tryphena's alleged intimacy with Hardy's friend, Horace Moule. (See the notes on "Standing by the Mantelpiece.") The mound is seen "by the rays of the moon," nearly always in Hardy's poetry a symbol for a cynical or realistic view.

LIDDELL AND SCOTT is a humorous memorial poem occasioned by the death of Henry George Liddell on January 18, 1898. Contemplation of Liddell and Scott's vast labors in writing *A Greek-English*

Lexicon probably reminded Hardy of Browning's "A Grammarian's Funeral," and perhaps lines like Browning's "While he could stammer / He settled *Hoti's* business" determined his colloquial treatment. Instead of presenting, like Browning, students' praise of the lexicographers, he let the men speak for themselves in amazement at their own audacity, amusement at their misgivings, and relief that the job is done.

During a visit to Oxford in 1893, when Liddell received an honorary degree, Hardy observed the ceremonies "from the undergraduates' gallery of the Sheldonian."[1] Liddell and Scott were both associated with places in Wessex. Hardy owned the fifth edition of *A Greek-English Lexicon* (Oxford, 1851), and in conversations with his linguist-friend, William Barnes, he may have spoken often of Liddell and Scott.

Dr. Henry George Liddell (1811-98), after education at Christ Church, Oxford, became in 1838 headmaster of Winchester School. He had already begun collaboration with Robert Scott on their *Lexicon*. The first edition appeared in 1843, and it became the standard authority. In 1855, Liddell became Dean of Christ Church, Oxford, from which he retired in 1891. Robert Scott (1811-87), born in Devonshire, was likewise educated at Christ Church. After collaboration with Liddell and publication of the *Lexicon*, he became master of Balliol College, Oxford, in 1854.

Liddell and Scott's *Lexicon* was based upon the Greek-German lexicon of Franz Ludwig Passow, published in 1819. It was intended to supersede that of James Donnegan, whose *New Greek and English Lexicon* (first edition, 1826) was also in Hardy's library.[2] The poem has Liddell refer to "old Donnegan" somewhat disparagingly.

The reference to ἄαατος, ἀαγής, and ὠώδης is to the first and last words of Liddell and Scott's work.

1. *Later Years*, p. 22; *Life*, p. 257.
2. Rutland, *Thomas Hardy*, p. 27.

CHRISTMASTIDE presents an ironic contrast between the poet's inner despondence, deepened by spirit-dampening weather, and a "sodden tramp's" Christmas cheer that ignores the weather as he heads toward the Casuals' gate of the "Union House." On Damers Road in Dorchester, it is now called Damers Hospital, the geriatric unit of the Dorset County Hospital. In Hardy's time any "casual" (pauper or tramp) could apply to the police for a ticket, with which he would be admitted for supper, a bed, and breakfast. "Christmastide" is a companion-poem to "A Nightmare and the Next Thing."

RELUCTANT CONFESSION tells in dialogue the story of an unmarried woman who committed aborticide to save her reputation. Mentioning a loss at cards as beginning a chain of desperate actions, the poem reflects Hardy's interest in gambling and the fateful chances that follow.

EXPECTATION AND EXPERIENCE is a monologue addressed, the second line suggests, to Hardy by a woman he did not know.

ARISTODEMUS THE MESSENIAN, a one-act drama, is based upon a story told by Pausanias, a Greek geographer-historian of the second century, A.D., in his *Description of Greece*. In Book IV, Chapters IX-XIII, Pausanias tells the story of Aristodemus, King of Messenia in the years 731-724, B.C. When the Messenians, at war with the Lacedaemonians (Spartans), found themselves harassed, they retired to the mountain district of Ithome. Under continued attack, they sent a messenger to the oracle at Delphi, who brought back the message that they might save themselves by sacrificing a virgin. The patriot Aristodemus offered to sacrifice his daughter to save the state. "A Messenian, whose name is not known, happened to be deeply in love with the daughter of Aristodemus, and was on the eve of marrying her. He at first disputed the right of Aristodemus to the maiden as he had betrothed her to him, and argued that he being her betrothed alone had right to her. And afterwards, when he found this argument unavailing, he invented a shameful story, that he had had an amour with her and that she was pregnant by him. And at last he wrought up Aristodemus to such a pitch that driven to madness in his anger he killed his daughter, and afterwards cut her up and found she was not pregnant . . . . the mass of the Messenians rushed forward to kill the girl's lover, as he had caused Aristodemus to commit a useless crime. . . . But this man was a very great friend of Euphaes [King of the Messenians]. Euphaes accordingly persuaded the Messenians that the oracle was fulfilled by the death of the girl, and that what Aristodemus had done was sufficient." The Lacedaemonians, fearing the prophecy of the oracle, retired. Six years later King Euphaes died, and Aristodemus was elected king. When the Lacedaemonians were again threatening the Messenians, Aristodemus saw a vision: "He dreamed that he was going out to battle fully armed . . . and his daughter appeared to him in a black dress with her breast and belly ripped up, and he thought she . . . took away his armour, and instead of it put upon him a golden crown and white robe. And as Aristodemus was dispirited, for he thought the dream announced to him the end of his life (for the Messenians buried their notable men in white raiment with crowns on their heads) . . . Aristodemus . . . cut his throat at his daughter's grave."[1]

In dramatizing this tale, Hardy followed a romantic tradition in making the lover an unknown beggar, rather than a friend of the king; he neglected Aristodemus's dream and suicide. He secured dramatic concentration by having King Euphaes killed in battle even before Aristodemus killed his daughter, and having the lover kill himself.

He may have written the poem while he was working on *The Dynasts.* In this epic-drama, the Prince Regent, the Emperor of Russia, and other guests attend the opera in London. There, "The curtain rises on the first act of the opera 'Aristodemo,' Madame Grassini and Signor Tramezzini being the leading voices." (Part Third, IV, viii.) Perhaps Hardy looked up the story behind the opera at this time. The theme of the opera has no bearing upon *The Dynasts,* except as historical fact.[2] He may have written the poem after some later reading of Pausanias's story.

The story, at least as Hardy concentrated it, suited his taste for irony, or for good intentions that result in tragedy. The play presents an exercise in "dramatic hendecasyllabics," or metrical lines of eleven syllables. In comment, Hickson says, "The 87 lines are in falling rhythm, varying between 4- and 5-stresses, with frequent use of rhythmical variations."[3]

1. Shilleto, *Pausanias' Description of Greece,* pp. 246, 253.
2. A number of plays and operas were written about Aristodemus, for instance, Claude Boyer's *Aristodème,* Paris, 1649; Carlo de' Dottori's *Aristodeme,* in the seventeenth century; and Catherine Crowe's *Aristodemus,* Edinburgh, 1838.
3. *The Versification of Thomas Hardy,* p. 88.

EVENING SHADOWS, first published in the *Daily Telegraph* on May 7, 1928,[1] seems suggested by the shadows of Hardy's home, Max Gate. The "neighbouring Pagan mound" is Conquer Barrow, a burial site of the ancient Britons. In the evening of his life, the shadows of time lengthen, but when he is dead the shadows will extend no farther than now. The shadows of yet-living faiths will stretch no farther: all present religions and cultures will fade away.

1. Purdy, *Thomas Hardy: A Bibliographical Study,* p. 254.

THE THREE TALL MEN was first published in the *Daily Telegraph* on August 9, 1928.[1] Perhaps the idea for this wryly humorous poem came to Hardy as he worked on the manuscript for *The Early Life.* He had recorded in his diary for March 13, 1883: "Our servant brings us a report . . . that the carpenter who made a coffin for Mr. W. who died the other day, made it too short. A bystander said satirically,

'Anybody would think you'd made it for yourself, John!' (the carpenter was a short man). The maker said, 'Ah—they would!' and fell dead instantly."[2] In his first manuscript, the poem was titled "The Two Tall Men"; it was written on the back of an announcement of the sale of Wembley Stadium and Racecourse Shares dated August 24, 1927. Hardy ended this version as at present: the tall carpenter died at sea.[3] The insertion of a third tall man illustrates his impish effort to deepen his irony. (For another example of this effort, see the notes on "Ah, Are You Digging on My Grave?")

1. Purdy, *Thomas Hardy: A Bibliographical Study*, p. 254.
2. P. 206; *Life*, pp. 158-59.
3. Weber, "An Important Hardy Manuscript," pp. 303-4.

THE LODGING-HOUSE FUCHSIAS was first published in the *Daily Telegraph* for August 13, 1928.[1] The poem, naming Mrs. Masters, seems based upon an incident in Hardy's life at Swanage. In July of 1875, he and his bride found lodgings in Swanage "at the house of an invalided captain of smacks and ketches" named Masters, and lived there until March of 1876.[2] In theme, the poem parallels a passage in *The Mayor of Casterbridge*. When Susan Henchard has died, Mother Cuxsom laments: "And all her shining keys will be took from her, and her cupboards opened; and little things a' didn't wish seen, anybody will see; and her wishes and ways will all be as nothing!" (Chapter XVIII.)

1. Purdy, *Thomas Hardy: A Bibliographical Study*, p. 254.
2. *Early Life*, pp. 141-42; *Life*, pp. 107-8.

THE WHALER'S WIFE may be based on fact. If so the "I" who tells it represents Hardy, and his source of information is the "ancient swain" of the ninth stanza. A disguise so slight as to seem revealing lies in the name of the inn and its location near a church. The name "The Ring of Bells" is so common for inns in the villages of Wessex that it may serve as a disguise for a similar name.

In Bridport, fifteen miles west of Dorchester and a mile and a half north of Bridport Harbor at West Bay, there is a picturesque old "pub" called "The Five Bells" on the road toward West Bay. The prominent "signpost" or inn-sign for "The Five Bells" has a colorful display on each side: on one side, five brazen bells, and on the other, five bell-ringers toiling at the ropes. "The Five Bells" is diagonally across the road from the parish church about a hundred yards farther from the town-center, so that people living in Bridport and attending the church would walk past the "pub" on their way home, as in the poem.

The story rests on the kind of irony that attracted Hardy: the simple and gullible whaler, home from the sea with a dream of settling down with a devoted wife as publican (in British usage, keeper of a "pub"), infers the worst from the tale of a Sunday morning toper, though the "we" of the story suggests the presence of nodding cronies.

THROWING A TREE was first published in the Winter, 1928, issue of the French magazine *Commerce,* under the title "Felling a Tree." On the facing page was published a French translation by Paul Valéry, with a note saying that the poem was sent to the magazine by Mrs. Hardy and that it was the last written by Hardy a short time before his death (January 11, 1928).[1]

The poem with its original title, "Felling a Tree," may have been suggested by William Barnes's "Vellèn the Tree," which Hardy chose for the edition of Barnes's poems he edited.[2] Though details differ, both poems are chiefly descriptive and both close with a similar conclusion. Barnes's last two lines read: "Zoo the gre't elem tree out in little hwome groun' / Wer a stannèn this mornèn, an' now's a-cut down." Perhaps Hardy changed his title to avoid calling attention to the similarity.

"Throwing a Tree" exhibits Hardy's feeling that the tree is in some way a suffering fellow-creature. Job and Ike are called "executioners," and as they cut into the tree, he uses such words as "gash," "shivers," and "quivers" as if to picture the tree's pain. No doubt he shared a feeling that Jude, in *Jude the Obscure,* had as a boy: "He could scarcely bear to see trees cut down or lopped, from a fancy that it hurt them; and late pruning, when the sap was up and the tree bled profusely, had been a positive grief to him in his infancy."[3]

The poem may be read as symbolizing Hardy's thought of himself as approaching the end of his life, when he might fall as the tree fell. This possibility is suggested by the feeling of old South in *The Woodlanders,* that his life-span was associated with that of the great tree seen from his window. (Chapter XIV.) The tree is located somewhere in the New Forest. (See the notes on "A Trampwoman's Tragedy.")

1. Certain circumstances suggest that "Felling a Tree" was by no means Hardy's last poem. In a letter dated March 11, without a year, the Princess Marguerite Di Bassiano wrote to Hardy requesting a poem for *Commerce,* which she was sponsoring. A letter from Leonard Woolf to Mrs. Hardy, dated January 3, 1927—probably a mistake for 1928—refers to Hardy's permission to Princess Di Bassiano to publish a French translation of a poem, but says that *Commerce* will publish the translation only if it is accompanied by the original. No other poem by Hardy first appeared in this magazine. (Letters are in the Dorset County Museum.)

Apparently, Mrs. Hardy sent the manuscript of "Felling a Tree" after Hardy's death. As Hardy had prepared the manuscript for *Winter Words*, presumably he then changed the title to "Throwing a Tree," and Mrs. Hardy must have sent an earlier manuscript.

2. *Select Poems of William Barnes*, London, 1908.

3. Part I, Chapter II. *The Woodlanders* is shot through with phrases that imply the suffering of trees as they sigh, rub each other into wounds, etc. See, for instance, Chapter VII.

THE WAR-WIFE OF CATKNOLL was first published in the *Daily Telegraph* for June 21, 1928.[1] Hardy's naming a place and a time (when a soldier has returned from France) suggests that this ballad-like drama is based upon fact. Catknoll seems Hardy's name for the village of Chetnole, which is on a country road about fourteen miles northwest of Dorchester. In the Middle Ages, this village was called "Chateknolle."[2] The unnamed road running through the village might well be called Chetnole ("Catknoll") Street. This road crosses a river named the Wriggle that also runs through the village. Though it normally has hardly enough water to invite suicide, it has steep banks. Hutchings says of it: "In spate after a heavy storm on the hills I am told it resembles a miniature 'Colorado River,' and makes almost as much commotion."[3]

In the 1920's, while gathering material for *The Early Life*, Hardy examined the parish registers of Melbury Osmund, where his mother was born. In the *Register of Baptisms* it is recorded that on June 30, 1817, George King was "Baptized privately," the son of Edith Wills, described as "Wife of James Wills, a Soldier who has been out of England more than two years." Hardy may have added fiction to dramatize the story: the return of the soldier from France and his wife's suicide. Perhaps to obscure any connection with his mother's family, Hardy moved the scene to Chetnole, disguised as Catknoll, which is situated less than two miles to the east of Melbury Osmund. The two villages are similar in size and in the fact that a small river runs through each.

The time of the soldier's return, in the winding up of the Napoleonic wars, is suggested in the phrase "she must be crowned," which Hardy footnotes as "Old English."

1. Purdy, *Thomas Hardy: A Bibliographical Study*, p. 254.
2. Fägersten, *The Place-Names of Dorset*, p. 222.
3. *Inside Dorset*, p. 159.

CONCERNING HIS OLD HOME was first published in the *Daily Telegraph* for August 16, 1928.[1] After the death of Hardy's mother in 1904, his brother Henry and his sisters Mary and Kate lived in the "old home" at Higher Bockhampton until the end of 1912, at which time they went to live at Talbothays, a farm-house near West Stafford.

In February, 1913, Hermann Lea moved into the homestead. Hardy told him: "I do not know anyone I would rather see there than you, for I feel you will respect the old associations of the place, and leave things as they are." Lea was a somewhat eccentric bachelor who, though interested in gardening, beekeeping, etc., probably did "leave things as they are" in the house and allow it to become dilapidated. Hardy visited Lea from time to time. Of a visit in 1918, Lea wrote: "I know that, in spite of his interests in the house and garden, a visit here was not without sadness to him, as he freely admitted to me more than once." Lea occupied the house until 1921,[2] when it passed into the hands of caretakers.

Of this visit, Mrs. Florence Hardy wrote to Sir Sydney Cockerell on April 18: "Strangely enough we cycled this afternoon (T. H. and I) to Bockhampton for the first time this year, and sat in the garden. . . . It was a heavenly afternoon—but somehow, the visit seemed sad. . . . And going towards the cottage he asked himself why he had come again to that old place—and thought he should go there no more."[3] Nevertheless he did return. *The Later Years* presents an entry in his diary for May 26, 1922, with a comment: "'Visited Stinsford and Higher Bockhampton. House at the latter shabby, and garden. Just went through into heath, and up plantation to top of garden.' It was becoming increasingly painful to Hardy to visit this old home of his, and often when he left he said that he would go there no more."[4]

The poem seems to present his reactions after this visit. It traces four moods that progress from pained observation of "that dismal place" to nostalgic memories of childhood. The progress is psychologically interesting. After the resolution of Mood I, Mood II wavers toward "just once more." In Mood III, mentioning the "green low door," Hardy's mind returns to Higher Bockhampton as it was in his childhood: "The domiciles were quaint, brass-knockered, and green-shuttered then, some with green garden-doors and white balls on the posts, and mainly occupied by lifeholders of substantial footing like the Hardys themselves." Mood IV, recalling the "flowers' rich store," advances to his romantic youth as pictured in his adolescent poem "Domicilium,"[5] wherein "Red roses, lilacs, variegated box / Are there in plenty, and such hardy flowers / As flourish best untrained."

1. Purdy, *Thomas Hardy: A Bibliographical Study*, p. 254.
2. Cox, ed., *Thomas Hardy Through the Camera's Eye*, pp. 28, 32, 33.
3. Meynell, ed., *Friends of a Lifetime*, p. 298.
4. P. 226; *Life*, p. 415. Apparently his final visit was on November 1, 1926, when he went with Cecil Hanbury "to look at fencing, trees, etc. with a view to tidying and secluding the Hardy house." Skilling, *Thomas Hardy and His Birth-place*, p. 15.
5. *Early Life*, pp. 3-4; *Life*, pp. 3-4.

HER SECOND HUSBAND HEARS HER STORY was first published in the *Daily Telegraph* for July 23, 1928.[1] It presents a bedtime dialogue in which a wife confides to her second husband how she had unintentionally (but without regret) murdered her drunken first husband. The wife's story is a confession to a kindly man whom she trusts with her secret. In some wonder at the wife's self-possession, he calls it a "cool queer tale."

Discussing Hardy's fondness for making poems of odd, scandalous facts, Blunden says: " 'It was a true story,' said Hardy eagerly. And that was for him full warrant for most of these anecdotes." In listing a number of them, Blunden includes "Her Second Husband Hears Her Story" and implies that the poem was based on fact.[2] I was assured by elderly people in Dorset that the event might well have occurred in some remote village.

1. Purdy, *Thomas Hardy: A Bibliographical Study*, p. 254.
2. *Thomas Hardy*, p. 247.

YULETIDE IN A YOUNGER WORLD was first published as a pamphlet by Faber & Gwyer, Ltd., of London. The manuscript was "sent to the publishers in May 1927 at the request of Richard de la Mare, son of the poet, to inaugurate a series of gift booklets. It was published 25 August 1927 in two forms simultaneously, a limited edition of 350 copies . . . and an ordinary edition of 5,000 copies."[1]

The poem presents the triumph of reason over literal faith in superstitions and the religiously miraculous. The loss of faith, making men "blinker-bound," has deadened the wonder of Christmas. The poem may be interpreted as a picture of the aging poet's feeling that he had been happy as a youth in his now-lost dreams. Perhaps realizing that the poem expressed only a passing fancy, he did not prize it. When Louis Untermeyer wished to include it in an anthology, Hardy wrote on September 21, 1927: "It is not a poem I value, and I should prefer, if I were making the selection, 'The Carrier,' or 'Waiting Both,' or 'Song to an Old Burden.' "[2]

1. Purdy, *Thomas Hardy: A Bibliographical Study*, pp. 249-50.
2. In the Lilly Library, Indiana University.

AFTER THE DEATH OF A FRIEND was first published in the *Daily Telegraph* for July 10, 1928.[1] The poem expresses Hardy's attitude toward death in the light of the attitude of an unnamed friend, probably Horace Moule, who committed suicide in 1873. Poems that clearly concern Moule name him only as a friend. Moule's dying words were "Easy to die," which Hardy parallels in "made but little of it." In spite of the phrase "Inexorable, insatiate one!" his attitude is summed up by Evelyn Hardy: "He once declared to a friend, in a peculiarly Donnian phrase, that dying seemed to him merely 'like stepping into the next room.' "[2]

1. Purdy, *Thomas Hardy: A Bibliographical Study*, p. 254.
2. *Thomas Hardy*, p. 333.

THE SON'S PORTRAIT was sent to Macmillan in March of 1924.[1] The theme of a wife's callousness toward her dead husband's portrait is paralleled in *Jude the Obscure*. After her desertion of Jude, Arabella sells his portrait, and Jude comes upon it in a broker's shop: "On the back was still to be read, *'Jude to Arabella,'* with the date. She must have thrown it in with the rest of her property at the auction." (Part I, Chapter XI.)   In the poem, the mother's shock is sharpened by her anguished burial of the portrait in place of the son, lost in the war.

1. Purdy, *Thomas Hardy: A Bibliographical Study*, p. 255.

LYING AWAKE was first published in the *Saturday Review* for December 3, 1927.[1] Presenting graphic images of what the poet knows, without looking, the world looks like at dawn, the poem pictures Hardy's characteristic ability to see vivid pictures in memory or reverie.

1. Purdy, *Thomas Hardy: A Bibliographical Study*, p. 255.

THE LADY IN THE FURS was first published as "The Lady in the Christmas Furs" in the *Saturday Review* for December 4, 1926.[1] The date in Hardy's note, 1925, the original title, and the date of first publication suggest that the poem was written about Christmas furs of 1925 and held until the Christmas season of the next year. The poem has a threefold theme: a scornful picture of a vain, proud, callous woman; a protest against the slaughter of animals for their furs; and an attack upon "sweatshop" labor in industry.

Quoting part of the poem, Weber says that Hardy "let the whole world know what he thought of ladies like Rebekah Owen."[2]   (See the notes on "To a Lady.")   Some particulars of the poem do not fit Miss Owen, who had no husband, though her wealth, inherited from her father, came from trade. Possibly Weber's comment rests upon letters that Mrs. Florence Hardy wrote to Miss Owen in 1915. On September 6, she wrote: "I am so glad you have that handsome coat —& I know that you look like a princess in it—a *handsome* princess. . . . My husband, who notices so little as a rule, always says how well & effectively you have always dressed." Miss Owen must have spoken of the coat again, for on October 1, Florence wrote: "I am quite sure that you will look so splendid in your new fur coat that you will

forget having paid more than you think it is worth."[3] An objection
to this identification is that the letters are dated 1915, and the poem,
1925.

Mrs. Gertrude Bugler, who was chosen by Hardy to play Tess and
other roles in the plays produced by the Hardy Players and who knew
the Hardy household well in the 1920's, told me, in a conversation
of May 9, 1967, that she knew from "personal knowledge" that "The
Lady in the Furs" portrayed Mrs. Cecil Hanbury of Kingston Maur-
ward, who had a fine fur coat, purchased with the money her husband
made in processing baby and invalid foods. Hardy and the Hanburys
had been friendly (see the notes on "To C. F. H."), but Mrs. Hardy
and Mrs. Hanbury had "fallen out."

1. Purdy, *Thomas Hardy: A Bibliographical Study*, p. 255.
2. *Hardy and the Lady from Madison Square*, p. 203.
3. In the Colby College Library.

CHILDHOOD AMONG THE FERNS was first published in the *Daily
Telegraph* for March 29, 1928.[1] The poem is autobiographical, de-
veloping a memory recorded in *The Early Life*. When Hardy was
less than eight years old, "He was lying on his back in the sun, think-
ing how useless he was, and covered his face with his straw hat. . . .
Reflecting on his experiences of the world so far as he had got, he
came to the conclusion that he did not wish to grow up. Other boys
were always talking of when they would be men; he did not want at
all to be a man, or to possess things, but to remain as he was, in the
same spot and to know no more people than he already knew (about
half a dozen)."[2]

He made use of this experience in describing the childhood of
Jude in *Jude the Obscure*. Lying on a heap of litter, Jude "pulled his
straw hat over his face, and peered through the interstices of the
plaiting at the white brightness, vaguely reflecting. Growing up
brought responsibilities, he found. . . . If he could only prevent him-
self growing up! He did not want to be a man." (Part I, Chapter
II.) "Childhood Among the Ferns" has been set to music in *Before
and After Summer* (London: Boosey & Hawkes, 1949).

1. Purdy, *Thomas Hardy: A Bibliographical Study*, p. 255.
2. Pp. 19-20; *Life*, pp. 15-16. The passage occurs just before a description of
Hardy's first school, which he entered in 1848.

A COUNTENANCE, Duffin says, is "a totally new, bizarre, modern
bit of portraiture."[1] The poem expresses the romantic idea that
some irregularity of feature enhances beauty, but with the realistic
question whether this element of charm would continue to be at-
tractive.

1. *Thomas Hardy*, p. 309.

A POET'S THOUGHT suggests that an intuition expressed in a poem "leapt all over the land" in the manner, perhaps, of "the winged shafts of truth" in Tennyson's "The Poet." The second stanza contrasts this romantic view with the reality (in Hardy's experience with reviewers) that popular interpretation distorted the thought out of all recognition.

SILENCES treats the depressing effect of silence in a place that the memory associates with sound. Hardy seems to be speaking of his birthplace in Higher Bockhampton after his sisters and brother and perhaps Hermann Lea had abandoned it. (See the notes on "Concerning His Old Home.")

"I WATCHED A BLACKBIRD" was first published in the *Daily Telegraph* for July 2, 1928.[1] Southworth comments that "The quality of observation in this poem is that of a trained naturalist."[2] Not a naturalist, Hardy was a devoted bird-watcher. The poem versifies an entry in his diary for April 15, 1900. In the typescript of *The Later Years* labelled "T. H. Vol. II. 1892 to end. 3rd Rough Copy," the entry is copied as: "Easter Sunday. Watched a blackbird on a budding sycamore near enough to see his tongue and even his coloured bill parting and closing as he sang. He flew down, picked up a stem of hay, and flew up to where he was building."[3] Perhaps Hardy wrote the poem at the time he inserted the entry, and then omitted it because he had "duplicated" it in the poem. Possibly, when Mrs. Hardy sent the poem to the *Daily Telegraph* after Hardy's death, she observed the duplication and omitted the passage then.

1. Purdy, *Thomas Hardy: A Bibliographical Study*, p. 255.
2. *The Poetry of Thomas Hardy*, p. 199.
3. In the Dorset County Museum. The passage, written on the back of a page, might have been inserted on p. 85 or 86 of the volume as published; *Life*, p. 306 or 307.

A NIGHTMARE, AND THE NEXT THING seems to describe Hardy's late-afternoon walk from Max Gate into downtown Dorchester on a dull, foggy Christmas day. If so, he observes first the houses in Fordington on the way to High East Street, and climbs this thoroughfare just as the lamps are lit. Three "casuals" pass him on the way to the Union House. (See the notes on "Christmastide.") Looking down the street, he sees a wagonette approaching, with six girls on the way to a dance.

The poem contrasts the "nightmare" mood of the poet with the gaiety of even "clammy casuals," who, like the girls, see no "gray nightmare." The nightmare is not defined (except as symbolized in the weather), but it may be surmised in view of the probable date. The Christmas cannot be that of 1927, for Hardy was ill then and barely able to get downstairs. It may be that of 1926 or 1925, when he had passed his middle eighties, was physically feeble, and, looking toward death as a release from life, was taking a last Christmas walk alone in the gloom. If the nightmare is a foreboding of death, the "next thing" may be death itself.

TO A TREE IN LONDON, though dated as written in "192—," was based upon Hardy's memory of his life in London in the summer of 1870. *The Early Life* says: "He seems to have passed the days in Town desultorily and dreamily . . ." with his mind occupied with Emma Gifford, whom he had met in March. He busied himself to some extent with architectural work. "He was welcomed by Mr. Blomfield, to whom he lent help in finishing some drawings. Being acquainted with another well-known Gothic architect, Mr. Raphael Brandon, Hardy assisted him also for a few weeks . . . and the old-world out-of-the-way corner of Clement's Inn where Brandon's offices were situate made his weeks with Brandon still more attractive to him, Knight's chambers in *A Pair of Blue Eyes* being drawn from Brandon's."[1]

The description of Knight's chambers in "Bede's" (Clement's) Inn includes the tree addressed in Hardy's poem: "Bede's Inn has this peculiarity, that it faces, receives from, and discharges into a bustling thoroughfare speaking only of wealth and respectability, whilst its postern abuts on as crowded and poverty-stricken a network of alleys as are to be found anywhere in the metropolis. . . . On the fine October evening on which we follow Stephen Smith to this place, a placid porter is sitting on a stool under a sycamore tree in the midst. . . . We notice the thick coat of soot upon the branches, hanging underneath them in flakes, as in a chimney. The blackness of these boughs does not at present improve the tree—nearly forsaken by its leaves as it is—but in the spring their green fresh beauty is made doubly beautiful by the contrast." (Chapter XIII.)

Clement's Inn is an office building in central London near the Royal Courts of Justice. A narrow lane and an iron railing separate it from the Law Courts. Beside the lane and the railing are two large plane (or sycamore) trees, surrounded by asphalt paving and smoke-darkened buildings, except for a small parking lot and a few small trees beside the Courts. The poem reflects Hardy's feeling of being cramped and stunted in London during the period when, hoping to make a reputation as a writer, he was edging away from architecture.

1. Pp. 101-2; *Life*, pp. 76-77.

THE FELLED ELM AND SHE in an early draft was called "The Thrown Elm."[1] This colloquial jingle expresses Hardy's fetishistic feeling that human lives are mysteriously linked with the lives of trees. This feeling underlies the story of old South in Chapter XIV of *The Woodlanders* and the poems "The Tree: An Old Man's Story," "The Tree and the Lady," and "Throwing a Tree."

1. Purdy, *Thomas Hardy: A Bibliographical Study*, p. 255.

HE DID NOT KNOW ME was first published in the *Daily Telegraph* for May 17, 1928.[1] This dialogue reported by a sorrowing woman seems an allegory to illustrate the epigram of the last two lines. It may in a general way allude to Hardy's failure to "know" his first wife in her later years. Her poetic and other literary effusions were optimistic in tone, while many of his were pessimistic. (See Cox, ed., *Poems and Religious Effusions by Emma Lavinia Hardy*.)

1. Purdy, *Thomas Hardy: A Bibliographical Study*, p. 255.

SO VARIOUS was first published in the *Daily Telegraph* for March 22, 1928.[1] It expresses Hardy's amused application of a thought recorded in his diary for December 4, 1890: "I am more than ever convinced that persons are successively various persons, according as each special strand in their characters is brought uppermost by circumstances."[2] Weber says that "This piece of self-analysis was quite true, and the preceding chapters of this book have shown Hardy acting as musician, architect, playwright, artist, editor, antiquary, poet, philosopher, and novelist."[3] He might have added a variety of personal traits evident in Hardy's poems: Hardy was a solitary, living secluded at Max Gate and fond of the country; a clubman, fond of evenings at the Savile in London; a misogynist deriding woman's vanity; an ardent lover even in old age—and so on.

The poem rests largely upon Hardy's long-continued tussle with reviewers. Sensitive to reviews, he apparently tried to keep abreast of them. Talking with Frederick Dolman in 1894, he pointed to a pile of current magazines and said, "What a mass of periodicals come here by the post!"[4] When *Jude the Obscure* was being viciously reviewed, he "with his quick sense of humour could not help seeing a ludicrous side to it all," but he was also hurt. He "underwent the strange experience of beholding a sinister lay figure of himself constructed by them [reviewers], which had no sort of resemblance to him as he was, and which he, and those who knew him well, would not have recognized as being meant for himself if it had not been called by his name."[5]

In a humorously satiric letter to Clement Shorter on August 8,

1907, he paralleled the theme of "So Various," saying: "I endeavour to profit from the opinions of those wonderful youths & maidens, my reviewers, & am laying to heart a few infallible truths taught by them: e.g.,—That T. H.'s verse is his only claim to notice. That T. H.'s prose is his only real work. That T. H.'s early novels are best. That T. H.'s later novels are best. That T. H.'s novels are good in plot & bad in character. That T. H.'s novels are bad in plot & good in character[n]. That T. H.'s philosophy is all that matters. That T. H.'s writings are good in spite of their bad philosophy. This is as far as I have got at present, but I struggle gallantly on."[6] Hardy kept a scrapbook of clippings from magazines and newspapers describing him, his home, and his opinions. Opposite many clippings he wrote "Lies" or "Invented."[7]

1. Purdy, *Thomas Hardy: A Bibliographical Study*, p. 256.
2. *Early Life*, p. 301; *Life*, p. 230.
3. *Hardy of Wessex*, 2nd ed., p. 238.
4. Dolman, "An Evening with Thomas Hardy," p. 76.
5. *Later Years*, p. 39; *Life*, p. 270.
6. In the British Museum.
7. Labelled "T. H. Personal" in the Dorset County Museum.

A SELF-GLAMOURER seems Hardy's meditation upon the "little happiness" of his life seen from the point of view of old age. Through labor to realize his youthful dreams, some "visions" have become "verities."

THE DEAD BASTARD was first published in the *Daily Telegraph* for September 7, 1928.[1] This soliloquy by a woman who suffered by the scandal of her child's birth but suffered more when the child died forms a part of Hardy's attack upon the convention that an unwed mother is "ruined" for life. In *Tess of the D'Urbervilles*, commenting upon Tess's agony when her child dies, he said ironically: "So passed away Sorrow the Undesired—that intrusive creature, that bastard gift of shameless Nature who respects not the social law." (Chapter XIV.) In "The Dark-Eyed Gentleman," he pictured the bastard child as a potential blessing.

1. Purdy, *Thomas Hardy: A Bibliographical Study*, p. 256.

THE CLASPED SKELETONS was first published in the *Daily Telegraph* for August 2, 1928.[1] The headnote, giving the "surmised date" as 1800 B.C. and the place as "an Ancient British Barrow near the writer's house," suggests that the clasped skeletons were found in Conquer Barrow, an ancient British burial site a few hundred yards east of Max Gate. In building the driveway, Hardy told William Archer, "We decapitated a row of five Roman soldiers or colonists in moving the earth to make the drive there. —*W. A.* And wasn't there a lady as well?—*Mr. Hardy.* Yes. I think I showed you the little bronze-gilt fibula that had fastened the fillet across her brow. I took it from her skull with my own hands, and it lies in the corner cupboard yonder."[2]

The poem implies that the skeletons were those of a man and a woman clasping one another as lovers. An instance is given in Hutchins's *History of Dorset.* In a barrow "about half-a-mile south of the Afflington Barn, upon the Swanage and Kingston Road" were found, among other interments, one that "had no wall of stone or protection of any kind, and contained the remains of a man and a woman." (I, 530.)

Assuming that love continues in the grave, the poem presents a list of lovers whose passion seems, by comparison, a thing of "yestertide." Paris and Helen were lovers who brought about the Trojan war before the sixth century B.C. King David committed adultery with Bathsheba in the eleventh century B.C. (2 Samuel 11.) Jael welcomed Sisera into her tent, but when he slept, murdered him, in the fourteenth century B.C. (Judges 4.) Aholah "committed whoredoms in Egypt" in the sixth century B.C., until she was slain. (Ezekiel 23.) Aspasia was the mistress of Pericles, ruler of Athens, in the fifth century B.C. Philip's son, Alexander the Great, loved the courtesan Thaïs and took her with him on his campaign in Asia in the fourth century B.C. Dryden's "Alexander's Feast" says that the "vanquished victor sunk upon her breast." Mark Antony was led to suicide by his passion for Cleopatra in the first century B.C. The Gospels say that, at Jesus's trial, Pilate's "wife [Procula] sent unto him, saying, Have thou nothing to do with that just man: for I have suffered many things this day in a dream because of him." In the twelfth century A.D., the monk Abélard, tutor of Héloise, became her lover, for which he was "scarred" (castrated) by her uncle.

1. Purdy, *Thomas Hardy: A Bibliographical Study,* p. 256.
2. Archer, "Real Conversations," p. 313.

IN THE MARQUEE was first published in the *Daily Telegraph* for July 16, 1928. "Hardy's rough notes for the poem are headed, 'The party at W[estbourne] P[ark] V[illas].' "[1] This fact suggests that the poem records a memory or a fictional idea that came to him during a party in a back garden when he was living at Westbourne Park Villas in 1863-1867.

1. Purdy, *Thomas Hardy: A Bibliographical Study,* p. 256.

AFTER THE BURIAL records the ironic juxtaposition of sorrow and joy in the varied processes of life. The "large tall tower" and the "jocund clangour" along the street suggest a dwelling near the center of Dorchester and St. Peter's Church.

THE MONGREL was first published in the *Daily Telegraph* for June 25, 1928.[1] "Havenpool" is Hardy's name for Poole Harbour, about twenty miles east of Dorchester. He took his fictional name from history; Hutchins records that in an earlier period the Burgesses of Pool [*sic*] called the harbor the "Haven of Pool." The scene by "the paved wharf-side" suggests the street that is also a quay where boats tie up. Because the harbor is large and the inlet narrow, the waters rushing seaward at ebb-tide provide a tow strong enough to overcome a dog's power to reach the shore. The passage in Hutchins that names the Haven of Pool is followed by "The tide rises nine feet perpendicular in the harbour, which has this peculiar in it, that the sea contrary to all other ports in England, ebbs and flows twice in the twenty-four hours."[2]

Hardy's indignation at human treachery toward animals is evident in the poem. The man destroys his faithful dog (presumably not salable, because a mongrel) to avoid paying a dog-tax. He does so through the dog's "ardent pride" in pleasing his master, held to be "a god enshrined." Then the poem presents the master through the dog's eyes, in which, realizing treachery, blind love turns to "a loathing of mankind."

1. Purdy, *Thomas Hardy: A Bibliographical Study*, p. 256.
2. *The History of Dorset*, I, 8-9.

CONCERNING AGNES was first published in the *Daily Telegraph* for May 21, 1928. Agnes was Lady Grove, who had died on December 7, 1926. The poem recalls Hardy's dancing with her at Rushmore in September, 1895. "The two kept up a friendship and correspondence, Lady Grove consulting Hardy about her writing and dedicating her book *The Social Fetich* (1907) to him."[1]

The Later Years describes the incident of the first two stanzas: "In September they [Mr. and Mrs. Hardy] paid a week's visit to General and Mrs. Pitt-Rivers at Rushmore. . . . It was on the occasion of the annual sports at the Larmer Tree, and a full moon and clear sky favouring, the dancing on the green was a great success. The local paper gives. . . : 'After nightfall the scene was one of extraordinary picturesqueness and poetry, its great features being the illumination of the grounds by thousands of Vauxhall lamps, and the dancing of hundreds of couples under these lights and the mellow radiance of the full moon. For the dancing . . . some country-dances were started by the house-party, and led off by the beautiful Mrs. Grove, the daughter of General Pitt-Rivers, and her charming sister-in-law, Mrs. Pitt.' . . . It may be worth mentioning that, passionately fond of dancing as Hardy had been from earliest childhood, this was the last occasion on which he ever trod a measure. . . . It was he who started the country dances, his partner being the above-mentioned Mrs. (afterwards Lady) Grove." *The Later Years* also describes Hardy's dancing with Lady Grove at the Imperial Institute in London in July of 1896: "Here one evening they met, with other of their friends, the beautiful Mrs., afterwards Lady, Grove; and the 'Blue Danube' Waltz being started, Hardy and the latter lady danced two or three turns to it among the promenaders, who eyed them with a mild surmise as to whether they had been drinking or not." [2]

Agnes Grove was the daughter of Lieutenant-General Augustus Pitt-Rivers of Rushmore, an estate fifteen miles southwest of Salisbury, near Farnham. General Pitt-Rivers had, in 1880, laid out pleasure-grounds for the recreation of the people of surrounding towns and villages; the grounds included gardens, lawns, a "Temple," and arbors for picnic parties, with a bandstand for a band that provided music every Sunday afternoon through the summer. "Larmer Avenue" is Larmer Road, which leads from Larmer Park to Minchington Cross on the Rushmore Estate. It is named for the Larmer Tree, on the boundary between Dorset and Wiltshire, a wych elm under which, according to tradition, King John assembled his huntsmen. (By the 1890's only the shell of the original tree remained, but General Pitt-Rivers had had an oak planted in the center of the shell, and it was called the Larmer Tree.) [3]

Hardy's recollection, as stated in *The Later Years*, that his dancing with Lady Grove was "the last occasion on which he ever trod a measure" is supported by his reply to a birthday greeting from her dated June 2, 1924. He wrote on the back of a letter to be copied by Mrs. Hardy: "Says I am to tell you he often thinks of you & does not forget that you are the last person he ever danced with (if his memory serves) at the Larmer Tree." [4]

The last two stanzas of "Concerning Agnes" picture her as beautiful in death, wherever she may lie, "in a nook I have never seen." Hardy imagines her as vaguely like any one of four Greek mythological figures: Aphrodite, goddess of love; Kalupso (Calypso), a nymph who entertained Ulysses for seven years; Amphitrite, a sea-goddess and wife of Poseidon; and one of the nine Muses. The phrasing suggests that he was thinking of a tomb that would bear Lady Grove's image with "features marble-keen."

1. Purdy, *Thomas Hardy: A Bibliographical Study*, p. 256.
2. Pp. 37-38, 53; *Life*, pp. 269, 281.

3. See Lieutenant-General Pitt-Rivers, *A Short Guide to the Larmer Grounds.* The Grounds are now closed to the public. The buildings intended for public entertainment are somewhat dilapidated; roads are rutted, but magnificent avenues of trees and the abandoned buildings indicate the splendor of a former time.

4. In the Dorset County Museum. Apparently Hardy's memory did not serve at the moment. He "danced for the last time in his life," with Mrs. Cecil Hanbury in December, 1919. See the notes on "To C. F. H." and *Later Years*, p. 198; *Life*, p. 394.

HENLEY REGATTA uses rain so to frustrate a woman's dreams that she loses her mind. Though an untimely rain is a common experience, Hardy often makes use of it as a force of nature that seems hostile to human plans. In *The Return of the Native*, the rain so dampens Eustacia's will to flee with Wildeve that it helps bring about her "abyss of desolation" on the heath and her death. (Book Fifth, Chapters VII and VIII.) In "The Satin Shoes" rain on a woman's wedding day leads to the bride's insanity.

The regatta, which originated as a rowing-contest between Oxford and Cambridge Universities, became in 1839 an annual event of June or July that attracts thousands of visitors. It is held at Henley-on-Thames, about six miles north and slightly east of Reading.

AN EVENING IN GALILEE is a soliloquy by Mary, the mother of Jesus, within "stage directions" that open and close the poem and that set it near Nazareth. From here she looks "far west towards Carmel" (Mount Carmel, about twenty miles away near the Mediterranean) and "east to the Jordan" River and the "smooth Tiberias' strand" (the Sea of Galilee), about fifteen miles away. That is, she surveys the world she knows. The time suggested is that of Jesus's ministry, not long before the crucifixion. This setting is related to Hardy's poem "Panthera." Mary's final look to the south "towards Jezreel" seems a reference to the direction from which Panthera had come.

Mary asks herself questions that any anxious mother might ask about a brilliant son whose ideas and actions are unconventional and inexplicable to her. Mary's question whether Jesus, certainly eccentric, is also mad rests upon experiences described in the Gospels. Including some apparent scorn for his mother, they would rankle in any mother's heart. Jesus's argument with the High-Priest is presented in Matt. 21:23-27, in which Jesus, asserting his authority to teach in the Temple, refused to state the basis for that authority. Mary recalls his rebuke at the marriage in Cana, "Woman, what have I to do with thee?" as in John 2:3-4. Hardy quoted Jesus's slight to Mary in asking, "Who is my mother?" from Matt. 12:48, or Mark 3:33. Her comment that he might have asked "Who is my father?" seems a reference to Panthera.

Mary does not approve Jesus's mingling with the "lowest folk," such fishermen as Simon Peter, James, and John, as in Luke 5, and she is dismayed that Jesus encourages "That woman of no good character," Magdalene, as in Luke 8 and elsewhere. Mary is puzzled that Jesus, who said "Keep the Commandments" (Matt. 19:17), should "smile upon" a prostitute. She feels that such signs of madness may lead Him to death.[1]

1. Perhaps, in centering Mary's thought upon Jesus's "madness," Hardy intended an ironic contrast to the "sweet reasonableness" of Jesus's message, so called in Matthew Arnold's *Literature and Dogma*.

THE BROTHER is a melodramatic poem spoken by a high-spirited brother so shamed by his sister's seduction that he murders her seducer, and, upon learning of her marriage, rushes off to kill himself. The story may rest upon some incident near Swanage when Hardy lived there in 1875. "Bollard Head" seems to be Ballard Point (sometimes called "Ballard Head"), where a cliff some 200 feet high juts out into the sea just north of Swanage.

WE FIELD-WOMEN is a reminiscence of Tess, in *Tess of the D'Urbervilles*, at Flintcomb-Ash Farm, where she became a "fieldwoman pure and simple, in winter guise; a gray serge cape, a red woollen cravat, a stuff skirt covered by a whitey-brown rough wrapper, and buff-leather gloves." (See the notes on "Tess's Lament.") "How it rained" in the poem is detailed in the novel: "It was so high a situation, this field, that the rain had no occasion to fall, but raced along horizontally upon the yelling wind, sticking into them like glass splinters till they were wet through. . . . But to stand working slowly in a field, and feel the creep of rain-water, first on legs and shoulders, then on hips and head, then at back, front, and sides, and yet to work on till the leaden light diminishes and marks that the sun is down, demands a modicum of stoicism, even of valour." "How it snowed" is pictured as: "The snow had followed the birds from the polar basin as a white pillar of a cloud, and individual flakes could not be seen. The blast smelt of icebergs, arctic seas, whales, and white bears, carrying the snow so that it licked the land but did not deepen on it." In the snow, Marian "arrived to tell her [Tess] that they were to join the rest of the women at reed-drawing in the barn till the weather changed." (Chapters XLII and XLIII.) Reeddrawing is the exhausting work of stripping wheat from the stalks to prepare the straw for thatching roofs.

"How it shone," however, indicates that Tess is not the speaker of the poem, who must be Marian or Izz Huett, for Tess does not return to Talbothays Dairy. King surmises that the poem "may have been written before the completion of the novel," as the poem implies Tess's return to Talbothays.[1]

1. "Verse and Prose Parallels in the Work of Thomas Hardy," p. 58.

A PRACTICAL WOMAN, Hogan says, is a humorous poem: "No subject is too sacred for his [Hardy's] oblique sense of humor. Motherhood itself is subjected to scrutiny in a risqué piece called 'A Practical Woman.' "[1] In the light of Hardy's interest in hereditary factors, as in "Heredity," "The Forbidden Banns," and *Jude the Obscure*, the device of the speaker of the poem to get a bright, healthy son seems a serious suggestion.

1. "Structural Design in Thomas Hardy's Poetry," p. 235.

SQUIRE HOOPER was first published in the *Daily Telegraph* for April 12, 1928.[1] It tells a story that Hardy found in Hutchins's *History of Dorset*. Squire Edward Hooper of Hurn Court in the parish of Christchurch, Hampshire, belonged to a family noted for hospitality. When King Charles II visited an earlier Edward Hooper, he was so jovially entertained that he knighted Hooper in the wine-cellar. The Edward Hooper of the poem was at one time a captain in the Dorset Militia. He "collected his company at his house at Boveridge,[2] where he hospitably entertained them a week, giving each man one shilling a day." In Edward Hooper's later life, "Hurn Court was his constant residence, where he enjoyed an uncommon [sic] happy state of health until past the age of ninety; when, being as it were worn out, he, one day after breakfast, politely took leave of his company, and retired to his chamber—to die; or rather to commence a blessed eternity. Obiit Sep. 16, 1795, aet 94." (III, 384.)

The poem has Hooper die at ninety instead of ninety-four, perhaps to save a syllable in the opening line, invents the nature of the "company" from whom Hooper took polite leave, an illness similar to Hardy's own haemorrhage of 1880,[3] and the conversation of the guests.

After the death of Edward Hooper, Hurn Court passed into the possession of his grandson, who became Lord Malmesbury; the estate is now the property of the Earl of Malmesbury, but the mansion and grounds around it are used for the Hurn Court School for Boys. The mansion still exhibits the Hooper coat of arms (fittingly, for a sporting family, three boars on a shield), as well as the arms of the Earls of Malmesbury. Trees of great age, the nearby Stour

River, and the mansion show the taste of men who lived vigorously in the grand manner of eighteenth-century gentlemen. The poem expresses admiration for the courageous pride in the code of the gentry.

1. Purdy, *Thomas Hardy: A Bibliographical Study*, p. 257.
2. A property in Dorset besides the estate in Hampshire.
3. *Early Life*, p. 187; *Life*, p. 145.

"A GENTLEMAN'S SECOND-HAND SUIT" was first published in *Harper's Monthly Magazine* (New York) for March, 1928. Hardy sent the poem to the magazine in December, 1927.[1] It is a humorous poem, apparently suggested by his musing upon a dress-suit seen beside a pawn-shop door. He probably thought of his own dancing-time, as presented in "Reminiscences of a Dancing Man."

1. Purdy, *Thomas Hardy: A Bibliographical Study*, p. 257.

"WE SAY WE SHALL NOT MEET" was first published in the *Daily Telegraph* for September 11, 1928.[1] The poem reflects with poignancy upon aged Hardy's meetings with old friends and their casual, wary farewells, for they may not meet again.

1. Purdy, *Thomas Hardy: A Bibliographical Study*, p. 257.

SEEING THE MOON RISE in a manuscript has the title "At Moonrise, or 'We used to go.'"[1] Perhaps Hardy changed the title to avoid confusion with "At Moonrise and Onwards," a companion poem that describes the moon seen over Heath-Plantation Hill. "Seeing the Moon Rise" regrets that he, eighty-seven in August, 1927, cannot go with friends to see the moon there, for in old age "Zest burns not so high!"

"Heath-Plantation Hill" and "Froom-hill Barrow" are two names for the same place, usually called Frome Hill. It rises about three quarters of a mile east of Hardy's home, Max Gate, along the road that leads to Lower Bockhampton. On the crest is a tumulus. From there one has a view of Dorchester to the west and of Stinsford Parish and "Egdon" Heath to the north and northeast. The hill descends northward to the valley of the Frome. Though the country road leading up the hill is now graded, it may have been a "pathway, steep and narrow" in 1927.

1. In the Dorset County Museum.

SONG TO AURORE was first published in the *Daily Telegraph* for May 3, 1928.[1] The poem seems a lament for the pain of loving; affection is preferable to possessive passion.

1. Purdy, *Thomas Hardy: A Bibliographical Study*, p. 257.

HE NEVER EXPECTED MUCH was first published in the *Daily Tele-graph* for March 19, 1928.[1] In a conversation with the World, Hardy says that even as a child he had not expected that "life would all be fair." *The Early Life* and many poems[2] indicate that he was normally happy in childhood and through much of a young manhood spangled with idealistic dreams. The stanza states the truth chiefly of such moods of reflective insight as that described in "Childhood Among the Ferns." In these moods, normal disappointments might seem dismal when set against starry dreams that life might *all* be fair. The moods led the poet to expect only the "neutral-tinted haps" that define an attitude more stoic than pessimistic. The poem "has a touch of the archiepiscopal warning, 'Above all, no enthusiasm.' Life, undeniably, is a mixture; he wishes to see it as it is."[3]

Repetition of part of the first line in the second of each stanza (as in "A Trampwoman's Tragedy," "Great Things," and elsewhere) gives the poem a hymn-like tone.

1. Purdy, *Thomas Hardy: A Bibliographical Study,* p. 257.
2. For instance, "Domicilium," written in boyhood, "I Was the Midmost," "Yuletide in a Younger World," and, with reference to young manhood, "In the Seventies."
3. McDowall, *Thomas Hardy,* p. 18.

STANDING BY THE MANTELPIECE is a dramatic monologue in which the speaker uses folk-lore to tell his listener that he is soon to die. The headnote identifies the speaker as Hardy's friend Horace Mosley Moule, who killed himself in his chambers at Cambridge University on September 21, 1873.

In folk-belief "a little column of tallow left standing after most of the candle has been consumed, fantastically like a coffin or winding shroud" forecasts a death. The speaker "sees the candle-wax taking the shape of a shroud, and accepts the omen by moulding it . . . to his fate."[1] *The Early Life* records Hardy's observation of candles taking the shape of shrouds when he attended a five o'clock service at King's Chapel, Cambridge, in October of 1880 and "the candles guttered in the most fantastic shapes I ever saw,—and while the wicks burnt down these weird shapes changed form. . . . They were stalactites, plumes, laces; or rather they were surplices,—frayed shreds from those of bygone 'white-robed scholars,' or from their shrouds—dropping bit by bit in a ghostly decay."[2]

Purdy says of the listener in the poem that "It is a woman addressed."[3] Evelyn Hardy agrees, adding the source of her information and an explication of the poem: "Shortly before his death, Sir Sydney Cockerell[4] . . . told me in person that Hardy had revealed to him that Horace had been engaged to an 'un-named lady of title.' Highly strung, subject to periods of depression and greatly overworked, he dined with his fiancée, took too much wine at table, considered that he had publicly disgraced her and later ended his life." In the poem, Hardy "envisaged Moule addressing his fiancée after his decision to end his life. . . . The second [stanza] clearly refers to Moule's intended marriage, June being the month for marriage in several Hardy poems. . . . In the third stanza, 'embitterment,' possibly a quarrel, is mentioned. The fourth implies that Moule had been frank about his failings and that she had accepted them. . . . In the fifth and sixth stanzas it is clear that some irrevocable words were spoken by the woman, probably the breaking of their engagement. . . . The woman . . . remains a nameless shadow."[5]

Rutland, indicating that the fourth stanza of the poem is inexplicable on the theory set forth by Purdy and Evelyn Hardy, has challenged their statements. He says: "Florence Emily Hardy told me, about 1933, that she knew nothing of its [the suicide's] circumstances. I believed that then, and I still do. . . . Sir Sydney Cockerell, about 1937, told me the same. Miss Evelyn Hardy now quotes him as 'shortly before his death' telling her a story which, considering Horace Moule's family upbringing and social status, is hardly credible."[6]

Deacon and Coleman set forth a second theory. Aware that Hardy was engaged to Tryphena Sparks before he met Emma Gifford, they surmise that during her teacher-training at Stockwell College in London between 1869 and 1871, Hardy introduced Tryphena to Moule without speaking of his engagement and that Moule fell in love with her, discovered that he had betrayed his friend, determined upon suicide, and announced his decision to Hardy.[7] Phelps presents an annotation in Hardy's Prayer-Book that may have some bearing upon this theory. Alongside Psalm 41, Hardy pencilled: "Day 8, St. Juliot, Sept. '72," a year before Moule's suicide. Verse 9 of the Psalm reads: "Yea, even mine own familiar friend, whom I trusted: who did also eat of my bread, hath laid great wait for me." Phelps asks: "Can this refer to his friend, Horace Moule, who, at some time during this period, appears to have rivalled Hardy in the affections of Tryphena Sparks?"[8]

Dates do not support this theory if the occasion of the poem was Hardy's visit to Moule in June of 1873.[9] By this time, presumably, Hardy was engaged to Emma Gifford, and Tryphena had been teaching school in Plymouth since January, 1872. Perhaps the occasion was in July of 1870, when Hardy and Moule were together in London. *The Early Life* says that by August of 1870 Moule "knew of the vague understanding" between Hardy and Miss Gifford. There is no record that Hardy saw Moule between this time and some time in 1872. He "had not consulted" Moule about *Desperate Remedies*, but when the novel was "slated" in the *Spectator* on April 22, 1871, Moule "wrote a brief line to Hardy bidding him not to mind the slating." Still the friends did not meet until by accident, in 1872, Hardy "met in the middle of a crossing by Trafalgar Square his friend Moule, whom he had not seen for a long time."[10] At the inquest in 1873, Horace's brother Charles deposed that "Years ago he had been in the habit of talking about suicide, but not of late."[11] Hardy's visit with Moule in June of 1873 is described as a happy one, suggesting a reconciliation.

Perhaps Moule threatened suicide in a quarrel with Hardy in 1870, but did not kill himself until 1873, whether or not because an "unnamed lady of title" rejected him then. If so, Hardy's date in the subtitle refers to the suicide, not to the occasion of the poem. In this interpretation, the fourth stanza says that Hardy encouraged the friendship of Tryphena and Moule, nearly twice her age, but expressed surprise that they fell in love. This situation is paralleled in *Jude the Obscure.* Jude is shocked to observe Phillotson place his arm around Sue's waist: "The ironical clinch to his sorrow was given by the thought that the intimacy between his cousin and the schoolmaster had been brought about entirely by himself." (Part II, Chapter V.)

1. Firor, *Folkways in Thomas Hardy*, pp. 14-15.
2. P. 184; *Life*, p. 141.
3. *Thomas Hardy: A Bibliographical Study*, p. 257.
4. Named in Hardy's will to serve with Mrs. Florence Hardy as his literary executor. Cox, ed., *Thomas Hardy's Will*, p. 4.
5. "Thomas Hardy and Horace Moule," p. 89.
6. Rutland, "Hardy and Moule," pp. 158-59.
7. This explanation is in Chapter 9 of *Providence and Mr Hardy*. The authors admit: "There is no direct evidence of any such relationship between Tryphena and Moule, but what we have is an interlacing pattern of hints." P. 112.
8. *Annotations by Thomas Hardy in His Bibles and Prayer-Book*, p. 10. This phrasing in *The Book of Common Prayer* is slightly different from that of the King James Bible.
9. *Early Life*, p. 123; *Life*, p. 93.
10. *Early Life*, pp. 102, 104, 111, 115; *Life*, pp. 77, 78, 84, 87.
11. See Moule in the Key to Persons.

BOYS THEN AND NOW may recall Hardy's childhood when he was the "midmost" of his rural world and daydreamed it the center of a cosmos made for him. (See "I Was the Midmost.") He was perhaps like little Johnny Nunsuch in *The Return of the Native*, to whom Diggory explains that he is a reddleman: "Yes, that's what I be. Though there's more than one. You little children think there's only one cuckoo, one fox, one giant, one devil, and one reddleman, when there's lots of us all." (Book First, Chapter VIII.)

THAT KISS IN THE DARK was first published in the *Daily Tele-graph* for September 13, 1928.[1] A woman explains an inadvertent kiss after a lover's quarrel in a country home.

1. Purdy, *Thomas Hardy: A Bibliographical Study*, p. 257.

A NECESSITARIAN'S EPITAPH, colloquially humorous in phrasing, presents life as like a dance of cats on hot bricks.

BURNING THE HOLLY was first published in the *Daily Telegraph* for August 20, 1928.[1] The story of this ballad-like poem seems narrated by a lodging-house keeper to his wife. He has been deeply affected by the tragedy of a lodger, "a famous dancer, / Much lured of men." This story is the melodrama of a woman seduced by a masterful villain, got with child, and abandoned, only to come "home" and disappear a second time. The fate of the child is not stated. The narrator compassionately suffers without having sinned.

The crisis occurs on Twelfth Night, the evening of January 6 that, in old observances, marked the Feast of the Epiphany and the end of the Christmas season. On this night the now-dried holly, ivy, and mistletoe are burned, and secular merrymaking breaks the religious solemnity of Christmas. In the symbolism of the poem, as the holly wastes to ashes, the dancer follows her false lover. The poem makes use of chant-like repetitions, perhaps to represent the old folk by the fire turning over and over the sad tale of the dancer they had loved.

1. Purdy, *Thomas Hardy: A Bibliographical Study*, p. 257.

SUSPENSE seems more concerned with the clammy weather (often typical of Dorset) than with any clear story. The point seems to be that, whatever the fate of the lovers, nature is indifferent.

THE SECOND VISIT was first published in the *Daily Telegraph* for May 31, 1928.[1] The descriptive details fit the old mill in the village of Upwey, about half a mile west of the road between Dorchester and Weymouth, or about three and a half miles southwest of Dorchester. A spring at this mill-site,[2] celebrated as a "wishing well," is the beginning of the River Wey, which is a brook before this addition to its waters. The second visit may be that of August, 1879, when Hardy and his wife, Emma, "spent a few days in going about the district . . . his mother coming to see them, and driving to Portland, Upwey, etc., in their company."[3] Hardy's biographies do not record any other visit. Deacon and Coleman, agreeing that the mill-site is Upwey, surmise that the first visit was by Hardy and Tryphena Sparks before 1873, and the second visit was that of 1879.[4]

The poem presents a memory of two scenes in the same place, alike in general, but different in details. The poet's memory leaps across the years to an early beloved who said, "You know I do!"

1. Purdy, *Thomas Hardy: A Bibliographical Study*, p. 257.

2. No longer an active mill, but a dwelling, though the banks of the millpond and its stone-work remain.

3. *Early Life*, p. 169; *Life*, p. 129. Hardy wrote to Mrs. Arthur Henniker on October 22, 1900: "I have been out on a little cycle tour with our niece, who is staying here—to Upwey, where there is a wishing well. We duly wished, & what will result remains to be seen." In the Dorset County Museum. The niece was Lilian Gifford, Mrs. Hardy's relative. This visit may be the second Hardy had in mind, but that of 1879 is hardly the first, with a sweetheart.

4. *Providence and Mr Hardy*, p. 121. Elsewhere Miss Deacon wrote: "We have been told by Nellie Tryphena Bromell, the daughter of Tryphena, that her mother had paid visits in her youth to Upwey Mill and the wishing-well." *That Mysterious Tragic Pair*, p. 5.

OUR OLD FRIEND DUALISM, opening with "All hail to him, the Protean!"[1] ironically mocks the dualistic concepts of God and the Devil. Spinoza[2] and the Monists[3] set forth rationalistic theories that Hardy found convincing for himself and, he supposed, most modern thinkers, the "We" of the poem. He stated this point of view in the Preface of *The Dynasts,* defending his concept of the Immanent Will by saying: "The wide prevalence of the Monistic theory of the Universe forbade, in this twentieth century, the importation of Divine personages from any antique Mythology as ready-made sources or channels of Causation, even in verse, and excluded the celestial machinery of, say, *Paradise Lost*, as peremptorily as that of the *Iliad* or the *Eddas*."

Dualism (personifying theologians and dualistic philosophers) cites the philosophies of Bergson[4] and James[5] in his support. In 1915, Hardy was reading Bergson. He devoted a page and a half of his "Literary Notes, II" to comments on Bergson's *Creative Evolution*.[6] To Dr. C. W. Saleeby, he wrote: Bergson's "theories are much pleasanter ones than those they contest, and I for one would gladly believe them; but . . . for his charming and attractive assertions he does not adduce any proofs whatever. . . . I fear his theory is, in the bulk, only our old friend Dualism in a new suit of clothes."[7] He wrote in 1924 to Ernest Brennecke in comment upon his *Thomas Hardy's Universe*: "You are quite right in asserting in the footnote at page 71 that I have never been influenced by Bergson . . . his views seeming to me to be only a re-hashing of the old creed of Dualism."[8] These statements explain "We argue them pragmatic cheats." Dualism agrees that Bergson, James, and pragmatism are "deceiving," but argues that "I must live," for "flamens" (priests of ancient Rome, here, ironically, theologians) declare the worth of dualistic concepts. Hardy seems more amused than disturbed.

1. A reference to Proteus, a Greek sea-god that assumed a variety of shapes.
2. Baruch Spinoza (1632-77), a Dutch rationalistic philosopher who postulated a monistic system.
3. Believers in Monism, that ultimate reality is one, as opposed to the dualists, who believe in the conflicting principles of good and evil, God and the Devil.
4. Henri Bergson (1859-1941), a French thinker who supported the dualistic principle of struggle between good and evil.
5. William James (1842-1910), an American psychologist and pragmatist.
6. In the Dorset County Museum.
7. *Later Years*, pp. 167-68; *Life*, pp. 369-70.
8. Hardy's pencil-draft of this letter is in the Dorset County Museum.

FAITHFUL WILSON was first published in the *Daily Telegraph* for April 16, 1926. "The poem was suggested by an epigram of Strato which Hardy found in his copy of *Select Epigrams from the Greek Anthology*, ed. J. W. Mackail."[1] The epigram that Hardy domesticates in application to Wilson and Fanny reads:

Τίς δύναται γνῶναι τὸν ἐρώμενον εἰ παρακμάξει,
πάντα συνὼν αὐτῷ μηδ' ἀπολειπόμενος;
Τίς δύνατ' οὐκ ἀρέσαι τὴν σήμερον, ἐχθὲς ἀρέσκων;
εἰ δ' ἀρέσει, τί παθὼν αὔριον οὐκ ἀρέσει.

Mackail translates it under the title "Love's Immortality": "Who may know if a loved one passes the prime, while ever with him and never left alone? who may not satisfy to-day who satisfied yesterday? and if he satisfy, what should befall him not to satisfy to-morrow?"

1. Purdy, *Thomas Hardy: A Bibliographical Study*, p. 258.

GALLANT'S SONG may have been originally titled "Dandy's Song." The evidence is a scrap of paper marked " 'Dandy's' altered to 'Gallant's' in pencil. . . . From Mrs. Hardy on 18 December, 1931."[1] The date, 1868, suggests Hardy's amused observation of woman's nature during his early manhood.

1. In the Miriam Lutcher Stark Library, University of Texas.

A PHILOSOPHICAL FANTASY was first published in the *Fortnightly Review* for January, 1927. The original title, "In the Matter of an Intent, A Philosophic Fantasy," seemed to the editor "a little abstract and remote." Hardy "agreed on the second title as denoting 'more clearly that the poem is rather of the nature of a dream than a consistent argument.' "[1] *The Later Years* says: "Hardy liked the year to open with a poem of this type from him in some leading review or newspaper. The quotation at the heading, 'Milton . . . made God argue,' gives the keynote, and the philosophy is much as he had set forth before, but still a ray of hope is shown for the future of mankind."[2]

The motto quoted from Bagehot's essay "John Milton"[3] throws light on Hardy's intention in the poem. It appears in a passage that anticipates several ideas in the poem: "Milton has selected for delineation exactly that part of the divine nature which is most beyond the reach of the human faculties, and which is also, when we try to describe our fancy of it, the least effective to our minds. He has made God *argue*. Now, the procedure of the divine mind from truth to truth must ever be incomprehensible to us."[4]

The poem seems Hardy's attempt, "in his own ironic way, to justify God's ways to man."[5] The God he presents, the "Causer" or the Absolute, is by no means Milton's anthropomorphic God; the justification is not Milton's assertion of human free will. It is a personification of the Immanent Will of *The Dynasts*. The theme includes the hope for evolutionary meliorism with which this epic-drama ends. Among other sources for Hardy's concept, Schopenhauer's *The World as Will and Idea* must be included. The *"unfulfilled intention"* of the Causer echoes the same term from Chapter VII of *The Woodlanders*, completed after he had read Schopenhauer. His "blind force persisting" translates Schopenhauer's "blinden Drang, ein finsteres, dumpfes Treiben"; and "purposeless propension," "erkenntnisloses Streben."[6]

Though the poem is in the form of a rambling conversation, it is concerned with why life exhibits injustices and imperfections. The answer lies in the nature of the Causer. The questioner assumes that the Causer is manlike and had some plan that He (or It) has not fulfilled. The Causer denies that He is manlike, is subject to human frustrations, or is anything conceivable by man. He had no aim in creation; He exists outside time; He feels no emotions. The ancient stories told of Him are "A mass of superstition / And monkish imposition." His treatment of matter is "scientific," without moral or ethical purpose. Men may know of right and wrong, but He does not; yet He is not "averse to be a learner." His actions are unconscious, for consciousness developed inadvertently in man. Perhaps for this reason the alleged injustices of life may be "mending." Life may develop in ways not of His "first dreaming."[7]

The poem presents philosophical ideas in the tone of the Gilbert and Sullivan operettas. The Causer jokes about His sexlessness, man's vanity in imagining himself like his Maker, eons as "stray-time," and the absurdity of man's religious concepts. The diction mixes colloquialisms ("I love procrastination") and quasi-religious archaisms (thee and thy). The poem exhibits doggerel rimes ("those all" and "disposal") in a varied pattern. Hardy is playing with profound ideas so familiar that they no longer bother him.

1. Purdy, *Thomas Hardy: A Bibliographical Study*, p. 258. Evelyn Hardy says that the poem was originally called "A Conversational Phantasy." *Thomas Hardy's Notebooks*, p. 114.

2. P. 252; *Life*, p. 436.

3. A review of David Masson's *Life of Milton*, published in *National Review*, IX (July, 1859), 150-86.

4. Quoted from Norman St. John-Stevas, ed., *The Collected Works of Walter Bagehot*, Cambridge, Mass.: Harvard University Press, 1956, II, p. 142. Milton does make God argue to "justify the ways of God to men." In Book III of *Paradise Lost*, ll. 80-134, God justifies to Christ His punishment of man on the basis that man has free will. Evelyn Hardy says that Hardy was acquainted with Bagehot's writing, or some of it, before going to London in 1862: "But in 1860-2 he and Horace Moule walked the Frome meadows, discussing *Essays and Reviews*, Bagehot's *Estimates*, and other books of a revolutionary nature fresh from the press." *Thomas Hardy*, p. 51.

5. Hynes, *The Pattern of Hardy's Poetry*, p. 35.

6. Bd. I, 5, 211, cited by Osawa, "Hardy and the German Men-of-Letters," pp. 504-44.

7. Hardy had previously treated all these ideas, not only in *The Dynasts*, but in such poems as "The Lacking Sense," "The Sleep-Worker," "Doom and She," "New Year's Eve," and "God's Education."

A QUESTION OF MARRIAGE was first published in the *Daily Telegraph* for September 26, 1928.[1] The poem may be read as a comment upon social stratification in English life, but Weber surmises that it may express Hardy's feeling at being sometimes snubbed by his first wife Emma. "She did not forget that her father was a solicitor, that her uncle was a canon of Worcester Cathedral and Archdeacon of London, that her brother-in-law was a rector. When Hamlin Garland visited Hardy's birthplace, the owner repeated to him the local belief that Mrs. Hardy had taken more pride in being the niece of an archdeacon than in being the wife of Thomas Hardy." Late in life, "he was still sensitive on the subject of 'those contrasting positions,'" and expressed his feeling in "A Question of Marriage."[2]

1. Purdy, *Thomas Hardy: A Bibliographical Study*, p. 258.

2. *Hardy of Wessex*, 1st ed., pp. 158-59.

THE LETTER'S TRIUMPH was first published in the *Daily Telegraph* for July 19, 1928. In the manuscript, the poem was followed by "Based on an incident," which was deleted.[1] One may surmise the incident as a man's remark upon posting a letter or a woman's comment upon a treasured letter kept close to her person.

1. Purdy, *Thomas Hardy: A Bibliographical Study*, p. 258.

A FORGOTTEN MINIATURE is a companion to "On a Discovered Curl of Hair." A locket containing a miniature portrait of Hardy's first wife Emma, as she was about 1870, and a curl of her hair were found in February, 1913, some three months after Emma's death. The final stanza of "A Forgotten Miniature" suggests that the poem was written long after its companion. Perhaps the miniature was laid away a second time and rediscovered when Hardy was working on notes for his biography.

WHISPERED AT THE CHURCH-OPENING was first published in the *Daily Telegraph* for June 4, 1928.[1] R. F. Dalton, former Curator of the Dorset County Museum, told me that he believed the last phrase of the poem, "a vicar still," referred to the Reverend Henry G. B. Cowley, Vicar of Stinsford Church from 1910 to 1933, an humble man whose "mind ran on charity and good will" and who was a close friend of Hardy's.

The poem may have been suggested by the Bishop of Wakefield's announcement in the newspapers that he had thrown *Jude the Obscure* into the fire. *The Later Years* says that the incident brought to Hardy's memory "a witty remark he had once read in a *Times* leading article, to the effect that the qualities which enabled a man to become a bishop were often the very reverse of those which made a good bishop when he became one."[2]

Johnson suggests that the poem may present in allegory Hardy's reflection upon reviewers' attacks upon his literary style: "Hardy's practice reveals that he must have thought of style as ornamental, inorganic, even mechanical, as something separate from and subordinate to the ideas expressed in the action or scene described. A late poem, 'Whispered at the Church-Opening,' makes this clear in its contrast between the 'eloquent' and successful bishop and the unsuccessful vicar, 'sincerest of all; / Whose words, though unpicked, gave the essence of things.' Like his vicar, Hardy is always sincere, often painfully so; but his words are rarely 'unpicked.' "[3]

1. Purdy, *Thomas Hardy: A Bibliographical Study*, p. 258.
2. P. 48; *Life*, p. 278.
3. "Hardy and Burke's 'Sublime,' " p. 56.

IN WEATHERBURY STOCKS, with its action dated 1850, may rest upon a memory of Hardy's childhood. *The Early Life* says that among his "childish memories were those of seeing men in the stocks."[1] He said to William Archer: "I have seen men in the stocks. . . . I remember one perfectly—when I was very young. It was in the village I have called Weatherbury. I can see him now, sitting in the blazing sun, with no other human being near except me. I can see his blue worsted stockings projecting through the leg-holes, and the shining nails in his boots. He was quite a hero in my eyes. I sidled up to him and said good-day to him, and felt mightily honoured when he nodded to me."[2]

"Weatherbury" is Hardy's name for Puddletown, about five miles east of Dorchester. In his boyhood stocks stood in the Town Square near the old court house and St. Mary's Church.[3] "Blooms-End" is his name for the home of Mrs. Yeobright and the site of the Christmas mumming in *The Return of the Native* (Book Second, Chapter V) ; it was drawn from "a farm-house called Bhompston" in a field near Lower Bockhampton.[4]

Jim may be the musician who plays the serpent in "The Country Wedding." There he is among the Stinsford musicians (the "Mellstock" choir) who are playing for a wedding in Puddletown. As he is not named in other mentions of these musicians, he may be a native of Puddletown. That he might get into the stocks for some misbehavior is suggested by his playing the serpent, which the "Mellstock" musicians do not consider an altogether virtuous instrument.[5]

1. P. 27; *Life*, p. 21.
2. Quoted by Copps, "The Poetry of Thomas Hardy," p. 763, from Archer, "Real Conversations."
3. Lea, *Thomas Hardy's Wessex*, p. 36. These stocks are mentioned in *Far from the Madding Crowd*, Chapter XLIV: boys play Prisoners' Base in the square near the church, "the old stocks conveniently forming a base facing the boundary of the churchyard."
4. Lea, *Thomas Hardy's Wessex*, p. 75.
5. *Under the Greenwood Tree*, Part the First, Chapter IV.

A PLACID MAN'S EPITAPH was first published in the *Daily Telegraph* for April 19, 1928.[1] To the extent that the poem is a self-portrait, Hardy suggests that in old age he achieved placid serenity. The close of each line with a double-rime ending in "it" suggests witty musing.

1. Purdy, *Thomas Hardy: A Bibliographical Study*, p. 258.

THE NEW BOOTS presents a gossipy conversation between the neighbor of a widow and a stranger who apparently does not know that the widow's husband has died, possibly of exposure to "rain and slush and slop."

THE MUSING MAIDEN had in an early manuscript the title "The Imaginative Maiden."[1] According to Hardy's footnote, the poem was written in his rooms in Westbourne Park Villas as one of his earliest poems. One image, at least, seems derivative from his strenuous reading at this time. The final stanza seems to echo John Donne's lines in "The Extasie": "Our eye-beames twisted, and did thred / Our eyes, upon a double string," which could have suggested the conceits throughout the poem.[2] Evelyn Hardy, however, suggests that in describing an "artless, country girl with a loving heart," Hardy may have had in mind "some Lizbie, or Louisa, of the Bockhampton lanes before he had gone to seek his fortune in London."[3]

1. Purdy, *Thomas Hardy: A Bibliographical Study*, p. 258.
2. Cited by Vinson, "Diction and Imagery in the Poetry of Thomas Hardy," p. 290.
3. "Some Unpublished Poems by Thomas Hardy," pp. 30-31. Miss Hardy is speaking primarily of "An Unplanted Primrose," but relates the two poems. See "To Lizbie Browne" and "To Louisa in the Lane."

LORNA THE SECOND "was suggested by an unusual marriage in 1927 in the family of Hardy's old friend, Bosworth Smith. A disappointed suitor of 'Lorna the First' married, eight years after her death, her young daughter. The reminiscence of *The Well-Beloved* could not have escaped the poet."[1]

Letters in the Dorset County Museum indicate the friendship of Hardy and the family of Reginald Bosworth Smith. In a letter of the 1870's (no exact date is given) he wrote to Mrs. Smith of his pleasure in a recent conversation with her and spoke of sending her a copy of *A Pair of Blue Eyes*. A letter of 1906 from Smith to Hardy commented on *The Dynasts*, mentioning "the copy you so kindly gave my daughter and which she values greatly," the daughter being "Lorna the First."[2] In this year Lorna was married to a German, Edwin Goldman, Professor of Surgery at the University of Freiburg, disappointing her family, who had encouraged an English suitor, Stewart Gore-Browne. Hardy attended the wedding. He wrote to Mrs. Smith on October 22, 1913: "Your daughter Lorna was greatly liked by my late wife—& I may add by myself. We were at her wedding, if you remember, & I was grieved when I learnt of her bereavement,"[3] presumably the death of Professor Goldman. Mrs. Goldman had a daughter whom she named Lorna, "Lorna the Second" of Hardy's poem.

Meanwhile, the disappointed suitor, Gore-Browne, went into the army. The rest of the story is told in the *Dorset County Chronicle* for July 28, 1927: "Fashionable Marriage.—The marriage was celebrated on Saturday [July 23] at St. George's, Hanover Square [London], of Lieut.-Colonel Steward Gore-Browne, D. S. O., late Royal Field-Artillery, of Oakley House, Abingdon, and Miss Lorna Bosworth Goldman, daughter of the late Professor Goldman, and ward of Major C. S. and the Hon. Mrs. Goldman, of Park-street. The bride is a granddaughter of the late Mrs. Bosworth Smith, of Bingham's Melcombe."[4]

There is some parallel between the idea of the poem and Hardy's novel *The Well-Beloved*. In it the hero, Jocelyn Pierston, falls in love with Avice Caro, but does not marry her; at the age of forty, seeing Avice imaged in her daughter Avice the Second, he wishes to marry her, but she marries another; and at the age of sixty, retaining his "ideal," he wishes to marry the daughter of Avice the Second, Avice the Third, but she elopes with a younger man.

Hardy's poem is written as a soliloquy by Lieutenant-Colonel Gore-Browne, who seems a little amused at himself, as in his forcing the rimes "scorn a," "mourn a," and "born a" to fit the treasured name, Lorna.

1. Purdy, *Thomas Hardy: A Bibliographical Study*, p. 259.
2. Ibid., p. 129.
3. In the Miriam Lutcher Stark Library, University of Texas.
4. Mrs. Smith had died on March 6, 1927. See also the *Times* for July 25, 1927. Mrs. Joan Cochrane of Milton Abbas, sister of Lorna the First and aunt of Lorna the Second, told me that, encouraged by the family, Stewart Gore-Browne proposed to Lorna the First, but was rejected, but that, keeping the ideal of Lorna in his heart, he found it realized in her daughter.

A DAUGHTER RETURNS seems a sequel to "The Ruined Maid." In both poems, gay raiment and ornaments are signs of sin, contrasted with the hardships of virtue; in both, the "ruined" girl speaks standard English (perhaps with a London accent, the "note of that voice"), in contrast with the old-fashioned "thee" and "thou" of country (Dorset) dialect; and though "The Ruined Maid" was written in 1866, it was published in *Poems of the Past and the Present* on November 17, 1901,[1] whereas "A Daughter Returns" is dated one month later, December 17, 1901. Perhaps upon reading over "The Ruined Maid" when published, it occurred to Hardy to write a sequel.

The poem seems to owe something, especially the outraged "heavy father," to the conventions of Victorian domestic melodrama. The melodrama made much of scenery: the unmarried mother with her babe wandered helpless through the falling snow. The final stanza shifts the scenery to the father's mental picture of *his* suffering in sleepless, dismal dawns. (It does not seem to occur to him, outraged by his daughter's finery, that he might forgive the erring girl.) It is possible to see the poem (like "The Ruined Maid") as humor and concealed satire.

1. Purdy, *Thomas Hardy: A Bibliographical Study*, p. 118.

THE THIRD KISSING-GATE was first published in the *Daily Telegraph* on July 30, 1928. "Four of the 5 stanzas (excepting stanza 4) are derived, with some revision, from 'The Forsaking of the Nest,' a poem of 9 stanzas printed . . . in *Nash's Magazine*, February 1912."[1]

Kissing gates are common in Dorset to allow easy passage for persons on foot but no passage for sheep or cattle. A kissing gate swings in a V-shaped enclosure with room enough for one person at a time to pass around its end, though an animal pushing against the gate would simply close it. A lover can block passage until his girl grants him a kiss.

The girl's route is a short-cut from Dorchester to Stinsford. She leaves High East Street ("down the town") in Dorchester and walks the London Road past Grey's Bridge. This road is lined with trees, but on the right an iron fence separates it from the meadows. Just past two small bridges over branches of the Frome River, the girl comes to a kissing gate in the fence and passes through it to a foot-path across the meadow ("Mellstock Leaze"). She follows the path across this hedge-enclosed field to a second kissing gate just south of the garden of Stinsford House, and then to a "third mead" through which branches of the Frome meander near the path; just before a third gate, she passes a waterfall.[2] A hedgerow leads from each side of the third gate. Her lover is evidently waiting behind a hedge. In "The Forsaking of the Nest," the girl is late in getting home.

1. Purdy, *Thomas Hardy: A Bibliographical Study*, p. 259.
2. Now the ruins of a broken dam, but a waterfall in Hardy's time.

DRINKING SONG was first published in the *Daily Telegraph* for June 14, 1928. The manuscript "suggests as sub-title, 'on Great Thoughts belittled.' "[1] This poem by an aging sage sets the substance of a university lecture to the rollicking rhythm of a student-chorus in a beer-hall. The poem is pessimistic in its assertions that the human mind through the ages has not been able to solve the riddle of the universe. The one certainty of the poem "conveyed by the image of the butterflies" is "the fragility, the delicacy, and the vulnerability of the human condition."[2] The poem is without despair; it rises to a climax in the theme, "We'll do a good deed nevertheless!"

Stanza by stanza, Hardy sums up the solutions great minds have offered to the riddle of existence, only to show that each insight, held valid for a time, penetrated no deeper than a surface. Thales (Greek geometer, naturalist, and philosopher, 640-546 B.C.) laid the foundations for Greek explanations of phenomena in terms of natural law in an earth-centered universe. Copernicus (Polish astronomer, 1473-1543) discovered that the earth rotates daily on its axis and that the planets (the earth among them) revolve in orbits around the sun. David Hume (Scottish philosopher and psychologist, 1711-76) undermined belief in miracles by arguing that God works through the laws of nature, of which miracles are a violation. Charles Darwin (English biologist, 1809-82) established the principle of evolution, showing that all animals and plants are descended from one prototype and that therefore (a doctrine important in Hardy's thinking) humanity and the lower animals are of one family. Thomas Kelly Cheyne (English biblical scholar, 1841-1915) employed the methods of rationalistic criticism to cast doubt upon the long-accepted story of the birth of Jesus from a virgin.[3] Albert Einstein (German-Swiss-American physicist, 1879-1955) established the highly mathematical and difficult theory of relativity as a basic principle in understanding the universe.[4]

1. Purdy, *Thomas Hardy: A Bibliographical Study*, p. 259.

2. Zietlow, "The Tentative Mode of Hardy's Poems," p. 118.

3. Hardy was interested in Cheyne's writings. In his "Literary Notes II" (in the Dorset County Museum, not paged at this point), he devotes half a page to summing up: *"Virgin Birth"* with quotations from the article on the subject in *"Encyclopaedia Biblica.* Ed. by Revd. T. K. Cheyne, D. Litt. DD. article by Prof. H. Usener." The gist of the article is that the story of the virgin birth of Jesus was "an unwelcome intrusion of heathen mythology into the substance of the gospels," at some time after Jesus's life on earth.

4. Hardy's description of Einstein's theory as "Not yet quite clear / To many here" suggests his own difficulties in understanding it. In "Literary Notes II" (see footnote above), he devoted a page to "Einstein on Time & Space," chiefly quotations from reviews. In a letter dated December 31, 1919, he wrote to Dr. J. Ellis MacTaggart: "I have of late been getting out of patience, if not with philosophers, with men of science. You probably, or I shd. say certainly, have grasped with ease all that Einstein has been telling us, which is more than I have done. Really after what he says the universe seems to be getting too comic for words. However, though one may think queerly of time and space I can see that motion is merely relative, & have long done so; & I feel that it is just as true to assert that the earth stands still & the rest of the universe moves as to assert the opposite: & who knows if we may not get to despise Galileo & applaud the views of the Holy Inquisition!" (Pencil-draft of letter in the Dorset County Museum.) Hardy's copy of *Relativity: The Special and the General Theory: A Popular Exposition* (London: Methuen, 1920) is in the Dorset County Museum. On June 12, 1921, Mrs. Florence Hardy wrote to Alda, Lady Hoare: "T. sends a message—or rather asks a question. Are you interested in Einstein's theory? He ponders over it in the night." (In the Stourhead Collection, the County Archives, Trowbridge, Wiltshire.) Archibald Henderson wrote in 1924: "Mr. Hardy said that he understood Relativity; and when his listeners indicated skepticism, he added: '—up to a point.'" ("Thomas Hardy in a New Role," p. 790.) An undated entry (about 1927) in Hardy's list of books purchased reads: *"Einstein and the Universe,* by C. Nordmann, Fisher Unwin, 10/6." (Evelyn Hardy, *Thomas Hardy's Notebooks*, p. 116.)

THE TARRYING BRIDEGROOM is a soliloquy by an anxious girl awaiting at the church the arrival of her betrothed. "Where the lane divides the pasture" suggests Stinsford Church, approached from the north by a narrow lane between fields and from the southeast by a footpath leading to pastures. The "pink shalloon" refers to the thin, twilled worsted cloth of which the country girl's dress was made. Whether or not with an intended meaning, the title suggests the parable of the ten virgins. In Matt. 25:5, the "bridegroom tarried."

THE DESTINED PAIR was first published in the *Daily Telegraph* for June 7, 1928.[1] The poem suggests that love and marriage are controlled by Fate rather than by free choice, compatibility, or foresight. It raises the question of a mismating, though the only reason for the question is that the fated pair are from different backgrounds, the man a farmer living in a village, and the woman living in a city. The archaic word "weet" means "know."

1. Purdy, *Thomas Hardy: A Bibliographical Study*, p. 259.

A MUSICAL INCIDENT, written in the first person and treating a basic trait in Hardy's temperament, may record an actual experience. On this assumption, Duffin says: "The man Hardy, the man who is seen in the poems . . . is almost incredibly sensitive. He is deeply disturbed by seeing a woman fall asleep while her friend plays to her, and hearing her murmur hypocritical appreciation afterwards."[1] The site of the poem may be Max Gate.

1. *Thomas Hardy*, p. 309.

JUNE LEAVES AND AUTUMN was first published in the *Daily Telegraph* for June 28, 1928.[1] The poem presents a thought that would occur to few but Hardy: compassion for dead leaves based upon the animistic feeling that the living leaves "joyed" in their "store of days to come," and the reflection in autumn that death comes to all, soon or late.

1. Purdy, *Thomas Hardy: A Bibliographical Study*, p. 259.

NO BELL-RINGING was first published in Dorchester on February 28, 1925, as a pamphlet for Mrs. Florence Hardy. It was illustrated with a photograph of the Tower of the church of Fordington St. George, Dorchester.[1] The poem is subtitled "A Ballad of Durnover," Hardy's name for Fordington. It was perhaps suggested by facts recorded in *The Early Life* and a tradition in one of his notebooks. He usually sat up on the night of December 31 to hear the church bells ring in the New Year. He had such interest in this custom that *The Early Life* records for December 31, 1884: "To St. Peter's belfry to the New-Year's-Eve ringing." Whenever he remained at Max Gate, the bells he would hear (at least, most clearly) would be those of Fordington St. George, the church closest to Max Gate. Without explanation, he records for December 31, 1887: "A silent New Year's Eve—no bell, or band, or voice."[2] On one New Year's Eve, late in life, he did not sit up to hear the bells; for December 31, 1917, *The Later Years* says: "*New Year's Eve.* Went to bed at eleven. East wind. No bells heard. Slept in the New Year."[3]

A tradition that may bear on "No Bell-Ringing" is copied into his notebook labelled "Facts," as follows: *Memories & Traditions. Recorded by L. C. Boswell-Stone. . . . It was Xmas Eve 1814, & the custom every year on that day for the clerk & sexton to decorate the ch. in the primitive manner of those times, after cleaning the brass furniture. . . . Branches of evergreen, holly & mistletoe were stuck in every available place; the largest branch of the last-named, being the rarest, was put in front of the Mayor. . . . Clerk Hardy, & Ambrose Hunt the sexton, after carefully locking themselves in, had been the best part of a winter's day engaged in this work, & sat down at last on a settee near the vestry, whence a view down the Ch. of St. Peter, esp. of the N. aisle, was obtained. Then a sudden temptn. seized these 2 men. It was very cold, a glass of wine wd. do them good; the wine was in the vestry, easily come at. So, having taken some appropriated for the Holy Commn. they seated thems., but had hardly tasted the wine when they became aware of a well-known figure seated between them —their late rector. [Rev. Nathanl. Templeman—died 1813.]*[4]* They did not see him come: he seemed to rise up suddenly. He looked from one to the other with a very angry countenance, shaking his head at them just as he did in life when displeased, but with a more solemn aspect. Then rising and facing them he slowly floated up the N. aisle & sank down gradually out of their sight. The clerk swooned, the sexton tried to say the Lord's Prayer, &, when the apparition vanished he after some trouble, unlocked the ch. door & got help for H. . . . The story spread through the town, soon reaching the ears of our rector M. Richman who determined to search into the truth, & submit the men to rigid examim. . . . They . . . never varied from their first account. Rector forgave them after exhortation. p. 20."*[5]* With changes, Hardy made use of such a tradition in Part V, Chapter VI, of *Jude the Obscure.* Jude and Sue are employed to reletter the Ten Commandments in a church near Aldbrickham. As they work, the vicar and his churchwarden enter to observe. The churchwarden tells a tale of workmen relettering the Ten Commandments and drinking to keep "up to their work." They set their rum-bottle on the communion table, drink from it there, fall asleep, and discover that while they slept the Devil had finished the Commandments with the "nots" left out. Possibly, in working on notes for *The Early Life* in 1925, Hardy combined the "silent New Year's Eve" of 1887, the material from "Facts," and the story of the Devil's appearance from *Jude,* to produce "No Bell-Ringing."

In the poem, the boy approaches the church along an empty "three-mile road." As Fordington St. George is on the eastern end of

Fordington (Dorchester), near Road A 352 that runs past Max Gate, the boy apparently comes from the country near West Stafford or perhaps Broadmayne. The church stands on the crest of a hill. Hardy's imagery when the boy arrives suggests something sinister, as in the image of "a dead man's bones on a gibbet-post." As usual in Hardy's poems, the moonlight is a sinister symbol.

The explanation from the bell-ringer, years later, suggests that when the ringers "swilled the Sacrament-wine" they inadvertently entered into a pact with the Devil;[6] and the narrator's realization that "we were accurst" supports this interpretation.

1. Purdy, *Thomas Hardy: A Bibliographical Study*, p. 233.
2. Pp. 221, 267; *Life*, pp. 169, 203.
3. Pp. 179-80; *Life*, p. 379. It is not clear whether he failed to hear the bells because the east wind blew from Max Gate toward the church or because he fell asleep.
4. The brackets are Hardy's.
5. "Facts," in the Dorset County Museum, is unpaged at this point. The tradition is partly copied from the source Hardy cites and partly paraphrased; it is found also in Metcalfe, *St. Peter's*, pp. 46-47.
6. See Firor, *Folkways in Thomas Hardy*, p. 295.

"I LOOKED BACK" was first published in the *Daily Telegraph* for May 24, 1928.[1] The poem presents a series of scenes, each haunted by the sense that it may be seen no more. The first is, apparently, of Max Gate on a recent evening; the second, of a former merrymaking; and the third, of a rendezvous with a "maid forgot" in Hardy's courting days. The moon of the first stanza, in his poetry a symbol of cold reality, suggests loss deeper than nostalgia.

1. Purdy, *Thomas Hardy: A Bibliographical Study*, p. 259.

THE AGED NEWSPAPER SOLILOQUIZES was first published, with the title "The Newspaper Soliloquises," in the *Observer* for March 14, 1926.[1] Its editor, J. L. Garvin, wrote Hardy on March 2: "The *Observer* on March 14 comes out as a larger paper with more literature and a row of reviews by eminent hands. . . . Have you a poem you could send me for that date as you used to send one now and then to the Outlook when edited by me twenty years ago?" Garvin wrote on March 6: "You made glad the Editor and the office whooped with pleasure when the happy lines came in. It is true. The *Observer* is 135 years old yet renewing itself as it has done again and again."[2]

1. Purdy, *Thomas Hardy: A Bibliographical Study*, pp. 259-60. Perhaps the editor changed Hardy's spelling of "Soliloquizes."
2. In the Dorset County Museum.

CHRISTMAS: 1924 was first published, with the title "Peace upon Earth," in the *Daily Telegraph* for June 18, 1928.[1] Hardy had been brooding upon the thought of the poem since the Boer War. He wrote to Mrs. Florence Henniker on February 25, 1900: "I met a religious man on Friday . . . & I said, We, the civilized world, have given Christianity a fair trial for nearly 2000 years, & it has not yet taught countries the rudimentary virtue of keeping peace: so why not throw it over, & try, say, Buddhism. . . . It shocked him for he could only see the unchristianity of Kruger."[2] Hardy believed in Jesus's message in the Sermon on the Mount, but he saw the ritual of mass as a substitution of the magic (or the miraculous in the Gospels) for Jesus's teachings.

1. Purdy, *Thomas Hardy: A Bibliographical Study*, p. 260.
2. In the Dorset County Museum.

THE SINGLE WITNESS seems a traditional story of a "county" family in Wessex. The tale may be one told in Heath's manuscript. (See the notes on "The Dame of Athelhall.") The date of the action is some time after Waterloo. The poem illustrates the lawless pride of the nobility of an earlier time. The poem may be compared with Hardy's short-story "What the Shepherd Saw" in *A Changed Man*.

HOW SHE WENT TO IRELAND "presumably refers to Dora Sigerson, Clement Shorter's wife, who died 6 January 1918 and was taken to Dublin for burial." At Shorter's request, Hardy wrote, after Mrs. Shorter's death, a preface for her book of sketches, *A Dull Day in London*, published in June, 1920.[1] He had evidently found in Mrs. Shorter a kindred spirit. His preface for her book says: "Many years ago when I chanced to be sitting by the sea in the company of the writer of the following charming sketches, I was struck by the evidences of her sympathy with the lower animal creation. . . . On opening, this week, these last pages of hers, the first thing I remark is the same sympathy further extended, till it seems to embrace all animate and inanimate nature."[2] The opening chapter of her book presents a playfully sympathetic treatment of birds, cats, and dogs.

1. Purdy, *Thomas Hardy: A Bibliographical Study*, pp. 260, 210.
2. Orel, *Thomas Hardy's Personal Writings*, pp. 86-87.

DEAD "WESSEX" THE DOG TO THE HOUSEHOLD was first published (in two stanzas only) in the *Daily Telegraph* for May 10, 1928.[1] The wire-haired terrier "Wessex" (see the notes on "A Popular Personage at Home") was not the first dog at whose death Hardy grieved. He wrote to Edmund Gosse on September 25, 1890: "We are quite in grief today. Our poor dog Moss died this morning, and we have buried her under the trees by the lawn. It was singular that your last photo included her. That happens to be the only portrait of any sort that was taken of her: so if you could let us have it when developed, (even if not a good picture in itself) we should be glad."[2]

"Dead 'Wessex' " is a soliloquy by the spirit of Wessex addressed to the "Wistful ones" who miss him, Hardy and his wife Florence. Wessex died on December 27, 1926, and was buried on the morning of December 28 by Bertie Stephens, Hardy's gardener, in the animals' graveyard at Max Gate, where "There were already some 12 or 13 dogs and cats . . . each with its own tombstone."[3] Hardy designed and erected a tombstone engraved: "The / Famous Dog / Wessex / August 1913—27 Dec. 1926 / Faithful. Unflinching."[4]

The Later Years says: "A sadness fell upon the household, for Hardy's dog, Wessex, now thirteen years old, was ill and obviously near his end. Two days after Christmas Hardy makes this entry: '27 *December*. Our famous dog "Wessex" died at ½ past 6 in the evening, thirteen years of age. 28. Wessex buried. 28. *Night*. Wessex sleeps outside the house the first time for thirteen years.' The dog lies in a small turfed grave on the west side of Max Gate."[5]

Hardy wrote to Sir Sydney Cockerell on December 29, 1926: "Of course he was merely a dog, and not a good dog always, but *thousands* (actually thousands) of afternoons and evenings I would have been alone but for him, and had always him to speak to. But I . . . hope no one will ask me about him or mention his name."[6]

1. Purdy, *Thomas Hardy: A Bibliographical Study*, p. 260.
2. A copy of this letter is in the Colby College Library. See *Early Life*, p. 300; *Life*, pp. 229-30.
3. Stephens, *Thomas Hardy in His Garden*, p. 10.
4. Hardy's drawings for the tombstone are in the Dorset County Museum.
5. Pp. 250-51; *Life*, pp. 434-35.
6. Meynell, ed., *Friends of a Lifetime*, p. 314. The letter is dated December 26 in error; see Purdy, *Thomas Hardy: A Bibliographical Study*, p. 260.

THE WOMAN WHO WENT EAST was first published in the *Daily Telegraph* for May 14, 1928. The manuscript has the deleted title "The Woman of the West."[1] This poem is a fantasy in dialogue between a "stranger Dame," and a "Good Sir" who is an "Old native" and an "old lover" of the questioning woman. Possibly Hardy had in mind an imaginary visit by his first wife Emma to Cornwall at some time before her death in 1912. The poem protests the decay of all things as they grow old, in contrast with the dream that if left alone a woman's beauty would not become a "skeleton that Time" alters.

1. Purdy, *Thomas Hardy: A Bibliographical Study*, p. 260.

NOT KNOWN in the manuscript has the deleted note at the end "1914: After reading criticism."[1] The poem expresses Hardy's irritation at the reviewers and journalistic critics who wrote about him in his later years, especially those who deduced his personality by misreading his poems. This irritation echoes his pencil-jottings beside the reviews pasted in "Reviews of T. H.'s Books (Poetry)" in the Dorset County Museum. Comments range from corrections of misprints, through charges of misreading and spite, to "Lies!" (See the notes on "So Various.")

1. Purdy *Thomas Hardy: A Bibliographical Study*, p. 260.

THE BOY'S DREAM was first published in the *Daily Telegraph* for July 12, 1928.[1] The poem portrays a sensitive, introspective boy being brought up in a provincial town (e.g., Plymouth, Bath, or Bristol). He is evidently of high-school age and lame (or at least physically weak). The boy resembles in temperament Father Time of *Jude the Obscure* and the boy of "Midnight on the Great Western," (See the notes on this poem.)

1. Purdy, *Thomas Hardy: A Bibliographical Study*, p. 260.

THE GAP IN THE WHITE, Lewis says, helps us understand Hardy's "unbounded sympathy," even if "gossip lures Hardy on to the most intractable subjects" for poetry.[1] His headnote dating the event as "178—" suggests that the poem rests on fact. Possibly it has some relation to a letter he wrote to Mrs. Arthur Henniker on August 13, 1899: "You will remember my saying I had never had any necessity for a dentist? As a judgement, about a fortnight ago a front tooth came out—absolutely without a flaw in it.—I have done nothing to remedy it, & do not intend to."[2]

The theme is characteristic: love may depend more on external beauty than on essential worth, and a lifetime of happiness may be wrecked by a trifling circumstance. Critics have found the technique characteristic. Who else than Hardy, says Shanks, "could have seen the tragedy implicit in this collocation of love and dentistry? . . . Who else, having chosen it, would have dared the ruthless prose of that parenthesis? The answer is: Only another man who loved the details of life even to greediness as Hardy did."[3]

1. "The Lyrical Poetry of Thomas Hardy," p. 164.
2. In the Dorset County Museum.
3. "Songs of Joy," p. 610.

FAMILY PORTRAITS was published as "The Portraits" in *Nash's and Pall Mall Magazine* for December, 1924. "It was subsequently much revised, the present fifth stanza added and the last 3 stanzas in particular rearranged and rewritten. This final version was first printed in the *Daily Telegraph*, 6 August 1928."[1] In the poem, three "picture-drawn people," "a maiden of mild wistful tone" (the "fair woman" of a later stanza), a "dark woman," and a "sad man—a man of much gloom," step from picture-frames to enact an obscure drama. The characters are Hardy's ancestors whose portraits one may suppose hung at Max Gate or at his birthplace in Higher Bockhampton. As the portraits from these homes do not fit the details of the poem, they may represent ancestors Hardy discovered in his search of parish registers and such other sources of information as tales told by his mother and his grandmother. (See "One We Knew.") The poem suggests marital irregularities among Hardy's forebears, but their nature was obscure to Hardy beyond the fact that he saw in them some determination of his own nature and experiences. If he had been fully aware of his "blood's tendance," he might have averted choices that had painful consequences.

Both before and during the time he was preparing notes for his biography, Hardy worked out various pedigrees, not only the pedigree published by Evelyn Hardy,[2] but also other versions now in the Dorset County Museum. From some of them he omitted facts that he certainly knew. In the pedigree that Evelyn Hardy published, he omitted the names of four of his mother's brothers and sisters and the names of all his father's brothers and sisters, though other pedigrees include these items. Lois Deacon, quoting from *The Early Life*, says: "'Jemima saw during girlhood and young womanhood some very stressful experiences of which she could never speak in her maturer years without pain.' It is inconceivable that Hardy would reveal these stressful matters while members of his family were still alive."[3]

Lurid experiences among Hardy's ancestors are suggested in the parish records Hardy consulted. Families in the villages of Wessex (isolated communities in the eighteenth and nineteenth centuries) tended to intermarry or interbreed without marriage. For instance, the "Banns of Marriage" for Melbury Osmund (Hardy's mother's birthplace) read: "Thomas Childs and Hannah Childs, both of Melbury Osmund, 1790; Edmund Childs and Frances Childs, both of Melbury Osmund, 1792; Thomas Childs and Sarah Childs, both of Melbury Osmund, 1813; Edmund Childs and Elizabeth Childs, both of Melbury Osmund, 1816," and so on. The registers list illegitimate births among various families: on October 17, 1830, Jemima Woods, daughter of Charlotte Childs, was baptized with no father named (presumably a man named Woods); on July 29, 1827, Caroline Childs, "base-born daughter of Charlotte Bird, Melbury Osmund" was baptized; on January 20, 1826, Ann, daughter of Mary Childs "single woman," was baptized, and so on. As Hardy's great-grandmother was born Maria Childs, these data interested him. Perhaps the drama of "Family Portraits" took place at Melbury Osmund.

He had ancestors elsewhere. His paternal grandmother was born Mary Head of Fawley in Berkshire. (This is the grandmother of "One We Knew.") He investigated the records of Fawley (the "Marygreen" of *Jude the Obscure*) and of nearby Chaddleworth, the villages of the Head family. In the early chapters of the manuscript of *Jude the Obscure*, the cousins Jude and Sue are given the same family name, Head, and an obscure drama of mixed emotions among their ancestors is suggested.[4] The parish records of Fawley and Chaddleworth, like those of Melbury Osmund, reveal marital irregularities: on July 2, 1820, Jesse, son of William Darling and Sarah Goddard, "his wife's sister," was baptized. The records of the Head family include: "Baptized John Stroude the natural son of Anne Head, March the 16th 1752." The irregularities touch Hardy's grandmother. Mary Head's father, James Head, was buried on May 6, 1772; Mary was born after her father's death, as she was baptized on October 30 of this year. Mary's mother, also Mary, had a son, William, baptized on April 25, 1779—with no father named.[5]

Whatever ancestral drama Hardy had in mind, the poem suggests that hereditary factors govern temperament and those choices among actions that determine consequences. The poem seems to foreshadow events in his life: his conflict in love between the dark-haired Tryphena Sparks (suggested in "a dark woman in former time known") and Emma Gifford, a "fair woman." As in Hardy's life, the characters move in "puppet-like movements" in response to a "strange allure." The compulsion of natural, sinister forces is suggested in symbols in the opening stanza: the "blast" and the "white-shrouded candles." (See the notes on "Heredity," "The Pedigree," and "Her Late Husband.")[6]

1. Purdy, *Thomas Hardy: A Bibliographical Study*, p. 260.

2. *Thomas Hardy*, facing p. 224.

3. *Hardy's Grandmother, Betsy, and Her Family*, p. 5; see *Early Life*, p. 9; *Life*, p. 8.

4. Though Jude's last name is changed to that of the village, Fawley, Sue's last name retains a suggestion of the original in Bride*head*.

5. From the parish registers of Fawley and Chaddleworth.

6. Hardy's term "blood's tendance" suggests that his ideas on heredity had a medical basis. Notes among his papers indicate that he regularly read the *Fortnightly Review*. There he possibly read two articles by Francis Galton, "The Anthropometric Laboratory" (XXXI, March, 1882, pp. 332-38) and "Medical Family Registers" (XXXIV, August, 1883, pp. 244-50). These articles discuss the bases for inherited family tendencies, traits, capacities, and weaknesses, the rise and decay of families, and inherited limitations upon free will.

THE CATCHING BALLET OF THE WEDDING CLOTHES tells a story in the rhythm of a ballet, partly in dialogue between a vain girl and a "white witch" and partly in narrative. The headnote indicates the time of the story as during the reign of William IV, 1830-37. The white witch is not an evil enchantress, but a woman whose advice is worldly wisdom.[1] The girl at first follows her impulses and marries Jack the sailor, but later abandons him for her wealthy suitor. To the extent that the poem is a parable, worldliness rules the girl's final choice, with the result that she was wealthy but unhappy.[2]

1. She resembles Elizabeth Endorfield of *Under the Greenwood Tree*, Part the Fourth, Chapter III.
2. The poem may have been suggested by a distantly similar story recorded in Hardy's journal for March 4, 1889. See *Early Life*, p. 285; *Life*, pp. 217-18.

A WINSOME WOMAN meditates that whatever the charms of the woman known to the poet, she must pass away and be forgotten.

THE BALLAD OF LOVE'S SKELETON presents a conversation between a callous, pleasure-loving Hanoverian baron of King George III's entourage and a woman of Weymouth so fascinated by his rank and person that she has no will of her own.

The time of the action is noted as "179—." George III visited Weymouth[1] in the summer of 1789 and was so pleased that he returned there for a vacation nearly every summer through 1805. In the early 1790's, he stayed at the Royal Hotel. Hardy had lunch there in August of 1890, and *The Early Life* says: "This was the Old Royal Hotel, now pulled down, where George III. and his daughters used to dance at the town assemblies, a red cord dividing the royal dancers from the townspeople. The sockets for the standards bearing the cord were still visible in the floor while the building was standing."[2] The hotel faced the esplanade along the beach, referred to in the poem as the "Royal Strand."

The opening proposal of the baron suggests the scene of the woman's seduction. Culliford Hill is a steep hilltop about three and a half miles north of Weymouth, from which one has a view of the town, the sea, and, to the north, Dorchester. A tree called Culliford Tree (among other trees) and ancient burial barrows mark the hilltop. Hardy perhaps intended readers who know of the barrows to find a sinister suggestion in the place, in ironic contrast to the baron's comment upon squirrels, sunny places, and shepherds' thyme. The baron's other proposals, to "strut the Royal Strand," "joy again" in a new dance, and "whirl to-night, / Forgetting all things save ourselves," indicate his self-centered love of pleasure. He has urged the woman to kill their unborn child to avoid soiling his "noble name."

His winning argument is the extra card he has that will admit the woman to dance among the aristocracy, apart from the "burgher-throng below." The woman is not entirely depraved. Some of her statements recall Hardy's view that a woman with an unwanted child might outlive shame.[3]

1. Hardy's "Budmouth," a coastal resort-city seven miles south of Dorchester.
2. P. 300; *Life*, p. 229. Later King George resided at the Gloucester Hotel.
3. The poem recalls a country girl's irresistible fascination by Baron Von Xanten in *The Romantic Adventures of a Milkmaid*.

A PRIVATE MAN ON PUBLIC MEN was first published in the *Daily Telegraph* for March 26, 1928.[1] The title of the poem is misleading. After eight lines on the strife of public men for wealth and fame, the poem turns to Hardy and his preference for privacy.

Undoubtedly he was shy. Though in the city often, he made his home in the country; he sought no public office. On the other hand, he was highly sensitive to critics' opinions of his work; his biography is full of his enjoyment of society, lists of prominent people he dined with, etc.; and he was proud of his honorary degrees and other honors. Perhaps the poem is partly an apology for an attitude he adopted in his later years. He was world-famous in the 1920's, and consequently journalists, publicists, promoters, sight-seers, and tourists pestered him, pried for personal facts to publish, and would not take silence for an answer. Often hiding from these people, he designated his wife Florence as his "chucker-out" and relied upon the fierce dog Wessex to help. When strangers did get through the barriers, he was sometimes brusque.

A second topic of the poem is his alleged pessimism. Much of his writing does present philosophic bases for pessimism; no doubt he was extraordinarily sensitive to the pains of life; he suffered much for himself and in compassion for others, but he was not the gloomy nay-sayer he was often labelled. Hundreds of reminiscences report that he was reasonably serene in old age, living through "years of moderate gladness / Mellowed by sundry days of sadness."

1. Purdy, *Thomas Hardy: A Bibliographical Study*, p. 261.

CHRISTMAS IN THE ELGIN ROOM was the last of Hardy's writings published during his life. *The Later Years*, speaking of an illness that began on December 11, 1927, says: "From then his strength waned daily. He was anxious that a poem he had written, 'Christmas in the Elgin Room' should be copied and sent to *The Times*. This was done, and he asked his wife anxiously whether she had posted it with her own hand. . . . Two days later he received a personal letter of thanks, with a warm appreciation of his work, from the editor of

The Times. This gave him pleasure, and he asked that a reply should be sent."[1] The poem appeared in the *Times* for December 24, 1927, and simultaneously as a pamphlet printed for Mrs. Hardy.[2]

The poem presents the fantasy of a conversation on Christmas Eve among the gods and goddesses of the Elgin Room in the British museum. The date given in the headnote is "early last century," before they had become acquainted with the meaning of Christmas. They view their replacement in "men's good will" with wonder and dismay.

The Elgin Marbles are sculptures taken from the ruins of the Parthenon, or temple to the goddess Athena on the Acropolis in Athens. Brought to England by Lord Elgin and in 1816 sold to the nation, they were housed in the British Museum in rooms called the Elgin rooms.

Themes implicit in the poem include the protest of the gods at being removed from their sunny home on "Athenai's Hill" to the gloom and chill of a northern land, and dismay at the substitution of a Christian deity and Christian values for the more radiant values of Athena and the Greek gods generally. These themes were by no means original with Hardy, and possibly he drew them more from romantic poetry than from reflection upon the marbles. Byron in "The Curse of Minerva" called Lord Elgin a "spoiler worse than both" the Turk and the Goth, who "basely stole what less barbarians won." In the second canto of "Childe Harold's Pilgrimage," he wrote of the marbles: "Curst be the hour when from their isle they roved" and British hands snatched Greece's "shrinking Gods to northern climes abhorr'd!" Keats's sonnet "On Seeing the Elgin Marbles" speaks of their beauty "That mingles Grecian grandeur with the rude / Wasting of old Time . . . / A sun—a shadow of a magnitude." The "Wasting of old Time" suggests the passing of old cultures and religions, replaced by new, as in Swinburne's "Hymn to Proserpine": "Thou hast conquered, O Pale Galilean, the world has grown grey from thy breath."[3]

In the British Museum in 1905, gathering material for *The Dynasts*, Hardy must have seen the Elgin marbles at the time he began the poem, but a letter to Edmund Gosse allows the surmise of influences more from the poets than from the marbles. Gosse wrote to Hardy upon seeing the poem: "I want very much to know *when* you wrote it."[4] Hardy replied: "I can only go by the dates attached in fixing their history: the poem having been begun in 1905 (probably when I was in the Elgin Room, though I don't remember being there) and then abandoned, and not finished till last year."[5]

In the poem, the "Borean" people are the English, as Boreas is the god of the north wind. Aurore refers to the rising sun, as Aurora is goddess of the dawn. Helios is god of the sun; Ilissus, god of a river near Athens; Demeter, goddess of agriculture; Poseidon, god of the sea; Persephone, goddess of the underworld; and Zeus, father of the gods.

1. P. 264; *Life*, pp. 444-45.
2. Purdy, *Thomas Hardy: A Bibliographical Study*, p. 251.
3. Hardy quotes this line in Part II, Chapter III of *Jude the Obscure*.
4. In the Dorset County Museum.
5. Gosse, "Mr. Hardy's Last Poem."

"WE ARE GETTING TO THE END" was first published in the *Daily Telegraph* for May 28, 1928.[1] The sonnet gives up hope in the "evolutionary meliorism" Hardy had postulated in the "Apology" of *Late Lyrics and Earlier*.

He suggests that his personal life is "spasmodically" pleasant, but that his dream that through reason men may improve the race is futile. Sassoon quotes a letter by Hardy that states the basis of this thought: "I fear . . . that what appears . . . evident is that it is getting worse and worse. All development is of a material and scientific kind —and scarcely any addition to our knowledge is applied to objects philanthropic and ameliorative."

The sestet applies this generalization to war as madness generated by "some demonic force." Sassoon, reporting a conversation with Hardy in the 1920's, states the basis for this despair: "I remember asking him—one evening when staying at Max Gate—whether he believed in the League of Nations or any such design for the prevention of war. Rather diffidently, he expressed his view that wars came about almost like atmospheric disturbances, adding that he had sometimes felt that they were caused by supernatural agencies and were beyond human control."[2]

1. Purdy, *Thomas Hardy: A Bibliographical Study*, p. 261.
2. *Siegfried's Journey*, pp. 223 and 120.

HE RESOLVES TO SAY NO MORE was written in 1927[1] and first published in the *Daily Telegraph* for September 18, 1928.[2] The "Pale Horse" of the first stanza symbolizes the approach of death, as in Rev. 6:8, "And I looked, and behold a pale horse: and his name that sat on him was Death, and Hell followed with him."

The poem conceals, as too horrible for men's minds to bear, the disintegrative forces that Hardy saw operative in the world during his last year of life. They may be surmised from earlier statements. In 1922, he wrote in the "Apology" for *Late Lyrics and Earlier*: "Whether owing to the barbarizing of taste in the younger minds by the dark madness of the late war, the unabashed cultivation of selfishness in all classes, the plethoric growth of knowledge simultaneously with the stunting of wisdom, 'a degrading thirst after outrageous stimulation' . . . we seem threatened with a new Dark Age." In a conversation of 1925 reported by Frederick Lefèvre, he repeated this thought: "I think rather that we are entering on a dark age whose port of entry was the abominable war we have just lived through. . . . The folly of the war and all the follies which it engendered, the appalling development of selfishness, the cult, if I may say so, of egoism, scientific development linked directly with a corresponding strangling of wisdom, the degrading thirst for disordered excitement, constitute such a menace for civilization that rationalism and religion ought to league themselves without delay to battle against the invading barbarism."[3]

Yet the poem is not without hope. Hardy's "rationalism and religion ought to league themselves . . . against the invading barbarism" implies that, by removing blinkers, they can do so. He "still holds that the only way that men can liberate their souls for the fashioning of all things fair is to know reality to be as dark as it has been revealed to him; and yet in his passionate pity he would spare them the vision."[4] It is implied that men of reason and religion, with courage to face the legions of the new barbarism, rather than evade them, have a chance. Hardy apparently died in the belief that the chance is slim.

1. *Later Years*, facsimile facing p. 262.
2. Purdy, *Thomas Hardy: A Bibliographical Study*, p. 261.
3. "An Hour with Thomas Hardy," pp. 100-102.
4. C. P., "Thomas Hardy's Last Poems."

Part Two

Notes on Hardy's Poems not Previously Published or not collected, Alternate Titles, The Dynasts, and The Queen of Cornwall

Each of Hardy's poems was, in his feeling, an expression of himself. Therefore, except for *The Dynasts* and *The Queen of Cornwall*, separately published, he collected into the eight volumes that underlie *Collected Poems* nearly all the poetry he wrote. Only a few incidental pieces escaped him or were rejected. Part Two offers notes on these poems.

Some of them are only stanzas or scraps, published in his novels and stories, as "Eunice" is published in *Desperate Remedies* and there attributed to the fictional character Aeneas Manston. Others are poems Hardy wrote for friends, as he wrote "A. H." for Mrs. Florence Henniker and "To J. M. B." for J. M. Barrie. He wrote "The Calf," "The Lizard," and "The Yellow-Hammer" to introduce Florence Dugdale's chapters on these creatures in her books for children. Besides pieces written for special purposes, he either overlooked or rejected for publication a few poems that Evelyn Hardy has published since his death. He apparently kept for years, but finally rejected another poem, untitled, that opens "When wearily we shrink away." Discovered in the Dorset County Museum, it is published for the first time in the present notes. On his death-bed Hardy wrote two poems, each called "Epitaph," one for G. K. Chesterton and one for George Moore. They are published here for the first time, with the permission and approval of Miss Irene Cooper Willis, speaking for the Trustees of the Hardy Estate. The only poems published here are ones either not published elsewhere, or published in a book not likely to be found in most libraries.

The following notes include comments on odds and ends of poems, for instance, Hardy's translations of foreign poems and his revision of a poem by someone else ("If you think"); on poems attributed to Hardy, but not by him ("Two Roses" and "The Old Clock"); and on lost poems known only by some reference to the title or the subject.

Hardy was much concerned to give his poems suitable titles, and on second thought he often changed the manuscript-title of a poem when he published it; sometimes he changed a title when he republished a poem. The following notes list the alternative titles. The list may have value for the student who comes upon references to a poem with the title it bore in manuscript or as published under a title different from the usual one.[1]

In developments from manuscript through various publications, Hardy often revised, sometimes by altering a word or phrase, but sometimes by adding or omitting a stanza or more. To examine these revisions is beyond the scope of the present study: a variorum edition would be useful, but it would be another book. Purdy points out and comments upon Hardy's significant revisions.

The arrangement of Part Two is alphabetical by title, with no classification to separate the long discussion of *The Dynasts*, for instance, from the preceding brief notation of "A Dream indeed?" Dates and details of publication under alternate titles are omitted; they may be found in the notes treating the poem as published in *Collected Poems*.

1. For this identification, I have not thought it necessary to examine all manuscripts, widely scattered in various libraries and among collectors; I have relied upon Professor Purdy's *Bibliographical Study*, though I have not footnoted each item taken from this source. I have relied upon this book also for alternate titles of poems as published in various places.

* * * * * * * *

A. H., 1855-1912

A laurelled soldier he; yet who could find
In camp or court a less vainglorious mind?
Sincere as bold, one read as in a book
His modest spirit in his candid look.

At duty's beckoning alert as brave,
We could have wished for him a later grave!
A season ere the setting of his sun
To rest upon the honours he had won. . .

Yet let us not lament. We do not weep
When our best comrade sinks in fitful sleep,
And why indulge regrets if he should fall
At once into the sweetest sleep of all?

Hardy contributed this poem to Mrs. Florence Henniker's *Arthur Henniker, A Little Book for His Friends* (London, 1912), a book of obituaries, reminiscences, and letters of sympathy. "The poem was left uncollected because of its personal nature and also because the last quatrain was simply a recasting of an old epitaph Hardy had suggested for Alfred Pretor in 1907 (see *Later Years*, p. 126)."[1]

Major-General Arthur H. Henniker was the husband of Hardy's close friend, Mrs. Florence Henniker. Educated at Cambridge, Henniker entered the Army as a lieutenant; he saw military action in Egypt and South Africa. He died of heart failure on February 6, 1912, at fifty-six. *The Later Years* records that on October 20, 1894, Hardy "Dined at the Guards' Mess, St. James's, with Major Henniker. After dinner went round with him to the sentries with a lantern."[2]

1. Purdy, *Thomas Hardy: A Bibliographical Study*, p. 316.
2. P. 34; *Life*, p. 266.

ABOVE THE YOUTH'S is two lines in *Jude the Obscure,* Part II, Chapter VI, translated (by Hardy?) from Heine's "Götterdämmerung" in Heine's *Buch der Lieder*: "Auf dem begeistert stolzen Jünglingshaupt / Seh ich die lachend bunte Schellenkappe."

AFTER THE BATTLE is the manuscript title of "Outside the Casement."

AGNOSTIC (EVENSONG:———CATHEDRAL), THE, is the manuscript title of "The Impercipient."

AMONG THE ROMAN GRAVEMOUNDS is the title of "The Roman Gravemounds" as published in the *English Review*.

AS IF NOT THERE is the manuscript title of "The Dream is—Which?"

AT A REHEARSAL OF ONE OF J. M. B.'S PLAYS is discussed in the notes on "To J. M. B."

AT AN EVENING SERVICE [SUNDAY] AUGUST 14, 1870 is the manuscript title of "The Young Churchwarden."

AT HIS FUNERAL is the title of "She at His Funeral" as published in *Selected Poems*.

AT LODGINGS IN LONDON is the manuscript title of "At Mayfair Lodgings."

AT MADAME TUSSAUD'S AND LATER is the manuscript title of "At Madame Tussaud's in Victorian Years."

AT MIDDLE-HILL GATE IN FEBRUARY is the manuscript title of "At Middle-Field Gate in February."

AT MOONRISE, OR "WE USED TO GO" is the manuscript title of "Seeing the Moon Rise."

AT NEWS OF A WOMAN'S DEATH is the title of "Thoughts of Phena" as published in *Selected Poems*.

AT ST. LAUNCE'S is the manuscript title of "St. Launce's Revisited."

AT THE CEMETERY LOOGE is the manuscript title of "The Supplanter."

AT THE WAR OFFICE AFTER A BLOODY BATTLE is the title of "At the War Office, London" as published in the *Sphere*.

AUTUMN [OCTOBER] AT THE HOMESTEAD is the manuscript title of "Shortening Days at the Homestead."

AUTUMN EVENING is the manuscript title of "At Day-Close in November."

AUTUMN IN MY LORD'S PARK is the title of "Autumn in King's Hintock Park" as published in the *Daily Mail Books' Supplement*.

AUTUMN IN THE PARK is the title of "Autumn in King's Hintock Park" as published in *Time's Laughingstocks*.

AUTUMN NIGHT-TIME is the manuscript title of "Night-time in Mid-Fall."

BATTUE, THE, is the title of "The Puzzled Game-Birds" in the Wessex Edition.

BENIGHTED TRAVELLER, THE, is the manuscript title of "The Wanderer."

BREAK O' THE DAY, THE, is a song, eight lines of which appear in Chapter XLIX of *Tess of the D'Urbervilles*. It is not Hardy's poem. Under the note "Old Song sung at Melbury Osmund about 1820," it appears in Hardy's manuscript-booklet *Country Songs of 1820 Onwards Killed by the Comic Song of the Music Hall*, in the Dorset County Museum.

BRIDEGROOM, THE, is the manuscript title of "The Pair He Saw Pass."

BUDMOUTH DEARS is from *The Dynasts*, Part Third, II, i, published separately as "Hussar's Song: 'Budmouth Dears'" in *Selected Poems*. The song has been set to music by Boynton Smith (in the program for production of *The Trumpet-Major* by the Dorchester Debating and Dramatic Society, 1912), Gerald Finzi (London: Oxford University Press, not dated), and Martin Shaw (London: J. Curwen and Sons, and Germantown, Pa.: Curwen, Inc., 1927).

BY MELLSTOCK CROSS AT THE YEAR'S END is the title of "By Henstridge Cross at the Year's End" as published in the *Fortnightly Review*.

BY THE CENTURY'S DEATHBED is the title of "The Darkling Thrush" as published in the *Graphic*.

BY THE ROMAN EARTHWORKS is the manuscript title of "The Roman Gravemounds."

You may have seen, in road or street
   At times, when passing by,
A creature with bewildered bleat
Behind a milcher's tail, whose feet
   Went pit-pat. That was I.

Whether we are of Devon kind,
   Shorthorns, or Herefords,
We are in general of one mind
That in the human race we find
   Our masters and our lords.

When grown up (if they let me live)
   And in a dairy-home,
I may less wonder and misgive
Than now, and get contemplative,
   And never wish to roam.

And in some fair stream, taking sips,
   May stand through summer noons,
With water dribbling from my lips
And rising halfway to my hips
   And babbling pleasant tunes.

Hardy wrote "The Calf" for E. J. Detmold and Florence E. Dugdale (later the second Mrs. Hardy), *The Book of Baby Beasts* (London, 1911, p. 105). The poem is not there attributed to Hardy, but is ascribed to him by Mrs. Hardy's sisters.[1] The poem is followed by Miss Dugdale's three-page essay on "The Calf."

1. Purdy, *Thomas Hardy: A Bibliographical Study*, p. 314.

CENTURY'S END, THE, is the manuscript title of "The Darkling Thrush."

CHANCE is the manuscript title of "Hap."

CHILDREN VERSUS SIR NAMELESS, THE, is the manuscript title of "The Children and Sir Nameless."

CHOIRMASTER'S FUNERAL, THE, is the manuscript title of "The Choirmaster's Burial."

CHORUS OF THE PITIES is from *The Dynasts*, Part Third, After Scene, separately published in *Selected Poems*.

CLOCK OF TIME, THE, is the manuscript title of "The Clock of the Years."

COMET AT YALBURY OR YELL'HAM, THE, is the title of "The Comet at Yell'ham" as published in *Poems of the Past and the Present.*

COMPLAINT OF THE COMMON MAN, THE, was in the manuscript of *Poems of the Past and the Present.* Purdy says: "From the table of contents it appears that one poem, 'The Complaint of the Common Man' (placed between 'The King's Experiment' and 'The Tree'), was removed from the collection. It is no longer identifiable if it appears elsewhere in Hardy's work."[1]

1. *Thomas Hardy: A Bibliographical Study*, p. 117-18.

CONVERSATIONAL PHANTASY, A, is the early title for "A Philosophical Fantasy." See Evelyn Hardy, *Thomas Hardy's Notebooks*, p. 114.

"CORNHILL'S" JUBILEE, THE, is the manuscript title of "The Jubilee of a Magazine."

DAIRYMAN DICK is a three-line rime to characterize Richard Crick in Chapter XVII of *Tess of the D'Urbervilles.*

DANDY'S SONG is the early title for "Gallant's Song."

DAY OF FIRST SIGHT is the title of "First Sight of Her and After" as published in *Moments of Vision.*

DE PROFUNDIS, I, II, AND III is the title of "In Tenebris," I, II, and III, as published in *Poems of the Past and the Present.*

DEAD DRUMMER, THE, is the title of "Drummer Hodge" as published in *Poems of the Past and the Present.*

DEAD FINGERS, THE, is the title of "Haunting Fingers" as published in the *New Republic* (New York).

DEAR MY LOVE is the opening phrase of a four-line translation (presumably Hardy's) stated to be from Heine's *Lieb Liebchen* in Chapter XI of *Two on a Tower.* It is in fact from Heine's *Junge Leiden*, "Lieder 4," as follows:

Lieb' Liebchen, leg's Händchen aufs Herze mein:—
Ach, hörst du, wie's pocht im Kämmerlein?
Da haust ein Zimmermann schlimm und arg,
Der zimmert mir einen Totensarg.

DECEMBER RAIN-SCENE, A, is the title of "An Autumn Rain-Scene" as published in the *Fortnightly Review*.

DEPARTURE, THE, is the title of "Embarcation" as published in the *Daily Chronicle*. The poem should not be confused with "Departure," which follows "Embarcation" in the *Collected Poems*.

DEPARTURE BY TRAIN, A, is a lost poem. *The Early Life* says of Hardy in 1868: "In the February following a memorandum shows that he composed a lyric entitled 'A Departure by Train,' which has disappeared."[1] Possibly this poem treats the departure of Tryphena Sparks from Puddletown for London. Tryphena was enrolled as a pupil-teacher in Puddletown School on November 7, 1866, and remained so until January or February, 1868. Entries in the log-book for the school during most of this period state that her work was satisfactory, except in Geography, but on January 16, 1868, the log-book records: "Reproved pupil teacher for neglect of duty–parents very angry in consequence, determine to withdraw her a month hence." On January 20, the log states that Tryphena had been replaced in the Girls' Department by Frances Dunman and had been sent to the Boys' Department. This is the final entry regarding her.[2] In connection with the theory that shortly after this time Tryphena gave birth to Hardy's alleged son Randy, Deacon and Coleman say of "A Departure by Train": "We know that he [Hardy] wrote many other poems which were lost, but this is the only one whose composition he notes. Why? What is so unusual about this piece? Did it commemorate the departure by train of Tryphena, to have her baby at some place away from home, so that its birth might be known to as few as possible?"[3]

1. P. 76; *Life*, p. 57.
2. For this information I am indebted to Frank Southerington, who examined the log-book of the Puddletown School and wrote me the information given above.
3. *Providence and Mr Hardy*, p. 191.

DISCORD, A, is the manuscript title of "The Sun on the Letter."

DOMICILIUM was first published in pamphlet-form by Clement Shorter in 1916, and in similar form for Mrs. Florence Hardy in 1918.[1] Written between 1857 and 1860, "Domicilium" was reprinted in *The Early Life* as a footnote to the opening description of Hardy's birthplace. The introductory comment says: "Some Wordsworthian lines ... give with obvious and naïve fidelity the appearance of the paternal homestead at a date nearly half a century before the birth of their writer, when his grandparents settled there, after his great-grandfather had built for their residence the first house in the valley."[2]

1. Purdy, *Thomas Hardy: A Bibliographical Study*, pp. 176-77 and 208. *Early Life*, speaking of some publications of Hardy's youth, says that "After this followed the descriptive verses 'Domicilium,' and accounts of church-restorations carried out by Hicks, which Hardy prepared for the grateful reporter of the *Dorset Chronicle*." P. 43; *Life*, p. 33. The biography seems mistaken in suggesting publication at this time. See Purdy, pp. 291 and 293.

2. P. 4; *Life*, p. 4. Describing the homestead as Hardy knew it in his childhood, the poem devotes nearly two-thirds of its lines to the wildness of the Heath, especially as his grandmother remembered it. In the introduction to her edition of the poem, Mrs. Hardy wrote: "The influence of Wordsworth, a favourite author of the youthful poet's, will be clearly perceived, also a strong feeling for the unique and desolate beauty of the adjoining heath." The lines bear comparison with portions of the opening chapter of *The Return of the Native*. Pictures of Hardy's birthplace and the nearby heath are presented opposite p. 14 of Pinion, *A Hardy Companion*.

DOWN WESSEX WAY is the title given to "The Spring Call" when it was reprinted in *The Society of Dorset Men in London Yearbook* for 1914-15.

DREAM INDEED?, A, is the manuscript title of "A Dream or No."

DYNASTS, THE, Hardy's epic-drama, is in length and complexity comparable to all the rest of his poetry together. The present notes only sketch its major features.[1]

Part First of *'The Dynasts,' A Drama of the Napoleonic Wars, In Three Parts, Nineteen Acts, and One Hundred and Thirty Scenes* was published on January 13, 1904; Part Second on February 9, 1906; and Part Third on February 11, 1908.[2] *The Dynasts* was not only Hardy's major achievement in poetry; it was also the realization of a plan that had been forming in his mind since boyhood. His grandfather, a volunteer in a local regiment, had subscribed to *A History of the Wars* with Napoleon. When eight-year-old Tommy found it in a closet, its lurid scenes "set him on the train of ideas" that led to *The Dynasts*. A year or so later at a harvest-supper and dance, he began his "extensive acquaintance with soldiers of the old uniforms and long service" that served him well in writing of the wars. As a young man in London in 1865, he heard "Palmerston . . . War Secretary during the decisive hostilities with Napoleon," which brought him "face to face . . . with one who had contributed to direct the affairs of that war." On June 17, 1868, he outlined a narrative poem on the Battle of the Nile. "It was never finished, but it shows that the war with Napoleon was even then in his mind as material for poetry." In the summer of 1870, he visited Chelsea Hospital and talked with "the old asthmatic and crippled men, many of whom . . . had fought at Waterloo, and some in the Peninsula." He took his bride, Emma, with him to Chelsea Hospital on Waterloo Day, 1875;

the record of the visit offers details from old soldiers' memories. Within the month Hardy made a note: "Mem: A Ballad of the Hundred Days. Then another of Moscow. Others of earlier campaigns—forming altogether an Iliad of Europe from 1789 to 1815."[3] In 1876, he was in Brussels exploring the field of Waterloo and looking for the site of the Duchess of Richmond's Ball. In June of 1877, he made a memorandum to abandon the ballad-sequence and "Consider a grand drama, based on the wars with Napoleon, or some one campaign." He began a correspondence with Mrs. Chatteris to gather facts about her father, Admiral Sir Thomas Hardy of Trafalgar. On October 27, 1878, he was again in Chelsea Hospital listening to tales of warfare in the Peninsula and at Waterloo. He attended the funeral of Louis Napoleon on July 12, 1879, and observed the Napoleonic profile in Prince Napoleon, said to resemble "Boney." Detailed research in the British Museum for *The Trumpet-Major* furnished material later used in *The Dynasts*.

In 1881, Hardy added something philosophic to his plan: "Mode for a historical Drama. Action mostly automatic, reflex movement, etc. Not the result of what is called *motive*, though always ostensibly so, even to the actors' own consciousness. Apply an enlargement of these theories to, say, 'The Hundred Days'!" On February 16, 1882, he noted: "Write a history of human automatism, or impulsion—viz., an account of human action in spite of human knowledge." He speculated on March 4, 1886, about telling a story "by rendering as visible essences, spectres, etc. the abstract thoughts of the analytic school. . . . The human race to be shown as a great network or tissue which quivers in every part when one point is shaken, like a spider's web if touched. Abstract realisms to be in the form of Spirits, Spectral figures, etc." By the autumn of this year, he was reading in the British Museum toward his epic-drama. Visiting Italy in 1887 and sitting on the roof of Milan Cathedral, he "conceived the Milan Cathedral scene in *The Dynasts*." By September of 1889, he concluded: "I feel continually that I require a larger canvas. . . . A spectral tone must be adopted. . . . Royal ghosts. . . . Title: 'A Drama of Kings.' " In April of 1890, he decided to "View the Prime Cause or Invariable Antecedent as 'It' and recount its doings." On June 26, 1892, he "Considered methods for the Napoleonic drama. Forces; emotions; tendencies. The characters do not act under the influence of reason."

He went again to Brussels in September, 1896, to examine Waterloo. At this time he jotted in his pocket-book: "Europe in Throes. Three Parts. Five Acts each. *Characters*: Burke, Pitt, Napoleon, George III, Wellington . . . and many others." More jotting continued along these lines with increasing intensity. He collected a Napoleonic library and spent much time at the British Museum.[4] Thus the concepts underlying *The Dynasts* developed from his boyhood fascination with uniforms and old soldiers' tales, through accretions of philosophic interpretation, into a study of history from a point of view that both surveyed the clash of empires and comprehended the human lot in the grip of cosmic forces.

Hardy's title indicates his theme.[5] Writing to Edmund Gosse on January 31, 1904, he explained that the title was the best and shortest one "I could think of to express the rulers of Europe in their desperate struggle to maintain their dynasties rather than to benefit their peoples."[6]

The dynasts of Europe, not only Napoleon but also the rulers of Prussia, Austria, Spain, Russia, and even, to some extent, England, all struggling to maintain their rule, are the antagonists, the villains, of the drama. The suffering peoples of Europe (the chief concern of the Spirit of the Pities) are the protagonists, the heroes. As Orel says, the selfish game that all the rulers play "is Napoleon's game. Their desire to aggrandize, to expand national boundaries, to join an alliance with Napoleon when he is up and to rend him when he is down, are desires that Napoleon can fully understand. It is an age of dynasts," to whom the suffering peoples are "puppets in a playing hand." Hardy, speaking through Pities, identifies himself "not with the conquerors and the dynasts . . . but with those who suffer, bleed, and all too often die before their time."[7] Observing how, for his own advantage, Francis of Austria betrays England, a Chorus of the Pities sings: "Each for himself, his family, his heirs; / For the wan weltering nations who concerns, who cares?" (I, VI, v.) Exhausted with slaughtering one another at Talavera, common soldiers of hostile armies drink together from a stream, "get to grasping hands across the rill, / Sealing their sameness as earth's sojourners," and return to their lines "to riddle one another through." (II, IV, v.) Thus do "The pale pathetic peoples still plod on / Through hoodwinkings to light!" (III, IV, iv.)

In the struggle among the dynasts, the chief protagonist is England, fighting for life against Napoleon's schemes to conquer the world. Only England, though misled by squabbling statesmen, never bows to Napoleon; and as the play advances to its climax, Wellington emerges as the English champion whose stubbornness is more than a match for Napoleon's once-brilliant scheming.

Another theme of *The Dynasts* is the degeneration of Napoleon as a servant of the Immanent Will. Hardy omitted much of the praiseworthy in his characterization of Napoleon, the emperor's love for order and his dreams of a unified Europe. He refers to him as the savior of the French Revolution, the champion of liberty, only when Pities whispers to him in Milan Cathedral, "Lieutenant Bonaparte, / Would it not seemlier be to shut thy heart / To these unhealthy splendours?—helmet thee / For her thou swar'st-to first, fair Liberty?" (I, I, vi.) Hardy chose to present Napoleon as a violent eruption of the Will in history, he being Its[8] analogue and agent. He opened the drama after Napoleon had already begun to usurp the Revolution and to embark upon his adventures toward making himself master of the world. When Napoleon seizes the crown of empire from the Church and places it on his own head, he starts psychologically and morally, in spite of later victories, on an inescapable downhill road. The rest of the drama might be called a study in Nemesis. In the play, Napoleon feels himself a victim of the Will. He says in apologizing to Queen Louisa for his selfishness: "Some force within me, baffling mine intent, / Harries me onward, whether I will or no. / My star, my star is what's to blame—not I." (II, I, viii.) [9] As agent of the Will, or its victim, he continues to wreak havoc through all Europe for selfish ends.

Hardy symbolizes Napoleon's degeneration in the gradual weakening of his physical vigor. When Napoleon meets with Alexander of Russia on the River Niemen, "The EMPEROR looks well, but is growing fat." (II, I, vi.) This deterioration is an increasing obstacle to the success of the Will operating through him; for example, when Napoleon is defeated, deserted, and forced to abdicate, Years observes: "How heavily grinds the Will upon his brain, / His halting hand, and his unlighted eye." This image of reluctant gears connects Napoleon's physical condition with the difficulty of the Will in driving him toward triumph. Napoleon speaks of his own mind at this time as a "flaccid brain." (III, IV, iv.) When he is ill, despondent, or weary, he cannot serve the Will effectively and conquer.

"Napoleon's cynicism, deepening with time, disgusted Hardy. . . . Part Third is, above all, Napoleon's story. The effrontery of the man who invaded Muscovy with 600,000 men because 'circumstance' compelled him; who gilded the dome of the Invalides 'in best gold leaf, and on a novel pattern' to distract the Parisians from the massacre of the troops he left behind in eastern Europe . . . holds our shocked attention for scene after scene."[10] Even Years, who understands that Napoleon is victim of the Will, speaks to him at last in contempt: "Such men as thou, who wade across the world / To make an epoch, bless, confuse, appal, / Are in the elemental ages' chart / Like meanest in-

sects on obscurest leaves." (III, VII, ix.) This is Hardy's view, justi-
fied in the historical facts he selected.

Hardy interpreted the human action of *The Dynasts* in an allegory
of symbols. The symbols are an Immanent Will and personified ab-
stractions called spirits. The Immanent Will is his term for what
philosophers call the "Ding an sich," the thing-in-itself, or the ulti-
mate metaphysical reality.[11] In relation to human action, the Will is
an energy that operates through impulses in the unconscious, non-
rational, reflex, instinctive, or involuntary portions of the mind.[12]
The Will is "personified" as an all-inclusive Brain, and (though in-
visible to human sight) is exhibited in operation six times in *The
Dynasts*. The displays and the comments of the spirits indicate that
It works not as an engine or even an insensate force (e.g., gravitation),
but as a living organism. It is both transcendent, existing throughout
the universe, and immanent, existing in each particle of matter. It
is omniscient, but unconscious (as a computer may "know" the data
it contains, without awareness). Its timeless omniscience includes
the past, present, and future as cause and necessitated consequence. It
is constantly "thinking."

Its thought is that of a dream. One asleep cannot control a dream;
one "watches" it. Yet its course is fixed by the contents of the mind.
In this way the Will dreams "a fixed foresightless dream." (III, VII,
viii.) Its dream forms a pattern of impulses and hence actions in Its
puppets, men. This pattern bears no relation to the reason or welfare
of the person It inhabits. It has, therefore, no morality in any human
sense; It is unaware of right, wrong, pleasure, or pain in Itself or Its
creatures.

The Will acts within Its human puppets through impulses and
hungers that are nakedly selfish. Only men capable of disinterested
reason, selfless compassion, and moral courage can resist the impulses
of the Will. Resistance is possible because man has reflective con-
sciousness fed by sensations. Reflection allows man to choose on the
basis of reason instead of impulse Thus some freedom of the Will
(or freedom *from* the Will) is possible. In the allegory of *The Dy-
nasts,* man's consciousness may even awaken in the Will (which in-
habits man) some conscious awareness. To a minute extent, man is
a variable in the equations of the Will's determinism. This is the
basis for the allegory of "evolutionary meliorism" that concludes *The
Dynasts*.

The Will and Its action in the human drama are observed and
interpreted by personified abstractions called spirits. They are symbols
for various attributes of the human mind. Each separate spirit is an

aspect of the mind, or of Hardy's mind. No one of them reflects all of his thought, though the Spirit of the Years seems to reflect his reason, and the Spirit of the Pities, his feeling and temperament.

The most impressive of the spirits is Years. He represents experience, reason, and a scientific and philosophic understanding of the world. As "showman" of the Will, he sets human life against the backdrop of the universe known to Victorian thinkers. Like many of them, he is a determinist. The propositions that he states and defends derive from his speech in the Fore Scene:

> In the Foretime, even to the germ of Being,
> Nothing appears of shape to indicate
> That cognizance has marshalled things terrene,
> Or will (such is my thinking) in my span.
> Rather they show that, like a knitter drowsed,
> Whose fingers play in skilled unmindfulness,
> The Will has woven with an absent heed
> Since Life first was; and ever will so weave.

Years "speaks for the rationalistic side of Hardy's mind, the side which could not be content with anything less than a full look at the worst."[13]

The Spirit of the Pities stands for Hardy's (or all compassionate) feeling. This spirit, called "a mere juvenile—who only came into being in what the earthlings call their Tertiary Age," feels in himself the suffering he witnesses. Told to be quiet in his protests and "heed the Cause of things," Pities replies to Years, "I feel, Sire, as I must!" (I, I, vi.) Affected by the sensations from which consciousness is formed, he receives impulses from perception of suffering, and hence tries to inspire unselfish acts in resistance to the selfish Will. Throughout the drama, he seeks to awaken men, the other spirits, and even the Will to awareness and compassion. Because man is wrought on by events as well as impulses from the Will, Pities reasons that there are *two* sources of action and believes that man may choose.

Other spirits, Sinister (the perversity in human nature), Ironic (an aloof intellectual, but capable of pity), Rumours, and Recording Angels give variety of interpretation to the drama. The feminine Shade of the Earth (Mother Nature) suffers, but is bound in inexplicable thraldom. She is, however, "not averse" to amelioration in the human lot; that is, nothing in the natural world would positively block the development of compassion.

The spirits debate the meaning of the human drama. As Years is showman of the Will, Pities is showman of suffering. Years reports facts, and Pities the feeling about facts. Pities speaks for man-the-victim and for man's hopes and dreams. As the drama progresses, Pities grows in experience, assurance, and stature.

Pities's basic point of view, in opposition to the determinism of Years, is stated in the Fore Scene as a utopian (or Christian) dream: "We would establish those of kindlier build, / In fair Compassions skilled, / . . . Those, too, who love the true, the excellent, / And make their daily moves a melody." The question is whether human feeling and reason influenced by feeling can overcome the forces represented by the dynasts, including the impulse to regard war as romantic: "Accoutred in kaleidoscopic hues / That would persuade us war has beauty in it!" (III, VII, iv.)

Feeling in himself the suffering he witnesses, Pities protests the irrational action of the Will in permitting the development of consciousness in life: "But O, the intolerable antilogy / Of making figments feel!" (I, IV, v) —while Itself remaining unconscious and suffering nothing. Yet the fact of suffering is a ground for hope. Through suffering, understood by reason, man may develop compassion and come to love "the true, the excellent."

The debate among the spirits is inconclusive. Though the final Chorus sings the hope "That the rages / Of the ages / Shall be cancelled, and deliverance offered from the darts that were, / Consciousness the Will informing, till It fashion all things fair!" it seems doubtful whether human reason may ever overcome self-centered, aggressive impulses—or whether, in the symbolism of the play, reason and suffering may ever influence the Will. Apparently Hardy, at least now and then, believed it possible that in the long evolution of the ages, compassion, developed into instinct, might overcome the selfish impulses of human nature. This is what (in sober common sense, with the symbolism laid aside) he meant by his often-repeated "evolutionary meliorism."

Using his spirits as choruses, he gave *The Dynasts* something of the form and meaning of a Greek drama, though history limited him to the actions and sequences of fact. He sought to give his drama authenticity consistent with the hundreds of histories, memoirs, biographies, and letters that he read.[14] From these materials, he was able to select facts to fit his interpretation. The materials included traditions of his childhood, well-known scenes and events in Wessex, tales told by his grandmother, and personal stories of the old campaigners in Chelsea Hospital and elsewhere. These items helped him give verisimilitude to his characters, a strong sense of life to his action.

Hardy strikingly anticipated the techniques of moving pictures in his use of spirits as aerial viewers and commentators and in his panoramic stage-directions. Crowds and armies are seen from lofty heights: marching troops seem caterpillar shapes and individuals seem insects. Battle scenes crowded and confused in turmoil are then broken into individualized parts. The spirits magnify small matters, or contrarily make great events seem petty. Scenes blur and fade in clouds, rain, or darkness.

The poetry is extremely varied. "From Campbell and Scott, from the hymn-book, from Browning and Swinburne and Tennyson's 'Maud' Hardy caught metrical impulses which he knew would be appropriate to his vast argument and which he converted into his own manner of stress and current and shock."[15] Lyrics vary from marching songs like "Budmouth Dears" to the magnificent protest of the spirit-choruses against the spoliation of the earth at Waterloo: "The green seems opprest, and the Plain afraid." Many poems are adaptations of folk-airs, like the "Mad Soldier's Song" of the Russian campaign. Blank verse, standard for drama, gives dignity (if not high lyric quality) to scenes like the debate in Parliament.

Hardy's prose, in stage-directions and in many scenes treating common soldiers or peasant characters, is rapid and condensed, slangy, or vulgar, fitting the scene. Much of it is realistically humorous, like the scene of the deserters in the cellar near Astorga; it is humorous in a more satiric tone in the high comedy of the Prince Regent and his wives at Carlton House. Some humor is folksily grotesque, like the tale of broaching the cask in which Nelson's body was preserved. The diction in the philosophic speeches of Years and the other spirits is both scientific-abstract and concrete in its imagery, with many coinages like "pulsion of the Byss" (impulses from the Will). Critics have objected to Hardy's philosophic vocabulary, but it was characteristic of him to coin a word to picture something he saw clearly, so that the reader might see it. If the Will acts with clock-like laws, then men are aptly "jackaclocks," a word that drew a picture for Hardy because he knew jackaclocks in Wessex churches. He wrote with an attempt at vividness, using words that may require many a reader to use a dictionary, its etymologies, and his imagination. His style includes a good deal of irony, not only in the speeches of the Spirit Ironic, but in numerous double meanings in scene and commentary. A good example is the scene on the field of Borodino, when Napoleon commands his soldiers to march reverently past the image of his infant son, but immediately afterwards scoffs at the Russian soldiers kneeling to the icons their priests take through the ranks.[16]

1. For books and articles treating *The Dynasts* in some detail consult the bibliography for titles by Bailey, Brennecke, Chakravarty, Clifford, Dóbree, Fair-

child, Hopkins, Horsman, Korg, Miller, Morcos, Morrell, Orel, Pinion, Reed, Roberts, Sherman, Stedmond, Stewart, Waldock, and Wright.

2. Though all titles spoke of 130 scenes, Hardy changed plans as he proceeded. The drama contains 131 scenes besides the Fore Scene and the After Scene. See Purdy, *Thomas Hardy: A Bibliographical Study*, pp. 127-34.

3. Following the plan of telling the Napoleonic story in ballads, Hardy wrote "Valenciennes," "San Sebastian," "Leipzig," "The Peasant's Confession," and "The Alarm."

4. Items above are drawn from *Early Life*, pp. 20-21, 25, 67, 76, 103, 139-40, 146, 150, 154, 161-62, 168, 191, 197-98, 232, 240, 256, 290, 294; *Later Years*, pp. 9, 57; *Life*, pp. 16-17, 19, 50-51, 57-58, 78, 106, 110, 114, 117, 123-24, 128, 148, 152, 177, 183, 195, 221, 225, 247, 284.

5. It is taken from the Greek of the Magnificat, translated by a Chorus of the Pities in Part Third, After Scene, as "Thee . . . Who hurlest Dynasts from their thrones." Subsequent references to *The Dynasts* will be placed in parenthesis after a quotation and abbreviated; for example, I, II, iv would indicate Part First, Act II, scene iv.

6. Photostat in the Colby College Library.

7. *Thomas Hardy's Epic-Drama*, pp. 80, 90.

8. Hardy capitalized the pronoun It in reference to the Immanent Will.

9. Chakravarty remarks concerning this speech: "So Napoleon too has another 'Will,' and an 'intent' which he pitifully fails to carry out." *"The Dynasts" and the Post-War Age in Poetry*, p. 46.

10. Orel, *Thomas Hardy's Epic-Drama*, p. 60.

11. Hardy's term Will was taken from Schopenhauer's *The World as Will and Idea* and Von Hartmann's *Philosophy of the Unconscious*. The sources of Hardy's concept are analyzed in book-length studies.

12. The Will is also the energy that underlies all matter and all life; It is the "First Cause" and "Prime Mover" of all existence and all the processes of nature.

13. Hynes, *The Pattern of Hardy's Poetry*, p. 169.

14. Hardy's sources have been recently examined by Wright in *The Shaping of The Dynasts*.

15. Blunden, *Thomas Hardy*, p. 233.

16. For dramatic productions of portions of *The Dynasts*, see Roberts, *Hardy's Poetic Drama and the Theatre*.

EJECTED MEMBER'S WIFE, THE, is the title of "The Rejected Member's Wife" as published in the *Spectator*.

EMLEEN is the original title in the manuscript of "At a Fashionable Dinner."

END OF THE OLD YEAR is the manuscript title of "End of the Year 1912."

EPIGRAM ON EXISTENCE is the manuscript title of "A Young Man's Epigram on Existence."

EPILOGUE is the manuscript title of "Exeunt Omnes."

EPILOGUE (of *The Dynasts*) was written for a stage production. When Harley Granville-Barker produced scenes from *The Dynasts* at the Kingsway Theatre on November 25, 1914, he asked Hardy for a "Prologue" and an "Epilogue," which the Reader recited before and after the play, respectively. "The Prologue was printed in the programme from the first and was reprinted, under the title 'A Poem on the War,' in *The Sphere*, 5 December 1914 . . . the Epilogue was first printed here [in *The Sphere*] and added to the programme in later (undated) issues."[1] *The Dynasts, Prologue and Epilogue* was printed as a pamphlet by Clement Shorter in 1914. The poems may be found in Roberts, *Hardy's Poetic Drama and the Theatre*, pp. 38-39 and 42-43.

The "Epilogue," eighteen lines in length, sums up the action of the scenes presented, calls attention to World War I, then raging, and expresses the hope that "May such reminders soon forever pass, / And war be but a shade on memory's glass."

1. Purdy, *Thomas Hardy: A Bibliographical Study*, p. 173.

EPITAPH (for G. K. Chesterton) is in an envelope in the Dorset County Museum labelled "Last lines dictated by T. H., referring to George Moore and G. K. Chesterton" and also labelled "Two epitaphs —on G. Moore and G. K. Chesterton—dictated by Hardy on his deathbed." The envelope is signed "F. E. Hardy" and dated "January, 1928." The two poems it contains seem to be in Mrs. Hardy's handwriting. The epitaph for Chesterton reads:

> Here lies nipped in this narrow cyst
> The literary contortionist
> Who prove & never turn a hair
> That Darwin's theories were a snare
> He'd hold as true with tongue in jowl
> That Nature's geocentric rule
> . . . . true & right
> And if one with him could not see
> He'd shout his choice word "Blasphemy."[1]

The basis for the poem is apparently Chesterton's attack upon Hardy in 1913, in *The Victorian Age in Literature*. Chesterton wrote in comment upon "free-thinking" among Victorian novelists: "Hardy went down to botanize in the swamp, while Meredith climbed towards the sun. Meredith became, at his best, a sort of daintily dressed Walt Whitman: Hardy became a sort of village atheist brooding and blaspheming over the village idiot."[2] This aphorism was quoted in reviews and newspaper stories antagonistic to Hardy.

He suffered from the abuse of reviewers. Sir George Douglas wrote in 1928, after Hardy's death: "The savage assault made upon him by the critics and the public after the publication of 'Jude' distressed him far more bitterly than the world will ever know."[3] Hardy

wrote to Alfred Noyes on December 19, 1920: "I very seldom do give
critics such trouble [as writing to them], usually letting things drift,
though there have been many occasions when a writer who has been
so much abused for his opinions as I have would perhaps have done
well not to hold his peace."[4]

Always conservative and dogmatic in his views, Chesterton in 1922
became a Roman Catholic and tended more than ever to disparage
"liberalism." By an irony that might have pained Hardy, Chesterton
(in ignorance of the poem's existence) wrote several obituary notices
on Hardy's death, in which he praised him and offered excuses for
his opinions that differed from his own. One such obituary is "Thom-
as Hardy" in the *Illustrated London News*, January 21, 1928.

1. This poem and "Epitaph" (for George Moore) are here printed for the first
time by permission of Miss Irene Cooper Willis, speaking for the Trustees of the
Hardy Estate.
2. In the 1966 edition, p. 62.
3. Typescript in the National Library of Scotland, Edinburgh, p. 3.
4. *Later Years*, p. 216; *Life*, p. 408.

EPITAPH (for George Moore) is partly treated in the notes on
"Epitaph" (for G. K. Chesterton). The epitaph for Moore reads:

"No mortal man beneath the sky
Can write such English as can I
They say it holds no thought my own
What then, such beauty (perfection) is not known."

Heap dustbins on him:
They'll not meet
The apex of his self conceit.

Moore's attacks upon Hardy express an obsession: he waged a
long-continued, one-sided feud. His first sneer at Hardy appeared in
Confessions of a Young Man, published in 1886. He began by saying:
"Hardy seemed to me inferior to George Eliot: 'One of George Eliot's
miscarriages,' I said, laying aside 'Far from the Madding Crowd,' and
abandoned myself to dreams of what English narrative prose was and
what it might be." (The *bon mot*, "One of George Eliot's miscar-
riages," delighted certain of Hardy's reviewers, who quoted it over
the years.) Comments upon *Far from the Madding Crowd* go on to
disparage the structure of the book, its "hare-hearted" development,
and Bathsheba's marriage with Oak, "a conclusion which of course
does not come within the range of literary criticism."[1] In *Conversa-
tions in Ebury Street* (1924), Moore devoted Chapters VI and VII to
ridicule. Hardy's poetry "popularised pessimism and coaxed his

readers into drinking from an old tin pot a beverage that had hitherto only been offered to them in golden and jewelled goblets." Calling Hardy's prose the worst written in the nineteenth century, Moore mocked his grammar, diction, and imagery. Concerning his plots, he charged that he "shrank from the essential" from "lack of invention, brain paralysis, something of the sort." Summing up Hardy's novels, he wondered "why the public should have selected for their special adoration ill-constructed melodramas, feebly written in bad grammar."

When Middleton Murry wrote a reply to Moore's attacks, Hardy wrote a letter of thanks to Murry, in which he said of Moore: "I doubt if he was worth such good powder and shot as you give him! . . . Somebody once called him a putrid literary hermaphrodite, which I thought funny, but it may have been an exaggeration. The reviewers . . . have timidly waited till you came along to show at any rate that (to change the image) this lion, so great at roaring, is only Snug the Joiner."[2] Hardy then entered in his notebook for April 1, 1924: "George Moore. *The Times* in its notices of the monthly reviews agrees with Mr. Middleton Murry, in *The Adelphi*, in the latter's smashing criticism of that ludicrous blackguard George Moore's book called *Conversations in Ebury Street*, in which I believe I am libelled wholesale, though I have not seen the book."[3] Moore's criticisms imply, as the poem does ironically, that Moore wrote in an exquisite style beside which Hardy's was uncouth. Oddly, whether or not disparaging her husband's style, Mrs. Florence Hardy admired Moore's. In a letter to Rebekah Owen on December 17, 1915, she wrote of Moore: "The things he generally writes about are disgusting & he is a horrible (though amusing) man—but sometimes he writes the most exquisite, the most *peerless* English."[4] Mrs. Hardy told Newman Flower of the "Epitaph" for Moore, and Flower wrote that, regarding Moore's attacks, "Hardy took no notice. But when he was dying he did take notice. For the first time the rancour he had endured brought resentment to him. He felt the strive [*sic*] to answer—even though he lay now on his deathbed. . . . He groped for his note-book, and wrote a poem; his last.[5] In that verse he flayed George Moore. . . . That poem was never published. Florence Hardy told me that it was brilliant—the more brilliant since it was written by one who wished to express his retort before Death."[6]

1. Pp. 199-200 in the Putnam edition of 1959.
2. In the Berg Collection, New York Public Library.
3. Evelyn Hardy, *Thomas Hardy's Notebooks*, p. 104.
4. In the Colby College Library.
5. The envelope containing the poem says that Hardy dictated it.
6. *Just As It Happened*, p. 103.

EPITAPH BY LABOURERS ON JAS. is a four-line poem, first published in Pinion, *A Hardy Companion* (1968), p. 140.

EUNICE is twice printed in Hardy's first-published novel, *Desperate Remedies* (in Chapters XVI, 4, and XVII, 3) as written by the character Aeneas Manston. Presumably Hardy wrote the poem as one of the poems of the 1860's that publishers rejected. The Preface to the 1912 edition of *Desperate Remedies* says: "The readers may discover . . . that certain scattered reflections and sentiments therein are the same in substance with some of the *Wessex Poems* and others, published many years later. The explanation of such tautology is that the poems were written before the novel." Then "Eunice" is the first of Hardy's poems to be published. Rutland points out that the original title of his first, unpublished novel was *The Poor Man and the Lady / A Story with no Plot / Containing some original Verses,* and surmises that "Eunice" may have been "one of the 'original verses' alluded to in the discarded title of *The Poor Man.*"[1]

1. *Thomas Hardy,* pp. 111, 139.

EVADERS, THE, is the manuscript title of "The Dissemblers."

EVE OF WATERLOO, THE, is the title given to Choruses of the Years and the Pities beginning "The eyelids of eve fall together at last" from *The Dynasts* (III, VI, viii) as separately published in *Selected Poems.*

EXHORTATION, AN, is the manuscript title of "A Young Man's Exhortation."

FACE IN THE MIND'S EYE, THE, is the title of "In the Mind's Eye" in *Selected Poems.*

FAIR VAMPIRE, THE, is the manuscript title of "The Vampirine Fair."

FALL OF THE LEAF, THE, is the deleted manuscript title of "The Best She Could."

FAMOUS TRAGEDY OF THE QUEEN OF CORNWALL, THE, is a one-act verse-drama to be associated with Hardy's courtship of Emma Gifford. It is dedicated to four persons, three of whom played roles in that romance. In his gift-copy of "1st Edition: 1st copy" of the play to his wife Florence, Hardy wrote in parenthesis after the initials dedicating the play, E. L. H., C. H., H. C. H., and F. E. H., respectively: 'Emma Lavinia Hardy, née Gifford; Caddell Holder, Rector of St. Juliot,

Cornwall; Helen Catherine Holder, née Gifford," and "Florence Emily Hardy, née Dugdale."[1]

The Cornwall of Hardy's romance is called "Lyonnesse" in "When I Set Out for Lyonnesse" and "the region of dream and mystery" in the Preface of *A Pair of Blue Eyes*. Hardy met Emma at St. Juliot Rectory on the evening of March 7, 1870. His diary for March 9 records: "Drove with Mrs. Holder and Miss Gifford to Boscastle, and on to Tintagel."[2] In the following August, when Hardy again visited Emma, "His hosts drove him to various picturesque points . . . among others to King Arthur's Castle, Tintagel, which he now saw for the first time;[3] and where, owing to their lingering too long among the ruins, they found themselves locked in, only narrowly escaping being imprisoned there for the night by much signalling with their handkerchiefs. . . . The lingering might have been considered prophetic, seeing that, after it had been smouldering in his mind for between forty and fifty years, he constructed *The Famous Tragedy of the Queen of Cornwall* from the legends connected with that romantic spot." In August of 1872, Hardy was again in Cornwall, at which time "He walked to Tintagel Castle and sketched there a stone altar, having an Early-English ornamentation on its edge." Later in the year, he "was at Bockhampton finishing *A Pair of Blue Eyes*, the action of which . . . proceeds on the coast near 'Lyonnesse'—not far from King Arthur's Castle at Tintagel." Hardy and his wife Florence made a journey to Cornwall in September of 1916, visiting Tintagel, "that romantic spot," and attending Tintagel Church. These visits (and perhaps others, not recorded) provided the setting for Hardy's play. When he had finished it, in May of 1923 he "made, with infinite care, his last drawing, an imaginary view of Tintagel Castle. . . . It was used as an illustration when *The Queen of Cornwall* was published."[4] He wrote to Alfred Noyes on November 17, 1923, that his "little play" had been "53 years in contemplation," that is, since his second visit to Emma Gifford.[5] He wrote with relief to Sir George Douglas that *The Queen of Cornwall* "has been obstructing the way for a long time: & I am glad it is finished—though I liked doing it, the place & its associations being so familiar."[6]

As a letter to Sir Sydney Cockerell on September 20, 1916, says, Hardy began the play after his visit to Tintagel in 1916, but apparently he found the task exhausting: "Alas, I fear your hopes of a poem on Iseult—the English, or British, Helen—will be disappointed. I visited the place 44 years ago with an Iseult of my own, and of course she was mixed in the vision of the other."[7] He laid the work aside until the spring of 1923, but had the manuscript in the hands of Macmillan by the end of August.

His treatment of the Tristram story is original, though it makes use of the basic action found in many versions and, presumably, known to any audience. He wrote: "I have tried to avoid turning the rude personages of say, the fifth century into respectable Victorians, as was done by Tennyson, Swinburne, Arnold, etc. On the other hand it would have been impossible to present them as they really were, with their barbaric manners and surroundings."[8] Hardy was well acquainted with earlier versions. "It is clear from the markings in his copy of Malory . . . that he had carefully familiarized himself with that version of the story."[9] Perhaps he was acquainted with the researches of Joseph Bédier: his motto, quoted from "The Monk Thomas," seems taken from Bédier. As he commented in some detail on Wagner's music,[10] he was probably acquainted with *Tristran und Isolde*. As treatments of the story from the Middle Ages onward have varied, he was free to adapt the story to fit his theme.

In most versions, when Tristram was on his death-bed in Brittany, he sent for Queen Iseult to come to him. If the returning envoy should hoist a white sail it would tell Tristram that the Queen was on board; if a black one, that she could not come. Iseult of the White Hands, learning of this plan, told the ailing Tristram that the white sail was a black one. Tristram died in despair. When the Queen arrived, she embraced the dead Tristram and died also. Other versions have Tristram murdered by King Mark, but not under the circumstances of Hardy's play. Hardy, to tell the whole complex story within the classical unities of time and place, has it enacted at Tintagel; he brings the two Iseults together there in the last hour before the characters are to die. Bopp sums up his additions: "The appearance and swoon of Iseult of the White Hands, the damsel with the letter, the Queen's embittered upbraidings, Tristram's gentle efforts to soothe her, and finally the slaying of Mark at his wife's hand are original matters added by the author." Hardy "produced for the story a conclusion which is entirely his own."[11] Where most versions flame with passion, his version has only one love-song ("Let's meet again to-night, my Fair") ; the rest of the talk of love is wary in tone, with a good deal of bickering. Whatever Hardy intended, audiences were more sympathetic toward Iseult the Whitehanded than moved by the Queen's passion. "The entry of the hapless Iseult the Whitehanded touched an even greater depth of feeling, in which pity for one of the saddest figures in romance found full expression. In a scene which fairly quivered with emotion, and in which her anguished *cri du coeur* brought the tears to many eyes, the deserted wife . . . makes a brave struggle to win her beloved lord back to her." [12]

This result seems a consequence of Hardy's view of the story. In all versions, Tristram and Iseult are victims of a love-potion, magic outside their own wills. Hardy so stresses this point that the tragedy seems not one of passion, but of fate. "Iseult the Queen, Iseult the wife, Mark, and Tristram, are swept along by a will without themselves which in working to accomplish its own issues renders the dispositions of the characters jealous, deceptive, cruel, or desperate." [13] As in *The Dynasts*, the characters are puppets. The emotion aroused by the drama is pity, and Iseult the Whitehanded, who had sinned least, is most to be pitied.

For the form of his play, Hardy chose an approach to Greek tragedy. He wrote: "The unities are strictly preserved. . . . The change of persons on the stage is called a change of scene, there being no change of background. My temerity in pulling together into the space of an hour events that in the traditional stories covered a long time will doubtless be criticized. . . . I felt free to adapt it to my purpose in any way—as, in fact, the Greek dramatists did in their plays. . . . Wishing it to be thoroughly English I have dropped the name of Chorus for the conventional onlookers, and called them Chanters, though they play the part of a Greek Chorus to some extent. I have also called them Ghosts (I don't for the moment recall an instance of this in a Greek play)." [14] Hardy begins the action just before the catastrophe, in the manner of Greek drama, and uses the Chanters to remind the audience of the preceding passion. Chanters who are also Ghosts have the effect of undermining passion. This effect is deepened when the Ghosts are not only "Shades of Dead Old Cornish Men" and "Dead Cornish Women" but also Mummers who speak in a "recitative" monotone. [15] These items add to the effect of Greek tragic form the sense of a macabre dream.

The wizard Merlin in a Prologue and an Epilogue introduces and closes the play. He is "a phantasmal figure with a white wand," seen in a "blue light." At the time the Hardy Players produced the play, "Hardy added the prologue and epilogue for the character of Merlin, Mr. Boughton says, 'for no artistic reason, but' . . . so that Mr. Tilley, veteran actor, stage manager, and writer for the Hardy Players, would not be omitted from the cast." [16] Merlin suggests that love in itself is sorrow, with fatality in its conclusion. He asks the audience to judge "not harshly" characters "witlessly" (not of their own wills) caught "in a love / Whose hold on them was strong."

To present the antique romance with meaning for the reflective modern mind, though he used archaic words, Hardy sought realism in characterization, seeking truth rather than exalted passion in the conflict of the contrasted Iseults and the clash of the soured king and ardent but irresolute Tristram. At the same time, he recalled his experience with Emma and perhaps Tryphena Sparks. He turned to memories of the 1870's, found lovers' spats more sharply set forth in *A Pair of Blue Eyes* than he could create them at the age of eighty-three, and lifted a number of passages from the novel with only slight changes. For example, we may compare Elfride's pleading with Knight not to desert her and Iseult of the White Hands's pleading with Tristram:

Elfride: What meaning have you, Harry? You only say so, do you? . . . You are not in earnest, I know—I hope you are not? Surely I belong to you, and you are going to keep me for yours? (Chapter XXXIV.)	*Iseult the White Handed*: How, Tristram mine? / What meaning mete you out by that to me? / You only say it, do you? You are not, / Cannot be, in true earnest—that I know! / I hope you are not in earnest?—Surely I, / This time as always, do belong to you, / And you are going to keep me always yours? (Scene XVI.)

Other passages exhibit the same "plagiarism," intended, it seems, to give reality to the scene.[17]

The style seems labored, a mixture of medieval terms and furniture and modern tones, as in Brangwain's "My Lady, when I cast eye waterwards / From the arrow-loop, just as the keel ground in / Against the popplestones, it seemed a woman's; / But she was wimpled close." (Scene XII.) Archaic terms and syntax seem patched on to modern meanings. Where, in *A Pair of Blue Eyes*, Knight says to Elfride, who has followed him to London: "Not hate you, Elfride . . . but you cannot stay here now, just at present, I mean," Tristram says, "Not hate you, Iseult. / But, hate or love, lodge here you cannot now." Such terms as "dalliances," "sans tarriance," "certes," and "half amort" (half-dead), proper in a fully realized medieval setting, seem questionable to indicate the medieval in a play thematically and psychologically modern. The variety and intricacy of verse-patterns seem remarkable for a poet eighty-three years old.[18]

The Queen of Cornwall was produced by the Hardy Players in Dorchester on November 28-30, 1923, and in London on February 21, 1924. The most important production was an operatic version by Rutland Boughton, at Glastonbury, Malvern, Bournemouth, and

Bath. Boughton (working in collaboration with Hardy) "cut the prologue and the epilogue, and in the place of the latter he substituted Hardy's lyric, 'A Spot,' sung by the Chorus of Shades at the end of the work. He included five other lyrics from Hardy's collected poems in order to develop the emotion as one always does in setting a piece to music. They were: 'Bereft she thinks she dreams,' 'When I Set Out for Lyonnesse,' 'The End of the Episode,' 'If It's Ever Spring Again,' and 'Beeny Cliff.' " Hardy went to see the operatic version at Glastonbury, after which he observed "that in the play the sympathies of the audience were with White Hands, while in the opera the sympathies are with the Queen of Cornwall."[19]

Boughton's Opera, *The Queen of Cornwall*, was published (London: Joseph Williams, 1923). C. A. Speyer set "Tristram's Song" to music (in manuscript in the Dorset County Museum) ; E. W. Smerdon of the Hardy Players set this song to music for their production. Music for "Could he but come to me," for use in a production of 1936, is in the Colby College Library.

1. In the Dorset County Museum. Helen Holder, wife of Caddell Holder, was Emma's sister.

2. Tintagel, a town on the Cornish coast about three miles southwest of Boscastle, is near Tintagel Castle, the ruins of which remain on a high cliff overlooking the Atlantic. This castle is traditionally associated with King Arthur. In fact, "The Castle was built about 1145 by Reginald, Earl of Cornwall" long after King Arthur's time, and "No evidence whatever has been found to support the legendary connection of the Castle with King Arthur." Ministry of Public Buildings and Works, *Tintagel Castle*, pp. 5-6.

3. The Castle is about half a mile west of the town; apparently Hardy did not visit it on March 9.

4. *Early Life*, pp. 98, 103, 120, 121; *Later Years*, pp. 172, 230; *Life*, pp. 75, 78, 91, 92, 373, 419. In addition to his own drawing, he had inserted into the program for the Hardy Players' production of the play a watercolor drawing of Tintagel which Emma Gifford had made before her marriage.

5. In the Miriam Lutcher Stark Library, University of Texas.

6. Dated January 4, 1924; in the National Library of Scotland, Edinburgh.

7. Meynell, ed., *Friends of a Lifetime*, p. 284.

8. *Later Years*, pp. 235-36; *Life*, p. 423.

9. Purdy, *Thomas Hardy: A Bibliographical Study*, p. 229.

10. *Early Life*, p. 237; *Later Years*, pp. 117-18; *Life*, pp. 181, 329-30.

11. "The Famous Tragedy of the Queen of Cornwall," pp. 18-19.

12. Review in *Dorset County Chronicle*, November 29, 1923.

13. Bopp, "The Famous Tragedy of the Queen of Cornwall," p. 21.

14. *Later Years*, p. 235; *Life*, pp. 422-23.

15. The stage-direction says that they shall be costumed "as in the old mumming shows."

16. Roberts, *Hardy's Poetic Drama and the Theatre*, p. 88.

17. Snell, in "A Self-Plagiarism by Thomas Hardy," presents the parallel above and seven others.

18. See Hickson, "The Versification of Thomas Hardy," pp. 89-91, for an analysis of the verse. Deacon and Coleman have suggested that *The Queen of Corn-*

wall presents an allegory of Hardy's conflict between his love for Emma Gifford (indicated in the dedication) and his earlier love for Tryphena Sparks. See *Providence and Mr Hardy*, pp. 137-38, and Deacon, *Hardy's Sweetest Image*, p. 23.

19. For details of dramatic productions outside the scope of these notes see Roberts, *Hardy's Poetic Drama and the Theatre*, pp. 81-107, from which the quotations above are taken.

FAR FROM THE MADDING CROWD is a couplet labelled "Times, 1910," clipped from a newspaper and pasted into a scrapbook labelled "T. H. Personal" in the Dorset County Museum. The news item reads: "Thomas Hardy Pottery.—Mr. Thomas Hardy has approved the production of a series of Dorset ware illustrating his novels. The various designs, including a sketch portrait of 'Tess,' were provided by Mr. Hardy himself who wrote several couplets. Beneath a line drawing of 'Tess' are the words 'No girl in Wessex rivalled Tess / In beauty, charm, and tenderness.' On a vase bearing a representation of Sergeant Troy and Bathsheba Everdene, there is the couplet—'Far from the madding crowd / Where lovers' hearts beat loud.' There is a third couplet on a vase on which is depicted Gabriel Oak represented in a pose of humility before Bathsheba—'To his scornful love comes Gabriel Oak / And asks to be one of her shepherd folk.' . . . The Hardy ware is made and painted by hand."

FELLING A TREE is the title of "Throwing a Tree" as printed in *Commerce* (Paris).

FIDDLER'S STORY, THE, is the title of "The Country Wedding" as published (together with "A Jingle on the Times") in pamphlet-form for Mrs. Florence Hardy.

FINE LADY, THE, is the manuscript title of "A Leader of Fashion."

FIRE AT TRANTER SWEATLEY'S, THE, is the title of "The Bride-Night Fire" as published in the *Gentleman's Magazine* and in *Wessex Poems*.

FOREBODINGS is the manuscript title of "Premonitions."

FORSAKING OF THE NEST, THE, is a poem of nine stanzas published in *Nash's Magazine* for February, 1912, later revised into a poem of five stanzas, "The Third Kissing-Gate." The original poem is more complex than the revision; it includes a description of the girl's anxious father awaiting her return home.

FUNERAL OF JAHVEH, THE, is the alternative title for "God's Funeral" as submitted to the *Fortnightly Review*.

G. M. is the title of "George Meredith" as published in the *Times* and in *Time's Laughingstocks*.

GLASS IN THE STREAM, THE, is the manuscript title of "Under the Waterfall."

GLASS-STAINER, THE, is presumably "The Young Glass-Stainer," called "The Glass-stainer" in *The Later Years*.[1]

1. P. 26; *Life*, p. 260.

GLIMPSE FROM THE TRAIN, A, is the title of "Faintheart in a Railway Train" as published in the *London Mercury*.

GREAT ADJUSTMENT, THE, is the manuscript title of "There Seemed a Strangeness."

HANGMAN'S SONG, THE, is the alternate title of "The Stranger's Song."

HATBAND, THE, was evidently prepared for *Winter Words*, but was not included in the volume. It was published with a commentary by Evelyn Hardy in "Some Unpublished Poems by Thomas Hardy" in the *London Magazine*. Twenty-eight lines long, in six stanzas, it describes the struggle of two young men for the honor of wearing a funeral-hatband in mourning for a dead maiden. One man is her lover, the other a friend. The lover wins the hatband, but engages in sport while wearing it. The friend mourns that he would not have desecrated it in this way.

HE PREFERS THE EARTHLY is the manuscript title of "He Prefers Her Earthly."

HE VIEWS HIMSELF AS AN AUTOMATON is presumably "He Wonders About Himself" as mentioned in *The Later Years*.[1]

1. P. 26; *Life*, p. 260.

HIS EDUCATION is the title of "God's Education" as published in *Time's Laughingstocks*.

HIS LOVE BRINGS LITTLE PLEASURE is the manuscript title of "How Great My Grief."

HOPE SONG OF THE SOLDIER'S SWEETHEARTS AND WIVES is the title of "Song of the Soldiers' Wives and Sweethearts" in a soldiers' magazine, *Khaki*.

HOW HE LOOKED IN AT THE DRAPER'S is the title of "At the Draper's" as published in the *Saturday Review*.

HUMOUR IN THE SERVANTS' QUARTERS is the manuscript title of "In the Servants' Quarters."

HUNDRED YEARS SINCE, A, was published in the *North American Review* for February, 1915. It is in thirteen stanzas of three rimed lines each. It was written to celebrate the centenary of this magazine. Hardy was grateful to it for first publishing "A Trampwoman's Tragedy," which he considered "upon the whole, his most successful poem,"[1] after it had been rejected by the *Cornhill* as unsuitable for a family periodical. Invited by Colonel George Harvey to contribute to the centenary number, Hardy replied in September, 1914, that he would send a contribution, "though it will probably take the shape of verse, as I do not print prose nowadays." On December 20, he sent the verses with the hope that they "may be of a character suited to its celebration."[2]

The poem reviews the career of the magazine through years of strife, warfare, and empire-building and ends with the hope that it may "expand and last, / And make for binding Satan[3] fast / Ere one more hundred years have passed."

1. *Later Years*, p. 93; *Life*, p. 312.
2. In the Harvard University Library.
3. In context, the war-spirit.

HUSSAR'S SONG: "BUDMOUTH DEARS" is identified in the notes on "Budmouth Dears."

IF I HAD KNOWN is the manuscript title of "If You Had Known," with the poem in the first person.

IF YOU THINK is Hardy's revision of a poem by James Smellie, Mayor of Dudley, who on September 23, 1925, wrote to ask Hardy's opinion of some verses to be placed on a Memorial Clock Tower in honor of heroes of World War I. He proposed: "If you think, have a kindly thought / If you speak, have a kindly word / For the heroes, who for your freedom fought / And died, that you might live." Hardy replied on September 25 with a revision, as: "If you think, have a kindly thought, / If you speak, speak generously / Of those who as heroes fought / And died, to keep you free."[1]

1. Smellie's letter and a draft of Hardy's reply are in the Dorset County Museum. The Mayor of Dudley in 1966, C. E. Clarke, wrote me that neither Smellie's verse nor Hardy's revision was inscribed on the Clock Tower.

IMAGINATIVE MAIDEN, THE, is the manuscript title, deleted, for "The Musing Maiden."

IMPROMPTU TO THE EDITOR, AN, is the title of "The Jubilee of a Magazine" as published in the *Cornhill Magazine*.

IN A CHURCHYARD is the manuscript title or subtitle of "Transformations."

IN A EWELEAZE is the title of "In a Eweleaze near Weatherbury" as published in *Selected Poems*.

IN AN OLD PLACE OF RESORT AFTER MANY YEARS is the manuscript title of "In a Former Resort after Many Years."

IN A LONDON LODGING is the manuscript title of "In a London Flat."

IN MEMORIAM, F. T. is mentioned in *The Later Years*, which says of 1924: "On January 5 a poem by Hardy, 'In Memoriam, F. T.,' appeared in *The Times*, a last tribute to an old friend."[1] The poem was published as "In the Evening."

1. P. 237; *Life*, p. 424.

IN MEMORY OF SERGEANT M————. DIED 184— is the manuscript title of "San Sebastian."

IN ST. PAUL'S: 1869 is the manuscript title of "In St. Paul's a While Ago."

IN THE CRYPTED WAY is the title of "In the Vaulted Way" as published in *Time's Laughingstocks*.

IN THE MATTER OF AN INTENT, A PHILOSOPHIC FANTASY is the title for "A Philosophical Fantasy" rejected by the editor of the *Fortnightly Review*.

IN THE TIME OF WAR AND TUMULTS is the title of "In Time of Wars and Tumults" as published in the *Sphere*.

IN TIME OF SLAUGHTER is the title of "Quid Hic Agis?" as published in the *Spectator*.

INQUIRY, AN, is the manuscript title, deleted, of "A Dream Question" (not to be confused with "An Inquiry" published in *Human Shows*).

JINGLE ON THE TIMES, A, is Hardy's reply to Elizabeth Asquith, who wrote him on December 5, 1914, to request a poem for "an album in aid of the Arts Fund." She said: "Artists have been the worst sufferers from the war up to now, the economical retrenching in beauty before anything else." The album would be sold to relieve distress among artists. A letter of December 21 thanks Hardy for the verses, saying, "They are perfect for the album."[1] The album did not appear, but Mrs. Florence Hardy included the poem with "The Fiddler's Story" (collected as "The Country Wedding") in a privately printed pamphlet issued in October, 1917. The poem has not been reprinted.

It is a poem of seventy-two lines in nine stanzas. It presents a painter, a sculptor, a poet, a musician, an actor, an architect, and a preacher, who offer their wares. Each is ironically rebuked for bringing his gifts to a world that has no use for trifles in time of war. The poem ends: "Fighting, smiting, / Running through; / That's now the civilized / Thing to do."

1. In the Dorset County Museum.

LADY CLO is the manuscript title of "Lady Vi."

LADY IN THE CHRISTMAS FURS, THE, is the title of "The Lady in the Furs" as published in the *Saturday Review*.

LADY REVISITS ALONE THE CHURCH OF HER MARRIAGE, A, is the manuscript title of "She Revisits Alone the Church of Her Marriage."

LAMENT, A, is the manuscript title of "Tess's Lament."

LAST CHORUS is the title of the concluding chorus of *The Dynasts* as published in *Selected Poems*.

LAST LEAVING, A, is the title of "A Leaving" in a separate manuscript of the poem.

LATTER-DAY CHORUS, A, is the title of "A Last Chorus" (from *The Dynasts*) as published in the *Nation*.

LAVINE is a manuscript title (originally "Emleen") of "At a Fashionable Dinner."

LET ME is the title of "Let Me Believe" as published in *Human Shows*.

LIFE'S OPPORTUNITY is the title of "The Unborn" as published in *Wayfarer's Love*.

LIZARD, THE, is a poem Hardy wrote for E. J. Detmold and Florence E. Dugdale (later the second Mrs. Hardy), *The Book of Baby Pets*, issued in London in March, 1915. Not signed, but attributed to him by Mrs. Hardy, it reads:

If on any warm day when you ramble around
Among moss and dead leaves, you should happen to see
A quick trembling thing dart and hide on the ground,
And you search in the leaves, you would uncover me.

It is followed by Miss Dugdale's chapter "About Lizards."

LONDON NIGHTS is the covering title for "The Two Rosalinds" and "Reminiscences of a Dancing Man" as a pair published in *Collier's* (New York) and in the *English Review*.

LONG-AGO SUNRISE AT DOGBURY GATE, A, is the manuscript title for "Life and Death at Sunrise."

LOOKING BACK is a poem in the manuscript of *Time's Laughingstocks* that was left unpublished, its place being taken by "In the Crypted Way." It is an eight-line poem in two stanzas, published for the first time by Purdy, *Thomas Hardy: A Bibliographical Study*, page 149. The poem treats the fading of love with the passage of time.

MANY A ONE HAS LOVED AS MUCH AS I is a lost poem. *The Early Life* says of Hardy's poems written in London in 1866-67: "Some had been sent to magazines, one sonnet that he rather liked, which began 'Many a one has loved as much as I,' having been lost, the editor never returning it and Hardy having kept no copy."[1]

1. P. 71; *Life*, p. 54.

MARBLE MONUMENT, THE, is the manuscript title of "The Marble Tablet."

MIDNIGHT REVEL, THE, is the title of "The Paphian Ball" as published in *McCall's Magazine* (New York).

MISERY OF THAT MOMENT, THE, is the manuscript title of "That Moment."

MY LOVE'S GONE A-FIGHTING is the song concluding Part III, V, vi, of *The Dynasts*, published as a separate poem in *Selected Poems*. Hardy told Vere H. Collins on December 27, 1920, that he had thought of reprinting the lyrics from *The Dynasts*. He said: "Two or three of them—for example 'Trafalgar' and 'My Love's Gone a-fighting'—are as good as anything in the *Collected Poems*."[1] The poem has been set to music by Charles Speyer (London: Schott & Co., 1921).

1. Collins, *Talks with Thomas Hardy at Max Gate*, p. 30.

NEWSPAPER SOLILOQUISES, THE, is the title of "The Aged Newspaper Soliloquizes" as published in the *Observer*.

NIGHT IN A SUBURB is the title of "Beyond the Last Lamp" as published in *Harper's Monthly Magazine* (New York).

NIGHT OF TRAFALGAR, THE, is the title of a song in *The Dynasts*, I, V, vii, as separately published in *Selected Poems*. The song is sung by "Second Boatman" at Weymouth in celebration of the British victory.

1918 is the manuscript title of "The Peace Peal."

NISI DOMINUS FRUSTRA is the manuscript title of "The Church-Builder."

NO GIRL IN WESSEX is treated in the notes on the poetic item "Far from the Madding Crowd."

NOBLE LADY'S STORY, THE, is the title of "The Noble Lady's Tale" as published in *Harper's Weekly* (New York).

NOT A LINE OF HER WRITING HAVE I is the opening line of "Thoughts of Phena." *The Early Life* refers to this poem by quoting the line without naming the title.[1]

1. P. 293; *Life*, p. 224.

NOT AGAIN is the manuscript title of "Best Times."

O JAN! O JAN! O JAN! was sung and danced by the Hardy Players when they produced *The Queen of Cornwall* at the Corn Exchange in Dorchester, November 28-30, 1923. Hardy's copy is labelled "Operetta. Being a Rescension of a Wessex Folk-piece, with additions by Thomas Hardy. (As played in Dorsetshire houses—about 1844 to 1847. *Note.* There appear to be several versions of this old performance.)"[1] The piece is a dramatic poem in seventy-two lines to be sung by three actors. The theme of the skit is a gentleman's effort to win a lady's heart by offering her everything from a silken gown to, finally, his heart, which she accepts. Between offers the gentleman, his adviser (a farmer), and the lady dance a three-handed reel. It is not clear what Hardy added to this folk-piece partly remembered from his childhood.[2] Under the usual title of "No John, No John" a version was popular for many years. The lyric may be found in any good music libraray.

1. Marked "T. H.'s copy" in the Dorset County Museum. Music is appended with the notation: "Tune for three-handed reel: any dance in 2/4 time—such as Calder Fair, Nancy's Fancy, Fairy Dance, Soldier's Joy, Speed the Plough, etc."
2. An account of the background and the performance is in Mardon, *Thomas Hardy as a Musician.*

OH THE OLD OLD CLOCK is a poem of three twelve-line stanzas with Hardy's signature and the date December 19, 1855, discovered inside a grandfather's clock which had been in Hardy's Bockhampton home during his boyhood. It was published in the *Times Literary Supplement* on August 23, 1947, with the title "Hardy's Earliest Verse." Then it was discovered to be "The Old Cottage Clock" by Charles Swain, the Manchester poet (1801-74), presumably copied by fifteen-year-old Hardy.

OLD CLOCK, THE, is the title of "Oh the old old clock" as published by Weber. (See the bibliography.)

OLD MASON, THE, is the manuscript title of "The Old Workman."

OLD PATHS, THE, is the manuscript title, deleted, of "Paths of Former Time."

OLD PORTRAIT, THE, is the manuscript title of "An Old Likeness."

ON DURNOVER MOOR is the manuscript title of "On Martock Moor."

ON J. M. B. is the manuscript title of "To J. M. B."

ON STOURCASTLE FOOT-BRIDGE (1877) is the manuscript title of "On Sturminster Foot-Bridge."

ON THE DOORSTEP is a poem of twelve lines published as number X in the series of twelve "Satires of Circumstance" in the *Fortnightly Review* for April 1, 1911, but withdrawn when Hardy republished the series in the volume *Satires of Circumstance*. (The poem is not to be confused with "On the Doorstep" published in *Moments of Vision*.) In two six-line stanzas, the poem presents a quarrel between a husband and wife, during which the father of the wife strikes the husband. The wife curses the father. Though the characters are not named, the situation recalls that of *The Woodlanders* in which the father Melbury injures the husband Fitzpiers because Fitzpiers mistreats the daughter Grace, who is angered with her father for injuring her husband. (Chapter XXXV.)

ONE WHO OUGHT NOT TO BE THERE is the manuscript title of "The Interloper."

ORPHANED, A POINT OF VIEW is the title of "Unrealized" as published in *The Queen's (Christmas) Carol* in 1905.

PALE WAS THE DAY is the opening phrase of "two well-known lines from one of Ethelberta's poems" in *The Hand of Ethelberta*, Chapter VIII.

PATHETIC FALLACY, THE, is the manuscript title of "The Seasons of Her Year."

PEACE UPON EARTH is the title of "Christmas: 1924" as published in the *Daily Telegraph*.

PEASANT'S PHILOSOPHY, A, is the manuscript title, deleted, of "The Bedridden Peasant."

PEDESTRIAN, THE, is the manuscript title, deleted, of "The Weary Walker." (The poem is not to be confused with "The Pedestrian" published in *Moments of Vision*.)

PHANTOM, THE, is the title of "In the Mind's Eye" as published in *Time's Laughingstocks*.

PLAINT OF A PUPPET, THE, is the manuscript title of "A Plaint to Man."

PLAINT OF CERTAIN SPECTRES, THE, is the title of "Spectres that Grieve" as published in the *Saturday Review*.

PLAY OF ST. GEORGE, THE, is a traditional mummers' play, fragments of which are presented in Book Second, Chapter V, of *The Return of the Native*, where it brings Eustacia and Clym face to face for the first time. Hardy drew the lines and action from his memory of the play as he had seen it as a boy. When the Hardy Players put the novel on the stage in November, 1920, he provided an expanded version; on Christmas night the "carol singers and mummers came to Max Gate . . . the latter performing the *Play of Saint George*, just as he had seen it performed in his childhood."[1] In April of 1921, Mrs. Hardy had this version published with the title "The Play of Saint George as Aforetime Acted by the Dorsetshire Christmas Mummers. . . . Collocated and Revised by Thomas Hardy." Roger S. Loomis republished the play in 1928.[2] Hardy's letter of permission said: "I have great pleasure in permitting you to reprint the recension of the 'Play of St. George' that I managed to concoct from my memories of it as acted in my boyhood." The play is Hardy's poem only as he may have filled out gaps in his memory.

1. *Later Years*, p. 220; *Life*, p. 411.
2. New York: Samuel French. It was published with a prefatory sketch-history of the traditional mummers' play and a modernized version by Loomis.

POEM ON THE WAR, A, is the title of the "Prologue" of *The Dynasts* as published in the *Sphere*. (See the notes on "Epilogue" of *The Dynasts*.)

POEMS IMAGINATIVE AND INCIDENTAL is the manuscript title of *Human Shows* when sent to the publisher.

POEMS OF FEELING, DREAM, AND DEED is the manuscript title of *Poems of the Past and the Present* as phrased in Hardy's contract with the publisher.

POINT DU JOUR, LE, is Clym's song in *The Return of the Native*, Book Fourth, Chapter II. It was taken from Charles-Guillaume Étienne's *Gulistan*, an opera, Act II, scene viii.[1]
1. Roche, "Thomas Hardy and C.-G. Étienne," p. 173.

PORTRAITS, THE, is the title of "Family Portraits" as published in *Nash's and Pall Mall Magazine*.

PRETTY PINK FROCK is the title of "The Pink Frock" as named in *The Later Years*.[1]
1. P. 31; *Life*, p. 264.

PROLOGUE (of *The Dynasts*) is treated in the notes on "Epilogue" of *The Dynasts*. On December 1, 1914, Hardy wrote to Edmund Gosse: "I return the playbill with the Prologue signed as you wished. . . . I am afraid the lines were hardly worth signing, having nothing to do with the drama as a whole, & being just an effusion for the nonce to help the performance of what was staged mainly for patriotic & practical objects."[1]
1. In the British Museum.

PROTEAN LADY, THE, is the manuscript title of "The Protean Maiden."

QUEEN OF CORNWALL, THE, is treated in the notes on *The Famous Tragedy of the Queen of Cornwall*.

QUESTIONS is the manuscript title, deleted, of "To the Moon."

QUIET TRAGEDY, A, is the title of "The Satin Shoes" as published in *Harper's Monthly Magazine* (New York).

RAIN ON HER GRAVE is the manuscript title of "Rain on a Grave."

REJECTED ONE'S WIFE, THE, is the manuscript title of "The Rejected Member's Wife."

REMEMBRANCE is the title of "One We Knew" as published in *Harper's Weekly* (New York). The editor substituted the title "Remembrance."

RENCOUNTER, A, is the manuscript title of "The Two Soldiers."

RETURN FROM FIRST BEHOLDING HER, THE, is the title of "First Sight of Her and After" as published in *Selected Poems*.

RETURN TO ATHELS-HALL, THE, is the manuscript title of "The Dame of Athelhall."

SEDUCER MUSES, THE, is the manuscript title of "Rake-hell Muses."

SHE is the title of "She at His Funeral" in *Wessex Poems*, where "At His Funeral" is in the position of a subtitle.

SHE THINKS SHE DREAMS is the manuscript title of "Bereft, She Thinks She Dreams."

SHE WOULD WELCOME OLD TRIBULATIONS was published with a commentary by Evelyn Hardy in "Some Unpublished Poems by Thomas Hardy." The poem is twenty-one lines long, in three stanzas. It presents an elderly woman's nostalgic memories of her childhood by the seashore. Dating the poem before the death of Emma, Hardy's first wife, Evelyn Hardy says that it was written "from the woman's point of view, this time from that of Emma Hardy, when sixty years old, looking back on a childhood experience in Plymouth, the city of her birth, to which she remained deeply attached all her life." (P. 32.)

SICK GOD, THE, is the title of "The Sick Battle-God" in *Poems of the Past and the Present*.

SLEEPING PALACE, A, is the manuscript title of "A Spellbound Palace."

SNOW AT UPPER TOOTING is the erased manuscript title of "Snow in the Suburbs."

SONG is the title of an "old draft" (1868) of "Retty's Phases."

SONG OF THE SOLDIERS is the title of "Men Who March Away" as published in the *Times Literary Supplement* and in pamphlet form by Clement Shorter.

SONG OF THE SOLDIERS' WIVES is the title of "Song of the Soldiers' Wives and Sweethearts" as published in the *Morning Post* and in *Poems of the Past and the Present*.

SONNET ON THE BELGIAN EXPATRIATION is the title of "On the Belgian Expatriation" as published in *King Albert's Book*.

SOUND OF HER, THE, is an unidentified poem listed in the manuscript of the Table of Contents of *Moments of Vision*, but not included in the volume.

STAYING AND GOING is the manuscript title, deleted, of "On the Doorstep" as published in *Moments of Vision*.

T——A. AT NEWS OF HER DEATH. (DIED 1890) is the manuscript title of "Thoughts of Phena."

THEY ARE GREAT TREES is published in *The Later Years*. Hardy's journal for May 8, 1918, reads: "A letter from Sir George Douglas carries me back to Wimborne and the time when his brother Frank lived opposite us there in the Avenue." Then a six-line poem, beginning "They are great trees, no doubt, by now," is quoted. The entry continues: "Whether any more of this poem was written is not known."[1] Hardy lived in a house called "Llanherne" in the Avenue, Wimborne, from June 25, 1881, until June, 1883.

1. Pp. 186-87; *Life*, p 386.

THOUGHTS FROM SOPHOCLES is a sonnet published by Evelyn Hardy in "Some Unpublished Poems by Thomas Hardy" (p. 39), together with notes that discuss Hardy's reading of Sophocles toward the end of his life. The notes present Jebb's prose translation of the passage Hardy versifies (*Oedipus Coloneus*, 1200-50) and comment upon Hardy's diction. The passage Hardy condensed concerns the welcome approach of death.

THOUGHTS OF PH——A is the title of "Thoughts of Phena" as published in *Wessex Poems*.

THREE BURGHERS, THE, is the manuscript title of "The Burghers."

THROWN ELM, THE, is the title of "The Felled Elm and She" in a manuscript given by Hardy to Mrs. St. John Hornby. "It is an earlier draft with alterations and alternative readings."[1]

1. Purdy, *Thomas Hardy: A Bibliographical Study*, p. 255.

TIME'S LAUGHINGSTOCKS, A SUMMER ROMANCE is the title of "The Revisitation" as published in the *Fortnightly Review*.

TO A BRIDEGROOM is a poem of twenty-four lines, in eight stanzas, published by Evelyn Hardy in "Some Unpublished Poems by Thomas Hardy," pp. 36-37. It is dated "1866 (abridged)." Evelyn Hardy's notes state the theme of the poem as "the evanescence of woman's beauty, and physical decay" and compare it with "Amabel."

TO AN ORPHAN CHILD is the title of "To a Motherless Child" as published in *Wessex Poems*.

TO EXTERNAL NATURE is the manuscript title of "To Outer Nature."

TO HIM is the title of "She, to Him," II, as published in *Selected Poems*.

TO HIS SCORNFUL LOVE is treated in the notes on the poem "Far from the Madding Crowd."

TO J. M. B. is a poem of eight lines in two stanzas addressed to J. M. Barrie and published beneath his portrait on the frontispiece of *The Plays of J. M. Barrie*. The poem was written when Hardy attended a rehearsal of Barrie's *Mary Rose*. *The Later Years*, under an entry for April 21, 1920, says: "This was Hardy's last visit to London. He, with his wife, stayed for two nights only at J. M. Barrie's flat, so near the house in Adelphi Terrace where he had worked as an architect's assistant nearly sixty years before."[1]

1. P. 211; *Life*, p. 404.

TO LADY ———. OFFENDED BY SOMETHING THE AUTHOR HAD WRITTEN is the manuscript title of "To a Lady."

TO MY FATHER'S FIDDLE is the manuscript title of "To my Father's Violin."

TO THE UNKNOWN GOD is a translation of the title " 'ΑΓΝΩΣΤΩι ΘΣΩι."

TRAMP'S TRAGEDY, THE, is the title of "A Trampwoman's Tragedy" as published in the *North American Review* (New York).

TWO RED LIPS is the manuscript title of "Two Lips."

TWO ROSES is an eighteen-line poem in three stanzas published in *London Society* for August, 1882, and signed "Thomas Hardy." It was not by Hardy, who wrote to the publisher in protest. A disclaimer was published in *Figaro* on August 19.[1]

1. See Adams, "Another Man's Roses."

TWO TALL MEN, THE, is an early version of "The Three Tall Men."[1]

1. See Weber, "An Important Hardy Manuscript."

UNPLANTED PRIMROSE, THE, is a poem of twenty-eight lines in four stanzas, published by Evelyn Hardy in "Some Unpublished Poems by Thomas Hardy," pp. 35-36. The poem is dated "1865-67 Westbourne Park Villas. (From old MS)." It is a woman's soliloquy about a rooting of a primrose that she gave her lover to plant. On her return to the garden a year later, she could not find the plant growing, but discovered its "withered skeleton" on a seat where the lover had laid it. The poem may describe an event in Hardy's life, perhaps (though the dates do not fit exactly) in his courtship of Tryphena Sparks, or it may be a fiction to symbolize any neglected love-token. The fair copy with the note "From old MS." suggests that it was intended for *Winter Words*.

UPPER LEAVES, THE, is the manuscript title of "The Upper Birch-Leaves."

VICAR'S YOUNG WIFE, THE, is the manuscript title of "In the Days of Crinoline."

VICTORIAN REHEARSAL, A, is a poem of thirty lines in two stanzas, published by Evelyn Hardy in "An Unpublished Poem by Thomas Hardy." The poem realistically describes a drab, lackadaisical morning-rehearsal, with comments upon scandalous gossip about the private life of the leading lady. It seems to reflect Hardy's brief experience on the stage and his disillusionment with it as described in *The Early Life*: "Mark Lemon . . . rather damped the young man's [Hardy's] ardour by reminding him that the elder Mathews had said that he would not let a dog of his go on the stage, and that he himself . . . would rather see a daughter of his in her grave than on the boards of a theatre. In fact almost the first moment of his sight of stage realities disinclined him to push further in that direction; and his only actual contact with the stage at this time was his appearance at Covent Garden as a nondescript in the pantomime of 'The Forty Thieves,' and in a representation of the Oxford and Cambridge boat-race."[1]

1. Pp. 71-72; *Life*, p. 54.

VOICES FROM THINGS GROWING is the title of "Voices from Things Growing in a Churchyard" as published in the *London Mercury* and in a pamphlet for Mrs. Hardy.

WAITING is the manuscript title of "A Wife Waits."

[669]

WAR-SHADOW is the title of "At the War Office, London" as published in a wartime anthology, *Lest We Forget*, 1915.

WASTED ILLNESS (OVERHEARD), A, is the title of "A Wasted Illness" in the Wessex edition of Hardy's works.

WET EASTER MORNING, A, is the manuscript title of "A Drizzling Easter Morning."

WHEN I WEEKLY KNEW is the title of "Quid Hic Agis?" as published in a pamphlet for Mrs. Hardy in 1916.

WHEN WEARILY WE SHRINK AWAY is the opening phrase of a poem, never published, that exists in manuscript in the Dorset County Museum. Without a title, it is labelled "Probably by Thomas Hardy. Compare writing in Notes, p. 518, 520-522, 524, at the beginning of Commonplace Book I." If the poem is Hardy's, it was probably written about 1865, as suggested by the handwriting. It has "Suggested by M. H." at the end, probably indicating Hardy's sister Mary. The poem reads:

When wearily we shrink away
  From comrades forward striving,
And drop behind where once we strove
  High schemes no more contriving
Though feeling but chance contact bred
  Their slight concern about us,
Still seems it sad they all whirl on
  Nor think they whirl without us.

When worn by fondness unrepaid,
  We class all friends together,
As passage birds who leave us lone
  At close of summer weather;
Nor ask or hear of them, and they
  Ne'er ask or hear about us,
The punishment is hard, to see
  They love so well without us.

'Tis not that, lacking us, they love
  Which touches then most keenly,
But that, un-noting whom they lack
  They still love on serenely:
That e'en they fail to note they lack
  Their own old thoughts about us;

> That hardly would they, might they note
> They thus love on without us.

The poem apparently expresses Hardy's feeling during his early years in London about friends left behind in Dorchester.

WHILE DRAWING ARCHITECTURE IN A CHURCHYARD is the manuscript title of "While Drawing in a Churchyard."

WHITE AND BLUE is Hardy's version of a poem by William Barnes. For Thomas Humphry Ward, ed., *The English Poets*, Vol. V, *Browning to Rupert Brooke*, Hardy wrote a preface to his selection of ten poems by Barnes. He "translated" two of the ten, "White and Blue" and "The Wind at the Door," from Barnes's Dorset dialect into "common English."[1]

1. See Purdy, *Thomas Hardy: A Bibliographical Study*, p. 320, and Orel, *Thomas Hardy's Personal Writings*, p. 85.

WIDOW, THE, is the title of "The Widow Betrothed" as published in *Poems of the Past and the Present*.

WIDOW'S THOUGHT, THE, is the manuscript title of "She Hears the Storm."

WIND AT THE DOOR, THE, is treated in the notes on "White and Blue" above.

WOMAN OF THE WEST, THE, is the manuscript title of "The Woman Who Went East."

WORDS ON THE BRASS, THE, is the manuscript title of "The Inscription."

WORLD'S VERDICT, THE. A MORALITY-RIME is the manuscript title of "The Two Men."

YELLOW-HAMMER, THE, was written for E. J. Detmold and Florence E. Dugdale (later the second Mrs. Hardy), *The Book of Baby Birds* (London, 1912, p. 75). The poem is not there attributed to Hardy, but is ascribed to him by Purdy, *Thomas Hardy: A Bibliographical Study*, p. 316. The poem reads:

> When, towards the summer's close,
> Lanes are dry,
> And unclipt the hedgethorn rows,
> There we fly!

While the harvest waggons pass
  With their load,
Shedding corn upon the grass
  By the road.

In a flock we follow them,
  On and on,
Seize a wheat-ear by the stem,
  And are gone. . . .

With our funny little song,
  Thus you may
Often see us flit along,
  Day by day.

The poem introduces Miss Dugdale's four-page essay on the yellow-hammer.

YOUNG HOPE (SONG) is the manuscript title of "Song of Hope."

Bibliography
and
Index

Bibliography

The following bibliography is not a list of the scholarship treating Hardy's works. It is a list giving data about publications quoted in the present study and cited in the footnotes.

Adams, Frederick B., Jr. "Another Man's Roses," *New Colophon*, II (June, 1949), 107-12.

Andersen, Carol Reed. "Time, Space, and Perspective in Thomas Hardy," *Nineteenth-Century Fiction*, IX (December, 1954), 192-208.

Anshutz, Herbert Leo. "The Road to Nirvana: A Study of Thomas Hardy's Novels and Poems. . . ." Ph. D. dissertation, University of Washington, 1949.

Archer, William. "Real Conversations: Conversation I.—With Mr. Thomas Hardy,'" *Critic*, XXXVIII (April, 1901), 309-18.

Ashe, Geoffrey. *King Arthur's Avalon*. London: Collins, 1957.

Asquith, Lady Cynthia. "Thomas Hardy at Max Gate," *Listener*, LV (June 7, 1956), 753-54.

Atkinson, C. T. *The Dorsetshire Regiment*. 2 vols. Oxford: University Press, 1947.

B., R. G. "Cerne Abbas Church Inventory, 1634," *Notes and Queries for Somerset and Dorset*, XIX (March, 1928), 98-99.

Baedeker, K. *Italy: Handbook for Travellers. First Part: Northern Italy*. Seventh Remodelled Edition. Leipsic: Karl Baedeker, 1886.

———. *Italy: Handbook for Travellers. Second Part: Central Italy and Rome*. Seventh Revised Edition. Leipsic: Karl Baedeker, 1881.

Bailey, J. O. "Evolutionary Meliorism in the Poetry of Thomas Hardy," *Studies in Philology*, LX (July, 1963), 569-87.

———. *Thomas Hardy and the Cosmic Mind: A New Reading of "The Dynasts."* Chapel Hill: University of North Carolina Press, 1956.

Baker, Howard. "Hardy's Poetic Certitude," *Southern Review*, VI (Summer, 1940), 49-63.

Barnes, John H. *Forty Years on the Stage*. London: Chapman and Hall, 1914.

[Bartelot], "Stinsford and the Hardy Family," *Somerset and Dorset Notes and Queries*, XIX (March, 1928), 106-9.

Bartlett, Phyllis. "Hardy's Shelley," *Keats-Shelley Journal*, IV (Winter, 1955), 15-29.

Bax, Hugh. "How Great Is Hardy?" in *Official Handbook Thomas Hardy Festival*. Dorchester: Thomas Hardy Festival Society, 1968, pp. 9-12.

Baxter, Lucy. *The Life of William Barnes*. London and New York: Macmillan and Co., 1887.

Beatty, C. J. P., ed. *The Architectural Notebook of Thomas Hardy*, Dorchester: Dorset Natural History and Archaeological Society, 1966.

———. "Hardy as Architect," in *Official Handbook Thomas Hardy Festival*. Dorchester: Thomas Hardy Festival Society, 1968, pp. 88-89.

———. *Stinsford—A Hardy Church*. St. Peter Port, Guernsey: Toucan Press, 1967.

"Bishop Analyzes Hardy's Religion, The," *Dorset County Chronicle*, June 6, 1940.

Blackmur, R. P. "The Shorter Poems of Thomas Hardy," in *The Expense of Greatness*, New York: Arrow Editions, 1940, pp. 37-73. Same essay in *Southern Review*, VI (Summer, 1940), 20-48.

Blathwayt, Raymond. "A Chat with the Author of 'Tess,'" *Black and White*, IV (August 27, 1892), 238-40.

Blunden, Edmund. *Thomas Hardy*. London: Macmillan and Co., 1942.

Blunt, Wilfrid. *Cockerell: Sydney Carlyle Cockerell, Friend of Ruskin, etc.* London: Hamish Hamilton, 1964.

Blyton, W. J. *We Are Observed: A Mirror to English Character*. London: John Murray, 1938.

Bopp, Dorothy G. "*The Famous Tragedy of the Queen of Cornwall*: A Study of Hardy's Play." M.A. thesis, Columbia University, 1925.

Boswell-Stone, L. C. *Memories and Traditions*. London and Bungay: Richard Clay and Sons, 1895.

Bowden, Ann. "The Thomas Hardy Collection," *Library Chronicle of the University of Texas*, VII (Summer, 1962), 6-14.

Bowra, C. M. "The Lyrical Poetry of Thomas Hardy," in *Inspiration and Poetry.* London: Macmillan & Co., and New York: St. Martin's Press, 1955, pp. 220-41.

Brennecke, Ernest, Jr., ed. *Life and Art by Thomas Hardy.* New York: Greenberg, 1925.

———. *The Life of Thomas Hardy.* New York: Greenberg, 1925.

———. *Thomas Hardy's Universe: A Study of a Poet's Mind.* London: T. Fisher Unwin, 1924.

Brown, Douglas. *Thomas Hardy.* London: Longmans, Green and Co., 1961.

Brown, Janet. "Thomas Hardy's Poem on Donaghadee," *Belfast Telegraph,* July 25, 1953.

Calhoun, Philo. "An Old Architect's Last Draft," *Colby Library Quarterly,* V (December, 1959), 61-69.

Cecil, David. *Hardy the Novelist: An Essay in Criticism.* London: Constable and Co., 1943.

Chakravarty, Amiya. *"The Dynasts" and the Post-War Age in Poetry.* London and New York: Oxford University Press, 1938.

Chew, Samuel C. *Thomas Hardy: Poet and Novelist.* New York: Russell & Russell, 1964 (first published, 1921).

Clifford, Emma. "The Child: The Circus: and 'Jude the Obscure,'" *Cambridge Journal,* VII (1954), 531-46.

———. "The Impressionistic View of History in *The Dynasts,*" *Modern Language Quarterly,* XXII (March, 1961), 21-23.

———. "Thomas Hardy and the Historians," *Studies in Philology,* LVI (October, 1959), 654-68.

———. *"War and Peace* and *The Dynasts,*" *Modern Philology,* LIV (August, 1956), 33-44.

Clinton-Baddeley, V. C. "The Written and the Spoken Word," *Essays and Studies,* XVIII (1965), 73-82.

Cockerell, Sydney. "A Memorial to Thomas Hardy," London *Times,* October 27, 1928.

Colby Library Quarterly. *A Descriptive Catalogue of the Grolier Club Centenary Exhibition, 1940, of the Works of Thomas Hardy.* Waterville, Maine, 1940.

Coleman, Terry, letter to the London *Times Literary Supplement,* January 30, 1969, pp. 110-11.

Collins, Vere H. "The Love Poetry of Thomas Hardy," *Essays and Studies by Members of the English Association,* XXVIII (1942), 69-83.

———. *Talks with Thomas Hardy at Max Gate, 1920-1922.* Garden City, New York: Doubleday, Doran, 1928.

Colvin, Sir Sidney. *John Keats.* New York: Charles Scribner's Sons, 1917.

Compton-Rickett, Arthur. "Thomas Hardy, O. M.: A Recollection," in *Portraits and Personalities.* London: Selwyn & Blount, 1937, pp. 21-32.

Copps, Abbie M. "The Poetry of Thomas Hardy." M.A. thesis, Cornell University, 1929.

Cox, Charles J. *The Royal Forests of England.* London: Methuen, 1905.

Cox, J. Stevens, ed. *Poems and Religious Effusions by Emma Lavinia Hardy.* St. Peter Port, Guernsey: Toucan Press, 1966.

——. *Thomas Hardy Through the Camera's Eye.* Beaminster, Dorset: Toucan Press, 1964.

——. *Thomas Hardy's Will and Other Wills of His Family.* St. Peter Port, Guernsey: Toucan Press, 1967.

Daniell, E. S. *The Valley of the Bride.* Dorchester: Longman's, 1950.

Davis, F. Hadland. "The Music of Thomas Hardy," in *The Dorset Year Book, 1922.* Weymouth, England: Society of Dorset Men, 1922, pp. 70-74. Same essay in *Musical Times,* LXII (April 1, 1921), pp. 255-58.

Deacon, Lois. *Hardy's Grandmother, Betsy, and Her Family.* St. Peter Port, Guernsey: Toucan Press, 1966.

——. *Hardy's Summer Romance.* St. Peter Port, Guernsey: Toucan Press, 1967.

——. *Hardy's Sweetest Image.* Ingledene, Chagford, Devon: privately printed, 1964.

——. "That Mysterious Tragic Pair," in manuscript, 1966.

——. *The Chosen.* St. Peter Port, Guernsey: Toucan Press, 1966.

——. *The Moules and Thomas Hardy.* St. Peter Port, Guernsey: Toucan Press, 1968.

——. "Thomas Hardy and Tryphena: Her Immortality," in manuscript, 1966.

——. *Tryphena and Thomas Hardy.* Beaminster, Dorset: Toucan Press, 1962.

——. *Tryphena's Portrait Album.* St. Peter Port, Guernsey: Toucan Press, 1967.

—— and Terry Coleman. *Providence and Mr Hardy.* London: Hutchinson & Co., 1966.

"Death of Mrs. Thomas Hardy," *Dorset County Chronicle,* October 21, 1937.

Dobrée, Bonamy. "The Dynasts," *Southern Review,* VI (Summer, 1940), 109-24.

Dodge, Theodore Ayrault. *Napoleon.* 4 vols. London: Gay and Bird, 1907.

Dolman, Frederick. "An Evening with Thomas Hardy," *Young Man,* VIII (March, 1894), 74-79.

Douglas, Sir George. "Thomas Hardy: Some Recollections," *Hibbert Journal,* XXVI (April, 1928), 385-98.

Duffin, H. C. *Thomas Hardy: A Study of the Wessex Novels, the Poems, and the Dynasts.* Manchester, England: University Press, 1962 (first edition, 1916).

Edgren, C. Hobart. "A Hardy-Housman Parallel," *Notes and Queries,* CXCIX (March, 1954), 126-27.

Edmonds, J. M., ed. *Lyra Graeca.* London: William Heineman, and New York: G. P. Putnam's Sons, 1922.

Eliot, George, Trans. *The Life of Jesus Critically Examined* by Dr. David Friedrich Strauss, Translated from the Fourth German Edition. 3 vols. London: Swan Sonnenschein & Co.; New York: Macmillan & Co., 1898.

Elliott, Albert Pettigrew. *Fatalism in the Works of Thomas Hardy.* Philadelphia: 1935.

Elliott, G. R. "Spectral Etching by Thomas Hardy in the Shorter Poems," in *The Cycle of Modern Poetry.* Princeton: Princeton University Press, 1929, pp. 91-111.

Ellis, S. M. "Some Personal Recollections of Thomas Hardy," *Fortnightly Review,* N.S. CXXIII (March, 1928), 393-406.

Ervine, St. John. "Thomas Hardy and the Maid from Donaghadee," *Belfast Telegraph,* July 16, 1953.

Evans, Evelyn L. *The Homes of Thomas Hardy.* St. Peter Port, Guernsey: Toucan Press, 1968.

Fackler, Miriam Ernestine. "Death: Idea and Image in Some Later Victorian Lyrists." Ph.D. dissertation, University of Colorado, 1955.

Fägersten, Anton. *The Place-Names of Dorset.* Uppsala: Lundequistska, 1953.

Fairchild, Hoxie Neale. *Gods of a Changing Poetry,* Vol. V of *Religious Trends in English Poetry.* New York and London: Columbia University Press, 1962.

———. "The Immediate Source of *The Dynasts,*" *PMLA,* LXVII (March, 1952), 43-64.

Fea, Allan. *King Monmouth.* London and New York: John Lane, 1902.

Felkin, Elliott. "Days with Thomas Hardy: from a 1918-1919 Diary," *Encounter,* XVIII (April, 1962), 27-33.

Firor, Ruth A. *Folkways in Thomas Hardy*. Philadelphia: University of Pennsylvania Press, 1931, and New York: A. S. Barnes & Co., 1962.

FitzGerald, Eileen M. "Science in the Poetry of Tennyson, Hardy, and Meredith." M.A. thesis, Mount Holyoke College, 1929.

Flower, Newman. *Just As It Happened*. New York: William Morrow and Company, 1950.

——. "Our First President: Some Recollections of Sir Frederick Treves," in *The Dorset Year Book for 1954-55*. Weymouth, England: Society of Dorset Men, 1954, pp. 17-21.

——. "Walks and Talks with Hardy," *Countryman*, XXXIV (Winter, 1946), 193-95.

Ford, Ford Madox. "Thomas Hardy, O. M. Obiit 11 January, 1928," New York *Herald-Tribune Books*, January 22, 1928, pp. 1-3.

Foster, J. J. *Wessex Worthies*. London: Dickinson, 1920.

Freeman, John. "Thomas Hardy" in *The Moderns: Essays in Literary Criticism*. London: Robert Scott, 1916, pp. 103-59.

Friedman, Barton R. " 'When There Is Nothing': Hardy's *Souls of the Slain*," *Renascence*, XVII (Spring, 1965), 121-27.

Ghent, Percy. "Thomas Hardy Note Is Mainly Concerned with Canadian Babe," *Evening Telegram* (Toronto, Canada), September 8, 1941.

Gierasch, Walter. "Hardy's *On the Departure Platform*," *Explicator*, IV (1945), item 10.

Gifford, Henry. "Thomas Hardy and Emma," *Essays and Studies*, N.S. XIX (1966), 106-21.

Gilder, Jeannette L. "Thomas Hardy Makes a New Departure," New York *World*, December 8, 1895.

Gorman, Herbert S. "Hardy and Housman," in *The Procession of Masks*, Boston: B. J. Brimmer Co., 1923, pp. 171-83.

Gosse, Edmund. *The Life of Algernon Charles Swinburne*. London: Macmillan and Co., 1917.

——. "The Lyrical Poetry of Thomas Hardy" in *Some Diversions of a Man of Letters*. New York: Charles Scribner's Sons, 1919, pp. 233-58.

——. "Mr. Hardy's Last Poem," London *Times*, January 13, 1928.

——. "Mr. Hardy's Lyrical Poems," *Edinburgh Review*, CCXXVII (April, 1918), 272-93.

——. Review of *Human Shows*, *Living Age*, CCCXXVIII (Feb. 6, 1926), 336-38.

Graves, Robert. *Good-Bye to All That: An Autobiography*. New York: Jonathan Cape & Harrison Smith, 1930.

Grew, Eva Mary. "Thomas Hardy as Musician," *Music and Letters,* XXI (April, 1940), 120-42.

Grey, Rowland. "A Letter from Thomas Hardy," *Great Thoughts,* No. 2386, pp. 225-26.

Griffith, Philip Mahone. "The Image of the Trapped Animal in Hardy's *Tess of the D'Urbervilles," Tulane Studies in English,* XIII (1963), 85-94.

Gross, Harvey. *Sound and Form in Modern Poetry: A Study of Prosody from Thomas Hardy to Robert Lowell.* Ann Arbor: University of Michigan Press, 1965.

Guerard, Albert J. "The Illusion of Simplicity: The Shorter Poems of Thomas Hardy," *Sewanee Review,* LXXII (Summer, 1964), 363-88.

Haeckel, Ernst. *The Riddle of the Universe at the Close of the Nineteenth Century,* trans. by Joseph McCabe. 2nd ed. London: Watts & Co., 1901.

Haggard, H. Rider. *The Days of My Life.* London: Longmans, Green, 1926.

Hamilton, Cosmo. "Thomas Hardy: Fruitless Conflicts," in *People Worth Talking About,* New York: Robert M. McBride, 1933, pp. 245-52.

Hansford, F. E. "A Heart of Pity," *Schoolmaster and Woman Teacher's Chronicle* (March 22, 1928), p. 573.

Hardy, Emma L. *Poems and Religious Effusions by Emma Lavinia Hardy,* ed. by J. Stevens Cox. St. Peter Port, Guernsey: Toucan Press, 1966.

——. *Spaces: An Exposition of Great Truths by a New Treatment.* Dorchester: Longman, 1912.

Hardy, Evelyn. "Plots for Five Unpublished Short Stories," *London Magazine,* V (November, 1958), 33-54.

——. "Some Unpublished Poems by Thomas Hardy," *London Magazine,* III (1956), 28-39.

——. *Thomas Hardy: A Critical Biography.* London: Hogarth Press, 1954.

——. "Thomas Hardy and Horace Moule," London *Times Literary Supplement,* January 29, 1969, p. 89.

——. *Thomas Hardy's Notebooks and Some Letters from Julia Augusta Martin.* London: Hogarth Press, 1955.

——. "An Unpublished Poem by Thomas Hardy," London *Times Literary Supplement,* June 2, 1966, p. 504.

—— and Robert Gittings, eds. *Some Recollections by Emma Hardy.* London: Oxford University Press, 1961.

Hardy, Florence Emily. *The Early Life of Thomas Hardy: 1840-1891.* New York: Macmillan Company, 1928.

——. *The Later Years of Thomas Hardy: 1892-1928.* New York: Macmillan Company, 1930.

——. *The Life of Thomas Hardy: 1840-1928.* London: Macmillan and Company, 1962. (*The Life* is a one-volume publication of *The Early Life* and *The Later Years.*)

[Hardy, Thomas]. "Death of Miss Mary Hardy," *Dorset County Chronicle,* December 2, 1915.

——. "Recollections of 'Leader Scott,' " *Dorset County Chronicle* and London *Times* November 27, 1902.

"Hardys and Keatses," *Dorset Year Book, 1928,* pp. 135-37.

Harrison, Frederic. "Novissima Verba," *Fortnightly Review,* CVII (February, 1920), 177-86.

Hartmann, Eduard von. *Philosophy of the Unconscious,* trans. by W. C. Coupland. 3 vols. London: Kegan, Paul, Trench, Trübner, & Co., 1890.

Harvey, John. *Gothic England.* London: B. T. Batsford, 1947.

Harvey, O. D. *Puddletown the Weatherbury of "Far from the Madding Crowd."* Dorchester: Privately printed, 1958.

Heath, F. R., and Sidney Heath. *Dorchester and Its Surroundings.* Dorchester: Longman, 1905-6.

Hedgcock, F. A. *Thomas Hardy: Penseur et Artiste.* Paris: Hachette & Cie., 1911.

Helps, Arthur L. *St. Mary's Church Puddletown.* Dorchester: Longman, 1955.

Henderson, Archibald. "Thomas Hardy in a New Role," *Forum,* LXXI (June, 1924), 783-90.

[Henniker, Florence]. *Arthur Henniker: A Little Book for His Friends.* London: Arthur L. Humphreys, 1912.

Hickson, Elizabeth Cathcart. *The Versification of Thomas Hardy.* Philadelphia: University of Pennsylvania Press, 1931.

Hill, Charles J. "George Meredith and Thomas Hardy," *Notes and Queries,* CXCVIII (1953), 69-71.

Hoare, Dorothy M. "The Tragic in Hardy and Conrad," in *Some Studies in the Modern Novel.* London: Chatto & Windus, 1938, pp. 113-32.

Hodgins, James Raymond. "A Study of the Periodical Reception of the Novels of Thomas Hardy, George Gissing, and George Moore." Ph.D. dissertation, Michigan State University, 1960.

Hogan, Donald Joseph. "Structural Design in Thomas Hardy's Poetry." Ph.D. dissertation, University of Minnesota, 1958.

Holland, Clive. "My Walks and Talks in Wessex with Thomas Hardy," *John O'London's Weekly* (March 30, 1951), pp. 170-71.

————. "The Thomas Hardy I Knew," *Christian Science Monitor* (magazine section), May 18, 1940.

————. *Thomas Hardy, O. M.: The Man, His Works and the Land of Wessex.* London: Herbert Jenkins, 1933.

————. *Thomas Hardy's Wessex Scene.* Dorchester: Longman, 1948.

————. "When I Cycled and Talked with Hardy," *Chambers's Journal* (November, 1945), pp. 571-75.

Holmes, Lawrence Richard. "Hardy's *Her Father*," *Explicator*, XIV (1956), item 53.

Homer, Christine Wood. *Thomas Hardy and His Two Wives.* Beaminster, Dorset: Toucan Press, 1964.

Hopkins, Annette B. "*The Dynasts* and the Course of History," *South Atlantic Quarterly*, XLIV (1945), 432-44.

Horsman, E. A. "The Language of *The Dynasts*," *Durham University Journal*, XLI (December, 1948), 11-16.

Houghton, Walter E. *The Victorian Frame of Mind, 1830-1870.* New Haven and London: Yale University Press, 1957.

Housman, Laurence. *My Brother, A. E. Housman.* New York: Charles Scribner's Sons, 1938.

Howe, Irving. *Thomas Hardy.* New York: Macmillan Company, 1967.

Hudson, W. H. *Nature in Downland.* London and New York: Longmans, Green, and Co., 1900.

Hutchings, Monica. *Dorset River.* London: MacDonald, 1956.

————. *Inside Dorset.* Sherborne: Abbey Press, 1965.

————. *Inside Somerset.* Sherborne: Abbey Press, 1963.

Hutchins, John. *The History and Antiquities of the County of Dorset.* 4 vols. 3rd ed. Westminster: John Bowyer Nichols and Sons, 1861-73.

Huxley, Thomas H. "Evolution and Ethics," in *Collected Essays.* New York: D. Appleton & Co., 1899, IX, 46-86.

Hynes, Samuel. *The Pattern of Hardy's Poetry.* Chapel Hill: The University of North Carolina Press, 1961.

Jackman, Douglas. *300 Years of Baptist Witness in Dorchester, 1645-1945.* Dorchester: Privately printed, 1945.

Johnson, S. F. "Hardy and Burke's 'Sublime,'" in *Style in Prose Fiction*, ed. by Harold C. Martin. New York: Columbia University Press, 1959, pp. 55-86.

Jones, Bernard, ed. *The Poems of William Barnes.* 2 vols. Carbondale, Ill.: Illinois Southern University Press, 1962.

Jones, Doris Arthur. *The Life and Letters of Henry Arthur Jones.* London: Victor Gollancz, 1930.

Kennedy, X. J. *An Introduction to Poetry.* Boston and Toronto: Little, Brown and Co., 1966.

Ketcham, Carl H. " 'A Vixen Voice': Hardy and Thackeray," *Colby Library Quarterly*, Series VIII (September, 1965), 130.

King, R. W. "The Lyrical Poems of Thomas Hardy," *London Mercury*, XV (December, 1926), 157-70.

———. "Verse and Prose Parallels in the Work of Thomas Hardy," *Review of English Studies*, N.S. XIII (1962), 52-61.

Knott, Olive. "Dorset Superstitions," in *The Dorset Year-Book, 1961-1962.* Weymouth, England: Society of Dorset Men, p. 73.

———. *Hardy's Sturminster Home.* St. Peter Port, Guernsey: Toucan Press, 1968.

Knowles, David. "The Thought and Art of Thomas Hardy," *Dublin Review*, CLXXXIII (1928), 208-18.

Korg, Jacob. "Hardy's *The Dynasts*: A Prophecy," *South Atlantic Quarterly*, LIII (January, 1954), 24-32.

Kramer, Dale. "Repetition of Imagery in Thomas Hardy," *Victorian Newsletter*, No. 23 (Spring, 1963), 26-27.

———. "Revisions and Vision," a study of *The Woodlanders* read in manuscript.

Kreuzer, James R. *Elements of Poetry.* New York: Macmillan Company, 1955.

Lake, W. E. *Cerne Abbas of Dorset.* Cerne Abbas, 1952.

Lea, Hermann. *A Handbook to the Wessex Country of Thomas Hardy's Novels and Poems.* London: Kegan Paul, and Bournemouth: Holland Rowbottom, 1904.

———. *Thomas Hardy's Wessex.* London: Macmillan and Co., 1913.

Lefèvre, Frédéric, "An Hour with Thomas Hardy," *Living Age*, CCCXXV (April 11, 1925), 98-103.

Lewis, C. Day. "The Lyrical Poetry of Thomas Hardy," *Proceedings of the British Academy*, XXXVII (1951), 155-74.

Lord, Walter. *A Night to Remember.* London, New York: Longmans, Green and Co., 1956.

Lowell, Amy. *John Keats.* 2 vols. Boston and New York: Houghton, Mifflin Co., 1925.

Lowes, John Livingston. "Two Readings of Earth," *Yale Review*, XV (April, 1926), 515-39.

Lubbock, Percy, ed. *The Diary of Arthur Christopher Benson.* New York: Longmans, Green and Co., 1926.

Lucas, E. V. *The Colvins and Their Friends.* New York: Charles Scribner's Sons, 1928.

Mackail, Denis. *Barrie: The Story of J. M. B.* New York: Charles Scribner's Sons, 1941.

Maitland, Frederic William. *The Life and Letters of Leslie Stephen.* New York: G. P. Putnam's Sons, and London: Duckworth and Co., 1906.

Mardon, J. Vera. *Thomas Hardy as a Musician.* Beaminster, Dorset: Toucan Press, 1964.

Marrot, H. Vincent. *The Life and Letters of John Galsworthy.* New York: Scribner's, 1936.

Mayers, D. E. "Dialectical Structures in Hardy's Poems," *Victorian Newsletter*, No. 27 (Spring, 1965), 15-18.

McCutcheon, George Barr. *The Renowned Collection of First Editions of Thomas Hardy, Rudyard Kipling, Robert Louis Stevenson.* New York: American Art Association, 1925.

McDowall, Arthur. *Thomas Hardy: A Critical Study.* London: Faber and Faber, 1931.

McGregor, John James. *History of the French Revolution.* Waterford, England: John Bull, 1817. (Vol. III tells the story of Valenciennes, as in Hardy's poem.)

McWilliam, W. "In Thomas Hardy's Wessex," *Geographical Magazine*, XI (May, 1940), 36-49.

Metcalfe, Rev. A. *A Popular and Illustrated Guide to St. Peter's Church Dorchester.* Dorchester: Longman and Ling, 1907.

Meynell, Viola, ed. *Friends of a Lifetime: Letters to Sydney Carlyle Cockerell.* London: Jonathan Cape, 1940.

Mill, John Stuart. "Nature" in *Three Essays on Religion.* London, 1874, republished in many editions.

——. *On Liberty.* London, 1859, republished in many editions.

Miller, Edward Shepard. "Hardy's Venerable Drama," *Studies in English Literature* [journal of the English Literary Society of Japan], XVII (October, 1937), 568-81.

Mills, D. C. "Thomas Hardy's Association with Wimborne," *Wyvern* [Wimborne, Dorset: Wimborne County Modern School] (1960), pp. 12-14.

Ministry of Public Buildings and Works. *Tintagel Castle.* London: Her Majesty's Stationery Office, 1939.

Morcos, Louis. " 'The Dynasts' and the Bible," *Annual Bulletin of English Studies* [Ein Shams University, Cairo, Egypt] (1955), pp. 29-65.

——. "The Manuscript of Thomas Hardy's *The Dynasts*," *Annals of the Faculty of Arts* [Ein Shams University, Cairo, Egypt], III (January, 1955), 1-37.

Morrell, Roy. " 'The Dynasts' Reconsidered," *Modern Language Review*, LVIII (April, 1963), 161-71.

———. *Thomas Hardy: The Will and the Way*. Kuala Lumpur: University of Malaya Press, 1965.

Moule, G. H. *Stinsford Church and Parish*. Dorchester: Henry Ling, 1940.

Moule, Rev. G. W. H. *A Revised List of the Birds of Dorset, Up to 1962* (pamphlet reprinted from *Proceedings* of the Dorset Natural History and Archaeological Society, LXXXVI, 1965), 66-85.

Moule, H. J. *Dorchester Antiquities*. Dorchester: Henry Ling, 1906.

———. "Monolith on Batcombe Hill," *Notes and Queries for Somerset and Dorset*, I (1890), 247-48.

Moule, Handley C. G. *Memories of a Vicarage*. London: Religious Tract Society, 1913.

[Moule, Horace]. Review of *Under the Greenwood Tree, Saturday Review*, XXXIV (September 28, 1872), 417-18.

Mundy, Harriot Georgiana, ed. *The Journal of Mary Frampton*. London: Sampson Low, Marston, Searle, & Rivington, 1885.

Murry, J. Middleton. *The Letters of Katherine Mansfield*. New York: Alfred A. Knopf, 1932.

———. *The Problem of Style*. London: Oxford University Press, 1922.

———. "Thomas Hardy," in *Katherine Mansfield and Other Literary Portraits*. London: Peter Nevill, 1949, pp. 215-29.

Neiman, Gilbert. "Thomas Hardy, Existentialist," *Twentieth Century Literature*, I (January, 1956), 207-14.

Neumeyer, Peter F. "The Transfiguring Vision," *Victorian Poetry*, III (Autumn, 1965), pp. 263-66.

Nevinson, Henry W. *Changes and Chances*. New York: Harcourt, Brace and Company, 1923.

———. *More Changes More Chances*. New York: Harcourt, Brace and Company, 1925.

———. *Thomas Hardy*. London: George Allen & Unwin, 1941.

Newton, A. Edward. *Thomas Hardy, Novelist or Poet?* Philadelphia: privately printed, 1929.

Norman, Sylva. "Thomas Hardy" in *The Great Victorians*, ed. by H. J. and Hugh Massingham. Garden City, New York: Doubleday, Doran & Company, 1932, pp. 209-25.

Noyes, Alfred. "The Poetry of Thomas Hardy," *North American Review*, CXCIV (July, 1911), 96-105.

Oliphant, Mrs. M. "The Anti-Marriage League," *Blackwood's Edinburgh Magazine*, CLIX (January, 1896), 135-49.

Oliver, Constance M. *Thomas Hardy Proposes to Mary Waight*. Beaminster, Dorset: Toucan Press, 1964.

Olivero, F. "The Poetry of Hardy," *Poetry Review*, XX (January, 1929), 1-22.

Orel, Harold. *"The Dynasts* and *Paradise Lost,"* South Atlantic Quarterly, LII (July, 1953), 355-60.

———. *Thomas Hardy's Epic-Drama: A Study of "The Dynasts."* Lawrence, Kansas: University of Kansas Press, 1963.

———. *Thomas Hardy's Personal Writings*. Lawrence, Kansas: University of Kansas Press, 1966.

O'Rourke, May. *Thomas Hardy: His Secretary Remembers*. Beaminster, Dorset: Toucan Press, 1965.

Osawa, Mamoru. "Hardy and the German Men-of-Letters," *Studies in English Literature*, XIX (October, 1939), 504-44.

Oswald, Arthur. "A Somerset Village: Tintinhull and Its Houses," *Country Life*, CXIX (April 12, 1956), 736-39.

———. "Tintinhull House, Somerset," *Country Life*, CXIX (April 19, 1956), 798-99.

P., C. "Thomas Hardy's Last Poems," *Manchester Guardian Weekly*, XIX (October 5, 1928), 273.

Parker, W. M. "Hardy's Letters to Sir George Douglas," *English*, XIV (Autumn, 1963), 218-25.

Pascoe, Charles Eyre. *The Dramatic List*. London: Hardwicke and Bogue, 1880.

Peirce, Walter. "Hardy's Lady Susan and the First Countess of Wessex," *Colby Library Quarterly*, Series II (February, 1948), 77-82.

Pentin, Rev. Herbert. "Dorset Children's Doggerel Rhymes," *Proceedings of the Dorset Natural History and Antiquarian Field Club*, XXXVIII, 112-32.

Perkins, David. "Hardy and the Poetry of Isolation," *ELH: Journal of English Literary History*, XXVI (1959), 253-70.

Perrine, Laurence. "Thomas Hardy's 'God Forgotten,'" *Victorian Poetry*, VI (Summer, 1968), 187-88.

Phelps, Kenneth. *Annotations by Thomas Hardy in His Bibles and Prayer-Book*. St. Peter Port, Guernsey: Toucan Press, 1966.

Phelps, William Lyon. *Autobiography with Letters*. New York, London, Toronto: Oxford University Press, 1939.

Pinion, F. B. *A Hardy Companion*. London: Macmillan and Co., 1968.

Pitt-Rivers, Lieutenant-General. *A Short Guide to the Larmer*

Grounds, Rushmore; King John's House; and the Museum at Farnham, Dorset. London: Harrison and Sons, [*c.* 1896].

Pope, Alfred. *The Old Stone Crosses of Dorset.* London: Chiswick Press, 1906.

Powys, Llewelyn. *Dorset Essays.* London: John Lane, 1935. (The essays include "Stinsford Churchyard," pp. 183-87.)

Purdy, Richard Little. *"Thomas Hardy: A Bibliographical Study,* London, New York, Toronto: Oxford University Press, 1954, reprinted 1968.

R., H. "Max Gate: Memories of Thomas Hardy's Home," *Birmingham Post* (England), June 15, 1938.

Ransome, John Crow. "Hardy—Old Poet," *New Republic,* CXXVI (May 12, 1952), 16 and 30-31.

——. "Honey and Gall," *Southern Review,* VI (Summer, 1940), 2-19.

——. "Thomas Hardy's Poems and the Religious Difficulties of a Naturalist," *Kenyon Review,* XXII (Spring, 1960), 169-93.

——, ed. *Selected Poems of Thomas Hardy,* New York: Macmillan Company, 1961.

Rawlins, S. W. "Napper of Tintinhull," *Somerset and Dorset Notes and Queries,* XXVIII (August, 1960), 277-85.

Reed, Henry. "The Making of 'The Dynasts,'" in *The Penguin New Writing,* No. 18, ed. John Lehman. Harmondsworth, England, and New York: Penguin Books, 1943, pp. 136-47.

Richards, I. A. *Practical Criticism: A Study of Literary Judgment.* London: Kegan Paul, Trench, Trübner & Co., 1929.

Roberts, Marguerite. "The Dramatic Element in Hardy's Poetry," *Queen's Quarterly,* LI (December, 1944), 429-38.

——. *Hardy's Poetic Drama and the Theatre.* New York: Pageant Press, 1965.

——. *Tess in the Theatre.* Toronto: University of Toronto Press, 1950.

Roche, Charles Edward. "Thomas Hardy and C.-G. Étienne," *Modern Language Notes,* LXVIII (1953), 173.

Routley, Erik. *University Carol Book.* Brighton, England: H. Freeman & Co., 1961.

Rutland, William R. "Hardy and Moule," London *Times Literary Supplement,* February 13, 1969, pp. 158-59.

——. *Thomas Hardy: A Study of His Writings and Their Background.* Oxford: Basil Blackwell, 1938, and reprinted, New York: Russell and Russell, 1962.

Sanders, Gerald D., and John H. Nelson, eds. *Chief Modern Poets of England and America.* New York: Macmillan, 1947.

Sassoon, Siegfried. *Meredith.* New York: Viking Press, 1948.

——. *Siegfried's Journey: 1916-1920.* New York: Viking Press, 1946.

Schwartz, Delmore. "Poetry and Belief in Thomas Hardy," *Southern Review,* VI (Summer, 1940), 64-77.

Scudamore, Joyce. *Florence and Thomas Hardy.* Beaminster, Dorset: Toucan Press, 1964.

Shanks, Edward. "Songs of Joy," *Saturday Review,* CXLVI (November 10, 1928), 610.

Sherman, Elna. "Music in Thomas Hardy's Life and Work," *Musical Quarterly,* XXVI (October, 1940), 419-45.

——. "Thomas Hardy: Lyricist, Symphonist," *Music and Letters,* XXI (April, 1940), 143-71.

——. *Wessex Tune Book.* London: Schott & Co., 1963.

Sherman, George Witter. "The Influence of London on *The Dynasts,*" *PMLA,* LXIII (September, 1948), 1017-28.

——. "A Note on One of Thomas Hardy's Poems," *Colby Library Quarterly,* Series III, No. 6 (May, 1952), 99-100.

——. "Thomas Hardy and Professor Edward Beesly," *Notes and Queries,* CXCVIII (1953), 167-68.

——. "Thomas Hardy and the Lower Animals," *Prairie Schooner,* XX (1946), 304-9.

——. "The Wheel and the Beast: The Influence of London Life on Thomas Hardy," *Nineteenth-Century Fiction,* IV (1949), 209-19.

Sherren, Wilkinson. *The Wessex of Romance.* London: Chapman and Hall, 1902.

Shilleto, Arthur Richard. *Pausanias' Description of Greece.* London: George Bell and Sons, 1900.

Siegel, Paul N. "Hardy's 'Convergence of the Twain,'" *Explicator,* XI (1952), item 13.

Skilling, James. "Hardy's Birthplace—That's Our Home," in *Thomas Hardy Festival Supplement, Dorset Evening Echo,* July 6, 1968, p. 9.

—— and M. R. Skilling. *Thomas Hardy and His Birthplace.* Ditchling, Sussex: National Press, 1968.

Slack, Robert C. "The Text of Hardy's *Jude the Obscure,*" *Nineteenth-Century Fiction,* XI (March, 1957), 261-75.

Smith, E. P. "A Critical Study of the Poetry of Thomas Hardy," B.L. thesis, Oxford University, 1963.

Snell, Reginald. "A Self-Plagiarism by Thomas Hardy," *Essays in Criticism,* II (January, 1952), 114-17.

Sotheby & Co. *Catalogue of Valuable Printed Books . . . Autograph Letters* for sale on June 22 and 23, 1959, London.

Southerington, F. R. *The Early Hardys*. St. Peter Port, Guernsey: Toucan Press, 1968.

——. *Hardy's Child: Fact or Fiction*. St. Peter Port, Guernsey: Toucan Press, 1968.

——. "Hardy's Poetic Vision," in manuscript, 1967.

——. "Human Behaviour and Responsibility in the Prose Works of Thomas Hardy." Ph.D. dissertation, Magdalen College, Oxford University, 1968.

Southworth, James Granville. *The Poetry of Thomas Hardy*. New York: Columbia University Press, 1947.

Sparks, James. "Piddletown Volunteer Broadside," *Somerset and Dorset Notes and Queries*, XX (1930), 58.

Spencer, Marjorie. "A Maid from the County Down," *Belfast Telegraph*, July 13, 1953.

Squire, J. C. "Mr. Hardy's Old Age," *Essays on Poetry*. London: Hodder and Stoughton, n.d.

——. "Thomas Hardy's Verse," *Land and Water*, LXX (December 13, 1917), 17.

Stedmond, J. M. "Hardy's *Dynasts* and the 'Mythical Method,'" *English*, XII (Spring, 1958), 1-4.

Stephens, Bertie Norman. *Thomas Hardy in His Garden*. Beaminster, Dorset: Toucan Press, 1963.

Stevenson, Lionel. "Thomas Hardy," *Darwin among the Poets*. Chicago: University of Chicago Press, 1932, pp. 237-97.

Stewart, Agnes. "'The Dynasts': A Psychological Interpretation," *English Review*, XXXVIII (May, 1924), 666-80.

Stewart, J. I. M. "Hardy," in *Eight Modern Writers*, Vol. XII of *The Oxford History of English Literature*, eds. F. P. Wilson and Bonamy Dobrée. Oxford: Clarendon Press, 1963, pp. 19-70.

Stickland, Dorothy. *Thomas Hardy at Cattistock*. St. Peter Port, Guernsey: Toucan Press, 1968.

Strachey, Lytton. "Mr. Hardy's New Poems," in *Literary Essays*, New York: Harcourt Brace and Co., 1949, pp. 220-25. Also in *New Statesman*, December 19, 1914.

Strauss, David Friedrich: *The Life of Jesus Critically Examined*, trans. by George Eliot. 3 vols. London: Chapman, 1846.

Taylor, Alfred J., and R. E. M. Wheeler. *The Roman Baths of Bath*. Bath: Mendip Press, 1954.

Terrot, Charles. *Traffic in Innocents*. New York: E. P. Dutton Co., 1960.

Thompson, C. W. *Records of the Dorset Yeomanry*. Dorchester: Dorset County Chronicle Printing Works, 1894.

Tuttleton, June Martin. "Thomas Hardy and the Christian Religion." Ph.D. dissertation, the University of North Carolina at Chapel Hill, 1964.

Van Doren, Mark. "The Poems of Thomas Hardy" in *Four Poets on Poetry*, ed. by Don Cameron Allen. Baltimore: Johns Hopkins Press, 1959, pp. 83-107.

Vincent, Benjamin. *Haydn's Dictionary of Dates*. 18th ed. London: Ward, Lock, & Co., 1885.

Vinson, Grace Esther. "Diction and Imagery in the Poetry of Thomas Hardy." Ph.D. dissertation, University of Wisconsin, 1953.

Von Hartmann. *See* Hartmann.

Voss, Harold Lionel. *Motoring with Thomas Hardy*. Beaminster, Dorset: Toucan Press, 1963.

Waldock, A. J. A. "Thomas Hardy and 'The Dynasts,' " in *James, Joyce, and Others*. London: Williams and Norgate, 1937, pp. 53-78.

Weber, Carl J. "Ainsworth and Thomas Hardy," *Review of English Studies*, XVII (April, 1941), 193-200.

——. *"Dearest Emmie": Thomas Hardy's Letters to His First Wife*. London: Macmillan and Co., 1963.

——. "From Belmount Hall to Colby," *Colby Mercury*, VII (May, 1942), 85-93.

——. *Hardy and the Lady from Madison Square*. Waterville, Maine: Colby College Press, 1952.

——. *Hardy in America: A Study of Thomas Hardy and His American Readers*. Waterville, Maine: Colby College Press, 1946.

——. *Hardy Music at Colby*. Waterville, Maine: Colby College Library, 1945.

——. *Hardy of Wessex*. New York: Columbia University Press, 1940.

——. *Hardy of Wessex: His Life and Literary Career*. 2nd ed. New York: Columbia University Press, and London: Routledge and Kegan Paul, 1965.

——. *Hardy's Love Poems*. London: Macmillan and Co., 1963.

——. "An Important Hardy Manuscript," *Colby Library Quarterly*, IV (1958), 303-4.

——. *The Letters of Thomas Hardy*. Waterville, Maine: Colby College Press, 1954.

——. *The Old Clock by Thomas Hardy*. Portland, Maine: The Southworth-Anthoensen Press, 1946.

——. "Thomas Hardy's 'Song in *The Woodlanders*,'" *ELH: A Journal of English Literary History*, II (November, 1935), 242-45.

Webster, Harvey Curtis. *On a Darkling Plain: The Art and Thought of Thomas Hardy*. Chicago: University of Chicago Press, 1947.

Wedel, Theodore O. "Our Pagan World," *Theology*, XXXIX (November, 1939), 333-43.

Weygandt, Cornelius. *The Time of Yeats: English Poetry of Today against an American Background*. New York and London: D. Appleton-Century Co., 1937.

Wheeler, H. B. F., and A. M. Broadley. *Napoleon and the Invasion of England*. 2 vols. London, 1907.

Williams, Charles. "Thomas Hardy," in *Poetry at Present*. Oxford: Clarendon Press, 1931, pp. 1-16.

Willis, Irene Cooper. "Thomas Hardy," a 31-page typescript, 1940, in the Colby College Library.

Wilson, Carroll Atwood. *Thirteen Author Collections of the Nineteenth Century*. 2 vols. New York: Scribner's, 1950. (Hardy: I, 39-117.)

Windle, Bertram C. A. *The Wessex of Thomas Hardy*. London: John Lane, 1925. (First published in 1902.)

Wing, George. *Hardy*. Edinburgh and London: Oliver and Boyd, 1963.

Wright, Walter F. *The Shaping of "The Dynasts": A Study in Thomas Hardy*. Lincoln, Nebraska: University of Nebraska Press, 1967.

Yale University Library. *Thomas Hardy, O. M. Catalogue of a Memorial Exhibition*. New Haven, 1928.

Young, Ernest W. *Dorchester: Its Ancient and Modern History*. Dorchester: Henry Ling, and London: Simpkin, Marshall and Co., 1886.

——. *Dorchester: Its Principal Buildings and Institutions, and Its Neighbourhood*. Dorchester: Henry Ling, and London: Simpkin, Marshall and Co., 1886.

Zachrisson, Robert E. *Thomas Hardy as Man, Writer, and Philosopher*. Stockholm: Almquist & Wiksells, 1928.

Zietlow, Paul. "The Tentative Mode of Hardy's Poems," *Victorian Poetry*, V (Summer, 1967), 113-26.

——. "Thomas Hardy and William Barnes: Two Dorset Poets," *PMLA*, LXXIV (March, 1969), 291-303.

Zimmerman, Michael. "Thomas Hardy and the Modern Tradition in Poetry," *Kanazawa English Studies*, No. 11, Kanazawa University, Japan, 1968.

Index

This index lists each mention of Hardy's poems and the writers, scientists, and philosophers who influenced Hardy. Hardy is omitted, for his name appears on nearly every page, but members of his family are listed except for incidental mentions. Cities, towns, villages, buildings, rivers, and persons (both fictional and actual) are listed when they throw significant light on Hardy's realism. Hardy's themes are so numerous and varied that only such wide-ranging topics as "Animals," "Bible" (quotations from scriptures), and "Love, idealization in" are listed to consolidate items. Since alternate titles of poems are alphabetically listed in Part II, they are omitted. Poems, short stories, and essays are listed in quotation marks, whether or not so published.